When should I travel to get the best airfare?
Where do I go for answers to my travel questions?
What's the best and easiest way to plan and book my trip?

frommers.travelocity.com

Frommer's, the travel guide leader, has teamed up with **Travelocity.com**, the leader in online travel, to bring you an in-depth, easy-to-use resource designed to help you plan and book your trip online.

At **frommers.travelocity.com**, you'll find free online updates about your destination from the experts at Frommer's plus the outstanding travel planning and purchasing features of Travelocity.com. Travelocity.com provides reservations capabilities for 95 percent of all airline seats sold, more than 47,000 hotels, and over 50 car rental companies. In addition, Travelocity.com offers more than 2,000 exciting vacation and cruise packages. Travelocity.com puts you in complete control of your travel planning with these and other great features:

Expert travel guidance from Frommer's - over 150 writers reporting from around the world!

Best Fare Finder - an interactive calendar tells you when to travel to get the best airfare

Fare Watcher - we'll track airfare changes to your favorite destinations

Dream Maps - a mapping feature that suggests travel opportunities based on your budget

Shop Safe Guarantee - 24 hours a day / 7 days a week live customer service, and more!

Whether traveling on a tight budget, looking for a quick weekend getaway, or planning the trip of a lifetime, Frommer's guides and Travelocity.com will make your travel dreams a reality. You've bought the book, now book the trip!

Travelocity.com
A Sabre Company

Frommer's

Also available from Hungry Minds, Inc.:

the Unofficial Guide® to Las Vegas 2002

Bob Sehlinger
with Deke Castleman

Hungry Minds™

Best-Selling Books • Digital Downloads • e-Books • Answer Networks • e-Newsletters
Branded Web Sites • e-Learning

New York, NY ✦ Cleveland, OH ✦ Indianapolis, IN

In memory of Dan Wallace, a Gamblin' Man

Every effort has been made to ensure the accuracy of information throughout this book. Bear in mind, however, that prices, schedules, etc., are constantly changing. Readers should always verify information before making
final plans.

Hungry Minds, Inc.
909 Third Avenue
New York, NY 10022

Produced by Menasha Ridge Press

ISBN 0-7645-6422-6

ISSN 1064-5640

Manufactured in the United States of America

10 9 8 7 6 5 4 3 2 1

2002 Edition

Contents

List of Illustrations

Acknowledgments

The people of Las Vegas love their city and spare no effort to assist a writer trying to dig beneath the facade of flashing neon. It is important to them to communicate that Las Vegas is a city with depth, diversity, and substance. "Don't just write about our casinos," they demand, "take the time to get to know us."

We made every effort to do just that, enabled each step of the way by some of the most sincere and energetic folks a writer could hope to encounter. Myram Borders of the Las Vegas News Bureau provided us access to anyone we wanted to see, from casino general managers to vice cops. Cam Usher of the Las Vegas Convention and Visitors Authority also spared no effort in offering assistance and contacts. Thanks to Nevada expert Deke Castleman for his contributions to our entertainment, nightlife, buffet, and hotel coverage.

Restaurant critic Muriel Stevens ate her way through dozens of new restaurants but drew the line when it came to buffet duty. Jim McDonald of the Las Vegas Police Department shared his experiences and offered valuable suggestions for staying out of trouble. Jack Sheehan evaluated Las Vegas golf courses, and forest ranger Debbie Savage assisted us in developing material on wilderness recreation.

Purple Hearts to our field research team, who chowed down on every buffet and $2 steak in town, checked in and out of countless hotels, visited tourist attractions, and stood for hours in show lines:

Mike Jones	K'-Lynne Cotton	Nicole Jones	Marty Newey
Julie Newey	Holly Cross	Shirley Gutke	Dan Cotton
Joan Burns	Lee Wiseman	Molly Merkle	Leslie Cummins
Grace Walton	Sean Ross	Chris Mohney	

Much gratitude to Gabbie Oates, Russell Helms, Annie Long, Dianne DiBlasi, Steve Jones, and Jan Mucciarone, the pros who somehow turned all this effort into a book.

Introduction

On a Plane to Las Vegas

I never wanted to go to Las Vegas. I'm not much of a gambler and have always thought of Las Vegas as a city dedicated to separating folks from their money. As it happens, however, I have some involvement with industries that hold conventions and trade shows there. For some years I was able to persuade others to go in my place. Eventually, of course, it came my turn to go, and I found myself aboard a Delta jumbo jet on my first trip to Las Vegas.

Listening to the banter of those around me, I became aware that my fellow passengers were divided into two distinct camps. Some obviously thought themselves on a nonstop flight to nirvana and could not have been happier. Too excited to remain seated, they danced up and down the aisles clapping one another on the back in anticipation. The other passengers, by contrast, groused and grumbled, swore under their breath, and wore expressions suggesting a steady diet of lemons. These people, as despondent as Al Capone en route to a tax audit, lamented their bad luck and cursed those who had made a trip to such a place necessary.

To my surprise, I thoroughly enjoyed Las Vegas. I had a great time without gambling and have been back many times with never a bad experience. The people are friendly, the food is good, hotels are a bargain, it's an easy town to get around in, and there is plenty to do (24 hours a day, if you are so inclined).

It's hard to say why so many folks have such strong feelings about Las Vegas (even those who have never been there). Among our research team we had people willing to put their kids in boarding school for a chance to go, while others begged off to have root canal surgery or prune their begonias. A third group wanted to go very badly but maintained the pretense of total indifference. They reminded me of people who own five TVs yet profess never to watch television; they clearly had not mustered the courage to come out of the closet.

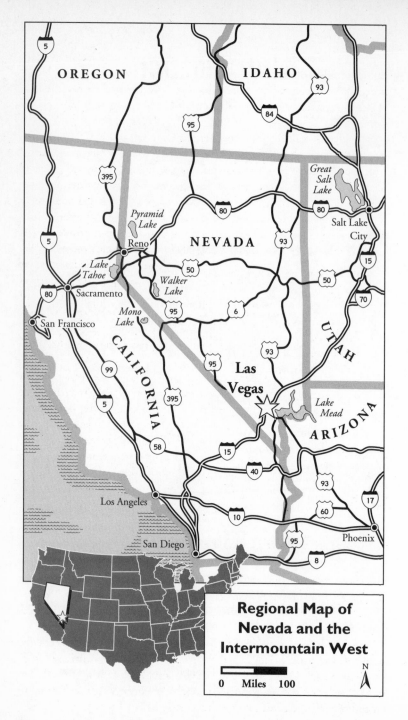

OREGON

IDAHO

NEVADA

Great
Salt
Lake

Pyramid
Lake

Reno

Salt Lake
City

Lake
Tahoe

Sacramento

Walker
Lake

San Francisco

CALIFORNIA

Mono
Lake

UTAH

Las
Vegas

Lake
Mead

ARIZONA

Los Angeles

San Diego

Phoenix

**Regional Map of
Nevada and the
Intermountain West**

0   Miles   100

N

What I discovered during my first and subsequent visits is that the non-gambling public doesn't know very much about Las Vegas. Many people cannot see beyond the gambling, cannot see that there could possibly be anything of value in Las Vegas for nongamblers or those only marginally interested in gambling.

When you ask these people to describe their ideal vacation, they wax eloquent about lazy days relaxing in the sun, playing golf, enjoying the luxury of resort hotels, eating in fine restaurants, sight-seeing, shopping, and going to the theater. Outdoor types speak no less enthusiastically about fishing, boating, hiking, and, in the winter, skiing. As it happens, Las Vegas offers all of these diversions and probably at the lowest prices available anywhere. Gambling is just the tip of the iceberg in Las Vegas, but it's all many people can see.

Las Vegas is, of course, about gambling, but there's much more. Las Vegas has sunny, mild weather two-thirds of the year, some of the finest hotels and restaurants in the world, the most diversified celebrity and production show entertainment to be found, unique shopping, internationally renowned golf courses, and numerous attractions. For the outdoor enthusiast, Red Rock Canyon National Conservation Area, Lake Mead National Recreation Area, and Toiyabe National Forest offer some of the most exotic and beautiful wilderness resources in North America.

This guide is designed for those who want to go to Las Vegas and for those who *have* to go to Las Vegas. If you are a recreational gambler and/or enthusiastic vacationer, we will help you pour champagne over the iceberg. We will show you ways to have more fun, make the most of your time, and spend less money. If you are one of the skeptics, unwilling spouses or companions of gamblers, business travelers, or people who think they would rather be someplace else, we will help you discover the nine-tenths of the Las Vegas iceberg that is hidden. We will demonstrate that you can have the time of your life in this friendly city and never bet that first nickel.

Looking Back, Looking Ahead

In 1946, Bugsy Siegel opened the Flamingo Hotel, kicking off the metamorphosis that changed three miles of mostly barren desert into what is now the Las Vegas Strip. The original Flamingo was an eyepopper in its day and established a baseline that all subsequent casinos had to at least match, if not improve upon.

As new hotels appeared in the neon Valhalla, each contributed something different, and occasionally something better, raising the bar (to use a high jumping metaphor) incrementally. Two properties, the Desert Inn and Caesars Palace, advanced the standard significantly, but because they catered to an exclusive clientele, their competitors chose not to follow suit.

Then came the Mirage, a large hotel and casino offering the spectacle of Caesars and the refined taste of the Desert Inn (almost), but, more important, it targeted not the carriage trade but rather the average tourist. The Mirage was equal parts tourist attraction, hotel, and casino, and each part was executed with imagination and flair. Not many Las Vegas tourists could afford the Mirage's expensive guest rooms, but the place was nonetheless a must-see on every visitor's touring itinerary.

The Mirage's success demonstrated that gamblers, contrary to prevailing opinion, actually paid attention to their gaming environment and, if given a choice, preferred an interesting, dynamic, and attractive setting to the cramped, noisy, monochromatic boiler room that was the norm. Beyond a doubt, the Mirage was in a class by itself. Observers waited impatiently to see if any competitor would challenge the Mirage, though most believed the standard was impossibly high.

But the answer was not long in coming. A veritable explosion of new developments was rushed from the drawing board to the construction zone. First was the Excalibur in 1990. It was big, plastic, gaudy, and certainly no direct competitor to the Mirage, but its Knights-of-the-Round-Table theme played exceptionally well with the blue-collar and family markets. Next came the class of 1993, which included the pyramid-shaped Luxor, Treasure Island (sister property to the Mirage), and the MGM Grand Hotel and Theme Park. Though the MGM Grand Theme Park was a bust, the hotel and casino were immediately successful. Likewise, the Luxor and Treasure Island, with their knockout themes, rocketed up the pop chart.

In the three years before the next wave of new hotels opened in 1996, the vital signs of the newer and older properties were monitored closely. The MGM Grand was the largest hotel-casino in the world, Excalibur was a close second, and the other new hotels offered more than 2,500 rooms each. As with the bull stock market in the 1990s, there was endless speculation and debate about how long the building boom could last. But the preliminary data seemed to indicate that the new properties were responsible for increasing the aggregate market. Room occupancy rates remained high.

Though more visitors were coming to Las Vegas, the lion's share of the business was going to the newer, high-profile hotels. Older properties, including some of the Strip's most established casinos, found themselves increasingly in the margins. So too, downtown Las Vegas was in a tailspin, with gaming revenues down, or flat, year after year. The new marching orders, avoided or ignored for so long, were crystal clear: If you want to play in the big league, you have to upgrade, and upgrading meant approximating the Mirage standard.

The response of downtown Las Vegas was to combine the Fremont Street casinos into a mega-gaming venue, a new Glitter Gulch, tied together by a pedestrian plaza under the canopy of the Fremont Street Experience electric light show. Back on the Strip, older properties, including Bally's, the Desert Inn, the Flamingo, Harrah's, the Sahara, the Boardwalk, Circus Circus, and the Riviera, scrambled to upgrade. One property, Vegas World, was razed to make room for a whole new hotel-casino. The venerable Caesars Palace alone managed to stay ahead of the game, making improvements each year to maintain its position at or near the top of the Strip food chain.

In 1996 the Stratosphere Hotel and Casino, with the tallest observation tower in the U.S., opened at the old Vegas World site. Farther south on the Strip, the Monte Carlo hit the scene, a joint venture between Circus Circus Enterprises and Mirage Resorts. Then in 1997, New York–New York opened its doors. With more than 100,000 people a day visiting during its first weeks of operation, New York–New York quickly dispelled the notion that the Strip was overbuilt. In typical Las Vegas go-for-broke style, the Dunes, the Sands, and the Hacienda were blown up to make room for yet more gargantuan gambling palaces.

The boom proceeded at warp speed, with a construction frenzy that through 2001 has added a whopping 23,000 new rooms to Las Vegas' inventory (now totaling roughly 130,000). Bellagio (opened in 1998) draws its inspiration from Italy's Lake Como, adding 3,000 rooms to the Mirage Resorts galaxy, and catering to the upscale market. Across the street is the 2,900-room Paris Casino Resort with its own 50-story Eiffel Tower. Just south is the new Aladdin, a 2,600-room complex with an ancient desert kingdom theme. On the site of the old Sands is the Venetian. An all-suite property with 3,000 suites in its first building phase, the Venetian features a shopping complex in a Venice canal setting complete with gondola rides. And at the southern end of the Strip on the old Hacienda property, the 3,700-room Mandalay Bay, a Mandalay Resort Group (formerly Circus Circus Enterprises) hotel-casino for an adult clientele, opened in early 1999.

Not all of the new development is on the Strip or downtown. More and more new casinos are being built around town in an effort to cater to the local population without forcing them to battle the traffic of the Strip. In just the past nine years we have witnessed the opening of the Fiesta, Texas Station, Silverton, the Hard Rock, the Reserve, the Orleans, Arizona Charlie's East, Suncoast, and Sunset Station. To the west of the Strip, Regent International premiered Regent Las Vegas, a 550-room spa and golf resort in the Summerlin residential area of Las Vegas, in 1999. In December 1999, Hyatt completed its 500-room hotel-casino, the Hyatt Las Vegas, in nearby Henderson. The development is surrounded by a manmade lake and a Jack Nicklaus–designed golf course.

Both the Hilton and the Regent Las Vegas have had a tough time luring visitors away from the Strip. In a marketing flip-flop, the Regent gave up on out-of-towners and began targeting the locals. The Hilton is trying (fairly successfully) to fill its rooms with meeting attendees and golfers.

Then there's the mergers and acquisitions. In 2000, Steve Wynn, the visionary behind the Mirage and the Las Vegas transformation it kicked off, sold the Mirage, Bellagio, Treasure Island, Golden Nugget, and half of Monte Carlo to MGM-Grand for $6.4 billion. MGM-Grand immediately closed Bellagio's celebrated art gallery and sold much of the art. Wynn, meanwhile, purchased the venerable Desert Inn. He says he intends to build a 3,000-room non-themed resort on the DI site, stating ironically that "themes are a thing of the past." Wynn always seems to be one step ahead of the pack, and he might be correct about themes. Still, it's like Dr. Spock saying that children are a thing of the past.

Only months earlier, Hilton's casino subsidiary, Park Place Entertainment, bought Caesars Palace and O'Shea's, adding them to a line-up that already included the Las Vegas Hilton, Bally's, Paris, and the Flamingo. The Circus Circus/Mandalay Resort Group owns a good chunk of what's left including Luxor, Mandalay Bay, Excalibur, Circus Circus, and half of the Monte Carlo. In other merger activity, Harrah's acquired the Rio and Station Casinos bought the Fiesta and the Reserve.

If you wonder where it will all end, you're not alone. Critics of growth point out that the infrastructure is not keeping pace with the new development. The Strip is the most sclerotic traffic artery imaginable, making 45-minute slogs out of a one-mile trip. Relief in the form of viable mass transit options is currently being stymied by casino owners. Water also is a problem (look around, it's a desert out there!). Casino owners duck the blame for spiraling water consumption by insisting that it's the expanding local population that accounts for most of the usage. This is a bit disingenuous given that it's the building boom and the new casinos that are driving the population growth. New properties currently under construction will create almost 16,000 new jobs. That's a lot of thirsty people, dogs to bathe, and lawns to water.

For you, the Las Vegas visitor, the news is mixed. Room rates, which have been cycling upward for several years, have leveled off, and responding to a sluggish economy, might decline. More rooms have come on line in 2001, which may help with this somewhat, but don't look for incredible deals at the new, high-profile properties—(except, perhaps, the Aladdin) especially those on the Strip between Spring Mountain and Tropicana. Other, more welcome news, particularly in conjunction with the stabilizing rates, is the much improved quality of hotel rooms in Las Vegas. The rooms of the newer properties are quite nice, and many of the older hotels have renovated or refurbished their rooms.

The dining scene is another plus. Buffets continue to improve as competition sharpens, and there is now a branch of seemingly every big-name restaurant in Las Vegas (Four Seasons, Le Cirque, Aqua, Delmonico Steak House, Lawry's, Morton's, The Palm, Wolfgang Puck, Brennan's, Commander's Palace, and on and on). Although theme dining continues to proliferate, the public has weeded out the weak sisters. It's fine to have a theme, but patrons are appropriately voting their palate. Proprietary restaurants are holding their own, but just barely. The bad news is that, aside from buffets, it costs more to dine in Las Vegas now, especially in the new, brand-name joints. Still, compared to other cities with dynamic restaurant scenes, Las Vegas remains a bargain.

Production and celebrity headliner shows are not the bargain they once were. In fact, the average price of a ticket is up almost 96% since 1992! On the other side of the coin, the quality of the average show has also trended up. Las Vegas promoters claim prices are a bargain compared to entertainment elsewhere, but that's wishful thinking. Probably half of the shows in town are overpriced.

A few years back the big buzz was Las Vegas as a family destination. Insiders understood, however, that all the talk was just that. At most the family thing was a PR exercise to make Las Vegas appear more wholesome. It was tacitly understood that the big dogs would never allow theme parks and other family oriented attractions to actually compete with the casinos for a visitor's time. Lost in the backwash of this hollow debate, however, was the exponential burgeoning of theme shopping. Although undoubtedly there will be some retail casualties, the case can be made that shopping is fast becoming as potent an attraction in Las Vegas as gambling. On the Strip alone are 3 huge theme shopping venues (Forum Shops, Grand Canal Shops, and Desert Passage) and a comparatively white bread mall, but one that's buttressed with every name department store in North America. For the first time, there is something powerful enough to suck the players right out of the casinos, and it arrived on the scene as stealthily as a Trojan horse.

The economy in 2001 cast a shadow over the entire Las Vegas tourism environment causing a number of big projects to be put on at least temporary hold. Meanwhile occupancy rates remained high, spurred by an uptick in convention business. Even so, developers worried that hotel room supply was outpacing demand and that maybe there wouldn't be enough visitors to fill all those new malls and designer restaurants. Simply put, the bull in Las Vegas was every bit as headstrong as the bull in the 1990's stock market, and if anything, even more difficult to corral. Today, for the first time in a decade, casino companies are really managing their growth, and in an economic climate that's uncharted waters for many, are behaving more like an IBM than a runaway dotcom. Whether high ticket shows, expense account restaurants, boutique retailers and $200 room rates will survive the shakedown is a toss up, even for the handicappers. The only certainty is that the casinos have placed huge bets in a game of economic roulette. Now, like every sweaty-palmed player in their casinos, they wait anxiously to see where the roulette ball will fall.

About This Guide

HOW COME "UNOFFICIAL"?

Most "official" guides to Las Vegas tout the well-known sights, promote the local casinos, restaurants, and hotels indiscriminately, and leave out a lot of good stuff. This guide is different.

Instead of pandering to the tourist industry, we'll tell you if a well-known restaurant's mediocre food is not worth the wait. We'll complain loudly about overpriced hotel rooms that aren't convenient to the places you want to be, and we'll guide you away from the crowds and congestion for a break now and then.

We sent in a team of evaluators who toured the casinos and popular attractions, reviewed the production shows, ate in the area's best restaurants, performed critical evaluations of its hotels, and visited the best nightclubs. If a restaurant serves bad food or a show is not worth the admission price, we can say so—and, in the process, hopefully make your visit more fun, efficient, and economical.

CREATING A GUIDEBOOK

We got into the guidebook business because we were unhappy with the way travel guides make the reader work to get any usable information. Wouldn't it be nice, we thought, if we were to make guides that are easy to use?

Most guidebooks are compilations of lists. This is true regardless of whether the information is presented in list form or artfully distributed through pages of prose. There is insufficient detail in a list, and prose can present tedious helpings of nonessential or marginally useful information. Not enough wheat, so to speak, for nourishment in one instance, and too much chaff in the other. Either way, these types of guides provide little more than departure points from which readers initiate their own quests.

Many guides are readable and well researched, but they tend to be difficult to use. To select a hotel, for example, a reader must study several pages of descriptions with only the boldface hotel names breaking up large blocks of text. Because each description essentially deals with the same variables, it is difficult to recall what was said concerning a particular hotel. Readers generally must work through all the write-ups before beginning to narrow their choices. The presentation of restaurants, shows, and attractions is similar except that even more reading is usually required. To use such a guide is to undertake an exhaustive research process that requires examining nearly as many options and possibilities as starting from scratch. If any recommendations are actually made, they lack depth and conviction. These guides compound rather than solve problems by failing to boil travelers' choices down to a thoughtfully considered, well-distilled, and manageable few.

How Unofficial Guides Are Different

Readers care about the authors' opinions. The authors, after all, *are* supposed to know what they are talking about. This, coupled with the fact that the traveler wants quick answers (as opposed to endless alternatives), dictates that authors should be explicit, prescriptive, and above all, direct. The *Unofficial Guide* tries to do just that. It spells out alternatives and recommends specific courses of action. It simplifies complicated destinations and attractions and helps the traveler feel in control in the most unfamiliar environments. The objective of the *Unofficial Guide* is not to have the most information or all of the information; it aims to have the most accessible, useful information, unbiased by affiliation with any organization or industry.

An *Unofficial Guide* is a critical reference work that focuses on a travel destination that appears to be especially complex. Our authors and research team are completely independent from the attractions, restaurants, and hotels we describe. *The Unofficial Guide to Las Vegas* is designed for individuals and families traveling for the fun of it, as well as for business travelers and convention-goers, especially those visiting Las Vegas for the first time. The guide is directed at value-conscious, consumer-oriented adults who seek a cost-effective, though not Spartan, travel style.

How This Guide Was Researched and Written

While much has been written about Las Vegas, very little has been evaluative. Some guides practically regurgitate the hotels' and casinos' own promotional material. In preparing this work, we took nothing for granted. Each casino, hotel, restaurant, show, and attraction was visited at different times throughout the year by a team of trained observers. They conducted detailed evaluations and rated each property and entertainment according to formal, pretested rating criteria. Interviews were conducted to determine what tourists of all ages enjoyed most *and least* during their Las Vegas visit.

While our observers are independent and impartial, they do not claim to have special expertise. Like you, they visited Las Vegas as tourists or business travelers, noting their satisfaction or dissatisfaction.

The primary difference between the average tourist and the trained evaluator is the evaluator's skills in organization, preparation, and observation. The trained evaluator is responsible for much more than simply observing and cataloging. While the average tourist is being entertained by the magic of *Siegfried & Roy*, for instance, the professional is rating the performance in terms of theme, pace, continuity, and originality. The evaluator also checks out the physical arrangements: Is the sound system clear and audible without being overpowering? Is seating adequate? Can everyone in the audience clearly see the staging area? And what about the performers: Are they competent and professional; Are they compelling and engaging? Does the performance begin and end on time? Does the show contain the features described in the hotel's promotional literature? These and many other considerations figure prominently in the rating of any staged performance. Observer teams use detailed checklists to analyze casinos, attractions, hotel rooms, buffets, and restaurants. Finally, evaluator ratings and observations are integrated with tourist reactions and the opinions of patrons for a comprehensive quality profile of each feature and service.

In compiling this guide, we recognize that tourists' ages, backgrounds, and interests will strongly influence their taste in Las Vegas offerings and will account for a preference for one show or casino over another. Our sole objective is to provide the reader with sufficient description, critical evaluation, and pertinent data to make knowledgeable decisions according to individual tastes.

LETTERS, COMMENTS, AND QUESTIONS FROM READERS

We expect to learn from our mistakes, as well as from the input of our readers, and to improve with each book and edition. Many of those who use the *Unofficial Guides* write to us to ask questions, make comments, or share their own discoveries and lessons learned in Las Vegas. We appreciate all such input, both positive and critical, and encourage our readers to continue writing. Readers' comments and observations will be frequently incorporated in revised editions of the *Unofficial Guide* and will contribute immeasurably to its improvement.

How to Write the Author:

Bob Sehlinger
The Unofficial Guide to Las Vegas
P.O. Box 43673
Birmingham, AL 35243

When you write, be sure to put your return address on your letter as well as on the envelope—sometimes envelopes and letters get separated. And remember, our work takes us out of the office for long periods of time, so forgive us if our response is delayed.

Reader Survey

At the back of this guide you will find a short questionnaire that you can use to express opinions concerning your Las Vegas visit. Clip the questionnaire out along the dotted line and mail it to the above address.

HOW INFORMATION IS ORGANIZED: BY SUBJECT AND BY GEOGRAPHIC ZONES

To give you fast access to information about the *best* of Las Vegas, we've organized material in several formats.

Hotels   Because most people visiting Las Vegas stay in one hotel for the duration of their trip, we have summarized our coverage of hotels in charts, maps, ratings, and rankings that allow you to quickly focus your decision-making process. We do not go on page after page describing lobbies and rooms which, in the final analysis, sound much the same. Instead, we concentrate on the specific variables that differentiate one hotel from another: location, size, room quality, services, amenities, and cost.

Restaurants   We provide a lot of detail when it comes to restaurants. Since you will probably eat a dozen or more restaurant meals during your stay, and since not even *you* can predict what you might be in the mood for on Saturday night, we provide detailed profiles of the best restaurants in Las Vegas.

Entertainment and Nightlife   Visitors frequently try several different shows or nightspots during their stay. Because shows and nightspots, like restaurants, are usually selected spontaneously after arriving in Las Vegas, we believe detailed descriptions are warranted. All continuously running stage shows, as well as celebrity showrooms, are profiled and reviewed in the entertainment section of this guide. The best nightspots and lounges in Las Vegas are profiled alphabetically under nightlife in the same section (see pages 264–276).

Geographic Zones   Though it's easy to get around in Las Vegas, you may not have a car or the inclination to venture far from your hotel. To help you locate the best restaurants, shows, nightspots, and attractions convenient to where you are staying, we have divided the city into geographic zones:

- Zone 1   The Las Vegas Strip and Environs
- Zone 2   Downtown Las Vegas
- Zone 3   Southwest Las Vegas

- Zone 4   North Las Vegas
- Zone 5   Southeast Las Vegas and the Boulder Highway

All profiles of hotels, restaurants, and nightspots include zone numbers. For example, if you are staying at the Golden Nugget and are interested in Italian restaurants within walking distance, scanning the restaurant profiles for restaurants in Zone 2 (downtown) will provide you with the best choices.

Comfort Zones   Because every Las Vegas hotel-casino has its own personality and attracts a specific type of customer, for each property we have created a profile that describes the casino's patrons and gives you a sense of how it might feel to spend time there. The purpose of the comfort-zone section is to help you find the hotel-casino where you will feel most welcome and at home. Comfort-zone descriptions begin on page 87.

Las Vegas: An Overview

GATHERING INFORMATION

Las Vegas has the best selection of complimentary visitor guides of any American tourist destination we know. Available at the front desk or concierge table at almost every hotel, the guides provide a wealth of useful information on gaming, gambling lessons, shows, lounge entertainment, sports, buffets, meal-deals, tours and sight-seeing, transportation, shopping, and special events. Additionally, most of the guides contain coupons for discounts on dining, shows, attractions, and tours.

What's On is the most comprehensive of the visitor guides. *Today in Las Vegas* is also very comprehensive, but is organized somewhat differently. Because both formats come in handy, we always pick up a copy of each magazine.

Both guides are published weekly and are distributed on a complimentary basis in Las Vegas. If you want to see a copy before you leave home, subscriptions or single issues are available as follows:

Today in Las Vegas
Lycoria Publishing Company
3626 Pecos McLeod Dr., Suite 14
Las Vegas, NV 89121
(702) 385-2737
www.todayinlv.com

What's On Magazine
4425 Industrial Road
Las Vegas, NV 89103
(702) 891-8811
www.ilovevegas.com

Other publications include *Showbiz Magazine,* published by the *Las Vegas Sun* newspaper, and *Where Las Vegas.* Both have much of the same information discussed above plus feature articles.

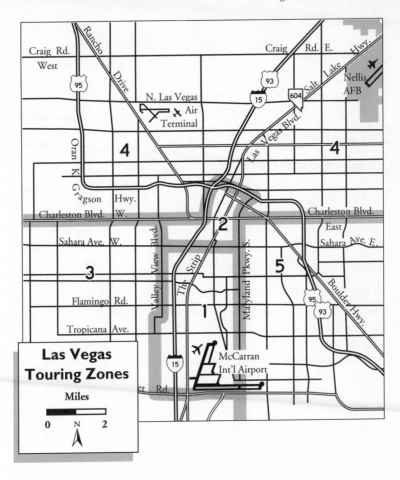

The *Las Vegas Advisor* is a 12-page monthly newsletter containing some of the most useful consumer information available on gaming, dining, and entertainment, as well as taking advantage of deals on rooms, drinks, shows, and meals. With no advertising or promotional content, the newsletter serves its readers with objective, prescriptive, no-nonsense advice, presented with a sense of humor. At a subscription rate of $50 a year, the *Las Vegas Advisor* is the best investment you can make if you plan to spend four or more days in Las Vegas each year. If you are a one-time visitor but wish to avail yourself of all this wisdom, single copies of the *Las Vegas Advisor* can be purchased for $5 at the Gambler's Book Club store at 630 South 11th Street, (702) 382-7555. To speed delivery of the first issue (which includes discount coupons), send a self-addressed, legal-sized envelope with 77 cents postage along with your request. For additional information, write:

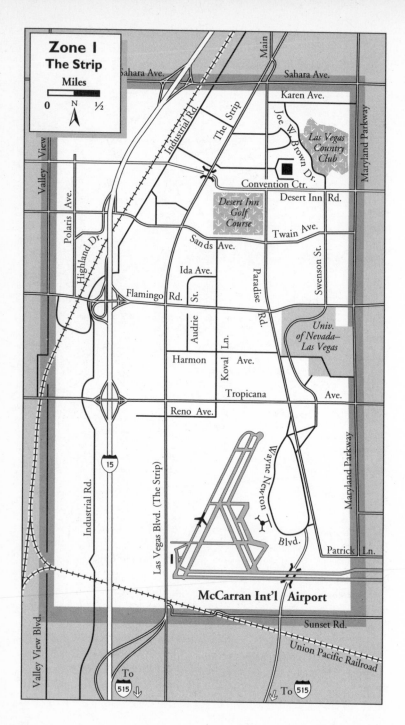

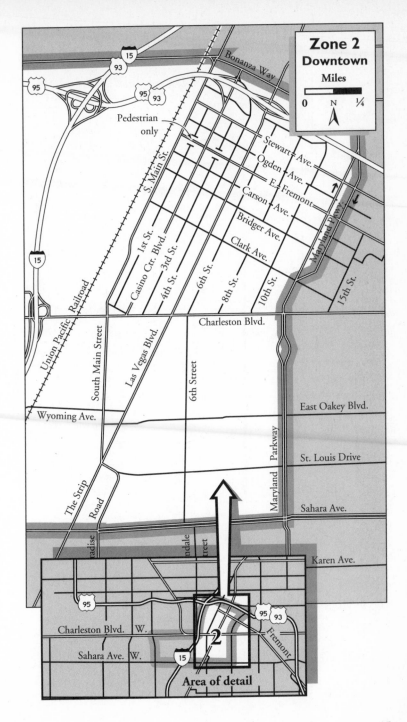

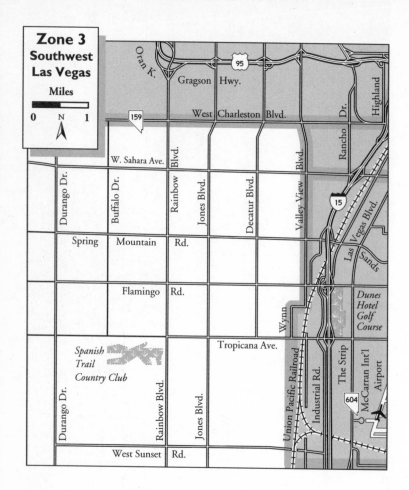

Zone 3
Southwest Las Vegas

Miles

0   N   1

Oran K.

95

Gragson Hwy.

West Charleston Blvd.

Highland

159

Rancho Dr.

W. Sahara Ave.

Rainbow Blvd.

Jones Blvd.

Decatur Blvd.

Valley View Blvd.

15

Durango Dr.

Buffalo Dr.

Las Vegas Blvd.

Spring Mountain Rd.

Sands

Flamingo Rd.

Wynn

Dunes Hotel Golf Course

Tropicana Ave.

Spanish Trail Country Club

Durango Dr.

Rainbow Blvd.

Jones Blvd.

Union Pacific Railroad

Industrial Rd.

The Strip

604

McCarran Int'l Airport

West Sunset Rd.

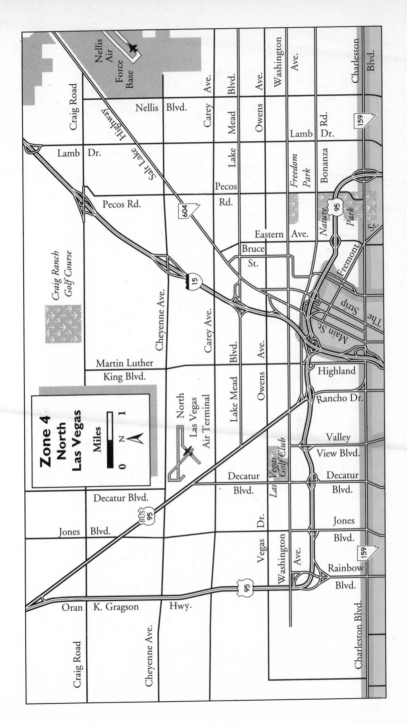

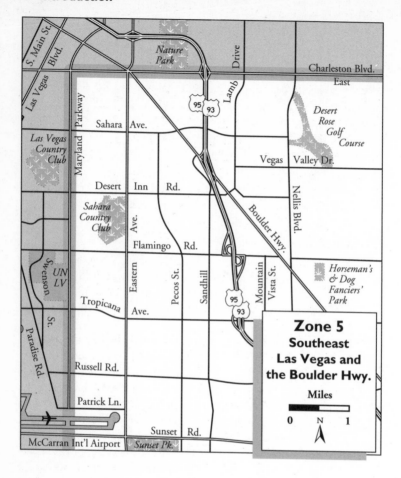

Las Vegas Advisor
Huntington Press
3687 South Procyon Ave., Suite A
Las Vegas, NV 89103
(702) 252-0655 or (800) 244-2224
www.lasvegasadvisor.com

Las Vegas and the Internet

The explosive growth of Las Vegas is not only physical, but also virtual. Three years ago at this time, Las Vegas casinos had a minimal presence on the World Wide Web; this year, there are too many sites to list. The following are the best places to go on the Web to launch yourself into Las Vegas cyberspace. Use the directories to surf the many individual sites.

The official website of the Las Vegas Convention and Visitors Authority is www.lasvegas24hours.com.

For the largest selection of Las Vegas casinos on the Web, look up www.intermind.net, then hit Hotels & Casinos.

An extensive site aimed at people relocating to Las Vegas or interested in investing in Las Vegas real estate is at www.lasvegas4sale.com.

Other Las Vegas on-ramps include:

www.vegas.com	www.lasvegas.com
www.pcap.com	www.casinogambling.about.com
www.lasvegasadvisor.com	www.ilovevegas.com

WHEN TO GO TO LAS VEGAS

The best time to go to Las Vegas is in the spring or fall, when the weather is pleasant. If you plan to spend most of your time indoors, it doesn't matter what time of year you choose; if you intend to golf, play tennis, run, hike, bike, or boat, try to go in March, April, early May, October, November, or early December.

Because spring and fall are the nicest times of year, they are also the most popular. The best time of year for special deals and bargain room rates is in December (after the National Finals Rodeo in early December and excluding the week between Christmas and New Year's), January, and during the scorching months of the summer, particularly July and August.

Weather in December, January, and February can vary incredibly. While high winds, cold, rain, and snow are not unheard of, chances are better that temperatures will be mild and the sun will shine. Though the weather is less dependable than in spring or fall, winter months are generally well suited to outdoor activities. We talked to people who in late February water-skied on Lake Mead in the morning and snow-skied the same afternoon at Lee Canyon up in the mountains. The winter months provide an unbeatable combination of good value and choice of activities. From mid-May through mid-September, however, the heat is blistering. During these months it's best to follow the example of the gambler and the lizard—stay indoors or under a rock.

Crowd Avoidance

In general, weekends are busy and weekdays are slower. The exceptions are holiday periods and when large conventions or special events are being held. Most Las Vegas hotels have a lower guest-room rate for weekdays than for weekends. For a stress-free arrival at the airport; good availability of rental cars; and a quick, easy hotel check-in, try to arrive Monday afternoon through Thursday morning (Tuesday and Wednesday are best).

Las Vegas hosts huge conventions and special events (rodeos, prize fights) that tie up hotels, restaurants, transportation, showrooms, and traffic for a week at a time. If you prefer to schedule your visit at a time when things are a little less frantic, we provide a calendar listing the larger citywide conventions and regularly scheduled events to help you avoid the crowds. Note that two or three medium-sized conventions meeting at the same time can impact Las Vegas as much as one big citywide event.

Because conventions of over 12,000 attendees can cause problems for the lone vacationer, the following list will help you plan your vacation dates. Included are the convention date, the number of people expected to attend, and the convention location (with hotel headquarters, if known at the time of publication). If you would like to have a more complete convention calendar mailed to you, call the Las Vegas Convention and Visitors Authority at (702) 892-0711 or (702) 892-7576.

Arriving and Getting Oriented

If you drive, you will have to travel through the desert to reach Las Vegas. Make sure your car is in good shape. Check your spare tire and toss a couple gallons of water in the trunk, just in case. Once en route, pay attention to your fuel and temperature gauges.

Virtually all commercial air traffic into Las Vegas uses McCarran International Airport (www.mccarran.com). At McCarran, a well-designed facility with good, clear signs, you will have no problem finding your way from the gate to the baggage claim area, though it is often a long walk. Fast baggage handling is not the airport's strongest suit, so don't be surprised if you have to wait a long time on your checked luggage. If you are renting a car from a rental company with a counter at the airport, you can often complete the paperwork before your checked baggage arrives. Once you have picked up your bags, you will have to produce the baggage claim check before you're allowed to exit the building.

If you do not intend to rent a car, getting from the airport to your hotel is no problem. Shuttle services are available starting at $4.50 one-way and $9 round-trip. Sedans and "stretch" limousines range from about $28 to $35 one-way. Cabs are also available. The fare to Las Vegas Strip locations ranges from $9 to $18 one-way plus tip. One-way taxi fares to downtown run about $16 to $23. The limo service counters are in the hall just outside the baggage claim area. Cabs are at the curb. Additional information concerning ground transportation is available on the McCarran International Airport website, www.mccarran.com.

Month	Average a.m. Temp.	Average p.m. Temp.	Pools O=Open	Recommended Attire
				Las Vegas Weather and Dress Chart
January	57	32		Coats and jackets are a must.
February	50	37		Dress warmly: jackets and sweaters.
March	69	42	O	Sweaters for days, but a jacket at night.
April	78	50	O	Still cool at night—bring a jacket.
May	88	50	O	Sweater for evening, but days are warm.
June	99	68	O	Days hot and evenings are moderate.
July	105	75	O	Bathing suits.
August	102	73	O	Dress for the heat—spend time at a pool!
September	95	65	O	Days warm, sweater for evening.
October	81	53	O	Bring a jacket or sweater for afternoon.
November	67	40		Sweaters and jackets, coats for night.
December	58	34		Coats and jackets a must: dress warmly!

Convention and Special Events Calendar

Dates	Convention/Event	Number of Attendees	Location/HQ
2001			
Aug 27–30	Magic International	90,000	Conv Ctr/ Hilton
Aug 27–31	Gentlemen's Club	2,700	Mandalay Bay
Sept 5–8	North American Bridal Association	5,000	Tropicana
Sept 5–16	Senior Softball World Championship	15,000	Various Complexes
Sept 9–12	National Beer Wholesalers Association	3,200	Paris LasVegas
Sept 10–12	Packaging Machinery Manufacturers	18,000	Sands Expo Ctr
Sept 10–12	Yamaha Motor Corp.	2,800	Mandalay Bay
Sept 13–15	General Motors Corp.	18,000	Conv Ctr/ MGM Grand
Sept 16–21	Laborers Int'l Union of North America	5,000	Hilton
Sept 23–25	Primetime Fall Marketplace & Conference	5,000	Conv Ctr/Hilton
Sept 24–26	Machine Tool Show	7,000	Conv Ctr/Multiple
Sept 24–26	PGA Int'l Golf Show	23,300	Conv Ctr/Mirage
Sept 30– Oct 3	Interbike Expo	27,000	Sands Expo Ctr/ Multiple
Oct 1–2	Western Food Industry Expo	5,000	Conv Ctr
Oct 1–3	American Gaming Assoc.	6,000	Conv Ctr
Oct 1–3	Int'l Assoc. for the Leisure and Entertainment Industry	6,500	Conv Ctr/Mirage
Oct 4–6	Amusement and Music Operators Association	7,500	Conv Ctr/Hilton
Oct 8–10	Household Goods Forwarders Assoc. of America	2,500	Paris LasVegas
Oct 9–12	Tru*Serv	22,000	Conv Ctr/Hilton
Oct 10–11	Western Nursery & Garden Expo	6,500	Conv Ctr/Multiple
Oct 11–13	Art Las Vegas Show	11,000	Sands Expo Ctr/ Venetian
Oct 12–13	JLC Live–Construction Training Show	7,000	Conv Ctr/Riviera
Oct 12–14	AMA U.S. Open of Supercross	10,000	MGM Grand

Convention and Special Events Calendar (continued)

Dates	Convention/Event	Number of Attendees	Location/HQ
2001			
Oct 15–18	12 Technologies	10,000	Sand Expo Ctr/ Venetian
Oct 16–18	Western Rental Equipment Expo	3,500	Conv Ctr/Hilton
Oct 17–19	World Gaming Congress	23,000	Sands Expo Ctr
Oct 19–20	California Glass Assoc.	2,500	Cashman Ctr/ Golden Nugget
Oct 21–23	National Assoc. of Convenience Stores Inc.	22,000	Conv Ctr/Hilton
Oct 23–25	Bass Hotels & Resorts	12,000	Conv Ctr
Oct 23–25	GSE Int'l Expo LLC	3,000	Rio
Oct 23–25	Metalcon International	8,500	Conv Ctr/Hilton
Oct 24–27	American Supply Assoc.	5,400	Hilton
Oct 25–28	NHRA Points Event	30,000	LV Motor Speedway
Oct 25–28	PBR BudLight Cup World Championships	55,000	Thomas&Mack Ctr
Oct 29–31	Western Carwash Assoc.	2,500	Rio
Oct 30–31	Pennzoil World of Outlaws	10,000	LV Motor Speedway
Oct 30– Nov 2	Automotive Aftermarket Industry Week	85,000	Conv Ctr/Multiple
Oct 30– Nov 2	Tire Association of North America	5,000	Conv Ctr/Aladdin
Nov 1–3	Las Vegas Antique Arms Show	5,000	Riviera
Nov 12–16	Comdex Fall(Housing)	225,000	Sands Expo Ctr
Nov 13–19	National Industrial Fastener Show and Conference	3,500	Paris Las Vegas
Nov 14–18	Champion Enterprises	2,800	Venetian
Nov 18–28	American Contract Bridge League	8,000	Hilton
Nov 22–25	Public Affairs Int'l	3,000	Aladdin
Nov 28–30	Supplyside West Int'l Trade Show and Conference	2,500	Venetian
Nov 30– Dec 2	Int'l Autobody Congress & Exposition	42,000	Conv Ctr/Multiple
Dec 7–16	National Finals Rodeo	170,000	Thomas&Mack Ctr
Dec 11–13	Power–Gen	12,500	Conv Ctr/Hilton
Dec 14–16	Int'l Coin & Stamp Collectors Society	5,000	Tropicana

Convention and Special Events Calendar (continued)

Dates	Convention/Event	Number of Attendees	Location/HQ
2002			
Jan 8–11	2002 Int'l CES	20,000	Conv Ctr/Hilton
Jan 8–11	Video Software Dealers Assoc.	10,000	Sands Expo Ctr/ Venetian
Jan 11–18	Int'l Solid Surface Fabricators Assoc.	6,000	Mirage
Jan 22–25	National Assoc. of Television Program Executives	20,000	Conv Ctr/Hilton
Jan 28– Feb 5	Las Vegas Antique Arms Show	5,000	Riviera
Feb 11–13	Awards and Recognition Assoc.	6,500	Conv Ctr/Hilton
Feb 11–13	National Grocers Assoc.	4,000	Conv Ctr/ Paris LasVegas
Feb 11–14	American Fence Assoc. Inc.	6,000	Conv Ctr/Multiple
Feb 18–21	Builder Marts of America	2,800	Paris LasVegas
Feb 19–22	Magic International	100,000	Conv Ctr/Hilton
Mar 1–6	Snowsports Industries America	25,000	Conv Ctr/Hilton
Mar 3–6	Truckload Carriers Assoc.	2,100	Bellagio
Mar 4–6	Nightclub & Bar Convention & Trade Show	21,000	Conv Ctr/Aladdin
Mar 5–7	Int'l Security Conference	15,930	Conv Ctr/Hilton
Mar 10–14	Institute of Scrap Recycling Industries	3,000	Bellagio
Mar 16–18	Limousine and Chauffeured Transportation	4,000	ParisLasVegas
Mar 19–23	Conexpo–CON/AGG	150,000	Conv Ctr/Hilton
Mar 20–23	Safari Club Int'l	22,000	Sands Expo Ctr/ Venetian
Mar 21–24	National Open Chess Tournament	2,000	Riviera
Apr 7–11	National Franchisee Assoc. Inc.	2,200	MGM Grand
Apr 8–11	National Assoc. of Broadcasters	125,000	Conv Ctr/Hilton
Apr 13–16	American Truck Dealers Assoc.	2,000	Conv Ctr/Hilton
Apr 13–16	National Automobile Dealers Association Truck Conference	2,600	Hilton

Convention and Special Events Calendar (continued)

Dates	Convention/Event	Number of Attendees	Location/HQ
2002			
Apr 22–25	National Council of Teachers of Mathematics	21,000	Venetian
Apr 23–26	McDonald's Corporation	18,000	Conv Ctr/Hilton
May 13–15	WasteExpo	15,000	Conv Ctr/LasVegas
May 13–19	Int'l Reprographic Association	2,400	ParisLasVegas
May 14–16	Intershow/ The Money Show	11,500	Bally's
May 19–23	National Assoc. of Orthopaedic Nurses	2,500	MGM Grand
Jun 1–3	Int'l Esthetics, Cosmetic & Spa Conference	13,500	Conv Ctr/Hilton
Jun 1–3	Int'l Hair & Nail Conference	5,500	Conv Ctr
Jun 3–9	UAW Constitutional Convention	6,500	MGM Grand
Jun 5–9	Las Vegas Antique Arms Show	2,500	Riviera
Jun 6–8	National Nutritional Foods Assoc.	11,500	Conv Ctr/Hilton
Jun 10–14	National Assoc. of Credit Management	2,500	Bally's
Jun 11–13	Internet Entertainment Expo	20,000	Conv Ctr
Jun 12–14	Satellite Broadcasting & Communications Assoc.	7,500	Conv Ctr/Hilton
Jun 13–15	Int'l Communications Industries Association	2,200	Sands Expo Ctr/ Venetian
Jun 18–19	Bowling Proprietors Association of America	6,500	Conv Ctr
Jun 18–19	ISA–The Instrumentation, Systems, and Automation Society	8,000	Conv Ctr
Jun 19–21	Las Vegas Int'l Hotel Restaurant Gaming Expo	8,000	Conv Ctr/Multiple
Jun 23–27	Int'l SL–1 Users Association Inc. (Nortel)	5,000	Sands Expo Ctr/ Venetian
Jun 23–28	American Federation of State, County, and Municipal Employees (AFL/CIO)	6,500	Bally's
Jun 25–27	Int'l Trucking Show	30,000	Conv Ctr/Hilton
Jun 27–29	Construction Specs. Institute	12,000	Conv Ctr/Hilton

Convention and Special Events Calendar (continued)

Dates	Convention/Event	Number of Attendees	Location/HQ
2002			
Jul 2–7	Vietnam Helicopter Pilots Association	2,300	Riviera
Jul 7–15	National Strength & Conditioning Assoc.	3,500	Riviera
Jul 18–20	Billiard Congress of America	8,000	Conv Ctr/Riviera
Jul 21–25	American Culinary Federation	2,000	MGM Grand
Jul 22–25	Retail Tobacco Dealers of America	5,000	Sands Expo Ctr/ Venetian
Aug 1–3	National Business Media Inc.	8,000	Conv Ctr
Aug 3–19	Int'l Association of Fire Fighters	4,000	Mandalay Bay
Aug 12–15	United Steelworkers of America	2,500	Conv Ctr
Aug 26–29	Magic International	100,000	Conv Ctr/Hilton
Aug 29– Sept 1	Italian Catholic Federation	4,000	Tropicana
Sept 9–11	PGA International Golf Show	23,300	Conv Ctr/Mirage
Sept 17–22	Bass Hotels & Resorts	15,000	Conv Ctr/Multiple
Sept 23–24	Western Food Industry Expo	5,000	Conv Ctr
Sept 23–25	American Public Transportation Association	15,000	Conv Ctr/Hilton
Sept 24–26	Internet Commerce Expo	20,000	Conv Ctr
Oct 1–3	National Assoc. of Elevator Contractors	6,000	Conv Ctr/Hilton
Oct 8–10	Western Rental Equipment Expo	4,000	Conv Ctr/Hilton
Oct 16–18	Int'l Sanitary Supply Assoc.	12,000	Conv Ctr/Hilton
Oct 20–22	Int'l Assoc. for the Leisure	6,500	Sands Expo Ctr/ Mirage
Oct 23–24	Western Nursery & Garden Expo	9,000	Conv Ctr/Multiple
Oct 25–27	Lighting Dimensions Int'l.	15,000	Conv Ctr/Multiple
Oct 27–29	Medical Group Mgmt. Assoc.	8,000	Conv Ctr/Multiple
Oct 29– Nov 2	Urban Land Institute	3,200	Bellagio
Nov 5–8	Automotive Aftermarket Industry Week	85,000	Sands Expo Ctr/ Multiple
Nov 18–22	Comdex Fall	225,000	Conv Ctr/Multiple
Dec 9–12	Bank Administration Institute	10,000	Conv Ctr/Multiple

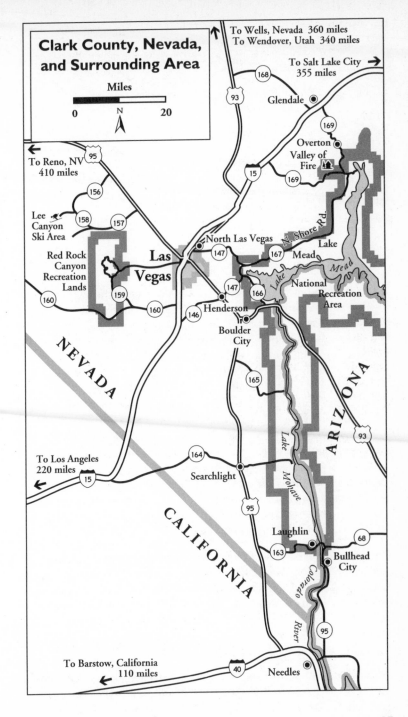

Clark County, Nevada, and Surrounding Area

Miles
0   N   20

To Wells, Nevada 360 miles
To Wendover, Utah 340 miles

To Salt Lake City
355 miles

168

93

Glendale

To Reno, NV
410 miles

95

156

158

157

Lee
Canyon
Ski Area

Red Rock
Canyon
Recreation
Lands

160

159

160

169

Overton
Valley of
Fire

169

15

147

North Las Vegas

167

Lake
Mead

N. Shore Rd.

Lake
Mead

Las
Vegas

147

166

Lake
Mead

National
Recreation
Area

146

Henderson

Boulder
City

NEVADA

165

ARIZONA

93

To Los Angeles
220 miles

15

164

Searchlight

95

Lake
Mohave

Laughlin

163

68

Bullhead
City

95

CALIFORNIA

Colorado
River

To Barstow, California
110 miles

40

Needles

Rental Car Agencies	
At the Terminal	**Off-Airport**
Airport Car Rental	Alamo
All State	Enterprise
Avis	Ladki International
Budget	Practical
Dollar	Resort
Hertz	US Rent-A-Car
National	
Savmor	
Thrifty	

If you rent a car, you will need to catch your rental company's courtesy vehicle at the middle curb of the authorized vehicle lanes. These lanes are at ground level between the baggage claim building and the main terminal.

If someone is picking you up in their car, you should proceed on ground level to the opposite side of the baggage claim building (away from the main terminal) to the baggage claim/arrivals curb. If the person picking you up wants to park and meet you, the best place to hook up is on the ground level of the baggage claim building near the car rental counters where the escalators descend from the main terminal.

There are two ways to exit the airport by car. You can depart via the old route, Swenson Street, which runs north-south roughly paralleling the Strip; or you can hop on the new spur of Interstate 515. Dipping south from the airport, I-515 connects with I-15. We recommend using I-515 if you are headed downtown or to any of the hotels west of the Strip. Swenson Street is a better route if you are going to the Las Vegas Convention Center, to UNLV, or to hotels on or east of the Strip.

Convenience Chart   To give you an idea how convenient your hotel is to common destinations such as the Strip, downtown, the Las Vegas Convention Center, UNLV, and the airport, we have provided a section on getting around. Included in that chapter is a "convenience chart" that lists estimated times by foot and cab from each hotel to the destinations outlined above (see pages 47–49). In the same section are tips for avoiding traffic congestion and for commuting between the Strip and downtown.

Rental Cars   All of the national car rental companies have operations in Las Vegas, and there are also a few local companies. If you rent cars frequently in the course of business or leisure travel, or want to pick up bonus miles on your frequent-flyer account, we recommend patronizing whichever company you normally use.

Each year we observe how long it takes each of the Las Vegas rental car agencies to process customers' paperwork and send them on their way. Interestingly, the car rental agencies with counters at the airport are much faster than agencies located outside the airport. At the airport, most companies complete the paperwork and have you on your way in a zippy five to ten minutes. Outside the airport, processing time ranges from 12 to 20 minutes. For those customers using the off-airport agencies, the processing time is in addition to any time spent waiting for the agency's courtesy vehicle and commuting to the off-airport location. (Courtesy vehicles pick up passengers at the center curb outside the baggage claim building about every 10 to 15 minutes.) The processing time also excludes time spent waiting in line at the rental agency before being served. As a relevant aside to the on- and off-airport comparison, county officials levy a surcharge amounting to 8% of your rental fee if you use an agency not physically located at the airport. With 7% sales tax, 6% state surcharge, and 8% airport fee, rental car taxes can add up to an additional 21% on top of your bill.

At the airport, the process of disembarking from the plane, walking to the baggage area, waiting for and claiming luggage, and proceeding to the car rental counter had the effect of evenly distributing car rental customers. Queues at the airport car rental counters would ebb and flow, but almost never exceeded six to eight customers. The longest airport queues were at the Avis and Hertz counters, but these moved quickly, with enough agents to keep waiting time to a minimum.

In contrast to agencies in the airport, customers of agencies outside the airport were massed into groups as they were picked up by the shuttle buses. Therefore, instead of arriving in a more or less continuous, manageable flow (as at the airport), customers of off-airport agencies frequently descended in veritable platoons.

In the dollar and cents department, prices fluctuate so much from week to week that it's anyone's guess who will offer the best deal during your visit. Our advice is to have your travel agent check rates at all of the rental agencies for the dates in question. Rental car companies list their most competitive rates on the airline computer systems that travel agents use. Also, rental companies will give you better service when they are accountable to two persons: you and your travel agent, who is a potential source of additional business.

Be aware that Las Vegas is a feast-or-famine city when it comes to rental car availability. On many weekends, or when a citywide convention is in town, it may be impossible to get a rental car unless you reserved way in advance. If, on the other hand, you come to town when business is slow, the rental agencies will practically give you a car. We have been able to rent from the most expensive companies for as little as $22 a day under these circumstances. If you are certain that you are visiting during a slow time, reserve a car in advance to cover yourself and then, on arrival, ask each rental company to quote you its best price. If you can beat the price on your reserved car, go for it.

When you (or your travel agent) call to reserve a rental car, ask for the smallest, least expensive car in the company's inventory, even if you ultimately intend to rent a larger vehicle. Chances are you will be upgraded without charge when you arrive. If not, rental agencies frequently offer on-site upgrade incentives that beat any deals you can make in advance. Always compare daily and weekly rates.

If you decline insurance coverage on the rental car because of protection provided by your credit card, be aware that the coverage provided by the credit card is secondary to your regular auto insurance policy. In most situations the credit card coverage only reimburses you the deductible on your regular policy. Also be aware that some car rental contracts require that you drive the car only in Nevada. If you, like many tourists, visit Hoover Dam or trek out to the Grand Canyon, you will cross into Arizona. Another item to check in advance, if applicable, is whether your rental agency charges for additional drivers.

When you rent your car, make sure you understand the implications of bringing it back empty of fuel. Some companies will charge $3 or more per gallon if they have to fill the tank on return. We returned a car with between a third and a half tank of gas remaining and were charged $36, the same as if we had coasted in with a completely empty tank. Also, beware of signs at the car rental counters reading "Gas Today—$1.35 per gallon" or some such. That price usually applies to the gas already in the car when you rent it, not the price per gallon of a fill-up should you return the car empty. The price per gallon for a fill-up on return will be somewhere in the fine print of your rental contract.

Another rental car problem we encountered involved a pinhead-sized chip on the windshield. Understanding the fine print of rental car contracts, and because we always decline the insurance offered by the agencies, we inspect our cars thoroughly for any damage before accepting the car and leaving the lot. In this instance, as always, we inspected the car thoroughly and did not notice any windshield flaws. When we returned the car after three days, we were requested to remain at the counter to complete an "accident report." Insisting that we were unaware of any damage, we requested that the car be retrieved for our inspection. Still unable to find the alleged damage, we asked the counter agent to identify it for us. The agent responsible for the accident report then had to scrutinize the windshield for half a minute before she could find the mark, even though she knew its exact location from the employee who checked the car in. The conclusion to be drawn here is that if you decline coverage, the rental agency may hold you responsible for even the tiniest damage, damage so slight that you may never notice it. Before you leave the lot, inspect your rental car with care, scrutinizing every inch, and have the agency record anything you find. This will not inhibit them from charging you for damage sustained while the car is in your possession, but at least you will have the peace of mind of knowing that they are not putting one over on you.

Some rental companies will charge you for "loss of use" if you have an accident that takes the car out of use. Since some car insurance policies do not pay loss-of-use charges, check your coverage with your insurance agent before you rent. Finally, if you use a credit card to pay for your rental car, be aware that Diner's Club offers the best supplemental insurance coverage.

LAS VEGAS CUSTOMS AND PROTOCOL

In a town where the most bizarre behavior imaginable is routinely tolerated, it is ironic that so many visitors obsess over what constitutes proper protocol. This mentality stems mainly from the myriad customs peculiar to gaming and the *perceived* glamour of the city itself. First-timers attach a great deal of importance to "fitting in." What makes this task difficult, at least in part, is that half of the people they are trying to fit in with are first-timers too.

The only hard rules for being accepted downtown or on the Strip are to have a shirt on your back, shoes on your feet, some manner of clothing below the waist, and a little money in your pocket. Concerning the latter, there is no maximum. The operational minimum is bus fare back to wherever you came from.

This notwithstanding, there are three basic areas in which Las Vegas first-timers tend to feel especially insecure:

Gambling The various oddities of gaming protocol are described under the respective casino games in the chapter on gambling (see page 287). Understand, however, that despite appearances, gambling is very informal. While it is intelligent not to play a game when/if you do not know how, it is unwarranted to abstain because you are uncertain of the protocol. What little protocol exists (things like holding your cards above the table and keeping your hands away from your bet once play has begun) has evolved to protect the house and honest players from cheats. Dealers (a generic term for those who conduct table games) are not under orders to be unfriendly, silent, or rigid. Observe a game that interests you before you sit down. Assure yourself that the dealer is personable and polite. Never play in a casino where the staff is surly or cold; life's too short.

Eating in Gourmet Restaurants These are mostly meat and potatoes places with fancy names, so there is no real reason to be intimidated. Men will feel more comfortable in sport coats, but ties are optional. Women turn up in everything from slacks and blouses to evening wear. When you sit down, a whole platoon of waiters will attend you. Do not remove your napkin from the table. In gourmet rooms, only the waiters are allowed to place napkins in the laps of patrons. After the ceremonial placement of the napkin, the senior waiter will speak. When he concludes, you may order cocktails, consider the menu, sip your water, or engage in conversation. If there are women in your party, their menus will not have prices listed. If your party is totally comprised of women, a menu with prices listed will be given to the woman who looks the oldest. When you are ready to order, even if you only want a steak and fries, do not speak until the waiter has had an opportunity to recite in French from the menu. To really please your waiters, order something that can be prepared tableside with dramatic flames and explosions. If your waiters seem stuffy or aloof, ask them to grind peppercorns or Parmesan cheese on something. This will usually loosen them up.

There will be enough utensils on the table to perform a triple bypass. Because these items are considered expendable, use a different utensil for each dish, surrendering it to the waiter along with the empty plate at the end of the course. If there are small yellow sculptures on the table, they are probably butter.

Tipping   Because about a third of the resident population of Las Vegas are service providers in the tourist industry, there is no scarcity of people to tip. From the day you arrive until the day you depart, you will be interacting with redcaps, porters, cabbies, valet parking attendants, bellhops, waiters, maître d's, dealers, bartenders, keno runners, housekeeping personnel, room service, and others.

Tipping is an issue that makes some travelers very uncomfortable. How much? When? To whom? Not leaving a tip when one is customary makes you feel inexperienced. Not knowing how much to tip makes you feel vulnerable and out of control. Is the tip you normally leave at home appropriate in Las Vegas?

The most important thing to bear in mind is that a tip is not automatic, nor is it an obligation. A tip is a reward for good service. The following suggestions are based on traditional practices in Las Vegas:

Porters and Redcaps   A dollar a bag.

Cab Drivers   A lot depends on the service and the courtesy. If the fare is less than $8, give the cabbie the change and $1. On a $4.50 fare, in other words, give him the 50 cents change plus a buck. If the fare is more than $8, give the cabbie the change and $2. If you are asking the cabbie to take you only a block or two, the fare will be small, but your tip should be large ($3–

5) to make up for his wait in line and to partially compensate him for missing a better-paying fare. Add an extra dollar to your tip if the cabbie does a lot of luggage handling.

Valet Parking   Two dollars is correct if the valet is courteous and demonstrates some hustle. A dollar will do if the service is just OK. Only pay when you take your car out, not when you leave it. Because valet attendants pool their tips, both of the individuals who assist you (coming and going) will be taken care of.

Bellmen   When a bellhop greets you at your car with one of those rolling carts and handles all of your bags, $5 is about right. The more of your luggage that you carry, of course, the less you should tip. Sometimes bellhops who handle only a small bag or two will put on a real performance when showing you your room. I had a bellhop in one Strip hotel walk into my room, crank up the air conditioner, turn on the television, throw open the blinds, flick on all the lights, flush the commode, and test the water pressure in the tub. Give me a break. I tipped the same as if he had simply opened the door and put my luggage in the room.

Waiters   Whether in a coffee shop, a gourmet room, or ordering from room service, the standard gratuity for acceptable service is 15% of the total tab, before sales tax. At a buffet or brunch where you serve yourself, it is customary to leave $1–2 for the folks who bring your drinks and bus your dishes.

Cocktail Waiters/Bartenders   Here you tip by the round. For two people, $1 a round; for more than two people, $2 a round. For a large group, use your judgment: Is everyone drinking beer, or is the order long and complicated? In casinos where drinks are sometimes on the house, it is considered good form to tip the server $1 per round or per every couple of rounds.

Dealers and Slot Attendants   If you are winning, it is a nice gesture to tip the dealer or place a small bet for him. How much depends on your winnings and on your level of play. With slot attendants, tip when they perform a specific service or when you hit a jackpot. In general, unless other services are also rendered, it is not customary to tip change makers or cashiers.

Keno Runners   Tip if you have a winner or if the runner really provides fast, efficient service. How much to tip will vary with your winnings and with your level of play.

Showroom Maître d's, Captains, and Servers   There is more to this than you might expect. If you are planning to take in a show, see our suggestions for tipping in the chapter on entertainment (see page 209).

Hotel Maids   On checking out, leave $1–2 for each day you stayed, providing the service was good.

How to Look and Sound Like a Las Vegas Old-Timer   If you wish to appear as if you are a real Las Vegas veteran, there are several affectations that will give you credibility:

- Never refer to Las Vegas as "Vegas."

- Lament the disappearance of the Elvis statue from the front of the Boardwalk.

- Comment often and disparagingly about traffic on the Strip.

- Knowledgeably discuss Las Vegas's six big implosions (Dunes, Landmark, Hacienda, Aladdin, Sands, El Rancho).

DOES ANYONE KNOW WHAT'S GOING ON AT HOME? (DOES ANYONE REALLY CARE?)

If you are more interested in what you are missing at home than what is going on in Las Vegas, Borders Book Shop at 2323 South Decatur Boulevard stocks Sunday papers from most major cities. To find out whether Borders stocks your favorite newspaper, call (702) 258-0999.

Las Vegas as a Family Destination

Occasionally the publisher sends me around to promote the *Unofficial Guide* on radio and television, and every year I am asked the same question: Is Las Vegas a good place for a family vacation?

Objectively speaking, Las Vegas is a great place for a family vacation. Food and lodging are a bargain, and there are an extraordinary number of things, from swimming at Wet 'n Wild to rafting through the Black Canyon on the Colorado River, that the entire family can enjoy together. If you take your kids to Las Vegas *and forget gambling,* Las Vegas compares favorably with every family tourist destination in the United States. The rub, of course, is that gambling in Las Vegas is pretty hard to ignore.

The marketing gurus, as you may have observed, have tried mightily to recast the town's image and to position Las Vegas as a family destination. The strategy no doubt attracts some parents already drawn to gambling but previously unwilling to allocate family vacation time to a Las Vegas trip. Excepting these relatively few families, however, it takes a lot more than hype to convince most parents that Las Vegas is a suitable destination for a family vacation.

For years, Las Vegas has been touted as a place to *get away* from your kids. For family tourism to succeed in Las Vegas, that characterization has to be changed, or at least minimized. Next, and much more unlikely, gambling must be relegated to a position of secondary importance. There is gambling on cruise ships, for example, but gambling is not the primary reason people go on cruises. Las Vegas, similarly, cannot develop as a bona fide family destination until something supersedes gambling as the main draw. Not very likely. The MGM Grand Adventures Theme Park and Adventuredome at Circus Circus represent a start, but they are only a fraction of what Las Vegas will require to achieve critical mass as a family vacation venue.

To legitimately appeal to the family travel market, the city must consider the real needs of children and parents. Instead of banishing children to midway and electronic games arcades, hotels need to offer substantive, educational, supervised programs or "camps" for children. The Station casinos are breaking some new ground in this area. Additionally, and equally important, Las Vegas must target and sell the family tourist trade in nontraditional geographic markets. Though Southern California is Las Vegas's largest and most lucrative market, it's not reasonable to expect families with Disneyland, SeaWorld, and Universal Studios in their backyard to travel to Las Vegas to visit a theme park.

TAKING YOUR CHILDREN TO LAS VEGAS TODAY

Las Vegas today is a fairly adult tourist destination. As a city (including the surrounding area), however, it has a lot to offer children. What this essentially means is that the Strip and downtown have not been developed with children in mind, but if you are willing to make the effort to venture away from the gambling areas there are a lot of fun and wholesome things for families to do. As a rule, however, people do not go to Las Vegas to be continually absent from the casinos.

Persons under age 21 are not allowed to gamble, nor are they allowed to hang around while *you* gamble. If you are gambling, your children have to be somewhere else. On the Strip and downtown, the choices are limited. True, most Las Vegas hotels have nice swimming pools, but Las Vegas summer days are much too hot to stay out for long. While golf and tennis are possibilities, court or greens fees are routinely charged, and you still must contend with limitations imposed by the desert climate.

After a short time, you will discover that the current options for your children's recreation and amusement are as follows:

1. You can simply allow your children to hang out. Given this alternative, the kids will swim a little, watch some TV, eat as much as

their (or your) funds allow, throw water balloons out of any hotel window that has not been hermetically sealed, and cruise up and down the Strip (or Fremont Street) on foot, ducking in and out of souvenir stores and casinos.

2. If your children are a mature age ten or older, you can turn them loose at the Adventuredome at Circus Circus or at the Wet 'n Wild swimming park. At both parks, however, the kids will probably cut bait and go cruising after two hours of Grand Slam and about four hours of Wet 'n Wild.

3. You can hire a baby-sitter to come to your hotel room and tend your children. This works out pretty much like option 1 without the water balloons and the cruising.

4. You can abandon the casino (or whatever else you had in mind) and "do things" with your kids. Swimming and eating (as always) will figure prominently into the plan, as will excursions to places that have engaged the children's curiosity. You can bet that your kids will want to go to the Adventuredome at Circus Circus and probably to the Wet 'n Wild swimming park. The white tigers, dolphins, and exploding volcano at the Mirage; the naval battle at Treasure Island; the MGM Grand Lion Habitat; the high-tech attractions at the Luxor, the Sahara, the Forum Shops, and the Las Vegas Hilton; and the Stratosphere Tower are big hits with kids. The Excalibur offers a sort of movie/ride in which you feel as if you are riding a real roller coaster. New York–New York and the Sahara each feature a real roller coaster. If you have two children and do a fraction of all this stuff in one day, you will spend $80 to $250 for the four of you, not counting meals and transportation.

If you have a car there are lots of great, inexpensive places to go—enough to keep you busy for days. We recommend Red Rock Canyon and Hoover Dam for sure. On the way to Hoover Dam, you can stop for a tour of the Ethel M. Chocolate Factory.

A great half-day excursion (during the spring and fall) is a guided raft trip through the Black Canyon on the Colorado River. This can easily be combined with a visit to Hoover Dam. Trips to the Valley of Fire State Park (driving, biking, hiking) are also recommended during the more temperate seasons.

Around Las Vegas there are a number of real museums and museum-cum–tourist attractions. The Lied Discovery Children's Museum (just north of downtown) is worthwhile, affordable, and a big favorite with kids age 14 and younger. While you are in the neighborhood, try the Natural History Museum directly across the street.

5. You can pay someone else to take your kids on excursions. Some in-room sitters (bonded and from reputable agencies) will take your kids around as long as you foot the bill. For recommendations, check with the concierge or front desk of your hotel. Another option, if your kids are over age 12, is to pack them off on a guided tour, advertised by the handful in the various local visitor magazines.

Hotels That Solicit Family Business

Only Circus Circus and the Excalibur actively seek the family trade with carnival game midways where children and adults can try to win stuffed animals, foam rubber dice, and other oddities. A great setup for the casinos, the midways turn a nice profit while innocuously introducing the youngsters to games of chance. In addition, Circus Circus operates the Adventuredome theme park and offers free circus acts each evening, starring top-notch talent, including aerialists (flying trapeze). The Excalibur provides family-oriented production shows, as well as impromptu magic, puppet, and comedy shows in its second-floor Medieval Village. Both hotels offer reasonably priced rooms and inexpensive food and drink. The Excalibur has the better swimming pool of the two, but Circus Circus offers the nicer guest rooms (Excalibur bathrooms are equipped with a shower only, i.e., no tub).

Parents traveling with children are welcome at all of the larger hotels, though certain hotels are better equipped to deal with children than others. If your children are water puppies and can enjoy being in a swimming pool all day, Mandalay Bay, Venetian, Aladdin, Flamingo, Monte Carlo, MGM Grand, Mirage, Rio, Tropicana, Caesars Palace, Bellagio, and Treasure Island have the nicest pools in town. The Las Vegas Hilton and Hard Rock Hotel, among others, also have excellent swimming facilities.

If your kids are older and into sports, the MGM Grand, along with Caesars Palace, the Las Vegas Hilton, and Bally's, offer the most variety. During the warmer months you can't beat Santa Fe Station, with its hockey-sized ice skating rink (open all year) and huge bowling complex.

When it comes to childcare and special programs, the MGM Grand, Sunset Station, Venetian, Orleans, Suncoast, and Gold Coast along with the Hampton Inn provide childcare facilities.

Tours and Excursions

For the most part, the various bus sight-seeing tours available in Las Vegas offer two things: Transportation and drivers who know where they're going. In our opinion, if you have a car and can read a map, you will save both money and hassle by going on your own.

Special Events

There is almost always something fun going on in Las Vegas outside of gambling. Among other things, there are minor league baseball, rodeos, concerts, UNLV basketball and football, and, of course, movies. If you are traveling with children, it's worth the effort to pick up a local newspaper and check out what's going on.

Part One

Lodging and Casinos

Where to Stay: Basic Choices

THE LAS VEGAS STRIP AND DOWNTOWN

From a visitor's perspective, Las Vegas is more or less a small town and fairly easy to get around in. Most of the major hotels and casinos are in two areas: Downtown and on Las Vegas Boulevard, known as the Strip.

The downtown hotels and casinos are often characterized as older and smaller than those on the Strip. While this is true in a general sense, there are both large and elegant hotels downtown. What really differentiates downtown is the incredible concentration of casinos and hotels in a relatively small area. Along Fremont Street, downtown's main thoroughfare, the casinos present a continuous, dazzling galaxy of neon and twinkling lights for more than four city blocks. Known as Glitter Gulch, these several dozen gambling emporiums are sandwiched together in colorful profusion in an area barely larger than a parking lot at a good-sized shopping mall.

Contrast in the size, style, elegance, and presentation of the downtown casinos provides a varied mix, combining extravagant luxury and cosmopolitan sophistication with an Old West boom-town decadence. Though not directly comparable, downtown Las Vegas has the feel of New Orleans's Bourbon Street: alluring, exotic, wicked, sultry, foreign, and above all, diverse. It is a place where cowboy, businessperson, showgirl, and retiree mix easily. And like Bourbon Street, it is all accessible on foot.

If downtown is the French Quarter of Las Vegas, then the Strip is Plantation Row. Here, huge resort hotel-casinos sprawl like estates along a four-mile section of Las Vegas Boulevard South. Each hotel is a vacation destination unto itself, with casino, hotel, restaurants, pools, spas, landscaped grounds, and even golf courses. While the downtown casinos are fused into a vibrant, integrated whole, the huge hotels on the Strip demand individual recognition.

While the Strip is literally a specific length of Las Vegas Boulevard South, a larger area is usually included when discussing hotels, casinos, restaurants, and attractions. East and parallel to the Strip is Paradise Road, where the Las Vegas Convention Center and several hotels are located. Also included in the Strip area are hotels and casinos on streets intersecting Las Vegas Boulevard, as well as properties positioned to the immediate west of the Strip (on the far side of I-15).

Choosing a Hotel

The variables that figure most prominently in choosing a hotel are price, location, your itinerary, and your quality requirements. Downtown, on Boulder Highway, on the Strip, and elsewhere in Las Vegas, there is a wide selection of lodging with myriad combinations of price and value. Given this, your main criteria for selecting a hotel should be its location and your itinerary.

The Strip vs. Downtown for Leisure Travelers

Though there are some excellent hotels on the Boulder Highway and elsewhere around town, the choice for most vacation travelers is whether to stay downtown or on (or near) the Strip. Downtown offers a good choice of hotels, restaurants, and gambling, but only a limited choice of entertainment, and fewer amenities such as swimming pools and spas. There are no golf courses and only four tennis courts downtown. If you have a car, the Strip is an 8- to 15-minute commute from downtown via I-15. If you do not have a car, public transportation from downtown to the Strip is as efficient as Las Vegas traffic allows and quite affordable.

If you stay on the Strip, you are more likely to need a car or require some sort of transportation. There are more hotels to choose from on the Strip, but they are spread over a much wider area and are often (but not always) pricier than downtown. On the Strip, one has a sense of space and elbow room, as many of the hotels are constructed on a grand scale. The selection of entertainment is both varied and extensive on the Strip, and Strip recreational facilities rival those of the world's leading resorts.

Downtown is a multicultural, multilingual melting pot with an adventurous, raw, robust feel. Everything in this part of town seems intense and concentrated, an endless blur of action, movement, and light. Diversity and history conspire in lending vitality and excitement to this older part of Las Vegas, an essence more tangible and real than the monumental, plastic themes and fantasies of many large Strip establishments.

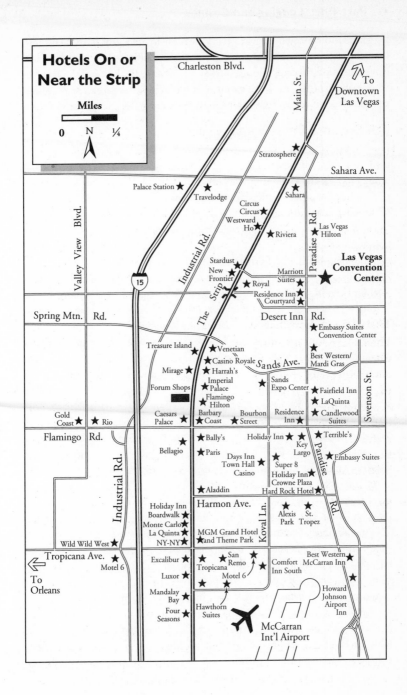

Hotels On or Near the Strip

Miles

0   N   ¼

Charleston Blvd.

Main St.

To Downtown Las Vegas

Stratosphere ★

Sahara Ave.

Palace Station ★   ★
         Travelodge ★
                  Circus
                  Circus ★   Sahara ★
              Westward
              Ho ★
                     ★ Riviera   Las Vegas ★ Hilton

Valley View Blvd.

Industrial Rd.

15

The Strip

Paradise Rd.

Stardust ★
New ★
Frontier ★
         ★ Royal
              Marriott
              Suites ★
         Residence Inn ★
              Courtyard ★

Las Vegas Convention Center ★

Spring Mtn. Rd.

Desert Inn   Rd.
              ★ Embassy Suites
                 Convention Center

Treasure Island ★
         ★ Venetian
         ★ Casino Royale   Sands Ave.
Mirage ★   ★ Harrah's
         Imperial
Forum Shops   ★ Palace   Sands
              Flamingo   Expo Center
              ★ Hilton
Gold   Barbary   Bourbon   Residence
Coast ★   ★ Rio   Caesars ★ Coast ★ ★ Street   Inn ★
              Palace

★ Best Western/
   Mardi Gras

Swenson St.

★ Fairfield Inn
★ LaQuinta
★ Candlewood
   Suites

Flamingo   Rd.

Industrial Rd.

Bellagio ★
         ★ Bally's   Holiday Inn ★ ★   ★ Terrible's
         ★ Paris   Key
              Days Inn   Largo
              Town Hall ★   ★   ★ Embassy Suites
              Casino   Super 8
                        Holiday Inn ★
                        Crowne Plaza
         ★ Aladdin   Hard Rock Hotel ★

Paradise Rd.

Harmon Ave.
Holiday Inn
Boardwalk ★   ★   ★
Monte Carlo ★   Alexis   St.
La Quinta ★   Park   Tropez
NY-NY ★   MGM Grand Hotel
              and Theme Park

Koval Ln.

Wild Wild West ★

Tropicana Ave.
              ★
         Motel 6
To Orleans

Excalibur ★   ★ ★ San ★   Best Western ★
         Tropicana Remo   Comfort   McCarran Inn
Luxor ★   ★ Motel 6   Inn South   ★
Mandalay ★   Howard
Bay   Johnson
Hawthorn ★   Airport
Four ★ Suites   Inn
Seasons

McCarran Int'l Airport

41

Though downtown caters to every class of clientele, it is less formal and, with exceptions, more of a working man's gambling town. Here the truck driver and welder gamble alongside the secretary, the Realtor, and the rancher. The Strip, likewise, runs the gamut but tends to attract more high rollers, middle-class suburbanites, and business travelers going to conventions.

The Fremont Street Experience

For years, downtown casinos watched from the sidelines as Strip hotels turned into veritable tourist attractions. There was nothing downtown, for example, to rival the exploding volcano at the Mirage, the theme parks at Circus Circus, the pirate battle at Treasure Island, or the view from the Stratosphere Tower. As gambling revenue dwindled and more customers defected to the Strip, downtown casino owners finally got serious about mounting a counterattack.

The counterattack, known as the Fremont Street Experience, was launched at the end of 1995. Its basic purpose was to transform downtown into an ongoing event, a continuous party, a happening. Fremont Street through the heart of Glitter Gulch was forever closed to vehicular traffic and turned into a park with terraces, street musicians, and landscaping. An aesthetically pleasing environment, Las Vegas–style, the project united all of the casinos in a sort of diverse gambling mall.

Transformative events on the ground aside, however, the main draw of the Fremont Street Experience is up in the air. Four blocks of Fremont Street are covered by a 1,400-foot-long, 90-foot-high "space frame"—an enormous, vaulted, geodesic matrix. This futuristic structure totally canopies Fremont Street. In addition to providing nominal shade from the blistering sun, the space frame serves as the stage for a nighttime attraction that has definitely improved downtown's fortune. Set into the inner surface of the space frame are 2.1 million tiny lights, which come to life in a computer-driven, multisensory show. The small lights are augmented by 40 speakers on each block, booming symphonic sound in syncopation with the lights.

That the Fremont Street Experience turns downtown Las Vegas into a unique urban theater is beyond dispute. What remains to be seen is whether visitors, the vast majority of whom lodge on the Strip, will continue to venture downtown to enjoy the show. This writer's guess is that they will want to but may not because of Las Vegas's increasingly horrendous traffic.

We at the *Unofficial Guide* enjoy and appreciate downtown Las Vegas, and all of us hope that the Fremont Street Experience will continue to have a beneficial effect. We are amazed and appalled, however, by the city's general lack of commitment to improving its infrastructure, particularly the

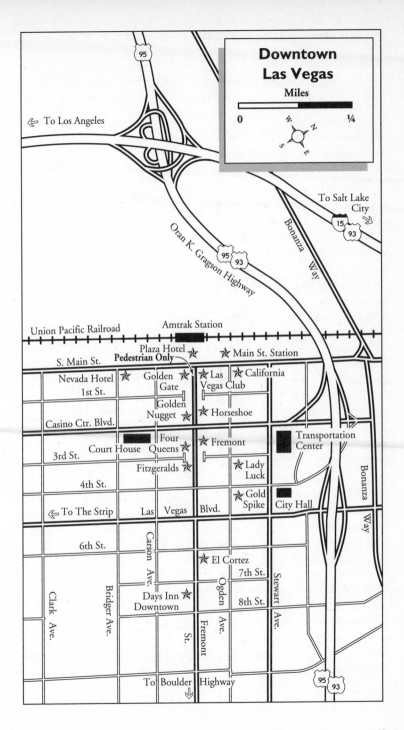

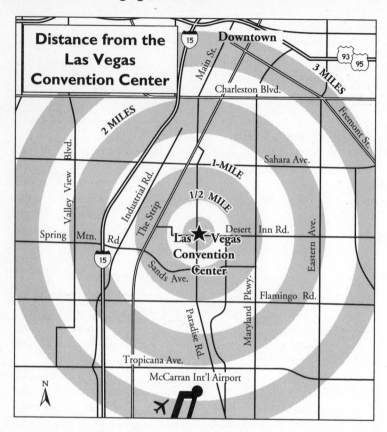

traffic situation. The market, in terms of aggregate numbers of gamblers, is undeniably located out on the Strip. To create an attraction sufficiently compelling to lure this market downtown is to fight only half the battle. The other half of the battle is to make it easy for all those folks on the Strip to get downtown, and on this front the war is being lost.

If You Visit Las Vegas on Business

If you are going to Las Vegas for a trade show or convention, you will want to lodge as close as possible to the meeting site, ideally within easy walking distance. Many Strip hotel-casinos, including the Riviera, Stardust, Flamingo, Venetian, Paris, Bellagio, Mandalay Bay, Aladdin, Las Vegas Hilton, MGM Grand, Treasure Island, Tropicana, Sahara, Mirage, Caesars Palace, Harrah's, and Bally's, host meetings of from 100 to 2,000 attendees, offer lodging for citywide shows and conventions held at the Las Vegas Convention Center, and have good track records with business travelers.

Our maps should provide some assistance in determining which hotels and motels are situated near your meeting site.

Because most large meetings and trade shows are headquartered at the Convention Center or on the Strip, lodging on the Strip is more convenient than staying downtown. Citywide conventions often provide a shuttle service from the major hotels to the Las Vegas Convention Center, and, of course, cabs are available, too. Las Vegas traffic is a mess, however, particularly in the late afternoon, and there are a finite number of cabs. The best bet, if you can swing it, is either to stay in the convention's host hotel or within walking distance. One alternative to staying near your meeting site is to find a good deal on a room elsewhere around town and commute to your meeting in a rental car. Often the savings on the room will pay for the transportation.

Large Hotel-Casinos vs. Small Hotels and Motels

Lodging properties in Las Vegas range from tiny motels with a dozen rooms to colossal hotel-casino-resort complexes of 5,000 rooms. As you might expect, there are advantages and drawbacks to staying in either a large or small hotel. Determining which size is better for you depends on how you plan to spend your time in Las Vegas.

If your leisure or business itinerary calls for a car and a lot of coming and going, the big hotels can be a real pain. At the Luxor, Excalibur, and Las Vegas Hilton, for example, it can take as long as 15 minutes to get from your room to your car if you use the self-parking lot. A young couple staying at the Las Vegas Hilton left their hotel room 40 minutes prior to their show reservations at the Mirage. After trooping to their van in the Hilton's distant self-parking lot, the couple discovered they had forgotten their show tickets. By the time the husband ran back to their room to retrieve the tickets and returned to the van, only five minutes remained to drive to the Mirage, park, and find the showroom. As it turned out, they missed the first 15 minutes of the performance.

Many other large hotels have multistory, self-parking garages that require lengthy and dizzying drives up and down ramps. If you plan to use the car frequently and do not want to deal with the hassle of remote parking lots, big garages, or the tipping associated with valet parking, we recommend that you stay in a smaller hotel or motel that provides quick and convenient access to your car.

Quiet and tranquility can also be reasons for choosing a smaller hotel. Many Las Vegas visitors object to passing through a casino whenever they go to or leave their room. Staying in a smaller property without a casino permits an escape from the flashing lights, the never-ending clanking of coins, and the unremitting, frenetic pace of an around-the-clock gambling town. While they may not be as exciting, smaller hotels tend to be more restful and homelike.

The ease and simplicity of checking in and out of smaller properties has its own appeal. To be able to check in or pay your bill without standing in a line, or to unload and load the car directly and conveniently, all significantly diminish the stress of arriving and departing. When we visited the registration lobby of one of the larger hotels on a Friday afternoon, for example, it reminded us of Kennedy International Airport shut down by a winter storm. Guests were stacked dozens deep in the check-in queues. Others, having abandoned any hope of registering in the near future, slept curled up around their luggage or sat reading on the floor. The whole lobby was awash in suitcases, hanging bags, and people milling about. Though hotel size and check-in efficiency are not always inversely related, the sight of a registration lobby fitted out like the queuing area of Disneyland's Jungle Cruise should be enough to make a sane person think twice.

Along similar lines, a large hotel does not ensure more comfortable or more luxurious accommodations. In Las Vegas there are exceptionally posh and well-designed rooms in both large and small hotels, just as there are threadbare and poorly designed rooms in properties of every size. A large establishment does, however, usually ensure a superior range of amenities, including on-site entertainment, room service, spas or exercise rooms, concierge services, bell services, valet parking, meeting rooms, baby-sitting, shoe shining, dry cleaning, shopping, 24-hour restaurants, copy and fax services, check cashing, and, of course, gambling.

If you plan to do most of your touring on foot or are attending a convention, a large hotel in a good location has its advantages. There will be a variety of restaurants, entertainment, shopping, and recreation close at hand. In case you are a night owl, you will be able to eat or drink at any hour, and there will always be lots going on. Many showrooms offer 11 p.m. or midnight shows, and quite a few hotels (Sam's Town, Castaways, Suncoast, Gold Coast, Orleans, Santa Fe Station) have 24-hour bowling.

For visitors who wish to immerse themselves in the atmosphere of Las Vegas, to live in the fast lane, and to be where the action is, a large hotel is recommended. These people feel they are missing something unless they stay in a large hotel-casino. For them, it is important to know that the excitement is only an elevator ride away.

Getting Around:
Location and Convenience

LAS VEGAS LODGING CONVENIENCE CHART

The following chart will give you a feel for how convenient specific hotels and motels are to common Las Vegas destinations. Both walking and cab commuting times are figured on the conservative side. You should be able to do a little better than the times indicated, particularly by cab, unless you are traveling during rush hour or attempting to navigate the Strip on a weekend evening.

Commuting Time in Minutes				
From:	**To:**			UNLV Thomas
Hotel	Las Vegas Strip	Convention Center	Down-town	McCarran Airport	& Mack Center
Aladdin	on Strip	8/cab	15/cab	7/cab	8/cab
Alexis Park	5/cab	8/cab	15/cab	5/cab	6/cab
AmeriSuites	4/cab	5/walk	15/cab	10/cab	9/cab
Arizona Charlie's East	19/cab	18/cab	12/cab	21/cab	20/cab
Arizona Charlie's West	12/cab	18/cab	12/cab	20/cab	22/cab
Bally's	on Strip	8/cab	15/cab	7/cab	7/cab
Barbary Coast	on Strip	10/cab	15/cab	8/cab	9/cab
Bellagio	on Strip	12/cab	15/cab	11/cab	12/cab
Best Western Mardi Gras	6/cab	10/walk	15/cab	9/cab	7/cab
Best Western McCarran Inn	6/cab	9/cab	15/cab	4/cab	7/cab
Boardwalk Holiday Inn	on Strip	12/cab	15/cab	11/cab	12/cab
Boulder Station	19/cab	18/cab	12/cab	21/cab	20/cab
Bourbon Street	4/walk	8/cab	15/cab	7/cab	7/cab
Caesars Palace	on Strip	10/cab	12/cab	10/cab	10/cab
California	13/cab	15/cab	downtown	19/cab	19/cab
Casino Royale	on Strip	9/cab	14/cab	10/cab	10/cab
Castaways	19/cab	18/cab	12/cab	21/cab	20/cab
Circus Circus	on Strip	5/cab	13/cab	14/cab	13/cab
Comfort Inn	3/cab	9/cab	15/cab	4/cab	6/cab-
Courtyard	4/cab	5/walk	15/cab	9/cab	8/cab

Commuting Time in Minutes (continued)

From: Hotel	To: Las Vegas Strip	Convention Center	Down-town	McCarran Airport	UNLV Thomas & Mack Center
El Cortez	11/cab	15/cab	6/walk	16/cab	17/cab
Excalibur	on Strip	13/cab	14/cab	7/cab	8/cab
E-Z 8 Motel	4/cab	9/cab	12/cab	9/cab	10/cab
Fairfield Inn	5/cab	5/cab	15/cab	9/cab	8/cab
Fiesta Hotel	18/cab	18/cab	10/cab	22/cab	22/cab
Fitzgeralds	14/cab	15/cab	downtown	17/cab	17/cab
Flamingo Hilton	on Strip	9/cab	13/cab	8/cab	8/cab
Four Queens	15/cab	15/cab	downtown	19/cab	17/cab
Four Seasons	on Strip	14/cab	15/cab	7/cab	13/cab
Fremont	15/cab	15/cab	downtown	19/cab	17/cab
Frontier	on Strip	8/cab	13/cab	11/cab	10/cab
Gold Coast	4/cab	13/cab	14/cab	10/cab	10/cab
Gold Spike	14/cab	15/cab	4/walk	18/cab	17/cab
Golden Gate	14/cab	15/cab	downtown	19/cab	18/cab
Golden Nugget	14/cab	15/cab	downtown	18/cab	19/cab
Green Valley Ranch Station	15/cab	18/cab	16/cab	15/cab	14/cab
Hard Rock Hotel	4/cab	6/cab	15/cab	6/cab	6/cab
Harrah's	on Strip	9/cab	15/cab	10/cab	10/cab
Holiday Inn Crowne Plaza	5/cab	5/cab	14/cab	8/cab	6/cab
Holiday Inn Emerald Springs	4/cab	8/cab	15/cab	7/cab	7/cab
Horseshoe	14/cab	15/cab	downtown	19/cab	19/cab
Howard Johnson	4/cab	14/cab	14/cab	9/cab	11/cab
Howard Johnson Airport	5/cab	7/cab	15/cab	3/cab	5/cab
Imperial Palace	on Strip	9/cab	15/cab	10/cab	10/cab
King 8	4/cab	13/cab	14/cab	8/cab	10/cab
Lady Luck	14/cab	15/cab	3/walk	19/cab	18/cab
Las Vegas Club	14/cab	15/cab	downtown	19/cab	18/cab
Las Vegas Hilton	5/cab	5/walk	13/cab	10/cab	8/cab
Luxor	on Strip	13/cab	15/cab	8/cab	10/cab
Main Street Station	14/cab	15/cab	downtown	19/cab	19/cab
Mandalay Bay	on Strip	14/cab	16/cab	7/cab	13/cab
Marriott Suites	14/cab	5/walk	15/cab	10/cab	9/cab
Maxim	4/walk	8/cab	15/cab	7/cab	7/cab
MGM Grand	on Strip	12/cab	15/cab	9/cab	9/cab

Commuting Time in Minutes (continued)

From: Hotel	To: Las Vegas Strip	Convention Center	Down-town	McCarran Airport	UNLV Thomas & Mack Center
Mirage	on Strip	11/cab	15/cab	11/cab	10/cab
Monte Carlo	on Strip	12/cab	15/cab	11/cab	12/cab
Motel 6 (Tropicana)	3/cab	12/cab	15/cab	6/cab	8/cab
Nevada Hotel	14/cab	15/cab	downtown	19/cab	18/cab
Nevada Palace	21/cab	26/cab	21/cab	19/cab	18/cab
New York– New York	on Strip	12/cab	15/cab	11/cab	12/cab
Orleans	4/cab	15/cab	14/cab	11/cab	11/cab
Palace Station	5/cab	10/cab	10/cab	14/cab	15/cab
Palm	5/cab	13/cab	14/cab	10/cab	10/cab
Paris	on Strip	9/cab	15/cab	8/cab	8/cab
Plaza Hotel	14/cab	15/cab	downtown	19/cab	18/cab
Quality Inn	5/walk	8/cab	15/cab	8/cab	8/cab
Regent Las Vegas	18/cab	21/cab	15/cab	23/cab	24/cab
Reserve	18/cab	17/cab	19/cab	17/cab	15/cab
Residence Inn	4/cab	6/cab	15/cab	12/cab	12/cab
Rio	5/cab	14/cab	13/cab	10/cab	10/cab
Riviera	on Strip	4/cab	14/cab	11/cab	10/cab
Royal Hotel	3/walk	5/cab	14/cab	13/cab	11/cab
Sahara	on Strip	4/cab	13/cab	13/cab	11/cab
St. Tropez	5/cab	6/cab	15/cab	7/cab	6/cab
Sam's Town	20/cab	25/cab	20/cab	18/cab	17/cab
San Remo	5/walk	11/cab	15/cab	6/cab	8/cab
Santa Fe Station	27/cab	30/cab	23/cab	33/cab	36/cab
Silverton	10/cab	17/cab	20/cab	12/cab	17/cab
Stardust	on Strip	4/cab	13/cab	12/cab	10/cab
Stratosphere	3/cab	7/cab	9/cab	14/cab	14/cab
Suncoast	18/cab	21/cab	15/cab	23/cab	24/cab
Sunrise Suites	19/cab	24/cab	19/cab	17/cab	16/cab
Sunset Station	18/cab	17/cab	18/cab	16/cab	15/cab
Terrible's	5/cab	6/cab	15/cab	6/cab	6/cab
Texas Station	17/cab	16/cab	13/cab	22/cab	22/cab
Treasure Island	on Strip	11/cab	14/cab	11/cab	10/cab
Tropicana	on Strip	11/cab	15/cab	6/cab	9/cab
Vacation Village	8/cab	18/cab	18/cab	8/cab	12/cab
Venetian	on Strip	9/cab	14/cab	8/cab	8/cab
Westward Ho	on Strip	5/cab	15/cab	13/cab	12/cab

Commuting to Downtown from the Strip

Commuting from the Strip to downtown is a snap on I-15. From the Strip you can get on or off I-15 at Tropicana Avenue, Flamingo Road, Spring Mountain Road, or Sahara Avenue. Once on I-15 heading north, stay in the right lane and follow the signs for downtown and US 95 South. If you exit onto Casino Center Boulevard, you will be right in the middle of downtown with several large parking garages conveniently at hand. Driving time to downtown varies from about 14 minutes from the south end of the Strip (I-15 via Tropicana Avenue) to about 6 minutes from the north end (I-15 via Sahara Avenue).

Commuting to the Strip from Downtown

If you are heading to the Strip from downtown, you can pick up US 95 (and then I-15) by going north on either Fourth Street or Las Vegas Boulevard. Driving time from downtown to the Strip takes 6–14 minutes, depending on where you are going on the Strip.

Free Connections

Traffic on the Strip is so awful that the hotels, both individually and in groups, are creating new alternatives for getting around.

1. A monorail connects Bally's, Paris Las Vegas, and the MGM Grand on the east side of the Strip, while an elevated tram (that looks like a monorail) links the Bellagio and Monte Carlo on the west side. Farther south on the west side, a shuttle tram serves the Excalibur, Luxor, Mandalay Bay, and Four Seasons.

2. The Rio operates a shuttle from the Rio Visitor's Center, just south of Paris Las Vegas on the Strip, to the Rio, about a half-mile west of the Strip on West Flamingo Road. Shuttles are also available linking the Barbary Coast on the northeast corner of the Strip and Flamingo to the Gold Coast about a mile west.

3. Free shuttle service from the nongaming Polo Towers near the Aladdin to the Stratosphere runs on the hour northbound to the Stratosphere and on the half hour for the southbound return from 9 a.m. until 11 p.m.

PUBLIC TRANSPORTATION

Las Vegas's Citizen's Area Transit (CAT) provides reliable bus service at reasonable rates. Although one-way fares along the Strip are $2, one-way fares

Commonly Used Public Transportation Routes

	Round-trip from/to	Hours of Operation	Frequency of Service	Fare
Citizen's Area Transit Bus # 301	Vacation Village/ Downtown Transportation Center	24 hours	Every 15 minutes	$2
Citizen's Area Transit Bus # 302 (Strip Express) Northbound	Vacation Village/ Downtown Transportation Center	10 a.m. to 1 a.m.	Every 20 minutes	$2
Citizen's Area Transit Bus # 302 (Strip Express) Southbound	Downtown Transportation Center/Vacation Village	10 a.m. to 1 a.m.	Every 20 minutes	$2
Citizen's Area Transit Bus # 303	Vacation Village/ Las Vegas Factory	5:35 a.m. to 1:25 a.m.	Once an hour	$2
	Outlet Stores	10 a.m. to 6 p.m.	On the half hour	
Las Vegas Strip Trolley Route	Luxor/ Stratosphere	9:30 to 1:30 a.m.	Every 15 minutes	$1.50

in residential areas are only $1.25. Children age five and under ride all routes for free. All public transportation requires exact fare. Transfers are free on all routes but must be used within two hours of issue. All CAT buses are equipped with wheelchair lifts and bicycle racks, both of which are provided at no extra charge. Handicapped persons requiring door-to-door service should call ahead for reservations. For general route and fare information, to request a schedule through the mail, or to make reservations for door-to-door service, call (702) 228-7433.

The Las Vegas Strip Trolley Company is privately owned and provides transportation along the Strip and between the Strip and downtown. These buses are styled to look like San Francisco cable cars, and they cost a little less than CAT buses. Children age four and under ride free. Call (702) 382-1404 for more information.

What's in an Address?

DOWNTOWN

The heart of the downtown casino area is Fremont Street between Fourth Street (on the east) and Main Street (on the west). Hotel-casinos situated along this quarter-mile four-block stretch known as Glitter Gulch include the Plaza Hotel, Golden Gate, Las Vegas Club, Binion's Horseshoe, Golden Nugget, Sam Boyd's Fremont, Four Queens, and Fitzgeralds. Parallel to Fremont and one block north is Ogden Avenue, where the California, Lady Luck, and the Gold Spike are located. Main Street Station is situated on Main Street at the intersection of Ogden.

All of the downtown hotel-casinos are centrally positioned and convenient to the action, with the exception of the El Cortez, which sits three blocks to the east. While there is a tremendous difference in quality and price among the downtown properties, the locations of all the hotels (except the El Cortez) are excellent. When you stay downtown, everything is within a five-minute walk. By way of comparison, on the Strip it takes longer to walk from the entrance of Caesars Palace to the entrance of the Mirage, next door, than to cover the whole four blocks of the casino center downtown.

THE STRIP

While location is not a major concern when choosing from among the downtown hotels, it is of paramount importance when selecting a hotel on the Strip.

I once received a promotional flyer from a Las Vegas casino proudly proclaiming that it was located "right on the Strip." It supported the claim with a color photo showing its marquee and those of several other casinos in a neat row with their neon ablaze. What recipients of this advertisement (except those familiar with Las Vegas) never would have guessed was that the photo had been taken with a special lens that eliminated all sense of distance between the casinos. While the advertised casino appeared to be next door to the other casinos in the picture, it was in reality almost a mile away.

A common variation on the same pitch, but without the photo, is "Stay Right on the Las Vegas Strip at Half the Price." Once again, the promoter is attempting to deceive by taking advantage of the recipient's ignorance of Strip geography. As it happens, the Las Vegas Strip (Las Vegas Boulevard South) starts southwest of the airport and runs all the way downtown, a distance of about seven miles. Only the four-mile section between Mandalay Bay and the Stratosphere contains the large casinos and other attractions of interest to visitors. South of Mandalay Bay "on the Strip" is the airport boundary and some nice desert. North of the Stratosphere en route to downtown, the Strip runs through a recently resurgent commercial area sprinkled with wedding chapels, fast-food restaurants, and small motels.

The Best Locations on the Strip

Beware of hotels and motels claiming to be on the Strip but not located between Mandalay Bay and the Stratosphere. They might be nice properties, but chances are you will be disappointed with the location.

If you stay on the Strip, you want to be somewhere in the Mandalay Bay to Stratosphere stretch, and even there, some sections are much more desirable than others. The Mandalay Bay basically anchors the south end of the Strip, about a quarter-mile from the Luxor, its closest neighbor. Likewise, at the other end, the Stratosphere and the Sahara are somewhat isolated. In between, there are distinct clusters of hotels and casinos.

Strip Cluster 1: The Cluster of the Giants   At the intersection of the Strip (Las Vegas Boulevard South) and Tropicana Avenue are five of the world's largest hotels. The MGM Grand Hotel is the largest hotel in the United States. Diagonally across the intersection from the MGM Grand is the Excalibur, the third largest hotel in the United States. The other two corners of the intersection are occupied by New York–New York and the Tropicana. Nearby to the south is the Luxor (second largest) and to the north is the Holiday Inn Boardwalk and Monte Carlo (all on the Strip). The San Remo is situated on Tropicana across from the MGM Grand. From the intersection of the Strip and Tropicana, it is a half-mile walk south to Mandalay Bay and a three-tenths-mile hike north to the Aladdin. The next cluster of major hotels and casinos is at the intersection of Flamingo Road, one mile north. With the opening of New York–New York and the Monte Carlo in 1996, Strip Cluster 1 challenged the status, at least in terms of appeal and diversity, of Strip Cluster 2. Progress always has its dark side, however. Here it is the phenomenal increase of traffic and congestion on East Tropicana Avenue as it approaches the Strip.

Strip Cluster 2: The Grand Cluster   From Flamingo Road to Spring Mountain Road (also called Sands Avenue, and farther east, Twain Avenue) is the greatest numerical concentration of major hotels and casinos on the Strip. If you wish to stay on the Strip and prefer to walk wherever you go, this is the best location. At Flamingo Road and Las Vegas Boulevard are Bally's, Caesars Palace, Barbary Coast, Paris, and Bellagio. Heading east on Flamingo are Bourbon Street and Maxim. Toward town on the Strip are the Flamingo, O'Shea's, Imperial Palace, Mirage, Harrah's, Casino Royale, the Venetian, and Treasure Island. Also in this cluster are the Forum Shops and the Grand Canal Shoppes, Las Vegas's most unique shopping venues.

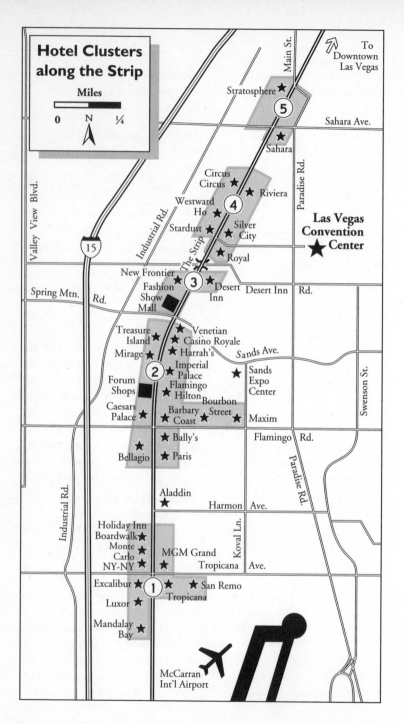

Hotel Clusters along the Strip

Miles

0   N   ¼

To Downtown Las Vegas

Main St.

Stratosphere ★

5

Sahara Ave.

Sahara ★

Paradise Rd.

Circus Circus ★

★ Riviera

Westward Ho ★

4

Stardust ★

★ Silver City

Valley View Blvd.

Industrial Rd.

The Strip

Las Vegas Convention ★ Center

★ Royal

15

New Frontier ★

3

Desert Inn

Desert Inn Rd.

Spring Mtn.   Rd.

Fashion Show Mall

Treasure Island ★

★ Venetian
★ Casino Royale

Mirage ★

★ Harrah's

Sands Ave.

2

★ Imperial Palace

Sands Expo Center

Forum Shops

★ Flamingo
★ Hilton

★

Swenson St.

Caesars Palace ★

★ Barbary Coast

Bourbon Street ★

★ Maxim

★ Bally's

Flamingo   Rd.

Bellagio ★

★ Paris

Paradise Rd.

Aladdin ★

Harmon   Ave.

Holiday Inn Boardwalk ★
Monte Carlo ★
NY-NY ★

Koval Ln.

MGM Grand ★

Tropicana   Ave.

Industrial Rd.

Excalibur ★

1

★   ★ San Remo

Luxor ★

Tropicana

Mandalay Bay ★

McCarran Int'l Airport

A leisure traveler could stay a week in this section (without ever getting in a car or cab) and not run out of interesting sights, good restaurants, or good entertainment. On the negative side, for those with cars, traffic congestion at the intersection of the Strip and Flamingo Road is the worst in the city.

Strip Cluster 3   Another nice section of the Strip is from Spring Mountain Road up to the New Frontier and what was the Desert Inn. This cluster, pretty much in the center of the Strip, is distinguished by its easy access. The New Frontier can be reached by two different roads. Visitors who prefer a major hotel on the Strip but want to avoid the daily traffic snarls could not ask for a more convenient location. Though the New Frontier is about a quarter mile from the nearest cluster of casinos in either direction, it is situated within a four-minute walk of Fashion Show Mall, one of the most interesting and diversified upscale shopping centers in the United States. There are also some very good restaurants in this section, including Chin's in the mall and Margarita's at the New Frontier. Finally, this cluster is a 4-minute cab ride (or a 16-minute walk) from the Las Vegas Convention Center.

Strip Cluster 4   The next cluster up the Strip is between Convention Center Drive and Riviera Boulevard. Arrayed along a stretch just over a half-mile long are the Stardust, Westward Ho, Riviera, and Circus Circus with its Adventuredome theme park. Great for people-watching and enjoying the lights, this area contains the third largest concentration of major hotels and casinos. Casinos and hotels in this cluster are considerably less upscale than those in the "grand cluster" but offer acceptable selections for dining and entertainment, as well as proximity to the Las Vegas Convention Center. Traffic along this section of the Strip is also woefully congested.

Strip Cluster 5   Finally, near the intersection of Las Vegas Boulevard and Sahara Avenue there is a relatively isolated cluster that contains Wet 'n Wild (a water theme park), the Sahara, and, about a third of a mile toward town, the Stratosphere. Though fairly isolated if you intend to walk, for visitors with cars this cluster provides convenient access to the Strip, the Convention Center, and downtown.

Just off the Strip

If you have a car, and if being right on the Strip is not a big deal to you, there are some excellent hotel-casinos on Paradise Road, and to the east and west of the Strip on intersecting roads. The Rio and Gold Coast on Flamingo Road, Palace Station on Sahara Avenue, and Orleans on Tropicana Avenue offer exceptional value; they are all less than a half mile from the Strip and are situated at access ramps to I-15, five to ten minutes from downtown.

Boulder Highway, Green Valley, Summerlin and North Las Vegas

Twenty minutes from the Strip in North Las Vegas are Texas Station, the Fiesta, and, on the edge of civilization, Santa Fe Station. All three have good restaurants, comfortable guest rooms, and lively, upbeat themes. Hotel-casinos on Boulder Highway southeast of town include Castaways, Boulder Station, Sam's Town, Arizona Charlie's East, and Nevada Palace. Also to the southeast are Sunset Station and the Reserve in Green Valley. Like the North Las Vegas trio, the Boulder Highway and Green Valley properties cater primarily to locals. Northwest of town is the posh new Regent Las Vegas, with two upscale hotels and the Tournament Player's Club (TPC) at the Canyons Golf Course. Nearby is the new Suncoast Casino.

THE LIGHTS OF LAS VEGAS: TRAFFIC ON THE STRIP

During the past decade, Las Vegas has experienced exponential growth—growth that unfortunately has not been matched with the development of necessary infrastructure. If you imagine a town designed for about 300,000 people being inundated by a million or so refugees (all with cars), you will have a sense of what's happening in Las Vegas.

The Strip (Las Vegas Boulevard South), where a huge percentage of the local population works and where more than 80% of tourists and business travelers stay, has become a clogged artery in the heart of the city. The heaviest traffic on the Strip is between Tropicana and Sahara Avenues, where most of the larger hotels are located. Throughout the day and night, local traffic combines with gawking tourists, shoppers, and cruising teenagers to create a 3-mile-long, bumper-to-bumper bottleneck.

When folks discuss the "lights of Las Vegas," it used to be that they were talking about the marquees of the casinos. More recently, however, the reference is to the long, multifunctional traffic lights found at virtually every intersection on the Strip. These lights, which flash a different signal for every possible turn and direction, combine with an ever-increasing number of vehicles to ensure that nobody goes anywhere very fast. Also affected are the major traffic arteries that cross the Strip east to west; the worst snarls occur at the intersection of the Strip and Flamingo Avenue.

Strip traffic is the Achilles heel of the current Las Vegas development boom. It is sheer lunacy to believe you can plop a litter of megahotels on the Strip without compounding an already horrific traffic situation. While city government and the hospitality industry dance around the issue, traffic gets worse and worse. Approximately 48,000 hotel rooms were added along the Strip during the nineties, and about 26,000 more are scheduled to come on line by 2001. Clearly, an elevated train or some other form of fast, efficient public transportation is needed, but the city leaders and the hoteliers are now so far behind the curve that nothing is likely to save the Strip from massive gridlock.

Sneak Routes

Fortunately, most of the large hotels along this section of the Strip have back entrances that allow you to avoid the insanity of the main drag. Industrial Road and I-15 run parallel to the Strip on the west side, providing backdoor access to hotels situated on the west side of Las Vegas Boulevard. Paradise Road and Koval Lane run parallel to the Strip on the east side.

Room Reservations: Getting a Good Room, Getting a Good Deal

Because Las Vegas is so popular for short weekend getaways, weekend occupancy averages an astounding 92% of capacity for hotels and 70% of capacity for motels. Weekday occupancy for hotels is a respectable 83%, and for motels, 63%. What these figures mean, among other things, is that you want to nail down your lodging reservations before you leave home.

Also, consider that these occupancy percentages are averages. When a large convention is in town or when Las Vegas hosts a championship prizefight, the National Finals Rodeo, or any other major event, rooms become hard to find. If you are heading to Las Vegas purely for fun and relaxation, you may want to avoid going when the town is packed. For more information about dates to avoid, see pages 19–20.

THE WACKY WORLD OF LAS VEGAS HOTEL RESERVATIONS

Though there are almost 130,000 hotel rooms in Las Vegas, getting one is not always a simple proposition. In the large hotel-casinos there are often five or more separate departments that have responsibility for room allocation and sales. Of the total number of rooms in any given hotel, a number are at the disposal of the casino; some are administered by the reservations department at the front desk; some are allocated to independent wholesalers for group and individual travel packages; others are blocked for special events (fights, Super Bowl weekend, etc.); and still others are at the disposal of the sales and marketing department for meetings, conventions, wedding parties, and other special groups. Hotels that are part of a large chain (Holiday Inn, Hilton, etc.) have some additional rooms administered by their national reservations systems.

At most hotels, department heads meet each week and review all the room allocations. If rooms blocked for a special event, say a golf tournament, are not selling, some of those rooms will be redistributed to other departments. Since

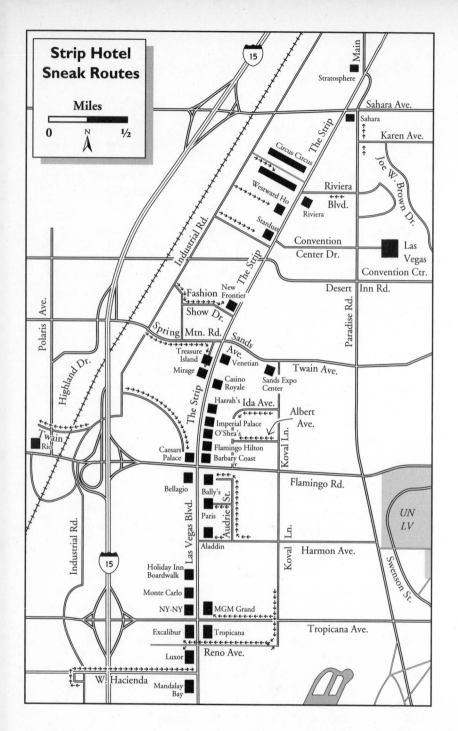

Strip Hotel Sneak Routes

Miles

0   N   ½

15

Stratosphere

Main

Sahara Ave.

The Strip

Sahara

Karen Ave.

Circus Circus

Joe W. Brown Dr.

Westward Ho

Riviera

Blvd.

Riviera

Stardust

Convention

Center Dr.

Las Vegas Convention Ctr.

Industrial Rd.

The Strip

Desert

Inn Rd.

Fashion

New Frontier

Paradise Rd.

Show Dr.

Spring Mtn. Rd.

Sands

Ave.

Polaris Ave.

Treasure Island

Venetian

Twain Ave.

Highland Dr.

Mirage

Casino Royale

Sands Expo Center

Harrah's

Ida Ave.

Albert Ave.

The Strip

Imperial Palace

O'Shea's

Twain

Rio

Caesars Palace

Flamingo Hilton

Barbary Coast

Koval Ln.

Bellagio

Bally's

St.

Flamingo Rd.

Paris

Audrie

UN LV

Las Vegas Blvd.

Aladdin

Koval Ln.

Harmon Ave.

Industrial Rd.

15

Holiday Inn Boardwalk

Monte Carlo

NY-NY

MGM Grand

Swenson St.

Excalibur

Tropicana

Tropicana Ave.

Luxor

Reno Ave.

W. Hacienda

Mandalay Bay

Sneak Routes for Hotels on the West Side of the Strip

The Stratosphere's self-park garage is off Baltimore Street, which connects to Las Vegas Blvd.

Circus Circus, Westward Ho, and the *Stardust* can be reached via Industrial Road.

The New Frontier has an entrance off Fashion Show Drive, which connects to Industrial Road.

The Mirage and *Treasure Island* are accessible by taking Industrial Road or I-15 and then turning east on Spring Mountain Road.

Caesars Palace can be accessed from Industrial Road.

The Holiday Inn Boardwalk and the *Monte Carlo* must be accessed from the Strip.

New York–New York can be reached via Tropicana Avenue.

Bellagio has an entrance off Flamingo Road (heading east).

Excalibur, Luxor, and *Mandalay Bay* can be reached by turning south off Tropicana onto Koval Lane and then turning right onto Reno Avenue. Reno Avenue intersects the Strip at a traffic light, allowing you to cross to Excalibur and Luxor. An alternate route is to take Industrial Road south, turning right on Connector Road and then right again on West Hacienda.

Sneak Routes for Hotels on the East Side of the Strip

The Sahara has an entrance on Paradise Road.

The Riviera can be reached by turning west on Riviera Boulevard from Paradise.

The Venetian is accessible from Koval Lane.

Harrah's Las Vegas, the *Imperial Palace, O'Shea's,* and the *Flamingo Hilton* each have a back entrance off Audrie Street, a small thoroughfare branching off Flamingo Road. Audrie Street can also be reached by turning west on Albert or Ida avenues from Koval Lane.

Sneak Routes for Hotels on the East Side of the Strip (cont'd)

The *Aladdin* is accessible from westbound Harmon Road.

The *Barbary Coast* is the only major hotel on the east side of the Strip that is truly stuck. If you want to go to the Barbary Coast, park somewhere else and walk over. Don't even think about arriving at or departing from the Barbary Coast's parking lot between 3:30 p.m. and 8 p.m.

Bally's and *Paris* can be reached by turning north off Harmon Avenue onto an isolated section of Audrie Street.

The *MGM Grand* is accessible by heading west (toward the Strip) on Tropicana Avenue or by turning west off Koval Lane.

The *Tropicana* is accessible by turning south off Tropicana Avenue onto Koval Lane and then turning right onto Reno Avenue.

---

special events and large conventions are scheduled far in advance, the decision makers have significant lead time. In most hotels, a major reallocation of rooms takes place 40–50 days prior to the dates for which the rooms are blocked, with minor reallocations made right up to the event in question.

If you call the reservations number at the hotel of your choice and are informed that no rooms are available for the dates you've requested, it does not mean the hotel is sold out. What it does mean is that the front desk has no more rooms remaining in their allocation. It is a fairly safe assumption that all the rooms in a hotel have not been reserved for guests. The casino will usually hold back some rooms for high rollers, the sales department may have some rooms reserved for participants in deals they are negotiating, and some rooms will be in the hands of tour wholesalers or blocked for a citywide convention. If any of these remaining rooms are not committed by a certain date, they will be reallocated. So a second call to the reservations department may get you the room that was unavailable when you called two weeks earlier.

GETTING THE BEST DEAL ON A ROOM

Compared to that in other destinations, lodging in Las Vegas is so inexpensive that the following cost-cutting strategies may seem gratuitous. If you are accustomed to paying $120 a night for a hotel room, you can afford 70% of the hotels in town, and you may not be inclined to wade through all the options listed below to save $20 or $30 a night. If, on the other hand, you would like to obtain top value for your dollar, read on.

Beating Rack Rates

The benchmark for making cost comparisons is always the hotel's standard rate, or rack rate. This is what you would pay if, space available, you just walked in off the street and rented a room. In a way, the rack rate is analogous to an airline's standard coach fare. It represents a straight, nondiscounted room rate. In Las Vegas, you assume that the rack rate is the most you should have to pay and that with a little effort you ought to be able to do better.

To learn the standard room rate, call room reservations at the hotel(s) of your choice. Do not be surprised if there are several standard rates, one for each type of room in the hotel. Have the reservationist explain the difference in the types of rooms available in each price bracket. Also ask the hotel which of the described class of rooms you would get if you came on a wholesaler, tour operator, or airline tour package. This information will allow you to make meaningful comparisons among various packages and rates.

The Season

December and January are roller-coaster months for Las Vegas. In December, the town is empty except for National Finals Rodeo week in early December and Christmas/New Year's week. Similarly, in January, the town is packed during the Consumer Electronics Show and the Super Bowl weekend, and pretty much dead the rest of the time. During the slow parts of these months, most of the hotels offer amazing deals on lodging. Also, hotels sometimes offer reduced rates in July and August. While the list below stands up pretty well as a general guide, one type of deal or package might beat another for a specific hotel or time of year.

Sorting Out the Sellers and the Options

To book a room in a particular hotel for any given date, there are so many different in-house departments, as well as outside tour operators and wholesalers selling rooms, that it is almost impossible to find out who is offering the best deal. This is not because the various deals are so hard to compare but, rather, because it is so difficult to identify all the sellers.

Though it is only a rough approximation, here is a list of the types of rates and packages available, ranked from the best to the worst value.

Room Rates and Packages	Sold or Administered by
1. Gambler's rate	Casino or hotel
2. December, January, and summer specials	Hotel room reservations or marketing department

3. Wholesaler packages   Independent wholesalers

4. Tour operator packages   Tour operators

5. Reservation service discounts   Independent wholesalers
                                       and consolidators

6. Half-price programs   Half-price program operators

7. Commercial airline packages   Commercial airlines

8. Hotel packages   Hotel sales and marketing

9. Corporate rate   Hotel room reservations

10. Hotel standard room rate   Hotel room reservations

11. Convention rate   Convention sponsor

The room rate ranking is subject to some interpretation. A gambler's rate may, at first glance, seem to be the least expensive lodging option available, next to a complimentary room. If, however, the amount of money a guest is obligated to wager (and potentially lose) is factored in, the gambler's rate might be by far the most expensive.

Complimentary and Discounted Rooms for Gamblers

Most Las Vegas visitors are at least peripherally aware that casinos provide complimentary or greatly discounted rooms to gamblers. It is not unusual, therefore, for a business traveler, a low-stakes gambler, or a nongambling tourist to attempt to take advantage of these deals. What they quickly discover is that the casino has very definite expectations of any guest whose stay is wholly or partially subsidized by the house. If you only want a gambler's discount on a room, they will ask what game(s) you intend to play, the amount of your average bet, how many hours a day you usually gamble, where (at which casinos) you have played before, and how much gambling money you will have available on this trip. They may also request that you make an application for credit or provide personal information about your occupation, income, and bank account.

If you manage to bluff your way into a comp or discounted room, you can bet that your gambling (or lack thereof) will be closely monitored after you arrive. If you fail to give the casino an acceptable amount of action, you will probably be charged the nondiscounted room rate when you check out.

Even for those who expect to do a fair amount of gambling, a comp or discounted room can be a mixed blessing. By accepting the casino's hospitality, you incur a certain obligation (the more they give you, the bigger the obligation). You will be expected to do most (if not all) of your gambling in the casino where you are staying, and you will also be expected to play a certain number of hours each day. If this was your intention all along, great.

On the other hand, if you thought you would like to try several casinos or take a day and run over to Hoover Dam, you may be painting yourself into a corner.

Taking Advantage of Special Deals

When you call, always ask the reservationist if the hotel has any package deals or specials. If you plan to gamble, be sure to ask about "gambling sprees" or other gaming specials. If you do not anticipate gambling enough to qualify for a gambling package, ask about other types of deals. If the reservationist is not knowledgeable, don't conclude that the hotel offers no packages or special deals of its own. Instead, have the reservationist transfer your call to the sales and marketing department and ask them.

If you have a lot of lead time before your trip, write or call the hotel and ask about joining their slot club. Though only a few hotels will send you a membership application, inquiring about the slot club will get you categorized as a gambler on the hotel's mailing list. Once in Las Vegas, sign up for the slot clubs of hotel-casinos that you like. This will ensure that you receive notification of special deals that you can take advantage of on subsequent visits. Also, being a member of a hotel's slot club can also come in handy when rooms are scarce. Once, trying to book a room, we were told the hotel was sold out. When we mentioned that we had a slot card, the reservationist miraculously found us a room. If you are a slot club member, it is often better to phone the slot club member services desk instead of the hotel reservations desk.

If you enjoy window shopping on the Internet, log onto the homepage of hotels that interest you. As far as rooms go, however, it's rare in our experience to find a deal on the hotel's website that's better than the ones they quote you on the phone. A reservationist on the phone knows she has a good prospect on the line and will work with you within the limits of her authority. On the Web there's no give or negotiation: it's a take-it-or-leave-it deal. Finally, most hotels, including many of the new super properties, really haven't learned how to merchandise rooms through their website.

Having shopped the hotel for deals, start checking out tour operator and wholesaler packages advertised in your local newspaper, and compare what you find to packages offered in the Sunday edition of the *Los Angeles Times*. Next, check out packages offered by the airline tour services (American Airlines Fly-Away, Delta Vacations, etc.). When working with the airline tour services, always ask if they have any special deals going on with particular hotels.

Take the better deals and packages you discover, regardless of the source, and discuss them with a travel agent. Explain which one(s) you favor and ask if he or she can do any better. After your travel agent researches the options, review the whole shooting match and select the deal that best fits your schedule, requirements, and budget.

Since Las Vegas room rates are among the most reasonable in the country, you may not want to go to all of this effort. If you are working with a restricted budget, or plan to visit Las Vegas once or more each year, it is probably worth the hassle to check the rate and package options. If, conversely, you are used to paying $65–125 a night for a hotel room, you may prefer to choose a hotel and leave it to your travel agent to get you the best deal available.

Timing Is Everything

Timing is everything when booking a guest room in Las Vegas. If a particular hotel has only a few rooms to sell for a specific date, it will often bounce up the rate for those rooms as high as it thinks the market will bear. Conversely, if the hotel has many rooms available for a certain date, it will lower the rate accordingly. The practice remains operative all year, although the likelihood of hotels having a lot of rooms available is obviously greater during "off-peak" periods. As an example, we checked rates at an upscale nongaming hotel during two weeks in October. Depending on the specific dates, the rate for the suite in question ranged from $75 (an incredible bargain) to $200 (significantly overpriced) per night.

Which day of the week you check in can also save or cost you some money. At some hotels a standard room runs 20% less if you check in on a Monday through Thursday (even though you may stay through the weekend). If you check into the same room on a weekend, your rate will be higher and may not change if you keep your room into the following week. A more common practice is for the hotel to charge a lower rate during the week and a higher rate on the weekend.

Helping Your Travel Agent to Help You

A travel agent friend told me once, "Las Vegas is our least favorite destination." What she meant, essentially, is that travel agents cannot make much money selling trips to Las Vegas. Airfares to Las Vegas are among the lowest in the country, and hotel rooms frequently go for less than $50 a night. On top of this, the average stay in Las Vegas is short. To a travel agent this adds up to a lot of work with little potential for a worthwhile commission. Because an agent derives only a small return for booking travel to Las Vegas, there isn't much incentive for the travel agent to become product knowledgeable.

Except for a handful of agents who sell Las Vegas travel in volume (usually in Las Vegas's primary markets), there are comparatively few travel agents who know much about Las Vegas. This lack of information translates into travelers not getting reservations at their preferred hotel, paying more than is necessary, or being placed in out-of-the-way or otherwise undesirable lodging.

When you call your travel agent, ask if he or she has been to Las Vegas. Firsthand experience means everything. If the answer is no, either find another agent or be prepared to give your travel agent a lot of direction. Do not accept any recommendations at face value. Check out the location and rates of any suggested hotel and make certain that the hotel is suited to your itinerary.

Because travel agents tend to be unfamiliar with Las Vegas, your agent may try to plug you into a tour operator's or wholesaler's preset package. This essentially allows the travel agent to set up your whole trip with a single phone call and still collect an 8–10% commission. The problem with this scenario is that most agents will place 90% of their Las Vegas business with only one or two wholesalers or tour operators. In other words, path of least resistance for them, and not much choice for you.

Often, travel agents will use wholesalers who run packages in conjunction with airlines, like Delta's Vacations or American's Fly-Away Vacations. Because of the wholesaler's exclusive relationship with the carrier, these trips are very easy for travel agents to book. However, they will probably be more expensive than a package offered by a high-volume wholesaler, who works with a number of airlines in a primary Las Vegas market.

To help your travel agent get you the best possible deal, do the following:

1. Determine where you want to stay in Las Vegas (the Strip, downtown, Boulder Highway, etc.), and if possible choose a specific hotel. This can be accomplished by reviewing the hotel information provided in this guide, by writing or calling hotels that interest you, or by checking out your selected hotels on the Internet.

2. Check out the Las Vegas travel ads in the Sunday travel section of your local newspaper and compare them to ads running in the newspapers of one of Las Vegas's key markets (i.e., Los Angeles, San Diego, Phoenix, Chicago). See if you can find some packages that fit your plans and that include a hotel you like.

3. Call the wholesalers or tour operators whose ads you have collected. Ask any questions you might have concerning their packages, but do not book your trip with them directly.

4. Tell your travel agent about the packages you find and ask if he or she can get you something better. The packages in the paper will serve as a benchmark against which to compare alternatives proposed by your travel agent.

5. Choose from among the options uncovered by you and your travel agent. No matter which option you elect, have your travel agent book it. Even if you go with one of the packages in the newspaper, it will probably be commissionable (at no additional cost to you) and will provide the agent some return on the time invested on your behalf. Also, as a travel professional, your agent should be able to verify the quality and integrity of the package.

No Room at the Inn (Maybe)   If you are having trouble getting a reservation at the hotel of your choice, let your travel agent assist you. As discussed, the agent might be able to find a package with a wholesaler or tour operator that bypasses the hotel reservations department. If this does not work, he or she can call the sales and marketing department of the hotel and ask them, as a favor, to find you a room. Most hotel sales reps will make a special effort to accommodate travel agents, particularly travel agents who write a lot of Las Vegas business. Do not be shy or reluctant about asking your travel agent to make a special call on your behalf. This is common practice in the travel industry and affords the agent an opportunity to renew contacts in the hotel's sales department.

If your travel agent cannot get you a room through a personal appeal to the sales department and does not know which tour operators and wholesalers package the hotel you want, have the agent call hotel room reservations and:

1. Identify him- or herself as a travel agent.

2. Inquire about room availability for your required dates; something might have opened up since their (or your) last call.

3. If the reservationist reports that there are still no rooms available, have your travel agent ask for the reservations manager.

4. When the reservations manager comes on the line, have your agent identify him- or herself and ask whether the hotel is holding any space for wholesalers. If the answer is yes, have your agent request the wholesalers' names and phone numbers. This is information the reservations manager will not ordinarily divulge to an individual but will release to your travel agent. Armed with the names and numbers of wholesalers holding space, your agent can start calling the listed wholesalers to find you a package or a room.

No Room at the Inn (for Real)   More frequently than you would imagine, Las Vegas hotels overbook their rooms. This happens when guests do not check out on time, when important casino customers arrive on short notice, and when the various departments handling room allocations get their signals crossed. When this occurs, guests who arrive holding reservations are told that their reservations have been canceled.

To protect yourself, always guarantee your first night with a major credit card (even if you do not plan to arrive late), send a deposit if required, and insist on a written confirmation of your reservation. When you arrive and check in, have your written confirmation handy.

Precautions notwithstanding, the hotel still might have canceled your reservation. When a hotel is overbooked, for whatever reason, it will take care of its serious gambling customers first, its prospective gambling customers (leisure travelers) second, and business travelers last. If you are informed that you have no room, demand that the hotel honor your reservation by finding you a room or by securing you a room at another convenient hotel. Should the desk clerk balk at doing this, demand to see the reservations manager. If the reservations manager stonewalls, go to the hotel's general manager. Whatever you do, do not leave until the issue has been resolved to your satisfaction.

Hotels understand their obligation to honor a confirmed reservation, but they often fail to take responsibility unless you hold their feet to the fire. We have seen convention-goers, stunned by the news that they have no room, simply turn around and walk out. Wrong. The hotel owns the problem, not you. You should not have to shop for another room. The hotel that confirmed your reservation should find you a room comparable to or better than the one you reserved, and for the same rate.

WHERE THE DEALS ARE

Hotel room marketing and sales is confusing even to travel professionals. Sellers, particularly the middlemen, or wholesalers are known by a numbing array of different and frequently ill-defined terms. Furthermore, roles overlap, making it difficult to know who specifically is providing a given service. Below we try to sort all of this out for you and encourage you to slog through it. Understanding the system will make you a savvy consumer and will enable you to get the best deals regardless of your destination.

Tour Operators and Wholesalers

Las Vegas hotels have always had a hard time filling their rooms from Sunday through Thursday. On the weekends, when thousands of visitors arrive from Southern California, Phoenix, and Salt Lake, the town comes alive. But on Sunday evening, as the last of the Los Angelenos retreat over the horizon line, Las Vegas lapses into the doldrums. The Las Vegas Convention and Visitors Authority, along with hotel sales departments, seek to fill the rooms on weekday nights by bringing meetings, conventions, and trade shows to town. While collectively they are very successful, on many weekdays there remain a lot of empty hotel rooms.

Recognizing that an empty hotel room is a liability, various travel entrepreneurs have stepped into the breach, volunteering to sell rooms for the hotels and casinos. These entrepreneurs, who call themselves tour operators, inbound travel brokers, travel wholesalers, travel packagers, or receptive operators, require as a quid pro quo that the hotels provide them a certain number of rooms at a significantly reduced nightly rate, which they in turn resell at a profit. As this arrangement extends the sales outreach of the hotels, and as the rooms might otherwise go unoccupied, the hotels are only too happy to cooperate with this group of independent sales agents. Though a variety of programs have been developed to sell the rooms, most are marketed as part of group and individual travel packages.

This development has been beneficial both to the tourist and the hotel. Predicated on volume, some of the room discount is generally passed along to consumers as an incentive to come to Las Vegas during the week or, alternatively, to stay in town beyond the weekend. Wholesalers have made such a positive contribution to the Las Vegas hotel occupancy rate that rooms are now made available to them for weekends as well as weekdays.

By purchasing your room through a tour operator or wholesaler, you may be able to obtain a room at the hotel of your choice for considerably less than if you went through the hotel's reservations department. The hotel commits rooms to the wholesaler at a specific deep discount, usually 18–30% or more off the standard quoted rate, but makes no effort to control the price the wholesaler offers to his customers.

Wholesalers holding space at a hotel for a specific block of time must surrender that space back to the hotel if the rooms are not sold by a certain date, usually 7–14 days in advance. Since the wholesaler's performance and credibility is determined by the number of rooms filled in a given hotel, the wholesaler is always reluctant to give rooms back. The situation is similar to when the biology department at a university approaches the end of the year without having spent all of its allocated budget. The department head reasons that if the remaining funds are not spent (and the surplus is returned to the university), the university might reduce the budget for the forthcoming year. Tour wholesalers depend on the hotels for their inventory. The more rooms the hotels allocate, the more inventory they have to sell. If a wholesaler keeps returning rooms unsold, it is logical to predict that the hotel will respond by making fewer rooms available in the future. Therefore, the wholesaler would rather sell rooms at a bargain price than give them back to the hotel unsold.

Taking Advantage of Tour Operator and Travel Wholesaler Deals
There are several ways for you to tap into the tour operator and wholesaler market. First, check the travel sections of your Sunday paper for travel packages or tours to Las Vegas. Because Las Vegas hotels work with tour operators and wholesalers from all over the country, there will undoubtedly be someone in your city or region running packages to Las Vegas. Packages generally consist of room, transportation (bus or air), and often other features such as rental cars, shows, etc. Sometimes the consumer can buy the package for any dates desired; other times the operator or wholesaler will specify the dates. In either event, if a particular package fits your needs, you (or your travel agent) can book it directly by calling the phone number listed in the ad.

If you cannot find any worthwhile Las Vegas packages advertised in your local paper, go to a good newsstand and buy a Sunday paper, preferably from Los Angeles, but alternatively from San Diego, Phoenix, Salt Lake City, Denver, or Chicago. These cities are hot markets for Las Vegas, and their newspapers will almost always have a nice selection of packages advertised. Because the competition among tour operators and wholesalers in these cities is so great, you will often find deals that beat the socks off anything offered in your part of the country.

Find a package that you like and call for information. Do not be surprised, however, if the advertised package is not wholly available to you. If you live, say, in Nashville, Tennessee, a tour operator or wholesaler in Los Angeles may not be able to package your round-trip air or bus to Las Vegas. This is because tour operators and wholesalers usually work with bus and air carriers on a contractual basis, limiting the transportation they sell to round trips originating from their market area. In other words, they can take care of your transportation if you are flying from Southern California but most likely will not have a contract with an airline that permits them to fly you from Nashville. What they sometimes do, however, and what they will be delighted to do if they are sitting on some unsold rooms, is sell you the "land only" part of the package. This means you buy the room and on-site amenities (car, shows, etc.), if any, but will take care of your own travel arrangements.

Buying the "land only" part of a package can save big bucks because the wholesaler always has more flexibility in discounting the "land" part of the package than in discounting the round-trip transportation component. One of the sweetest deals in travel is to purchase the "land only" part of a package at a time when the airlines are running a promotion. We combined a two-for-one air special from Delta with a "land only" package from a wholesaler and chalked up a savings of 65% over separate quoted rates and a 22% savings over the full air/land package offered by the wholesaler.

Tour Operators and Travel Wholesalers

Some of the following businesses will deal directly with consumers while others will not. Concerning the latter, have your travel agent call for you.

A & P Tours
East McKeesport,
Pennsylvania
(412) 351-4800
(Deals directly with
consumers)

American Travel
Kansas City, Kansas
(913) 788-7997 or
(800) 827-7997
(Deals directly with
consumers)

America West Vacations
Tempe, Arizona
(800) 356-6611
(Deals directly with
consumers)

Funjet Vacations
Milwaukee, Wisconsin
(800) 558-3050
and
Southfield, Michigan
(248) 827-4050
(Deals directly with
consumers)

Kingdom Vacations
Plains, Pennsylvania
(800) 626-8747

Mile High Tours
Denver, Colorado
(303) 758-8246 or
(800) 777-TOUR
(Deals directly with
consumers)

MLT Vacations
Minnetonka, Minnesota
(612) 474-2540 or
(800) 328-0025

North American Leisure Group
Toronto, Ontario
(416) 485-1700

Premier Vacations
Honolulu, Hawaii
(808) 596-0030

Sunquest Vacations West
Richmond, British
Columbia
(604) 714-5141

Travel by Us
Seattle, Washington
(800) 841-4321
(Deals directly with
consumers)

Half-Price Programs

The larger discounts on rooms in nongaming properties (hotels without casinos), in Las Vegas or anywhere else, are available through half-price hotel programs, often called travel clubs. Program operators contract with an individual hotel to provide rooms at a deep discount, usually 50% off rack rate, on a "space available" basis. In practice, space available generally means that you can reserve a room at the discounted rate whenever the hotel expects to be at less than 80% occupancy. A little calendar sleuthing to help you avoid citywide conventions and special events will increase the chances of choosing a time for your visit when the discounts are available.

Most half-price programs charge an annual membership fee or directory subscription charge of $25 to $125. Once enrolled, you are mailed a membership card and a directory listing all the hotels participating in the program. Examining the directory, you will notice immediately that there are a lot of restrictions and exceptions. Some hotels, for instance, "black out" certain dates or times of year. Others may only offer the discount on certain days of the week or require you to stay a certain number of nights. Still others may offer a much smaller discount than 50% off rack rate.

Some programs specialize in domestic travel, some in international travel, and some specialize in both. The more established operators offer members up to 4,000 hotels to choose from in the United States. All of the programs have a heavy concentration of hotels in California and Florida, and most have a very limited selection of participating properties in New York City or Boston. Offerings in other cities and regions of the United States vary considerably. The programs with the largest selection of hotels in Las Vegas are Encore, Travel America at Half Price (Entertainment Publications), International Travel Card, and Quest.

One problem with half-price programs is that not all hotels offer a full 50% discount. Another slippery problem is the base rate against which the discount is applied. Some hotels figure the discount on an exaggerated rack rate that nobody would ever have to pay. A few participating hotels may deduct the discount from a supposed "superior" or "upgraded" room rate, even though the room you get is the hotel's standard accommodation. Though the facts can be hard to pin down, the majority of participating properties base discounts on the published rate in the *Hotel & Travel Index* (a quarterly reference work used by travel agents) and work within the spirit of their agreement with the program operator. As a rule, if you travel several times a year, you will more than pay for your program membership in room rate savings.

A noteworthy addendum to this discussion is that deeply discounted rooms through half-price programs are not commissionable to travel agents.

Half-Price Programs	
Encore	(800) 638-0930
Entertainment Publications	(800) 285-5525
International Travel Card	(800) 342-0558
Quest	(800) 638-9819

In practical terms this means that you must ordinarily make your own inquiry calls and reservations. If you travel frequently, however, and run a lot of business through your travel agent, he or she will probably do your legwork, lack of commission notwithstanding.

Players Club

The most visible discount travel club selling Las Vegas is Players Club. Players Club advertises savings of 25–60% on lodging, cruises, shows, and dining. In addition to Las Vegas, Players Club also sells Atlantic City, Lake Tahoe, Reno, the Caribbean, Hawaii, Mexico, and five cruise lines.

Players Club costs $192 (plus a $10 handling fee) a year for membership. In Las Vegas, Players Club uses Bally's, San Remo, the Flamingo Hilton, the Las Vegas Hilton, the Luxor, the Holiday Inn Boardwalk, and the Stardust. The Club also offers a three-month no-risk guarantee during which you can cancel your membership and receive a full refund of all fees.

An extremely determined person who knows Las Vegas can probably find a deal that beats Players Club but will have to invest a lot of time for a package only marginally less expensive. By joining Players Club, we were able to secure rooms in hotels that were otherwise sold out and to realize discounts of 18–45%. Since discounts apply to weekends and weekdays, as well as any length of stay, Players Club can be a real godsend for anyone traveling to Las Vegas to attend a convention or trade show. The savings we describe above are based on discounting standard rates quoted by the hotel. If you figure the percentage discount on convention rates, you can save in excess of 60%.

Savings on shows ranged as high as 50%, though most discounts in this category were in the 25% range. A nice extra, however, is that Players Club membership allows you "Invited Guest" privileges at participating shows, which means no waiting in show lines. Savings of up to 25% on meals applies only to designated restaurants, but there are some pretty decent restaurants on the list.

Though Players Club also offers discount airfares, we were able to beat their prices pretty regularly, but only with nonrefundable advance purchase

Reservation Services

Hotel Reservations Network   (800) 96-HOTEL
    www.hotelreservationsnetwork.com
 	
Reservations Plus   (800) 733-6644
    www.resplus.com
 	
RMC Travel Center   (800) 782-2674 or (800) 245-5738
 	
Accommodations Express   (800) 444-7666
    www.accomodationsexpress.com

tickets. If you purchase air travel from Players Club, you will pay a little more ($20–55) but will gain the advantage of being able to cancel your reservations with only a nominal penalty.

If you are interested in Players Club, you can call (800) 275-6600, but they are not always accepting new members. When you call, an operator will take your name, address, and phone number. Later an aggressive tele-marketer will call you back and try to sign you and your credit card up over the phone. If you ask for membership information, they will likewise try to respond over the phone. State that you do not have time to listen to an oral sales presentation, and insist that a complete written description of the club be mailed to you. Incidentally, if you join and later decide to cancel, Players Club will honor their money-back guarantee without any hassle.

Reservation Services

When wholesalers and consolidators deal directly with the public, they frequently represent themselves as "reservation services." When you call, you can ask for a rate quote for a particular hotel, or alternatively, ask for their best available deal in the area where you prefer to stay. If there is a maximum amount you are willing to pay, say so. Chances are the service will find something that will work for you, even if they have to shave a dollar or two off their own profit.

The discount available (if any) from a reservation service depends on whether the service functions as a consolidator or a wholesaler. Consolidators are strictly sales agents who do not own or control the room inventory they are trying to sell. Discounts offered by consolidators are determined by the hotels with rooms to fill. Consolidator discounts vary enormously depending on how desperate the hotel is to unload the rooms. When you deal with a room reservation service that operates as a consolidator, you pay for your room as usual when you check out of the hotel.

Wholesalers, as we discussed above, have long-standing contracts with hotels that allow the wholesaler to purchase rooms at an established deep discount. Some wholesalers hold purchase options on blocks of rooms while others actually pay for rooms and own the inventory. Because a wholesaler controls the room inventory, it can offer whatever discount it pleases consistent with current demand. In practice, most wholesaler reservation-service discounts fall in the 10–40% range. When you reserve a room with a reservation service that operates as a wholesaler, you must usually pay for your entire stay in advance with your credit card. The service then sends you a written confirmation and usually a voucher (indicating prepayment) for you to present at the hotel.

Our experience has been that the reservation services are more useful in finding rooms in Las Vegas when availability is scarce than in obtaining deep discounts. Calling the hotels ourselves, we were often able to beat the reservation services' rates when rooms were generally available. When the city was booked, however, and we could not find a room by calling the hotels ourselves, the reservation services could almost always get us a room at a fair price.

Hotel-Sponsored Packages

In addition to selling rooms through tour operators, consolidators, and wholesalers, most hotels periodically offer exceptional deals of their own. Sometimes the packages are specialized, as with golf packages, or are only offered at certain times of the year, for instance, December and January. Promotion of hotel specials tends to be limited to the hotel's primary markets, which for most properties is Southern California, Arizona, Utah, Colorado, Hawaii, and the Midwest. If you live in other parts of the country, you can take advantage of the packages but probably will not see them advertised in your local newspaper.

Some of the hotel packages are unbelievable deals. Once, for instance, one hotel offered three nights' free lodging, no strings attached, to any adult from Texas; and the Stardust ran a $32 special that included a room, a show, and a buffet for two people. And on certain dates in November, December, and January, the Flamingo offered a deal that included a room for two or more nights at $35 per night (tax inclusive), with two drinks and a show thrown in for good measure. In July of 2000, 27 hotels offered rates less than $40. Look for the hotel specials in Southern California newspapers, or call the hotel and ask.

An important point regarding hotel specials is that the hotel reservationists do not usually inform you of existing specials or offer them to you. In other words, *you have to ask.*

Exit Information Guide

A company called EIG (Exit Information Guide) publishes a book of discount coupons for bargain rates at hotels throughout California and Nevada. These books are available free of charge in many restaurants and motels along the main interstate highways. Since most folks make reservations prior to leaving home, picking up the coupon book en route does not help much. For $3 ($5 Canadian), however, EIG will mail you a copy (third class) before you make your reservations. Properties listed in the guide for Las Vegas are generally smaller, nongaming hotels. If you call and use a credit card, EIG will send the guide first class for an additional charge. Write or call:

Exit Information Guide
4205 N.W. Sixth Street
Gainesville, FL 32609
(352) 371-3948
www.roomsaver.com

HOW TO EVALUATE A TRAVEL PACKAGE

Hundreds of Las Vegas package trips and vacations are offered to the public each year. Almost all include round-trip transportation to Las Vegas and lodging. Sometimes room tax, transportation from the airport, a rental car, shows, meals, welcome parties, and/or souvenirs are also included.

In general, because the Las Vegas market is so competitive, packages to Las Vegas are among the best travel values available. Las Vegas competes head-to-head with Atlantic City for Eastern travelers and with Reno, Lake Tahoe, Laughlin, and other Nevada destinations for Western visitors. Within Las Vegas, downtown competes with the Strip, and individual hotels go one-on-one to improve their share of the market. In addition to the fierce competition for the destination traveler, the extraordinary profitability of gambling also works in the consumer's behalf to keep Las Vegas travel economical. In almost every hotel, amazing values in dining and lodging are used to lure visitors to the casino.

Packages should be a win/win proposition for both the buyer and the seller. The buyer (or travel agent) only has to make one phone call and deal with a single salesperson to set up the whole trip: transportation, lodging, rental car, show admissions, and even golf, tennis, and sightseeing. The seller, likewise, only has to deal with the buyer one time, eliminating the need for separate sales, confirmations, and billings. In addition to streamlining selling, processing, and administration, some packagers also buy airfares in bulk on contract like a broker playing the commodities market. Buying or guaranteeing a large number of airfares in advance allows the packager to buy them at a significant savings from posted fares. The same practice is also applied to hotel rooms. Because selling packaged trips is an efficient way of doing business, and the packager can often buy individual components (airfare, lodging) in bulk at a discount, savings in operating expenses realized by the seller are sometimes passed on to the buyer. So the package is not only convenient but an exceptional value. In any event, that is the way it is supposed to work.

In practice, the seller occasionally realizes all of the economies and passes none of the savings along to the buyer. In some instances, packages are loaded with extras that cost the packager next to nothing but run the retail price of the package sky-high. While this is not as common with Las Vegas packages as those to other destinations, it occurs frequently enough to warrant some comparison shopping.

When considering a package, choose one that includes features you are sure to use. Whether you use all the features or not, you will most certainly pay for them. Second, if cost is of greater concern than convenience, make a few phone calls and see what the package would cost if you booked its individual components (airfare, lodging, rental car) on your own. If the package price is less than the à la carte cost, the package is a good deal. If the costs are about the same, the package is probably worth it for the convenience.

An Example   My niece and her husband were looking at a package they found with Delta Vacations. The package included round-trip airfare (on Delta) from Atlanta, four nights' lodging (Friday through Monday) at the Luxor, airport transfers (transportation to and from the airport), and about 20 "bonus features," including:

- 2-for-1 admission to Hoover Dam tours

- Free admission to the Imperial Palace Auto Collection

- 2-for-1 cocktails at New York–New York

- 2-for-1 admission to Spellbound

- A free Planet Hollywood souvenir

- Discounted Lake Mead Boat Cruises

The price, tax included, was $548 per person, or $1,096 all together. Checking the Luxor and a number of airlines, they found the following:

Same room at the Luxor, two people to a room, for four nights with room tax included	$519
Transportation to and from the airport	$14
Subtotal	$533

Subtracting the $533 (lodging and airport transfers) from the cost of Delta's package total of $1,096, they determined that the air and "bonus features" portion of the package was worth $563 ($1,096 – $533 = $563). If they were not interested in using any of the bonus features, and they could fly to Las Vegas for less than $563, they would be better off turning down the package.

Scouting around, the lowest fare they could find was $320 on American Airlines with an advance purchase ticket. This piece of information completed their analysis as follows:

Option A: Delta Vacation package for two · · · · · · · · · · · · · · · $1,096

Option B: Booking their own air and lodging

Lodging, including tax	$519
Airfare on American Airlines for two	$640
Transportation to and from hotel	$14
Total	$1,173

For Business Travelers
CONVENTION RATES: HOW THE SYSTEM WORKS

Business travelers, particularly those attending trade shows or conventions, are almost always charged more for their rooms than leisure travelers. For big meetings, called citywide conventions, huge numbers of rooms are blocked in hotels all over town. These rooms are reserved for visitors attending the meeting in question and are usually requested and coordinated by the meeting's sponsoring organization in cooperation with the Las Vegas Convention and Visitors Authority.

Individual hotels negotiate a nightly rate with the convention sponsor, who then frequently sells the rooms through a central reservations system of its own. Since the hotels would rather have gamblers or leisure travelers than people attending conventions (who usually have limited time to gamble), the negotiated price tends to be high, often $10 to $50 per night above the rack rate.

Meeting sponsors, of course, blame convention rates on the hotels. Meanwhile the hotels maintain a stoic silence, not wishing to alienate meeting organizers. Following the publication of an earlier edition of this guide, the publisher received the following irate letter from a major convention sponsor:

> *Mr. Sehlinger writes that the convention sponsors often charge what they think the market will bear. Therefore, if the convention-goer gets gouged on a room, it is the doing of the convention sponsor, not the*

*hotel. This statement is completely false and misleading and puts [con-
vention sponsors] in a false light. [Our organization] does not make any
profit on hotel rooms. . . . The general practice is to charge our members
exactly what the hotel charges us. Each member pays his or her own
hotel bill when leaving Las Vegas, and [we] receive no commission,
kickback, or other payment from the hotel.*

To be fair, convention sponsors should be given some credit simply for having their meeting in Las Vegas. Even considering the inflated convention rates,
meeting attendees will pay 20–60% less in Las Vegas for comparable lodging
than in other major convention cities. As for the rest, well, let's take a look.

Sam Walton taught the average American that someone purchasing a
large quantity of a particular item should be able to obtain a better price (per
item) than a person buying only one or two. If anyone just walking in off
the street can buy a single hotel room for $50, why then must a convention
sponsor, negotiating for 900 rooms for five nights in the same hotel (4,500
room-nights in hotel jargon), settle for a rate of $60 per night?

Many Las Vegas hotels take a hardline negotiating position with meeting
sponsors because (1) every room occupied by a convention-goer is one less
room available for gamblers, and (2) they figure that most business travelers
are on expense accounts. In addition, timing is a critical factor in negotiating
room rates. The hotels do not want business travelers occupying rooms on
weekends or during the more popular times of the year. Convention sponsors who want to schedule a meeting during high season (when hotels fill
their rooms no matter what) can expect to pay premium rates. In addition,
and regardless of the time of year, many hotels routinely charge stiff prices to
convention-goers as a sort of insurance against lost opportunity. "What if we
block our rooms for a trade show one year in advance," a sales manager asked,
"and then a championship prizefight is scheduled for that week? We would
lose big-time."

A spokesman for the Las Vegas Convention and Visitors Authority indicated that the higher room rates for conventioneers are not unreasonable
given a hotel's commitment to the sponsor to hold rooms in reserve. But reserved rooms, or room blocks as they are called, fragment a hotel's inventory
of available rooms, and often make it harder, not easier, to get a room in a
particular hotel. The bottom line is that convention-goers pay a premium
price for the benefit of having rooms reserved for their meeting—rooms that
would always be cheaper, and often easier to reserve, if the sponsor had not
reserved them in the first place. For a major, citywide convention, it is not
unusual for attendees to collectively pay in excess of $1 million for the peace
of mind of having rooms reserved.

Whether room blocking is really necessary is an interesting question. The Las Vegas Convention and Visitors Authority works with convention sponsors to ensure that there is never more than one citywide meeting in town at a time and to make sure that sponsors do not schedule their conventions at a time when Las Vegas hotels are otherwise normally sold out (National Finals Rodeo week, Super Bowl weekend, New Year's, and so on). Unfortunately for meeting planners, some major events (prizefights, tennis matches) are occasionally scheduled in Las Vegas on short notice. If a meeting planner does not block rooms and a big fight is announced for the week the meeting is in town, the attendees may be unable to find a room. This is such a nightmare to convention sponsors that they cave in to exorbitant convention rates rather than risk not having rooms. The actual likelihood of a major event being scheduled at the same time as a large convention is small, though the specter of this worst-case scenario is a powerful weapon in the bargaining arsenal of the hotels.

On balance, meeting sponsors negate their volume-buying clout by scheduling meetings during the more popular times of year or, alternatively, by caving in to the hotels' "opportunity cost" room pricing. Conversely, hotels play unfairly on the sponsor's fear of not having enough rooms, and they charge premium rates to cover improbable, ill-defined opportunity losses. Is there collusion here? Probably not. The more likely conclusion is that both hotels and sponsors have become comfortable with an inflexible negotiating environment, but one that permits meeting sponsors to distribute the unreasonable charges pro rata to their attendees.

Working through the Maze

If you attempt to bypass the sponsoring organization and go directly through the hotel, the hotel will either refer you to the convention's central reservations number or quote you the same high price. Even if you do not identify yourself as a convention-goer, the hotel will figure it out by the dates you request. In most instances, even if you lie and insist that you are not attending the convention in question, the hotel will make you pay the higher rate or claim to be sold out.

By way of example, we tried to get reservations at the Riviera for a major trade show in the spring, a citywide convention that draws about 30,000 attendees. The show runs six days plus one day for setting up, or seven days total, Saturday through Friday. Though this example involves the Riviera, we encountered the same scenario at every hotel we called.

When we phoned reservations at the Riviera and gave them our dates, they immediately asked if we would be attending a convention or trade show. When we answered in the affirmative, they gave us the official sponsor's central reservations phone number in New York. We called the sponsor and learned that a single room at the Riviera (one person in one room) booked through them would cost $91 per night including room tax. The same room (we found from other sources) booked directly through the Riviera would cost $80 with tax included.

We called the Riviera back and asked for the same dates, this time disavowing any association with the trade show, and were rebuffed. Obviously skeptical of our story, the hotel informed us that they were sold out for the days we requested. Unconvinced that the hotel was fully booked, we had two different members of our research team call. One attempted to make reservations from Wednesday *of the preceding week* through Tuesday of the trade show week, while our second caller requested a room from Wednesday of the trade show week through the following Tuesday. These respective sets of dates, we reasoned, would differ sufficiently from the show dates to convince the Riviera that we were not conventioneers. In each case we were able to make reservations for the dates desired at the $80-per-night rate.

It should be stressed that a hotel treats the convention's sponsoring organization much like a wholesaler who reserves rooms in a block for a negotiated price. What the convention, in turn, charges its attendees is out of the hotel's control. Once a hotel and convention sponsor come to terms, the hotel either refers all inquiries about reservations to the sponsor or accepts bookings at whatever nightly rate the sponsor determines. Since hotels do not want to get in the way of their convention sponsors (who are very powerful customers) or, alternatively, have convention attendees buying up rooms intended for other nonconvention customers, the hotel reservations department carefully screens any request for a room during a convention period.

Strategies for Beating Convention Rates

There are several strategies for getting around convention rates:

1. Buy a package from a tour operator or a wholesaler This tactic makes it unnecessary to deal with the convention's central reservations office or with an individual hotel's reservations department. Many packages allow you to buy extra days at a special discounted room rate if the package dates do not coincide perfectly with your meeting dates.

Packages that use air charter services operate on a fixed, inflexible schedule. As a rule these packages run three nights (depart Thursday, return Sunday; or depart Friday, return Monday) or four nights (depart Monday, return Friday; or depart Sunday, return Thursday). Two-night, five-night, and seven-night charter packages can also be found. Charter air packages offer greater savings, but usually less flexibility, than packages that use commercial carriers.

Since the Riviera would not give us their standard rate for the trade show dates, our remaining alternatives were to either find a package or book through the sponsor's central reservations. We wanted to travel from Birmingham, Alabama, and stay at the Riviera for the seven nights of the show. For one person, the options were as follows:

Option A: Reservations through show's official sponsor

Riviera for seven nights at $91 per night (tax included)	$637
plus round-trip airfare from Birmingham, Alabama	$344
Total	$981

Option B: Charter package

Riviera for seven nights, all taxes, round-trip direct flights, two breakfasts, two dinner buffets, and three shows

Total	$798

Option C: Airline tour service's package

American's Fly-Away Vacations offered round-trip airfare, seven nights' lodging, taxes included, to the Riviera for $789 but were sold out for the required dates when we called six weeks in advance. They were able to offer the same package for the Las Vegas Hilton at $873. The Las Vegas Hilton is within easy walking distance of both the Riviera and the Convention Center.

Total	$789 or $873

Delta Vacations did not use the Riviera but had a package with round-trip airfare and seven nights' lodging, all taxes included, available for the desired dates at two hotels *not* within walking distance of the Riviera or the Las Vegas Convention Center:

Flamingo	$769
Harrah's	$879

United's Vacation Planning Center, whose wholesaler is Funway Holidays, had a package with round-trip airfare, seven nights' lodging at the Riviera, taxes, and airport transfers available for the dates of the show.

Total	$851

If you are able to beat the convention rate by booking a package or getting a room from a wholesaler, don't blow your cover when you check in. If you walk up to the registration desk in a business suit and a convention ID badge, the hotel will void your package and charge you the full convention

Strip Hotels That Rarely Participate in Room Blocks		
Circus Circus	Luxor	Westward Ho
Excalibur		

Downtown Hotels That Seldom Participate in Room Blocks		
Binion's Horseshoe	Fitzgeralds	Lady Luck
California	Four Queens	
El Cortez	Fremont	

rate. If you are supposed to be a tourist, act like one, particularly when you check in and check out.

2. Find a hotel that does not participate in the convention room blocks
Many of the downtown, North Las Vegas, and Boulder Highway hotels, as well as a few of the Strip hotels, do not make rooms available in blocks for conventions. If you wish to avoid convention rates, obtain a list of your convention's "official" hotels from the sponsoring organization and match it against the hotels listed in this guide. Any hotel listed in this book that does not appear on the list supplied by the meeting sponsors is not participating in blocking rooms for your convention. This means you can deal with the nonparticipating hotels directly and should be able to get their regular rate.

Most citywide trade shows and conventions are held at the Las Vegas Convention Center. Of all the nonparticipating hotels, only Circus Circus and Westward Ho are within a 15-minute walk. If you stay at any of the other hotels, you will have to commute to the Convention Center by shuttle, cab, or car.

3. Reserve late Thirty to sixty days prior to the opening of a citywide convention or show, the front desk room reservations staff in a given hotel will take over the management of rooms reserved for the meeting from the hotel's sales and marketing department. "Room Res," in conjunction with the general manager, is responsible for making sure that the hotel is running at peak capacity for the dates of the show. The general manager has the authority to lower the room rate from the price negotiated with the sponsor. If rooms are not being booked for the convention in accordance with the hotel's expectations, the general manager will often lower the rate for attendees and, at the same time, return a number of reserved rooms to general inventory for sale to the public. A convention-goer who books a room at the last minute might obtain a lower rate than an attendee who booked early through the sponsor's central housing service. Practically speaking, however, do not expect to find rooms available at the convention headquarters hotel or at most of the hotels within easy walking distance. As a rule of thumb, the farther from the Convention Center or headquarters a hotel is, the better the chances of finding a discounted room at the last minute.

THE LAS VEGAS CONVENTION CENTER

The Las Vegas Convention Center is the largest single-level convention and trade show facility in the United States. Almost 2 million square feet of exhibit space are divided into two main buildings: the brand new South Hall and the older North Hall. A pedestrian bridge over Desert Inn Road connects the halls. Trade shows that crowd facilities in Washington, San Francisco, and New York fit with ease in this immense Las Vegas complex. In addition to the exhibit areas, the Center has a new lobby and public areas, a kitchen that can cater a banquet for 12,000 people, and 89 meeting rooms. Serving as headquarters for shows and conventions drawing as many as 250,000 delegates, the Convention Center is on Paradise Road, one very long block off the Las Vegas Strip and three miles from the airport.

For both exhibitors and attendees, the Las Vegas Convention Center is an excellent site for a meeting or trade show. Large and small exhibitors can locate and access their exhibit sites with a minimum of effort. Numerous loading docks and huge bay doors make loading and unloading quick and simple for large displays arriving by truck. Smaller displays transported in vans and cars are unloaded on the north side of the main hall and can be carried or wheeled directly to the exhibit area without climbing stairs or using elevators. The exhibit areas and meeting rooms are well marked and easy to find.

The Las Vegas Convention and Visitors Authority also operates Cashman Field Center, home of Las Vegas's AAA baseball team. In addition to a baseball stadium, the Center contains a 2,000-seat theater and 100,000 square feet of meeting and exhibit space. For more information, call (702) 892-0711.

Lodging within Walking Distance of the Las Vegas Convention Center

While participants in citywide conventions lodge all over town, a few hotels are within easy walking distance of the Convention Center. Next door, and closest, is the huge Las Vegas Hilton, with over 3,100 rooms. The Hilton routinely serves as headquarters for meetings and shows in the Convention Center and provides, if needed, an additional 220,000 square feet of exhibit, ballroom, banquet, special event, and meeting room space. Many smaller

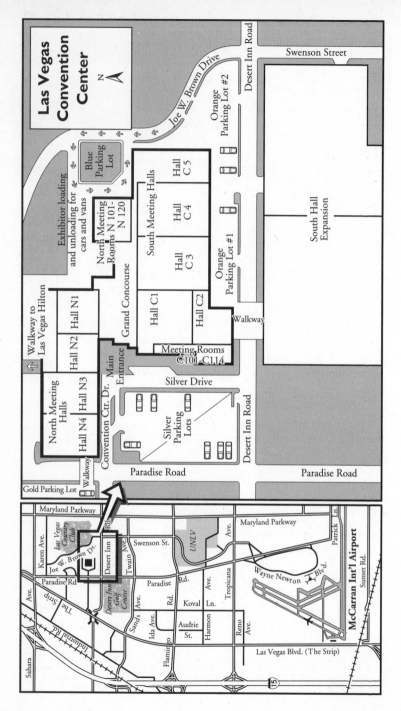

Hotels within a 20-Minute Walk of the Convention Center		
AmeriSuites	202 suites	7-minute walk
Circus Circus	3,741 rooms	15-minute walk
La Concha	352 rooms	15-minute walk
Las Vegas Courtyard (Marriott)	149 rooms	6-minute walk
Las Vegas Hilton	3,174 rooms	5-minute walk
Mardi Gras Inn (Best Western)	314 suites	12-minute walk
Marriott Suites	255 suites	9-minute walk
New Frontier	988 rooms	20-minute walk
Residence Inn (Marriott)	192 suites	7-minute walk
Riviera Hotel	2,075 rooms	10-minute walk
Royal Hotel	220 rooms	12-minute walk
Stardust	2,500 rooms	15-minute walk

conventions conduct all their meetings, including exhibits, at the Hilton. The walk from the lobby of the Hilton to the Convention Center is about five minutes for most people.

A long half block away (to its rear entrance) is the 2,075-room Riviera Hotel. Like the Las Vegas Hilton, the Riviera is often the headquarters for large shows and meetings at the Convention Center. With 158,000 square feet of meeting and banquet space, the Riviera, like the Hilton, hosts entire meetings and provides supplemental facilities for events at the Convention Center. The walk from the rear (eastern) entrance of the Riviera to the Convention Center takes about ten minutes.

Parking at the Las Vegas Convention Center

In all, there are approximately 6,000 parking space in nine color-coded lots. Gold Lots 1–4 make up the bulk of visitor parking; the Gold Lots are located in front of the complex off of Paradise Road. Across Paradise Road from the Gold Lots, between Convention Center Drive and Desert Inn Road, are two Silver Lots. Visitors will want to explore the Gold and Silver lots first.

There are two Orange Lots located off of Desert Inn Road, which runs between the older part of the convention center and the new South Hall expansion. As of press time, parking in the Orange Lots was partially closed off due to construction with the balance reserved for employees. A single, small Blue Lot located behind the complex off of Joe W. Brown Drive is currently used by employees and may have little or no space available for conventioneers. So, although the front lots most likely will be packed, check there first (at least until the Orange Lots are cleared of construction duty).

Though access to the exhibit floor varies from meeting to meeting, attendees are often required to enter through the Convention Center's main entrance off Paradise Road. If not parked in the Gold or Silver lots, convention-goers must hike around the south side of the complex in order to reach the front door, a seven- to ten-minute walk. For other meetings, properly credentialed attendees (i.e., those with registration badges) are permitted to enter the exhibit halls by one of several doors along the south side of the Convention Center. As a rule, getting out is not as hard as getting in, and attendees are usually permitted to exit through the south-side doors.

Cabs and Shuttles to the Convention Center

Large, citywide conventions often provide complimentary bus service from major hotels to the Convention Center. If you are staying at a smaller hotel and wish to use the shuttle bus, walk to the nearest large hotel on the shuttle route. Though cabs are plentiful and efficient in Las Vegas, they are sometimes in short supply at convention or trade show daily opening and closing times. Public transportation—CAT buses ($2) and the Las Vegas Strip Trolley ($1.50)—is also available from the larger hotels. Exact fare is required.

Your best bet is to stay within walking distance of the Convention Center. If you end up staying too far away to walk, a car is usually less hassle than depending on cabs and shuttle buses.

Lunch Alternatives for Convention and Trade-Show Attendees

The Convention Center food service provides a better than average lunch and snack selection. As at most convention centers, however, prices are high. Outside of the Convention Center, but within walking distance, are the buffet and coffee shop at the Hilton, and Nippon, a Japanese restaurant and sushi bar (a ten-minute walk). The better restaurants at the Las Vegas Hilton are not open for lunch.

The restaurants mentioned above provide decent food and fast service but are bustling eateries not particularly conducive to a quiet business lunch. At 3900 Paradise Road, however, there is a small shopping center (only three minutes from the Convention Center by cab) that has several quiet, high-quality ethnic restaurants. Shalimar, a good Indian restaurant, offers a lunch buffet. Across the parking lot are Yolie's, a Brazilian steak house, and its neighbor Beijing, one of the city's better Chinese restaurants. Also located in the shopping center is a sandwich shop.

Comfort Zones: Matching Guests with Hotels

I have a good friend, a single woman of 32, who, in search of a little romance, decided to take a Caribbean cruise. Thinking that one cruise was pretty much like any other, she signed up for a cruise without doing much shopping around. She ended up on a boat full of retired married folks who played bingo or bridge every evening and were usually in the sack by 10:30 p.m. My friend mistakenly assumed, as have many others, that cruises are basically homogeneous products. In fact, nothing could be farther from the truth. Each cruise provides a tailored experience to a specific and narrowly defined market. If my friend had done her homework, she could have booked passage on a boat full of young, single people and danced and romanced into the night.

In Las Vegas, it is likewise easy to assume that all the hotels and casinos are fairly similar. True, they all have guest rooms, restaurants, and the same mix of games in the casino, but each property molds its offerings to appeal to a well-defined audience. This concerted effort to please a specific population of guests creates what we call a "comfort zone." If you are among the group a hotel strives to please, you will feel comfortable and at home and will have much in common with the other guests. However, if you fail to determine the comfort zone before you go, you may end up like my friend— on the wrong boat.

Visitors come to Las Vegas either to vacation and play or to attend a meeting or convention. While these reasons for coming to Las Vegas are not mutually exclusive, there is a marked difference between a recreational visitor and a business traveler. The vacationer is likely to be older (45 years and up), retired, and from the Midwest, Southern California, Arizona, Colorado, or Hawaii. The business traveler is younger on average and comes from just about anywhere. Individual hotels and casinos pay close attention to these differences and customize their atmosphere, dining, and entertainment to satisfy a specific type of traveler.

The California Hotel, downtown, for example, targets Hawaiians and maintains a specialty food store and restaurants that supply their clientele with favorite snacks and dishes from the islands. On the Boulder Highway, Sam's Town is geared toward cowboys and retired travelers. Entertainment at Sam's Town consists of bowling and country-western dancing. Circus Circus on the Strip attracts the RV crowd (with its own RV park) but also offers large, low-priced rooms, buffets, free circus acts, and an amusement park to lure families. The Las Vegas Hilton and the Venetian, both next door to the convention centers, go the extra mile to make business travelers feel at home.

Some hotels are posh and exclusive, while others are more Spartan and intended to appeal to younger or more frugal visitors. Each property, however, from its lounge entertainment to its guest room decor or the dishes served in its restaurants, is packaged with a certain type of guest in mind.

Because Las Vegas is basically a very informal town, you will not feel as out of place as my friend did on her cruise if you happen to end up in the wrong hotel. In any given property there is a fairly broad range of clientele. There always will be hotels where you experience a greater comfort level than at others, however. In a place as different as Las Vegas, that added comfort can sometimes mean a lot.

Democracy in the Casinos

While Las Vegas hotels and casinos continue to be characterized as appealing to "high rollers" or "grinds," the distinction has become increasingly blurred. High rollers, of course, are wealthy visitors who come to gamble in earnest, while grinds are less affluent folks who grudgingly bet their money a nickel or quarter at a time. For many years, the slot machine was symbolic of the grinds. Unable to join the action of the high-stakes table games, these blue-collar gamblers would sit for hours pumping the arms of the slots. More recently, however, the slots are the symbol of casino profitability, contributing anywhere from 40–100% of a given casino's bottom line.

The popularity of the slot machine among gamblers of all types has democratized the casino. The casinos recognize that the silver-haired lady at the quarter slots is an extremely valuable customer and that it is good business to forgo the impression of exclusivity in order to make her comfortable. In Las Vegas there are casinos that maintain the illusion of an upper-crust clientele while quietly practicing an egalitarianism that belies any such pretense. By virtue of its economic clout, the slot machine has broadened the comfort zone of the stuffiest casinos and made Las Vegas a friendlier, more pleasant (albeit noisier) place.

The Feel of the Place

Las Vegas's hotel-casinos have distinctly individual personalities. While all casinos contain slot machines, craps tables, and roulette wheels, the feel of each particular place is unique, a product of the combined characteristics of management, patrons, and design. This feel, or personality, determines a hotel-casino's comfort zone, the peculiar ambience that makes one guest feel totally at home while another runs for the exit.

The Author's Bias Openly Admitted   As you read the hotel-casino descriptions that follow, you will perhaps intuit that the author is a little claustrophobic. I do not understand why so many casinos are dark, noisy, and confining; they are more like submarines than places of recreation. Why, I'd like to know, isn't there a casino in a nice, rooftop atrium where you can watch the sun set and the birds fly over? Is there a reason why we should be blinded by blinking lights or deafened by clanking coins in gloomy tunnels upholstered with red Naugahyde?

Apparently there is some casino marketing theory which postulates that customers will gamble longer and more aggressively if their circadian rhythms are disturbed, their natural clocks unplugged. Zoos confuse nocturnal animals this way to make them rummage around when they should be sleeping. Casino customers, like these animals, are never supposed to know if it is day or night. This is patently ridiculous, of course, because unlike bats and lemurs, almost every gambler has a watch or can tell what time it is by the type of food on the buffet.

Why do I worry about this, you ask? Isn't doubling down on any two cards and re-splitting pairs in blackjack more important than how low the ceiling is? Maybe to you, my friend, but not to me. I want to gamble where I can breathe, stand up straight, and not smell the person playing at the next machine. I'd like for my pupils to be the same size for more than three consecutive seconds, and I'd like to be able to conduct a conversation without using a megaphone. I'd even like to know whether or not it's raining outside. And while I'm aware that it is perfectly possible to play craps in an alley, that's not why I go to Las Vegas. We've got plenty of alleys at home.

This is not to imply that I gamble in the departure concourse at the airport but to warn you about my natural bias against hotels and casinos that feel like velveteen U-boats. If, in the following descriptions, I talk about "ceiling height" a lot, I hope you will understand.

Hotels with Casinos

How to Avoid Reading the Hotel-Casino Descriptions   If you don't care how a place "feels" but just want to know whether it has room service and tennis courts, or when check-out time is, you can skip to the alphabetically arranged Hotel Information Chart at the end of this chapter.

Aladdin   (www.aladdincasino.com)

With the distinction of being the only strip hotel to be imploded and then rebuilt on the same site, the new Aladdin Resort and Casino is the Las Vegas version of Phoenix rising. The question for the moment, however, is how high can this bird fly? The theme, of course, draws its inspiration from the

Arabian Nights tales, which in turn are based on the Islamic culture and folklore of North Africa and the eastern Mediterranean.

The casino and hotel present the theme in whimsical storybook fashion with some Las Vegas neon and glitter tossed in for good measure. A two-story, football-field-long mural over the strip entrance, for example, twinkles with fiber-optic flowers, not something you'd likely see in the desert, even with a good buzz. The size of the mural typifies the oversize proportions of the casino and hotel public areas where scale dominates detail. The hotel lobby occupies the lower level, with the casino on the second floor. Continuing upward there is a mezzanine level and third floor overlooking the entire gaming area. The casino's more interesting details include ebony Pegasus flying horse sculptures at the entrance to the sports book and an Aladdin's lamp the size of a small locomotive atop the Lamp Bar. Another attention getter, the Roc Bar, sits beneath the watchful eye of a mammoth, raven-like bird from the Sinbad story.

In addition to the main casino, there is a casino for elite patrons and high rollers called the London Club. Here the casino's most valued customers can gamble and dine in elegant closed-door surroundings without being bothered by, well, the rest of us.

Ringing the casino except on the west is the Desert Passage shopping venue. Built to human scale and more realistically rendered than the fanciful casino, Desert Passage consists of 130 upscale stores and restaurants situated along the streets of a mythical Arabian city. Incorporating the icons and architecture of the Arab world from Istanbul to Marrakech, Desert Passage streets reside in perpetual twilight beneath sky murals painted on an arched ceiling. The overall effect is well done, much in the image of the Forum Shops at Caesars Palace and the Grand Canal Shops at the Venetian. You can enter Desert Passage from the strip or from two entrances connecting the shopping complex with the casino.

Guest rooms at the Aladdin are roomy and come equipped with two phone lines and a complete computer set up that allows guests to go online without bringing along their own computers. The lobby for the hotel is on the lowest level and can be accessed from Harmon Avenue. Elevators serving the guestroom floors are adjacent to the lobby eliminating the usual inconvenient trek through the casino with all of your luggage.

The swimming complex, situated six floors up, is spacious and offers the usual amenities, but is not visually very interesting. The spa and health club were still struggling to open when the *Unofficial Guide* went to press.

Entertainment at the Aladdin includes the Aladdin Theatre for the Performing arts, a huge venue that hosts headliners, concerts, and theater productions, and the Blue Note Jazz Club. Even with its prestigious New York parentage, the Blue Note is a huge disappointment. For starters, parking is remote, it's hard to access the club from the shopping area or the casino, and there are lots of incidental charges that quickly add up to an exorbitantly expensive evening.

Dining at the Aladdin is good, with something for every budget. Though staying power is sometimes a problem with new buffets, the Aladdin Spice Market buffet was one of the best in town when we went to press. All together there are 21 restaurants on site. They range from national chains such as P.F. Chang's to clones of celebrated eateries in other cities like Anasazi, IBIZA, and Commanders Palace. During our last visit, however, some of the restaurants were struggling (as were a number of the Desert Passage retailers) so expect a few changes in the line-up.

There's a lot at the Aladdin (as there is at most new casinos) that needs fixing: no odds board in the sports book*; low pay slots and video poker machines; $2 valet parking fee (plus tip) for Desert Passage; remote self-parking; price gouging at the Blue Note; no real anchor store in the shopping venue; etc. Market pressure will probably take care of most problems—Las Vegas is a very competitive town. The other, less appealing, scenario is that the Aladdin is one super property too many.

The Aladdin targets the Southwestern US, European, Middle Eastern, and Asian markets as well as convention and business visitors.

Arizona Charlie's *East and West*   (www.azcharlies.com)

Patronized primarily by locals, Arizona Charlie's are working person's casinos with a Southwestern ranch flavor. Everything is informal, a sort of shirtsleeves place. And it's busy. There is an energy, a three-ring circus feel of much going on at once—lots of slots, some table games, a sports book, burgers and beer, and a lounge that often features big-name (OK, medium-name) entertainment. The hotel rooms are passable, but the real reason to patronize Arizona Charlie's is the video poker—they're the best machines in town, and considering what town you're in, this means they're among the best machines anywhere. The original Arizona Charlie's is on Decatur, west of the Strip. A new Arizona Charlie's East opened in 2000 on the Boulder Highway.

Bally's   (www.ballyslv.com)

A complete resort, Bally's is blessed with exceptional restaurants, one of the better buffets in Las Vegas, and *the* best Sunday champagne brunch. Entertainment likewise is top-quality, with an outstanding production show, *Jubilee!* Guest rooms are large and comfortable, and the hotel, although quite spread out, is easy to find your way around in. Amenities include a health club and spa and a large, diversified shopping arcade.

*A sports book is a casino facility, sometimes simple, often elaborate, where wagers are taken on sporting events.

The casino is immense, open, and elegantly modern—sophisticated in a formal, understated way, like a tuxedo. Active without being claustrophobic, and classy without being stiff, Bally's captures the style of Continental casinos without sacrificing American informality.

Bally's caters to meetings and conventions and is one of the few hotels where you will not feel out of place in a business suit. Guests are frequently under age 40 here and come from all over, but particularly Southern California, Chicago, and elsewhere in the Midwest. Bally's also has a loyal Spanish-speaking clientele.

Demonstrating legitimate concern about the traffic congestion on the Strip, Bally's joined with the MGM Grand in constructing a monorail that connects Bally's with the MGM Grand Hotel and theme park. It is the hope of Bally's and the MGM Grand that the city will continue the initiative, extending the monorail the length of the Strip and perhaps even downtown. In a separate project, Bally's has built a series of moving walkways to transport guests from Las Vegas Boulevard into the casino. In a Las Vegas first, Bally's also offers moving walkways *out* of the casino. Maybe this is the only way, short of a forklift, that Bally's could get the bulk loaders out of the buffet.

Barbary Coast   (www.barbarycoastcasino.com)

The Barbary Coast is an old-fashioned casino for real gamblers. Appointed in dark wood embellished with murals in stained glass, this small hotel-casino serves a loyal clientele of locals and serious gamblers. With the feel of an exclusive and tasteful gentleman's club, the Barbary Coast's offerings are straightforward and simple. Table games still reign supreme in the casino, and the gourmet restaurant, Michael's, is regarded by many locals as the most dependable in town. There is no showroom, no swimming pool, no sauna or whirlpool, and most of the 200 hotel rooms (decorated in a San Francisco-turn-of-the-century style) are reserved for regular customers.

Bellagio   (www.bellagiolasvegas.com)

It's no secret that Steve Wynn established a new standard for Las Vegas hotel-casinos when he opened the Mirage in 1989. While it's doubtful that Wynn foresaw the impact the Mirage would have on Las Vegas, it's certain that he relishes his role as an instrument of change. Now, like an author trying to build on the success of an earlier work, Wynn took another shot in 1999 at bumping up the standard. The vehicle for Wynn's aspirations this time is Bellagio, situated on the site of the old Dunes hotel and golf course. Quite simply, Wynn intended for it to be the best hotel in the world, a hotel that will rewrite the concept of hospitality. In 2000, however, in a move that took everyone by surprise, Wynn sold the Bellagio along with his other casino properties to MGM Grand for $6.4 billion in cash. Wynn's latest attempt to rock the Las Vegas status quo will take place sometime during the next three years on the site of the venerable Desert Inn. For now, though, back to the Bellagio.

With its main entrance off the Strip just south of Flamingo Road, the Bellagio is inspired by an Italian village overlooking Lake Como in the sub-Alpine north of Italy. The facade of the Bellagio will remind you somewhat of the themed architecture Wynn employed at Treasure Island, only this time it's provincial Italian instead of Caribbean. The Bellagio village is arrayed along the west and north sides of a man-made lake, where dancing fountains provide allure and spectacle, albeit more dignified than the Mirage's exploding volcano or Treasure Island's buccaneer carnage.

Rising behind the village facade in a gentle curve is the 3,000-room hotel, complete with casino, restaurants, shopping complex, complete spa, and pool. Imported marble is featured throughout, even in the guest rooms and suites, as are original art, traditionally styled furnishings, and European antiques. Guest rooms and meeting rooms also feature large picture windows affording views of lushly landscaped grounds and formal gardens.

Surprisingly, the Italian village theme of Bellagio's lakefront facade is largely abandoned in the hotel's interior. Though a masterpiece of integrated colors, textures, and sightlines, the interior design reflects no strong sense of theme. In two steps, passing indoors, you go from a provincial village on a very human scale to a monumentally grand interior with proportions reminiscent of national libraries. You've heard it's lovely, and naturally it is, but somehow in a very different way than you might have anticipated. The vast spaces are exceedingly tasteful and unquestionably sophisticated, yet they fail to evoke the fun, whimsy, and curiosity so intrinsic to the Mirage and Treasure Island.

Perhaps because Las Vegas has conditioned us to a plastic, carnival sort of stimulation, entering the Bellagio is like stepping from the midway into the basilica. The surroundings impress but do not engage our emotions—except, of course, for the art, and that is exactly the point. Seen as a rich, neutral backdrop for the extraordinary works of art displayed throughout Bellagio, the lapse of thematic continuity is understandable. No theme could compete, and none should.

Truly the art is everywhere, even on the ceiling of the registration lobby, where a vibrantly colorful blown glass piece by Dale Chihuly hangs. Some wonderful works are showcased in the Bellagio's restaurants. Thirteen original Picassos, for example, are on exhibit in the restaurant of the same name.

Architecturally, Bellagio's most creative and interesting spaces are found in its signature conservatory and botanical gardens (where the flowers and plants are changed regularly) and in its restaurants. If you spend time at the Bellagio, visit each of the restaurants for a moment, if only to take in their stunning design. All Bellagio's restaurants, including a Las Vegas branch of Le Cirque, feature panoramic views. Some offer both indoor and outdoor dining experiences. In addition to the restaurants, Bellagio serves one of Las Vegas's best— and not unexpectedly one of the city's most expensive—buffets. With the exception of the buffet and coffee shop, Bellagio's restaurants require reservations, preferably made a month to six weeks before you leave home.

The Bellagio's showroom hosts a new production of the justly acclaimed *Cirque du Soleil.* Though terribly expensive, the show is *Cirque's* most challenging production yet, featuring a one-of-a-kind set that transforms seamlessly from hard surface to water. Like Bellagio itself, the *Cirque* production *"O"* (from the pronunciation of the French word *eau* for water) lacks the essential humor and humanness of *Cirque's Mystere* at Treasure Island, but is nonetheless heartrendingly beautiful.

Meant to be luxurious, the Bellagio seeks to establish itself as the prestige address of Las Vegas. For example, retailers in the shopping venue include Chanel, Hermes, Tiffany, Gucci, and Fred Leighton. Rates for guest rooms and suites are among the highest ever seen on the Strip, and its purported target market includes high rollers and discriminating business travelers who often eschew gaming properties. It's hard, however, to discuss exclusivity and personal service in the same breath with 3,000 rooms. Also, there's a lot of both new and old competition for the upscale market, including Caesars, the Venetian, and Mandalay Bay, to name a few. What's more, Bellagio guests do not have to look far to make comparisons: All north-facing guest rooms peer directly down on the stunning pool complex at Caesars Palace.

Room rates have bounced all over the place during Bellagio's first three years and in the future may bounce to a level that you find acceptable. If you stay at the Bellagio you will find the same basic informality typical of the rest of the Strip, and, surprisingly, you will encounter more people like you in the hotel than you will the super rich. Expressed more directly, Bellagio is a friendly place to stay and gamble and not at all pretentious. I did have a funny experience, however, in one of its retail shops. For three days I passed the same men's clothing shop and never saw a soul in it. Suspecting that it was being avoided because of the Bellagio's reputation for expensive boutique shopping, I ventured in. As a test I chose a cotton shirt-jacket almost identical in appearance to one I had seen in a Banana Republic catalog for $68. Not finding a price tag, I inquired of the helpful salesperson and was informed that this garment sold for a mere $1,490. When I laughed out loud, he explained in all seriousness that the shirt was made in Italy. Indeed, and no doubt hand delivered via the Concorde!

Boardwalk   (www.hiboardwalk.com)

The Boardwalk, though completely upgraded, remains a modest casino by Las Vegas standards. Blessed with a good location next to the Monte Carlo, the Boardwalk is a jumping-off place for guests heading to more imposing surroundings up and down the Strip. Acquired in 1994 by Holiday Inn, the casino was expanded and rebuilt from scratch with a light, airy, Coney Island–boardwalk theme. In 1998, the Boardwalk was bought by Mirage, and in summer 2000 was acquired by MGM Grand. Though all table games are represented, the emphasis is definitely on slots. A new-ish hotel tower (built while under Holiday Inn's ownership) offers guest rooms that live up to the Holiday Inn standard, but won't quite meet that of MGM. No telling what changes MGM will affect. On the down side, at present dining is limited to counter service, a buffet, and a small coffee shop. Because the only entrance to the Boardwalk is via the Strip, auto accessibility is also a problem. Owing to the Holiday Inn connection, guests at the Boardwalk run the gamut.

Boulder Station   (www.boulderstation.com)

Boulder Station is a clone of Palace Station, sharing its railroad theme and emphasis on good food and lounge entertainment. Located on Boulder Highway not far from the Showboat, Boulder Station features a roomy casino with a Western town motif (more in the image of turn-of-the-century Denver than of Dodge City). Tastefully done, with much attention to detail, the casino includes one of the nicest sports books in Las Vegas. Thirty-three big-screen, high-resolution monitors make the Boulder Station sports book a superb place for spectators. Like its sister properties, Boulder Station is an oasis for the hungry, with a great buffet, several good full-service restaurants, and possibly the best selection of fast food found in any casino. Guest rooms in the 300-room hotel tower are modest but comfortable, with good views. There is a swimming pool, but it is small and stark. Clientele consists primarily of locals and Southern Californians.

Comparing Boulder Station to Palace Station, we like the casino much better at Boulder Station but prefer the guest rooms at Palace Station's tower. The buffets and restaurants run pretty much a dead heat, but Boulder Station is much less crowded.

Bourbon Street   (www.bourbonstreethotel.com)

Bourbon Street is located a block east of the Strip on Flamingo. Known locally as an "overflow" joint, Bourbon Street offers a small casino, a lounge, a coffee shop quality restaurant, and inexpensive guest rooms within easy walking distance of the Strip.

Caesars Palace   (www.caesars.com)

Of Las Vegas's theme hotels and casinos, Caesars Palace was the first to fully realize its potential. As an exercise in whimsical fantasy and excess, Caesars'

Roman theme has been executed with astounding artistry and attention to detail. Creating an atmosphere of informality in surroundings too pretentious to believe is hard to pull off, but that is exactly what Caesars Palace has done. Somehow the vaulted ceilings, classic statuary, and graceful arches accommodate the clanking of coins and the activity of the pits. Gambling at Caesars feels a little like pitching horseshoes in the Supreme Court, but, incredibly, it works.

Caesars Palace provides two spacious and luxurious casinos, excellent restaurants, beautiful landscaping, top celebrity entertainment, exquisite guest rooms, and all of the services and amenities of a world-class resort. The adjoining Forum Shops, opened in 1992 and expanded in 1997 and again in 2000, give Caesars Palace the distinction of offering one of the most unique themed shopping complexes in the United States.

In 2000 Caesars embarked on a complete renovation and face lift to compliment the 1997 expansion that included a new 29-floor hotel tower with a 20,000-square-foot health spa and fitness center. Guest rooms in the new tower (floors five and up) offer some of the best views on the Strip. Outside there is an elaborate new "Roman bath" swimming complex with four large pools and two outdoor whirlpool spas. Caesars Palace offers a broad assortment of entertainment options. R&B, blues, and oldies rock groups entertain in the Forum Casino lounge, while modern rock and disco are served up for dancing on Cleopatra's Barge nightspot. For the less energetic, there are the Forum Shops and the 3-D simulator *Race For Atlantis* attraction.

Originally designed for high-rollers, Caesars is now enjoyed by a broad range of clientele from the East, the Midwest, and Southern California. Popular with Asian and Hispanic visitors, Caesars also hosts small meetings and caters to business travelers. Though a myth persists that Caesars' employees are as imperious as their surroundings, we find Caesars Palace to be a friendly, easygoing, albeit pricey place to play. As a tourist attraction in its own right, Caesars Palace should be on every visitor's must-see list.

California   (www.thecal.com)

The California is a pleasant, downtown hotel-casino with excellent, moderately priced restaurants and a largely Hawaiian and Filipino clientele. It is a friendly, mellow place to stay or gamble—unpretentious, but certainly comfortable. The casino rambles but, like most downtown casinos, does not allow much elbowroom. The decor is subdued and tasteful, with wood paneling and trim. The shops, menus, and services work to make visiting Pacific Islanders feel as much at home as visitors from Kansas City or Tampa. While some hotel-casinos are spectacles or happenings, the California is simply a nice, relaxed place to spend some time.

Casino Royale   (www.casinoroyalhotel.com)

Located across the Strip from the Mirage, the diminutive Casino Royale has about 150 guest rooms. Small, accessible, and unpretentious, Casino Royale provides bargain lodging in the Strip's high-rent district. While the crowded and slot-heavy casino will make downtown gamblers feel right at home, the Casino Royale's newest feature is its second-floor Italian restaurant, Trilussa. The property's clientele runs the gamut from tour groups to convention-goers on a tight budget to folks who could not get rooms at other hotels on the block.

Castaways   (www.showboat-lv.com)

Castaways, formerly the Showboat, is on Boulder Highway not far from downtown and about 12 minutes from the Strip. To many of its local patrons, Castaways is a huge bowling alley with a hotel and casino on the side. Not that there is anything dinky about the hotel or casino, but with over 100 lanes and inexpensive charges per game, plus its status as the largest bowling complex in the country, the bowling complex gives Castaways its informal, sporty identity. The casino, which includes an elaborate and immense bingo parlor, is decorated like a working man's Mirage with rattan, bright floral accents, and high ceilings. Though the casino is usually busy, there is little sensation of congestion or overcrowding. Restaurants at Castaways offer a good value for the dollar, with an excellent buffet, coffee shop, and Italian eatery. There is also good lounge entertainment.

Circus Circus   (www.circuscircus.com)

Circus Circus was the first hotel on the Strip to actively pursue family trade. Children, young adults, retirees, and the novice (or modest) gambler are welcome here. The labyrinthine casino has low ceilings and is frenetic, loud, and always busy. On a positive note, it was redecorated in lighter colors in 1998, and is now a much more pleasant place to gamble. Dollar blackjack and nickel slots abound. The circus theme, both exciting and wholesome at the same time, is extended to every conceivable detail of the hotel's physical space and operation. Entertainment consists of live, top-quality circus acts (free) and a games midway.

Circus Circus has a very good steak house (the only escape from the circus theme); a huge, inexpensive buffet; an RV park; and a monorail shuttle that connects the property's two main buildings. And, to give credit for great innovation, Circus Circus was the first casino to set aside a nonsmoking gaming area. In 1993, Circus Circus launched what is now the Adventuredome, formerly Grand Slam Canyon, a desert canyon–themed amusement park totally enclosed in a giant pink dome. Here guests can enjoy a roller coaster, a flume ride, robotic dinosaurs, and more. A detailed description of

Adventuredome can be found in Part Five: "Shopping and Seeing the Sights", on page 376.

In 1997 Circus Circus opened a new hotel tower as well as a shopping and restaurant arcade adjoining Adventuredome. As concerns the new restaurants, they provide Circus Circus with some much-needed alternatives to the steak house and the buffet.

Desert Inn   (www.thedesertinn.com)

Steve Wynn, after selling the Mirage, Golden Nugget, and Bellagio, purchased the Desert Inn. Within three months he closed the venerable casino and is currently in the process of replacing the DI with a new 2600-room resort.

El Cortez   (www.elcortez.net)

Situated several blocks east of the central downtown casino area, El Cortez caters to seniors, motor coach tours, and blue-collar locals. The large, rambling casino is congested and bustling; the slots are the major draw. The oldest original casino in Las Vegas, El Cortez has the aesthetic appeal of a garment factory, with narrow aisles, low ceilings, and slot machines packed into every conceivable crevice. Food and drink are bargains, however, and the loose slots give patrons a lot of play for their money. Also, there is considerable Las Vegas history in El Cortez; one section of the original building appears just as it did when the casino opened in 1941. While guest rooms at El Cortez have not been recently renovated, they're quite nice, and an exceptional value.

Excalibur   (www.excaliburcasino.com)

The Excalibur is owned by Mandalay Resort Group (formerly Circus Circus Enterprises) and is designed to attract an upscale family business. By combining a Knights of the Round Table theme, restaurants with giant portions, family-oriented entertainment, and moderate costs, the Excalibur "packs 'em in," especially on weekends. A Las Vegas rendition of a medieval realm, the Excalibur is oversized, garish, and more in the image of Kmart than of King Arthur.

Situated on three levels, the Excalibur's restaurants and shops are integrated into a medieval village theme area on the top floor. On the lower floor is a midway-type games arcade, the Excalibur's showroom (where jousting tournaments are featured), and a now-primitive motion simulator (it was the first virtual ride in Las Vegas, and it's never been upgraded). The cavernous middle level contains the casino, a roomy and festive place with a 1950s art deco decor, meant no doubt to approximate the best in Dark Ages interior design. The atmosphere is supposed to be courtly and regal but has more the feel of an aircraft hangar decorated by Ozzie and Harriet.

The Excalibur is the third largest hotel in the United States (the MGM Grand and Luxor are larger), and it certainly features the world's largest hotel parking lot (so far removed from the entrance that trams are dispatched to haul in the patrons). If you can get past the parking lot commute, the plastic execution of its medieval theme, and the fact that most guest rooms have showers only (no tubs), and you do not object to joining the masses, there is good value to be had at the Excalibur. The food is good and economically priced, as is the entertainment. The staff is friendly and accommodating, and you won't go deaf or blind, or become claustrophobic, in the casino. If you need a change of pace, a covered walkway connects the Excalibur with the Luxor next door, pedestrian bridges provide direct access to New York–New York and the Tropicana, and an overhead train runs to Luxor and Mandalay Bay.

Fiesta   (www.fiestacasinohotel.com)

The Fiesta, which opened in 1994, was the first of two casinos to be situated at the intersection of Rancho Drive and Lake Mead Boulevard in North Las Vegas (the other is Texas Station). With 100 guest rooms and a video poker–packed, 40,000-square-foot casino (including the Spin City annex), the Fiesta features an Old Mexico theme. Entertainment includes a country dance hall. Restaurants specializing in southwestern food and steaks are the Fiesta's major draw. An excellent buffet features a mesquite grill. On Sunday there is a good Margarita Brunch. In 1997, the Fiesta finally got around to putting in a swimming pool, and in 1999, it expanded the casino and added a food court. The food court allowed them to expand the southwestern restaurant, add an oyster bar and a tequila bar (300 different margaritas, olé!), and open one of the best pizza parlors in town. Not only does the place serve excellent pizza, but it houses the 16-ton pipe organ rescued from the Roxy Theater in New York and restored, which a world-class organist plays every night. How's *that* for atmosphere? The Fiesta, acquired by rival Station Casinos, depends primarily on local clientele.

Fitzgeralds   (www.fitzgeralds.com)

Located downtown, Fitzgeralds anchors the east end of the Glitter Gulch section of Fremont Street. The casino is large and compartmentalized with gold press-metal ceilings, mirrored columns, and print carpet with little Irish hats. Completely renovated, the casino has largely abandoned its signature "luck of the Irish" theme. While the new look is more consistent with the clean, polished style pioneered by the Golden Nugget, Fitzgeralds has sacrificed much of its traditional warmth and coziness.

Rooms on the upper floors of the Fitz afford some of the best views in town, and corner rooms with hot tubs are a great bargain. The Fitzgeralds's registered guests tend to be older travelers and retirees from the Midwest. In the casino, the crowd is a mixed bag of regulars and bargain hunters lured by ads for free gifts in the local visitor guides.

Flamingo (www.flamingolv.com)

Built with gangster money in the 1940s and acquired by the Hilton Hotel chain in 1970, the Flamingo is a curious blend of Las Vegas hyperbole and corporate pragmatism. Once a tourist attraction in itself, this venerable hotel was the first super-resort on the Strip. Today, with its 3,642 rooms, four towers, and prime location, it is the centerpiece of the Strip's most prestigious block, surrounded by Bally's, the Barbary Coast, the Imperial Palace, Caesars Palace, Harrah's, and the Mirage. In 1995, the Flamingo renovated its guest rooms and added a stunning central swimming and garden complex complete with rock grottos and wildlife habitats. In 1997, the Flamingo's Strip facade was face-lifted and a large, comfortable sports book was opened in the inner casino.

Hilton, as you might expect, curbed the excesses of the colorful previous owners and transformed the Flamingo from a Las Vegas exaggeration into a very dependable chain hotel. Flashier than the Las Vegas Hilton and Bally's (its sister properties), the Flamingo is also less formal, offering an ambience comfortable to leisure and business travelers alike. The large, bustling casino retains the bright Miami pinks, magentas, and tangerines that established the Flamingo's identity more than four decades ago, but the hotel lobby, rooms, and services are standard Hilton. The Flamingo has consistent restaurants, a pretty good seafood buffet, a fine production show, truly creative lounge entertainment, and one of the top swimming areas in town.

Thanks to the Hilton national reservations system, the hotel's clientele comes in all colors and sizes, and from all over the country (but especially Southern California). The Flamingo actively cultivates the Japanese market and also does a strong business with tour wholesalers. Because it has one of the most diverse customer bases of any Las Vegas hotel, the Flamingo likewise has a very broad comfort zone.

Four Queens (www.fourqueens.com)

The Four Queens, situated in the heart of downtown, offers good food, respectable hotel rooms, and a positively cheery casino. Joining its neighbor, the Golden Nugget, as a member of the "All Right to Be Bright Club," the Four Queens casino was among the first to abandon the standard brothel red in favor of a glistening, light decor offset by a tropical print carpet. The result, as at the Golden Nugget, is a gaming area that feels fun, upbeat, and clean. Loyal Four Queens hotel guests tend to be middle-aged or older and come from Southern California, Texas, Hawaii, and the Midwest. The Four

Queens also caters to the motor coach tour market. In the casino there is a mix of all ages and backgrounds. Locals love Hugo's Cellar restaurant, but the Four Queens's top-quality lounge has been closed.

Four Seasons   (www.fourseasons.com/lasvegas)

Four Seasons Hotels and Mandalay Resort Group have combined to introduce a new concept to Las Vegas: the hotel-within-a-hotel. The Four Seasons is an exclusive, 400-room, noncasino hotel contained by the greater Mandalay Bay megaresort.

You can get to Four Seasons from within Mandalay Bay, but just barely: You walk almost behind the front desk, pass through two sets of double service doors, climb down a spiral staircase, and blunder into the Four Seasons lobby. Signs are few and small. This is the "back" entrance; Four Seasons prefers you to use the main, front, valet entrance, which is right off the Strip, a little south of Mandalay Bay's entrance.

You can access Mandalay Bay from Four Seasons by backtracking or by taking the private elevator to the casino level. You can also walk up the stairs at the Four Seasons elevator bay (the elevators are a pretty long hike from the front desk).

The lobby area has a plush feel, decorated with wood, Victorian sofas and easy chairs, a grand piano, and even a fireplace—a 1930s, New York atmosphere that's very different (and pleasingly so) from Las Vegas in the new millennium. Off the lobby is a 60-seat sitting area and a second lounge that fronts the First Floor Grill gourmet room. There's also the Verandah Cafe, the most exclusive coffee shop in town—giant French doors open onto the Four Seasons' private pool area, where you can also dine al fresco. The pool has lush foliage, a spa, and cabanas, which are kept cool and refreshing by misters.

Four Seasons' 400 rooms are on the 35th–39th floors of the Mandalay Bay tower. Private express elevators deliver guests to the Four Seasons' floors. Rates start at $250 for a superior king, but if you haggle a little, you can land a moderate king for less. However, it will still come at a hefty premium over Mandalay Bay's rooms, which are nearly identical. The main difference between the two standard rooms is the Four Seasons' fully stocked "private bar" (you'll pay $2.75 for a can of Coke, $4 for a pack of Lifesavers, $6 for an airline-sized bottle of liquor, and $19 for a small bottle of wine). Clear out the beverages from the mini-refrigerator and store your own drinks and snacks. Housekeepers provide turn-down service before bedtime.

Four Seasons will appeal to ultra-upscale travelers looking for a mini-oasis that insulates them from the hullabaloo of Las Vegas. But it doesn't come cheaply. You're paying for the brandness as much as the grandness, and there's plenty of better values nearby (even in the same building).

Fremont   (www.fremontcasino.com)

The Fremont is one of the landmarks of downtown Las Vegas. Acquired by the Boyd family in 1985, the Fremont offers good food, budget lodging, and a robust casino. Several years ago they redecorated and considerably brightened up the casino, which is noisy and crowded. The table games are roomily accommodated beneath a high ceiling ringed in neon, while the slots are crammed together along narrow aisles like turkeys on their way to market. Locals love the Fremont, as do Asians, Hawaiians, and the inevitable Southern Californians. The Fremont, like all Boyd properties, is friendly, informal, and comfortable.

Frontier, The New   (www.frontierlv.com)

If ever a Las Vegas hotel has been through the wringer, it's the Frontier . . . oops, make that the NEW Frontier. Though mostly forgotten, this is the hotel that essentially launched Siegfried & Roy in Las Vegas, the hotel with a super location smack in the middle of the Strip, and the hotel with owners, the Elardi family, who allowed the Frontier to get embroiled in a labor dispute and strike that lasted six and a half years. In 1998, the Elardis sold the Frontier to Phil Ruffin, who quickly settled the strike and christened the property the New Frontier. Ruffin poured a couple million into repairs and improvements. Some, like the new roof, you probably won't notice, but others, such as the new Chinese and Italian restaurants and the addition of a Gilley's Saloon (the bar with the mechanical bull from the film *Urban Cowboy*), stand out proudly. However, Ruffin is about to tear the whole place down and build San Francisco, a $500-million Bay Area–themed megaresort, though he faces an uphill battle, since the designer is suing Ruffin and will probably win.

In the meantime, the New Frontier stands, and may yet survive for some time. It is easily accessed from Fashion Show Drive or the Strip and is within easy walking distance of some of the best shopping in town. Through the improvements, the New Frontier has retained that unpretentious feel that has made it popular with both visitors and locals for over 40 years.

Gold Coast   (www.goldcoastcasino.com)

The Gold Coast, a half mile west of the Strip on Flamingo, is a favorite hangout for locals. A casual inspection of the Gold Coast reveals nothing unique: No fantasy theme, no special decor or atmosphere. But the Gold Coast does pay attention to detail and has the local market wired. The Gold Coast serves one of the best breakfast specials in town, provides lounge entertainment at all hours of the day, offers headliners and modest production shows in its showroom, and makes sure it has the locals' favorite kind of slots. To top things off, there is also a two-screen movie complex and a huge bowling alley. Free transportation is provided throughout the day to the casino's sister property, the Barbary Coast, on the Strip.

Gold Spike   (www.goldspikehotelcasino.com)

Situated downtown and about a four-minute walk from the heart of Fremont Street, the Gold Spike is basically a slot joint. Congested, loud, and smoky, with all the ambience of a boiler room, the Gold Spike lures customers with low minimums, cheap food, and $20 rooms.

Golden Gate   (www.goldengatecasino.net)

Another downtown casino devoted primarily to slots, the Golden Gate is crowded and dingy but redeems itself in part by offering one of the best shrimp cocktail specials in Las Vegas. On the western end of Glitter Gulch on Fremont Street, the Golden Gate has 106 budget hotel rooms.

Golden Nugget   (www.goldennugget.com)

The undisputed flagship of the downtown hotels and one of the most meticulously maintained and managed properties in Las Vegas, the Golden Nugget is smack in the middle of Glitter Gulch. The hotel offers bright, cheery rooms with tropical decor, a first-rate, though infrequently used, showroom, plus lounge entertainment, excellent restaurants, a large pool, a first-rate spa, a shopping arcade, and a workout room. The casino is clean and breezy with white enameled walls and white lights. The feel here is definitely upscale, though comfortable and informal. There is breathing room at the Golden Nugget, and an atmosphere that suggests a happy, more fun-filled approach to gambling.

If you stay or gamble at the Golden Nugget you are likely to meet people from New York, Dallas, Chicago, Los Angeles, and San Diego, as well as visitors from Taiwan, Hong Kong, and Japan. Younger travelers (ages 28–39) like the Golden Nugget, as do older tourists and retirees, many of whom arrive on motor coach tours.

Green Valley Ranch Station

The newest of the Station casinos, Green Valley Ranch Station is located about 15 minutes east of the Strip at the intersection of Green Valley Parkway and the Beltway in an upscale residential area. The property offers a 200-room hotel, a casino with 40 table games and almost 2,500 slot and video poker machines, six restaurants including a buffet, a spa, and a 10-screen cinema complex. Like all Station casinos, Green Valley Ranch Station provides locals with high-pay slots, good dining value, an excellent slot club, and high quality lounge entertainment.

Hard Rock Hotel (www.hardrockhotel.com)

Located off the Strip on Harmon near Paradise, the Hard Rock is billed as the world's first rock and roll hotel and casino. Like the adjoining Hard Rock Cafe, the 668-room hotel and domed casino are loaded to the gills with rock memorabilia and artifacts. Everywhere it's rock, rock, rock, from lounge music to the casino, which features piano-shaped roulette tables and chandeliers made from gold saxophones. The guest rooms, which offer a nice view, are surprisingly tasteful, with a Danish-modern European feel. The pool area likewise is comfortable, nicely designed, and was recently enlarged. Other strengths include five restaurants and The Joint, Las Vegas's most intimate venue for live rock. The Hard Rock Hotel targets baby boomers and younger folks from Southern California as well as from the Midwest and the big Northeastern cities.

Harrah's Las Vegas (www.harrahslasvegas.com)

Harrah's occupies the middle of the Strip's most prestigious block and is within easy walking distance of Bally's, the Flamingo, the Mirage, Caesars Palace, Paris, Bellagio, the Venetian, and Treasure Island. Unpretentious and upbeat, Harrah's offers tasteful guest rooms as well as a beautiful showroom, a comedy club, above-average restaurants and buffet, a pool, an exercise room, and a spa. The L-shaped casino is bright and roomy, and there is a feeling of lightheartedness and fun that is missing in far too many gambling halls. Best of all, the staff at Harrah's, from dealers to desk clerks, is exceptionally friendly and helpful. Though it is hard to imagine anyone not feeling comfortable at Harrah's, its clientele tends to be older visitors from the Midwest and Southern California, as well as business and convention travelers.

In 1996, Harrah's elected to forgo its highly successful riverboat theme for a new theme celebrating carnival and Mardi Gras. An ambitious expansion accompanied the re-theming, including a new hotel tower and a totally new facade featuring two giant gold-leaf court jesters hefting a 10-ton, 22-foot-diameter globe. The casino has been enlarged by 30% and redecorated with brightly colored confetti-patterned carpet, ceiling murals, and jazzy fiber-optic lighting. Other additions include a renovated swimming area, a new bar/restaurant with an outdoor patio, a steak house with a view of the Strip, and Carnival Court, an outdoor plaza with fountains and street entertainment.

Horseshoe (www.binions.com)

The Horseshoe, or more correctly Binion's Horseshoe, is one of the anchors of Glitter Gulch. The casino is large and active, with row upon row of slots clanking noisily under a suffocatingly low ceiling. The table games are less congested, occupying and an extended vertical space canopied by mirrors. With an Old West theme executed in the obligatory reds and lavenders, the Horseshoe is dark, but not dark enough to slow the enthusiasm of the locals and "real gamblers" who hang out there. One of the city's top spots for poker and craps, the Horseshoe is famous for not having any maximum bet limitations. You can bet a million dollars on a single roll of the dice if you wish.

On the lower (basement) level, is the coffee shop and what may be one of the most pleasant bars in the city; it, too, is dark but for once is paneled in rich woods. Twenty or so stories up from the cellar is the Ranch Steak House restaurant and lounge, offering a great view of the city. Also offering a great view is the Horseshoe's rooftop pool.

Imperial Palace   (www.imperial-palace.com)

The Imperial Palace has a large, active casino lavishly executed with mammoth chandeliers and carved beams. There is a lovely swimming and sunbathing area complete with waterfall, and a Nautilus-equipped exercise room and spa. *Legends in Concert,* one of the hottest shows in Las Vegas, plays nightly at the Imperial Palace's showroom, and the on-site auto museum is a first-rate tourist attraction in its own right. Situated just south of Harrah's, no hotel in Las Vegas has a better location than the Imperial Palace.

Most of the guest rooms at the Imperial Palace are modern and of Holiday Inn–level quality. The food at the Imperial Palace is on a par with most neighboring hotels, and the Embers restaurant can hold its own with the top steak houses in town.

Lady Luck   (www.ladyluck.com)

The Lady Luck is located downtown a block north of Fremont Street. It offers nice rooms (or small suites) at a great price, and it has an excellent restaurant (the Burgundy Room), and a large, uncomplicated casino. Not afraid to be different, the Lady Luck is one of the few casinos anywhere to have wall-sized plate-glass windows. If you are claustrophobic and looking for a casino where you won't feel cooped up, the Lady Luck might be your place. The staff is personable and the atmosphere informal. If you want variety, Glitter Gulch is a four-minute walk away.

The Lady Luck appeals to a diverse clientele, including Filipinos, Asian Americans, Californians, motor coach tourists, and locals.

Las Vegas Club   (www.playatlvc.com)

The Las Vegas Club is a downtown hotel-casino with a sports theme. The corridor linking the casino with the sports bar is a veritable sports museum and has dozens of vintage photos of boxing, baseball, and basketball legends. The casino itself, with its high, mirrored ceilings, is modest but feels uncrowded. It also has some of the more player-friendly blackjack rules around. If you plan on staying at the Las Vegas Club, ask for a room in the new North Tower. The food is good and consistent. The Las Vegas Club draws from Hawaii and the Midwest but also does a big business with bus groups and seniors.

Las Vegas Hilton   (www.lv-hilton.com)

Next door to the Las Vegas Convention Center, the Hilton does more meeting, trade show, and convention business than any other hotel in town. There are days at the Hilton when it's rare to see someone not wearing a convention badge. As you might expect, the Hilton is accommodating but not glitzy and provides a comfortable, neutral environment for its business clientele.

A 10- to 12-minute walk from the Strip, the Hilton operates under the valid assumption that many of its guests may never leave the hotel during their Las Vegas stay (except to go to the Convention Center). Thus the Hilton is an oasis of self-sufficiency and boasts lounges, a huge pool (remodeled in 1999), an exercise room, a shopping arcade, a buffet, and a coffee shop.

The Las Vegas Hilton has some of the best restaurants in town and features enough ethnic and culinary variety to keep most guests happy. The showroom at the Hilton occasionally hosts big name headliners. In 1998, the Hilton premiered *Star Trek: The Experience,* an interactive video and virtual reality amusement center featuring a space-flight simulation ride.

The casino, like the hotel itself, is huge and tastefully businesslike in its presentation but by no means formal or intimidating. The Hilton sports book is one of the largest in Las Vegas. If you can afford it, the Hilton is the most convenient place to stay in town if you are attending a trade show or convention at the Las Vegas Convention Center. If, however, you are in Las Vegas for pleasure, staying at the Hilton is like being in luxurious exile. Anywhere you go, you will need a cab or your own car. If you park in one of the Hilton's far-flung, self-parking lots, it will take you as long as 15 minutes to reach your car from your guest room.

Luxor   (www.luxor.com)

The Luxor is on the Strip south of Tropicana Road next to the Excalibur. Representing Mandalay Resort Group's first serious effort to attract a more upscale, less family-oriented clientele, the Luxor is among the more tasteful of Las Vegas's themed hotels. Though not originally believed to be on a par with Treasure Island and the MGM Grand, the Luxor may well be the most distinguished graduate of the much-publicized hotel class of 1993. While the MGM Grand is larger and Treasure Island more ostentatious, the Luxor demonstrates an unmatched creativity and architectural appeal.

Rising 30 stories, the Luxor is a huge pyramid with guest rooms situated around the outside perimeter from base to apex. Guest room hallways circumscribe a hollow core containing the world's largest atrium. Inside the atrium, inclinators rise at a 39° angle from the pyramid's corners to access the guest floors. While the perspective from inside the pyramid is stunning, it is easy to get disoriented. Stories about hotel guests wandering around in search of their rooms are legion. After reviewing many complaints from readers, we seriously recommend carrying a small pocket compass.

The Luxor's main entrance is from the Strip via a massive sphinx. From the sphinx, guests are diverted into small entryways designed to resemble the interior passages of an actual pyramid. From these tunnels, guests emerge into the dramatic openness of the Luxor's towering atrium. Rising imposingly within the atrium is an ancient Egyptian city, flanked incongruously on the left by a New York skyline.

Proceeding straight ahead at ground level from the main entrance brings you into the casino. Open and attractive, the 100,000-square-foot casino is tasteful by any standard.

One level below the casino and the main entrance is the Luxor's main showroom. One floor above the entry/casino level, on a mezzanine of sorts, is an array of structures representing the past, present, and future. Reaching high into the atrium, these dramatic buildings and monuments transform the atrium into a surrealistic vision, anachronistic yet powerful. The past is represented by an Egyptian temple and obelisk and the apparent excavation of an archaeological dig. In stark contrast nearby, representing the present, is a New York skyscraper scene. Finally, across a plaza is a grouping of futuristic structures. Here you'll find an attraction designed by Douglas Trumbull, creator of the *Back to the Future* ride at Universal Studios Florida, and an IMAX theater. In addition to the attractions, three restaurants, a huge electronic games arcade, and a collection of retail shops are on this level.

Flanking the pyramid are two new hotel towers that were part of a $300-million expansion completed in 1997; the expansion also included a new health spa and fitness center, and additional meeting and conference space.

The biggest surprise of all (to anyone who has ever stayed in a Mandalay Resort Group property) are the Luxor's large, tasteful guest rooms. Decorated in an understated Egyptian motif with custom-made furniture, the standard guest rooms are among the most nicely appointed in town. The only disappointment is that many of the guest rooms do not have tubs. In all, the Luxor offers 4,474 guest rooms, making it the second largest hotel in Las Vegas.

The Luxor's large, attractive pool complex, surrounded by private cabanas, desperately needs some additional plants and trees. Self-parking is as much a problem at the Luxor as at most large properties. Valet parking is quick and efficient, however, and well worth the $1 or $2 tip. The Luxor is within a 5- to 12-minute walk of the Excalibur, the Tropicana, and the MGM Grand. A moving walkway connects the Luxor to the Excalibur and an overhead "cable-liner" (read: shuttle) connects it with Mandalay Bay.

Main Street Station   (www.mainstreetcasino.com)

Situated on Main Street between Ogden and Stewart in downtown Las Vegas, Main Street Station originally opened in 1992 as a paid-admission nighttime entertainment complex with a casino on the side. Owned and managed by an Orlando, Florida, entrepreneur with no casino experience, it took Main Street Station less than a year to go belly-up. The property was acquired several years later by Boyd Gaming, which used Main Street Station's hotel to accommodate overflow guests from the California across the street. In 1997, the Boyds reopened the casino, restaurants, and shops, adding a brew pub in the process.

The casino is one of the most unusual in town (thanks largely to the concept of the original owner), with the feel of a turn-of-the-century gentleman's club. Though not as splendid now as in its original incarnation, the casino still contains enough antiques, original art, and oddities to furnish a museum. With its refurbished guest rooms, brew pub, steak house, excellent buffet, and unusual casino, Main Street Station is both interesting and fun, adding some welcome diversity to the downtown hospitality mix.

Mandalay Bay   (www.mandalaybay.com)

Mandalay Resort Group's Mandalay Bay opened on March 1, 1999, on the site of the old Hacienda, imploded on New Year's Day 1998. It completes the Mandalay Bay "Miracle Mile," which stretches along the Strip south from Monte Carlo, bypassing New York–New York, and continuing with Excalibur and Luxor. A "cable liner" (a monorail propelled by a cable à la San Francisco cable cars) connects Excalibur, Luxor, and Mandalay Bay every 15 minutes, 24 hours a day (it stops at Luxor on the northbound leg only).

Mandalay Bay itself is a megaresort in the true sense of the overworked word. Its 3,700 guest rooms rank it as the fifth largest hotel in Las Vegas (sixth largest in the world); interestingly, four out of the first five in town are Mandalay Bay resorts (Luxor, Excalibur, Circus Circus, and Mandalay Bay). Within the sprawling complex are the 43-story, three-wing tower; a 12,000-seat arena; an 1,800-seat theater; a 1,700-seat concert venue; a dozen restaurants; an 11-acre water park; and three large lounges. In fact, Mandalay Bay is so big that it has Las Vegas's only actual hotel-within-a-hotel on the property: the 400-room Four Seasons. The whole schmear cost a cool billion.

But that's not the half of it, because Mandalay Bay isn't your standard megaresort. It's clear that the planners and designers set out to take a few risks and appeal to a young, hip, fun-seeking market—as opposed to Bellagio, which has targeted a more refined, sophisticated, older clientele. If Bellagio is the crowning culmination of the Las Vegas of the twentieth century, Mandalay Bay might be Las Vegas's first foray into the twenty-first century. All the different ideas jammed into Mandalay Bay might not always add up to a cohesive whole, but so many parts of the sum are unique that it makes for an interesting series of sights.

The signature spectacle is the four-story wine tower at Manhattan–celebrity chef Charlie Palmer's restaurant, Aureole. This nearly 50-foot-tall glass and stainless structure stores nearly 10,000 bottles of wine. Lovely, athletic women dressed all in black—spandex tights, racing gloves, hard hats—manipulate the motorized cable, one on each of the four sides, that raises them up to retrieve a selected bottle and lowers them back down to deliver it.

The China Grill Cafe, the bar-and-grill annex to Mandalay Bay's Oriental room, China Grill, has a centerpiece 34-seat bar which is circled by a rubber conveyor. The belt goes round and round between the bar sitters and the open kitchen, carrying plates of "Zen Sum" appetizers.

Red Square Russian restaurant has a one-of-a-kind refrigerated walk-in showcase, open to the public, which stores 150 different varieties of vodka at 15 degrees. Drinks are served on a long bar top that has a thick strip of ice running its length (basically it keeps the bottom of the glasses chilled and provides a great medium for leaving fingerprints). Red Square also has a 16-foot-tall statue of Vladimir Lenin out front; the howl of criticism over the questionable taste of such a display prompted Mandalay to lop off Lenin's head, and the statue now has a big hole at the neck. Inside, Red Square sports a curious Communist theme, a paean to the Soviet 1930s when Joe Stalin was slaughtering tens of millions of the nation's civilians. Huge heroic posters of Russian intellectuals and professionals carrying shovels and pipe and automatic weapons fill the walls, and plentiful hammer-and-sickles symbolize the former Soviet Union no less than a swastika represents the Third Reich.

Rumjungle, a Polynesian dining and nightclub combo, is fronted by a huge "wall of fire": 80 small gas-fed flames surround two big flames at the entrance. The House of Blues restaurant and entertainment complex serves food (Southern style and Creole/Cajun), has the world's largest collection of Deep South folk art, and a strange dark bar with a crucifix theme. House of Blues also puts on a Sunday gospel brunch and holds rock and pop concerts in its 1,800-seat theater. Wolfgang Puck's Trattoria del Lupo (serving Italian fare), a Mexican restaurant, a noodle room, a coffee shop, a buffet, and ice cream and coffee counters round out the dining possibilities at Mandalay Bay. A main attraction at Mandalay Bay is Shark Reef, a 90,000 square foot aquarium exhibit with a walk-through acrylic tunnel. The aquarium is home to about 2,000 marine species including Nile crocodiles, moray eels, stingrays, and, of course, sharks.

The Coral Reef Lounge is one of the largest and most interesting bars in Las Vegas. Taking up a good part of an acre of the property, the Coral Reef is surrounded by lush tropical "foliage" (though fake, it's very effective) and has three distinct sitting areas: the 25-seat marble video poker bar; the lounge itself, with a big stage and good enough acoustics that the bands can crank it up; and a wooden deck away from the main noise, where you sit amongst the virtual vegetation, rock waterfalls, and lily ponds.

Speaking of acreage, the casino is typically monumental, with plenty of elbow room between machines and tables. The race and sports book boasts the largest screen in town, which is only right, since the book is so big the screen must be seen from long distances. The 80-seat (each one an over-sized, velour-covered easy chair) Turf Lounge and the large poker room are connected.

The pool area is also imaginative. The 11-acre Mandalay Beach has a lazy river, a placid pool, a beachfront cafe and bar, and the wedding chapel. The centerpiece, however, is a huge wave pool. The surf can be cranked up from one to eight feet, but there seems to be a little problem with the big water—it floods the sandy beach! Apparently, even machine-made seas can get too high. For the surfing lessons, the beach area is cleared so sunbathers don't get drenched.

All in all, Mandalay Bay accomplishes what every new megacasino-hotel sets out to do—deliver an inventive and hip experience that sets a new standard for all the megajoints that follow.

MGM Grand
Hotel, Casino, and Theme Park (www.mgmgrand.com)

When Steve Wynn opened the Mirage, he combined the amenities of a world-class resort with the excitement and visual appeal of a tourist attraction. At the Mirage, Treasure Island, and Bellagio, however, the attraction component is rendered in terms of nonparticipatory visual spectacle: at the Mirage, an exploding volcano; at Treasure Island, a naval battle; and at Bellagio, dancing fountains. The attraction is peripheral, no more or no less than a powerful and eye-popping way to generate traffic for the casino.

At Kirk Kerkorian's MGM Grand, the evolutionary combination of gambling resort and attraction was carried to the next logical stage, the development of a theme park ostensibly, if not actually, on an equal footing with the casino. This elevation of a nongaming attraction to a position of prominence signaled the first significant tourism product diversification in Las Vegas since the dawn of the luxury resort hotel-casinos in the 1950s. Make no mistake, the purpose of the theme park was to funnel patrons into the casino. What is different is that the theme park offered a recreation alternative intended to attract nongamblers as well as gamblers. As it happened, however, the theme park was highly publicized but pitifully designed. In 2000, after 7 years of limping along, the MGM (not so) Grand Adventures park closed. Probably, in retrospect, the park served its purpose, that is, to draw attention to the MGM Grand Hotel and Casino in its opening year.

With the exception of Walt Disney World, the MGM Grand combines more facilities and recreational opportunities than any other resort in the United States. It claims the distinction of being both the largest hotel in the United States (with 5,036 rooms) and the world's largest casino. Within the 112-acre complex, there is a 21-acre movie- and entertainment-themed amusement park; a 15,200-seat special-events arena; 380,000 square feet of convention space; an enormous swimming area; four tennis courts; a health spa; and a multilevel parking facility.

There's a small new casino, just opened, outside the lobby of the Mansion, MGM's ultra-upscale whale digs, and a new 6.6-acre pool-and-spa complex took over a chunk of the amusement park along with the dedicated convention center. The MGM Grand is on the northeast corner of Tropicana Avenue and the Strip. The Strip entrance passes beneath a 45-foot-tall MGM Lion atop a 25-foot pedestal, all surrounded by three immense digital displays. The lion entrance leads to a domed rotunda with table games and a Rainforest Cafe (situated right next to a new lion habitat), and from there to the MGM Grand's four huge casinos. All of the casinos are roomy and plush, with high ceilings and a comfortable feeling of openness.

A second entrance, with a porte-cochere 15 lanes wide, serves vehicular traffic from Tropicana Avenue. For all practical purposes, this is the main entrance to the MGM Grand, permitting you to go directly to the hotel lobby and its 53 check-in windows without lugging your belongings through the casinos. Just beyond the registration area is the elevator core, with 35 elevators servicing 30 guest floors.

Beyond the elevator core, a wide passageway leads toward five of the MGM Grand's eight distinct restaurants (not counting theme-park restaurants or fast food). Among the upscale restaurants are La Scala, serving Italian cuisine; the Brown Derby, offering beef and seafood; Gatsby's, serving California-style French cuisine; Emeril's, offering Creole/Cajun dishes; Coyote Cafe, featuring southwestern cuisine; and Dragon Court, a Chinese restaurant. More informal dining is available at the Wolfgang Puck Cafe and the Rainforest Cafe. (The MGM Grand has assembled an impressive team of chefs!) The MGM Grand's buffet (disappointing), 24-hour cafe, and pizza kitchen adjoin the casinos between the porte-cochere and lion entrances. For fast food there is a food court housing McDonald's, Mamma Ilardo's, and Hamada's Oriental Express.

There are two showrooms at the MGM Grand (exclusive of live entertainment in the theme park). The 630-seat Hollywood Theater features headliners, while the larger (1,700-seat) Grand Theater is home to a high-energy production show. Entertainment is also offered at the Catch a Rising Star comedy club, and in the casino's four lounges. In addition, the MGM Grand's special-events arena can accommodate boxing, tournament tennis, rodeo, and basketball, as well as major exhibitions.

Amenities at the MGM Grand, not unexpectedly, are among the best in Las Vegas. The swimming complex is huge—23,000 square feet of pool area, with five interconnected pools graced with bridges, fountains, and waterfalls. Other highlights of the complex include a floating stream, a poolside bar, and luxury cabanas. Adjoining the swimming area are a complete health club and spa and four lighted tennis courts. For those to whom recreation means pumping quarters into a machine, there is an extensive electronic games arcade supplemented by a "games of skill" midway. The newest addition to the entertainment mix is Lion Habitat, where you can watch live lions.

A first at the MGM Grand is a youth center that provides supervised programs for children (ages 3–12) of hotel guests both day and night. Only 50 or so children can be accommodated in the center, with a maximum five-hour stay.

Guest rooms at the MGM Grand are comfortable, with large baths. Almost all of the rooms have a small sitting area positioned by a large window. Rooms on the higher floors have exceptional views. Part of the old MGM Marina Hotel was incorporated into the new MGM Grand. Rooms in the old structure have been renovated but are not comparable in size or quality to the new rooms.

The MGM Grand's biggest problem, weekend hotel registration and check-out, has been addressed with a registration desk at the airport where guests can check in and pick up room keys while waiting for their baggage.

Drawing from a wide cross-section of the leisure market, the MGM Grand derives 80% of its business from individual travelers and tour and travel groups, with only 10% coming from trade show and convention attendees. The youth center, PG-rated showroom entertainment, and theme park make the MGM Grand a natural for families. Room rates in the $90–140 range make the MGM Grand accessible to a broad population. Geographically, the MGM Grand targets Southern California, Phoenix, Denver, Dallas, Houston, Chicago, and the Midwest.

Mirage   (www.themirage.com)

The Mirage has had an impact on the Las Vegas tourist industry that will be felt for years to come. By challenging all the old rules and setting new standards for design, ambience, and entertainment, the Mirage precipitated the development of a class of super-hotels in Las Vegas, redefining the thematic appeal and hospitality standard of hotel-casinos in much the same way Disney did theme parks. And with the recent sale of the Mirage to MGM Grand, we expect the Mirage to remain the standard.

Exciting and compelling without being whimsical or silly, the Mirage has demonstrated that the public will respond enthusiastically to a well-executed concept. Blending the stateliness of marble with the exotic luxury of tropical greenery and the straightforward lines of polished bamboo, the Mirage has created a spectacular environment that artfully integrates casino, showroom, shopping, restaurants, and lounges. Both lavish and colorful, inviting and awe-inspiring, the Mirage has avoided cliché. Not designed to replicate a famous palace or be the hotel version of "Goofy Golf," the Mirage makes an original statement.

An atrium rainforest serves as a central hub from which guests can proceed to all areas of the hotel and casino. Behind the hotel's front desk, a 60-foot-long aquarium contains small sharks, stingrays, and colorful tropical fish. In the entranceway from Las Vegas Boulevard is a natural-habitat zoological display housing rare white Bengal tigers. Outside, instead of blinking neon, the Mirage has a 55-foot-tall erupting volcano that disrupts traffic on the Strip every half hour. There is also a live dolphin exhibit and a modern showroom that is among the most well-designed and technologically advanced in Las Vegas.

The restaurants at the Mirage are special, especially Kokomo's, with its seafood specialties; Renoir, a Mobile 5-star winner; and Samba, a Brazilian steakhouse. For bulk eaters, there is an ample and affordable buffet. Illusionists Siegfried and Roy are the headliners in one of two showrooms. Impressionist Danny Gans performs in the other. Siegfried and Roy's show took Las Vegas entertainment (and prices) into the twenty-first century. Amenities at the Mirage include a stunning swimming and sunning complex with waterfalls, inlets, and an interconnected series of lagoons; a stylish shopping arcade; and a spa with exercise equipment and aerobics instruction. The casino is huge and magnificently appointed, yet informal, with its tropical motif and piped-in Jimmy Buffett music. Most guest rooms at the Mirage have been completely renovated and are now among the nicest in town.

Though registered guests pay premium prices (by Las Vegas standards) for the privilege of staying at the Mirage, the hotel is not an exclusive retreat of the wealthy. With its indoor jungle, live tigers and sharks, and traffic-snarling volcano, the Mirage remains one of Clark County's top tourist attractions. Whether by foot, bus, trolley, cab, or bicycle, every Las Vegas visitor makes at least one pilgrimage. The Mirage has become the Strip's melting pot and hosts the most incredible variety of humanity imaginable. Visitors wander wide-eyed through the casino at all hours of the day and night.

Monte Carlo   (www.monte-carlo.com)

The Monte Carlo opened on June 21, 1996. With 3,002 guest rooms, the Monte Carlo ranks as the seventh largest hotel in Las Vegas (and eighth in the world). The megaresort is modeled after the Place du Casino in Monte Carlo, Monaco, with ornate arches and fountains, marble floors, and a Gothic glass registration area. If the Monte Carlo fails as a resort, the building will be a perfect place to relocate the Nevada State Capitol.

On the surface, it's yet another huge hotel in the Las Vegas Age of the Megaresort. But scratch the surface just a little and you glimpse the future of Monopoly-board Las Vegas and the gambling business in general. Monte Carlo is a joint venture between Mirage Resorts, now owned by MGM Grand (which put up the land and a small amount of cash) and Mandalay Resort Group (which put up the rest of the cash and will run the joint), two of the largest casino competitors in the world. By combining their resources, Mirage and Mandalay were able to finance, design, and construct a monumental hotel-casino in record time (15 months from start to finish) and can operate it without taxing their individual infrastructures.

The guest rooms, furnished with marble entryways and French period wall art, are mid- to upper-priced (to compete with MGM Grand). There is an elaborate swimming complex with slides, a wave pool, and a man-made stream. There is also an exceptional health and fitness center, an interesting shopping arcade, and a brew pub with live entertainment. The casino, about a football field long and similarly shaped, is capped with simulated skylights and domes. The showroom is designed especially for illusionist Lance Burton, who signed a long-term contract to perform there. Restaurants cover the usual bases, offering steak, Italian, and Asian specialties respectively, with a nice brew pub thrown in for good measure.

Compared to the powerful themes of New York–New York, Treasure Island, and the Luxor, the Monte Carlo's turn-of-the-century Monacan theme fails to stimulate much excitement or anticipation. Besides being beyond the tourist's frame of reference, the theme lacks any real visceral dimension. The word *grand* comes to mind, but more in the context of a federal courthouse or the New York Public Library. Simply put (and this may be a big plus), the Monte Carlo is an attractive hotel-casino as opposed to a crowd-jammed tourist attraction.

New York–New York   (www.nynyhotelcasino.com)

When it opened in December 1996, this architecturally imaginative hotel-casino set a new standard for the realization of Las Vegas megaresort themes.

It's a small joint by megaresort standards ("only" around 2,000 rooms), but the triumph is in the details. The guest rooms are in a series of distinct towers reminiscent of a mini–Big Apple skyline, including the Empire State, Chrysler, and Seagrams buildings. Though the buildings are connected, each offers a somewhat different decor and ambiance.

A half-size Statue of Liberty and a replica of Grand Central Station lead visitors to one entrance, while the Brooklyn Bridge leads to another. The interior of the property is broken into themed areas such as Greenwich Village, Wall Street, and Times Square. The casino, one of the most visually interesting in Las Vegas, looks like an elaborate movie set. Table games and slots are sandwiched between shops, restaurants, and a jumble of street facades.

The street scenes are well executed, conveying both a sense of urban style and tough grittiness. New York–New York sacrificed much of its visual impact, however, by not putting in an imitation sky. At Sunset Station, by way of contrast, the Spanish architecture is augmented significantly by vaulted ceilings, realistically lighted and painted with clouds. This sort of finishing touch could have done wonders for New York–New York.

Like its namesake, New York–New York is congested in the extreme, awash day and night with curious sight-seers. There are so many people just wandering around gawking that there's little room left for hotel guests and folks who actually came to gamble. Because aisles and indoor paths are far too narrow to accommodate the crowds, New York–New York succumbs periodically to a sort of pedestrian gridlock.

Manhattan rules, however, do not apply at New York–New York: it's OK here to make eye contact and decidedly rude to shove people out of the way to get where you want to go. If you find yourself longing for the thrill of a New York cab ride, go hop on the roller coaster. New York–New York's coaster is the fourth one on the Strip, but it's the only one where you can stand on the street and hear the riders scream.

Guest rooms at New York–New York approximate the Holiday Inn standard but are somewhat disappointing for a hotel with such a strong, resonant theme. Likewise, the swimming area and health and fitness center are just average. Full-service restaurants are a little better than average, offering both variety and quality, while counter-service fast food is quite interesting, if not altogether authentic New York.

Nevada Palace   (www.nvpalace.com)

The Nevada Palace is a small, recently renovated Boulder Highway property patronized primarily by locals and by seniors who take advantage of its 168-space RV park. Pleasant, with a new pool, spa facilities, two decent restaurants, and fair room rates, the Nevada Palace is a friendly, less hectic alternative to staying downtown or on the Strip.

Orleans   (www.orleanscasino.com)

Opened in 1997, Orleans is situated just west of I-15 on Tropicana Avenue and is owned by Coast Resorts, which also run the Barbary Coast, the Suncoast, and the Gold Coast. Marketed primarily to locals, Orleans has a New Orleans/bayou theme executed in a hulking cavern of a building. The casino is festive with bright carpets, high ceilings, a two-story replication of a French Quarter street flanking the table games, and a couple of nifty bars. Orleans has a celebrity showroom that is attracting great musical talent (The Doobie Brothers, Willie Nelson, Ray Charles) and several restaurants that have little to do with the Louisiana theme. The buffet, which does serve Creole/Cajun dishes, has come a long way but can't quite match Louisiana standards. Upstairs, over the slots and buffet area, is a 70-lane bowling complex. An 840-room hotel tower completes the package.

Orleans struggled in its first year, prompting the addition of additional restaurants, a movie complex, a games arcade, and a childcare center.

Palace Station   (www.palacestation.com)

Located four minutes off the Strip on West Sahara, Palace Station is a local favorite that attracts some attention from tourists. With dependable restaurants that continuously offer amazing specials, a tower of handsome guest rooms, good prices, and a location that permits access to both downtown and the Strip in less than ten minutes, Palace Station has arrived. Decorated in a railroad theme, the casino is large and busy and places heavy emphasis on the slots (which are supposedly loose—i.e., having a high rate of payoff). There is also first-rate lounge entertainment.

The Palms   (www.thepalmslasvegas.com)

Located west of the Strip on Flamingo roughly across the street from the Gold Coast, Palms opens in late 2001. Though it primarily targets a youthful local market, Palms offers the size and amenities of many Strip casinos, including a roomy 95,000 square foot casino, a 42-story hotel tower, several entertainment venues, and a 14-screen cinema. Key is a centrally situated pool complex that will be ground zero for hip, younger guests. A bar on top of the hotel tower, six restaurants, plus a possible Top-Ten contender buffet rounds out the batting order. Entertainment had not been announced at press time, but you can bet that it will go head-to-head with the Rio and the Hard Rock Hotel.

Paris Las Vegas   (www.paris-lv.com)

On the Strip next to Bally's and across from Bellagio, Paris trots out a French Parisian theme in much the same way New York–New York caricatures the Big Apple. Paris has its own 50-story Eiffel Tower (with a restaurant halfway up), and an Arc de Triomphe. Thrown in for good measure are the Champs Elysée, Parc Monceau, and the Paris Opera House.

Like New York–New York, Paris presents its iconography in a whimsical way, contrasting with the more realistic Venetian or the Forum Shops at Caesars Palace. The casino resides in a park-like setting roughly arrayed around the base of the Eiffel Tower, three legs of which protrude through the roof of the casino. There's no live poker at Paris and the video poker schedules are lackluster, but the casino offers all of the usual table games and features the only authentic French roulette game in the country.

Flanking the tower and branching off from the casino are dining and shopping venues designed to re-create parisian and rural petit-village street scenes. Though spacious, the casino and other public areas at Paris are exceedingly busy, bombarding the senses with color, sound, and activity. While at the Venetian you have the sense of entering a grand space, at Paris the feeling is more of envelopment.

The hotel towers, with their almost 3,000 guest rooms, rise in an L shape framing the Eiffel Tower. The rooms are quite stunning, and rank along with the dining as one of Paris's most outstanding features.

Like the Venetian, the pool complex is situated on the roof. The facility is spacious but rather plain and underdeveloped in comparison with the rest of the property. One of the better spas and health clubs in Las Vegas connects both to the pool area and to the hotel.

The dining scene at Paris is a work in progress, though most of the property's restaurants opened to great acclaim. The flagship restaurant, French, of course, is situated 11 stories above the Strip in the Eiffel Tower. Several other restaurants, closer to the ground, and including the buffet also feature French cuisine. A Chinese restaurant, a "new world Caribbean," the Italian/ French La Provencal, and what passes for a coffee shop and late night restaurant round out the dining offerings. This last, called Mon Ami Gabi, serves until 2 a.m. on an outdoor terrace overlooking the Strip.

Back inside there's the Rue de la Paix shopping venue, not as large or impressive as the Canal Shops or the Forum Shops, but offering exclusive boutique shopping. The showroom hosts headliners. Le Cabaret is the happening lounge along with Tres Jazz, a jazz, drinking, and dining venue. And, of course, if you don't mind a little waiting, you can take an elevator ride to the top of the Eiffel Tower for a knockout view of the Strip.

Plaza (www.plazahotelcasino.com)

The Plaza has the distinction of being the only hotel in Las Vegas with its own railroad station (though the passenger trains no longer run on this stretch of track). Not too long ago, the hotel was run-down and about what you would expect for a downtown property attached to a train terminal. However, the Plaza renovated its tower rooms and now offers nice accommodations at very good prices. The only downtown hotel to provide on-site tennis, the Plaza also has one of only two downtown Las Vegas showrooms, featuring production shows and, periodically, live theater (invariably comedy). The property houses a domed restaurant with a view straight down the middle of Glitter Gulch and the Fremont Street Experience. The view (as opposed to the food) is the main attraction here. If you go, reserve a table by the window.

The casino's table gaming area is very pleasant, with its high, dark green ceiling punctuated by crystal chandeliers. Patrons include downtown walkins, attendees of small meetings and conventions, and Southern Californians.

Quality Inn
and Key Largo Casino   (www.keylargocasino.com)

The Quality Inn is a great compromise property. Though small, it has all the essentials (mini-casino, restaurant, gift shop, lounge, pool). The Quality offers quiet and simplicity with most of the amenities of a large resort; a wet bar and a refrigerator are standard in every room. The Quality's crowning glory is a green and extraordinarily peaceful central courtyard and pool complex. Its location permits easy access to the Strip and the airport.

Reserve   (www.vegas.com/resorts/reserve)

The Reserve, targeting the local market, is an African safari–themed hotel-casino located southeast of Las Vegas at the intersection of I-515 and Lake Mead Boulevard. Although the safari theme is well executed with faux baobab trees, jungle sound effects, and lurking predators (stuffed, of course), the Reserve reminds many people of a Rainforest Cafe with gambling. In any event, with its safari theme, a 42,000-square-foot casino, a hot lounge, a good buffet, several restaurants (try the steak house), and adequate guest rooms, the Reserve is different enough to lure most locals for a look-see. In 2000, the Reserve was acquired by Station casinos, thus ending some very consumer friendly competition between the Reserve and nearby Sunset Station.

Regent Las Vegas   (www.regentlasvegas.com)

The Regent Las Vegas is the first of several new upscale properties to offer a Scottsdale/Palm Beach resort experience as an alternative to the hype and madness of the Strip. Situated west of town near Red Rock Canyon, the Regent Las Vegas consists of two southwestern-style hotels built around the TPC golf course. The resort offers a classy, comfortable casino with 1200 slots and 40 table games, an 11-acre garden and a large swimming complex. Restaurants serve oriental, continental, and beef fare respectively. The buffet here is one of the better spreads in town. Although the lounges, including an "Irish Pub," offer live entertainment, there is no showroom. While guest rooms are spacious and among the nicest in Las Vegas, the real draw here is the golf and the spa. Guests include destination golfers, business travelers, and conference attendees, but the core market is locals.

Rio   (www.playrio.com)

The Rio is one of Las Vegas's great treasures. Tastefully decorated in a Latin American carnival theme, the Rio offers resort luxury at local prices. The guest rooms (all plush one-room suites) offer exceptional views and can be had for the price of a regular room at many other Las Vegas hotels. The combination of view, luxury, and price makes the Rio our first choice for couples on romantic getaways or honeymoons.

On Flamingo Road three minutes west of the Strip, the Rio also allows easy access to downtown via I-15. With 13 excellent restaurants, two great buffets, high-energy entertainment, a huge shopping arcade, a workout room, and an elaborate multipool swimming area, the Rio offers exceptional quality in every respect. Festive and bright without being tacky or overdone, the enlarged casino also offers a comfortable sports book.

In a phased expansion over the past six years, the Rio has quadrupled its guest room inventory, doubled the size of its swimming complex, beefed up its lineup of restaurants, and in the process turned into a true destination resort. Masquerade Village, a retail, restaurant, and specialty shopping venue that rings the casino, is home to the *Masquerade in the Sky,* a parade featuring floats and performers suspended from tracks high above the casino floor.

The Rio staff ranks very high in terms of hospitality, warmth, and an eagerness to please. The Rio is one of the few casinos to successfully target both locals and out-of-towners, particularly Southern Californians.

Riviera   (www.theriviera.com)

Extending from the Strip halfway to Paradise Road (and the Las Vegas Convention Center), the Riviera is well positioned to accommodate both leisure and business travelers. Though not isolated, the Riviera provides so much in the way of gambling, entertainment, and amenities that many guests never feel the need to leave the property. The Riviera has more long-running shows (four) than any other hotel in Las Vegas and offers a highly varied entertainment mix. These include a production show, a comedy club, a striptease show, a female impersonator show, as well as celebrity entertainers and lounge acts.

While some hotels may serve better food, there are few that offer more variety, especially to the informal diner. Guests on the move can choose from a number of fast-food restaurants in the Food Court or go for the Riviera's buffet. Upscale restaurants round out the package and supply ethnic diversity. As for amenities, the Riviera provides a spacious pool and sunbathing area, tennis courts, a shopping arcade, and a wedding chapel. Guest rooms, particularly in the towers, are more comfortable than the public areas suggest.

The casino is huge (big enough to get lost in on the way to the rest room) and somewhat of a maze. There is always a lot of noise and light, and a busy, unremitting flurry of activity. Walk-in traffic mixes with convention-goers, retirees on "gambling sprees," and tourists on wholesaler packages. Asians, Asian-Americans, and Southern Californians also patronize the Riviera.

Sahara   (www.saharahotelandcasino.com)

The Sahara, sporting a Moroccan theme after an extensive renovation, is situated at the far north end of the Strip (toward downtown). A complex of buildings and towers, the Sahara offers a casino, a convention hall, a showroom, a decent buffet, a shopping arcade, two upscale restaurants, and a swimming pool. Fronting the building along the strip is two attractions worth noting: Speedworld, a virtual reality racecar "ride," and Speed, a roller coaster. The Sahara is a little remote for anyone who wants to walk, but if you have a car, it is nicely positioned in relation to the Strip, downtown, and the Convention Center.

The Sahara is comfortable, but not flashy. Guest rooms are modern, and the new casino, with its Moroccan styling, is both tasteful and visually exciting. For the most part, the Sahara caters to businessmen attending meetings or conventions and to leisure travelers from Southern California and the Southwest.

Sam's Town   (www.samstownlv.com)

About 20 minutes east of the Strip on the Boulder Highway, Sam's Town is a long, rambling set of connected buildings with an Old West mining-town motif. In addition to the hotel and casino, there are a bowling alley, a very good buffet, one of Las Vegas's better Mexican eateries, a steak house, a great 1950s-style diner, and two RV parks. The lounge features live country-western music and dancing and is popular with both locals and visitors. A new events center and an 18-screen movie theater were added in 2000.

Other pluses include a free-form pool, a sand volleyball court, a child-care center, and a spa. Joining the "let's be an attraction" movement, Sam's Town offers an atrium featuring plants, trees, footpaths, waterfalls, and even a "mountain." A waterfall in the atrium is the site of a free but very well done fountains-and-light show (keep your eye on the robotic wolf). Frequent customers, besides the locals, include seniors and cowboys.

San Remo   (www.sanremolasvegas.com)

The San Remo sits next door to the Tropicana and across Tropicana Avenue from the MGM Grand Hotel and Theme Park. Since it is close to the airport and the southern end of the Strip, the San Remo's traditional market has been business travelers as well as Southern Californians, Southwestern leisure travelers, and Japanese "package-tourists."

The San Remo has a chandeliered casino, an OK restaurant, an average buffet, decent prime rib specials, and a good sushi bar. Dark hardwood furniture contrasts pleasantly with light wallpaper and patterned accessories in the well-appointed guest rooms. A central courtyard and pool complete the package.

Santa Fe Station   (www.stationsantafe.com)

Santa Fe Station is about 20 minutes northwest of Las Vegas, just off US 95. Like Sam's Town, the Rio, and the Showboat, Santa Fe Station targets both locals and tourists. Acquired by Station Casinos in 2000, the name was changed from Santa Fe to Santa Fe Station. Bright and airy, with a warm southwestern decor, Santa Fe Station is one of the more livable hotel-casinos in Las Vegas.

Santa Fe Station offers a spacious casino, a better-than-average buffet, and an all-purpose restaurant featuring steak, prime rib, and Mexican specialties. Santa Fe Station doesn't have a showroom, but live entertainment is provided in the lounge. In addition to a pool, there is a bowling alley and, amazingly, a hockey-sized ice-skating rink. Guest rooms, also decorated in a southwestern style, are nice and a good value.

Silverton   (www.silvertoncasino.com)

Southwest of Las Vegas at the Blue Diamond Road exit off I-15, Silverton opened in 1994 as Boomtown with a nicely executed Old West mining-town theme. The casino is visually interesting, with rough-hewn beams, mine tunnels, overhead mine car tracks, and a sizable array of prospecting and mining artifacts. The buffet is better than average, as is the coffee shop. The lounge features country music and dancing. Ten minutes from the Strip, Silverton is in a great position to snag Southern Californians. Silverton also targets the RV crowd with a large, full-service RV park.

Stardust   (www.stardustlv.com)

Situated on the Strip at the intersection with Convention Center Drive, the Stardust caters to the tour and travel market, meeting and trade show attendees, and locals. With a location that affords easy access to the Riviera and Circus Circus, the Stardust is well placed for Strip action and is about a 15-minute walk from the Las Vegas Convention Center. A high-rise tower with handsome guest rooms has doubled the number of rooms available at the Stardust, while new meeting facilities have elevated the property's status with business travelers. Amenities include a shopping arcade and a heated pool. The Stardust has consistent, high-quality restaurants such as William B's, which features some of Las Vegas's better prime rib.

The lounge entertainment is better than average at the Stardust, and Wayne Newton signed a contract with the Stardust guaranteeing he will perform his show here exclusively. The casino was renovated to the tune of $24 million in 1999 and is much more livable but just as spread out as ever.

Stratosphere (www.stratlv.com)

The Stratosphere Tower is the brainchild of Vegas World owner Bob Stupak, the quintessential Las Vegas maverick casino owner. Vegas World had been one of the last sole-proprietorship casinos in Las Vegas, but the lack of financing to complete the tower forced Stupak to sell 75% of his company to Lyle Berman and Grand Casinos of Minnesota and Mississippi (not to be confused with Las Vegas's MGM Grand). Stupak's original idea was to attach a tourist attraction (the tower) to Vegas World. Berman, however, realized that such a juxtaposition would be like locating the Washington Monument next to a Texaco station and insisted that Vegas World be bulldozed. The resort that has risen from the rubble happily combines Stupak's vision with Berman's taste.

The Stratosphere hotel-casino opened on April 30, 1996, and Las Vegas hasn't been the same since. At 1,149 feet, Stratosphere Tower is the tallest building west of the Mississippi—taller than the Eiffel Tower (the real one). It houses indoor and outdoor observation decks, a 360-seat revolving restaurant, and meeting rooms. The 360° view is breathtaking day (a life-size relief map of Las Vegas Valley and beyond) and night (the shimmering blaze of a billion bulbs).

Also at the top (hang on to your hats!) are two thrill rides. The world's highest roller coaster is also the world's slowest and shortest. It's a yawner, barely worth the 50 seconds of your time. However, if you try it, be sure to step out to the right! The other ride, however, a gravity/thrill experience called The Big Shot, is a monster: It rockets you straight up the tower's needle with a force of four Gs, then drops you back down with no Gs. And it all happens, mind you, at 1,000 feet in the air!

A second construction phase, including another 1,000 rooms and a new pool area were completed in 2001.

During the prior four-year construction of the tower itself, politicos, pundits, and industry bigwigs pegged their hopes on the tower attraction to revitalize the northern end of the Strip, which has long needed some modernizing. So far, however, the only project completed nearby is the expansion of the Sahara. Two new resorts rumored to be in the works for the vacant lots on either side of the Sahara, and a small casino called Chicago–Chicago planned for the site now occupied by Holy Cow!, have failed to materialize. A proposal (enter again Bob Stupak) for a hotel-casino housed in a full-scale replica of the *Titanic* was torpedoed by the City Council. But for the first time since 1992 (when it closed), The El Rancho site is the object of definite plans. Bought by Turnberry Place, who will build a billion-dollar condo complex, the El Rancho was imploded in September of 2000.

Suncoast   (www.suncoastcasino.com)

Like most of the Coast casinos, Suncoast is designed to attract locals. Located west of Las Vegas in Summerlin near some of the area's best golf courses, Suncoast offers high return slots and video poker, a surprisingly good (for a locals joint) fitness center, 64 lanes of bowling, and a 16-screen movie complex. In the food department, there's a decent buffet as well as restaurants serving Italian, Mexican, and big wads of meat respectively. The casino is open and uncrowded rendered in a southwest mission style. A showroom that features name bands, a new pool, and a child care center round out the offerings. For its size (440 rooms/78,000-square-foot casino), the Suncoast offers a pretty amazing array of attractions and amenities.

Terrible's   (www.terribleherbst.com/ett-gaming/casino-hotel)

Terrible's is the product of a well done $65 million renovation of the dilapidated old Continental Hotel and Casino. Located a couple of blocks off the Strip at the intersection of Paradise and Flamingo Roads, Terrible's offers excellent value with totally refurbished guest rooms, a good buffet, and a casino that's clean, bright, and busy. Terrible, incidently, is a person, Terrible Herbst to be exact. The Herbst family is well know locally for their gas stations and for auto racing. Terrible's targets local but is a good choice, by virtue of its location and easy parking, for anyone who has a car and intends to use it.

Texas Station   (www.texasstation.com)

Owned by Station Casinos which also owns and operates Palace Station, Sunset Station, Boulder Station, the Reserve, and the Fiesta, Texas Station has a single-story full-service casino with 91,000 square feet of gaming space, decorated with black carpet sporting cowboy designs such as gold, boots, ropes, revolvers, covered wagons, etc. The atmosphere is contemporary Western, a subtle blend of Texas ranch culture and Spanish architecture. This property offers seven restaurants, one of Las Vegas's best buffets, two bars, a dance hall called the Armadillo Honky Tonk, a 60 lane bowling center, childcare facilities, and a 12-screen theater showing first-run movies. Texas Station caters to locals and cowboys and is at the intersection of Rancho Drive and Lake Mead Boulevard in North Las Vegas.

Treasure Island   (www.treasureisland.com)

Treasure Island is one of three megacasino resorts to open during the fall of 1993. On the southwest corner of the Strip at Spring Mountain Road next door to the Mirage, Treasure Island is Caribbean in style, with a buccaneer theme. Though similar in amenities and services, Treasure Island targets a younger, more middle-class family clientele than the Mirage.

In the spirit of the Mirage, Treasure Island is an attraction as well as a hotel and casino. Crossing Buccaneer Bay from the Strip on a plank bridge, guests enter a pirate fort and seaside village reminiscent of Disney's Pirates of the Caribbean ride. Colorful and detailed, the village (which serves as the main entrance to the hotel and casino) is sandwiched between rocky cliffs and landscaped with palms. Every 90 minutes a British man-o'-war sails into the harbor and engages a pirate ship in a raging battle (firing over the heads of tourists on the bridge). Exceptional special effects, pyrotechnics, and a cast of almost two dozen pirates and sailors per show ensure that any Strip traffic not snarled by the Mirage's volcano (next door) will most certainly be stopped dead by Treasure Island's sea battle.

Passing through the main sally port, you enter the commercial and residential area of Buccaneer Bay Village, complete with town square, shops, restaurants, and, of course, the casino. The casino continues the old Caribbean theme, with carved panels and whitewashed, beamed ceilings over a black carpet, punctuated with fuschia, sapphire blue, and emerald green. The overall impression is one of tropical comfort: exciting, but easy on the eye and spirit. In addition to the usual slots and table games, a comfortable sports book is provided.

The hotel lobby and public areas are likewise elaborate and detailed. The lobby bar, a sort of building within a building, is especially eye-catching. Here, incredibly, a patio framed by exotic arches and columns is lit by chandeliers made from cast plastic human bones. The Treasure Island publicity people are quick to point out, however, that the various skulls, femurs, and scapulas are "finished in gold so that they don't look gory."

Pirate's Walk, the main interior passageway, leads to a shopping arcade, a steak house, and the buffet. Treasure Island's most upscale restaurant is the Buccaneer Bay Club overlooking the bay. Here you can enjoy a quiet, relaxing meal while watching the British and the pirates fire cannons at each other outside. Only in America.

Treasure Island amenities include a beautifully landscaped swimming area with slides, waterfalls, grottos, and tranquil pools. The pirate theme gives way to luxury and practicality in the well-equipped health club and spa. Larger than that of the Mirage, the facility features weight machines, free weights, a variety of aerobic workout equipment, large whirlpools, steam rooms, and saunas.

Treasure Island is home to the extraordinary *Cirque du Soleil,* which performs in a custom-designed, 1,500-seat theater. For the kids there is Mutiny Bay, an 18,000-square-foot electronic games arcade.

Guest rooms at Treasure Island are situated in a Y-shaped, coral-colored tower that rises directly behind the pirate village. Decorated in soft, earth-tone colors, the rooms provide a restful retreat from the bustling casino. Additionally, the rooms feature large windows affording a good view of the Strip or (on the west side) of the mountains and sunset. The balconies that are visible in photos of Treasure Island are strictly decorative and cannot be accessed from the guest rooms. Self-parking is easier at Treasure Island than at most Strip hotels. Valet parking is fast and efficient. An elevated tram connects Treasure Island to the Mirage next door.

Tropicana   (www.tropicanalv.com)

At the southern end of the Strip, the Tropicana sits across Las Vegas Boulevard from the Excalibur and opposite MGM Grand on Tropicana Avenue. With its Paradise and Island Towers and 1,910 rooms, the Tropicana is the oldest of the four hotels at the intersection of the Strip and Tropicana. It offers a full range of services and amenities, including tennis, an exercise room, meeting and convention space, and a shopping arcade. The Tropicana is also home to one of Las Vegas's most celebrated swimming and sun-bathing complexes. This facility, a system of lagoons and grottos embellished with flowing water, is less a swimming pool than a water park.

The Tropicana has four restaurants of merit that specialize, respectively, in steak and prime rib, Italian food, and Japanese teppan grill combinations. Entertainment offerings consist of a comedy club, a long-running production show, and lounge acts. The Tropicana's casino is bustling and bright, with multicolored floral carpeting and a stunning, 4,000-square-foot stained-glass canopy over the table games. Both festive and elegant, the Tropicana casino is an attraction in its own right and ranks as one of the city's more pleasant and exciting places to gamble, especially for table players.

Guest rooms are furnished in an exotic, tropical bamboo motif that (in some rooms) includes mirrors on the ceiling. Views from the upper rooms of both towers are among the best in town.

The Tropicana does a thriving business with the travel wholesalers and motor coach tours, and also aggressively targets the Japanese and Hispanic markets. In the casino you will find a more-youthful-than-average clientele, including a lot of guests from the nearby Excalibur enjoying the Trop's more luxurious and sophisticated style. The Tropicana's domestic market draws, not unexpectedly, from Southern California. It is particularly popular with slot players.

Vacation Village   (www.vacationvillage.com)

To say that Vacation Village is on the Strip is stretching a point. South of the airport at the southern end of Las Vegas Boulevard, Vacation Village is the most remote property on the south side of town. It provides budget accommodations and basic amenities to Californians taking the southernmost exit from I-15 onto the Strip. Vacation Village offers a nice Southwestern-style casino, pool, buffet, and Mexican restaurant. Though Vacation Village is friendly and informal and welcomes the family trade, its isolation makes it an inconvenient place to stay unless, for some reason, you enjoy the desert.

The Venetian   (www.venetian.com)

On the site of the fabled Sands Hotel across the Strip from Treasure Island, the Venetian is a gargantuan development being constructed in two phases. The first phase, the Venetian, drawing its theme from the plazas, architecture, and canals of Venice, Italy, opened in spring 1999. The Venetian follows the example of New York–New York, Mandalay Bay, Luxor, and Paris Las Vegas in bringing the icons of world travel to Las Vegas.

Visiting the Venetian is like taking a trip back to the artistic, architectural, and commercial center of the world in the 16th century. You cross a 585,000-gallon canal on the steep-pitched Rialto Bridge, shadowed by the Campanile Bell Tower, to enter the Doge's Palace. Inside, reproductions of famous frescoes, framed by 24-karat-gold molding, adorn the 65-foot domed ceiling at the casino entrance. The geometric design of the flat-marble lobby floor provides an M.C. Escher-like optical illusion that gives the sensation of climbing stairs—a unique and thoroughly delightful touch. Behind the front desk is a large illustrated map of the island city, complete with buildings, landmarks, gondolas, and ships. Characters in period costumes from the 12th to 17th centuries roam the public areas, singing opera, performing mime, and jesting.

Although the Venetian claims that its bread and butter customers are business travelers and shoppers, it hasn't neglected to include a casino in its product mix. In fact, the Venetian casino, at 116,000 square feet, is larger than that of most Strip competitors. When the Lido Casino comes on line with the completion of Phase II, the overall resort will top out at more than

200,000 square feet of casino, second only to the MGM-Grand (which weighs in at 175,000 square feet).

The Venetian Casino is styled to resemble a Venetian palace with architecture and decor representative of the city's Renaissance era. Period frescoes on recessed ceilings over the table games depict Italian villas and palaces. The huge and stupifyingly ornate casino offers 110 table games and 2,500 slot machines. The perimeter of the casino houses a fast-food court, along with French, Italian, and Southwestern restaurants, and what could be the fanciest coffee shop in town.

Upstairs is the Grand Canal Shoppes, with 65 stores, mostly small boutiques. The Escher-like floor design continues throughout the shopping venue, with different colors and shapes providing variations on the theme. The centerpiece of the mall is the quarter-mile Grand Canal itself, enclosed by brick walls and wrought-iron fencing and cobbled with small change. Gondolas ply the waterway, steered and powered by gondoliers who serenade the four passengers in each ($10 adults, $5 children). Passing beneath arched bridges, the canal ends at a colossal reproduction of St. Marks Square. Like The Forum Shops, the Grand Canal Shoppes are arranged beneath a vaulted ceiling painted and lighted to simulate the sky.

The Venetian's 16 restaurants, most designed by well-known chefs, provide a wide range of dining environments and culinary choice. Wolfgang Puck's Postino, Joachim Splichal's Pinot Brasserie, Emeril Lagasse's Delmonico Steakhouse, Steven Pyles' Star Canyon, Eberhard Müller's Lutece, and the Cheesecake Factory's Grand Luxe are some of the culinary powerhitters represented.

An all-suite hotel, the Venetian offers guest accommodations averaging 700 square feet and divided into sleeping and adjoining sunken living areas. The living room area contains adequate space from meetings, work, or entertaining, and is equipped with combination fax machine/copiers with a dedicated phone line. The development plan calls for two Y-shaped hotel towers, each with 3,000 suites and connected directly to the Sands Expo and Convention Center.

The five-pool swimming complex and spa area are situated on the rooftop over the shopping venue and are well insulated from the bustle of the strip. One of the largest of its kind in the country, the ultra-upscale bi-level Canyon Ranch Spa offers fitness equipment and classes, therapies, and sauna and steam, as well as a 40-foot indoor rock-climbing wall, medical center, beauty salon, and cafe.

The Venetian targets the convention market with its mix of high-end business lodging, power restaurants, unique shopping, and proximity to Sands Expo and Convention Center (with 1.7 million square feet, the Sands has more convention space than the Las Vegas Convention Center). The

Venetian will certainly welcome tourists and gamblers, who come mostly on the weekend, but the other five days will be monopolized by the trade show crowds.

Westward Ho   (www.westwardho.com)

A sprawling motel next to the Stardust, the Westward Ho offers a slot-oriented casino decorated in the usual dark colors. There are lounge entertainment, a couple of pools, palatable but undistinguished dining, good deals on drinks and snacks, and easy foot access to a number of nearby casinos.

Navigating the Land of the Giants

The grand hotels of Las Vegas are celebrated on television, in film, and of course, in countless advertisements. These are the prestige properties in a town that counts more hotel rooms than any other city in the world. Located along the center and southern end of the Strip, these hyper-themed mammoths beckon with their glamour and luxury. Specifically we're talking about:

Aladdin
Bellagio
Caesars Palace
Luxor
Mandalay Bay/Four Seasons
MGM Grand
Mirage
Monte Carlo
New York–New York
Paris Las Vegas
Treasure Island
Venetian

But can so many hotels actually mean less choice? From a certain perspective the answer is yes. The Strip, you see, is suffering a paroxysm of homogeneity. After you've chosen your preferred icon (Statue of Liberty, Eiffel Tower, Pyramid, Pirate Ship, Volcano, etc.), you've done the heavy lifting. Aside from theme, the big new hotels are pretty much the same. First, they're all so large that walking to the self-park garage is like taking a hike. Second, there are high quality guest rooms in all of the new properties, as well as at Caesars Palace, an older hotel that has kept pace. This is a far cry from ten years ago, say, when only a handful of hotels offered rooms comparable to what you'd find at a garden variety Hyatt or Marriott. Third, all of the mega-hotels are distinguished by designer restaurants, each with its big-name chef, that are too expensive for the average guest to afford. Ditto for most of the showrooms.

So let's say you're a person of average means and you want to stay in one of the new, glitzy super hotels. Location is not important to you as long as it's on the Strip. How do you choose? If you have clear preference for gondolas over pirate ships, or sphinx over lions, simply select the hotel with the theme that fires your fantasies. If, however, you're pretty much indifferent when it comes to the various themes, make your selection on the basis of price. Using the Internet, your travel agent, and the resources provided in this guide, find the colossus that offers the best deal. Stay there and venture out on foot to check all the other hotels. Believe us, once you're ensconced, having the Empire State Building outside your window instead of a statue of Caesar won't make any difference.

As it happens, there are also a number of very nice, but more moderately priced hotels mixed in among the giants, specifically:

Ballys
Barbary Coast
Boardwalk Holiday Inn
Casino Royale
Excalibur
Flamingo
Harrah's
Imperial Palace
Tropicana

Many of these hotels were the prestige addresses of the Strip before the building boom of the past decade. They are still great places, however, and properties where you can afford to eat in the restaurants and enjoy a show. Best of all, they are located right in the heart of the action. It's cool, of course, to come home and say that you stayed at Bellagio, but you could camp at the Excalibur for a week for what a Bellagio weekend would cost.

Suite Hotels

Suites

The term *suite* in Las Vegas covers a broad range of accommodations. The vast majority of suites consist of a larger-than-average room with a conversation area (couch, chair, and coffee table) and a refrigerator added to the usual inventory of basic furnishings. In a two-room suite the conversation area is normally in a second room separate from the sleeping area. Two-room suites are not necessarily larger than one-room suites in terms of square footage but are more versatile. One-room and two-room suites are often available in Las Vegas for about the same rate as a standard hotel room.

Larger hotels, with or without casinos, usually offer roomier, more luxurious multiroom suites. Floor plans and rates for these premium suites can be obtained for the asking from the hotel sales and marketing department.

There are some suite hotels that do not have casinos. Patronized primarily by business travelers and nongamblers, these properties offer a quiet alternative to the glitz and frenetic pace of the casino hotels. Because there is no gambling to subsidize operations, however, suites at properties without casinos are usually (but not always) more expensive than suites at hotels with casinos.

While most hotels with casinos offer suites, only the Rio and the Venetian are all-suite properties. At the Rio, the basic suite is a plush, one-room affair with wet bar and sitting area but no kitchen facilities. The Rio, on Flamingo Road just west of the I-15 interchange, sometimes makes its suites available at less than $110 per night and is one of the best lodging values in town. Suites at the Venetian average about 700 square feet, divided into a sunken living room, an adjacent sleeping area, and a bathroom. The suite configuration at the Venetian is rectangular, while the suites at the Rio are more square in layout. In both cases the sleeping area is open to the living area.

Suite Hotels without Casinos

AmeriSuites   (www.amerisuites.com)

At Paradise and Harmon, AmeriSuites offers tidy, but not luxurious, one-room suites at good prices. In addition to a small fitness center, an outdoor pool, and a few small meeting rooms, the AmeriSuites serves complimentary continental breakfast. By taxi, the AmeriSuites is about four minutes from the Strip and five minutes from the Las Vegas Convention Center.

Alexis Park   (www.alexispark.com)

The Alexis Park is the best known of the Las Vegas one- and two-room suite properties. Expensive, and therefore relatively exclusive, the Alexis offers most of the amenities of a large resort hotel, including a lovely pool, lighted tennis courts, and an exercise room. Pegasus, a continental restaurant at the Alexis, has been rated in past years by Mobil and others (though not by us) as the best gourmet restaurant in Las Vegas. Suites are upscale and plush, with a Southwestern decor. The hotel's staff is extremely friendly and not at all pretentious. Alexis Park's clientele includes executive-level business travelers and a good number of Southern California yuppies. Incidentally, the Alexis Park has filed a request to add a small casino. If this is a turn-off for you, call before you go.

Crowne Plaza Holiday Inn   (www.crowneplaza.com)

On Paradise Road, the Crowne Plaza is four minutes by cab to both the Strip and the Las Vegas Convention Center. There is a pool and a cafe, and a fine selection of ethnic restaurants are within easy striking distance. Suites are mostly of the two-room variety and are nicely, but not luxuriously, appointed.

Holiday Inn Emerald Springs   (www.holidayinnlasvegas.com)

The Holiday Inn, formerly the Emerald Springs Inn, two blocks east of the Strip on Flamingo Road, is a newer property offering moderately priced one- and two-room suites. Featuring pink stucco, marble, and large fountains both inside and out, the lobby, common areas, and rooms are tranquil and sedate by Las Vegas standards. The Veranda Cafe is the in-house coffee shop and serves a breakfast buffet. There is a lounge, heated pool, and spa.

Mardi Gras Inn *Best Western*   (www.bestwestern.com)

The Mardi Gras offers Spartan suites at good rates. Quiet, with a well-manicured courtyard and a pool, the Mardi Gras is only a short walk from the Las Vegas Convention Center. There is a coffee shop on the property, and a number of good restaurants are less than a half-mile away. Though a sign in front of the property advertises a casino, there is only a small collection of slot machines.

Marriott Suites   (www.marriott.com)

With an outdoor pool and hot tub, a fitness center, a full-service restaurant, and room service, the Marriott Suites offers the amenities you would expect from a Marriott. And the small building and easy access to parking make the Marriott Suites easy to navigate. Suites are tastefully decorated, though not as plush as some Marriott properties. At the southwest corner of Desert Inn and Paradise roads, the Marriott Suites is about a five-minute walk to the Convention Center and a five-minute cab ride to the Strip.

Residence Inn   (www.residenceinn.com)

Across from the Las Vegas Convention Center, the Residence Inn by Marriott offers comfortable one- and two-bedroom suites with full kitchens. Patron-ized primarily by business travelers on extended stays, the Residence Inn provides a more homelike atmosphere than most other suite properties. While there is no restaurant at the hotel, there is an excellent selection within a half-mile radius. Amenities include a pool, hot tubs, and a coin laundry. A second Residence Inn is about a mile away at the Hughes Center.

St. Tropez   (www.sttropezlasvegas.com)

The St. Tropez offers beautifully decorated one- and two-room suites at rates often less than $100 per night. Adjoining a small shopping mall, the St. Tropez provides a heated pool, a fitness center, VCRs in the suites, and a complimentary continental breakfast. The St. Tropez is within five minutes of the Strip and the airport, and about seven minutes from the Convention Center. Most guests are upscale business and convention travelers.

Las Vegas Motels

Because they must compete with the huge hotel-casinos, many Las Vegas motels offer great rates or provide special amenities such as a complimentary breakfast. Like the resorts, motels often have a very specific clientele. La Quinta Motor Inn, for instance, caters to government employees while the Best Western on Craig Road primarily serves folks visiting Nellis Air Force Base.

For the most part, national motel chains are well represented in Las Vegas. We have included enough chain and independent motels in the following ratings and rankings section to give you a sense of how these properties compare with hotel-casinos and all-suite hotels. Because chain hotels are known entities to most travelers, no descriptions are provided beyond the room quality ratings and summary charts. After all, a Comfort Inn in Las Vegas is pretty much like a Comfort Inn in Louisville, and we are all aware by now that Motel 6 leaves the light on for you.

Hotel-Casinos and Motels: Rated and Ranked

WHAT'S IN A ROOM?

Except for cleanliness, state of repair, and decor, most travelers do not pay much attention to hotel rooms. There is, of course, a discernible standard of quality and luxury that differentiates Motel 6 from Holiday Inn, Holiday Inn from Marriott, and so on. In general, however, most hotel guests fail to appreciate that some rooms are better engineered than other rooms.

Contrary to what you might suppose, designing a hotel room is (or should be) a lot more complex than picking a bedspread to match the carpet and drapes. Making the room usable to its occupants is an art, a planning discipline that combines both form and function.

Hotel/Motel Toll-Free Reservation Lines	
Best Western	(800) 528-1234 Continental U.S. & Canada
	(800) 855-1155 TDD
Comfort Inns	(800) 228-5150 Continental U.S.
Courtyard by Marriott	(800) 321-2211 Continental U.S.
Crowne Plaza	(800) 227-6963
Days Inn	(800) 325-2525 Continental U.S.
Fairfield Inn by Marriott	(800) 228-2800 Continental U.S.
Four Seasons	(800) 332-3442
Hilton	(800) 445-8667 Continental U.S.
	(800) 368-1133 TDD
Holiday Inns	(800) 465-4329 Continental U.S. & Canada
Howard Johnson	(800) 654-2000 Continental U.S. & Canada
	(800) 654-8442 TDD
La Quinta	(800) 687-6667
Motel 6	(800) 466-8356
Quality Inns	(800) 228-5151 Continental U.S. & Canada
Residence Inn by Marriott	(800) 331-3131 Continental U.S.
Super 8 Motels	(800) 843-1991 Continental U.S. & Canada
Travelodge	(800) 255-3050 Continental U.S. & Canada
TDD for all Marriott hotels	(800) 228-7014

Decor and taste are important, certainly. No one wants to spend several days in a room where the decor is dated, garish, or even ugly. But beyond the decor, there are variables that determine how "livable" a hotel room is. In Las Vegas, for example, we have seen some beautifully appointed rooms that are simply not well designed for human habitation. The next time you stay in a hotel, pay attention to the details and design elements of your room. Even more than decor, these are the things that will make you feel comfortable and at home.

Here are a few of the things we check that you may want to start paying attention to:

Room Size   While some smaller rooms are cozy and well designed, a large and uncluttered room is generally preferable, especially for a stay of more than three days.

Temperature Control, Ventilation, and Odor   The guest should be able to control the temperature of the room. The best system, because it's so quiet, is central heating and air conditioning, controlled by the room's own thermostat. The next best system is a room module heater and air conditioner, preferably controlled by an automatic thermostat, but usually by manually operated button controls. The worst system is central heating and air without any sort of room thermostat or guest control.

The vast majority of hotel rooms have windows or balcony doors that have been permanently secured shut. Though there are some legitimate safety and liability issues involved, we prefer windows and balcony doors that can be opened to admit fresh air. Hotel rooms should be odor-free and smoke-free and not feel stuffy or damp.

Room Security   Better rooms have locks that require an encoded plastic card instead of the traditional lock and key. Card and slot systems allow the hotel, essentially, to change the combination or entry code of the lock with each new guest who uses the room. A burglar who has somehow acquired a room key to a conventional lock can afford to wait until the situation is right before using the key to gain access. Not so with a card and slot system. Though larger hotels and hotel chains with lock and key systems usually rotate their locks once each year, they remain vulnerable to hotel thieves much of the time. Many smaller or independent properties rarely rotate their locks.

In addition to the entry lock system, the door should have a deadbolt, and preferably a chain that can be locked from the inside. A chain by itself is not sufficient. Doors should also have a peephole. Windows and balcony doors, if any, should have secure locks.

Safety   Every room should have a fire or smoke alarm, clear fire instructions, and preferably a sprinkler system. Bathtubs should have a nonskid surface, and shower stalls should have doors that either open outward or slide side-to-side. Bathroom electrical outlets should be high on the wall and not too close to the sink. Balconies should have sturdy, high rails.

Noise   Most travelers have occasionally been kept awake by the television, partying, amorous activities of people in the next room, or by traffic on the street outside. Better hotels are designed with noise control in mind. Wall and ceiling construction are substantial, effectively screening routine noise. Carpets and drapes, in addition to being decorative, also absorb and muffle sounds. Mattresses mounted on stable platforms or sturdy bed frames do not squeak even when challenged by the most passionate and acrobatic lovers. Televisions enclosed in cabinets, and with volume governors, rarely disturb guests in adjacent rooms.

In better hotels, the air conditioning and heating system is well maintained and operates without noise or vibration. Likewise, plumbing is quiet and positioned away from the sleeping area. Doors to the hall, and to adjoining rooms, are thick and well fitted to better keep out noise.

Darkness Control   Ever been in a hotel room where the curtains would not quite come together in the middle? In Las Vegas, where many visitors stay up way into the wee hours, it's important to have a dark, quiet room where you can sleep late without the morning sun blasting you out of bed. Thick, lined curtains that close completely in the center and extend beyond the dimensions of the window or door frame are required. In a well-planned room, the curtains, shades, or blinds should almost totally block light at any time of day.

Lighting   Poor lighting is an extremely common problem in American hotel rooms. The lighting is usually adequate for dressing, relaxing, or watching television but not for reading or working. Lighting needs to be bright over tables and desks and alongside couches or easy chairs. Since so many people read in bed, there should be a separate light for each person. A room with two queen beds should have an individual light for four people. Better bedside reading lights illuminate a small area so that if you want to sleep and someone else prefers to stay up and read, you will not be bothered by the light. The worst situation by far is a single lamp on a table between beds. In each bed, only the person next to the lamp will have sufficient light to read. This deficiency is often compounded by light bulbs of insufficient wattage.

In addition, closet areas should be well lit, and there should be a switch near the door that turns on lights in the room when you enter. A seldom seen, but desirable, feature is a bedside console that allows a guest to control all or most lights in the room from bed.

Furnishings   At bare minimum, the bed(s) must be firm. Pillows should be made with nonallergenic fillers and, in addition to the sheets and spread, a blanket should be provided. Bedclothes should be laundered with a fabric softener and changed daily. Better hotels usually provide extra blankets and pillows in the room or on request, and sometimes use a second topsheet between the blanket and the spread.

There should be a dresser large enough to hold clothes for two people during a five-day stay. A small table with two chairs, or a desk with a chair, should be provided. The room should be equipped with a luggage rack and a three-quarter- to full-length mirror.

The television should be color and cable-connected and, ideally, should have a volume governor and remote control. It should be mounted on a swivel base and preferably enclosed in a cabinet. Local channels should be posted on the set and a local TV program guide should be supplied.

The telephone should be TouchTone, conveniently situated for bedside use, and on it or nearby there should be easy-to-understand dialing instructions and a rate card. Local white and Yellow Pages should be provided. Better hotels have phones in the bath and equip room phones with long cords.

Well-designed hotel rooms usually have a plush armchair or a sleeper sofa for lounging and reading. Better headboards are padded for comfortable reading in bed, and there should be a nightstand or table on each side of the bed(s). Nice extras in any hotel room include a small refrigerator, a digital alarm clock, and a coffee maker.

Bathroom   Two sinks are better than one, and you can't have too much counter space. A sink outside the bath is great when two people are bathing and dressing at the same time. Sinks should have drains with stoppers.

Better bathrooms have both tub and shower with a nonslip bottom. Tub and shower controls should be easy to operate. Adjustable shower heads are

What the Ratings Mean		
★★★★★	*Superior Rooms*	Tasteful and luxurious by any standard
★★★★	*Extremely Nice Rooms*	What you would expect at a Hyatt Regency or Marriott
★★★	*Nice Rooms*	Holiday Inn or comparable quality
★★	*Adequate Rooms*	Clean, comfortable, and functional without frills—like a Motel 6
★	*Super Budget*	

preferred. The bath needs to be well lit and should have an exhaust fan and a guest-controlled bathroom heater. Towels should be large, soft, fluffy, and provided in generous quantities, as should hand towels and washcloths. There should be an electrical outlet for each sink, conveniently and safely placed.

Complimentary shampoo, conditioner, and lotion are a plus, as are robes and bathmats. Better hotels supply their bathrooms with tissues and extra toilet paper. Luxurious baths feature a phone, a hair dryer, sometimes a small television, or even a hot tub.

Vending There should be complimentary ice and a drink machine on each floor. Welcome additions include a snack machine and a sundries (combs, toothpaste) machine. The latter are seldom found in large hotels that have 24-hour restaurants and shops.

RATING THE HOTELS AND CASINOS

To help you select your Las Vegas hotel, we offer three different ratings:

1. Room Rating

2. Value Rating

3. Leisure, Recreation, and Services Rating

Although all three ratings will be defined in the following section, we should pause here to explain some changes from previous editions of this guide. The addition of so many luxury hotels in Las Vegas has necessitated an adjustment of our rating scales to allow for more meaningful comparison of the better hotels. Expressed differently, to make more room at the top, we had to adjust the entire scale. In terms of net effect, most hotels' ratings dropped slightly from last year. Generally speaking, however, this drop is the result of our adjustment as opposed to a shortcoming of the hotel.

ROOM RATINGS

To separate properties according to the relative quality, tastefulness, state of repair, cleanliness, and size of their standard rooms, we have grouped the hotels and motels into classifications denoted by stars. Star ratings in this guide apply to Las Vegas properties only and do not necessarily correspond to ratings awarded by Mobil, AAA, or other travel critics. Because stars have little relevance when awarded in the absence of commonly recognized standards of comparison, we have tied our ratings to expected levels of quality established by specific American hotel corporations.

Star ratings apply to *room quality only* and describe the property's standard accommodations. For almost all hotels and motels, a "standard accommodation" is a hotel room with either one king bed or two queen beds. In an all-suite property, the standard accommodation is either a one- or two-room suite. Also, in addition to standard accommodations, many hotels offer luxury rooms and special suites, which are not rated in this guide. Star ratings for rooms are assigned without regard to whether a property has a casino, restaurant(s), recreational facilities, entertainment, or other extras.

In addition to stars (which delineate broad categories), we also employ a numerical rating system. Our rating scale is 0–100, with 100 as the best possible rating, and zero (0) as the worst. Numerical ratings are presented to show the difference we perceive between one property and another. Rooms at the Luxor, Flamingo Hilton, and the Stardust, for instance, are all rated as ★★★½ (three and a half stars). In the supplemental numerical ratings, the Luxor and the Flamingo Hilton are rated 82 and 80, respectively, while the Stardust is rated 76. This means that within the three-and-a-half-star category, the Luxor and the Flamingo Hilton are comparable, and both have somewhat nicer rooms than the Stardust.

How the Hotels Compare

Here is a comparison of the hotel rooms in town. We've focused strictly on room quality and excluded any consideration of location, services, recreation, or amenities. In some instances, a one- or two-room suite can be had for the same price or less than that of a hotel room.

If you used an earlier edition of this guide, you will notice that many of the ratings and rankings have changed. These changes are occasioned by such positive developments as guest-room renovation, improved maintenance, and improved housekeeping. Failure to properly maintain guest rooms and poor housekeeping negatively affect the ratings. Finally, some ratings change as a result of enlarging our sample size. Because we cannot check every room in a hotel, we inspect a number of randomly chosen rooms. The more rooms we inspect in a particular hotel, the more representative our sample is of the property as a whole. Some of the ratings in this edition have changed as a result of extended sampling.

The guest rooms in many Las Vegas hotels can vary widely in quality. In most hotels the better rooms are situated in high-rise structures known locally as "towers." More modest accommodations, called "garden rooms," are routinely found in one- and two-story outbuildings. It is important to understand that not all rooms in a particular hotel are the same. When you make inquiries or reservations, always define the type of room you are talking about.

Finally, before you begin to shop for a hotel, take a hard look at this letter we received from a couple in Hot Springs, Arkansas:

We canceled our room reservations to follow the advice in your book [and reserved a hotel room highly ranked by the Unofficial Guide*]. We wanted inexpensive, but clean and cheerful. We got inexpensive, but [also] dirty, grim, and depressing. I really felt disappointed in your advice and the room. It was the pits. That was the one real piece of information I needed from your book! The room spoiled the holiday for me aside from our touring.*

Needless to say, this letter was as unsettling to us as the bad room was to our reader. Our integrity as travel journalists, after all, is based on the quality of the information we provide to our readers. Even with the best of intentions and the most conscientious research, however, we cannot inspect every room in every hotel. What we do, in statistical terms, is take a sample: we check out several rooms selected at random in each hotel and base our ratings and rankings on those rooms. The inspections are conducted anonymously and without the knowledge of the management. Although it would be unusual, it is certainly possible that the rooms we randomly inspect are not representative of the majority of rooms at a particular hotel. Another possibility is that the rooms we inspect in a given hotel are representative but that by bad luck a reader is assigned a room that is inferior. When we rechecked the hotel our reader disliked, we discovered that our rating was correctly representative, but that he and his wife had unfortunately been assigned to one of a small number of threadbare rooms scheduled for renovation.

The key to avoiding disappointment is to snoop around in advance. We recommend that you ask for a photo of a hotel's standard guest room before you book, or at least get a copy of the hotel's promotional brochure. Be forewarned, however, that some hotel chains use the same guest room photo in their promotional literature for all hotels in the chain; a specific guest room may not resemble the brochure photo. When you or your travel agent call, ask how old the property is and when your guest room was last renovated. If you arrive and are assigned a room inferior to that which you had been led to expect, demand to be moved to another room deserving of your expectations.

Cost estimates are based on the hotel's published rack rates for standard rooms, averaged between weekday and weekend prices. Each "$" represents $50. Thus a cost symbol of "$$$" means a room (or suite) at that hotel will cost about $150 a night.

How the Hotels Compare

Hotel	Star Rating	Quality Rating	Cost ($=$50)
Caesars Palace	★★★★½	95	$$$$–
Regent Las Vegas	★★★★½	95	$$$$–
Four Seasons at Mandalay Bay	★★★★½	94	$$$$$$–
Venetian	★★★★½	94	$$$$+
Mandalay Bay	★★★★½	92	$$$$+
Paris	★★★★½	91	$$$
Bellagio	★★★★	96	$$$$$–
Mirage	★★★★	89	$$$+
Alexis Park	★★★★	88	$$$–
Embassy Suites Convention Center	★★★★	88	$$$–
Hyatt at Lake Las Vegas	★★★★	88	$$$–
Aladdin	★★★★	87	$$–
Las Vegas Hilton	★★★★	87	$$–
MGM Grand	★★★★	87	$$$$–
St. Tropez	★★★★	87	$$–
Embassy Suites in Las Vegas	★★★★	86	$$+
Hard Rock Hotel	★★★★	86	$$$$–
Crowne Plaza	★★★★	85	$$$–
Golden Nugget	★★★★	85	$$+
Rio	★★★★	85	$$$$$–
Marriott Suites	★★★★	84	$$$–
Treasure Island	★★★★	84	$$$+
Residence Inn by Marriott	★★★★	83	$$$–
AmeriSuites	★★★½	82	$$+
Harrah's	★★★½	82	$$+
Luxor	★★★½	82	$$$–
New Frontier (Atrium Tower)	★★★½	82	$+
Sunset Station	★★★½	82	$$+
Bally's	★★★½	81	$$$+
Monte Carlo	★★★½	81	$$$+
Flamingo Hilton	★★★½	80	$+
Candlewood Suites	★★★½	79	$+
Stratosphere	★★★½	79	$+
Sam's Town	★★★½	78	$$–

How the Hotels Compare (continued)

Hotel	Star Rating	Quality Rating	Cost ($=$50)
Castaways	★★★½	77	$–
Courtyard by Marriott	★★★½	77	$$$+
Stardust	★★★½	76	$+
Arizona Charlie's East	★★★½	75	$+
Main Street Station	★★★½	75	$+
New Frontier (Garden Rooms)	★★★½	75	$+
New York–New York	★★★	74	$$+
Palace Station	★★★	74	$$–
Las Vegas Club (North Tower)	★★★	73	$+
Riviera	★★★	73	$$$–
Santa Fe Station	★★★	73	$+
Circus Circus (tower rooms)	★★★	72	$$+
The Reserve	★★★	72	$$+
Barbary Coast	★★★	71	$$–
Holiday Inn Emerald Springs	★★★	71	$$+
Texas Station	★★★	70	$$–
Sahara	★★★	69	$+
San Remo	★★★	69	$$–
Boulder Station	★★★	67	$+
California	★★★	67	$+
Comfort Inn South	★★★	67	$$–
Four Queens	★★★	67	$+
Orleans	★★★	67	$$–
Silverton	★★★	67	$–
Tropicana	★★★	67	$$$–
Excalibur	★★★	66	$$+
Fairfeild Inn	★★★	66	$$–
Arizona Charlie's West (Klondike Tower)	★★★	65	$+
Best Western Mardi Gras Inn	★★★	65	$$–
Holiday Inn Boardwalk	★★★	65	$$–
Imperial Palace	★★★	65	$$–
Sam Boyd's Fremont	★★★	65	$$–
Circus Circus (manor rooms)	★★★	59	$–
Bourbon Street	★★½	64	$–

How the Hotels Compare (continued)

Hotel	Star Rating	Quality Rating	Cost ($=$50)
Key Largo Casino	★★½	64	$+
La Quinta	★★½	64	$+
Maxim	★★½	64	$+
Fitzgeralds	★★½	63	$
Hawthorne Inn & Suites	★★½	63	$+
Terrible's	★★½	63	$+
El Cortez	★★½	62	$+
Fiesta	★★½	62	$+
Horseshoe (East Wing)	★★½	61	$–
Arizona Charlie's West (Meadows Tower)	★★½	60	$+
Plaza	★★½	60	$+
Lady Luck	★★½	59	$–
Nevada Palace	★★½	59	$+
Gold Coast	★★½	58	$$+
Las Vegas Club (South Tower)	★★½	58	$+
Best Western McCarran Inn	★★½	57	$+
Casino Royale	★★½	57	$+
Royal Hotel	★★½	56	$+
Horseshoe (West Wing)	★★½	53	$–
Days Inn Downtown	★★	53	$$–
Days Inn Town Hall Casino Hotel	★★	53	$$–
Vacation Village	★★	53	$$–
Howard Johnson Airport	★★	52	$+
Motel 6	★★	52	$+
Super 8	★★	52	$+
Howard Johnson	★★	50	$–
Travelodge Las Vegas Inn	★★	50	$+
Westward Ho	★★	50	$$–
Wild Wild West	★★	49	$

THE TOP 30 BEST DEALS IN LAS VEGAS

Having listed the nicest rooms in town, let's reorder the list to rank the best combinations of quality and value in a room. As before, the rankings are made without consideration of location or the availability of restaurant(s), recreational facilities, entertainment, and/or amenities. Once again, each lodging property is awarded a value rating on a 0–100 scale. The higher the rating, the better the value.

A reader recently complained to us that he had booked one of our top-ranked rooms in terms of value and had been very disappointed in the room. We noticed that the room the reader occupied had a quality rating of ★★½. We would remind you that the value ratings are intended to give you some sense of value received for dollars spent. A ★★½ room at $30 may have the same value rating as a ★★★★ room at $85, but that does not mean the rooms will be of comparable quality. Regardless of whether it's a good deal or not, a ★★½ room is still a ★★½ room.

Listed below are the best room buys for the money, regardless of location or star classification, based on averaged rack rates. Note that sometimes a suite can cost less than a hotel room.

The Top 30 Best Deals in Las Vegas

Hotel	Star Rating	Value Rating	Quality Rating	Cost ($=$50)
1. Castaways	★★★½	99	77	$–
2. St. Tropez	★★★★	78	87	$$–
3. Main Street Station	★★★½	77	75	$+
4. Stardust	★★★½	76	76	$+
5. Stratosphere	★★★½	75	79	$+
6. Las Vegas Hilton	★★★★	75	87	$$–
7. Silverton	★★★	72	67	$–
8. New Frontier (Atrium Tower)	★★★½	72	82	$+
9. Aladdin	★★★★	72	87	$$–
10. Candlewood Suites	★★★½	71	79	$+
11. Arizona Charlie's East	★★★½	67	75	$+
12. Sahara	★★★	66	69	$+
13. New Frontier (Garden Rooms)	★★★½	66	75	$+
14. Flamingo Hilton	★★★½	66	80	$+

The Top 30 Best Deals in Las Vegas (continued)

Hotel	Star Rating	Value Rating	Quality Rating	Cost ($=$50)
15. Las Vegas Club (North Tower)	★★★	65	73	$+
16. Circus Circus (manor rooms)	★★★	63	59	$−
17. Boulder Station	★★★	60	67	$+
18. Santa Fe Station	★★★	59	73	$+
19. Bourbon Street	★★½	57	64	$−
20. Golden Nugget	★★★★	57	85	$$+
21. Fitzgeralds	★★½	55	63	$
22. Horseshoe (East Wing)	★★½	55	61	$−
23. Four Queens	★★★	54	67	$+
24. Lady Luck	★★½	53	59	$−
25. Sam's Town	★★★½	52	78	$$−
26. Embassy Suites in Las Vegas	★★★★	51	86	$$+
27. California	★★★	50	67	$+
28. Arizona Charlie's West (Klondike Tower)	★★★	49	65	$+
29. Palace Station	★★★	49	74	$$−
30. Paris	★★★★½	48	91	$$$

Leisure, Recreation, and Services Rating of Hotel-Casinos

Many Las Vegas visitors only use their hotel rooms as a depository for luggage and a place to take a quick nap or shower. These folks are far more interested in what the hotel has to offer in terms of gambling, restaurants, live entertainment, services, and recreational pursuits.

Ranked below, in terms of the breadth and quality of their offerings, are Las Vegas hotels with full casinos. Using a weighted model, we have calculated a composite Leisure, Recreation, and Services Rating. The rating is designed to help you determine which properties provide the best overall vacation or leisure experience.

Interpreting the LR&S Ratings

Room quality is not considered in the Leisure, Recreation, and Services Rating (LR&S). Therefore a hotel with ordinary rooms may attain a high LR&S

score. A casino could have very ordinary guest rooms, for example, but score high in the LR&S rankings because it has a beautiful casino, excellent restaurants, a highly regarded buffet, shopping, and a good showroom.

Some hotels may score low because they offer little in the way of entertainment, recreation, or food service. If the property is somewhat isolated, like Vacation Village or El Cortez, these deficiencies pose serious problems. If, on the other hand, a hotel is situated in a prime location, the shortcomings hardly matter. The Barbary Coast does not have a showroom, but is within easy walking distance of showrooms at Caesars Palace, Bally's, the Mirage, Harrah's, the Imperial Palace, and the Flamingo. Likewise, the Four Queens, downtown, doesn't have a buffet but is within a three-minute walk of buffets at the Golden Nugget, Fremont, and Lady Luck.

Because the LR&S is a composite rating, its primary value is in identifying the properties that offer the highest quality and greatest variety of restaurants, diversions, and activities. The rating does not, however, indicate what those restaurants, diversions, or activities are. Bellagio and Caesars Palace have the highest LR&S ratings, but neither has a golf course. If you want to walk right out your door and tee off, you would do well to stay at the Regent Las Vegas. Use the LR&S evaluations as a general guideline. When you have identified several properties that seem interesting, check the alphabetized profiles in the Hotel Information Chart to make sure your preliminary selections offer the features that are important to you.

LR&S Rating for Hotels with Full Casinos

Rank	Hotel	Leisure, Recreation & Services Rating
1	Mandalay Bay	97
2	Bellagio	94
3	Caesars Palace	93
4	Mirage	93
5	MGM Grand	91
6	Aladdin	90
7	Rio	90
8	Treasure Island	90
9	Venetian	90
10	Paris	88
11	Luxor	87
12	Las Vegas Hilton	86

LR&S Rating for Hotels with Full Casinos (continued)

Rank	Hotel	Leisure, Recreation & Services Rating
13	Flamingo Hilton	83
14	Bally's	82
15	Monte Carlo	81
16	New York–New York	80
17	Harrah's	79
18	Stratosphere	78
19	Tropicana	78
20	Hard Rock Hotel	77
21	Regent Las Vegas	76
22	Golden Nugget	75
23	Excalibur	74
24	Sunset Station	74
25	Circus Circus	73
26	Orleans	73
27	Imperial Palace	72
28	Riviera	72
29	Sahara	71
30	Sam's Town	70
31	Texas Station	69
32	Main Street Station	68
33	Stardust	68
34	Palace Station	67
35	Santa Fe Station	67
36	New Frontier	66
37	Boulder Station	65
38	Fiesta	65
39	Gold Coast	64
40	Castaways	63
41	Lady Luck	62
42	Four Queens	61
43	Reserve	61
44	Suncoast	61
45	San Remo	60

Percentage Value of LR&S Components

Weight	Subject of Evaluation
20%	**Casino:** Design, quality, gaming variety, aesthetic appeal, and atmosphere.
20%	**On-Site Restaurants:** Quality, variety, aesthetic appeal, and atmosphere.
10%	**Showroom, Lounge, and Entertainment:** Availability, variety, and quality of live shows, movies, and other entertainment.
10%	**Hotel Services:** Valet parking, concierge, room service, check-in and check-out efficiency.
8%	**Sports and Recreational Offerings:** Availability, variety, and quality of on-site sports and recreational activities, including golf, tennis, racquetball, bowling, ice skating, weight lifting, stationary cycling, aerobics, jogging, and swimming.
8%	**Swimming and Sunbathing Area:** Quality, size, aesthetic appeal, and atmosphere of the pool and surrounding area.
6%	**Spa Facilities:** Availability, variety, and quality of on-site spa services, such as steam room, sauna, whirlpool, facials, massage, dietary services.
6%	**Buffet:** Availability and quality of a daily-offered buffet.
6%	**Shopping:** Availability, quality, and variety of shopping.
6%	**Landscaping and Upkeep:** Cleanliness, state of repair, and aesthetic appeal of buildings, facilities, and grounds.
100%	Leisure, Recreation, and Services Rating (LR&S)

LR&S Rating for Hotels with Full Casinos (continued)

Rank	Hotel	Leisure, Recreation & Services Rating
46	Silverton	60
47	Terrible's	60
48	Barbary Coast	59
49	California	59
50	Plaza	58
51	Arizona Charlie's East	57
52	Arizona Charlie's West	56
53	Horseshoe	56
54	Sam Boyd's Fremont	55
55	Las Vegas Club	54
56	Holiday Inn Boardwalk	53
57	Fitzgeralds	51
58	Nevada Palace	51
59	Westward Ho	51
60	Casino Royale	46
61	Wild Wild West	46
62	Bourbon Street	45
63	Days Inn Town Hall Casino	38
64	Vacation Village	38
65	El Cortez	31

When Only the Best Will Do

The trouble with profiles, including ours, is that details and distinctions are sacrificed in the interest of brevity and information accessibility. For example, while dozens of properties are listed as having swimming pools, we've made no qualitative discriminations. In the alphabetized profiles, a pool is a pool.

In actuality, of course, though most pools are quite basic and ordinary, a few (Mirage, Tropicana, Flamingo, Monte Carlo, MGM Grand, Aladdin, Mandalay Bay, Bellagio, Venetian, Regent Las Vegas, and the Rio) are pretty spectacular. To distinguish the exceptional from the average, we provide some best-of lists.

Best Dining (Expense No Issue)
1. Bellagio
2. Paris
3. Caesars Palace
4. Mandalay Bay
5. Venetian
6. Mirage
7. Rio
8. Aladdin

Best Dining (For Great Value)
1. Orleans
2. Suncoast
3. Main Street Station
4. Palace Station
5. Regent Las Vegas
6. Excalibur
7. California
8. Fiesta Station
9. Horseshoe
10. Boulder Station

Best Buffets
1. Sam's Town
2. Aladdin
3. Bellagio
4. Paris Le Village
5. Rio
6. Reserve
7. Orleans
8. Main Street
9. Fiesta
10. Sunset Station

Best Champagne Brunches
1. Bally's
2. MGM Grand (Brown Derby)
3. Circus Circus
4. Fiesta

5. MGM Grand (House of Blues)
6. Caesars Palace

Most Romantic Hotel-Casinos
1. Rio
2. Caesars Palace
3. Mirage
4. Mandalay Bay
5. Venetian

Best Guest-Room Baths
1. Caesars Palace
2. Bellagio
3. Venetian
4. Rio
5. Orleans

Most Visually Interesting Casinos
1. Luxor
2. Venetian
3. Caesars Palace
4. Main Street Station
5. Mandalay Bay
6. Mirage
7. New York–New York
8. Aladdin
9. Sunset Station
10. Rio

Best Views from Guest Rooms
1. Rio
2. Caesars Palace (Palace Tower)
3. Venetian (north-view rooms)
4. Bellagio
5. Mandalay Bay/Four Seasons
6. Stratosphere (upper south-view rooms)

7. Aladdin
8. Tropicana (towers)
9. Hard Rock Hotel
10. New York–New York
11. Fitzgeralds

Best for Shopping On-Site or within a Four-Minute Walk
1. Caesars Palace
2. Venetian
3. Mirage
4. Treasure Island
5. Aladdin

Best for Golf
Regent Las Vegas

Best for Tennis
1. MGM Grand
2 Bally's
3 Caesars Palace
4. Regent Las Vegas
5. Las Vegas Hilton

Best for Bowling
1. Castaways
2. Gold Coast
3. Sam's Town
4. Orleans
5. Santa Fe Station

Best for Jogging or Running
1. Mandalay Bay
2. Las Vegas Hilton

Best for Ice Skating
Santa Fe Station

Best Spas
1. Venetian
2. Regent Las Vegas
3. Caesars Palace

4. Bellagio
5. Mandalay Bay
6. Mirage
7. Paris
8. Monte Carlo
9. Treasure Island
10. Luxor

Best Swimming & Sunbathing
1. Mandalay Bay
2. Bellagio
3. Caesars Palace
4. Mirage
5. Venetian
6. Treasure Island
7. Tropicana
8. Flamingo
9. Monte Carlo
10. Hard Rock Hotel
11. Rio
12. Las Vegas Hilton
13. MGM Grand
14. Luxor

Best for Weight Lifting, Nautilus, Stationary Cycling, Stair Machines, & Other Indoor Exercise Equipment
1. Venetian
2. Caesars Palace
3. Mandalay Bay
4. Bellagio
5. Mirage
6. Paris
7. Treasure Island
8. MGM Grand
9. Luxor
10. Regent Las Vegas
11. Monte Carlo

Putting the Ratings Together

To complete the picture (for hotels with casinos), we need to combine the Room Quality Rating; the Room Value Rating; and the Leisure, Recreation, and Services (LR&S) Rating to derive an Overall Rating. In the first edition of this guide, we weighted each of these ratings equally and averaged them to obtain the Overall Rating. Subsequently, our readers indicated that the atmosphere, amenities, and services of their hotel-casino were as important to them as the quality and value of their guest room. Given this appreciated input, we have developed a new calculation for the Overall Rating. In our new calculation, guest room considerations (quality and value) account for half of the Overall Rating, while the LR&S Rating (reflecting the quality of the casino, restaurants, shows, physical plant, and services) accounts for the remaining half.

	Overall Ratings			
Hotel	50% LR&S Rating	25% Quality Rating	25% Value Rating	100% **Overall** **Rating**
Aladdin	90	87	72	85
Las Vegas Hilton	86	87	75	84
Caesars Palace	93	95	42	81
Mandalay Bay	97	92	33	80
Venetian	90	94	40	79
MGM Grand	91	87	48	79
Paris	88	91	48	79
Mirage	93	89	40	79
Bellagio	94	96	30	78
Flamingo Hilton	83	80	66	78
Stratosphere	78	79	75	78
Castaways	63	77	99	76
Treasure Island	90	84	35	75
Golden Nugget	75	85	57	73
Luxor	87	82	34	73
Rio	90	85	24	72
Main Street Station	68	75	77	72
Stardust	68	76	76	72

Hotel	50% LR&S Rating	25% Quality Rating	25% Value Rating	100% Overall Rating
Regent Las Vegas	76	95	38	71
Harrah's	79	82	44	71
New Frontier	66	79	70	70
Sahara	71	69	67	69
Bally's	82	81	31	69
Monte Carlo	81	81	30	68
Hard Rock Hotel	77	86	31	68
Sam's Town	70	78	51	67
New York–New York	80	74	33	67
Santa Fe Station	67	73	60	67
Circus Circus	73	66	50	66
Silverton	60	67	73	65
Palace Station	67	74	50	64
Boulder Station	65	67	60	64
Arizona Charlie's East	57	75	67	64
Suncoast	61	82	47	63
Tropicana	78	67	28	63
Orleans	73	67	37	63
Imperial Palace	72	65	41	62
Texas Station	69	70	41	62
Riviera	72	73	28	61
Four Queens	61	67	55	61
Excalibur	74	66	28	61
Lady Luck	62	59	53	59
California	59	67	51	59
Fiesta	65	62	42	59
Barbary Coast	59	71	42	58
Reserve	61	72	35	57
Las Vegas Club	54	66	55	57
Sunset Station	74	52	28	57
San Remo	60	69	37	57
Terrible's	60	63	40	56
Horseshoe	56	57	52	55
Fitzgeralds	51	63	56	55
Plaza	58	60	44	55

Overall Ratings (continued)

Overall Ratings (continued)

Hotel	50% LR&S Rating	25% Quality Rating	25% Value Rating	100% Overall Rating
Arizona Charlie's West	56	63	44	55
Sam Boyd's Fremont	55	65	39	53
Bourbon Street	45	64	58	53
Holiday Inn Boardwalk	53	65	41	53
Gold Coast	64	58	22	52
Nevada Palace	51	59	40	50
Casino Royale	46	57	37	46
Wild Wild West	46	49	35	44
Westward Ho	51	50	21	43
El Cortez	31	62	47	43
Days Inn Town Hall Casino	38	53	24	38
Vacation Village	38	53	20	37

Hotel	Room Star Rating	Zone	Street Address
Aladdin	★★★★	1	3667 Las Vegas Blvd., South Las Vegas, 89109
Alexis Park	★★★★	1	375 East Harmon Avenue Las Vegas, 89109
AmeriSuites	★★★½	1	4520 Paradise Road Las Vegas, 89109
Arizona Charlie's East	★★★½	5	4575 Boulder Highway Las Vegas, 89121
Arizona Charlie's West	★★½ /★★★*	3	740 South Decatur Blvd. Las Vegas, 89107
Bally's	★★★½	1	3645 Las Vegas Blvd., South Las Vegas, 89109
Barbary Coast	★★★	1	3595 Las Vegas Blvd., South Las Vegas, 89109
Bellagio	★★★★★	1	3600 Las Vegas Blvd., South Las Vegas, 89177
Best Western Mardi Gras Inn	★★★	1	3500 Paradise Road Las Vegas, 89109
Best Western McCarran Inn	★★½	1	4970 Paradise Road Las Vegas, 89119
Boulder Station	★★★	5	4111 Boulder Highway Las Vegas, 89121
Bourbon Street	★★½	1	120 East Flamingo Road Las Vegas, 89109
Caesars Palace	★★★★½	1	3570 Las Vegas Blvd., South Las Vegas, 89109
California	★★★	2	12 East Ogden Avenue Las Vegas, 89101
Candlewood Suites	★★★½	1	4034 South Paradise Road Las Vegas, 89109
Casino Royale	★★½	1	3411 Las Vegas Blvd., South Las Vegas, 89109
Castaways	★★★½	5	2800 East Fremont Street Las Vegas, 89104
Circus Circus	★★★ /★★★**	1	2880 Las Vegas Blvd., South Las Vegas, 89109
Comfort Inn South	★★★	1	5075 Koval Lane Las Vegas, 89109
Courtyard by Marriott	★★★½	1	3275 Paradise Road Las Vegas, 89109

*Meadows Tower/Klondike Tower; **manor rooms/tower rooms

Local Phone	Fax	Toll-Free Reservations	Discount Available	No. of Rooms	
(702) 736-0111	(702) 785-5511	(800) 634-3424		2600	⇨
(702) 796-3300	(702) 796-3354	(800) 582-2228	Gov't, military	500	⇨
(702) 369-3366	(702) 369-0009	(800) 833-1516	Senior, AAA	139	⇨
(702) 951-9000	(702) 951-9201	(817) 951-8002		300	⇨
(702) 258-5200	(702) 258-5192	(800) 342-2695	Gov't	225	⇨
(702) 739-4111	(702) 739-4405	(800) 634-3434	Gov't, AAA, senior	2,814	⇨
(702) 737-7111	(702) 693-8546	(888) BARBARY		200	⇨
(702) 693-7444	(702) 693-8546	(888) 987-6667		3,000	⇨
(702) 731-2020	(702) 731-4005	(800) 634-6501	Senior, military AAA, AARP	314	⇨
(702) 798-5530	(702) 798-7627	(800) 626-7575	Senior, military	100	⇨
(702) 432-7777	(702) 432-7730	(800) 683-7777		300	⇨
(702) 737-7200	(702) 734-3490	(800) 634-6956	Senior	166	⇨
(702) 731-7110	(702) 731-7172	(800) 634-6661	Senior, military, gov't	3,009	⇨
(702) 385-1222	(702) 388-2670	(800) 634-6255		781	⇨
(702) 836-3660	(702) 836-3661	none		160	⇨
(702) 737-3500	(702) 650-4743	(800) 854-7666		153	⇨
(702) 385-9123	(702) 383-9238	(800) 826-2800		450	⇨
(702) 734-0410	(702) 734-0410	(800) 634-3450	Senior	3,744	⇨
(702) 736-3600	(702) 736-0726	(800) 221-2222	Senior, military	106	⇨
(702) 791-3600	(702) 796-7981	(800) 321-2211	Gov't, military	149	⇨

Hotel	Ck. Out Time	Non-Smoking	Rack Rate	Room Quality	Room Value
Aladdin	11 a.m.		$$–	87	72
Alexis Park	11 a.m.	✓	$$$–	88	42
AmeriSuites	11 a.m.	Floors	$$+	82	43
Arizona Charlie's East	11 a.m.		$+	75	67
Arizona Charlie's West	11 a.m.	✓	$+/$+*	60/65*	38/50*
Bally's	11 a.m.	Floors	$$$+	81	31
Barbary Coast	Noon	✓	$$–	71	42
Bellagio	Noon	✓	$$$$$–	96	30
Best Western Mardi Gras Inn	Noon	✓	$$–	65	44
Best Western McCarran Inn	Noon	✓	$+	57	37
Boulder Station	Noon	✓	$+	67	60
Bourbon Street	Noon	✓	$–	64	58
Caesars Palace	Noon	Floors	$$$$–	95	42
California	Noon	✓	$+	67	51
Candlewood Suites	Noon	✓	$+	79	71
Casino Royale	Noon	✓	$+	57	37
Castaways	Noon	✓	$–	77	99
Circus Circus	11 a.m.	Floors	$–/$$+**	59/72**	64/36**
Comfort Inn South	11 a.m.	✓	$$–	67	45
Courtyard by Marriott	Noon	Floors	$$$+	77	29

*Meadows Tower/Klondike Tower; **manor rooms/tower rooms

Con-cierge	Convention Facilities	Meeting Rooms	Valet Parking	RV Park	Room Service	Free Breakfast
	✓	✓				
✓	✓	✓	✓		✓	
	✓	✓				✓
				✓	✓	
✓			✓			
✓	✓	✓	✓		✓	
✓	✓	✓	✓		✓	
✓	✓	✓	✓	✓	✓	
		✓				✓
						✓
✓	✓	✓	✓		✓	
		✓				
✓	✓	✓	✓		✓	
		✓	✓	✓	Breakfast	
	✓	✓	✓	✓	✓	
	✓	✓	✓	✓	Limited	
						✓
✓		✓			Dinner	Coffee

Hotel	Fine Dining/ Type of Food	Coffee Shop	24-hr. Café	Buffet	Deli
Aladdin	International				
Alexis Park	Continental	✓			
AmeriSuites					
Arizona Charlie's East	American		✓		
Arizona Charlie's West	Chinese, Steak	✓	✓	✓	✓
Bally's	Continental, Steak,	✓	✓	✓	
Barbary Coast	Continental,	✓	✓		
Bellagio	Continental,	✓	✓	✓	✓
Best Western Mardi Gras Inn		✓			
Best Western McCarran Inn					
Boulder Station	Steak/Seafood, Italian, Chinese	✓	✓	✓	✓
Bourbon Street			✓		
Caesars Palace	Asian, French, Italian, Japanese, Steak, Continental	✓	✓	✓	✓
California	Pasta/Seafood, Steak/Seafood	✓	✓ Breakfast		
Candlewood Suites					
Casino Royale		✓			
Castaways	Italian, Steak/Seafood	✓	✓	✓	
Circus Circus	Steak, Italian	✓	✓	✓	✓
Comfort Inn South		Adjacent			
Courtyard by Marriott		✓		✓	

Casino	24-hour Bar	Lounge	Showroom Entertainment	Gift Shop Drugs/News	Hair Salon	
			Headliners	✓	✓	⇨
		✓		✓	✓	⇨
						⇨
	Live music	✓				⇨
✓	✓	✓	Headliners	✓		⇨
✓	✓	✓	Production show, celebrity headliners	✓	✓	⇨
✓	✓	✓	Live music	✓		⇨
✓	✓	✓	Production show	✓	✓	⇨
Slots	✓	✓		✓	✓	⇨
						⇨
✓	✓	✓	Country-western performers	✓		⇨
Slots	✓	✓				⇨
✓	✓	✓	Celebrity headliner	✓	✓	⇨
✓	✓			✓		⇨
						⇨
✓	✓					⇨
✓	✓	✓		✓	✓	⇨
✓	✓	✓	Circus acts	✓	✓	⇨
						⇨
		✓				⇨

Hotel	Pool	Youth Activities	Exercise Rooms	Tennis & Racket Games
Aladdin	✓			
Alexis Park	✓ Heated		✓	
AmeriSuites	✓		✓	
Arizona Charlie's East	✓			
Arizona Charlie's West	✓ Seasonal			
Bally's	✓		Health spa	Tennis
Barbary Coast	✓			
Bellagio	✓		✓	
Best Western Mardi Gras Inn	✓			
Best Western McCarran Inn	✓			
Boulder Station	✓	✓		
Bourbon Street	Privileges		✓	
Caesars Palace	✓ Heated	✓	Health spa	✓
California	✓			
Candlewood Suites	✓		✓	
Casino Royale	✓			
Castaways	✓ Heated	✓		
Circus Circus	✓	✓		
Comfort Inn South	✓			
Courtyard by Marriott	✓ Heated		✓	Tennis

Golf	Other	Movie Theater	Sauna/Steam Whirlpool	Shopping Arcade	Elec Games Arcade
	Wedding gazebo		✓		
					✓
Privileges	Monorail		✓	✓	
Privileges					
Privileges	Wedding chapels	✓	✓	✓	
	Free shuttle		✓		✓
		✓			✓
Privileges		✓	✓	✓	
					✓
	Bowling, airport shuttle				✓
	Adventuredome, wedding chapel		✓	✓	✓
Privileges			✓		

Hotel	Room Star Rating	Zone	Street Address
Crowne Plaza	★★★★	1	4255 Paradise Road Las Vegas, 89109
Days Inn Downtown	★★	2	707 E. Fremont Street Las Vegas, 89101
Days Inn Town Hall Casino Hotel	★★	1	4155 Koval Lane Las Vegas, 89109
El Cortez	★★½	2	600 East Fremont Street Las Vegas, 89101
Embassy Suites Convention Center	★★★★	1	3600 South Paradise Road Las Vegas, 89109
Embassy Suites in Las Vegas	★★★★	1	4315 Swenson Street Las Vegas, 89119
Excalibur	★★★	1	3850 Las Vegas Blvd., South Las Vegas, 89109
Fairfeild Inn	★★★	1	3850 Paradise Road Las Vegas, 89109
Fiesta	★★½	3	2400 North Rancho Drive Las Vegas, 89130
Fitzgeralds	★★½	2	301 Fremont Street Las Vegas, 89101
Flamingo Hilton	★★★½	1	3555 Las Vegas Blvd., South Las Vegas, 89109
Four Queens	★★★	2	202 Fremont Street Las Vegas, 89101
Four Seasons at Mandalay Bay	★★★★½	1	3960 Las Vegas Blvd., South Las Vegas, 89119
Gold Coast	★★½	1	4000 West Flamingo Road Las Vegas, 89103
Golden Nugget	★★★★	2	129 East Fremont Street Las Vegas, 89101
Hard Rock Hotel	★★★★	1	4455 Paradise Road Las Vegas, 89109
Harrah's	★★★½	1	3475 Las Vegas Blvd., South Las Vegas, 89109
Hawthorne Inn & Suites	★★½	3	4975 S. Valley View Las Vegas, 89118
Holiday Inn Boardwalk	★★★	1	3750 Las Vegas Blvd., South Las Vegas, 89109
Holiday Inn Emerald Springs	★★★	1	325 East Flamingo Road Las Vegas, 89109

Local Phone	Fax	Toll-Free Reservations	Discount Available	No. of Rooms	
(702) 369-4400	(702) 369-3770	(800) 2-CROWNE	Senior, AARP	201	⇨
(702) 388-1400	(702) 388-9622	(800) 325-2344		147	⇨
(702) 731-2111	(702) 731-1113	(800) 634-6541	Senior, gov't, military	357	⇨
(702) 385-5200	(702) 385-1554	(800) 634-6703		401	⇨
(702) 893-8002	(702) 893-0378	(800) EMBASSY	AAA	286	⇨
(702) 795-2800	(702) 795-1520	(800) EMBASSY	AAA	220	⇨
(702) 597-7777	(702) 597-7040	(800) 937-7777		4,008	⇨
(702) 791-0899	(702) 791-2705	(800) 228-2800	AAA, gov't, AARP	129	⇨
(702) 631-7000	(702) 631-6588	(800) 731-7333		100	⇨
(702) 388-2400	(702) 388-2181	(800) 274-LUCK	Senior	638	⇨
(702) 733-3111	(702) 733-3353	(800) 732-2111	AAA, AARP,	642	⇨
(702) 385-4011	(702) 387-5122	(800) 634-6045	Military, gov't	690	⇨
(702) 632-5000	(702) 632-5222	(877) 632-5200		424	⇨
(702) 367-7111	(702) 367-8419	(888) 402-6278	Senior	711	⇨
(702) 385-7111	(702) 386-8362	(800) 634-3454	AAA	1,907	⇨
(702) 693-5000	(702) 693-5010	(800) 413-1638		667	⇨
(702) 369-5000	(702) 369-5008	(800) HARRAHS		2,700	⇨
(702) 798-7736	(702) 798-5951	(800) 780-7234		59	⇨
(702) 735-1167	(702) 739-8152	(800) HOLIDAY	Senior, military, AAA, gov't	654	⇨
(702) 732-9100	(702) 731-9784	(800) 732-7889	Senior, AAA gov't, military	150	⇨

Hotel	Ck. Out Time	Non-Smoking	Rack Rate	Room Quality	Room Value
Crowne Plaza	Noon	✓	$$$–	85	40
Days Inn Downtown	11 a.m.	✓	$$–	53	21
Days Inn Town Hall Casino Hotel	Noon	✓	$$–	53	24
El Cortez	11 a.m.	✓	$+	62	47
Embassy Suites Convention Center	11 a.m.	✓	$$$–	88	48
Embassy Suites in Las Vegas	11 a.m.	✓	$$+	86	51
Excalibur	11 a.m.	Floors	$$+	66	28
Fairfeild Inn	Noon	✓	$$–	66	44
Fiesta	Noon	✓	$+	62	42
Fitzgeralds	Noon	Floors	$	63	56
Flamingo Hilton	Noon	Floors/ Portion of casino	$+	80	66
Four Queens	Noon	Floors	$+	67	55
Four Seasons at Mandalay Bay	Noon	✓	$$$$$$–	94	27
Gold Coast	Noon	Floors	$$+	58	22
Golden Nugget	Noon	Floors	$$+	85	57
Hard Rock Hotel	Noon	Floors	$$$$–	86	31
Harrah's	Noon	Floors/ Part of casino	$$+	82	44
Hawthorne Inn & Suites	1 p.m.	✓	$+	63	40
Holiday Inn Boardwalk	Noon	✓	$$–	65	41
Holiday Inn Emerald Springs	Noon	Floors	$$+	71	33

Con-cierge	Convention Facilities	Meeting Rooms	Valet Parking	RV Park	Room Service	Free Breakfast
✓		✓			✓	Coffee ➡
						✓ ➡
						➡
		✓	✓		✓	➡
✓	✓	✓			✓	✓ ➡
	✓	✓			✓	✓ ➡
	✓	✓	✓		✓	➡
		✓				✓ ➡
		✓	✓			➡
		✓	✓		✓	➡
	✓	✓	✓		✓	➡
	✓	✓	✓		✓	➡
✓	✓	✓	✓		✓	➡
	✓	✓	✓		✓	➡
✓	✓	✓	✓		✓	➡
✓	✓	✓	✓		✓	➡
	✓	✓	✓		✓	➡
		✓				✓ ➡
		✓	✓		✓	➡
		✓			✓	➡

Hotel	Fine Dining/ Type of Food	Coffee Shop	24-hr. Café	Buffet	Deli
Crowne Plaza		✓			
Days Inn Downtown	American		✓		
Days Inn Town Hall Casino Hotel			✓		
El Cortez	Family/Steak	✓	✓		
Embassy Suites Convention Center	American				
Embassy Suites in Las Vegas					
Excalibur	Continental, Italian, Prime Rib	✓	✓	✓	
Fairfeild Inn					
Fiesta	Mexican, Steak	✓	✓	✓	✓
Fitzgeralds	Steak, Italian	✓	✓	✓	
Flamingo Hilton	Italian, Chinese, Gourmet, Continental, Japanese	✓	✓	✓	✓
Four Queens	American, Chinese	✓	✓		
Four Seasons at Mandalay Bay	American, Continental	✓			
Gold Coast	Steak, Italian, Seafood	✓	✓	✓	✓
Golden Nugget	Italian, Chinese	✓	✓	✓	
Hard Rock Hotel	Italian, Continental	✓	✓		
Harrah's	Steak/Seafood, Italian, Asian	✓	✓	✓	
Hawthorne Inn & Suites					
Holiday Inn Boardwalk		✓	✓	✓	✓
Holiday Inn Emerald Springs	American	✓			

Casino	24-hour Bar	Lounge	Showroom Entertainment	Gift Shop Drugs/News	Hair Salon	
		✓		✓		⇨
	✓	✓				⇨
✓	✓	✓		✓		⇨
✓	✓			✓	✓	⇨
		✓		✓		⇨
		✓				⇨
✓	✓	✓	Production show, King Arthur's Tournament	✓	✓	⇨
						⇨
✓	✓	✓	Live music	✓		⇨
✓	✓			✓		⇨
✓	✓	✓	Production show, Musical comedy	✓	✓	⇨
✓	✓			✓		⇨
		✓				⇨
✓	✓	✓	Dancing	✓	✓	⇨
✓	✓	✓	Production show	✓	✓	⇨
✓	✓	✓	Live music	✓	✓	⇨
✓	✓	✓	Production show, comedy show	✓		⇨
						⇨
✓	✓	✓	Variety shows	✓	✓	⇨
		✓				⇨

Hotel	Pool	Youth Activities	Exercise Rooms	Tennis & Racket Games
Crowne Plaza	✓Heated		✓	
Days Inn Downtown	✓			
Days Inn Town Hall Casino Hotel	✓Heated			
El Cortez				
Embassy Suites Convention Center	✓		✓	
Embassy Suites in Las Vegas	✓		✓	
Excalibur	✓Heated	✓		
Fairfeild Inn	✓			
Fiesta	✓Heated			
Fitzgeralds				
Flamingo Hilton	✓Heated		Health spa	Tennis
Four Queens				
Four Seasons at Mandalay Bay	✓		Health and fitness spa	
Gold Coast	✓Heated	✓	✓	
Golden Nugget	✓Heated		Health spa	
Hard Rock Hotel	✓Heated		Health spa	
Harrah's	✓	✓	✓	
Hawthorne Inn & Suites	✓		✓	
Holiday Inn Boardwalk	✓		✓	
Holiday Inn Emerald Springs	✓Heated		✓	

Golf	Other	Movie Theater	Sauna/Steam Whirlpool	Shopping Arcade	Elec Games Arcade
Privileges			✓		
			✓		
			✓		
					✓
	Wedding chapel		✓	✓	✓
					✓
			✓	✓	
	Wedding chapel		✓	✓	✓
	Bingo			Travelers' shop	✓
	Child-proofing of rooms, shark tank		✓		
	Bowling	✓	✓		✓
			✓	✓	✓
	Rock music, memorabilia		✓		✓
Privileges		✓	✓	✓	
			✓		
				✓	✓
	Complimentary shuttle to airport & strip			✓	

Hotel	Room Star Rating	Zone	Street Address
Horseshoe	★★ /★★½*	2	128 East Fremont Street Las Vegas, 89101
Howard Johnson	★★	1	3111 West Tropicana Avenue Las Vegas, 89103
Howard Johnson Airport	★★	1	5100 Paradise Road Las Vegas, 89119
Hyatt at Lake Las Vegas	★★★★	–	101 Montelago Blvd. Henderson, 89011
Imperial Palace	★★★	1	3535 Las Vegas Blvd., South Las Vegas, 89109
Key Largo Casino	★★½	1	377 East Flamingo Road Las Vegas, 89109
La Quinta	★★½	1	3970 Paradise Road Las Vegas, 89109
Lady Luck	★★½	2	206 North Third Street Las Vegas, 89101
Las Vegas Club	★★★ ★★½**	2	18 East Fremont Street Las Vegas, 89101
Las Vegas Hilton	★★★★	1	3000 Paradise Road Las Vegas, 89109
Luxor	★★★½	1	3900 Las Vegas Blvd., South Las Vegas, 89119-1000
Main Street Station	★★★½	2	200 North Main Street Las Vegas, 89101
Mandalay Bay	★★★★½	1	3950 Las Vegas Blvd., South Las Vegas, 89193-8880
Marriott Suites	★★★★	1	325 Convention Center Drive Las Vegas, 89109
Maxim	★★½	1	160 East Flamingo Road Las Vegas, 89109
MGM Grand	★★★★	1	3799 Las Vegas Blvd., South Las Vegas, 89109
Mirage	★★★★	1	3400 Las Vegas Blvd., South Las Vegas, 89109
Monte Carlo	★★★½	1	3770 Las Vegas Blvd., South Las Vegas, 89109
Motel 6	★★	1	195 E. Tropicana Las Vegas, 89109
Nevada Palace	★★½	5	5255 Boulder Highway Las Vegas, 89122

*West Wing/East Wing; **North Tower/South Tower

Local Phone	Fax	Toll-Free Reservations	Discount Available	No. of Rooms	
(702) 382-1600	(702) 384-1574	(800) 937-6537		354	⇨
(702) 798-1111	(702) 798-7138	(800) 300-7389	Senior, gov't, AAA	150	⇨
(702) 798-2777	(702) 736-8295	(800) 634-6439	AAA, gov't, senior	144	⇨
(702) 567-1234	(702) 567-6067	(800) 55-HYATT	AAA, gov't, senior	496	⇨
(702) 731-3311	(702) 735-8578	(800) 634-6441		2,700	⇨
(702) 733-7777	(702) 369-6911	(800) 634-6617	Senior	316	⇨
(702) 796-9000	(702) 796-3537	(800) NU-ROOMS	Senior	251	⇨
(702) 477-3000	(702) 477-3002	(800) LADY-LUCK		792	⇨
(702) 385-1664	(702) 387-6071	(800) 634-6532		410	⇨
(702) 732-5111	(702) 794-3611	(800) 732-7117	Senior, military, gov't	3,174	⇨
(702) 262-4000	(702) 262-4452	(800) 288-1000		4,407	⇨
(702) 387-1896	(702) 386-4421	(800) 465-0711		406	⇨
(702) 632-7777	(702) 632-7190	(877) 632-7000		3,276	⇨
(702) 650-2000	(702) 650-9466	(800) 244-3364	Senior, AAA	278	⇨
(702) 731-4300	(702) 735-3252	(800) 634-6987		800	⇨
(702) 891-1111	(702) 891-3036	(800) 929-1111		5,005	⇨
(702) 791-7111	(702) 791-7446	(800) 627-6667		3,049	⇨
(702) 730-7777	(702) 730-7200	(800) 311-8999		3,002	⇨
(702) 798-0728	(702) 798-5657	(800) 4-MOTEL-6		608	⇨
(702) 458-8810	(702) 458-3361	(800) 634-6283		209	⇨

Hotel	Ck. Out Time	Non-Smoking	Rack Rate	Room Quality	Room Value
Horseshoe	Noon		$–/$–*	53/61*	48/55*
Howard Johnson	11 a.m.	Floors	$–	50	45
Howard Johnson Airport	Noon	✓	$+	52	31
Hyatt at Lake Las Vegas	11 a.m.	✓	$$$–	88	48
Imperial Palace	Noon	Floors	$$–	65	41
Key Largo Casino	Noon	✓	$+	64	44
La Quinta	Noon	✓	$+	64	38
Lady Luck	Noon	✓	$–	59	53
Las Vegas Club	Noon	✓	$+/$+**	73/58**	66/44**
Las Vegas Hilton	Noon	✓	$$–	87	75
Luxor	11 a.m.	✓	$$$–	82	34
Main Street Station	11 a.m.	Floors	$+	75	77
Mandalay Bay	11 a.m.	Floors	$$$$+	92	33
Marriott Suites	Noon	✓	$$$–	84	46
Maxim	Noon	✓	$+	64	44
MGM Grand	11 a.m.	Floors	$$$$–	87	48
Mirage	Noon	Floors	$$$+	89	40
Monte Carlo	11 a.m.	Floors	$$$+	81	30
Motel 6	11 a.m.	✓	$+	52	31
Nevada Palace	Noon	✓	$+	59	40

*West Wing/East Wing; **North Tower/South Tower

Con-cierge	Convention Facilities	Meeting Rooms	Valet Parking	RV Park	Room Service	Free Breakfast
			✓		✓	
	✓	✓			✓	Coffee
		✓				
✓	✓	✓	✓		✓	
	✓	✓	✓		✓	
		✓				
		✓				✓
			✓		✓	
	✓	✓	✓		✓	
	✓	✓	✓		✓	
✓	✓	✓	✓		✓	
			✓	Privileges		
✓	✓	✓	✓		✓	
✓	✓	✓			✓	
	✓	✓	✓		✓	
✓	✓	✓	✓		✓	✓
✓	✓	✓	✓		✓	
✓	✓	✓	✓		✓	
	✓	✓		✓		

Hotel	Fine Dining/ Type of Food	Coffee Shop	24-hr. Café	Buffet	Deli
Horseshoe	Steak, Chinese	✓	✓	✓	✓
Howard Johnson		✓	✓		
Howard Johnson Airport					✓
Hyatt at Lake Las Vegas	American, Pacific	✓			
Imperial Palace	Steak, Seafood, Chinese, Ribs, Pizza	✓	✓	✓	
Key Largo Casino	American	✓	✓		
La Quinta					
Lady Luck	Steak/Seafood, Italian	✓	✓	✓	
Las Vegas Club	Steak/Seafood	✓	✓		✓
Las Vegas Hilton	French, Asian, Italian, Seafood, Mexican, Japanese	✓	✓	✓	
Luxor	American, Seafood, Steak	✓	✓	✓	✓
Main Street Station	Steak, Brewery	✓	✓	✓	
Mandalay Bay	American, Chinese, Fusion, Italian, Mexican, Southern	✓	✓	✓	✓
Marriott Suites	American/ Southwestern				
Maxim		✓		✓	
MGM Grand	Steak, Italian, Chinese, American, Seafood, Mexican	✓	✓	✓	✓
Mirage	French, Japanese, Steak/Seafood, Italian, Chinese	✓	✓	✓	
Monte Carlo	Steak, Chinese, Italian, French	✓	✓	✓	✓
Motel 6	American		✓		
Nevada Palace	Italian/Steak/ Seafood	✓	✓	✓	✓

Casino	24-hour Bar	Lounge	Showroom Entertainment	Gift Shop Drugs/News	Hair Salon	
✓	✓	✓		✓		⇨
✓	✓	✓	Variety, changes nightly			⇨
						⇨
✓	✓	✓		✓	✓	⇨
✓	✓	✓	Impersonator show	✓	✓	⇨
✓	✓	✓	Live music	✓		⇨
						⇨
✓	✓		Production show, magic, impersonator show	✓		⇨
✓	✓	✓		✓		⇨
✓	✓	✓	Production show	✓	✓	⇨
✓	✓	✓	Live entertainment changes nightly	✓	✓	⇨
✓	✓			✓		⇨
✓	✓	✓	Headliners, live music, sports	✓	✓	⇨
		✓		✓		⇨
		✓		✓		⇨
✓	✓	✓	Production show, celebrity headliner	✓	✓	⇨
✓	✓	✓	Production show, celebrity headliner	✓	✓	⇨
✓	✓	✓	Magic show	✓	✓	⇨
						⇨
✓	✓			✓		⇨

Hotel	Pool	Youth Activities	Exercise Rooms	Tennis & Racket Games
Horseshoe	✓			
Howard Johnson	✓			
Howard Johnson Airport	✓			
Hyatt at Lake Las Vegas	✓		✓	✓
Imperial Palace	✓		✓	
Key Largo Casino	✓Heated			
La Quinta	✓Heated		✓	
Lady Luck	✓			
Las Vegas Club	Privileges			
Las Vegas Hilton	✓Heated		✓	
Luxor	✓Heated		✓	
Main Street Station	Privileges			
Mandalay Bay	✓		✓	
Marriott Suites	✓Heated		✓	
Maxim	✓			
MGM Grand	✓Heated	✓	✓	✓
Mirage	✓Heated	✓	Health spa	
Monte Carlo	✓Heated		Health spa	✓
Motel 6	✓			
Nevada Palace	✓			

Golf	Other	Movie Theater	Sauna/Steam Whirlpool	Shopping Arcade	Elec Games Arcade
	Chapel				
					✓
	Free shuttle to Strip				✓
✓			✓		
	Auto collection, wedding chapel		✓	✓	✓
			✓		✓
	Airport shuttle (24-hour)	In rooms			
					✓
Privileges	Gated attraction	✓	✓	✓	
	Gated attractions	IMAX	✓	✓	✓
	11-acre water park, beach, river ride		✓	✓	
Privileges			✓		
				✓	✓
	Theme park, dance club	✓	✓	✓	✓
			✓	✓	✓
	Microbrewery, wedding chapel		✓	✓	✓
			✓		

Hotel	Room Star Rating	Zone	Street Address
New Frontier	★★★½ /★★★½*	1	3120 Las Vegas Blvd., South Las Vegas, 89109
New York–New York	★★★	1	3790 Las Vegas Blvd., South Las Vegas, 89109
Orleans	★★★	3	4500 West Tropicana Avenue Las Vegas, 89103
Palace Station	★★★	1	2411 West Sahara Avenue Las Vegas, 89102
Paris	★★★★½	1	3655 Las Vegas Blvd., South Las Vegas, 89109
Plaza	★★½	2	One Main Street Las Vegas, 89101
Regent Las Vegas	★★★★½	–	221 North Rampart Blvd. Las Vegas, 89128
The Reserve	★★★	–	777 West Lake Mead Drive Henderson, 89015
Residence Inn by Marriott	★★★★	1	3225 Paradise Road Las Vegas, 89109
Rio	★★★★	1	3700 West Flamingo Road Las Vegas, 89103
Riviera	★★★	1	2901 Las Vegas Blvd., South Las Vegas, 89109
Royal Hotel	★★½	1	99 Convention Center Drive Las Vegas, 89109
Sahara	★★★	1	2535 Las Vegas Blvd., South Las Vegas, 89109
Sam Boyd's Fremont	★★★	2	200 East Fremont Street Las Vegas, 89101
Sam's Town	★★★½	5	5111 Boulder Highway Las Vegas, 89122
San Remo	★★★	1	115 East Tropicana Avenue Las Vegas, 89109
Santa Fe Station	★★★	4	4949 N. Rancho Drive Las Vegas, 89130
Silverton	★★★	3	3333 Blue Diamond Road Las Vegas, 89139
St. Tropez	★★★★	1	455 East Harmon Avenue Las Vegas, 89109
Stardust	★★★½	1	3000 Las Vegas Blvd., South Las Vegas, 89109

*Atrium Tower/Garden Rooms

Local Phone	Fax	Toll-Free Reservations	Discount Available	No. of Rooms	
(702) 794-8200	(702) 794-8410	(800) 634-6966		986	⇨
(702) 740-6969	(702) 891-5285	(800) NY-FOR-ME		2,035	⇨
(702) 365-7111	(702) 365-7500	(800) ORLEANS		840	⇨
(702) 367-2411	(702) 221-6510	(800) 634-3101		1,028	⇨
(702) 946-7000	(702) 967-3830	(888) 266-5687	Senior, AAA	2,917	⇨
(702) 386-2110	(702) 382-8281	(800) 634-6575		1,052	⇨
(702) 869-7515	(702) 869-7771	(877) 869-8777		541	⇨
(702) 558-7000	(702) 567-7373	(800) 899-7770		224	⇨
(702) 796-9300	(702) 796-6571	(800) 331-3131	Senior, military	192	⇨
(702) 252-7777	(702) 253-6090	(800) PLAYRIO		2,563	⇨
(702) 734-5110	(702) 794-9451	(800) 634-6753		2,075	⇨
(702) 735-6117	(702) 735-2546	(800) 634-6118		236	⇨
(702) 737-2111	(702) 791-2027	(888) 696-2121	Senior, military, gov't	1,758	⇨
(702) 385-3232	(702) 385-6270	(800) 634-6182		447	⇨
(702) 456-7777	(702) 454-8014	(800) 634-6371		650	⇨
(702) 739-9000	(702) 736-1120	(800) 522-7366		711	⇨
(702) 658-4900	(702) 658-4919	(800) 872-6823	Military, gov't, corporate	200	⇨
(702) 263-7777	(702) 896-5635	(800) 588-7711		300	⇨
(702) 369-5400	(702) 369-1150	(800) 666-5400	Senior, military, AAA	149	⇨
(702) 732-6111	(702) 732-6257	(800) 824-6033		2,431	⇨

Hotel	Ck. Out Time	Non-Smoking	Rack Rate	Room Quality	Room Value
New Frontier	Noon	Floors	$+/$+*	82/75*	73/66*
New York–New York	11 a.m.	Floors	$$+	74	33
Orleans	Noon	Floors	$$−	67	37
Palace Station	Noon	Floors	$$−	74	50
Paris	11 a.m.	Floors	$$$	91	48
Plaza	Noon	✓	$+	60	44
Regent	Noon	✓	$$$$−	95	38
The Reserve	Noon	Floors	$$+	72	35
Residence Inn	Noon	✓	$$$−	83	42
Rio	Noon	Floors	$$$$$−	85	24
Riviera	11 a.m.	✓	$$$−	73	28
Royal Hotel	Noon	Floors	$+	56	45
Sahara	Noon	Floors	$+	69	67
Sam Boyd's Fremont	Noon	✓	$$−	65	39
Sam's Town	Noon	✓	$$−	78	51
San Remo	Noon	Floors	$$−	69	37
Santa Fe Station	Noon	✓	$+	73	60
Silverton	Noon	Floors	$−	67	73
St. Tropez	Noon	✓	$$−	87	78
Stardust	Noon	Floors	$+	76	76

*Atrium Tower/Garden Rooms

Con-cierge	Convention Facilities	Meeting Rooms	Valet Parking	RV Park	Room Service	Free Breakfast
		✓	✓		✓	
✓	✓	✓	✓		✓	
	✓	✓	✓		✓	
✓	✓	✓	✓		✓	
✓	✓	✓	✓		✓	
	✓	✓	✓		✓	
✓	✓	✓	✓	✓	✓	
			✓			
		✓			✓	✓
✓	✓	✓	✓		✓	Coffee
✓	✓	✓	✓		✓	
						Breakfast
		✓	✓		✓	
		✓	✓			Breakfast
	✓	✓	✓		✓	
	✓	✓	✓			
	✓	✓	✓	✓	✓	
✓		✓			✓	
	✓	✓	✓		✓	

Hotel	Fine Dining/ Type of Food	Coffee Shop	24-hr. Café	Buffet	Deli
New Frontier	Steak, Mexican	✓	✓	✓	✓
New York–New York	Steak, Chinese, Italian	✓	✓	✓	✓
Orleans	Italian, Steak	✓	✓	✓	
Palace Station	Seafood, Chinese, Mexican, Italian	✓	✓	✓	
Paris	French, American	✓	✓	✓	(Bakery)
Plaza	American/ Continental	✓	✓	✓	✓
Regent Las Vegas	Buffet, Health Food	✓	✓	✓	✓
The Reserve	Italian, Steak		✓	✓	
Residence Inn by Marriott					
Rio	Italian, Oyster Bar, Chinese, Southwestern, New Orleans, and more	✓	✓	✓	✓
Riviera	Steak/Seafood, Chinese, Italian	✓	✓	✓	
Royal Hotel		✓			
Sahara	Steak, Mexican	✓	✓	✓	
Sam Boyd's Fremont	Ribs, Gourmet	✓	✓	✓	
Sam's Town	Steak, Italian, American	✓	✓	✓	✓
San Remo	Italian, Japanese, Steak/Seafood	✓	✓	✓	✓
Santa Fe Station	Mexican, Steak French, Italian	✓	✓	✓	✓
Silverton		✓	✓	✓	✓
St. Tropez	Adjacent				
Stardust	Rib, Steak/Lobster, Mexican, Sushi	✓	✓	✓	✓

Casino	24-hour Bar	Lounge	Showroom Entertainment	Gift Shop Drugs/News	Hair Salon	
✓	✓		Country Western nightly	✓	✓	⇨
✓	✓	✓	Production show	✓	✓	⇨
✓	✓	✓	Celebrity headliners on weekends	✓	✓	⇨
✓	✓	✓	Live music	✓	✓	⇨
✓	✓	✓	Hunchback of Notre Dame in English	✓	✓	⇨
✓	✓	✓	Production show varies	✓	✓	⇨
✓	✓	✓	Entertainment in casino and restaurants	✓	✓	⇨
✓	✓	✓	Live music	✓		⇨
						⇨
✓	✓	✓	Live entertainment	✓	✓	⇨
✓	✓	✓	Production show, female impersonators, comedy club	✓	✓	⇨
✓	✓			✓		⇨
✓	✓	✓	Production shows variety	✓	✓	⇨
✓	✓	✓		✓		⇨
✓	✓	✓	Western dance hall/Production show	✓		⇨
✓	✓	✓	Production show	✓		⇨
✓	✓	✓		✓		⇨
✓	✓	✓	Live music	✓		⇨
						⇨
✓	✓	✓	Wayne Newton	✓	✓	⇨

Hotel	Pool	Youth Activities	Exercise Rooms	Tennis & Racket Games
New Frontier	✓Heated			
New York– New York	✓Heated	Family	Health spa, entertainment center	
Orleans	✓Heated	✓		
Palace Station	✓			
Paris	✓Rooftop	✓		
Plaza	✓Heated			Tennis
Regent Las Vegas	✓Heated	Limited	✓	✓
The Reserve	✓			
Residence Inn by Marriott	✓Heated		Privileges	
Rio	✓Heated		✓	
Riviera	✓Heated		✓	Tennis
Royal Hotel	✓			
Sahara	✓			
Sam Boyd's Fremont				
Sam's Town	✓	✓		
San Remo	✓Heated			
Santa Fe Station	✓	Nursery		
Silverton	✓			
St. Tropez	✓Heated		✓	
Stardust	✓Heated		✓	

Golf	Other	Movie Theater	Sauna/Steam Whirlpool	Shopping Arcade	Elec Games Arcade
			✓	✓	✓
	Roller coaster, wedding chapel		✓	✓	✓
	Bowling alley	✓	✓		✓
					✓
✓	Eiffel Tower		✓	✓	✓
	Wedding chapel			✓	✓
Putting green	Private gardens		✓	✓	
	Volleyball		✓		
	Grocery shopping service		✓		
Privileges		✓	✓	✓	
	Wedding chapel		✓	✓	✓
	Virtual reality racetrack	✓	✓	✓	✓
	Indoor park, 56-lane bowling center		✓		✓
	Wedding chapel				✓
Privileges	Bowling, ice skating	✓		✓	
			✓		✓
	Shuttle to the Strip & airport		✓		
			✓	✓	✓

Hotel	Room Star Rating	Zone	Street Address
Stratosphere	★★★½	1	2000 Las Vegas Blvd., South Las Vegas, 89104
Sunset Station	★★★½	5	1301 Sunset Road Las Vegas, 89014
Super 8	★★	1	4250 Koval Lane Las Vegas, 89109
Terrible's	★★½	1	4100 South Paradise Road Las Vegas, 89109
Texas Station	★★★	3	2101 Texas Star Lane Las Vegas, 89030
Travelodge Las Vegas Inn	★★	1	1501 West Sahara Las Vegas, 89102
Treasure Island	★★★★	1	3300 Las Vegas Blvd., South Las Vegas, 89109
Tropicana	★★★	1	3801 Las Vegas Blvd., South Las Vegas, 89109
Vacation Village	★★	1	6711 Las Vegas Blvd., South Las Vegas, 89119
The Venetian	★★★★★	1	3355 Las Vegas Blvd. South, Las Vegas, 89109
Westward Ho	★★	1	2900 Las Vegas Blvd., South Las Vegas, 89109
Wild Wild West	★★	1	3330 West Tropicana Avenue Las Vegas, 89103

Local Phone	Fax	Toll-Free Reservations	Discount Available	No. of Rooms	
(702) 380-7777	(702) 383-5334	(800) 99-TOWER	Senior, AAA	1,500	⇨
(702) 547-7777	(702) 432-7730	(888) SUNSET9		457	⇨
(702) 794-0888	(702) 794-3504	(800) 888-8000		290	⇨
(702) 733-7000	(702) 691-2423	(800) 640-9777		400	⇨
(702) 631-1000	(702) 631-8120	(800) 654-8888	AAA	200	⇨
(702) 733-0001	(702) 733-1571	(800) 578-7878	Senior, military, AAA	223	⇨
(702) 894-7111	(702) 894-7446	(800) 944-7444		2,900	⇨
(702) 739-2222	(702) 739-2469	(800) 634-4000		1,874	⇨
(702) 897-1700	(702) 361-6726	(800) 658-5000		313	⇨
(702) 733-5000	(702) 414-4805	(888) 2VENICE		3,000	⇨
(702) 731-2900	(702) 731-3544	(800) 638-6803		777	⇨
(702) 740-0000	(702) 736-7106	(800) 634-3488	Senior, AAA	300	⇨

Hotel	Ck. Out Time	Non-Smoking	Rack Rate	Room Quality	Room Value
Stratosphere	11 a.m.	Floors	$+	79	75
Sunset Station	Noon	Floors	$$+	82	47
Super 8	Noon		$+	52	28
Terrible's	Noon		$+	63	40
Texas Station	Noon	Floors	$$−	70	41
Travelodge Las Vegas Inn	Noon	✓	$+	50	30
Treasure Island	Noon	Floors	$$$+	84	35
Tropicana	Noon	Floors	$$$−	67	28
Vacation Village	Noon	✓	$$−	53	20
The Venetian	11 a.m.	Floors	$$$$+	97	40
Westward Ho	11 a.m.		$$−	50	21
Wild Wild West	Noon	✓	$	49	35

Con- cierge	Convention Facilities	Meeting Rooms	Valet Parking	RV Park	Room Service	Free Breakfast
✓		✓	✓		✓	⇨
✓	✓	✓	✓		✓	⇨
			✓			⇨
					✓	⇨
✓			✓		✓	⇨
		✓	✓		✓	⇨
✓	✓	✓	✓		✓	⇨
✓	✓	✓	✓		✓	⇨
✓		✓			✓	⇨
✓	✓	✓	✓		✓	⇨
					✓	⇨
						⇨

Hotel	Fine Dining/ Type of Food	Coffee Shop	24-hr. Café	Buffet	Deli
Stratosphere	Continental, Steak, Italian, American	✓	✓	✓	✓
Sunset Station	American, Steak/ Seafood, Mexican, Italian	✓	✓	✓	✓
Super 8					
Terrible's	American		✓	✓	
Texas Station	Seafood, Italian, Mexican, Steak, Chinese	✓	✓	✓	✓
Travelodge Las Vegas Inn					
Treasure Island	Seafood/Steak, American, Chinese, Italian	✓	✓	✓	✓
Tropicana	Steak, Chinese, Japanese, Italian	✓	✓	✓	✓
Vacation Village	Mexican/American	✓	✓		
The Venetian	Italian, Gourmet	✓	✓		✓
Westward Ho		✓	✓		
Wild Wild West		✓	✓		

Casino	24-hour Bar	Lounge	Showroom Entertainment	Gift Shop Drugs/News	Hair Salon	
✓	✓	✓	Production show	✓		⇨
			Live entertainment, concerts			⇨
✓	✓					⇨
		✓		✓		⇨
✓	✓	✓	Live entertainment nightly	✓		⇨
				✓		⇨
✓	✓	✓	Production show	✓	✓	⇨
✓	✓	✓	Production show, comedy club, magic	✓	✓	⇨
✓	✓	✓		✓	✓	⇨
✓	✓	✓	Headliners, live music	✓	✓	⇨
				✓		⇨
✓	✓	✓		✓		⇨

Hotel	Pool	Youth Activities	Exercise Rooms	Tennis & Racket Games
Stratosphere	✓Heated	✓		
Sunset Station	✓	✓	✓	
Super 8	✓		✓	
Terrible's	✓			
Texas Station	✓			
Travelodge Las Vegas Inn	✓			
Treasure Island	✓Heated		✓	
Tropicana	✓Heated		✓	
Vacation Village	✓			
The Venetian	✓		✓	✓
Westward Ho	✓			
Wild Wild West	✓			

Golf	Other	Movie Theater	Sauna/Steam Whirlpool	Shopping Arcade	Elec Games Arcade
	Big Shot (thrill ride)			✓	✓
	Daycare available	✓			✓
			✓		
	Daycare available	✓ 12 screens			✓
					✓
	Wedding chapels		✓	✓	✓
Privileges	Wedding chapel	✓	✓	✓	
					✓
Privileges	Fax machines in rooms		✓	✓	
			✓		

Part Two

Entertainment and Nightlife

Las Vegas Shows and Entertainment

Las Vegas calls itself the "Entertainment Capital of the World." This is arguably true, particularly in terms of the sheer number of live entertainment productions staged daily. On any given day in Las Vegas a visitor can select from dozens of presentations, ranging from major production spectaculars to celebrity headliners, from comedy clubs to live music in lounges. The standard of professionalism and value for your entertainment dollar is very high. There is no other place where you can buy so much top-quality entertainment for so little money.

That having been said, here's the bad news: The average price of a ticket to one of the major production shows topped $53 in 2001, a whopping 96% increase since 1992. To balance the picture, however, the standard of quality for shows has likewise soared. And variety, well, there's now literally something for everyone, from traditional Las Vegas feathers and butts to real Broadway musicals. And believe it or not, the value is still there. Maybe not in the grand showrooms and incessantly hyped productions, but in the smaller showrooms and lounges and in the main theaters of off-Strip hotels. There's more of everything now, including both overpriced tickets and bargains. Regarding the former, you'll be numbed and blinded by their billboards all over town. As concerns the latter, you'll have to scout around, but you'll be rewarded with some great shows at dynamite prices. Want to see the Doobie Brothers, Ray Charles, Crystal Gayle, or the Righteous Brothers? They're a mile from the Strip at the Orleans. Meanwhile catch Confederate Railroad or Jose Feliciano at Boulder Station's Railhead Saloon. *Second City*, a comedy act at the Flamingo, is one of the best buys in town at about $28, and there are always discount coupons floating around for productions at the downtown showrooms.

Almost a dozen major shows opened in the first two years of the new century. Although some forged new directions for Las Vegas entertainment, the most influential stem back to 1996 and to another style of entertainer. Impressionist Danny Gans opened the 870-seat Danny Gans Theatre, a converted ballroom at The Mirage (just after Mirage Resorts was acquired by MGM Grand, but before Steve Wynn actually surrendered ownership of the company).

After honing his act at corporate functions and trade shows, Gans, "went public" at the Stratosphere in 1996, later defected to the Rio, and now is a long-term fixture at the Mirage. His technical skills are unmatched; he touches upon more than 60 voices every show. But as his corporate background and Christian faith suggest, the act is inoffensive to the point of being a little bland; polished smooth of any sharp corners and shamelessly sentimental when it comes to recalling show business legends such as George Burns.

Gans is the first "resident headliner" to become a Las Vegas star without previous TV or movie fame since Wayne Newton, who also returned to the Strip in a long-term deal with the Stardust. The Stardust's vintage showroom makes a perfect match for Newton's leisurely paced evening of music and shtick, which hasn't changed much in at least 20 years. Oddly enough, the hotel had never hosted headliners for more than one- or two-night stands to spell its long running *Lido de Paris* and more recent *Enter the Night* revues. Newton still descends from a spaceship at the beginning of each show and lets the "MacArthur Park" rain come down on that cake at the end. The newest innovation for the Stardust perhaps comes from his years spent in Branson, Missouri—Newton gets out into the crowd and seems determined to shake every hand or kiss every cheek in the audience.

Gans' success opened the doors for other impressionists on the Strip. Andre Philippe Gagnon, who performs the Venetian, is a comedic singing impressionist who dwells in the 1980s era of MTV. He's a likeable, animated character who makes sure to have a strong punchline for voices (Mark Knopfler of Dire Straits or Axl Rose of Guns 'n Roses) that older audience members might not recognize. A third impressionist, Bill Acosta, serves up similar fare at the Flamingo.

Gans also led hotel buyers to make way for two other new arrivals, Clint Holmes and Rick Springfield. Harrah's decided to see if lightning could strike twice when it came to establishing another name on the Strip who has talent to spare, but no name recognition on the West Coast. But Clint Holmes had a good track record in Atlantic City and plenty of polished presence onstage. He's been in show business since 1971, when he scored the Top Ten novelty pop hit "Playground in My Mind." But the single didn't lead to a recording career, and he wound up in the showrooms, opening for the likes of Bill Cosby and Don Rickles. Harrah's longterm commitment to Holmes seemed risky at first, when attendance counts were low. But exit polls proved the hotel's intuition when it came to customer satisfaction, and now Holmes is on his way to joining Gans as another "resident headliner" on the Strip.

Veteran rocker Rick Springfield became the fourth lead in MGM Grand's mega-production EFX. He follows Michael Crawford, Tommy Tune, and David Cassidy.

Two shows, *Blue Man Group* at the Luxor and *De la Guarda* at the Rio, have taken aim at the under-35 age group, a generation that has embraced a new wave of nightclubs on the Strip, but hasn't warmed to its formal, ticketed entertainment. *Blue Man Group: Live at Luxor* was an off-Broadway hit for most of the 1990s, which made it as safe a bet as a surrealistic, avant-garde show on the Las Vegas Strip could be. As in New York, three silent pranksters in skullcaps and cobalt blue greasepaint play with their food, make music on PVC pipes, and teach the audience occasional lessons about science and technology. It's all funny and accessible, however, and the show—which features large-scale pieces not seen in other cities—seems to be on its way to a long run.

One of the *Blue Men's* neighbors in the realm of off-Broadway "nonverbal" theater, *De La Guarda* is an Argentinian troupe of aerialists and performance artists who soar above the heads of a standing audience while percussive club music works the crowd into the tribal experience of a rave or rock concert. The Rio built the troupe a custom venue, indicating the hotel's long-term commitment.

Magic and illusion are alive and thriving with two new major shows and a handful of small showroom and afternoon shows opening in 2001. Steve Wyrick opened at the Sahara in a new showroom that provides enough elbow room to perform his large object (as in airplanes) disappearing routines. Meanwhile, Melinda—the First Lady of Magic—returned to her hometown for a run at the Showroom at the Venetian. In late July, she was one of two tenants in a room that operates independently of the hotel, similar to the way gourmet chefs now lease restaurant space within the hotels. Owners of the busy showroom have a vested financial stake in impressionist Gagnon, but serve as landlord to Melinda.

Las Vegas showrooms became a little naughtier in 2001, reversing a four year trend of attrition among topless reviews. When we went to press there were eight such shows going strong, an increase of four over the previous year. Even the PG-13 Harrah's showroom fielded a topless show, the first to play there in more than a decade. Many of the new shows are late night affairs, taking over the main showrooms after hours.

Among new venues to open was the Blue Note Jazz Club (Aladdin), a place that operates like a nightclub but charges the admission of a show-room. Sam's Town launched a 1,100-seat multi-use showroom, scheduling a diverse array of headliners including Little Richard, Peabo Bryson, Bela Fleck, and Travis Tritt. The year 2001 also witnessed the groundbreaking on a new headliner room at Caesars Palace. The new room will replace the much-missed Circus Maximus, one of the prestige Las Vegas stages for a quarter of a century.

In 2000–2001 there were more changes in the Las Vegas showroom scene than in the previous ten years combined. Although old standards like *Jubilee!, Splash,* and the *Folies Bergere* continue to hold their own, and Las Vegas favored son Wayne Newton is home to stay, the definitive trend points in the direction of Broadway, albeit with a Las Vegas twist. And while you can expect to see ticket prices continue to rise, you'll also see more variety in the major showrooms, more limited-engagement concerts, and an increasing number of headliners appearing at intimate lounges around town.

Choices, choices, choices

Most Las Vegas live entertainment offerings can be lumped into one of several broad categories:

Celebrity Headliners	Impersonator Shows
Long-Term Engagements	Comedy Clubs
Production Shows	Lounge Entertainment

Celebrity Headliners   As the name implies, these are concerts or shows featuring big-name entertainers on a limited-engagement basis, usually one to four weeks, but sometimes for a one-night stand. Headliners are usually backed up by a medium-sized orchestra, and the stage sets and special production effects are kept simple. Performers such as Kenny Rogers, Wynonna, David Copperfield, and Tom Jones play Las Vegas regularly. Some even work on a rotation with other performers, returning to the same showroom for several engagements each year. Other stars, such as Barbra Streisand, play Las Vegas only rarely, transforming each rare appearance into a truly special event. While there are exceptions, the superstars are regularly found at the MGM Grand, Mandalay Bay, Aladdin, Las Vegas Hilton, and Bally's; sometimes at the Mirage and the Riviera; and occasionally at the Hard Rock. Big name performers in the city's top showrooms command premium admission prices of $25–90. Headliners of slightly lesser stature play at various other showrooms. Many of the newer hotels, including the Venetian, Mandalay Bay, Aladdin, Sam's Town, Suncoast, Sunset Station,

Texas Station, Orleans, Hard Rock, and MGM Grand, have concert and special event venues where artists ranging from John Lee Hooker to Sheryl Crow to the Rolling Stones perform, with World Championship Wrestling and Champions on Ice thrown in for balance.

Long-Term Engagements   These are shows by the famous and once-famous who have come to Las Vegas to stay. Wayne Newton, for example, has signed an exclusive 10-year contract for $25 million per year with the Stardust—he'll perform for 40 weeks and have 12 weeks off each year. Similarly, Clint Holmes has found a long-term home at Harrah's, and comic Rita Rudner has been trying to make a go of it at New York–New York.

Production Shows   These are continuously running, Broadway-style theatrical and musical productions. Cast sizes run from a dozen performers to well over a hundred, with costumes, sets, and special effects spanning a comparable range. Costing hundreds of thousands, if not millions, to produce, the shows feature chorus lines, elaborate choreography, and great spectacle. Usually playing twice a night, six or seven days a week, production shows often run for years.

Production shows generally have a central theme to which a more or less standard mix of choreography and variety acts (also called specialty acts) are added. Favorite central themes are magic/illusion—six such shows are currently running—and a "best of Broadway" theme, which figures prominently in four current shows.

In the most common format, the show will open with an elaborate production number featuring dancers and, often, topless showgirls. As the presentation continues, variety acts alternate with either magic or musical numbers, depending on the theme. Variety acts frequently integrated into production shows include stand-up comics, jugglers, acrobats, balancing artists, ventriloquists, martial arts specialists, bola-swinging gauchos, and even archers. Even if magic is not the central theme of the show, a magician or illusionist is usually included among the variety acts. As a rule, the show closes with a spectacular finale showcasing the entire cast in some unimaginably colossal set, augmented by an impressive array of costuming, lighting, and special effects. Special effects figure prominently in Las Vegas production shows, and even more prominently in advertisements for Las Vegas production shows. Special effects are defined as "better than regular effects." Nobody knows what regular effects are.

Las Vegas puts its own distinctive imprint on all this entertainment, imparting a great deal of homogeneity and redundancy to the mix of productions. The quality of Las Vegas entertainment is quite high, even excellent, but most production shows seem to operate according to a formula that fosters a numbing sameness. Particularly pronounced in the magic/illusion shows and the Broadway-style musical productions, this sameness discourages sampling more than one show from each genre. While it is not totally accurate to say that "if you've seen one Las Vegas production or magic show, you've seen them all," the statement comes closer to the truth than one would hope.

In the magic/illusion shows, the decade-long rage is to put unlikely creatures or objects into boxes and make them disappear. Some featured magicians repeat this sort of tiresome illusion more than a dozen times in a single performance, with nothing really changing except the size of the box and the object placed into it. Into these boxes go doves, ducks, turkeys, parrots, dwarfs, showgirls, lions, tigers, sheep dogs, jaguars, panthers, motorcycles (with riders), TV cameras (with cameramen), and even elephants. Sometimes the illusionist himself gets into a box and disappears, reappearing moments later in the audience. Generally the elephants and other animals don't reappear until the next performance. These box illusions are amazing the first time or two, but become less compelling after that. After they had seen all of the illusion shows in Las Vegas, our reviewers commented that they had witnessed the disappearance in a box of everything except Jerry Falwell. Food for thought.

The Broadway-style musical productions likewise lack differentiation, tending to merge after more than one sample into a great blur of bouncing bare breasts and fanciful, feathery costumes. It should be reiterated, however, that like the magic productions, most of the musicals are well done and extremely worthwhile. But like the magic productions, the musicals offer only slight variations of the same theme.

While they share a common format, production shows, regardless of theme, can be differentiated by the size of the cast and by the elaborateness of the production. Other discriminating factors include the creativity of the choreography, the attractiveness of the performers, the pace and continuity of the presentation, and its ability to build to a crescendo. Strength in these last-mentioned areas sometimes allows a relatively simple, lower-budget show such as *The Rat Pack is Back* (Sahara) to provide a more satisfying evening of entertainment than a lavish, long-running spectacular like *Splash* (Riviera).

Breaking new ground in the production show category are the magnificent, aquatic *Cirque du Soleil* production *"O"* at the Bellagio, Michael Flatley's *Lord of the Dance* stompfest at New York–New York, impressionist Danny Gans at the Mirage, percussionist *Blue Man Group* at the Luxor, and the gravity defying *De la Guarda*.

Impersonator Shows   These are usually long-running production shows, complete with dancers, that feature the impersonation of celebrities both living (Joan Rivers, Cher, Neil Diamond, Tina Turner, Madonna) and deceased (Marilyn Monroe, Elvis, Liberace, the Blues Brothers). In shows such as the Imperial Palace's *Legends in Concert, The Rat Pack Is Back* at the Sahara, and the Stratosphere's *American Superstars,* the emphasis is on the detail and exactness of the impersonation. In general, men impersonate male stars and women impersonate female stars (as you might expect). *La Cage* at the Riviera, however, features males impersonating female celebrities.

Comedy Clubs Stand-up comedy has long been a tradition in Las Vegas entertainment. With the success of comedy clubs around the country and the comedy club format on network and cable television, stand-up comedy in Las Vegas was elevated from lounges and production shows to its own specialized venue. Las Vegas comedy clubs are small- to medium-sized showrooms featuring anywhere from two to five comedians per show. As a rule, the shows change completely each week, with a new group of comics rotating in. Each showroom has its own source of talent, so there is no swapping of comics from club to club. Comedy clubs are one of the few Las Vegas entertainments that draw equally from both the tourist and local populations. While most production shows and many celebrity headliner shows are packaged for the over-40 market, comedy clubs represent a concession to youth. Most of the comics are young, and the humor is often raw and scatological, and almost always irreverent.

Lounge Entertainment Many casinos offer exceptional entertainment at all hours of the day and night in their lounges. For the most part, the lounges feature musical groups. On a given day almost any type of music, from oldies rock to country to jazz to folk, can be found in Las Vegas lounges. Unlike the production and headliner showrooms and comedy clubs, no reservations are required to take advantage of most lounge entertainment. If you like what you hear, just walk in. Sometimes there is a two-drink minimum for sitting in the lounge during a show, but just as often there are no restrictions at all. You may or may not be familiar with the lounge entertainers by name, but you can trust that they will be highly talented and very enjoyable. To find the type of music you prefer, consult one of the local visitor guides available free from the front desk or concierge at your hotel.

Lounge entertainment is a great barometer of a particular casino's marketing program; bands are specifically chosen to attract a certain type of customer. In general, if you find a casino with lounge entertainment that suits your tastes, you will probably be comfortable lodging, dining, and gambling there also.

As an alternative to high ticket prices in Las Vegas showrooms (a dozen shows now cost upwards of $70), several casinos have turned their nightclubs and lounges into alternative show venues with ticket prices in the $20–35 range. In 2000, Ra at the Luxor, The Nightclub at the Las Vegas Hilton, and Starlight Lounge at the Desert Inn all operated several nights each week as mini-showrooms. We've seen a number of marginal or unsuccessful clubs turned into showrooms over the years, but this is the first time we've observed highly successful nightspots converted. In the main, we don't care for this trend. True, it offers some low price shows, but at the cost of sacrificing some of the city's best lounges and nightclubs.

They Come and They Go

Las Vegas shows come and go all the time. Sometimes a particular production will close in one Las Vegas showroom and open weeks later in another. Some shows actually pack up and take their presentations to other cities, usually Reno/Lake Tahoe or Atlantic City. Other shows, of course, close permanently. During the past couple of years, we have seen the following productions disappear from the Las Vegas scene:

MADhattan (New York–New York)

Country Tonite (Aladdin)

Starlight Express (Las Vegas Hilton)

Country Fever (Golden Nugget)

Copacabana (Rio)

Melinda (Lady Luck)

Luck Is a Lady (Lady Luck)

Nudes on Ice (Plaza)

Lido de Paris (Stardust)

Showstopper (Desert Inn)

Thriller (Aladdin)

Tropical Heat (Rio)

Abracadabra (Aladdin)

Alakazaam (Aladdin)

Playboy's Girls of Rock & Roll (Maxim)

Comedy Cabaret (Maxim)

Fire & Ice (Hacienda)

Keep Smilin' America (Holiday)

Rodney's Place (El Rancho)

Cabaret Circus (Lady Luck)

Wild Things (Dunes)

Bare Essence (Sands)

Swing, Swing, Swing (Sands)

Hanky Panky (San Remo)

Brazilia (Rio)

Marty Allen & Steve Rossi (Vegas World)

Forbidden Vegas (Plaza)

Hot Stuff (Sands)

Winds of the Gods (Luxor)

City Lites (Flamingo)

Nashville USA (Boomtown)

Outrageous (San Remo)

Hell on Heels (Maxim)

Chicago (Mandalay Bay)

Enter the Night (Stardust)

Imagine (Luxor)

Great Radio Music Hall

Spectacular (Flamingo)

Spellbound (Harrah's)

Notre Dame de Paris (Paris)

At the Copa with David Cassidy (Rio)

The bottom line: it's hard to keep up with all this coming and going. Do not be surprised if some of the shows reviewed in this guide have bitten the dust before you arrive. Also do not be surprised if the enduring shows have changed.

Learn Who Is Playing before Leaving Home

The Las Vegas Convention and Visitors Authority publishes an entertainment calendar for all showrooms and many lounges. The brochure *Showguide,* organized alphabetically according to host hotel, tells who is playing, provides appearance dates, and lists information and reservation numbers.

The *Showguide* can be obtained without charge by writing or calling:

Las Vegas Convention and Visitors Authority
Visitor Information Center
3150 Paradise Road
Las Vegas, NV 89109-9096   (702) 892-7576 or (702) 892-0711

On the Internet, log onto ilovevegas.com and then click on "Limited Engagement." Note that only ten headliners at a time come up, so after checking the first ten click on "11–20" at the bottom of the screen to bring up the next batch.

Show Prices and Taxes

Admission prices for Las Vegas shows range from around $15 all the way up to $100 or more per person. Usually show prices are quoted exclusive of entertainment and sales taxes. Also not included are server gratuities.

As recently as 1990, there was no such thing as a reserved seat at a Las Vegas show. If you wanted to see a show, you would make a reservation (usually by phone) and then arrive well in advance to be assigned a seat by the showroom maître d'. Slipping the maître d' a nice tip ensured a better seat. Typically, the price of the show included two drinks, and you would pay at your table after you were served. While this arrangement is still practiced in a few showrooms, the prevailing trend is toward reserved seating. With reserved seating, you purchase your tickets at the casino box office (or by phone in advance with your credit card). As at a concert or a Broadway play, your seats are designated and preassigned at the time of purchase, and your section, aisle, and seat number will be printed on your ticket. When you arrive at the showroom, an usher will guide you to your assigned seat. Reserved seating, also known as "hard" or "box office" seating, sometimes includes drinks and sometimes does not.

A common package (once *the* most common package) is the cocktail show, where your admission usually includes the show and one or two drinks. If the quoted admission price for the cocktail show is $40 per person, your actual cost will be approximately as follows:

Cocktail show admission	$40.00
Entertainment and sales tax (17%)	$6.80
Total (before gratuities)	$46.80

If there are two performances per night, the early show is often (but not always) more expensive than the late show. In addition, some shows add a "surcharge" on Saturdays and holidays. If you tip your server a couple of bucks and slip the maître d' or captain some currency for a good seat (in a showroom without reserved seating), you can easily end up paying $27 or more for a $20 list-price show and $63 or more for a $50 list-price show.

Showrooms, like other Las Vegas hotel and casino operations, sometimes offer special deals. Sometimes free or discounted shows are offered with lodging packages. Likewise, coupons from complimentary local tourist magazines or casino funbooks (see page 12) provide discounts or "two for one" options. Since these specials come and go, your best bet is to inquire about currently operating deals and discounts when you call for show reservations. If you plan to lodge at a hotel-casino where there is a show you want to see, ask about room/show combination specials when you make your room reservations. When you arrive in Las Vegas, pick up copies of the many visitor magazines distributed in rental car agencies and at hotels. Scour the show ads for discount coupons.

HOW TO MAKE RESERVATIONS FOR LAS VEGAS SHOWS

Almost all showrooms take phone reservations. The process is simple and straightforward. Either call, using the reservation numbers listed in this book, or have your hotel concierge call. Most shows will accept reservations at least one day, and often several days or even weeks, in advance.

Some shows, when you call for reservations, will take only your name and the number of people in your party. Under this arrangement, you will either pay at the box office on the day of the show or, alternatively, pay in the showroom after you are seated.

An increasing number of shows will allow you to prepurchase your admission on the phone using a credit card. If you prepay, you will have to pick up your tickets at the box office before the show.

Hotel Lobby Ticket Sales

For some reason many people do not trust the phone reservation system, though it works perfectly well. These folks often purchase show tickets at booths operated by independent tour brokers in the hotel lobbies, paying substantial booking and gratuity surcharges for the privilege of having a ticket. Upon arriving at the showroom they discover that the ticket does not guarantee a reserved seat. In fact, they learn that it offers nothing except a mechanism for prepayment (sometimes at an inflated price). Further, at several showrooms, the ticket purchased earlier must be exchanged for one of the showroom's own tickets, thus necessitating another wait in line. Finally, not all shows are available through the brokers.

In some casinos there are both independent operators selling tickets to shows all over town and (in another location in the same casino) a reservations and ticket booth for the shows that are playing at that specific casino. The official reservations/ticket booth will usually only sell tickets or make reservations for the casino's own shows and, unlike the independent operator, will not tack on any extra charges.

When you pay your admission before entering the showroom, be sure to ask whether drinks and gratuities are included.

Trying to See a Show without a Reservation or Ticket

On Sunday through Thursday, you have a fair shot at getting into most Las Vegas shows just by asking the maitre d' to seat you or by purchasing a ticket at the box office if reserved seats are sold.

On most Fridays and Saturdays, however, it is a different story. If you decide on the spur of the moment that you would like to see the show at the casino where you have been dining or gambling, do not wait in line at the entrance to the showroom to make your inquiry. Instead, go directly to the box office, maître d', or to one of the other show personnel at the entrance and ask if they have room for your party. In some instances you may be asked to join the end of the guest line or stand by while they check for no-shows or cancellations. An amazing percentage of the time you will be admitted. Superstar celebrity headliner shows and performances of *Siegfried & Roy, Cirque du Soleil's Mystere* and *"O," Lord of the Dance,*

Blue Man Group, Danny Gans, Legends in Concert, EFX!, and *Tournament of Kings* are generally the most difficult shows to see on an impromptu basis.

DINNER SHOWS

Some dinner shows represent good deals, others less so. Be aware, however, that with all dinner shows, your drinks (if you have any) will be extra, and invariably expensive. Food quality at dinner shows varies. In general it can be characterized as acceptable, but certainly not exceptional. What you are buying is limited-menu banquet service for 300–500 people. Whenever a hotel kitchen tries to feed that many people at once, it is at some cost in terms of the quality of the meal and the service.

Tournament of Kings at the Excalibur does not provide the cocktail option. At *Tournament of Kings* all shows automatically include dinner of Cornish hen with soup, potatoes, vegetable, dessert, and choice of nonalcoholic beverage for about $45 per person, taxes and gratuities included. *Tournament of Kings* is described in detail below.

Several casions offer show-and-dinner combos where you get dinner and a show for a special price, but dinner is served in one of the casinos' restaurants instead of in the showrooms. The restaurants provide only coffee-shop ambience, but the food is palatable and a good deal for the money. At each casino you can eat either before or after the early show.

Early vs. Late Shows

If you attend a late show you will have time for a leisurely dinner prior to the performance. For those who prefer to eat late, the early show followed by dinner works best. Both shows are identical except that for some productions the early show is covered and the late show is topless. On weekdays, late shows are usually more lightly attended. On weekends, particularly at the most popular shows, the opposite is often the case.

PRACTICAL MATTERS
What to Wear to the Show

While it is by no means required, guests tend to dress up a bit when they go to a show. For a performance in the main showrooms at Bally's, Bellagio, Caesars Palace, the Las Vegas or Flamingo Hiltons, Mandalay Bay, or the Mirage, gentlemen will feel more comfortable in sport coats, with or without neckties. At the Las Vegas Hilton, Venetian, and Bally's, where there is a lot of convention traffic, men would not be overdressed in suits. Women generally wear suits, dresses, skirt and blouse/sweater combinations, and even semiformal attire.

Showrooms at the Luxor, the Stratosphere, Monte Carlo, New York–New York, Treasure Island, the MGM Grand, Harrah's, the Rio, Paris Las Vegas, Tropicana, Aladdin, the Riviera, the Sahara, and the Stardust are a bit less dressy (sport coats are fine, but slacks and sweaters or sport shirts are equally acceptable for men), while showrooms at the Excalibur, the Imperial Palace, the Orleans, Sam's Town, Suncoast, Sunset Station, Texas Station, the House of Blues at Mandalay Bay, the Golden Nugget, and the Hard Rock are the least formal of all (come as you are). All of the comedy clubs are informal, though you would not feel out of place in a sport coat or, for women, a dress.

Getting to and from the Show

When you make your reservations, always ask what time you need to arrive for seating, and whether you should proceed directly to the showroom or stop first at the box office. You are normally asked to arrive one hour before the curtain rises. If you are driving to another hotel for a show and do not wish to avail yourself of valet parking, be forewarned that many casinos' self-parking lots are quite distant from the showroom. Give yourself an extra 15 minutes to park, walk to the casino, and find the showroom. If you decide to use valet parking, be advised that the valet service may be swamped immediately following the show.

A show with a large seating capacity in one of the major casinos can make for some no-win situations when it comes to parking. At all of the mega-hotels, self-parking is either way off in the boonies or in a dizzying multistory garage, so your inclinations may be to use valet parking. After the show, however, 1,000–1,650 patrons head for home, inundating the valets, particularly after a late show. If you encounter this situation, your best bet is to use self-parking and give yourself some extra time, or use valet parking and plan to stick around the casino for a while after the show.

Invited Guests and Line Passes

Having arrived at the casino and found the showroom, you will normally join other show-goers waiting to be seated. If the showroom assigns reserved seats, the process is simple: just show your tickets to an usher and you will be directed to your seats. At showrooms without reserved seating, you will normally encounter two lines. One line, usually quite long, is where you will queue up unless you are an "Invited Guest." There is a separate line for these privileged folks that allows them to be seated without waiting in line or coming an hour early. Most invited guests are gamblers who are staying at that casino. Some have been provided with "comps" (complimentary admission) to the show. These are usually regular casino customers or high rollers. If you are giving the casino a lot of action, do not be shy about requesting a comp to the show.

Gamblers or casino hotel guests of more modest means are frequently given line passes. These guests pay the same price as anyone else for the show but are admitted without waiting via the Invited Guest line. To obtain a line pass, approach a floorman or pit boss (casino supervisory personnel are usually distinguished from dealers by their suits and ties) and explain that you have been doing a fair amount of gambling in their casino. Tell him or her that you have reservations for that evening's show and ask if you can have a line pass. Particularly if you ask on Sunday through Thursday, your chances of being accommodated are good.

If you are an invited guest under any circumstances, always arrive to be seated at least 30 minutes early.

Reservations, Tickets, and Maître d' Seating

If, like most guests, you do not have a line pass, you will have to go through the process of entering the showroom and being seated. A dwindling number of showrooms practice what is known as maître d' seating. This means that, except in the case of certain invited guests, no seats are reserved. If you called previously and made a reservation, that will have been duly noted and the showroom will have your party listed on the reservations roster, but you will not actually be assigned a seat until you appear before the maître d'. At some showrooms with maître d' seating, you are asked to pay your waiter for everything (show, taxes, drinks, etc.) once you have been seated and served.

At the comedy clubs and an increasing number of major showrooms you will be directed to a booth variously labeled "Tickets," "Reservations," "Box Office," or "Guest Services." The attendant will verify your reservation and ask you to go ahead and pay. Once paid, you will receive a ticket to show the maître d' on entering the showroom. This arrangement eliminates any requirement for paying the tab at your table (unless drinks are not included), thus simplifying service once you are seated. The ticket does not reserve you any specific seat; you still need to see the maître d' about that. Also, the ticket does not include gratuities for your server in the showroom unless specifically stated.

As discussed earlier, a growing number of showrooms have discarded maître d' seating in favor of "box office" or "hard" seating. At the Mirage, Bellagio, Orleans, the MGM Grand, the Luxor, Treasure Island, Monte Carlo, the Excalibur, the Stardust, Bally's, the Las Vegas Hilton, Mandalay Bay, Aladdin, New York–New York, Venetian, Paris, and Caesars Palace, specific reserved-seat assignments are designated on each ticket sold, as at a football game or on Broadway.

Most showrooms that issue hard (reserved-seat) tickets will allow you to charge your tickets over the phone using your credit card. If you charge your tickets over the phone, however, the quality of your seat assignments is at the mercy of the box office. On the other hand, if you take the trouble to buy your tickets in person at the hotel box office, you can review the seating chart and pick your seats from all seats available.

Where to Sit

When it comes to show seating, there are two primary considerations: visibility and comfort. The best accommodations in most showrooms are the plush, roomy booths, which provide an unencumbered view of the show. The vast majority of seats in many showrooms, however, and all in some, will be at banquet tables—a euphemism for very long, narrow tables where a dozen or more guests are squeezed together so tightly they can hardly move. When the show starts, guests seated at the banquet tables must turn their chairs around in order to see. This requires no small degree of timing and cooperation, since every person on the same side of the table must move in unison.

Showrooms generally will have banquet table seating right in front of the stage. Next, on a tier that rises a step or two, will be a row of plush booths. These booths are often reserved for the casino's best customers (and sometimes for big tippers). Many maître d's would rather see these booths go unoccupied than have high rollers come to the door at the last minute and not be able to give them good seats. Behind the booths but on the same level will be more banquet tables. Moving away from the stage and up additional levels, the configuration of booths and banquet tables is repeated on each tier.

In a trend that we greatly appreciate, many of the showrooms built during the last six years offer upholstered stadium seats, i.e., nice padded seats with armrests like you find in most upscale cinemas.

For a big production show on a wide stage like *Jubilee!*, *Siegfried & Roy*, *Cirque du Soleil*, the *Folies Bergere*, or *EFX!*, you want to sit in the middle and back a little. Being too close makes it difficult to see everything without wagging your head back and forth as if you were at a tennis match. Likewise, at a concert by a band or musical celebrity headliner (Tom Jones, Al Jarreau, B.B. King, etc.), partway back and in the center is best. This positioning provides good visibility and removes you from the direct line of fire of amplifiers and lights. This advice, of course, does not apply to avid fans who want to fling their underwear or room keys at the star.

For smaller production shows on medium-sized stages (*Lance Burton*, *Legends in Concert*, etc.), right up front is great. This is also true for headliners like Bill Cosby, Jerry Seinfeld, and David Copperfield. For female impersonators (*La Cage*), the illusion is more effective if you are back a little bit.

At comedy clubs and smaller shows, there are really no bad seats, though the *Comedy Stop* at the Tropicana has some columns in the showroom you want to avoid. Finally, be aware that comedians often single out unwary guests sitting down front for harassment, or worse, incorporate them into the act.

Getting a Good Seat at Showrooms with Maître d' Seating

1. Arrive early   No maître d' can assign you a seat that's already taken. This is particularly important for Friday and Saturday shows. We have seen comped invited guests (the casino's better customers) get lousy seats because they waited until the last minute to show up.

2. Try to go on an off night, i.e., Sunday through Thursday   Your chances of getting a good seat are always better on weeknights when there is less demand. If a citywide convention is in town, weekdays may also be crowded.

3. Try to know where (as precisely as possible) you would like to sit   In showrooms with maître d' seating, it is always to your advantage to specifically state your seating preferences.

4. Understand your tipping alternatives   Basically, you have three options:

- Don't tip

- Tip the maître d'

- Tip the captain (instead of the maître d')

Don't tip   Politely request a good seat instead of tipping. This option actually works better than you would imagine in all but a few showrooms, particularly Sunday–Thursday. If the showroom is not sold out and you arrive early, simply request a seat in a certain area. Tell the maître d', "We would like something down front in the center." Then allow the captain (the showroom staff person who actually takes you to your seat) to show you the seats the maître d' has assigned. If the assigned seat is not to your liking, ask to be seated somewhere else of your choosing. The captain almost always has the authority to make the seat assignment change without consulting the maître d'.

On slower nights, the maître d' will often "dress the showroom." This means that the maître d', not expecting a full house, will distribute patrons pretty equally throughout the showroom, especially nearer the stage. This procedure, which makes the audience look larger than it really is, is done for the morale of the performers and for various practical reasons, such as ensuring a near-equal number of guests at each server station. On these nights, you have a pretty good shot at getting the seats you want simply by asking.

Tip the maître d'   When you tip the maître d' it is helpful to know who you are dealing with. First, the maître d' is the man or woman in charge of the showroom. The showrooms are their domain, and they rule as surely as battalion commanders. Maître d's in the better showrooms are powerful and wealthy people, with some maître d's taking in as much as $1,650 a night. Even though these tips are pooled and shared in some proportion with the captains, it's still a lot of money.

When you tip a maître d', especially in the better showrooms, you can assume it will take a fairly hefty tip to impress him, especially on a busy night. The bottom line, however, is that you are not out to impress anyone; you just want a good seat. Somebody has to sit in the good seats, and those who do not tip, or tip small, have to be seated regardless. So, if you arrive early and tip $15–20 (for a couple) in the major showrooms, and $5–10 in the smaller rooms, you should get decent seats. If it is a weekend or you know the show is extremely popular or sold out, bump the tip up a little. If you arrive late on a busy night, ask the maître d' if there are any good seats left before you proffer the tip.

Have your tip in hand when you reach the maître d'. Don't fool around with your wallet or purse as if you are buying hot dogs and beer at the ball park. Fold the money and hold it in the palm of your hand, arranged so that the maître d' can see exactly how big the tip is without unfolding and counting the bills. State your preference for seating at the same time you inconspicuously place the bills in the palm of his hand. If you think all this protocol is pretty ridiculous, I agree. But style counts, and observing the local customs may help get you a better seat.

A variation is to tip with some appropriate denomination of the casino's own chips. Chips are as good as currency to the maître d' and implicitly suggest that you have been gambling with that denomination of chips in his casino. This single gesture, which costs you nothing more than your cash tip, makes you an insider and a more valued customer in the eyes of the maître d'.

Many maître d's are warm and friendly and treat you in a way that shows they appreciate your business. These maître d's are approachable and reasonable and will go out of their way to make you comfortable. There are also a number of maître d's and captains, unfortunately, who are extremely cold, formal, and arrogant. Mostly older men dressed in tuxedos, they usually have gray hair and a military bearing and can seem rather imposing or hostile. Do not be awed or intimidated. Be forthright and, if necessary, assertive; you will usually be accommodated.

Tip the captain   Using this strategy, tell the maître d' where you would like to sit but do not offer a tip. Then follow the captain to your assigned seats. If your seats are good, you have not spent an extra nickel. If the assigned seats are less than satisfactory, slip the captain a tip and ask if there might be something better. If you see seats you would like to have that are unoccupied, point them out to the captain. Remember, however, that the first row of booths is usually held in reserve.

Before the Show Begins

For years, the admission price to cocktail shows has included two drinks. For several years, however, this policy has been subject to experimentation, resulting in a confusing and constantly changing variety of drink inclusions and exclusions. While many showrooms continue to offer two drinks with admission, others have gone to either one drink or no drinks included.

The inclusion of drinks is not what makes Las Vegas shows a good entertainment value, but the absence of any standard practice in this regard certainly creates enough ill will and confusion to bias the customer's perception of value. From a consumer perspective, a package that includes drinks is straightforward, understandable, and a lot easier to administer in the showroom.

Some of the variations you will encounter are as follows: There will be a cash bar and no table service; if you want a drink before the show, you walk to the bar and buy it. At some showrooms, drinks are included but there is no table service. You take a receipt stub to the bar and exchange it for drinks.

In most other showrooms there is table service where you can obtain drinks from a server. If drinks are included, some slip of paper, a receipt stub, or other type of documentation will be deposited at your place by the captain when you are seated. This scrap of paper will alert your server that you have some drinks coming. When the server takes your order or, alternatively, when the drinks are delivered, he or she will remove the paper. If drinks are not included, there will usually be a small table sign or drink menu with prices listed.

In showrooms where there is table service, the servers run around like crazy trying to get everybody served before the show. Since all of the people at a given table are not necessarily seated at the same time, the server responsible for that table may make five or more passes before everyone is taken care of. If your party is one of the last to be seated at a table, stay cool. You *will* be noticed and you *will* be served.

Servers in showrooms are generally well organized and have their own way of getting things done. You can depend on your waiter or waitress to advise you when it is time to settle your tab. Until then, just relax. Do not try to offer the server a gratuity until the final bill is brought. Normally your server will collect for any drinks not included (and for your show admission in some showrooms with maître d' seating) just before the performance begins. On busy nights in large showrooms, the tab might not be presented until after the curtain has gone up. Most showrooms accept major credit cards and traveler's checks in addition to cash.

If you have prepaid for admission and drinks, your gratuity may have been included in your prepayment. If drinks and admission are prepaid, but not the gratuity, you should tip the server when your drinks are delivered (a dollar or two per person served is about right). If you are not sure whether drinks, gratuities, or anything else is included, ask.

Bladder Matters   Be forewarned that in most showrooms there is no rest room, and that the nearest rest room is invariably a long way off, reachable only via a convoluted trail through the casino. Since the majority of show-goers arrive early and consume drinks, it is not uncommon to start feeling a little pressure on the bladder minutes before show time. If you assume that you can slip out to the rest room and come right back, think again. If you are at the Las Vegas Hilton, Caesars, or the Tropicana, give yourself more than ten minutes for the round trip, and prepare for a quest. If you get to the can and back without getting lost, consider yourself lucky.

At most other showrooms, rest rooms are somewhat closer but certainly not convenient. The Riviera, the Imperial Palace, Luxor, Harrah's, the MGM Grand, Stratosphere, Venetian, and the Mirage, however, seem to have considered that show guests may not wish to combine emptying their bladders with a five-mile hike. Showrooms in these casinos are situated in close and much-appreciated proximity to the rest rooms.

Selecting a Show

Selecting a Las Vegas show is a matter of timing, budget, taste, and schedule. Celebrity headliners are booked long in advance but may play only for a couple of days or weeks. If seeing Tom Jones, Bob Dylan, or Jerry Seinfeld in concert is a big priority for your Las Vegas trip, you will have to schedule your visit to coincide with their appearances. If the timing of your visit is not flexible, as in the case of conventioneers, you will be relegated to picking from those stars playing when you are in town. To find out which shows and headliners are playing before you leave home, call the Las Vegas Convention and Visitors Authority at (702) 892-7576 and ask them to mail you a Las Vegas *Showguide*. On the Internet, log on to ilovevegas.com and then click on "Limited Engagement."

Older visitors are often more affluent than younger visitors. It is no accident that most celebrity headliners are chosen, and most production shows created, to appeal to the 40-and-over crowd. If we say a Las Vegas production show is designed for a mature audience, we mean that the theme, music, variety acts, and humor appeal primarily to older guests. Most Las Vegas production shows target patrons 40–50 years old and up, while a few appeal to audiences 55 years of age and older.

As the post–World War II baby boomers have moved into middle age and comparative affluence, they have become a primary market for Las Vegas. Stars from the "golden days" of rock and roll, as well as folk singers from the 1960s, are turning up in the main showrooms of the Hard Rock and Bally's with great regularity. On one occasion, Paul Revere and the Raiders, the Four Seasons, the Mamas and the Papas, the Temptations, the Four Tops, B. J. Thomas, and Arlo Guthrie were playing in different showrooms on the same night.

The two most hip, avant-garde shows in town are *Blue Man Group* (Luxor) and *De la Guarda* (Rio). Both target younger audiences, offering shows that are wild, loud, and conceptually quite different from anything else in town.

If you are younger than age 35 you will also enjoy the Las Vegas production shows, though for you their cultural orientation (and usually their music) will seem a generation or two removed. Several production shows, however, have broken the mold, in the process achieving a more youthful presentation while maintaining the loyalty of older patrons. *Splash* (Riviera) is a youthful, high-energy show—intensity, action, and volume personified. *Cirque du Soleil's Mystere* (Treasure Island) is an uproarious yet poignant odyssey in the European tradition, brimming over with unforgettable characters. Ditto for *Cirque's "O"* at the Bellagio. *Lance Burton* (Monte Carlo) is a smaller production but is extremely creative and work well for all ages. *Lord of the Dance* (New York–New York) is also high energy. And, again, the comedy clubs have a more youthful orientation.

LAS VEGAS SHOWS FOR THE UNDER-21 CROWD

An ever-increasing number of showrooms offer productions appropriate for younger viewers. Circus Circus provides complimentary, high-quality circus about once every half-hour, and *Tournament of Kings* at the Excalibur is a family dinner show featuring jousting and other benign medieval entertainments. Other family candidates include *Legends in Concert,* a celebrity impersonation show at the Imperial Palace; the magic-illusion shows *Siegfried & Roy* at the Mirage, and *Lance Burton* at the Monte Carlo; *Cirque du Soleil's Mystere* at Treasure Island and *"O"* at Bellagio; *Lord of the Dance* at New York–New York; and *EFX!* at the MGM Grand.

Many of the celebrity headliner shows are fine for children, and a few of the production shows offer a covered early show to accommodate families. Of the topless production shows, some operate on the basis of parental discretion while others do not admit anyone under age 21. Comedy clubs and comedy theater usually will admit teenage children accompanied by an adult. All continuously running shows are profiled later in this section. The profile will tell you whether the show is topless or particularly racy. If you have a question about a given showroom's policy for those under age 21, call the showroom's reservation and information number listed in the profile.

The Best Shows in Town: Celebrity Headliners

Choosing which celebrity headliner to see is a matter of personal taste, though stars like Wayne Newton and Engelbert Humperdink seem to have the ability to rev up any audience. We talked to people who, under duress, were essentially dragged along by a friend or family member to see Wayne Newton. Many of these folks walked into the showroom prepared to hate Wayne Newton. Yet despite their negative attitude, Newton delighted and amazed them.

My point is not to hype Wayne Newton but to suggest that the talent, presence, drive, and showmanship of many Las Vegas headliners often exceed all expectations, and that adhering to the limitations of your preferences may prevent you from seeing many truly extraordinary performers. Las Vegas is about gambling, after all. Do not be reluctant to take a chance on a headliner who is not readily familiar to you.

Most of the major headliners play at a relatively small number of showrooms. Profiles of the major celebrity showrooms and their regular headliners follow. The list is not intended to be all-inclusive but rather to give you an idea of where to call if you are interested in a certain headliner. Remember to check the "dark" entry to see when the showroom is closed.

Hard Rock Hotel—The Joint

Reservations and Information: (702) 693-5066 or (702) 226-4650

Frequent Headliners: Top current and oldies rock, pop, blues, folk, and world music stars

Usual Show Times: 8 p.m.

Approximate Admission Price: $15–180

Drinks Included: None

Showroom Size: 1,800 persons

Description and Comments   Have you ever been to a major rock concert in a facility so large that you needed binoculars to see the band? And did you wish that just once you could enjoy that band in a smaller, more intimate setting? Hard Rock Hotel's The Joint is that setting, a medium-sized two-level venue for rock and roll concerts, hosting the likes of Bob Dylan, the Black Crowes, Melissa Etheridge, the Eagles, and Seal. True, seeing Bob Dylan in a 1,400-person showroom is not as cozy as having him in your living room, but it sure beats Yankee Stadium. Because most performers playing The Joint are booked for short, limited engagements, each show is a special event.

On the floor, the tightly packed audience sits on folding chairs and barstools around small tables; there are 1,000 of these reserved seats. The stage is high and the floor is on an incline, so visibility is good. Acoustics are excellent, especially in the middle of the floor and in front of the balcony.

Consumer Tips   When the reserved seats are sold out (or if someone *wants* to stand), 400 or so "standing-room" tickets are sold. These entitle patrons to a spot toward the back of the floor (by the bar), the back of the balcony, or in "the pit." Visibility from a standing-room position on the balcony is limited (except from the first few rows, which are reserved). And stageside at The Joint, be prepared for ear-splitting, head-pounding, bone-quaking acoustics, not to mention being hemmed in by the crowd. If you don't want to be put in balcony Siberia where you can hear well enough but see nothing, or pinned against the stage for the whole show by a crush of sweaty rowdies, don't buy standing-room tickets. Book early for reserved seating—or shrug and say, "Oh well."

The Hard Rock Hotel box office sells reserved seats to shows at The Joint. You can purchase tickets via phone using your credit card or in person at the box office. Shows at The Joint are hot tickets in Las Vegas and sell out quickly, so buy your tickets as far in advance as possible.

Las Vegas Hilton—Hilton Theater

Reservations and Information: (702) 732-5111 or (800) 222-5361

Frequent Headliners: Trisha Yearwood, Johnny Mathis, Engelbert
   Humperdink, Dwight Yoakam, Wynonna, Tim Conway

Usual Show Times: Varies   *Dark:* Varies

Approximate Admission Price: Varies

Drinks Included: None

Showroom Size: 1,650 seats

Description and Comments   The Hilton Theater has been home to some of the biggest names to play Las Vegas, from Elvis to Wayne Newton with Bill Cosby along the way. Offerings run the gamut, including rock and country stars as well as top pop singers and comedians. Engagements run from a couple of days to two weeks.

Consumer Tips   Because of the Las Vegas Hilton's enormous size and boom-ing convention business, the showroom is almost as likely to sell out on a weekday as on a weekend. Reserved seat tickets can be purchased up to four weeks in advance over the phone with a credit card, or at the box office. While the Hilton will not guarantee the location of seats purchased over the phone, persons who come in person to the box office can choose from the avail-able seating as shown on the showroom diagram. If you use the Hilton's self-parking, give yourself at least ten minutes for the long walk to the showroom.

Mandalay Bay—House of Blues

Reservations and Information: (702) 632-7600 or (877) 632-7400;
   www.hob.com

Frequent Headliners: Current and former pop, rock, R&B, reggae, folk,
   and country stars

Usual Show Times: 8 p.m.

Approximate Admission Price: $12–100

Drinks Included: None

Showroom Size: 1,800 seats

Description and Comments   House of Blues is a newer Las Vegas concert hall, very different from The Joint at the Hard Rock, with which it competes head-on for performers and concert-goers. The House of Blues is more like an opera house (than the high school–gym Joint): Low ceiling, multitiered, and split-leveled, which gets the audience as close in to the act as possible. To that end, the acoustics are much better than the Joint's, but the House of Blues can get claustrophobic; the more crowded, the less comfortable it is. Also, the sight-lines are highly variable, even bizarre, especially for a new room—it's almost as if the designers were modifying an old theater rather than opening a new one. And it doesn't seem to have much to do with how much you pay for a seat: Some bad seats (in the nosebleed section and on the sides of the stage) don't cost much less than the best seats or much more than the cheapest tickets.

Live music is presented almost every night of the year. Major headliners, with tickets going for $30–100, appear once or twice a week at 8 p.m.; for these shows you must be 21 to attend; recent performers have included BB King, the Go-Go's, Peter Frampton, Chris Isaak, Ziggy Marley, and De la Soul. Filling in the booking gaps are minor shows, with tickets in the $12–30 range; check the hotline and website; you must be 18 or over for most of them (the few others are designated "all ages"). One recent line-up of minor artists consisted of the Low-Fidelity All-Stars, God Among Men, Orbital, and Angry Salad.

Consumer Tips   House of Blues ticket agents are very difficult to get by telephone; to save yourself an exorbitant phone bill, use the toll-free number listed above (and press 4). The box office is open 8 a.m.–midnight; the best time to call is right at 8 a.m. Once you have the operator (there's probably only one!) on the line, you'll often hear more bad news. The headliner shows sell out extremely fast, though you can usually pick up standing-room only tickets, where you'll be sardined in front of the stage (watch your wallet). If money is no object, try to get a VIP seat front and center in the balcony (the first ten rows are prime). If you can't, you might as well just opt for the cheap standing room, as the upper balcony and many of the loge seats aren't worth the extra money. Indeed, insiders tell us that many people give up their bad reserved seats to move down to the floor where they can see the whole stage!

Mandalay Bay—Mandalay Bay Theater

Reservations and Information: (702) 632-7580
Frequent Headliners: Broadway Musicals
Usual Show Times: 7:30 p.m.   *Dark:* Varies
Approximate Admission Price: $35–80
Drinks Included: None
Showroom Size: 1,700 seats

Description and Comments   The Mandalay Bay Theater opened with the hit musical *Chicago* for an engagement of over a year. More recently, the theater has hosted a number of traveling Broadway productions—including *Annie*. Occasionally the theater is used as a dance or concert venue.

Consumer Tips   The theater is new, gorgeous, and a little too big. With 1,700 seats, it's one-third larger than almost all Broadway houses. The floor and lower mezzanine seats are all good, but the upper mezzanine is pretty far away, especially for the price. If you go, spring for the extra $10 or $20 for the better seats.

Tickets can be ordered as far in advance as you want through the Mandalay Bay box office or Ticketmaster (phone (702) 474-4000). The cancellation policy is that there is none, so if you buy 'em you own 'em. You're given a confirmation number, which you're required to show when you pick up your tickets, along with a photo ID—that's for your own protection, they told us. Just in case someone overhears you making the reservations, cribs your confirmation number, picks your pocket, and shows up with your credit card for the tickets.

You can buy drinks at the bar in the theater lobby and carry them in; all the seats have cup holders. Beer starts at $4, mixed drinks at $6.50.

The intermission situation is interesting. Within 30 seconds of the curtain coming down, there's a long line at the rest room. It's best to pick up a re-entry pass and head into the casino; there's a bigger rest room just outside the theater.

MGM Grand—Garden Arena

Reservations and Information: (702) 891-7777 or (800) 646-7787;
   www.mgmgrand.com

Frequent Headliners: National acts, superstars, televised boxing, wrestling, and other sporting events

Usual Show Times: Varies   *Dark:* Varies

Approximate Admission Price: Varies

Drinks Included: None

Showroom Size: 17,157 seats

Description and Comments   This 275,000-square-foot special events center is designed to accommodate everything from sporting events and concerts to major trade exhibitions. The venue also offers auxiliary meeting rooms and ballrooms adjacent to the entertainment center. Barbra Streisand christened this venue with her first concert in more than 20 years on New Year's Eve, 1993. Championship boxing events, such as George Foreman vs. Michael Moorer (heavyweight championship of the world), and Mike Tyson's return to boxing, are favorite attractions at the Grand Garden Arena, as are the many big-name musical concerts.

Consumer Tips   Reserved-seat tickets can be purchased one to two months in advance with your credit card by calling the MGM Grand main reservations number or Ticketmaster outlets, for most but not all shows, (phone (702) 474-4000). If you are not staying at the MGM Grand, either arrive by cab or give yourself plenty of extra time to park and make your way to the arena.

MGM Grand—Hollywood Theater

Reservations and Information: (800) 646-7787

Frequent Headliners: Righteous Brothers, Liza Minnelli, Sheena Easton, Tom Jones, Don Rickles, Rodney Dangerfield, Engelbert Humperdink

Usual Show Times: Varies   *Dark:* Varies

Approximate Admission Price: $30–95

Drinks Included: None

Showroom Size: 650 seats

Description and Comments   A very modern and very comfortable show-room, with all front-facing seats, the Hollywood Theater hosts a wide range of musical and celebrity headliner productions for one- to three-week engagements.

Consumer Tips   Reserved-seat show tickets can be purchased one to two months in advance with your credit card by calling the MGM Grand's main reservations number. Children are allowed at most presentations; check first to make sure they are allowed. If you are not staying at the MGM Grand, either arrive by cab or give yourself plenty of extra time to park and make your way to the showroom.

Mirage—Theatre Mirage

Reservations and Information: (702) 792-7777 or (800) 963-9634;
   www.mirage.com

Frequent Headliners: *Siegfried & Roy,* Bill Cosby, Kenny Rogers, Paul
   Anka

Usual Show Times: Varies with performer, 7:30 and 11 p.m. for *Siegfried
   & Roy*

Dark: Wednesday and Thursday (for *Siegfried & Roy*)

Approximate Admission Price: $55–90; $100.50 for *Siegfried & Roy*

Drinks Included: 2 (tax, gratuity, and keepsake program included)

Showroom Size: 1,500 persons

Description and Comments   The *Siegfried & Roy* illusion and production show is featured at the Theatre Mirage the vast majority of the year. When Siegfried and Roy are off, other headliners are brought in for one- or two-week stands. The Theatre Mirage is one of the most modern showrooms in Las Vegas, with good visibility from every seat. All seats are reserved and preassigned.

Consumer Tips   Although it's assigned seating, no reservations are taken for any show in the Theatre Mirage. You must purchase tickets one to three days in advance of the performance at the Mirage box office. The only exception is for hotel guests at the Mirage, who are permitted to charge show tickets to their room. For more on obtaining tickets, see Consumer Tips under *Siegfried & Roy.*

Orleans—Orleans Showroom

Reservations and Information: (702) 365-7075

Frequent Headliners: Crystal Gayle, Rich Little, The Smothers Brothers

Usual Show Times: Varies with performer   *Dark:* Varies

Approximate Admission Price: Varies with performer

Drinks Included: None

Showroom Size: 800 seats

Description and Comments   This small but comfortable showroom offers tiered theater seats arranged in a crescent around the stage. Designed for solo performers and bands, the Orleans Showroom is an intimate venue for concerts with good visibility from anywhere in the house. The star lineup runs the gamut with a concentration in country-and-western singer celebrities.

Consumer Tips   This showroom features some great talent at bargain prices. All seats are reserved. Tickets can be purchased at the box office to the left of the showroom or over the phone using your credit card.

Stardust—Wayne Newton Theater

Reservations and Information: (702) 732-6325

Frequent Headliners: Wayne Newton, The Pointers, Manhattan Transfer, Marilyn McCoo and Billy Davis

Usual Show Times: Sunday–Thursday, 9 p.m.; Saturday, 8 and 11 p.m.   *Dark:* Friday

Approximate Admission Price: $50 (includes tax, tip, and 1 drink)

Drinks Included: 1

Showroom Size: 620 seats

Description and Comments   Vegas veteran Wayne Newton signed a multi-year contract in 2000, bringing headliner entertainment back to the Stardust for the first time in several decades. The consummate entertainer, Newton makes believers out of almost everyone who sees him; he's one of those phenoms whose stage presence and ability to work an audience make him dynamite to see live. You'll enjoy him more if you're over 50, of course, but even if you're 27 and Aunt Gladys makes you go, you'll have a great time. Other headliners appear during the 12 weeks each year when Wayne's off.

Consumer Tips   The Wayne Newton Theater is comfortable with good views from all seats, and is a near-perfect size for a headliner show. If you drive, be sure to give yourself some extra time to park and make your way to the theater.

Production Shows

LAS VEGAS PREMIER PRODUCTION SHOWS: COMPARING APPLES AND ORANGES

While we acknowledge that Las Vegas production shows are difficult to compare and that audiences of differing tastes and ages have different preferences, we have nevertheless ranked the continuously running shows to give you an idea of our favorites. This is definitely an apples-and-oranges comparison (how can you compare *Siegfried & Roy* to *De la Guarda?*), but one based on each show's impact, vitality, originality, pace, continuity, crescendo, and ability to entertain.

We would hasten to add that even the continuously running shows change acts and revise their focus periodically. Expect our list, therefore, to change from year to year. Also, be comforted by the knowledge that while some shows are better than others, there aren't any real dogs. The quality of entertainment among the continuously running production shows is exceptional. By way of analogy, we could rank baseball players according to their performance in a given All-Star game, but the entire list, from top to bottom, would still be All-Stars. You get the idea.

Production Show Hit Parade

Here's how we rank the Las Vegas production shows. Excluded from the list are short-run engagements (i.e., comedy clubs, comedy theater, and celebrity headliners) and afternoon-only shows. In addition to ranking the shows, we also have assigned each show a Value Rating as follows:

A Exceptional value, a real bargain

B Good value

C Absolutely fair, you get exactly what you pay for

D Somewhat overpriced

F Significantly overpriced

Show prices increased again during 2001, resulting in fewer bargains than in previous years. Prices in the 1990s escalated by more than 95%, with most of the increase in the last four years.

A Word about Small Showrooms

During the past couple of years, we have seen a number of casinos convert their lounge into a small showroom. Though the stage in these showrooms is routinely about the size of a beach towel, productions are mounted that include complex choreography, animal acts, and, in one notable case, an illusionist catching bullets in his teeth. In the case of musical revues, as many as four very thin or three average hula dancers can fit comfortably on the stage at one time. If the Mamas and the Papas had performed in one of these showrooms, Mama Cass would have had to join in from the hall.

A real problem with some smaller shows is that they often cost as much as productions in Las Vegas's major showrooms. We once reviewed *Hell on Heels* at the now defunct Maxim, for instance, and paid about $21 including tax and tip. Though *Hell on Heels* was a decent show and professionally performed, it could not compare in scope, talent, and spectacle to the lavish *Folies Bergere* at the Tropicana, available for only a few extra dollars.

Another problem is that small shows often play to even smaller crowds. We saw a performance of *That's Magic* at O'Sheas where the cast outnumbered the audience. Though the show featured talented illusionists, a good ventriloquist, and some dancers, the small facility made the production seem amateurish. It was heartrending to see professional entertainers work so hard for such a tiny audience. We felt self-conscious and uncomfortable ourselves, as well as embarrassed for the performers.

When it comes to smaller showrooms, simpler is better. That's why *Second City* and *Crazy Girls* work so well: Both shows take a minimalist approach. Additionally, both shows play in casinos large enough to draw an audience. Little showrooms in smaller casinos that attempt to mount big productions create only parody and end up looking foolish. Better that they revert to offering lounge shows, like those at New York–New York or Caesars Palace.

We have abandoned trying to cover the productions that play these small showrooms, mostly because the shows are very short-lived. If a small showroom production is exceptionally good and demonstrates staying power, however, we sometimes review it right along with the full-scale shows. In this edition, for example, we provide full reviews of *Crazy Girls* and *An Evening at La Cage* at the Riviera, and *Second City* at the Flamingo. This discussion, by the way, does not apply to comedy clubs, which work best in small rooms.

PRODUCTION SHOW PROFILES

Following is a profile of each of the continuously running production shows, listed alphabetically by the name of the show. If you are not sure of the name of a show, consult the previous section. Comedy clubs and celebrity headliner showrooms are profiled in separate sections. Prices are approximate and fluctuate about as often as you brush your teeth.

American Superstars

Type of Show: Celebrity impersonator production show
Host Casino and Showroom: Stratosphere—Broadway Showroom

Production Show Hit Parade

Rank	Show	Location	Value Rating
1.	Cirque du Soleil's Mystere	Treasure Island	B
2.	Cirque du Soleil's "O"	Bellagio	F
3.	De la Guarda	Rio	B
4.	EFX	MGM Grand	C
5.	Blue Man Group	Luxor	C
6.	Siegfried & Roy	Mirage	D
7.	The Rat Pack Is Back	Sahara	B
8.	Danny Gans	Mirage	D
9.	Legends In Concert	Imperial Palace	A
10.	Lance Burton	Monte Carlo	C
11.	Jubilee!	Bally's	C
12.	Takin' It Uptown w/ Clint Holmes	Harrah's	C
13.	Folies Bergere	Tropicana	C
14.	Andre-Phillippe Gagnon	Venetian	D
15.	Splash	Riviera	B
16.	American Superstars	Stratosphere	A
17.	Tournament of Kings	Excalibur	A
18.	Storm	Mandalay Bay	C
19.	Second City	Flamingo	B
20.	Melinda-First Lady of Magic	Venetian	D
21.	Steve Wyrick	Sahara	B
22.	The Scintas	Rio	C
23.	Bill Acosta: Lasting Impressions	Flamingo	F
24.	Crazy Girls	Riviera	D
25.	La Cage	Riviera	B
26.	Boy-lesque	New Frontier	B
27.	Skintight	Harrah's	D
28.	Men Are From Mars, Women Are From Venus	Flamingo	D
29.	Midnight Fantasy	Luxor	D
30.	Naked Angels	Plaza	D

Reservations and Information: (702) 382-4446 (reservations necessary)

Admission Cost with Taxes: $25.25 (ages 5–12); $32.95 (adults)

Cast Size: Approximately 24

Nights of Lowest Attendance: Sunday, Monday

Usual Show Times: 7 and 10 p.m. Wednesday, Friday, and Saturday;
  7 p.m. Sunday, Monday, and Tuesday   *Dark:* Thursday

Special Comments: Much enhanced on the larger stage

Topless: No

Author's Rating: ★★★ ½

Overall Appeal by Age Group:

Under 21	21–37	38–50	51 and older
★★★	★★★ ½	★★★★	★★★ ½

Duration of Presentation: An hour and a half

Description and Comments   *American Superstars* is a celebrity-impersonator show similar to *Legends in Concert* (Imperial Palace). Impersonated stars, which change from time to time, include Madonna, Michael Jackson, Gloria Estefan, the Spice Girls, and the ever-present Elvis. The impersonators, who do their own singing, are supported by a live band and (frequently upstaged) by an energetic troupe of dancers.

American Superstars is a fun, upbeat show. While the impersonations are, in general, not as crisp or realistic as those of *Legends in Concert,* the show exhibits a lot of drive and is a great night's entertainment.

Consumer Tips   *American Superstars* plays in the Stratosphere's main showroom, a change of venue that has allowed the production to improve and become truly competitive with *Legends in Concert.* Though tickets must be purchased in advance, seat assignment is at the discretion of the maître d'. Drinks are not included, but can be purchased at a bar outside the showroom. The showroom is situated at the end of the shopping arcade near the elevator bank for the Stratosphere Tower. *Note:* A $38 package is available including the show, drinks, buffet dinner, and tickets to the Tower.

Andre-Phillipe Gagnon

Type of Show: Musical impressionist

Host Casino and Showroom: Venetian—The Showroom

Reservations and Information: (702) 414-4300

Admission Cost with Taxes: $75–100

Cast Size: 6 (not counting Celine Dion)

Night of Lowest Attendance: Sunday
Usual Show Times: 8:30 p.m.   Dark: Tuesday and Thursday
Topless: No
Author's Rating: ★★★
Overall Appeal by Age Group:

Under 21	21–37	38–50	51 and older
★★★	★★★ ½	★★★★	★★★★

Duration of Presentation: An hour and a half

Descriptions and Comments A recent French-Canadian import, Andre-Phillipe Gagnon runs a close second only to Danny Gans as the best impressionist in Las Vegas. His vibe is a bit zanier and his act a bit more vaudeville than Gans; think of him as Jerry Lewis to Gans' smooth-operator Dean Martin. That said, his vocal talent and comic timing make him a star in his own right. In fact, Gagnon performs several unique variations on standard impressionist routines that you won't see elsewhere in Vegas, including a mutant "combination" impression of various celebrities chosen by the audience. Gagnon even does an impression of a randomly chosen audience volunteer—the two perform a bizarre "duet" in the "same" voice. The show closes with Gagnon rendering a duet with the looming videotaped image and voice of fellow Canadian Celine Dion.

Consumer Tips Gagnon's show is staged in the same ritzy, intimate theater at the Venetian as "Melinda, First Lady of Magic." Though this venue has fewer seats and about the same prices as the Danny Gans show at the Mirage, it's probably still an easier ticket to get due to Gans' extreme popularity. Gagnon is a viable, worthwhile alternative if you're jonesing for an impressionist show but can't find a seat for Gans. If nothing else, you'll be amazed at the quantity of bottled water Gagnon chugs during the show in order to keep his many voices fresh.

Bill Acosta: Lasting Impressions

Type of Show: Musical impressionist with some topless dancers
Host Casino and Showroom: Flamingo—Bugsy's Theater
Reservations and Information: (702) 733-3333
Admission Cost with Taxes: $49.95–69.95
Cast Size: 18
Night of Lowest Attendance: Tuesday (late show)
Usual Show Times: 10 p.m. (also 7:30 p.m. on Tuesday) Dark: Friday

Topless: Yes

Author's Rating: ★★ ½

Overall Appeal by Age Group:

Under 21	21–37	38–50	51 and older
—	★★★	★★★ ½	★★★★

Duration of Presentation: An hour and 20 minutes

Descriptions and Comments   Bill Acosta is a solid, old-school Las Vegas impressionist. A classy performer, his show and ensemble go for the kind of sweeping tributes typical of the Vegas heyday. Acosta is right at home in this atmosphere, and he's most comfortable (and most apt) doing impressions of Vegas legends like Frank Sinatra, Dean Martin, Sammy Davis, Jr., and so on. He stumbles a bit when attempting more contemporary celebs (his Ricky Martin is abysmal). Even so, his traditional show is well-produced and features a tight big-band orchestra and a talented troupe of dancers (some of whom are periodically topless). As a whole, Acosta's show is meant to combine a variety of classic Vegas-show elements, from chorus girls to showroom crooning. The standout routine is a startling "12 days of impressions," where Acosta rockets between voices as disparate as Ross Perot, Garth Brooks, Jack Nicholson, and more, all within seconds.

Consumer Tips   Less expensive than either Danny Gans or Andre-Phillipe Gagnon, Acosta's show hearkens back to the glitzier Vegas shows of yesteryear (there's even a golden staircase). The "young turk" impressionist shows focus more on the marquee performers as stars in their own right, while Acosta still has that reverential attitude of a lucky guy channeling the voices of the greats for your shared enjoyment and nostalgia. If you're into classic Las Vegas, you will more than likely prefer this show to Gans or Gagnon.

Blue Man Group

Type of Show: Performance art production show

Host Casino and Showroom: Luxor—Luxor Theatre

Reservations and Information: (702) 262-4400 or (800) 557-7428

Admission Cost with Taxes: $79 for floor seats, $69 for balcony seats

Cast Size: 3 plus a 15-piece band

Nights of Lowest Attendance: Sunday and Monday

Usual Show Times: Sunday and Monday at 7 p.m., Wednesday–Saturday, 7 and 10 p.m.   *Dark:* Tuesday

Topless: No

Special Comments: Teenagers will really like this show, but the blue guys, loud music, and dark colors could scare small children.

Author's Rating: ★★★★
Overall Appeal by Age Group:

Under 21	21–37	38–50	51 and older
★★★★	★★★★ ½	★★★★	★★★ ½

Duration of Presentation: 1 hour and 45 minutes

Description and Comments *Blue Man Group* gives Las Vegas its first large-scale introduction to that nebulous genre called "performance art." If you're from Mars and the designation "performance art" confuses you, relax—it won't hurt a bit. The Blue Man Group gives a stunning performance that can be appreciated by all kinds of folks.

The three blue men are just that—blue—and bald and mute. Their fast-paced show uses music and multi-media effects to make light of contemporary art and life in the information age. While the three blue men are the focus of the show, their antics are augmented by a 15-piece band and plenty of audience participation.

Funny, sometimes poignant, and always compelling, *Blue Man Group* pounds on complex instruments (made of PVC pipes) that could pass for industrial intestines. At times the mostly percussive music is overcome by eerie melodies, and the drumming blends with a seemingly spontaneous eruption of visual art rendered in mediums as diverse as marshmallows and goo-of-iffy-origin. *Blue Man Group* challenges the audience to keep up with them, sometimes forcing you to choose between three different areas of activity. This is effective, albeit frenetic, and not a little exhausting.

Staged in the 1,200-seat Luxor Theatre, the sound and lighting are technically awesome. The stage is set with large industrial shapes and lit with deep electric blues, blacks, and purples. Against these dark colors, the Blue men wield props, paints, and instruments, all in fluorescent whites, pinks, yellows, and blues. There are also a host of other costly and ultra high tech special effects, most notably an animated sculpture that dances with the help of strobe lights.

A 15-piece percussion band backs the *Blue Man Group* with a relentless and totally engrossing industrial dance riff. The band resides in a long dark alcove above the stage. At just the right moments, their loft is lit to reveal a group of neon-colored pulsating skeletons.

The Blue Men themselves play a group of instruments of their own creation, most of which are pipes of varying diameters and configurations with names like *tubulum* and *gyro shot*. Some resemble tubas, xylophones, or pipe organs. All are as stimulating visually as they are aurally.

Audience participation completes the *Blue Man* experience. The Blue Men often move into the audience and twice bring audience members on stage. One poor soul is offered a meal of industrial slime and becomes instrumental in the creation of a piece of art or an unfortunate stew—depending on your perspective. At the end of the show, the entire audience is involved in an effort to move a sea of paper across the theater. And a lot of folks can't help standing up to dance—and laugh.

Consumer Tips   This show is decidedly different and requires an open mind to appreciate. It also help to be a little loose, because like it or not, everybody gets sucked into the production. If you're uptight or believe that audiences should be passive rather than demonstrative, *Blue Man Group* will make you feel uncomfortable.

The Luxor Theater will knock you out. It's simply one of the best show venues in Las Vegas. All seats are reserved. If you don't want to get slimed by the Blue Men, ask to be seated five or six rows from the front of the stage. Tickets can be purchased at the box office, over the phone using your credit card, and through Ticketmaster. No drinks are included, but there is a cash bar outside the showroom.

Bottoms Up

Type of Show: Bawdy song, dance, and comedy
Host Casino and Showroom: Flamingo—Bugsy's Theater
Reservations and Information: (702) 733-3333
Admission Cost with Taxes: $14 (includes 1 drink)
Cast Size: 10
Usual Show Times: 2 p.m. and 4 p.m. daily
Special Comments: The only afternoon topless show in Las Vegas
Topless: Yes
Author's Rating: ½
Overall Appeal by Age Group:

Under 21	21–37	38–50	51 and older
—	★	★½	★★

Duration of Presentation: 1 hour (though it seems much, much longer)

Descriptions and Comments   *Bottoms Up* has been staged in a variety of forms for decades, in Las Vegas and elsewhere. In its current incarnation, it is quite likely the worst show in town. Imagine an ultra-corny series of excruciatingly stale comedy sketches, periodically interrupted by smarmy stand-up or awful lip-synched show tunes rendered by the wizened core performers. Many of the jokes and bits are lifted directly from ancient vaudeville, television shows, or endlessly circulated shaggy-dog jokes we all heard in grade school (and they weren't that funny then). In a town where anything goes, this production manages to find something to offend virtually everyone—when was the last time you chuckled at an unwed mother joke? Despite the show's relative brevity, you'll still get the feeling of being trapped in the showroom for a prolonged episode of torture. We can only hope that the abject humiliation of participating in this disaster will ultimately lead to better things for the younger performers, who possibly don't yet know any better.

Consumer Tips If it's imperative that you see a topless show in the afternoon, at least this one is very cheap. Otherwise, avoid *Bottoms Up* at all costs. As one dissatisfied customer complained, "I wish I'd spent my ticket money on the slot machines." Discount coupons are widely available in the visitor magazines, but no discount could be great enough to make this worthwhile. Consider yourself warned that the price of seeing this show is not strictly monetary.

Cirque du Soleil's Mystere

Type of Show: Circus as theater
Host Casino and Showroom: Treasure Island—*Cirque du Soleil* Showroom
Reservations and Information: (702) 894-7722 or (800) 392-1999
Admission Cost with Taxes: $88
Cast Size: 75
Nights of Lowest Attendance: Thursday
Usual Show Times: 7:30 and 10:30 p.m.   *Dark:* Monday and Tuesday
Special Comments: No table service (no tables!)
Topless: No
Author's Rating: ★★★★ ½
Overall Appeal by Age Group:

Under 21	21–37	38–50	51 and older
★★★★	★★★★★	★★★★★	★★★★½

Duration of Presentation: An hour and a half

Description and Comments *Mystere* is a far cry from a traditional circus but retains all of the fun and excitement. It is whimsical, mystical, and sophisticated, yet pleasing to all ages. The action takes place on an elaborate stage that incorporates almost every part of the theater. The original musical score is exotic, like the show.

Note: In the following paragraph, I get into how the show *feels* and why it's special. If you don't care how it feels, or if you are not up to slogging through a boxcar of adjectives, the bottom line is simple: *Mystere* is great. See it.

Mystere is the most difficult show in Las Vegas to describe. To categorize it as a circus does not begin to cover its depth, though its performers could perform with distinction in any circus on earth. *Cirque du Soleil* is more, much more, than a circus. It combines elements of classic Greek theater, mime, the English morality play, Dali surrealism, Fellini characterization, and Chaplin comedy. *Mystere* is at once an odyssey, a symphony, and an exploration of human emotions. The show pivots on its humor, which is sometimes black, and engages the audience with its unforgettable characters. Though light and uplifting, it is also poignant and dark. Simple in its presentation, it is at the same time extraordinarily intricate, always operating on multiple levels of meaning. As you laugh and watch the amazingly talented cast, you become aware that your mind has entered a dimension seldom encountered in a waking state. The presentation begins to register in your consciousness more as a seamless dream than as a stage production. You are moved, lulled, and soothed as well as excited and entertained. The sensitive, the imaginative, the literate, and those who love good theater and art will find no show in Las Vegas that compares with *Mystere* except *Cirque's* sister production *"O"* at the Bellagio.

Consumer Tips   Be forewarned that the audience is an integral part of *Mystere* and that at almost any time you might be plucked from your seat to participate. Our advice is to loosen up and roll with it. If you are too rigid, repressed, hungover, or whatever to get involved, politely but firmly decline to be conscripted.

Because *Mystere* is presented in its own customized showroom, there are no tables and, consequently, no drink service. In keeping with the show's circus theme, however, spectators can purchase refreshments at nearby concession stands. Tickets for reserved seats can be purchased seven days in advance at the *Cirque's* box office or over the phone using your credit card. For a comparison of *Mystere* and *Cirque de Soleil's "O"* at the Bellagio, see Description and Comments and Consumer Tips for *"O"* following this profile.

Cirque du Soleil's "O"

Type of Show: Circus and aquatic ballet as theater
Host Casino and Showroom: Bellagio—Bellagio Theater
Reservations and Information: (702) 693-7722
Admission Cost with Taxes: $121 main floor; $99 balcony
Cast Size: 74
Nights of Lowest Attendance: Sunday and Monday

Usual Show Times: 7:30 and 10:30 p.m.   *Dark:* Wednesday and Thursday
Topless: No
Author's Rating: ★★★★
Overall Appeal by Age Group:

Under 21	21–37	38–50	51 and older
★★★★	★★★★★	★★★★★	★★★★ ½

Duration of Presentation: An hour and a half

Description and Comments   I read an article a while back where *Cirque du Soleil* was described as "a circus without animals," a description so woefully inadequate that it really ticked me off. Truly, the writer who penned those words has the sensitivity of a slug. *Cirque* is not the sum of various tricks and stunts, rather it is an artistic theatrical collage replete with life and all of its meaning, emotion, and color. If a performer swings from rope or juggles a hoop it is as incidental, yet as integral, as a single dollop of paint on a Rembrandt canvas. It's not the single trick that matters, it's the context.

The title *"O"* is a play on words derived from the concept of infinity, with 0 (zero) as its purest expression, and from the phonetic pronunciation of *eau,* the French word for water. Both symbols are appropriate, for the production (like all *Cirque* shows) creates a timeless dream state and (for the first time in a *Cirque* show) also incorporates an aquatic dimension that figuratively and literally evokes all of the meanings, from baptism to boat passage, that water holds for us. The foundation for the spectacle that is *"O"* resides in a set (more properly an aquatic theater) that is no less than a technological triumph. Before your eyes, in mere seconds, the hard, varnished surface of the stage transforms seamlessly into anything from a fountain to a puddle to a vast pool. Where only moments ago acrobats tumbled, now graceful water ballerinas surface and make way for divers somersaulting down from above. The combined effect of artists and environment is so complete and yet so transforming that it's almost impossible to focus on specific characters, details, or movements. Rather there is a global impact that envelops you and holds you suspended. In the end you have a definite sense that you *felt* what transpired rather than having merely seen it.

Though *"O"* is brilliant by any standard and pregnant with beauty and expression, it lacks just a bit of the humor, accessibility, and poignancy of *Cirque's Mystere* at sister casino Treasure Island. Where *"O"* crashes over you like a breaking wave, *Mystere* is more personal, like a lover's arrow to the heart. If you enjoyed *Mystere,* however, you will also like *"O,"* and vice versa. What's more, the productions, while sharing stylistic similarities, are quite different. Though you might not want (or be able to afford) to see them both on the same Las Vegas visit, you wouldn't feel like you saw the same show twice if you did.

Consumer Tips   If you've never seen either of the Las Vegas *Cirque du Soleil* productions, we recommend catching *Mystere* first. For starters, it's $33 per person less expensive and, in our opinion, just as good (if not a smidge better). Plus, *Mystere* is more representative of *Cirque du Soleil's* hallmark presentation and tradition.

Unless you just went public with an Internet company, you're probably wondering if either of the *Cirque* productions are worth the hefty tariff. Truth be told, we've waffled on that question ourselves—$88–121 is a lot of money. In the final analysis, however, *Mystere* is so special that we think it's a fair value at $88. And although we understand why *"O"* is more expensive (technology, physical plant, etc.), we also believe that $121 ($99 for balcony seats) is pushing the envelope a little too hard. *"O"* is a great show and the Bellagio is a classy joint, but a hundred-bucks-plus? I dunno.

In any event, both shows are very popular. If you want to go, buy tickets via credit card over the phone before you leave home. If you decide to see *"O"* at the spur of the moment, try the box office about 30 minutes before show time. Sometimes seats reserved for comped gamblers will be released for sale.

Crazy Girls

Type of Show: Erotic dance and adult comedy
Host Casino and Showroom: Riviera—Mardi Gras Showrooms, second floor
Reservations and Information: (702) 794-9301 or (800) 634-3420
Admission Cost with Taxes: $25
Cast Size: 8
Nights of Lowest Attendance: Wednesday, Monday
Usual Show Times: 8:30 and 10:30 p.m., with a midnight show on
   Saturdays   *Dark:* Monday
Topless: Yes
Author's Rating: ★★★ ½
Overall Appeal by Age Group:

Under 21	21–37	38–50	51 and older
—	★★★ ½	★★★ ½	★★★ ½

Duration of Presentation: 1 hour

Description and Comments   *Crazy Girls* gets right to the point. This is a no-nonsense show for men who do not want to sit through jugglers, magicians, and half the score from *Oklahoma!* before they see naked women. The focus is on eight engaging, talented, and athletically built young ladies who bump and grind through an hour of exotic dance and comedy. The choreography (for anyone who cares) is pretty creative, and the whole performance is highly charged and quickly paced, though most vocals are lip-synched. The dancers are supported by a zany comedienne who doesn't shy away from X-rated humor. Solo routines (which may be dances or just sexy writhing) are shown in closeup on large video screens, but the videos are from previous performances, creating an odd disconnect when the video and onstage performer get out of synch.

Consumer Tips   The show is not really as dirty as the Riviera would lead you to believe, and the nudity does not go beyond topless and G-strings (how could it?). While designed for men, there is not much of anything in the show that would make women or couples uncomfortable. Men looking for total nudity should try the Palomino Club in North Las Vegas.

Ticket and box office information is the same as for *La Cage* (see Consumer Tips under *An Evening at La Cage*, page 238). VIP, up-close seating is available for old poots who forgot their glasses and includes a line pass. There are a few columns in the middle section that can obstruct views from back-center seats.

Danny Gans: Entertainer of the Year

Type of Show: Impressions and variety
Host Casino and Showroom: Mirage—Danny Gans Theater
Reservations and Information: (702) 791-7111 or (800) 963-9634
Admission Cost with Taxes: $75–99
Cast Size: Approximately 7
Nights of Lowest Attendance: Wednesday
Usual Show Times: 8 p.m.   *Dark:* Monday and Friday
Topless: No
Author's Rating: ★★★★
Overall Appeal by Age Group:

Under 21	21–37	38–50	51 and older
★★★	★★★½	★★★★	★★★★

Duration of Presentation: An hour and 10 minutes

Description and Comments   Danny Gans was well on his way to a promising career in major league baseball when he suffered a career-ending injury. Baseball's loss is Las Vegas entertainment's gain. This "man of many voices" is a monster talent. He does upwards of a hundred impressions during the show: Michael Jackson; Willie Nelson; James Stewart; Kermit the Frog; Pee Wee Herman; John Travolta; Peter Falk; Garth Brooks; Sammy, Frank, and Dino; Walter Cronkite with Presidents Clinton, Bush, Reagan, Carter, and Ford;

Billy Joel; Bruce Springsteen; Stevie Wonder; Ray Charles; Sylvester Stallone; Homer and Marge Simpson talking to Dr. Ruth's answering machine; Henry Fonda and Katharine Hepburn doing *On Golden Pond;* Paul Lynde; Wayne Newton; Neil Diamond; Sammy Davis Jr.; Natalie and Nat King Cole; Sarah Vaughan; The Artist Formerly Known as Prince; Bill Cosby; and, of course, Elvis. And that's a *short* list. At the end, he even does Danny Gans—typically a selection from his Christian pop album.

Gans not only does impressions, but also expressions. He captures his characters' faces, postures, and moves; he gets maximum effect from minimal props; he even plays a mean trumpet (for the Louis Armstrong bit). But that's not all. This is perhaps the tightest show in Las Vegas. Gans, his band, and the lighting are in perfect sync every note of the night. *Danny Gans* is great for Las Vegas. Tough luck for baseball.

In case you're wondering, Danny Gans is the best of the solo impressionists working Las Vegas Showrooms. We rank Andre-Phillipe Gagnon (Venetian) second, and Bill Acosta (Flamingo) third.

Consumer Tips Danny Gans is outstanding and a reasonable buy for the $75 seats. In any event, the show is more of an auditory than a visual experience, so leave the $99 seats (the first eight rows) to the high rollers and invited guests. The Mirage is a bustling place in the evenings so allow yourself an extra 15 minutes to park and get to the showroom.

De la Guarda

Type of Show: Interactive Melee'
Host Casino and Showroom: Rio—De la Guarda Theatre
Reservations and Information: (702) 252-7776
Admission Cost with Taxes: $45
Cast Size: 14
Nights of Lowest Attendance: Wednesday and Thursday
Usual Show Times: 9 p.m. Tuesday—Friday; 8 and 10:30 p.m. Saturday
Topless: No
Author's Rating: ★★★★ ½
Overall Appeal By Age Group:

Under 21	21-37	38-50	51 and older
★★★★ ½	★★★★ ½	★★★★ ½	★★★★

Duration of Presentation: About an hour

Description and Comments De La Guarda comes with more warnings than Space Mountain at Disneyland. The very first thing you're told when you inquire about this show is that "the audience must stand through the whole presentation and you may get wet." Both true. When you ask what the show is about you're told that it's really not about anything. Also true. If you want some information you can chew on, ask how much it costs to stand and get wet while watching a show about nothing. The answer to that one is $45.

Now that I've lulled you into thinking that this is a negative review, I'm going to tell you that this strange production is one of the best shows I've ever seen in Las Vegas. Why? Because it's gripping and powerful, because it's electric in its energy, because it's amazing in concept, and because on a very visceral level, it makes you happy to be alive.

De la Guarda roughly translates to guardian angel. And while the evolution of the show stems from the terror and chaos of years of military dictatorship in Argentina, you'll drive yourself batty trying to understand De la Guarda from a historic perspective. In fact, trying to understand De la Guarda at all is a needless waste of energy. De la Guarda, you see, is about feeling, not cognition. The best way to experience De la Guarda is to clear your mind and just let it wash over you.

So you ask, what exactly washes over you? Is that the getting wet part? Let's start at the beginning. First you enter what could be a hanger or a warehouse. There is a sort of muslin fabric that forms a ceiling about six feet over your head. The upper stories of the building, open to the roof support beams, are hidden by the cloth ceiling. Light and shadow images play on the cloth. Drops of water seep through it. What happens next we won't reveal, but it gathers you up, and truly takes you to a place you've never been. There is no plot to follow, and there are no characters. There is no stage and nothing separates the cast from the audience.

There is symbolism to be sure, but it's elemental rather than political: wind, water, gravity, sound; flight as a metaphor for transcendence. Pounding drums combine with freeform aerial dance and torrents of water in a baptism that envelopes both cast and audience resulting in an interaction that is the soul of the production.

By now, I'm sure you're thinking, "enough, enough already! Back off the existential stuff and spell out what happens." Sorry, but it's too good. I'm not going to spoil it for you. If you see a print ad for De la Guarda, it will show wet people swinging on a cable or jumping up and down. That's part of it, but only the tip of the iceberg. If you want to see the rest you'll have to take the dive.

Consumer Tips   We worried that nobody over 30 would like De la Guarda. Not true. Older patrons loved it as much as Gen X'ers. Standing, likewise was not a problem. You are so completely engrossed that you'd willingly stand an additional hour. As for getting wet, you can avoid the water by moving around a bit and (if you must) declining to embrace wet cast members. You can also take or leave the interaction according to your own comfort level. You'll enjoy the show more if you interact, but nobody's going to put you on the spot or make you do anything you don't want to do. Understand also, that pretty much the whole audience is interacting at the same time so there's no sense of being singled out or being put on display. Concerning dress, the box office will tell you to wear old clothes, but that's really overkill. We caught the show the first time after a dressy dinner and had no problem being both fully involved and staying clean and dry. Although, there's no one area of the building that provides a better view than another, we found the far left corner from the entrance to be our favorite vantage point. As you might expect, there's no smoking, eating, drinking, or photography.

EFX!

Type of Show: Grand-scale musical production show

Host Casino and Showroom: MGM Grand—Grand Theater

Reservations and Information: (702) 891-7777 or (800) 929-1111

Admission Cost with Taxes: $55 general admission, $75 preferred admission

Cast Size: 70

Nights of Lowest Attendance: Wednesday and Thursday

Usual Show Times: 7:30 and 10:30 p.m.   *Dark:* Sunday and Monday

Special Comments: Children's admission is $40 ages 12 years and under

Topless: No

Author's Rating: ★★★★ ½

Overall Appeal by Age Group:

Under 21	21–37	38–50	51 and older
★★★	★★★★ ½	★★★★ ½	★★★★

Duration of Presentation: An hour and a half

Description and Comments   *EFX!,* pronounced "Effects," is the MGM Grand's entry into the Las Vegas megashow competition. With a cast of 70 and a backstage support crew of 80, *EFX!* is designed to overwhelm. The production recently switched stars, losing Tommy Tune and gaining Rick Springfield. Like Michael Crawford, David Cassidy, and Tommy Tune before him, he brings his considerable talents to bear with infinite precision so that he complements the production instead of monopolizing or overwhelming it.

In *EFX!* Springfield guides the audience through an animatronic (robotic) and technological odyssey that is reported to have cost $30 million to produce. Broadway talent and aesthetics are integrated with cutting-edge, Hollywood special effects as Springfield takes the audience on a journey through time and space, appearing in the process as Merlin, H.G. Wells, P. T. Barnum, and Houdini.

We were surprised by how beautiful and aesthetically grounded *EFX!* is, and also by its delightful humor. Far from another Las Vegas monument to excess, the spectacle of *EFX!* fits its theme and operates in context. *EFX!* is a stunning and sensitive show that makes excellent use of its technology rather than being a numbing parade of special effects. There is nothing of the tail wagging the dog about *EFX!* The technology artfully augments the overall production and is integrated in a most unobtrusive way. *EFX!*, like *Cirque du Soleil's Mystere*, is most of all human, and like *Mystere*, it operates on multiple levels and engages many emotions. The score is lilting and uplifting and the choreography flawless. While the costumes and sets are staggering, they serve to create a theatrical environment that totally envelops the audience. The audience is one with the cast, and there are no feelings of boundaries or separation.

Consumer Tips We think *EFX!* has a stupid and misleading name that conveys none of its depth or artistry. *EFX!* is a must-see, ranking alongside *Cirque du Soleil's Mystere* and *"O"* as the best production shows in Las Vegas. While guests on the highest tiers are pretty far away from the stage, the only bad seats are those right up front where guests are periodically enveloped in fake fog. The better seats for *EFX!* are back about four tiers from the front and in the center. Reserved-seat tickets can be purchased over the phone with your credit card approximately two months in advance or in person at the Grand Theater box office. We recommend booking your seats a couple of weeks in advance. Children over five years old are welcome but must pay the stiff adult price. On the night of the show, give yourself an extra 20–30 minutes if you plan to use MGM Grand valet parking or self-parking.

An Evening at La Cage

Type of Show: Female-impersonator revue
Host Casino and Showroom: Riviera—Mardi Gras Showrooms, third floor
Reservations and Information: (702) 794-9433 or (800) 634-3420
Admission Cost with Taxes: $25
Cast Size: Approximately 20
Nights of Lowest Attendance: Sunday, Monday

Usual Show Times: 7:30 and 9:30 p.m.   *Dark:* Tuesday

Topless: No

Author's Rating: ★★★

Overall Appeal by Age Group:

Under 21	21–37	38–50	51 and older
—	★★★ ½	★★★	★★★

Duration of Presentation: 1 hour and 15 minutes

Description and Comments   La Cage re-creates the female-impersonator re-vue made famous by productions of the same name in New York and Los Angeles. A high-tempo show with a great sense of humor, *La Cage* is at once outrageous, lusty, weird, and sensitive. All of the performers, of course, are men. Celebrities impersonated include Joan Rivers, Tina Turner, Cher, Carol Channing, Shirley MacLaine, Bette Midler, and Madonna. A crew of dancers (also men impersonating women) give the presentation the feel of a quirky production show.

Some of the impersonators are convincing and pretty enough to fool just about anyone. Their costumes reveal slender, feminine arms and legs and hourglass figures. Others, however, look just like what they are—men in drag. The cast performs with great self-effacement and gives the impression that nobody is expected to take things too seriously. As one impersonator quipped, "This is a hell of a way for a 40-year-old man to be earning a living."

La Cage is kinky yet solid entertainment. It is also very popular and plays to appreciative heterosexual audiences. If you are curious, broad-minded, and looking for something different, give it a try. If the idea of a bunch of guys traipsing around in fishnet stockings and feather boas gives you the willies, opt for something more conventional.

Consumer Tips   La Cage and Boy-lesque (New Frontier) are similar in both content and quality. If you see one it would be redundant to see the other. If you are trying to choose, prices are comparable, so go with the show that's most conveniently located. In addition to La Cage, you can see the produc-tion show *Splash,* which plays off the main casino in the Versailles Theatre (see page 255). Shows can be purchased in conjunction with a meal, usually the buffet. The food on the show-dinner combos won't knock you out, but is a pretty good deal for the money. Also, it's quick and convenient. There is usually plenty of time to eat between shows.

Tickets for *La Cage* and the other Mardi Gras shows may be reserved up to 21 days in advance at the Riviera box office, or over the phone using your credit card up to 10 days in advance. Two cocktails are included in your ad-mission. Seating is by the maître d'. Once seated, you fetch your own drinks from the bar using your ticket stub as a voucher.

Folies Bergere (The Best of)

Type of Show: Music, dance, and variety production show
Host Casino and Showroom: Tropicana—Tiffany Theater
Reservations and Information: (702) 739-2411 or (800) 634-4000
Admission Cost with Taxes: $51.45 general; $62.45 VIP
Cast Size: Approximately 90
Nights of Lowest Attendance: Monday, Tuesday, Sunday
Usual Show Times: 7:30 p.m (allows ages 5 and up) and 10 p.m.
   Dark: Thursday
Topless: Late show only
Author's Rating: ★★★
Overall Appeal by Age Group:

Under 21	21–37	38–50	51 and older
★★	★★★	★★★	★★★★

Duration of Presentation: An hour and a half

Description and Comments   The *Folies Bergere,* a Las Vegas tradition modeled on the bawdy Parisian revue of the same name, has been playing at the Tropicana on and off since 1959. The show, which changes almost every year, is a classy dance and musical variety production with a large cast.

The *Folies Bergere* is pretty much what you would expect: exotically clad (or unclad) showgirls and cancan dancers, chorus lines, singers, and music with a fin-de-siecle French cabaret feel. The show runs through 14 different scenes, celebrating the music and dance traditions of Paris, Hollywood, and Las Vegas from the 1860s to the 1960s. The *Folies Bergere* is elaborate and colorful but not particularly compelling. The singing and dancing are competent and professional but, with one or two exceptions, not creative or exciting. The *Folies* has been successful for over 40 years, so it is understandable that the producers would be reluctant to tamper with the formula. The ante for competing in the big leagues, however, has gone up. The production innovations of *Siegfried & Roy* and the energy of *EFX!* have established new standards for action, tempo, and creativity in Las Vegas production shows. The *Folies Bergere* has failed to keep pace, and an extremely talented cast has been relegated to plugging its way through a staid and dated format.

In fairness, the Folies change and update various elements of the show every year. Recent changes make the show more appealing to the baby boomer generation who cut their teeth on rock (music, that is). Updated or not, however, Folies has become a sort of treasured relic, a nostalgic symbol of Las Vegas in those heady early days of the Strip.

Given the music and style of the *Folies*, you will be more likely to appreciate the production if you are over age 50. Younger patrons will fail to identify with the nostalgic music and dance of *la belle epoque,* or find much spontaneity in the overall *Folies* theme; the *Lion King* finale, for example, is strange and overwrought. But imaginative sets and costumes, elaborate staging, a diverse soundtrack, and the contemporary choreography that revs up near the end give this show some pop.

Consumer Tips   The *Folies* is presented on a wide stage in the nicely designed Tiffany Theater. There is a lot more booth seating than in most showrooms and a good view from practically every seat in the house. Dinner is no longer offered in the showroom, though there's a buffet show package for a few dollars extra. No drinks come with the price of the show. If you need to use the distant rest room before the show, allow yourself plenty of time.

Reservations can be made up to a month in advance, and all seats are reserved, so you can show up five minutes prior to show time and your seats will be waiting.

Hot Trix

Type of Show: Topless revue with comic and magician
Host Casino and Showroom: Plaza—Plaza Theater
Reservations and Information: (702) 386-2444
Admission Cost with Taxes: $30 (includes 1 drink)
Cast Size: Approximately 8
Night of Lowest Attendance: Thursday
Usual Show Times: 8 and 10 p.m.   *Dark:* Monday
Topless: Yes
Author's Rating: ★★ ½
Overall Appeal by Age Group:

Under 21	21–37	38–50	51 and older
—	★★ ½	★★★	★★★

Duration of Presentation: An hour and 20 minutes

Descriptions and Comments   The full name of this production is "Hot Trix with Special Guest Peter Barbutti and Karen Denise's Naked Angels," and it's often just called "Naked Angels." Barbutti, a grizzled comic and the nominal master of ceremonies, is a lounge lizard in true Las Vegas style. His act is a sort of cross between Jackie Mason and Don Rickles, mixing equal parts insult comic and cynical curmudgeon. He plays a mean piano too—with his face, we might add. Barbutti also serves as dirty ol' elder statesman to Karen Denise and her Naked Angels, who share the stage with him about half the time. Their solo and ensemble nude routines run the gamut, often involving erotic baths, gentle whip-teasing, or other kittenish play. One refreshing element is the total absence of any throwaway "framing" for the bare chests, which allows the performers to get right to business, as it were. Another occasional intermezzo is a sexy lady magician, who tries very hard but can't completely conceal the third-rate quality of some of her illusions.

Consumer Tips   Due to the stage design, sightlines in this small venue are slightly obstructed at the extreme front left and right; this also puts you uncomfortably close to the stage-mounted speakers, which buzz noticeably. Discount coupons are available at the casino and in visitor magazines.

Jubilee!

Type of Show: Grand-scale musical and variety production show

Host Casino and Showroom: Bally's—The Jubilee Theater

Reservations and Information: (702) 967-4567 or (800) 237-SHOW

Admission Cost with Taxes: $52–62.50 ($2.50 extra on credit card purchase)

Cast Size: 100

Nights of Lowest Attendance: Sunday, Thursday

Usual Show Times: 7:30 and 10:30 p.m.   *Dark:* Tuesday

Topless: Yes

Author's Rating: ★★★★

Overall Appeal by Age Group:

Under 21	21–37	38–50	51 and older
★★★	★★★	★★★ ½	★★★★

Duration of Presentation: An hour and a half

Description and Comments   *Jubilee!* is the quintessential, traditional Las Vegas production show. Faithfully following a successful decades-old formula, *Jubilee!* has elaborate musical production numbers, extravagant sets, beautiful topless showgirls, and quality variety acts. In *Jubilee!* you get what you expect—and then some.

With a cast of 100, an enormous stage, and some of the most colossal and extraordinary sets found in theater anywhere, *Jubilee!* is much larger than life. Running an hour and a half each performance, the show is lavish, very sexy, and well performed, but redundant to the point of numbing.

Two multiscene production extravaganzas top the list of *Jubilee!* highlights. The first is the sultry saga of Samson and Delilah, climaxing with Samson's destruction of the temple. Not exactly biblical, but certainly awe-inspiring. The second super-drama is the story of the *Titanic*, from launch to sinking. Once again, sets and special effects on a grand scale combine with nicely integrated music and choreography to provide an incredible spectacle.

In June 1997, *Jubilee!* unveiled a new $3 million, 16-minute opening act, based on a popular song by Jerry Herman, "Hundreds of Girls," and featuring 75 singers, dancers, and showgirls multiplied by gargantuan mirrors. The above-average specialty acts include an illusionist executing big-stage tricks, a juggler-acrobat couple whose main prop is a giant aluminum cube, and a strongman who performs mostly upside-down. The production concludes with "The Jubilee Walk," a parade of elaborately costumed showgirls patterned after the grand finale of the *Ziegfeld Follies*.

Consumer Tips   The 1,035-seat Jubilee Theater, with its high, wide stage and multitiered auditorium, is one of the best-designed showrooms in town. The Jubilee underwent a complete $2.5 million renovation in mid-1997. It now consists of seating at banquet tables at the foot of the stage (too close and cramped); one row of booths above the tables (more expensive but worth it); and 789 theater-style seats. The table and booth seats come with cocktail service; the theater-seat audience has to carry in their own drinks.

Reserved seats for *Jubilee!* can be purchased over the phone with a credit card up to six weeks in advance. Tickets can also be purchased in person at the Bally's box office. The price of a ticket covers admission and taxes.

Lance Burton: Master Magician

Type of Show: Magical illusion with dancing and specialty acts

Host Casino and Showroom: Monte Carlo—Lance Burton Theatre

Reservations and Information: (702) 730-7000 or (800) 311-8999

Admission Cost with Taxes: $54.95 balcony seating; $59.95 main-floor seating

Cast Size: 14

Nights of Lowest Attendance: Thursday, Friday

Usual Show Times: 7 and 10 p.m.   *Dark:* Sunday and Monday

Special Comments: No drinks included

Topless: No

Author's Rating: ★★★★

Overall Appeal by Age Group:

Under 21	21–37	38–50	51 and older
★★★★	★★★★	★★★★	★★★★

Duration of Presentation: An hour and a half

Description and Comments In a showroom designed especially for him, Lance Burton stars in an innovative and iconoclastic magic show, one of only two magic production shows in town to escape the curse of redundancy (see *Siegfried & Roy*). Performing in tight-fitting clothing with rolled-up sleeves (nothing can be concealed), Burton displays some extraordinary sleight of hand in a repertoire of illusions that cannot be seen in other showrooms. Augmented by comely assistants, a comedic juggler, and a talented dance troupe, Lance Burton delivers quality entertainment.

Consumer Tips The Lance Burton Theatre is an opulent imitation of a Parisian opera house and is both beautiful and comfortable. Theater seats ensure that no one gets wedged sideways at cramped banquet tables. On the down side, the venue is so large that it's hard to appreciate Burton's exquisite and subtle sleight of hand if you are seated in the boonies. Also, some illusions are difficult to see from the balcony seats. Try to get seats on the main floor close to the stage. Lance Burton tickets can be purchased over the phone or at the Monte Carlo box office up to two months in advance.

Legends in Concert

Type of Show: Celebrity-impersonator and musical production show

Host Casino and Showroom: Imperial Palace—Imperial Theatre

Reservations and Information: (702) 794-3261

Admission Cost with Taxes: $34.50 adults (includes tax, 2 drinks, and tip); $19.50 children (ages 12 and under)

Cast Size: Approximately 20

Nights of Lowest Attendance: Wednesday, Thursday

Usual Show Times: 7:30 and 10:30 p.m.   *Dark:* Sunday

Topless: No

Author's Rating: ★★★★

Overall Appeal by Age Group:

Under 21	21–37	38–50	51 and older
★★★★	★★★★	★★★★	★★★★

Duration of Presentation: An hour and a half

Description and Comments *Legends in Concert* is a musical production show featuring a highly talented cast of impersonators who re-create the stage performances of such celebrities as Elvis, Richie Valens, Prince, Cher, Rod Stewart, the Four Tops, and Gloria Estefan. Impersonators actually sing and/or play their own instruments, so there's no lip-syncing or faking. In addition to the Las Vegas production, *Legends in Concert* also fields a road show. The second show makes possible a continuing exchange of performers between the productions, so that the shows are always changing. In addition to the impersonators, *Legends* features an unusually hot and creative company of dancers, much in the style of TV's Solid Gold Dancers of old. There are no variety acts.

The show is a barn-burner and possibly, minute-for-minute, the fastest-moving show in town. The impersonations are extremely effective, replicating the physical appearances, costumes, mannerisms, and voices of the celebrities with remarkable likeness. While each show features the work of about eight stars, with a roster that ensures something for patrons of every age, certain celebrities (most notably Elvis) are always included. Regardless of the stars impersonated, *Legends in Concert* is fun, happy, and upbeat. It's a show that establishes rapport with the audience—a show that makes you feel good.

Consumer Tips   Admission includes two drinks. Payment must be made at the box office any time prior to the show. Arrive 40 minutes before show time for seating by the maître d'. If you drive to the Imperial Palace and intend to use the self-parking, give yourself a little extra time. Since *Legends* is very popular and almost always plays to a full house on weekends, be sure to make your reservations early.

Melinda

Type of Show: Magic and Illusion

Host Casino and Showroom: Venetian—Showroom at the venetian

Reservations and Information: (702) 948-3007

Admission Cost with Taxes: $38–77

Cast Size: 12

Nights of Lowest Attendance: Sunday and Monday

Usual Show Times: 6:30 and 8:30 p.m., Monday and Friday–Sunday;
    6:30 p.m., Tuesday and Thursday

Topless: No

Author's Rating: ★★★

Overall Appeal by Age Group:

Under 21	21-37	38-50	51 and older
★★★★	★★★ ½	★★★ ½	★★★ ½

Duration of Presentation: An hour and ten minutes

Description and Comments   We reviewed Melinda for almost a decade as she moved from casino to casino before she flew the coop from Las Vegas for a couple of years. She's back with a new show staged in the finest Las Vegas showroom she's ever worked. Her new show is grander (as fits its setting) than those of her past, and is also more PG-13 (no topless dancers), but otherwise the latest production is vintage Melinda. Over the years, Melinda has improved immensely in connecting with her audience and in projecting a sense of professional confidence—no more hesitant stumbling or awkward silences and gaps. Melinda is very much in charge. Melinda's shows have always (well, almost always) been fast paced. So it is with the current edition, except for an unfortunate interruption where the audience is subjected to a video showing Melinda escaping from a box of "deadly snakes" (actually scarlet king snakes and other harmless, venomous snake look-alikes).

The heart of the production, however, is the magic, or more correctly the illusions. Although Melinda doesn't break any new ground, her illusions are solid, and some of her props (a giant industrial drill on which she is impaled comes to mind) almost deserve a show of their own. What's really unique about Melinda, now and in the past, is that she always includes a couple of illusions that are so transparent that the most addled member of the audience can discern immediately how the trick is done. I don't to this day know if this transparency is purposeful or simply a matter of the illusions not being ready for prime time. Either way, it provides an interesting glimpse into the way illusionists perform their craft.

Consumer Tips   Melinda puts on a good show, but it's overpriced. You'll get better illusion and do less damage to your wallet at the Sahara (Steve Wyrick) or the Monte Carlo (Lance Burton). *Siegfried & Roy* charge over $100, but their illusion is merely the centerpiece of an eye-popping production show with a cast of almost 75. Finally, David Copperfield, although expensive, still delivers the most cutting-edge illusion and with the least redundancy.

The Showroom at the Venetian is a stunner, a great venue for both headliners and production shows. Although the box office sells various priced tickets, the line of sight is good from just about every seat. On Sundays and weekdays, when the show plays to less than a full house, ask for the lowest priced ticket. You'll often be upgraded at no extra charge. Drinks are not included but there's table service if you arrive early or a bar where you can fetch your own.

Men Are from Mars, Women Are from Venus

Type of Show: Broadway style musical comedy
Host Casino and Showroom: Flamingo
Reservations and Information: (702) 733-3333
Admission Cost with Taxes: $36, $44, $52

Cast Size: 10 plus musicians

Nights of Lowest Attendance: Sunday and Thursday

Usual Show Times: 7:30 p.m. Monday, Wednesday, Thursday, and Saturday; 7:30 and 10 p.m., Friday; 3 and 7:30 p.m., Sunday

Topless: No

Author's Rating: ★★

Overall Appeal by Age Group:

Under 21	21–37	38–50	51 and older
★★	★★ ½	★★ ½	★★ ½

Duration of Presentation: About an hour and a half (seems longer)

Description and Comments   Men Are from Mars, Women Are from Venus is a musical comedy about male/female relationships. The name of the show is taken from the famous pop psychology, self-help book of the same name by John Gray. Curiously, the book, though serious, is often very humorous. The musical comedy, on the other hand, falls flat in terms of both content and humor. Although the cast is exceptionally talented, they can't save the production from its lame plot, cliché'd humor, and immediately forgettable music. Simply put, this is a production that never gets off the ground. We recommend that you forget the show and read the book.

Consumer Tips   If for some reason you decide to see this show, purchase the least expensive ticket. Chances are you'll get a higher price seat as the maître d' "dresses the showroom," i.e., distributes guests equally around the room to make the theater look full.

Michael Flatley's Lord of the Dance

Type of Show: Celtic music and dance production

Host Casino and Showroom: New York–New York—Broadway Theater

Reservations and Information: (702) 740-6815

Admission Cost with Taxes: $59 Tuesday–Thursday; $68 Friday and Saturday

Cast Size: 44

Nights of Lowest Attendance: Wednesday

Usual Show Times: 7:00 and 10:00 p.m., Tuesday and Wednesday; 9 p.m., Thursday and Friday; 3 and 8 p.m., Saturday   *Dark:* Sunday and Monday

Special Comments: Michael Flatley does not dance.

Topless: No

Author's Rating: Rollicking fun; ★★★★

Overall Appeal by Age Group:

Under 21	21–37	38–50	51 and older
★★★★	★★★★	★★★★	★★★★

Duration of Presentation: An hour and a half

Description and Comments *Lord of the Dance* is a clone of *Riverdance,* the Celtic stepdance production that burst onto the world entertainment scene, astounding audiences with its energy and unerring footwork. Michael Flatley, once the male star of *Riverdance,* left the company and opened *Lord of the Dance* in Dublin in 1996. Since that time the two productions have been fierce competitors.

With its jubilant score, relentless pace, and exacting precision, *Lord of the Dance* is decidedly an upper—an evening's entertainment that leaves you curiously both energized and drained. Though the production operates within a story of good versus evil, and while there's great subtlety and delicacy at various points along the journey, it is when the entire cast of dancers is on stage at once with 80 feet thundering in flawless unison that *Lord of the Dance* realizes its potential. As the tempo builds and the pounding rhythm of shoes on hardwood echoes in your chest, you are drawn into such a spiraling, driving crescendo of energy that it's almost impossible to stay seated.

We like *Lord of the Dance* and think you will too. You don't have to be a ballet, or even a dance, fan to get excited about this production. On the other hand, it's not the typical Las Vegas show: There are no feathered showgirls, magicians, or jugglers. What you get is a mainline dose of Celtic music and dance. Believe us, that's enough.

Consumer Tips If you've seen a live performance of *Riverdance, Lord of the Dance* is essentially more of the same. If you've seen *Riverdance* only on video and liked it, we heartily recommend *Lord of the Dance.* The live production (of either show) has an impact and presence that can only be imagined by watching a video. *Lord of the Dance* sells out most nights, so purchase your tickets by phone with a credit card before leaving home. Try to get seats somewhere in the middle of the theater. The Broadway Theater is well designed, with good sight lines from most any seat, but for *Lord of the Dance,* you want to be at least 20 rows back from the stage.

Midnight Fantasy

Type of Show: Topless dance and comedy revue
Host Casino and Showroom: Luxor—Luxor Live Theater
Reservations and Information: (702) 262-4400
Admission Cost with Taxes: $29.95

Cast Size: Approximately 8

Nights of Lowest Attendance: Wednesday and Thursday

Usual Show Times: 8:30 p.m. (Tuesday, Thursday, Saturday, and Sunday) and 10:30 p.m. (Tuesday–Saturday)   *Dark:* Monday

Topless: Yes

Author's Rating: ★★★

Overall Appeal by Age Group:

Under 21	21–37	38–50	51 and older
—	★★★	★★ ½	★★

Duration of Presentation: An hour and 15 minutes

Descriptions and Comments   A breathy female voiceover starts things up, describing for the audience a sultry "midnight fantasy" of luxurious life in ancient Egypt (the Luxor's theme). So begins this largely incoherent show, which bounces from olden times to a cowgirl hoedown to a male Tina Turner impersonator. After the voiceover relates a particular scenario, dancers and singers come forth to sashay about in costumes appropriate for the scene. There's some half-naked cavorting, of course, but not as much as one might think from the suggestive nature of the show. And despite the panting over the loudspeakers, the dancing is not particularly erotic—it's almost like you're watching a normal, G-rated dance number where some of the performers just forgot their tops. The whole thing has a sort of dorky appeal, and it's pretty fun to watch as long as you're not dead-set on maximum nudity. Interludes between dance routines are filled by a DJ/MC/impressionist guy (who dragoons an audience member for a forced Elvis impression) and a standard-Vegas-issue foulmouthed comic.

Consumer Tips   Tickets for Midnight Fantasy must be purchased or picked up at the box office on the second floor of the Luxor, not at the one off the main casino floor. The large size of the stadium-style theater means there are lots of seats, but the higher rows can make good views of the distant stage problematic. The show is general admission, so just arrive a little early to insure a good seat.

The Rat Pack Is Back

Type of Show: Celebrity Impersonator

Host Casino and Showroom: Sahara—Congo Room

Reservations and Information: (702) 737-2515

Admission Cost with Taxes: $41

Cast Size: 20 including musicians

Nights of Lowest Attendance: Wednesday and Thursday

Usual Show Times: 7:30 and 10 p.m., Tuesday and Saturday; 8 p.m., Wednesday, Thursday, Friday, and Sunday

Topless: No

Author's Rating: ★★★★

Overall Appeal By Age Group:

Under 21	21-37	38-50	51 and older
★★ ½	★★★ ½	★★★★	★★★★½

Duration of Presentation: One hour and 20 minutes

Description and Comments　　The heart and soul of the original Rat Pack were crooners Frank Sinatra, Dean Martin, and Sammy Davis Jr., and comedian Joey Bishop. They all worked the Las Vegas showrooms of the 1960s, sometimes dropping in on each other's show and sometimes working together. Their late night antics at the old Sands, particularly, are among the richest of Las Vegas showroom legends.

The *Rat Pack Is Back* recreates a night when the acerbic Bishop and hard drinking Martin team up with Davis and Sinatra. Backed by a piano, bass, and drums trio, along with, get this, a 12-piece horn section, four talented impersonators take you back to a night at the Copa Room in 1963. The impersonations are riveting, almost spooky. Each impersonator not only nails his character's voice, singing style, and body language, but also bears a remarkable physical resemblance to the original. The casual interplay among the four effectively transports you back to the 1960s, and what you see is just how it was. The humor was racist, sexist, and politically incorrect, the showroom packed and smoky, and the music, well… drop dead brilliant.

As the show concludes, you inwardly hope they'll forget to introduce the actors playing the Rat Pack four. The recollection, the fantasy, is so complete that you desperately want to believe that it's really Frank, Dean, Joey, and Sammy up there. You're like the child at Disneyland who just knows that it's really Mickey he's meeting. When the impersonators are identified, as of course they are, it hurts a little.

Consumer Tips　　The *Rat Pack Is Back* is one of the few true bargains in the Las Vegas galaxy of shows. It's fitting that the show plays in the Congo Room, one of the town's older showrooms, and one just the right size to facilitate the necessary intimacy between audience and performers. Smoking is allowed, however, and guests seated close to the stage are really crammed in. Seats are assigned by the maître d', but for a $5 tip you can score just about any seat not reserved for the casino's high rollers. Ask for something about midway back. Obviously, *The Rat Pack Is Back* rates highest with folks

old enough to remember the originals. It's also a compelling show for anyone curious about the less polished, more informal Las Vegas of the early
1960s when lounge acts ruled.

Scintas

Type of Show: Musical and comedy review

Host Casino and Showroom: Rio—Copacabana Showroom

Reservations and Information: (702) 252-7776 or (800) PLAY-RIO

Admission Cost with Taxes: $38.50

Cast Size: 4

Nights of Lowest Attendance: Monday, Tuesday

Usual Show Times: Monday, Tuesday, Friday, and Sunday at 8 p.m., Saturday at 6 p.m. and 8:30 p.m., dark on Wednesday and Thursday

Topless: No

Author's Rating: ★★★

Overall Appeal by Age Group

Under 21	21–37	38–50	51 and older
★★	★★★	★★★ ½	★★★ ½

Duration of Presentation: An hour and a half

Description and Comments: Though the Scintas are also billed as a comedy
troupe, they shine most when playing music. With a heavy emphasis on
God and patriotism, this show would be more at home in Branson, Missouri.

The cast of Scintas includes siblings Frankie, Joe, and Chrissi Scinta.
Frankie Scinta provides much of the comedy and plays a variety of instruments, including keyboards. But his passion is the banjo. Joe Scinta is a
stereotypically dry bass player and sometime comedian. Baby sister Chrissi
sings a few numbers throughout the show, but isn't a constant stage presence. Italian pride notwithstanding, the group's drummer is handsome
Irishman Peter O'Donnell.

The Scintas enjoy performing comedy, but the comedy can be trite; comedy routines include Frankie Scinta covering Tom Jones songs with socks
stuffed down his pants. Some of the comedy is mildly racist and sexist—
undertones which might have played well 20 years ago, but now seem
unnecessary, not to mention odd juxtaposed with all of the God and Country stuff.

On the other hand, music is delivered with a great deal of warmth and
skill. The set list includes typical Las Vegas fare such as Dean Martin and
Elvis covers. But the Scintas also cover Billy Joel and Joe Cocker. Many

songs are performed as parts of seamless medleys. With a versatile and pleasant voice, Frankie Scinta does most of the singing. Sister Chrissi sings louder and longer than her brothers, delivering a patriotic medley as well as an emotional *I Will Always Love You* (penned by Dolly Parton and made famous by Whitney Houston).

Consumer Tips: The Copacabana Showroom is one of the best designed and most comfortable showrooms in Las Vegas. Though some seats are a bit distant, the line of site is uniformly excellent and the sound system is awesome. A cocktail waitress will visit your booth or table and there is a small snack kiosk near the entrance to the showroom. Less than $40, Scintas tickets are reasonably priced even though they don't include drinks or tips.

Second City

Type of Show: Sketch Comedy
Host Casino and Showroom: Flamingo—Bugsy's Celebrity Theatre
Reservations and Information: (702) 733-3333
Admission Cost with Taxes: $27.50
Cast Size: 5
Nights of Lowest Attendance: Monday, Tuesday
Usual Show Times: 8 and 10:30 p.m. nightly
Topless: No
Author's Rating: ★★★★
Overall Appeal by Age Group:

Under 21	21–37	38–50	51 and older
★★★ ½	★★★★	★★★★	★★★★

Duration of Presentation: One hour and 15 minutes

Description and Comments   *Second City* is a team of improvisational comedians, one of several franchised groups of comics playing around the country under the same name. The difference between an improvisational group and the stand-up comedians that work the Las Vegas comedy clubs is that the improv groups specialize in skits and songs as opposed to monologues. *Second City* is an amazingly talented lot individually and complement and balance each other well as a team. They do a crack job on the improvisational stuff, taking their cues from audience suggestions, but it's their set pieces that really demonstrate their genius.

Consumer Tips   Bugsy's Celebrity Theater is really an enclosed lounge, small and intimate, perfect for acts like *Second City*. Seating is by the maître d'. Because there really aren't any bad seats, tipping the maître d' is a waste of money unless you want to be right next to the stage. Sitting next to the stage at a comedy venue, however, is always risky because you might suddenly find yourself part of the show.

Siegfried & Roy

Type of Show: Magic and illusion show with choreography and great spectacle

Host Casino and Showroom: Mirage—Siegfried & Roy Theatre

Reservations and Information: (702) 792-7777 or (800) 456-4564

Admission Cost with Taxes: $100.50 (includes 2 drinks and gratuity)

Cast Size: Approximately 88

Nights of Lowest Attendance: Sunday, Monday

Usual Show Times: 7:30 and 11 p.m., Tuesday, Friday, Saturday; 7:30 p.m., Sunday and Monday   *Dark:* Wednesday and Thursday

Special Comments: All gratuities included in admission price

Topless: No

Author's Rating: ★★★★

Overall Appeal by Age Group:

Under 21	21–37	38–50	51 and older
★★★★★	★★★★★	★★★★★	★★★★★

Duration of Presentation: An hour and 40 minutes

Description and Comments   This show revolutionized Las Vegas production shows, paving the way for *Cirque du Soleil's Mystere, EFX!, and "O"*. Staged in a modern 1,500-person theater with good visibility from all seats, *Siegfried & Roy* delivers a great deal more than magic and illusion. With a cast of approximately 75, extraordinary costuming, and special effects comparable to those in *EFX!*, this Kenneth Feld production established new definitions for spectacle, impact, and energy.

A fantasy depicting archetypal good and evil provides story-line continuity to the varied illusions of *Siegfried & Roy.* The illusions involve (among other things) white tigers, elephants, and even mechanical dragons. Most illusions are incorporated into elaborate productions, with choreography and often an original score augmenting the skill of the illusionists. At the end of the show the fantasy is discarded to provide a glimpse of Siegfried and Roy as individuals and to showcase their famous white tigers. The production maintains continuity, pace, and focus throughout. Unlike most production shows, this one has no variety acts, no intrusions on the central theme.

The sets and special effects in this show are beyond belief, even overwhelming, with their rich profusion of color, shape, and image. But the presentation is still tasteful and sophisticated.

If there is a problem with *Siegfried & Roy,* it is the same problem that plagues most Las Vegas magic-illusion shows: redundancy. How many variations of making something in a box disappear can performers parade before a single audience without losing their impact? Does it really matter that the boxes and animals keep getting larger? Isn't it still the same illusion?

Siegfried & Roy is visually impressive. But are we drawn in and truly delighted or are we simply staggered by its size and scope? For most of us, it's a bit of both.

We recommend *Siegfried & Roy* as a landmark Las Vegas production show, as an example of what can be accomplished when a talented producer with extensive resources and advanced technology pulls out all the stops. Regardless of how you feel about the substance of the illusions, you will have witnessed in *Siegfried & Roy* a vision that established a new standard for Las Vegas production shows.

People in Las Vegas are peculiar about money. The same man who drops $500 in an hour at the craps table will canvas the entire city for the best $2 breakfast. The big question concerning *Siegfried & Roy* is whether the show is worth the hefty $100 admission. Because this show has moved its genre ahead a quantum leap, it deserves attention. *Mystere* (Treasure Island) and *EFX!* (MGM Grand), however, deliver comparable spectacle for less money, respectively, while *Lance Burton* and *David Copperfield* offer better illusion at half the price. When *Siegfried & Roy* was the only super-show in town (1992), it was easier to swallow the big price tag (then $67). But now, the quality of the competition suggests that *Siegfried & Roy* is significantly overpriced.

Consumer Tips   Even at $100 a pop in a theater with 1,500 seats, *Siegfried & Roy* sells out almost every night. Tickets are available over the phone and at the Mirage box office one week in advance. Though reserved seats are issued by computer, patrons can, to a limited degree, specify their seating preferences.

The best way to see *Siegfried & Roy* on short notice with the least hassle is to set your sights for the late show on a Sunday, Monday, or Tuesday. Try the box office between 2:30 and 5 p.m. On many days advance ticket buyers will not buy out both shows, and some same-day seats will be available. Obviously you will not have first choice of seats, but there really are no bad seats in this well-designed theater.

A second, but riskier, same-day strategy is to try the box office during the half hour before show time. With 1,500 seats it is almost invariable that there will be a small (sometimes very small) number of cancellations and no-shows. Additionally, the Siegfried & Roy Theatre, like all Las Vegas showrooms, reserves a number of seats for casino high rollers. Sometimes, and always at the last minute, some of these seats may be made available to paying guests.

Since all seats are reserved, you do not have to tip the maître d' or the captains. You also do not have to arrive an hour in advance. The showroom is well staffed, and guests are ushered to their assigned seats efficiently and usually without any waiting. We recommend entering the theater 25–30 minutes before show time. This will allow you plenty of time to get settled in and order the two drinks per person included in your admission. If you drive to the Mirage and use the self-parking, give yourself an extra 15 minutes for the long hike in from the parking lot.

If you are staying at the Mirage, you can call the box office from your room and reserve tickets. You may have the tickets charged to your hotel bill. Tickets for hotel guests can be picked up and paid for at the guest service window to the right of the box office at the theater entrance. If you fail to pick up your tickets, you will still be charged.

If you really enjoy magic and illusion but are unwilling to put up with the expense and hassle of buying a ticket to *Siegfried & Roy*, try *Lance Burton*. Though he lacks the elaborate production component of *Siegfried & Roy*, Burton performs comparable, if not superior, illusions, and with a great deal less redundancy.

Skintight

Type of Show: Topless dance show

Host Casino and Showroom: Harrah's—Harrah's Showroom

Reservations and Information: (702) 369-5111

Admission Cost with Taxes: $42

Cast Size: Approximately 16

Nights of Lowest Attendance: Sunday, Tuesday

Usual Show Times: 7:30 p.m. (Wednesday), 10:30 p.m. (Sunday, Monday, Tuesday, Friday), and midnight (Saturday)   *Dark:* Thursday

Special Comments: This is the only topless show permitting ages 18 and up, as opposed to ages 21 and up.

Topless: Yes

Author's Rating: ★★★ ½

Overall Appeal by Age Group:

Under 21	21–37	38–50	51 and older
★★★★*	★★★ ½	★★★	★★

* Under 18 not permitted

Duration and Presentation: An hour and a half

Descriptions and Comments An elaborately staged and choreographed production, *Skintight* gives the Riviera's *Crazy Girls* a run for its money as the best casino-based girlie show in Las Vegas. Still, unlike the largely unselfconscious *Crazy Girls*, *Skintight* has aspirations to putting on a bitchin' dance party. To that end, there's lots of pounding rock-and-pop dance numbers which are probably the aged producers' idea of what the kids on MTV are up to these days. Skin is frequently visible and widespread among the buff female and male cast, though it's still something of an afterthought even amid all the crotch-grabbing and pelvic grinds. The dancing and singing are nonetheless quite accomplished, helmed as they are by a talented vocalist and a lithe choreographer. In addition, extremely pneumatic former Playboy Playmate Cynthia Brimhall makes occasional appearances to sing a little or heckle the crowd. The most genuinely erotic and sensual moments, however, involve members of audience—the lucky goggle-eyed few dragged onstage for lap dances or an intimate bit of crooning from Brimhall herself.

Consumer Tips Sitting near the center aisle seems to increase one's chances of being selected for onstage antics. Discount coupons are available in the Harrah's casino and in visitor magazines.

Splash

Type of Show: Musical variety aquacade show
Host Casino and Showroom: Riviera—Versailles Theater
Reservations and Information: (702) 794-9301 or (800) 634-3420
Admission Cost with Taxes: $58 VIP, $47 general
Cast Size: Approximately 50
Nights of Lowest Attendance: Sunday, Tuesday, Wednesday
Usual Show Times: Daily, 7:30 and 10:30 p.m.
Special Comments: No drinks included
Topless: Late show only
Author's Rating: ★★★
Overall Appeal by Age Group:

Under 21	21–37	38–50	51 and older
★★★	★★★ ½	★★★ ½	★★★

Duration of Presentation: An hour and a half

Description and Comments When *Splash* first rolled into Las Vegas in 1985, it was like a peppy, young, jet-ski revue buzzing among ponderous cruise-ship extravaganzas. Though the ride was a bit bumpy—the show alternated frenetic production numbers with bizarre variety acts and you walked away with a mild case of whiplash—*Splash* managed to stay afloat for nearly ten years on rock and roll, great dancing, and pure exuberance. Meanwhile, however, a new wave of contemporary entertainment (*Siegfried & Roy, Mystere, "O,"* and *EFX!,* to name four) churned into town and left *Splash* bobbing in the wake.

The anticipation starts building as soon as you walk into the showroom, which is incorporated into the "supersubmarine" set, with ceiling misters, ushers and usherettes in nautical costumes, and a horseshoe-shaped runway with a metal-mesh grill, through which fountains and veritable walls of water are sure to drain.

The show is held together by a thin thread: the super-submarine visits the North Pole, the Bermuda Triangle, and Atlantis. On the way, though, it pauses at so many ports—four rip-roaring production numbers and a good dozen gimmicks and variety acts—that you wonder if anyone is steering the thing. The title and credits, to begin with, are displayed in 3-D. And then the performers come on like at a circus: an ice-skating duo, the world's only "prerecorded" comic (all body shtick, with the comedian riffing off of laser images, song snippets, and show sound bites), interactive laser tag with the VIP section of the audience, motorcycle daredevils, a juggling duo, and the water ballet in *Splash's* trademark 20,000-gallon tank.

One performance stands out: a break dancing and gangsta segment by the four Dragon Masters, who spin on every appendage (except one) and do some eye-popping acrobatics.

When it's all over, a few in the audience look a little disoriented, like they somehow missed the boat, and others seem to be suffering from culture shock, like they'll never use that travel agent again. But for most people, this is exactly the kind of entertainment they expect out of a Las Vegas extravaganza.

Consumer Tips   All seats are reserved and assigned in the order in which the reservations are received; the earlier you buy, the better your seats will be. Tickets may be purchased up to three weeks in advance over the phone or in person at the box office. Tickets may be picked up at the box office prior to the show. The Versailles Theater has been remodeled, and though it's still big and the back seats are as far away as ever, the VIP section has replaced the dreaded banquet tables (except for one row of four-seaters directly behind the VIPs)—in short, everyone in the audience has an unobstructed view.

Splash is four-walled (meaning the producer gets the "gate" or proceeds from the ticket sales, and leases the showroom from the hotel), and it seems the producer and the hotel weren't able to get together over the drink situation. Glassware is not allowed in the showroom. You must carry in your own fluid refreshments in plastic cups. There's a bar just outside the theater entrance that will provide you with the complimentary drink. Meal deals at the Riviera's Mardi Gras Food Court are often bundled with the show. See local visitor magazines for money-saving coupons.

Steve Wyrick, World-Class Magician

Type of Show: Magic and illusion production show

Host Casino and Showroom: Sahara—Sahara Theatre

Reservations and Information: (702) 737-2515 after 4:30 p.m. PST

Admission Cost with Taxes: $41

Cast Size: Approximately 12

Nights of Lowest Attendance: Sunday, Thursday

Usual Show Times: 7:30 and 10:30 p.m.   *Dark:* Tuesday

Special Comments: Top magic show for the ticket price

Topless: No

Author's Rating: ★★★ ½

Overall Appeal by Age Group:

Under 21	21–37	38–50	51 and older
★★★ ½	★★★ ½	★★★ ½	★★★ ½

Duration of Presentation: An hour and 15 minutes

Description and Comments   *Steve Wyrick, World-Class Magician* is the Las Vegas show scene's version of "we try harder." With four or five magic-themed production shows playing in town at any given time, it takes a fair amount of creativity to be different. Steve Wyrick digs deep and delivers some great illusion and sleight of hand that you won't see in other show-rooms. While his style and presentation, particularly his ability to connect with his audience, are reminiscent of Lance Burton, each illusion has a special twist that makes it unique. The showroom is large, maybe too large, for Wyrick's sleight of hand to be effective, but plenty big enough for Wyrick to pull off a couple of *Siegfried & Roy*–scale eyepoppers. If you go for the magic you won't be disappointed. Expect lots of flash and thunder—poly-technics, roaring engines, and a pounding soundtrack.

Consumer Tips   With a new show in a new, 875-seat theater, Steve Wyrick is able for the first time to offer a well-rounded production show, a show that goes beyond his more-than-capable illusion. Like Lance Burton, Steve Wyrick has a few things to learn about playing a large showroom, but you can't beat his show for innovation or for value. Compared to *Lance Burton* and *Siegfried & Roy*, Wyrick is a bargain at $41.

Storm

Type of Show: Special effects show set to Latin music
Host Casino and Showroom: Mandalay Bay–Storm Theatre
Reservations and Information: (702) 632-7580 or (877) 632-7400
Admission Cost with Taxes: $60.50–71.50
Cast Size: 50
Nights of Lowest Attendance: Sunday, Thursday
Usual Show Times: 7:30 p.m., Sunday, Monday, Wednesday, Thursday, and Saturday; 10:30 p.m., Wednesday, Friday, and Saturday *Dark:* Tuesday
Topless: No
Author's Rating: ★★½
Overall Appeal by Age Group:

Under 21	21–37	38–50	51 and older
★★★★*	★★★½	★★½	★★

   *Under 10 years old not admitted

Duration of Presentation: An hour and a half

Description and Comments   A hybrid of elements taken from a variety of other younger-skewing shows (like Cirque du Soliel and De La Guarda), Storm nearly blew itself out before its 2001 opening. After some rethinking and re-engineering, it has emerged as the newest gargantuan effects show on the Strip. Storm is ostensibly a show about the interaction of four natural forces—Fire, Ice, Wind, and Earth—as represented by the four principal actors/dancers/singers and their color-coordinated entourages. Prepare to disengage your brain completely: there's a frivolous theme of human passions, or emotions, or elements, or … hey, why aren't you DANCING? There's plenty of that, as the huge cast swings, swoops, and sashays around the stage to the tune of various Latin-themed cover songs. There's no doubt that it's a dazzling, tightly-run show, with plenty of flash. However, it's also a pretty incoherent mishmash of repeated climaxes and showstopping crescendos.

Storm is cheaper than either Cirque du Soliel show, is roughly equal in price to EFX! and Blue Man Group, and is more expensive than De La Guarda. However, other than the newness of its production and technology, it falls behind all those shows in terms of overall quality.

Consumer Tips   This show is one of the few where purchasing the VIP seats can make a dramatic difference in your experience. Upper auditorium seats are considerably removed from the stage and main action of the show. Additionally, performers move in among (and are sometimes suspended above) the lower auditorium seats, creating quite a spectacle for those down below. Props, effects, and other nearby technical gadgets also make lower-auditorium guests feel more included in the production.

Though Storm is not topless, note that suggestive elements, skimpy costumes, and sensual dancing mean that children under 10 years old are not admitted.

Takin' it Uptown Starring Clint Holmes

Type of Show: Live concert by Clint Holmes
Host Casino and Showroom: Harrah's—Harrah's Main Showroom
Reservations and Information: (702) 369-5111 or (800) 392-9002
Admission Cost with Taxes: $50
Cast Size: 14
Nights of Lowest Attendance: Monday, Tuesday
Usual Show Times: 7:30 p.m., Monday–Wednesday and Friday; 10 p.m.,
    Thursday and Saturday   *Dark:* Sunday
Topless: No
Author's Rating: ★★★ ½
Overall Appeal by Age Group:

Under 21	21–37	38–50	51 and older
★★ ½	★★★ ½	★★★★	★★★ ½

Duration of Presentation: An hour and a half

Description and Comments   *Takin' it Uptown Starring Clint Holmes* feels like an intimate concert performed by a seasoned jazz ensemble. There are no specialty acts, magicians, or contortionists, just a group of musicians giving it their all. Seating less than 600 people, Harrah's showroom is the perfect venue for the warm vocals of Clint Holmes. The locals seem to have embraced Holmes—he was recently voted "Best Singer in Las Vegas" according to the *Las Vegas Review-Journal,* the city's largest newspaper. Locals and tourists alike will appreciate this show, which epitomizes the trend towards family-friendly entertainment on the strip. You really could bring your children to this show and feel good about it, even if the sophisticated set-list will be most appreciated by those in their 40s and 50s.

You'll hear well-known jazz and blues standards, as well as pop favorites by Elton John, Jackson Browne, and others. The eclectic musical selection even includes a little samba. Holmes is complemented by an accomplished female vocalist, and the band, led by Bill Fayne, is at times fantastic, especially when the five-piece horn section struts it's stuff. The climax of the show is a jazz, rock, and pop medley-tribute to great singer-songwriters. Think great horns. Think Stevie Wonder.

Weaving heartfelt autobiographical storytelling into his show, Holmes graciously connects with the audience. His mother was a British opera singer and his father was an African American jazz musician. Holmes shares some thoughts on the challenge of his biracial identity and the blessing of growing up with music in his home. Pretty deep stuff for a Las Vegas production show.

Consumer Tips Harrah's Main Showroom has some booths and some free-standing chairs. The chairs are horribly uncomfortable, so ask for a booth. Drinks are available at a bar inside the showroom and the restrooms are clean and easy to access. At $50 per person, Clint Holmes tickets are reasonably priced

Tournament of Kings

Type of Show: Jousting and medieval pageant
Host Casino and Showroom: Excalibur—King Arthur's Arena
Reservations and Information: (702) 597-7600
Admission Cost with Taxes: $44, includes dinner
Cast Size: 35 (with 38 horses)
Nights of Lowest Attendance: Monday and Tuesday
Usual Show Times: 6 and 8:30 p.m.
Topless: No
Author's Rating: ★★★
Overall Appeal by Age Group:

Under 21	21–37	38–50	51 and older
★★★★	★★★★	★★★★	★★★★

Duration of Presentation: An hour and a half

Description and Comments *Tournament of Kings* is a retooled version of *King Arthur's Tournament,* which logged 6,000 performances (from Excalibur's opening night in June 1990 till late 1998). It's basically the same show, with a slightly different plot twist. If you saw one, the other will come as no surprise.

The idea is that Arthur summons the kings of eight European countries to a sporting competition in honor of his son Christopher. Guests view the arena from dinner tables divided into sections; a king is designated to represent each section in the competition. Ladies-in-waiting and various court attendants double as cheerleaders, doing their best to whip the audience into a frenzy of cheering for their section's king. The audience, which doesn't require much encouragement, responds by hooting, "huzzarring," and pounding on the dinner tables. Watch your drinks—all the pounding can knock them over.

Soup is served to the strains of the opening march. The kings enter on horseback. Precisely when the King of Hungary is introduced, dinner arrives (big Cornish hen, small twice-baked potato, bush of broccoli, dinner roll, and dessert turnover). The kings engage in contests with flags, dummy heads, javelins, swords, and maces and shields and joust a while, too. The horse work, fighting, and especially the jousting are exciting, and the music (by a three-man band) and sound effects are well executed.

Right on cue, Mordred the Evil One crashes the party, accompanied by his Dragon Enforcers. Arthur is mortally slain and all the kings are knocked out, leaving Christopher to battle the forces of evil and emerge—surprise!—victorious in the end.

Except that . . . it's not over. The coronation is the culmination, after some acrobatics and human-tower stunts from a specialty act. Finally, the handsome new king goes out in a (literal) blaze of glory. It's a bit anticlimactic and bogged down, which helps hurry you out so the crew can quickly set up for the second show or clean up and go home.

Consumer Tips　One of the few Las Vegas shows suitable for the whole family, and one of the fewer dinner shows, *Tournament of Kings* enjoys great popularity and often plays to a full house. Reserved seats can be purchased with a credit card up to six days in advance by calling the number listed above (there's an extra $2 charge if you order by phone). Or you can show up at the Excalibur box office, which opens at 8 a.m., up to six days ahead.

No matter where you sit, you're close to the action—and the dust and stage smoke. The air-conditioning system is steroidal, so you might consider bringing a wrap. Seating is reserved, so you can walk in at the last minute and don't have to tip any greeters or seaters.

Dinner is served without utensils and eaten with the hands, so you might want to wash up beforehand. Eating a big meal is a bit awkward with the show going on and all the cheering duties, so you might consider bringing some aluminum foil and a bag to take out the leftover bird. Beverage is limited to soda with dinner, but the food server will bring you water, and a cocktail waitress will bring you anything else. Service is adequate; no one tips, so you'll be a hero if you do.

Comedy Clubs

There is a lot of stand-up comedy in Las Vegas, and several of the large production shows feature comedians as specialty acts. In addition, there is usually at least one comedy headliner playing in town. Big names who regularly play Las Vegas include Bill Cosby, Jerry Seinfeld, Rodney Dangerfield, the Smothers Brothers, Joan Rivers, Andrew Dice Clay, George Carlin, Yakov Smirnoff, Don Rickles, and Rich Little. Finally, there are the comedy clubs.

A comedy club is usually a smaller showroom with a simple stage and two to five stand-up comics. In most of the Las Vegas comedy showrooms, a new show with different comedians rotates in each week. There are four bona fide Las Vegas comedy clubs:

Harrah's	*The Improv at Harrah's*
Riviera	*Comedy Club*
Tropicana	*Comedy Stop*
Excalibur	*Catch a Rising Star*

The comedy clubs, unlike the production showrooms, are never dark. There are two shows each night, seven days a week (except at the Riviera, where there are three performances nightly). The humor at the comedy clubs, as well as the audience, tends to be young and irreverent. A favorite and affordable entertainment for locals as well as for tourists, comedy clubs enjoy great popularity in Las Vegas.

The comedy club format is simple and straightforward. Comedians perform sequentially, and what you get depends on who is performing. The range of humor runs from slapstick to obscene to ethnic to topical to just about anything. Some comics are better than others, but all of the talent is solid and professional. There is no way to predict which club will have the best show in a given week. In fact, there may not be a "best" show, since response to comedy is a matter of individual sense of humor.

Comedy Stop

Type of Show: Stand-up comedy
Host Casino and Showroom: Tropicana—Comedy Stop Showroom
Reservations and Information: (702) 739-2714
Admission Cost with Taxes: $17.50 includes 2 drinks and gratuity
Cast Size: Usually 3 comedians
Nights of Lowest Attendance: Monday–Wednesday
Usual Show Times: 8 p.m. (non-smoking) and 10:30 p.m. (smoking)
Special Comments: Admission includes 2 drinks
Topless: No
Duration of Presentation: An hour and a half

Description and Comments To reach the Comedy Stop Showroom take the elevator (between the main casino and the shopping arcade) up one floor. The 400-person showroom is rectangular, with the stage on the long side. All seating is at banquet tables. Tickets may be purchased up to two weeks in advance by phone with a credit card, or admission can be prepaid at the Comedy Stop guest desk near the showroom entrance. After being seated, patrons trade their ticket stubs at a self-service bar for two drinks. If you use the Trop's self-parking lot, take an extra ten minutes to get to the showroom.

An Evening at the Improv

Type of Show: Stand-up comedy

Host Casino and Showroom: Harrah's—The Improv

Reservations and Information: (702) 369-5111

Admission Cost with Taxes: $27.45

Cast Size: 3–4 comedians

Nights of Lowest Attendance: Wednesday, Thursday

Usual Show Times: 8 and 10 p.m.   *Dark:* Monday

Topless: No

Description and Comments   Drinks are not included, but there is a self-serve cash bar. The showroom is on the second floor at the top of the escalator from the main casino. Reserved seats may be purchased by phone or in person up to 30 days in advance.

Riviera Comedy Club

Type of Show: Stand-up comedy

Host Casino and Showroom: Riviera—Mardi Gras Showrooms, second floor

Reservations and Information: (702) 794-9433

Admission Cost with Taxes: $21.95 general admission; $38.45 VIP (includes tax, tip, and 2 drinks); weekend late-night shows of more risqué "Extreme Comedy" are $16.50 and $24.75

Cast Size: Approximately 4

Nights of Lowest Attendance: Sunday–Wednesday

Usual Show Times: 8 and 10 p.m.; also Friday and Saturday, 11:45 p.m. (sometimes cancelled)

Topless: No

Description and Comments   Three shows—*Riviera Comedy Club, Crazy Girls,* and *La Cage*—are staged on the second and third floors above the Riviera casino in what are called the Mardi Gras Showrooms. In addition, the production show *Splash* plays off of the main casino in the Versailles Theater. It is not possible to schedule different shows back to back unless there is a minimum of an hour and a half between performances. Show tickets can also be purchased as a package with the Riviera's buffet. The food with the show-dinner combo is a good deal for the money but is not exactly a culinary breakthrough. The buffet is fast and convenient, however, and there is usually plenty of time to eat between shows.

Tickets for the *Comedy Club* may be purchased 21 days in advance at the Riviera box office located in the front center of the casino or by phone with a credit card. Seating is by the maître d'. There is no table service. After you are seated, proceed to the bar and turn in your ticket stub for drinks. Drinks are included even with the dinner combos.

Catch a Rising Star

Type of Show: Stand-up comedy

Host Casino and Showroom: Excalibur—Catch A Rising Star Showroom

Reservations and Information: (702) 597-7600

Admission Cost with Taxes: $17

Cast Size: Usually 2

Nights of Lowest Attendance: Sunday, Tuesday

Usual Show Times: 7:30 and 10 p.m. nightly

Topless: No

Duration of Presentation: About one hour

Description and Comments   Situated in a space previously occupied by a restaurant in the Medieval Village on the floor above the casino, Catch a Rising Star can accommodate almost 350 people. There are usually only two comedians, but each perform for 40–45 minutes.

Consumer Tips: Comics rotate in and out each week. Because the showroom is too large for a comedy club, you should arrive early on weekends to get a good seat. On weekdays, also due to the showroom size, Catch a Rising Star is a good bet if you decide at the last minute that you'd like to take in a show.

Las Vegas Nightlife

When it comes to nightspots, visitors and locals tend to go in different directions. With the exception of patronizing the comedy clubs, locals stay away from the Strip; visitors, conversely, almost never leave it. Both groups are missing out on some great nightlife.

Happily, lounges and clubs all over town are friendly and open, welcoming anyone who walks through the door. Visitors can feel comfortable in places primarily frequented by locals and vice versa. This kind of acceptance allows for a wide range of choices when it comes to nightlife.

Since you don't have to worry about feeling unwanted or out of place, you can select your nighttime entertainment on the basis of personal taste. Listed alphabetically below are profiles of the better nightspots in town.

Celebrity headliner shows, production shows, and comedy clubs are detailed in the preceding section. Striptease shows (for men and women) are also described in the following section, "Las Vegas below the Belt." Microbreweries also offer a fine choice for an evening of entertainment. Check out "The Best Brewpubs" section in Part Six, "Dining and Restaurants."

BABY'S

Dance
Who Goes There: 21–29; college students

4455 Paradise Rd. (Hard Rock Hotel); (702) 693-5000
Strip Zone 1

Hours: 11 p.m.–4 a.m., Thursday, Friday, and Saturday
Cover: Ladies, free; men, $10 Thursday, $25 Friday and Saturday
Minimum: None
Mixed drinks: $6+

Wine: $5–7
Beer: $4
Dress: Casual to sexy (no baggy, ripped, or torn jeans, or questionable attire)
Specials: Advertised
Food available: In casino

What goes on: After the last performance, The Joint showroom changes its attitude and caters to "Baby's." Male and female go-go dancers gyrate on stage as the dance floor fills with a young, hip crowd. The deejay deftly plays an eclectic mix of retro, funk, and pop that the crowd loves. The focus is on music, dancing, new friends, and fun. Each Thursday Baby's flies in a different international DJ.

Setting & atmosphere: A deejay booth adorned with the Hard Rock's blazing phoenix emblem highlights the stage. The lighting system vibrantly colors the black room, and the two bars jam with business. High tables are scattered near the entrance, with tables and chairs closer to the dance floor.

If you go: Use valet or take a cab because parking at the Hard Rock can be limited on busy nights. The Hard Rock's main bar is also a happenin' place to meet new friends and watch the casino action.

THE BEACH

Dance music of the 1970s, 1980s, and 1990s
Who Goes There: 21–40+; locals, visitors, conventioneers (cosmopolitan mix)

365 Convention Center (corner of Paradise and Convention Center,
across from the Convention Center); (702) 731-1925
Strip Zone 1

Hours: Varies according to entertainment. Sports bar, open 24
hours; dance bar open 10 p.m.–4
a.m., Sunday–Thursday; and until
6 a.m. Friday and Saturday
Cover: Varies; $5 weekdays; usually
$10 for out-of-state guests on
weekends; ladies are never charged.
Minimum: None
Mixed drinks: $4 and up

Beer: $4 and up
Dress: Very specific and strict (call
for restrictions)
Specials: Friday is Hurricane Beach
party; Thursday is Aquadance; call
for concert information; ladies
night Sunday, Monday, and
Wednesday
Food available: Lunch only

What goes on: These beach lovers don't miss the sand or the surf because
all the action is indoors. On the main floor, singles, couples, and new friends
alike dance, drink, eat, and laugh the night away in this "local's favorite"
party club. The fun is so contagious that even the bartenders and cocktail
waitresses join in the dancing. From the second-floor sports bar, patrons
watch games on over 60 TVs (including 5 big screens); play slots, video
poker, or pool; and view the action on the main floor. The Beach is an unpretentious and fun-loving spot that radiates positive energy and vibes.

Setting & atmosphere: Neon beer lights, palm fronds, coconuts, surf-
boards, and brightly painted murals give the club a beach flavor without
adding salt or sand. The wood walls offer excellent acoustics for live performances and the deejay's music. The main floor has five bars, high-table seating, and a dance area. Adjacent to the upstairs sports bar is a room available
for private parties or extra party space. ATM machines are on each floor.

If you go: Long lines begin at 9 p.m. and continue well past 2 a.m. on
weekends. Also, please note that the four-story garage is reserved for valet
on weekends, so use the Convention Center parking lot across the street.
Plan to arrive very early or take a cab. Smoke can be heavy in some corners
of the club. Women on their own can expect to find company. Call ahead
for special events information.

CLUB PARADISE

Upscale topless bar
Who Goes There: Men 21–65; professionals and conventioneers

4416 Paradise Rd.; (702) 734-7990
Strip Zone 1

Hours: Monday–Friday, 4 p.m.–
  6 a.m.; Saturday and Sunday,
  6 p.m.–6 a.m.
Cover: $10
Minimum: None
Mixed drinks: $6.25 and up
Wine: $6 and up
Beer: $5.25 and up
Dress: Casual to dressy
Specials: None
Food available: Appetizer menu and
  flambé/gourmet dining in the VIP
  room

What goes on: Club Paradise is a very plush, upscale topless bar featuring more than 50 dancers in a setting designed to make executives feel at ease. Featured dancers perform on an elevated stage, while others dance at patrons' tables. A showgirl dance revue with taped music provides a nightly interlude. There is a special VIP section that has its own small dance stage. To sit in the VIP section you must commit to purchasing a minimum of $200 in drinks per table during the course of the evening, in addition to the cover charge.

Setting & atmosphere: The club is tastefully decorated with upholstered armchairs, dark carpet, erotic wall art, and elegant fixtures.

If you go: Parking is valet only. Seating is by the maître d'. Though Club Paradise bills itself as a gentleman's club, women patrons are welcome.

CLUB RIO

Nightclub—Top 40 music
Who Goes There: 25–35 professionals; locals and visitors

3700 W. Flamingo (Rio Hotel); (702) 252-7777
Strip Zone 1

Hours: Wednesday–Saturday,
  10:30 p.m. until the crowd thins,
  or 3 a.m., whichever comes first
Cover: Local ladies, free; men, $10;
  out-of-state ladies, $5
Minimum: None
Mixed drinks: $5 and up
Wine: $4.25 and up
Beer: $3.75 and up
Dress: Collared shirts for men; no
  jeans, shorts, tennis shoes, or
  sandals
Specials: Wednesday, Fantasmic Universe night; Thursday, Latin Libido
  night; Friday and Saturday, DJ
  music
Food available: Restaurants on
  property

What goes on: Sexy and stylish, Club Rio is the hottest nightclub for successful singles and the chic well-to-do. Dancers fill the spacious dance floor. Couples snuggle in the showroom's comfy booths, while others mingle with potential partners. Although the music is loud and pulsating, there's little trouble conversing with new friends or ordering drinks from the attractive cocktail waitresses.

Setting & atmosphere: After the last show, the Copacabana showroom is transformed into a cosmopolitan nightclub with table lamps, mosaic laser lights, and giant video panels. Selected sections of booth seating are reserved for casino players. The sound system is clean, clear, and loud, but not too loud.

If you go: Arrive early to avoid the long lines after 11 p.m. The dress code encourages stylish attire (jackets for the men and dresses for the women). Watch your step along the showroom's terraced levels as you make your way to and from the dance floor. The club is located off the new Masquerade Village.

DYLAN'S SALOON & DANCE HALL

Recorded country music
Who Goes There: 25–50; urban and rodeo cowboys

4660 S. Boulder Hwy.; (702) 451-4006
Southeast Zone 5

Hours: Thursday–Saturday, 7 p.m.
  till dawn
Cover: None
Minimum: None
Mixed drinks: $3 and up
Wine: $3 and up

Beer: $2.50 and up
Dress: Jeans and cowboy hats
Specials: Line-dance lessons,
  7:30–9 p.m.
Food available: Typical bar fare

What goes on: Whether it's doing the two-step, shooting a game of pool, or enjoying a warm summer evening under the star-filled sky, the young and lively crowd whoops it up on the weekends. From ballads to rockabilly and honky-tonk, the deejay mixes the music to the crowd's delight. Seating around the dance floor is at a premium as singles look to meet new partners.

Setting & atmosphere: This dance hall has a spacious, 2,400-square-foot, silky smooth dance floor, two bars, friendly folks, and the usual rodeo decor. The party flows onto the patio and, on busy nights, the chain-linked, floodlit, dirt area adjacent to the parking lot. As the night parties on, the odors of beer and cigarette smoke get thicker.

If you go: The attitude is looser and hipper than Sam's Town Dance Hall. Arrive early for good seating. Because the parking lot is quite dark in areas, women on their own are advised to ask for an escort to their car.

GILLEY'S SALOON, DANCE HALL, AND BARBECUE

Live country and rock and roll
Who Goes There: 21–55; real and urban cowboys, locals and tourists

3120 Las Vegas Blvd., S. (New Frontier); (702) 794-8200
Strip Zone 1

Hours: 4 p.m. till the cows come
home; food available 4–9 p.m.
Cover: None
Minimum: None
Mixed drinks: $3 and up
Beer and Wine: $2 and up

Dress: Come as you are; in too-long
jeans, too-tight boots and too-big
hats you'll feel right at home
Specials: Line dance lessons,
Sunday–Thursday
Food available: Full menu of chuck-
wagon fare

What goes on: The six-piece Gilley's All-Star Band starts at 9 p.m. Tuesday–Saturday; a deejay spins the tunes on Sunday and Monday. The band plays two-minute country tunes, complete with pedal-steel guitar and fiddle, during the late dinner sets then cranks up the tempo later in the evening. The big dance floor gets crowded with two-steppers and line-dancers (lessons are offered Thursday and Saturday at 7:30 p.m.). Watchers sit at bar tables munching free peanuts from galvanized buckets.

Setting & atmosphere: The smell of beer-battered onion rings, rotisserie chicken, and hickory-smoked pork permeates the place from the kitchen on one end. On the other end are the two bars. In between are the dance floor, eating areas, and mechanical bronc. Bales of hay, a Mickey Gilley logo counter, and peanut shells on the floor complete the scene. The atmosphere is as heavily country as anywhere else in town—the heaviest on the Strip.

If you go: As long as it stands, the price is right no matter what mood you're in, but it helps to either be in, or ready for, cowboy hats, silver buckles, and fringed blouses. The joint is sedate till late, when everyone's finished eating, but then gets rocking and fun. Round about 11 p.m. (except on Mondays, when it closes at midnight) Gilley's loses its barbecue feel and lives up to the rest of its handle: saloon and dance hall.

THE NIGHTCLUB

Top 40/show combination
Who Goes There: 30–50; visitors, locals, convention-goers/businesspeople

3000 Paradise Rd., (Las Vegas Hilton); (702) 732-5755 or (702) 732-5422
Strip Zone 1

Hours: 8 p.m.–2 a.m. weeknights,
   till 3 a.m Friday and Saturday
Cover: None (after show)
Minimum: Varies, usually one drink
   per set
Mixed drinks: $5–6.75

Wine: $4.50
Beer: $2.50
Dress: Upscale casual
Specials: Live entertainment starts at
   8 p.m. (changes regularly)
Food available: In casino

What goes on: Couples and friends boogie to good live renditions of pop music on the small, curvy dance floor. Others are content to watch the leather-clad dancers on stage cavorting with the musicians. Meanwhile, onlookers admire the whole scene. Singles can either sit back and enjoy the show or meet new friends.

Setting & atmosphere: A combination of a Las Vegas showroom and a New York dance club, The Nightclub is a trendy art deco hot spot. The bar, situated in the rear of the 450-seat lounge, serves up libations and hosts more intimate conversation. On the wall to the left of the stage is a mutely painted mural of an art deco cityscape. The second floor provides a bird's-eye view of the band and offers a bit more seating space. On some nights a reserved ticket show is performed in the venue. At the conclusion of the show, the dance club cranks up.

If you go: Arrive early for choice seating. Cocktail service tends to be relaxed in this no-pressure environment. Because of the long hike from the public parking areas, take a cab or use valet for convenience. Dress is upscale yet casual.

OLYMPIC GARDEN

Topless bar
Who Goes There: Men 21–65; locals, visitors, and conventioneers

1531 Las Vegas Blvd. S.; (702) 385-8987
Strip Zone 1

Hours: Open 24 hours
Cover: $20 after 6 p.m., includes
   2 drinks
Minimum: None
Mixed drinks: $5 and up
Wine: $5 and up
Beer: $5 and up

Dress: Casual, but no tank tops or
   cutoffs
Specials: Male revue Tuesday,
   Wednesday, and Thursday, 9 p.m
   –1 a.m.; Friday 8 p.m.–4 a.m.
Food available: Order from Italian or
   Mexican menus

What goes on: Connoisseurs consider Olympic Garden the finest topless joint in Las Vegas. It's not the classiest club in town, but it is one of the most relaxed and least aggressive. And the women are top of the line. At any given time, 50 of the most eye-popping strippers in varying degrees of undress are on display. Four dancers in bikini bottoms or t-backs occupy the four center stages, playing the stageside audiences for tips, with some very explicit moves. Other showgirl-quality women gyrate in laps, walk to and from the dressing rooms, or just hang around the main entrance. You won't have any trouble getting entertained at Olympic Garden. Tuesday through Friday there's a male strip show on the second floor for local and visiting ladies (men must be accompanied by a woman).

Setting & atmosphere: Olympic Garden is basically a large, dimly lit room with booths against the walls and tables on the floor. Near the front door is a clothing shop with a large selection of lingerie. There's a video poker bar in the back.

If you go: Parking is free in the large, well-lit lot (usually crowded). Seating is by the cocktail waitress.

PALOMINO CLUB

Totally nude dance club
Who Goes There: Men 21–65; tourists, locals, conventioneers

1848 Las Vegas Blvd., N.; (702) 642-2984
North Las Vegas Zone 4

Hours: 1:30 p.m.–4 a.m.	Beer: $7
Cover: $15	Dress: Casual
Minimum: One drink	Specials: None
Mixed drinks: $7	Food available: None
Wine: $7	

What goes on: Because it is situated in North Las Vegas, in a different jurisdiction from the Strip, the Palomino can offer both nude dancing and alcohol. In Las Vegas (city and county), clubs can offer either total nudity or alcohol, but not both. Go figure. Anyway, about nine professionals and an equal number of so-called amateurs strip completely nude each night. A stand-up comic spells the dancers from time to time and provides the patrons with a good excuse to increase their alcohol consumption.

Setting & atmosphere: Unpretentious but comfortable, the emphasis at the Palomino is definitely on the performers, not the decor.

If you go: The Palomino has its own lighted self-parking lot. Seating is by the maître d'. Once you have paid the cover charge and ordered your drink, you can stay all night as long as you are well behaved. For what it's worth, women are welcome.

PEPPERMILL INN'S FIRESIDE LOUNGE

Romantic and quiet
Who Goes There: 25–55; locals and tourists

2985 Las Vegas Blvd. S. (across from the Stardust, next to La Concha)
Restaurant; (702) 735-4177; Lounge, (702) 735-7635
Strip Zone 1

Hours: Open 24 hours
Cover: None
Minimum: None
Mixed drinks: $4 and up
Wine: $4 and up

Beer: $3 and up
Dress: Casual
Specials: None
Food available: Appetizers available;
restaurant adjacent

What goes on: The Peppermill has been a longtime favorite of the locals. Couples and friends relax on plush, circular sofas while enjoying conversation and munchies. The peacefulness of the Fireside Lounge is a great escape from the frantic pace of the casinos.

Setting & atmosphere: One doesn't expect a lounge like this in a 24-hour coffee shop. It's inviting, quiet, and even tranquil. Tropical greenery creates secluded alcoves of privacy. The unique fireplace with gas flames dancing on a small pool of water can be hypnotizing. Taped soft rock and popular music play over a modest sound system.

If you go: Be warned—Las Vegas Boulevard car traffic is congested on weekends, making it preferable to walk or let a cabbie fight the traffic for you. Drinks are a bit pricey and vary in quality depending on the bartender. Service can be as relaxed as the atmosphere. If you really need to unwind, order your first drink from the bartender.

RA

Top 40, techno, and dance
Who Goes There: 21–35; locals and tourists,
college students to professionals

3900 Las Vegas Blvd. S. (Luxor); (702) 262-4000
Strip Zone 1

Hours: 10 p.m.–5 a.m., Wednesday–
Sunday
Cover: Local ladies, free; out-of-town
ladies, $10; men, $15

Minimum: None
Mixed drinks: $4.50
Wine: $4.75–6
Beer: $3.50

Dress: Club attire (no athletic shoes or work boots; no hats; no baggy, ripped, or torn jeans)
Specials: None

Food available: Hamada of Japan sushi bar is next to nightclub; restaurants in casino

What goes on: Ever wonder what the Egyptian sun god does after a hard day's work? He parties with the night-worshipping crowd until the wee hours of the morning. Singles line up at the railing for the best view of the dance floor. Couples and friends enjoy themselves at the booths and the two huge bars. On each end of the stage, go-go dancers lead the dancing throngs to the rhythmic music. Cigar aficionados can enjoy their evening in one of two lounges.

Setting & atmosphere: Journey through the misty temple entrance, pay homage (admission) at the gate, then enter the futuristic Egyptian-themed nightclub. Huge Ra statues adorn the two bars at each end of the room. All seating focuses on the dance floor and center stage during live performances. State-of-the-art lighting and sound systems complete the ambience.

If you go: Because RA is located off the main entrance, use valet for convenient parking. Lines are long by midnight, so arrive early or be prepared to wait (hotel guests can use the VIP line). Call ahead for special events such as cage dancing contests and 1980s nights.

SAND DOLLAR BLUES LOUNGE

Rhythm and blues
Who Goes There: Bikers to yuppies

3355 Spring Mountain Rd. (at Polaris); (702) 871-6651
Southwest Zone 3

Hours: Open 24 hours; music starts at 10 p.m. nightly
Cover: $3, Tuesday–Thursday; $5, Friday and Saturday; free, Monday
Minimum: None
Mixed drinks: $3 and up

Wine: $3 and up
Beer: $2.50 and up
Dress: Casual
Specials: Drink specials and prices depend on the event
Food available: Packaged snack food—no kitchen

What goes on: Everyone from attorneys to bikers sits back for an evening full of moody and marvelous blues by popular Las Vegas or out-of-town bands. It's standing-room only on Friday, Saturday, and special-event nights. Strip musicians gather for various jam sessions. In the back, pool players croon to the blues.

Setting & atmosphere: The exterior is nondescript. Both the interior and the patrons are earthy and full of character. The low ceiling keeps the lounge quite smoky. The U-shaped bar separates the dance floor from the pool tables. Nautical rope, worn wood pilings, small fishing nets, and sand dollars add to the bar's salty character. Neon beer signs and handwritten flyers dot the walls.

If you go: The club's unshaven appearance may deter some solo ladies from experiencing a night of great blues. The regulars make sure everything stays cool. The Sand Dollar is hard to spot at night, so arrive early or come by cab.

STUDIO 54

Dance, Top 40
Who Goes There: 25–40; locals, tourists, and trendy people

3799 Las Vegas Blvd., S. (MGM Grand); (702) 891-1111
Strip Zone 1

Hours: Tuesday–Saturday, 10 p.m. –5 a.m.
Cover: Ladies, free; men, $10–20
Minimum: None
Mixed drinks: $4.50–8
Wine: $5

Beer: $4–5.50
Dress: Club attire is enforced; collared shirt or sports coat for men; no baggy jeans, flannel shirts, T-shirts, sandals, or sneakers
Food available: In casino

What goes on: The New York club that set the standard during disco's heyday in the 1970s comes to Las Vegas. Stylish, beautiful people gather for a night of high energy, music, dance, and socializing.

Setting & atmosphere: It's three stories tall with dance floors, bars, and conversation areas on each level. The black-girder-and-steel-grate flooring and exposed elevator lifts give the club an industrial, high-tech feel. Black-and-white photographs of celebrities and trendsetters visiting the New York Studio 54 line the walls on the second floor.

If you go: If you love a club with an attitude then Studio 54 is for you. If you prefer a bit more fun and friendliness, try RA or Club Rio. Studio 54 is located at the Tropicana and Las Vegas Boulevard entrance—it's a long walk from both valet and the parking garages.

TOMMY ROCKER'S CANTINA AND GRILL

Top 40 and Jimmy Buffett–style music
Who Goes There: 25–30; professionals and career starters

4275 S. Industrial Blvd.; (702) 261-6688
Strip Zone 1

Hours: Open 24 hours
Cover: None
Minimum: None
Mixed drinks: $1.75–3.25;
wide selection of tequilas and rums
Wine: $2.75
Beer: $1.50–3; many microbrew
draft selections
Dress: Casual to sporty

Specials: Happy hour 4–7 p.m. and 4–7 a.m. with $1 off all drinks and appetizers, 50¢ off imports and domestic drafts; they are also the official Jimmy Buffett fan club location—call for special event information
Food: Sports bar–type food

What goes on: Singles and couples gather to check out the music and gregarious repartee of Tommy Rocker, the club's owner and professional musician when he's in town. Otherwise, they enjoy meeting new friends, singing Jimmy Buffett songs, shooting a friendly game of pool, cheering their favorite team on the big-screen TV, and indulging in the tasty libations and food fare.

Setting & atmosphere: An eclectic mix of Indian petroglyph images, palm trees, parrots, and neon gives Tommy Rocker's Cantina and Café a refreshing twist to the beach-style bar scene. In addition to the big-screen TV and two pool tables, the club offers a small dance floor, a nonsmoking party area, patio seating, and a standard center bar complete with progressive slot machines and a palm cabana roof.

If you go: Voted best live music club in a local survey, Tommy Rocker's offers plenty of parking, friendly yet professional security, and a great attitude. The music is loud but not deafening, allowing for conversation. Come early for best seating.

VOODOO Café AND LOUNGE

Restaurant and lounge with live entertainment
Who Goes There: 25+; upscale visitors and locals

3700 W. Flamingo Rd., (Rio Hotel); (702) 252-7777, ext. 8090
Southwest Zone 3

Hours: 9 p.m.–3 a.m.
Dinner: 5–11 p.m.
Entertainment: 9 p.m.–2 a.m.
(*Dark:* Monday)
Cover: Sunday–Thursday, $5; local ladies free weekdays; Friday and Saturday, $5 ladies; $10 men
Minimum: 2 drinks, Friday and Saturday
Mixed drinks: $3 and up
Wine: $2.75 and up

Beer: $2 and up
Dress: Casual to dressy; no hats, T-shirts, sport sandals, tank tops, tennis shoes, jean shorts, or torn/baggy jeans
Specials: None
Food available: Appetizers, $5–13; Creole/Cajun- and Louisiana-style soups, salads, and entrées in restaurant. Dinner prices: $21–35.95

What goes on: Sweethearts, friends, and colleagues enjoy conversation, decent regional cuisine, and live music. The lounge crowd grows as the evening approaches midnight and the VooDoo Café diners and late-night party-goers ascend to the 51st floor (really the 41st floor). Music lovers relax and enjoy the jazz and blues beat in the lounge. Adventurous souls party on the open-air patio, amazed at the electrifying view of the famous Strip and the surrounding Las Vegas valley.

Setting & atmosphere: The trendy decor is complete with black ceilings, mysterious paintings illuminated by black light, and animal-skin chair furnishings. Both the 50th-floor restaurant and the 51st-floor lounge are surrounded by glass windows and connected by a center staircase. The restaurant's staff is friendly, attentive, and knowledgeable about the menu. At the centralized bar, bartenders offer little conversation, as they efficiently serve the packed crowd. Conversation can be strained due to the ambient noise and entertainment and it can get *really* smoky as the night progresses.

If you go: While gusty desert winds are normal in Las Vegas, expect stronger winds in the spring and fall months and during weather changes. If the weather is questionable, call ahead to confirm that the patio will be open. After 10 p.m. on Friday and Saturday, expect a long line at the VooDoo elevators (managed by a humorless staff) and a very smoky lounge upstairs. Park in the "Masquerade Village" parking garage for easy access. If your evening plans include dancing, go to Club Rio. The glass elevators to VooDoo are a mini–thrill ride.

Las Vegas Below the Belt
DON'T WORRY, BE HAPPY

In many ways, Las Vegas is a bastion of hedonism. Just being there contributes to a lessening of inhibitions and a partial discarding of the rules that apply at home. Las Vegas exults in its permissiveness and makes every effort to live up to its image and to give its visitors freedom to have fun. Las Vegas has a steaminess, a sophisticated cosmopolitan excitement born of excess, an aura of risk and reward, a sense of freedom. The rules are different here; it's all right to let go.

Behind the illusion, however, is a community, and more particularly, a police department that puts a lot of effort into making it safe for visitors to experience the liberation of Las Vegas. It is hard to imagine another city where travelers can carry such large sums of money so safely. A tourist can get robbed or worked over in Las Vegas, but it is comparatively rare, and more often than not is due to the tourist's own stupidity. The Strip and downtown, especially, are well patrolled, and most hotels have very professional in-house security forces.

In general a tourist who stays either on the Strip or downtown will be very safe. Police patrol in cars, on foot, and, interestingly, on mountain bikes. The bikes allow the police to quickly catch pickpockets or purse snatchers attempting to make their escape down sidewalks or through parking lots. Streets that connect the Strip with Paradise Road and the Las Vegas Convention Center are also lighted and safe. When tourists get robbed, they are commonly far from downtown or the Strip, and often are trying to buy drugs.

ORGANIZED CRIME AND CHEATING

Very few visitors walk through a casino without wondering if the games are rigged or the place is owned by the mafia. During the early days of legalized gambling, few people outside of organized crime had any real experience in managing gaming operations. Hence a fair number of characters fresh from Eastern gangs and crime families came to work in Nevada. Since they constituted the resource pool for experienced gambling operators, the state suffered their presence as a necessary evil. In 1950, Tennessee senator Estes Kefauver initiated an attack on organized crime that led (indirectly) to the formation of the Nevada Gaming Commission and the State Gaming Control Board. These agencies, in conjunction with federal efforts, were ultimately able to purge organized crime from Las Vegas. This ouster, coupled with the Nevada Corporate Gaming Acts of 1967 and 1969 (allowing publicly held corporations such as Hilton, Holiday Inn, Bally, and MGM to own casinos), at last brought a mantle of respectability to Las Vegas gambling.

Today the Gaming Control Board oversees the activities of all Nevada gaming establishments, maintaining tight control through frequent unannounced inspections of gambling personnel and equipment. If you ever have reason to doubt the activity or clout of the Gaming Control Board, try walking around the Strip or downtown in a dark business suit and plain black shoes. You will attract more attention from the casino management than if you entered with a parrot on your head.

Cheating exists in Las Vegas gambling to a limited degree but is seldom perpetrated by the house itself. In fact, most cheating is done at the expense of the house, though honest players at the cheater's table may also get burned. Sometimes a dealer, working alone or with an accomplice (posing as a player), will cheat, and there are always con artists ready to take advantage of the house and legitimate players.

Skin Games—Sex in Las Vegas   Though nudity, prostitution, and pornography are regulated more tightly in Las Vegas than in many Bible Belt cities, the town exudes an air of sexual freedom and promiscuity. Las Vegas offers a near-perfect environment for marketing sex. Over 50% of all visitors are men, most between the ages of 21 and 59. Some come to party, and many, particularly convention-goers, are lonely. Almost all have time and money on their hands.

Las Vegas evolved as a gambling man's city, proudly projecting the image of a trail town where a man could be comfortable and just about anything could be had for a price. It was not until strong competition developed for the gambling dollar that hotels sought to enlarge their market by targeting women and families. Today, though there is something for everyone in Las Vegas, its male orientation remains unusually strong.

Las Vegas, perhaps more than any other American city, has objectified women. A number of Las Vegas production shows continue to feature topless showgirls and erotic dance, even though audiences are mostly couples. Lounge servers and keno runners are almost exclusively women, invariably attired in revealing outfits. Showroom comedians, after 30 years, persist in describing Las Vegas as an adult Disneyland.

Stripping on the Strip   Compared to the live adult entertainment in many cities, "girlie" (and "boy") shows in Las Vegas, both downtown and on the Las Vegas Strip, are fairly tame. In some of the larger showrooms, this is an accommodation to the ever-growing percentage of women in the audience. More often, however, it is a matter of economics rather than taste, the result of a curious City of Las Vegas law that stipulates that you can offer totally nude entertainment or you can serve alcoholic beverages, but not both.

More often than not, topless showgirls are a mere embellishment to a production that features song, dance, and variety acts. For the most part, the partial nudity is incidental and unimportant. While a half-dozen continuously running shows include a steamy, highly erotic dance number, these acts are not the focal point. Las Vegas entertainment is slowly moving away from nudity and eroticism, though for the moment, the genre is in no imminent danger of extinction. Some shows have de-emphasized bare breasts, and a few shows offer both a topless and a "covered" performance.

If you want to see stunning topless showgirls and dancers, the most erotic of the continuously running productions are *Crazy Girls* at the Riviera, followed by *Jubilee!* at Bally's. *Crazy Girls* is a topless, all-girl revue. The other show is a production spectacular that has prettier-than-average showgirls and sultrier-than-average dance numbers.

Although there are a number of other topless shows whose ads plaster the local visitor magazines, only Skintight at Harrah's is worth the cost of admission, and Skintight is a distant runner up to Crazy Girls.

Male Strippers   Economics and the market have begun to redress (or undress) the inequality of women's erotic entertainment in Las Vegas. Spearheaded by the now-extinct Dunes, which featured (Chippendales) male strippers for lengthy engagements, and empowered by the ever-growing number of professional women visiting Las Vegas for trade shows and conventions, the rules for sexual objectification are being rewritten. Today in Las Vegas, if watching a young stud flex his buns is a woman's idea of a good time, that experience is usually available (see the Olympic Garden on page 270).

Expensive Voyeurism   Just off the Strip are a number of adult entertainment nightspots that feature total nudity. One bills itself as the "only totally nude show in Las Vegas" and promises to "leave nothing to your imagination." Its claim is justified when it comes to the girls; they are indeed beautiful, young, and plentiful. What is left to the imagination, however, is the alcohol in your drink—there isn't any! And beyond your imagination is the price tag on these nonalcoholic concoctions. Never again will you have the opportunity to pay so much for a glass of fruit punch.

As expensive as the fruit punch is, there are other Las Vegas nude nightspots that can be far more expensive, not to mention embarrassing. Most of the clientele is funneled to these places by cab drivers who get a kickback for every customer delivered. Usually, as the scenario goes, a lonely tourist or businessman asks the cabbie about places where he can pick up a girl, or, more explicitly, find a prostitute. For a hefty tip the naive fellow is delivered to a sex-tease nightclub, which the cabbie describes as a "swinger's club: the hottest place in town—just what you are looking for." Inside the lights are low and there are a number of alluring young women, some nude, and some clad in negligees or other scanty attire. On the walls, barely readable in the dim light, are signs that state, "Prostitution Is Illegal in Las Vegas," and "No Alcoholic Beverages Shall Be Served or Consumed on These Premises."

There is no entertainment other than taped music or perhaps a jukebox; no dancers, no performers, no show. After paying a cover charge of up to $50 and being seated, the customer is invariably joined by a woman who gives every impression that she is prepared to have sex with him. In getting acquainted, she encourages him to buy her a drink, once again some astronomically priced nonalcoholic potion. If the fellow consents, she strings him along, ordering more drinks and promising great things to come. Later, she suggests that he buy a bottle of champagne (nonalcoholic), and they retire to a private back room.

In the back room she continues to come on to him and play him for additional bottles of champagne. This continues as long as he is willing to keep buying. Should he become impatient and demanding, insist on sex or refuse to buy more champagne, she will excuse herself on the pretext of using the rest room. Moments later, one or more bouncers enter the private room and forcibly eject the fellow from the club. Because of his complicity in soliciting the services of a prostitute, the customer has no legal recourse without incriminating or at least embarrassing himself.

The Palomino Club   While the Can Can Room claims to have the only totally nude show in Las Vegas, this is only true in a narrowly defined geographic sense. In North Las Vegas, a separate jurisdiction, there is no prohibition against nude entertainment and alcoholic beverages under the same roof. At the Palomino Club, ten minutes from downtown, the customer can have it all.

The Palomino Club is not inexpensive, but at least they're up front about what they're selling, and best of all, you do not have to drink Shirley Temples all night. There is a $10 cover charge and a two-drink minimum, at $7 a drink, for $24 total. To get one of the better seats, you should arrive before 10 p.m. and tip the maître d'. Once you have purchased your two drinks, you can stay as long as you can stand it—all night if you wish.

An average of seven professionals dance every night, performing in rotation and stripping completely nude. The pros are supplemented by four or more alleged amateurs who compete for prize money and tips in a strip contest held nightly at 11 p.m. All of the women, both pro and amateur, are attractive, well-built, and athletic. A stand-up comic rounds out the entertainment. The Palomino is without pretense. It delivers some of the best erotic dancing in town for about the same cost as a production show on the Strip. Conventioneers, tourists, and locals are the usual clientele.

Topless Bars   The main difference between a topless bar and a totally nude nightclub (aside from the alcohol regulations) is a G-string. Unless you're a gynecology intern, you might be satisfied with a topless bar. If you have more than a few drinks, the topless bars aren't less expensive than the Palomino but are often more conveniently located. Downtown, on Fremont Street, is the Girls of Glitter Gulch. There's no cover charge, but drinks average a stiff (no pun intended) $6.75 each, with a one-drink minimum. A U-shaped stage/runway ensures a good view from most seats.

A very upscale and elegant topless bar is Club Paradise at 4416 Paradise Road, not far from the Strip. Catering to a professional clientele, high rollers, and conventioneers, Club Paradise is the Rolls Royce of topless bars. The cover charge is $10 and there is a two-drink minimum, unless you elect to sit in the VIP section, where you are obligated to consume at least $80 worth of drinks. Fortunately, because drinks go for $4.75 and up, this is not difficult.

Another plush topless bar is Cheetah's, at 2112 Western Avenue. Cover is $10 with a two-drink minimum, and drink prices start at about four bucks. An equally upscale venue is the Olympic Garden at 1531 South Las Vegas Boulevard. Considered by locals and connoisseurs to be the best topless club in town, the Olympic Garden is the only club that also features male strippers for its female customers (in a separate showroom). The cover for Cheetah's is $10 with a two-drink minimum. Olympic Garden charges a $20 cover but the price includes two drinks. The Palomino, Club Paradise, and the Olympic Garden are profiled in the Nightlife section of this guide.

PROSTITUTION: NOW YOU SEE IT, NOW YOU DON'T

The people of Nevada have always maintained a practical and essentially laissez-faire attitude toward prostitution. For years prostitution was allowed to flourish and was accorded an implicit legal status by a body of some 50 statutes enacted to regulate it. The circumstances were similar to an equally confusing situation on Mississippi's Gulf Coast 35 years ago.

Mississippi was a dry state, but along the coast there were bars everywhere, recognized as a necessary adjunct to the developing tourist industry. It was laughable to watch the local police attempt to structure and regulate an illegal industry. How do you make rules for something that is against the law?

The history of prostitution in Nevada is essentially the same story. Prostitution was against the law, yet was administered as conscientiously as tax collection. Nevadans, while of conservative, principled, pioneer origins, always accepted prostitution as a practical reality, something as predictable and inevitable as cactus in the desert. Prostitution both filled a need and, by way of payoffs, augmented the meager income of law enforcement officials, county commissioners, and others. Prostitution was making great strides as a growth industry in Nevada, moving rapidly in the direction of total legalization, until it had a head-on collision with another growth industry—gambling.

At first glance, prostitution and gambling looked like a perfect team. The legalization of gambling perpetuated the Wild West, mining-town atmosphere of Nevada cities. There had always been women to take care of the prospectors, the speculators, the railroad workers, and later the dam builders and soldiers. It seemed the most natural thing in the world, completely in keeping with the state's robust, pragmatic Western image, for gambling and prostitution to work hand in glove to stimulate the burgeoning tourism industry.

The gaming czars, however, saw it differently. They were trying to get gambling out of the back room and install it as a respectable form of recreation (like bowling or shuffleboard, only more lucrative). Elderly ladies, married couples, and even Episcopal priests could enjoy a little innocent gambling, but prostitution was a different story. There was no way to make prostitution innocent, no way to separate it from infidelity, syphilis, and gonorrhea.

On the practical side, casino owners recognized that legal or illegal, prostitution was a fact of life (if not an out-and-out necessity) in every major convention and tourist city in the United States. The owners also realized that the wild, "anything goes" Western tradition (the thematic foundation of all Nevada tourism) demanded that sex be a part of the gambling-town product mix. The real question, as the gaming industry perceived it, was, how do you impart a little sexual sauciness to your operation without actually providing for the satisfaction of appetites aroused? In other words, what were you going to do with 5,000 conventioneers who had been fed a steady diet of topless showgirls and provocatively clad lounge waitresses and keno runners? Gambling and sex were like Siamese twins, an unfortunate pairing that defied separation. Reid and Demaris did not mince words in their classic *Green Felt Jungle* when they wrote, "Money mysteriously breeds prostitutes the way decaying flesh breeds maggots. Where there's easy money there's whores; it's that basic. And where there's gambling, there's easy money."

The uneasy conclusion was that prostitution had to be illegal, yet available. Gambling, with its newfound respectability, had to distance itself from prostitution without precipitating its demise. Las Vegas, in particular, had to have the best, most efficient prostitution system in the world while appearing as wholesome as Disneyland. When it came to sex, part of the market needed to be assured that Las Vegas was not pure form with no underlying substance. Another part of the market needed to believe that Vegas was a clean resort town, that gambling was a legitimate form of recreation, and that the tourism industry and the police were doing their best to stamp out prostitution.

This paradox was reconciled, incredibly, through a curious combination of legislation and role-playing. The casinos and the convention authority came down on prostitution with the righteous wrath of the Moral Majority. Joined by the conservative, largely Mormon local population, they used their combined clout to have prostitution outlawed in counties with a census of over 250,000 residents. In addition, the gaming commission was persuaded to further accentuate the difference between wholesome recreational gambling and the carnality of whoring by denying gambling licenses to hotels or other properties that engaged in or supported prostitution. Later, with the election of John Moran as Clark County sheriff in the early 1980s, the streetwalkers were effectively run off the Strip.

As intended, prostitution remained alive and healthy. So-called legal prostitution, symbolized by the large brothels, was just chased over the county line into Nye County where it was allowed to operate under stringent state regulation, but basically without interference. In Las Vegas and Clark County (where prostitution was declared illegal), the world's oldest profession simply switched to an entrepreneurial base. Where hotels and casinos previously had a virtual oligopoly in procuring women, they now stepped aside to permit a broad freelance trade to develop. A quintessential case of having your cake and eating it too, prostitution had been removed from sight without otherwise being harmed.

The flaw in the plan, predictably, was that the ever-increasing corps of sexual entrepreneurs could not be controlled. Part of the original procurement business devolved from hotel top management to any number of bellmen, pitmen, and other small operatives who kept male guests as happy as ever but did it quietly and discreetly, with nothing required of the host property. It was the other players, the small prostitution rings, the freelancers, and the "weekend warriors," who managed to unsettle the status quo.

Unlike the bellmen and other hotel personnel, who worked without fanfare from a private list of known and highly recommended professional courtesans, the freelancers were as visible as a Kmart grand opening, taking out ads in the Las Vegas Yellow Pages and distributing free "adult entertainment" magazines up and down the Strip. Las Vegas was again becoming a Sodom and Gomorrah, with gambling looking less all-American as a function of guilt by association.

What's in a Name?

Since it is against the law to promote and advertise prostitution in Las Vegas, the inventive carnal entrepreneurs started off by listing themselves as massage parlors. This, of course, outraged legitimate professional masseurs ("We don't do genitals"), who forced the state to pass standards and licensing legislation. Unable to meet the standards, the freelancers reappeared as escort or dating services. Once again, stringent licensing standards were applied, and the freelancers disappeared temporarily from sight. When they next surfaced, they were private dancers, entertainers, or party services. This most recent, and highly visible, reincarnation continues to this day. The Las Vegas Yellow Pages are chock-full of lurid ads.

Sensuous XXX Rated Dancers

Let Us Explore Your Fantasies . . .

Nude Strippers Direct to Your Room

24 Hours—Most Major Credit Cards Accepted

For tourists who do not sit around reading the Yellow Pages, adult entertainment newsprint tabloids, with the same ads, are distributed gratis up and down the Strip.

A couple of visiting businessmen, slightly inebriated and in high spirits, decided to call a number from one of the ads and have a stripper sent over. Both men, being married and absolutely terrified of sexually transmitted disease, had no intention of having intercourse. They simply wanted, as the ad promised, "sizzling hot erotic dancing, direct to your room." What they expected was a naughtier-than-average version of the wholesome young ladies, available in every city, who perform tasteful striptease at yuppie birthday parties. What they got was a sullen prostitute who made it abundantly clear (the ad notwithstanding) that if they wanted to see dancing, they could "march right over and buy a ticket to the *Folies Bergere*."

In a similar situation, three unsophisticated conventioneers from Little Rock phoned a private dancer service and requested information and prices. What the callers understood was that they could buy an hour of private dancing for $125, payable in advance with cash or credit card. What they were told, however, quite deliberately, was that the fee was $125 for "up to an hour" of private dancing. When the prostitute arrived and discovered, to her amazement, that these guys really wanted dancing, she obligingly took their money and launched into a perfunctory disrobing, without music or other artistic embellishment. In five minutes she was gone with the $125.

The most recent variation on the theme, taking advantage of growing consumer outrage, is "adult entertainment information services." These operations, ostensibly consultation services that "assist you in getting what you want without being ripped off," are nothing more than referral services, owned and operated by the prostitution agencies. It's only a matter of time, of course, before the authorities force prostitution into yet another metamorphosis, perhaps "Plumbing by the Hour" or "Gynecology Made Easy."

Unofficial Guide co-author Deke Castleman speculates that in future phone books, we may find prostitutes variously listed as "Bedroom Accessories," or "Temporary Services," or even "All-Purpose Rentals." The possibilities are endless.

Who's on First?

The cast of players in the Las Vegas prostitution game is a little confusing. At the top of the caste are select call girls with a small, but extremely lucrative, regular clientele. Another population of respected, highly recommended professionals work quietly on an on-call basis at the request of bell captains, pit bosses, and maître d's. Next come a cadre of seasoned and novice, but less exclusive, prostitutes whose services are marketed by cab drivers, bartenders, and even convenience store clerks. Tied with these are the entertainers, the contingent that forms the stable of the private dancers and other operations that deal directly with customers. At the bottom of the heap are the streetwalkers, often past their prime, diseased, or drug-addicted. Driven off the streets by the law, streetwalkers work out of lounges, lobbies, transportation terminals, and hotel shopping arcades, but only rarely on the street.

A final category that defies any ranking is that of the weekend warriors. These are working girls and professional women (teachers, nurses, sales clerks) from Utah, Southern California, and Arizona who augment their income by turning tricks in Las Vegas on weekends. While some of these women develop connections with specific procurers, most work alone and free-lance out of casino lounges and singles bars. Nicely dressed and usually intelligent, they have a style more like that of a single woman cruising than that of a prostitute soliciting business. When it comes to striking a deal, however, they play hardball as well as their full-time sisters. There are no free samples.

Pay Now, Pay Again Later

All prostitutes plying their trade in Las Vegas and Clark County operate illegally. Regardless of their exclusivity or clientele, these women are not regulated by the standards applied to prostitutes working for the legal brothels in less-populated counties. Women of this latter group are checked weekly by a physician for communicable disease and work under very strict guidelines on the premises of their employer.

In Las Vegas, sexually transmitted diseases, including syphilis, gonorrhea, genital herpes, and AIDS, are routinely passed from prostitute to client; customers of streetwalkers are most at risk. Las Vegas police work incessantly to identify disease-carrying prostitutes and get them off the street, but it's like excavating a bottomless pit. At the time this book went to press, the police were tracking 68 prostitutes known to have AIDS.

Be forewarned that it is just as illegal in Las Vegas for you to solicit the services of a prostitute as it is for them to solicit you, and that sometimes policewomen work undercover. If you are determined to have a sexual adventure, you had better drive to the lawful Nye County brothels.

Deadly Games People Play

Not all of the sex games played in Las Vegas involve prostitution. In Las Vegas, as in any resort town, many men and women keep their eyes open for a little romance. Frequently lonely and vulnerable, these tourists fall prey to any number of deceptions.

Women who allow themselves to come under the influence of an unknown male risk the possibility of being robbed and/or raped. Sometimes the crime is premeditated, but more often it is a variation of date rape, where the man, rejected, refuses to take no for an answer. To many men, tourists and locals alike, the Las Vegas female stereotype is a bimbo showgirl, good only for sex and decoration. If a woman looking for companionship hooks up with a guy who subscribes to this myth, she might well be in for a rough time.

Interestingly, middle-aged men are the most common victims of sex scams in Las Vegas. In a common scenario, a comely, well-dressed woman will make eye contact with a middle-aged man at the gaming tables. Always subtle, she may favor him with a smile when he wins or an expression of consolation when he loses. Working slowly and deliberately, sharing the moment and perhaps exchanging a few innocent words, she becomes an unintroduced friend. She does not push or direct, but instead allows the man to take the initiative. He likes her, invites her to grab a bite to eat or have a drink. They talk about their jobs, music, food, and all the other things people discuss when getting acquainted. If things proceed as she hopes, he finally asks her to his room for a drink. Making all the pro forma protestations, she ultimately pretends to be persuaded. Once in the room, he makes drinks. Talking and passing the time, she waits until he uses the rest room, then takes advantage of his absence to slip a powerful, quick-acting drug into his drink. A half hour later he is in dreamland. Usually with a male accomplice, the woman searches the room as the victim slumbers. Everything of value is stolen. The victim of this drug-induced trick roll commonly sleeps anywhere from 8 to 20 hours. Occasionally, if the victim is hypersensitive to the drug or has a medical condition, he dies.

How Felons Choose Their Victims   Felons choose their marks by observing a potential victim's attire and behavior. Wearing lots of jewelry and flaunting big bills is a sure way to attract attention. Stupid bets suggest inexperience, and excessive drinking lowers inhibitions and defenses. Playing without friends suggests that you are a solitary business traveler or on vacation and perhaps hungry for companionship.

If you meet somebody interesting, resist the urge to rush the relationship. In Las Vegas, as in any city, you should exercise caution. Proceed slowly with your new friendship. No matter what, keep the drinking under control and do not go anywhere to be alone. If you have a nice evening in the casino or over drinks or dinner, you can arrange to meet again tomorrow.

In the behavior department, learn the table games before you play, and make sensible bets. Go light on glitzy jewelry and refrain from flaunting your bankroll. Limit your alcohol intake and do not drink on an empty stomach. Beware of loners of either sex. Do not divulge your room number. Do not extend an invitation to come to your room or accept an invitation to go to the other party's room. If you are traveling alone, keep that to yourself.

Part Three

Gambling

The Way It Is

Gambling is the reason Las Vegas (in its modern metamorphosis) exists. It is the industry that fuels the local economy, paves the roads, and gives the city its identity. To visitors and tourists, gambling may be a game. To those who derive their livelihood from gambling, however, it is serious business.

There is an extraordinary and interesting dichotomy in the ways gambling is perceived. To the tourist and the gambler, gambling is all about luck. To those in the business, gambling is about mathematics. To the visitor, gambling is a few hours a day, while to the casinos, gambling is 24 hours a day, all day, every day. The gambler *hopes* to walk away with a fortune, but the casinos *know* that in the long run that fortune will belong to the house. To visitors, gambling is recreation combined with risk and chance. To the casinos, gambling is business combined with near certainty.

The casino takes no risk in the games themselves. In the long run the house will always win. The games, the odds, and the payoffs are all carefully designed to ensure this outcome. Yet the casino does take a chance and is at risk. The casino's bet is this: that it can entice enough people to play.

Imagine a casino costing millions of dollars, with a staff numbering in the hundreds. Before a nickel of profit can be set aside, all the bills must be paid and the payroll must be met. Regardless of the house's overwhelming advantage at the tables, it cannot stay in business unless a lot of people come to play. Ten players, 20 players, even 30 are not enough; the larger the casino, the more gamblers are required. If the casino can fill the tables with players, the operation will succeed and be profitable, perhaps incredibly so. On the other hand, if the tables go empty, the casino will fail.

The casino business is competition personified. Every owner knows how absolutely critical it is to get customers (gamblers) through the door. It is literally the sine qua non: No players, no profit. The casinos are aggressive and creative when it comes to luring customers, offering low-cost buffets, dollar shrimp cocktails, stage shows, lounge entertainment, free drinks, gambling tournaments, and slot clubs.

The most recent tactic for getting customers through the door is to package the casino as a tourist attraction in its own right. Take the Mirage, for example. There are exploding volcanoes in the front yard, white tigers in the entrance hall, palm trees in the living room, and live sharks in the parlor. Who, after all, wants to sip their free drink in a dingy, red-Naugahyde-upholstered catacomb when they could be luxuriating in such a resplendent tropical atrium?

The Short Run

If you ask a mathematician or a casino owner if you can win gambling in a casino, the truthful answer is yes, but only in the short run. The longer you play, the more certain it is that you will lose.

I learned about the short run (and the long run) on a road trip when I was in the fifth grade. My family lived in Kentucky, and every year we were fortunate enough to take a vacation to Florida. This particular year I was permitted to invite a schoolmate to come along.

As the long drive progressed, we became fidgety and bored. To pass the time, we began counting cars traveling in the opposite direction. Before many miles had passed, our counting evolved into a betting game. We each selected a color and counted the cars of that color. Whoever counted the most cars of his chosen color would win.

My friend chose blue as his color. I was considering red (my favorite) when I recalled a conversation between my mother and a car salesman. The salesman told my mother that white was by far the most popular color "these days." If this were true, I reasoned, there should be more white cars on the road than blue cars. I chose white.

As we rumbled through the hilly Kentucky countryside between Elizabethtown and Bowling Green my friend edged ahead. This puzzled me and I began to doubt the word of the car salesman. By the time we made Bowling Green, my friend Glenn was ahead by seven cars. Because I was losing, I offered to call it quits and pay up (a nickel for each car he was ahead). Glenn, not unexpectedly, was having a high time and insisted we continue playing.

By the time we crossed the Tennessee line I had pulled even. Once again I suggested we quit. Glenn would have none of it. Gloating enormously, he regained a three-car lead halfway to Nashville. Slowly, however, I overtook him, and by Nashville I was ahead by four cars. Tired of the game, I tried once more to end it. Since he was behind, Glenn adamantly demanded that we play all the way to Atlanta. We did, and by the time we got there Glenn owed me almost $4.

After a night in Atlanta and a great deal of sulking on Glenn's part, we resumed our travels. To my amazement, Glenn insisted—demanded, in fact—the opportunity to win back his previous day's losses. There would be one great "do-or-die battle, blues against whites," he said, all the way to our destination (St. Augustine, Florida). As we drove south, I went ahead by a couple of cars, and then Glenn regained the lead by a small margin. By the time we made St. Augustine, however, Glenn owed me another $5.40.

Outraged (and broke), Glenn exercised the only option remaining—he complained to my parents. Shaking his head, my father said, "Give Glenn his money back. Everybody knows that there are more white cars than blue cars." Not so. Glenn didn't.

While Glenn's behavior is not particularly unusual for a preadolescent, you would assume that adults have better sense. Everybody knows there are more white cars than blue cars, remember? In Las Vegas, however, the casinos are full of Glenns, all over age 21, and all betting on blue cars.

I nailed Glenn on the cars because I knew something that he didn't. In casino games, patrons either do not understand what they are up against, or alternatively (and more intelligently), they do understand, but chalk up their losses as a fair price to pay for an evening's entertainment. Besides, in the short run, there's a chance they might actually win.

Glenn's actions on our trip mirrored almost exactly the behavior of many unfortunate casino gamblers:

1. He did not understand that the game was biased against him.

2. He did not take his winnings and quit when he was ahead in the short run.

3. On losing, he continued playing and redoubled his efforts to pull even or win, ultimately (in the long run) compounding his losses.

Eagles and Robins

If on our drive I had said, "Let's count birds. You take eagles and I'll take robins," Glenn would have laughed in my face, instantly recognizing that the likelihood of spotting an eagle was insanely remote. While the casinos will not offer a fair game (like betting even money on the flip of a coin), they do offer something a bit more equitable than eagles and robins.

I had another friend growing up who was big for his age. Whenever I went to his house to play, he would beat me up. I was not a masochist, so I finally stopped going to his house. After a few days, however, he asked me to come back, offering me ice cream and other incentives. After righteously spurning his overtures for a time, I gave in and resumed playing at his house. True to his word, he gave me ice cream and generously shared his best toys, and from that time forward he beat me up only once a week.

This is exactly how the casinos operate, and why they give you a better deal than eagles vs. robins. The casinos know that if they hammer you every time you come to play, sooner or later you will quit coming. Better to offer you little incentives and let you win every once in a while. Like with my big friend, they still get to beat you up, but not as often.

The Battle and the War

In casino gambling, the short run is like a battle, and either player or casino can win. However, the casino always wins the war. The American Indians never had a chance against the continuing encroachment of white settlers. There were just too many settlers and too few Indians for the outcome ever to be in doubt. Losing the war, however, did not keep the Indians from winning a few big battles. So it goes in casino gambling. The player struggles in the face of overwhelming odds. If he keeps slugging it out, he is certain to lose. If, on the other hand, he hits and runs, he may come away a winner. It's like a commando raid: the gambler must get in, do some damage, and get out. Hanging around too long in the presence of superior force can be fatal.

To say that this takes discipline is an understatement. It's hard to withdraw when you are winning, and maybe even harder to call it quits when you are losing. Glenn couldn't do either, and a lot of gamblers are just like Glenn.

THE HOUSE ADVANTAGE

If casinos did engage in fair bets, they would win about half the bets and lose about half the bets. In other words, the casino (and you), on average, would break even, or at least come close to breaking even. While this arrangement would be more equitable, it would not, as a rule, generate enough money for the casino to pay its mortgage, much less foot the bill for the white tigers, pirate battles, lounge shows, $2 steaks, and free drinks.

To ensure sufficient income to meet their obligations and show a profit, casinos establish rules and payoffs for each game to give the house an advantage. While the house advantage is not strictly fair, it is what makes bargain rates on guest rooms, meals, and entertainment possible.

There are three basic ways that the house establishes its advantage:

1. The rules of the game are tailored to the house's advantage In blackjack, for instance, the dealer by rule always plays his own hand last. If any player busts (attains a point total over 21), the dealer wins by default without having to play out his hand.

2. The house pays off at less than the actual odds Imagine a carnival wheel with ten numbers. When the wheel is spun, each number has an equal chance of coming up. If you bet a dollar on number six, there is a one in ten chance that you will win and a nine in ten chance that you will lose. Gamblers express odds by comparing the likelihood of losing to the likelihood of winning. In this case, nine chances to lose and one to win, or nine to one. If the game paid off at the correct odds, you would get $9 every time you won (plus the dollar you bet). Each time you lost you would lose a dollar.

Let's say you start with $10 and do not win until your tenth try, betting your last dollar. If the game paid off at the correct odds, you would break even. Starting with $10, you would lose a dollar on each of your first nine attempts. In other words, you would be down $9. Betting your one remaining dollar, you win. At nine to one, you would receive $9 and get to keep the dollar you bet. You would have exactly the $10 you started with.

As we have seen, there is no way for a casino to play you even-up and still pay the bills. If, therefore, a casino owner decided to install a wheel with ten numbers, he would decrease the payoff. Instead of paying at the correct odds (nine to one), he might pay at eight to one. If you won on your last bet and got paid at eight to one (instead of nine to one), you would have lost $1 overall. Starting with $10, you lose your first nine bets (so you are out $9) and on your last winning bet you receive $8 and get to keep the dollar you bet. Having played ten times at the eight-to-one payoff, you have $9 left, for a total loss of $1. Thus the house's advantage in this game is 10% (one-tenth).

The house advantage for actual casino games ranges from less than 1% for certain betting situations in blackjack to in excess of 27% on keno and some slots. Although 1% doesn't sound like much of an advantage, it will get you if you play long enough. Plus, for the house it adds up.

Because of variations in game rules, the house advantage for a particular game in one casino may be greater than the house advantage for the same game in another casino. In most Las Vegas casinos, for instance, the house has a 5.26% advantage in roulette. At Sam's Town, however, because of the elimination of 00 (double zero) on certain roulette wheels, the house advantage is pared down to about 2.7%.

Rule variations in blackjack swing the house advantage from almost zero in single-deck games (surrender, doubling on any number of cards, dealer stands on soft 17, etc.), to more than 6% in multiple-deck games with draconian rules. Quite a few mathematicians have taken a crack at computing the house's advantage in blackjack. Some suggest that the player can actually gain an advantage over the house in single-deck games by keeping track of cards played. Others claim that without counting cards, a player utilizing a decision guide known as "basic strategy" can play the house nearly even. The reality for

95% of all blackjack players, however, is a house advantage of between 0.5% and 5.9%, depending on rule variations and the number of decks used.

Getting to the meat of the matter: blackjack played competently, baccarat, and certain bets in craps minimize the house advantage and give the player the best opportunity to win. Keno and wheel of fortune are outright sucker games. Slots, video poker, and roulette are not much better.

How the house advantage works in practice causes much misunderstanding. In most roulette bets, for example, the house holds a 5.26% advantage. If you place a dollar on black each time the wheel is spun, the house advantage predicts that, on average, you will lose 5.26 cents per dollar bet. Now, in actual play you will either lose one whole dollar or win one whole dollar, so it's not like somebody is making small change or keeping track of fractional losses. The longer you play, however, the greater the likelihood that the percentage of your losses will approximate the house advantage. If you played for a couple of hours and bet $1,000, your expected loss would be about $53.

All right, you think, that doesn't sound too bad. Plus, you're thinking: I would never bet as much as $1,000. Oh, yeah? If you approach the table with $200 and make 20 consecutive $10 bets, it is not very likely that you will lose every bet. When you take money from your winning bets and wager it, you are adding to your original stake. This is known as "action" in gambling parlance, and it is very different from bankroll. Money that you win is just as much yours as the stake with which you began. When you choose to risk your winnings in additional betting, you are giving the house a crack at a much larger amount than your original $200. If you start with

House Advantages	
Baccarat	1.17% on bank bets, 1.36% on player bets
Blackjack	0.5% to 5.9% for most games
Craps	1.4% to almost 17%, depending on the bet
Keno	20% to 35%
Roulette	5.26% to 7.89%, depending on the bet
Slots	2% to 25% (average 4% to 14%)
Video poker	1% to 12% (average 4% to 8%)
Wheel of fortune	11% to 24%

$200, win some and lose some, and keep playing your winnings in addition to your original stake until you have lost everything, you will have given the house (on average) about $3,800 worth of action. You may want to believe you only lost $200, but every penny of that $3,800 was yours.

3. The house takes a commission   In all casino poker games and in certain betting situations in table games, the house will collect a commission on a player's winnings.

Sometimes the house combines its various advantages. In baccarat, for instance, rules favor the house; payoffs are less than the true odds; and in certain betting situations, the house collects a commission on the player's winnings.

GAMES OF CHANCE AND THE LAW OF AVERAGES

People get funny ideas about the way gambling works. In casinos there are games of chance (roulette, craps, keno, bingo, wheel of fortune, slots, baccarat) and games of chance *and* skill (poker and blackjack).

A game of chance is like flipping a coin or spinning a wheel with ten numbers. What happens is what happens. A player can guess what the outcome will be but cannot influence it. Games of chance operate according to the law of averages. If you have a fair coin and flip it ten times, the law of averages leads you to expect that approximately half of the tosses will come up heads and the other half tails. If a roulette wheel has 38 slots, the law of averages suggests that the ball will fall into a particular slot one time in 38 spins.

The coin, the roulette ball, and the dice, however, have no memory. They just keep plugging along doing their thing. If I toss a coin and come up with heads nine times in a row, what are my chances of getting heads on the tenth toss? The answer is 50%, the same chance as getting heads on any toss. Each toss is completely independent of any other toss. When the coin goes up in the air that tenth time, it doesn't know that tails has not come up for a while, and certainly has no obligation to try to get the law of averages back into whack.

Though most gamblers are familiar with the law of averages, not all of them understand how it works. The operative word, as it turns out, is "averages," not "law." If you flip a coin a million times, there is nothing that says you will get 500,000 heads and 500,000 tails, no more than there is any assurance you will get five heads and five tails if you flip a coin ten times. What the law of averages *does* say is that, *in percentage terms,* the more times you toss the coin, the closer you will come to approximating the predicted average.

If you tossed a coin ten times, for example, you would not be surprised to get six tails and four heads. Six tails is only one flip off the five tails and five heads that the law of averages tells you is the probable outcome. By percentage, however, tails came up 60% (six of ten) of the time, while heads only came up 40% (four of ten) of the time. If you continued flipping the coin for a million tries, would you be surprised to get 503,750 tails and only 496,250 heads, a difference of 7,500 more tails than heads? The law of averages stipulates that the more we toss (and a million tosses are certainly a lot more than ten tosses) the closer we should come to approximating the average, but here we are with a huge difference of 7,500 more tails. What went wrong?

Nothing went wrong. True, after ten flips, we had only two more tails than heads, while after a million flips we had 7,500 more tails than heads. But in terms of percentage, 503,750 tails is 50.375% of one million, only about one-third of a measly percent from what the law of averages predicts. The law of averages is about percentages. Gambling is about dollars out of your pocket. If you had bet a dollar on heads each toss, you would have lost $2 after ten flips. After a million flips you would have lost $7,500. The law of averages behaved just as mathematical theory predicted, but that's probably not much consolation for going home broke.

Games of Chance and Skill

Blackjack and poker are games of chance and skill, meaning that the knowledge, experience, and skill of the player can have some influence on the outcome. All avid poker players or bridge players can recall nights when they played for hours without being dealt a good hand. That's the chance part. In order to win (especially in blackjack, where there is no bluffing), you need good cards. There is usually not much you can do if you are dealt a bad hand. As the Nevada mule drivers say, "You can't polish a turd."

If you are dealt something to work with, however, you can bring your skill into play and try to make your good hand even better. In casino poker, players compete against each other in the same way they do at Uncle Bert's house back home. The only difference is that, in the casino, the house takes a small percentage of each winning pot as compensation for hosting the game (are you listening, Uncle Bert?). Although not every casino poker player is an expert, your chances of coming up against an expert in a particular game are good. Our advice on casino poker: if you are not a tough fish, better not try to swim with the sharks.

Blackjack likewise combines chance and skill. In blackjack, however, players compete against the house (the dealer). Players have certain choices and options in blackjack, but the dealer's play is completely bound by rules. Much has been written about winning at blackjack. It's been said that by keeping track of cards played (and thereby knowing which cards remain undealt in the deck), a player can raise his or her bets when the deck contains a higher-than-usual percentage of aces, tens, and picture cards. In practice,

---

The Intelligence Test

If you have been paying attention, here is what you should understand by now:

1. That all gambling games are designed to favor the house, and that in the long run the house will always win.

2. That it costs a lot to build, staff, and operate a casino, and that a casino must attract many players in order to pay the bills and still make a profit.

3. That casinos compete fiercely for available customers and offer incentives ranging from 50-cent hot dogs to free guest rooms to get the right customers to their gaming tables.

Question: Given the above, what kind of customer gets the best deal?

Answer: The person who takes advantage of all the incentives without gambling.

Question: What kind of customer gets the next best deal?

Answer: The customer who sees gambling as recreation, gambles knowledgeably, makes sensible bets, sets limits on the amount he or she is prepared to wager, and enjoys all of the perks and amenities, but stays in control.

Question: What kind of customer gets the worst deal?

Answer: The person who thinks he or she can win. This person will foot the bill for everyone else.

---

however, the casino confounds efforts to count cards by combining several decks together, "burning" cards (removing undisclosed cards from play), and keeping the game moving at a fast pace. If an experienced gambler with extraordinary memory and power of concentration is able to overcome these obstacles, the casino will simply throw this person out.

In blackjack, as in every other casino game, it is ludicrous to suggest that the house is going to surrender its advantage. Incidentally, a super-gambler playing flawlessly in a single-deck game and keeping track of every card will gain only a nominal and temporary advantage over the house. On top of playing perfectly and being dealt good cards, the super-gambler must also disguise his play and camouflage his betting so the house won't know what he's up to. If you really want to make money on blackjack, write a book about it.

Playing It Smart

Experienced, noncompulsive, recreational gamblers typically play in a very disciplined and structured manner. Here's what they recommend:

1. *Never gamble when you are tired, depressed, or sick.* Also, watch the drinking. Alcohol impairs judgment and lowers inhibitions.

2. *Set a limit before you leave home on the total amount you are willing to lose gambling.* No matter what happens, do not exceed this limit.

3. *Decide which game(s) interest you and get the rules down before you play.* If you are a first-timer at craps or baccarat, take lessons (offered free at the casinos most days). If you are a virgin blackjack player, buy a good book and learn basic strategy. For all three games, spend an hour or two observing games in progress before buying in. Stay away from games like keno and wheel of fortune, in which the house advantage is overwhelming.

4. *Decide how long you want to play and work out a gambling itinerary consistent with the funds you set aside for wagering.* Let's say you plan to be in Las Vegas for two days and want to play about five hours each day. If you have $500 gambling money available for the trip, that's $250 a day. Dividing the $250 a day by five hours, you come up with $50 an hour.

   Now, forget time. Think of your gambling in terms of playing individual sessions instead of hours. You are going to play five sessions a day with $50 available to wager at each session.

5. *Observe a strategy for winning and losing.* On buying in, place your session allocation by your left hand. Play your allotted session money only once during a given session. Any time you win, return your original bet to the session-allocation stack (left hand), and place your winnings in a stack by your right hand. Never play any chips or coins you have won. When you have gone through your original allocation once, pick up the chips or coins in your winning stack (right hand) and quit. The difference between your original allocation and what you walk away with is your net win or loss for the session.

   During the session, bet consistently. If you have been making $1 bets and have lost $10, do not chase your losses by upping your bets to $10 in an effort to get even in a hurry.

   If you were fortunate and doubled your allocated stake during the session (in this case, walked away with $100 or more), take everything in excess of $100 and put it aside as winnings, not to be touched for the remainder of your trip. If you won, but did not double your money, or if you had a net loss (quit with less than $50 in your win stack), use this money in your next playing session.

6. *Take a break between sessions.* Relax for a while after each session. Grab a bite to eat, enjoy a nap, or go for a swim.

7. *When you complete the number of sessions scheduled for the day, stop gambling.* Period.

INDECENT EXPECTATIONS

Each month the *Las Vegas Advisor* (a newsletter published by Huntington Press—(702) 252-0655) runs a feature on gambling. The following article from a past issue will give you an idea what gamblers talk about at cocktail parties.

"The Odds against Woody Harrelson and Demi Moore"

By now, you've probably heard the basis of the plot of the hit movie *Indecent Proposal.* A young couple (Woody Harrelson and Demi Moore) find themselves desperate for money, and head to Las Vegas. There, they meet up with a "billionaire" gambler played by Robert Redford. Redford offers Moore a million dollars, and all she has to do is spend the night with him. Moore and Harrelson decide to accept the offer. The talk-show circuit went wild with discussions about morality and relationships, but we were more intrigued by an interesting and pertinent gambling question buried within the plotline. Namely: What are the chances of turning a little money into a lot by gambling?

In the movie, the couple takes a $5,000 stake to Las Vegas in an attempt to turn it into $50,000. What were the odds against their achieving their goal? By applying an optimal strategy of "bold" play at craps (line bets) or baccarat, the odds would have been about 9.5 to 1 against them. Bold play requires betting the entire $5,000 on a single coup, then rebetting the original wager, plus winnings, until either reaching the $50,000 goal or going broke (see chart). Any departure from this strategy raises the odds against success. Unfortunately for our heroes, they departed dramatically. Though it cannot be determined from the movie what the exact wagers were, it appears that the couple split their stake and made multiple wagers of $300 to $400 per coup, a decision that doomed their chances. Given this method, the odds against their winning the $50,000 were greater than *one million to one!*

The analysis above deals with a concept known as "gambler's ruin" and has implications for virtually all recreational gamblers, who find that they must choose between (1) optimizing their chances of winning and (2) getting in playing time at their game of choice.

BOLD-PLAY STRATEGY

Bet entire $5,000.

If lose, go home; if win, bet $10,000.

If lose, go home; if win, bet $20,000.

If lose, go home; if win, bet $10,000 (of $40,000 total).

If win, succeed; if lose, bet $20,000 (of $30,000 total).

If win, succeed; if lose, begin again betting entire $10,000.

There's a clearly defined trade-off. Assuming you want to win a specific amount of money, your best strategy is to bet as much as you can on as few wagers as possible until you reach your goal. You'll either go broke or reach your win figure—quickly. The first outcome is obviously undesirable. But so is the second (for most), since this strategy dictates that you now refrain from gambling any more.

If you divide your stake and make smaller bets, you are assured of gambling longer, but your chances of winning are diminished. Faced with this dilemma, most turn to the mystical idea of money management. Unfortunately, no system of money management can earn a profit (long-term) in a negative expectation game. In fact, most money-management systems require that you divide your stake into many units, and we've already seen that this leads to ultimate doom.

So, you have two choices:

1. Play only positive expectation games—certain blackjack (for expert card counters) and video poker games, promotions, coupons, the things we tell you about in the *LVA*. Dividing your stake is desirable when you have the advantage.

2. Accept the fact that you gamble for entertainment value and are destined to pay a fee (your losses) for "admission," just as surely as you must pay to see a concert or a sporting event.

In a sidebar to the *Las Vegas Advisor* article, mathematician and gambling author Peter Griffin had this to add:

The best the couple [Woody and Demi] could have done is apply a complicated combination of bold play and a betting method that utilizes 10 × odds [at a craps table]. This betting method is "99 and 44/100% pure," i.e., it gives .09944 chance of success (only about 9 to 1 against, which are the lowest odds achievable given Las Vegas's negative expectation gambling options).

What about blackjack at a casino like the New Frontier where favorable rules afford a basic strategy player [with perfect play] a slight edge?

The couple needed $50,000 quickly, else they might have gone to work and saved (probably ruled out by the Hollywood media elite since they don't want to encourage such values). This also rules out playing blackjack. Playing $1 per hand (perfect basic strategy), they would be virtually assured of turning their $5,000 into $50,000. However, it would take about 30 million hands. At 1,000 hands per day, both playing, that's about 40 years. At $5 per hand, they would reach their goal about 97% of the time, and it would take about six million hands or about eight years. Plus, they'd win New Frontier free-room tokens redeemable for nearly 30,000 nights.

GAMING INSTRUCTION AND RESOURCES

Most casino games are actually fairly simple once you know what's going on. A great way to replace inexperience and awkwardness with knowledge and confidence is to take advantage of the free gaming lessons offered by the casinos. Friendly, upbeat, and fun, the lessons introduce you not only to the rules, but also to the customs and etiquette of the respective games. Going slow and easy, the instructors take you step by step through the play and the betting without your actually wagering any money. Many casinos feature low-minimum-bet "live games" following the instruction. We also recommend the lessons to nonplaying companions of gamblers. For folks who usually spend a fair amount of time as spectators, casino games, like all other games, are more interesting if you know what is going on.

No matter how many books you have read, take a lesson in craps before you try to play in a casino. You don't need to know much to play baccarat, but *understanding* it is a different story. Once again, we strongly recommend lessons. Though you can learn to play blackjack by reading a book and practicing at home, lessons will make you feel more comfortable.

When "new games" are added to the traditional selection, casinos often offer instruction for a limited time. The latest rages are Red Dog poker and, owing to the increasing number of Asian gamblers, Pai Gow and Pai Gow poker. Lessons are also available in traditional poker. The San Remo offers regularly scheduled gaming lessons in Japanese.

Where to Go for Lessons

Baccarat	Caribbean Stud	Sam's Town	Poker
Bally's		Stardust	Monte Carlo
Caesars Palace	Harrah's		
MGM Grand	MGM Grand	**Let It Ride**	**Roulette**
Riviera	Riviera	Harrah's	Bally's
	Stardust	MGM Grand	Caesars Palace
Blackjack		Riviera	Circus Circus
Bally's	**Craps**	Stardust	Excalibur
Caesars Palace	Bally's		Harrah's
Circus Circus	Caesars Palace	**Pai Gow and**	Luxor
Excalibur	Circus Circus	**Pai Gow**	MGM Grand
Harrah's	Excalibur	**Poker**	Riviera
Lady Luck	Flamingo	Bally's	Stardust
Luxor	Harrah's	Caesars Palace	
MGM Grand	Lady Luck	Harrah's	**Video Poker**
Riviera	Luxor	MGM Grand	Fiesta
Sahara	MGM Grand	Stardust	
Silverton	Riviera		
Stardust	Sahara		

Written References and the Gambler's Book Club   Most libraries and bookstores offer basic reference works on casino gambling. If you cannot find what you need at home, call the Gambler's Book Club at (800) 634-6243 for a free catalog. If you would like to stop in and browse while you are in Las Vegas, the club's store is located at 630 South 11th Street, just off East Charleston Boulevard. The local phone is 382-7555. Before you buy, check our list of recommended reading on page 497. Gambler's Book Club, incidentally, sells single issues of the *Las Vegas Advisor,* quoted above.

Funbooks, Matchplay, and Understanding the Marquees

Casino games, not unexpectedly, are entrenched in jargon. Most of the terminology you can figure out intuitively, and much of the rest is useless in any event. The terms below, however, keep popping up in ads, in coupons, and on marquees, and manage to confuse a lot of people.

Crapless Craps   In crapless craps, dice totals of 2, 3, 11, and 12 count as point numbers. For information on the rules of craps, see pages 327–332.

Double Exposure 21   A version of blackjack in which both of the dealer's cards are dealt face up.

Double Odds   The option in craps of making an odds bet twice the size of your line bet. See "Craps," pages 327–332.

Funbooks   Little booklets of coupons available without charge from certain casinos. The coupons in funbooks vary widely from casino to casino but usually include coupons for souvenir gifts, discount show tickets, discount meals, two-for-one or free drinks, and matchplay (see below). Some funbooks offer exceptional value, while others are nothing more than a hustle. Coupons for keno and slots, for example, are practically worthless, while matchplay coupons for table games can be valuable. On balance, coupon books are worth checking out.

Loose Slots   Slot machines that are programmed to pay off more frequently. The term is usually applied to machines with a return rate of 94% or higher, meaning that the house advantage is 6% or less.

Matchplay Coupons   Coupons from funbooks or print ads that can be redeemed for matchplay chips. The matchplay chips must be combined with an equal amount of your own money on certain table game bets. If you win, you are paid off for the entire bet in real money. If you bet $5 in matchplay chips and $5 of your bankroll on the color black in roulette, you will win $10 of real money if the ball lands in a black slot. When you are paid off, the dealer collects your matchplay chips, which can only be used once, but you keep the $5 in real money you bet. If you lose, of course, the dealer will take both the real money and the matchplay chips.

Megabucks Slots   A statewide progressive slot machine network with grand jackpots in excess of $5 million. For additional information on progressive slot systems, see page 307.

Single-Deck Blackjack   Blackjack dealt from a single deck as opposed to two or more decks shuffled together.

Triple Odds   The option in craps of making an odds bet three times the size of your line bet. See "Craps," page 327–332.

WHERE TO PLAY

We receive a lot of mail from readers asking which casino has the loosest slots, the most favorable rules for blackjack, and the best odds on craps. We directed the questions to veteran gambler and tournament player Anthony Curtis, publisher of the *Las Vegas Advisor*. Here's Anthony's reply:

Where's the best casino in Las Vegas to play blackjack, video poker, and the rest of the gambling games? It could be almost anyplace on any given day due to spot promotions and changing management philosophies. A few casinos, however, have established reliable track records in specific areas. Absent a special promotion or change in policy, I recommend the following casinos as the best places to play each of the games listed:

Blackjack
Binion's Horseshoe

Almost 50 single-deck games with a skinny 0.15% casino edge versus basic strategy. Not as loose as they used to be with comps, but still a great place to play and be treated well for low stakes.

Quarter Slots
Sunset Station

Caters to discriminating local clientele. Good slot club with frequent multiple point days.

Dollar Slots
Las Vegas Hilton

Over 1% cash back, plus free tournaments and juicy offers for slot club members.

Craps
Casino Royale

One of only two casinos in Las Vegas that still offer 100 X odds, but Casino Royale's limits are lowest, requiring a minimum wager of $2 on the line.

Quarter Video Poker
Regent Las Vegas

Fantastic array of 100%+ schedules, including at least one, a 10/6 double double bonus game, that has not been seen elsewhere in Las Vegas.

Dollar Video Poker
Orleans

Good schedules for dollar players, including progressives that often surpass the breakeven point (i.e. exceed a 100% return). Improved slot club.

Roulette
Monte Carlo

Single zero in the heart of the Strip. The absence of the usual double zero lowers the casino's edge from 5.26% to 2.7%.

Baccarat
Binion's Horseshoe

This recommendation stems from the fact that the mini-baccarat tables on the first floor charge a 4% commission on winning bank bets as compared to the standard 5%. This concession lowers the house edge from 1.06% to 0.6%.

Keno Silverton	A comparison of keno return percentages shows casinos that target locals offer the best chance of winning.
Bingo Arizona Charlie's West	Converted big showroom to bingo hall, 24-hour schedule, some of the biggest jackpots in town generated by heavy action.
Poker Stardust	Lower stakes in this room but reasonable action and promotions. Good place to start.
Race and Sports Betting Imperial Palace	Famous for their wild proposition bets on big events. You can bet on more things here than anywhere else in town. Also a drive-through ticket window.
Let It Ride O'Shea's	Consistent low-minimum games. Waitresses deliver Irish beers to the table.
Caribbean Stud Binion's Horseshoe	High reset on progressive with low minimums.
Pai Gow Poker Gold Coast	Lots of action around the clock, and low minimums.

CHANGES IN ATTITUDE, CHANGES IN LATITUDE

Most people who love to gamble are not motivated by greed. Usually it is the tension, excitement, and anticipation of the game that they enjoy. Misunderstanding this reality has led many naive and innocent people into the nightmare of addictive gambling.

Ed was attending a convention on his first visit to Las Vegas. One evening, he decided to try his luck at roulette. Approaching the table, Ed expected to lose ("I'm not stupid, after all"). His intentions were typical. He wanted to "try" gambling while in Nevada, and he was looking for an adventure, a new experience. What Ed never anticipated was the emotional impact gambling would have on him. It transcended winning and losing. In fact, it wasn't about winning or losing at all. It was the *playing* that mattered. The "action" made him feel alive, involved, and terribly sophisticated. It also made him crazy.

The "high" described by the compulsive gambler closely parallels the experience of drug or alcohol abusers. In fact, there is a tendency for chemical addiction and gambling compulsion to overlap. The compulsive gambler attempts to use "the action" as a cure for a variety of ills, in much the same way that people use alcohol and drugs to lift them out of depression, stem anxiety or boredom, and make them feel more "in control."

Some people cannot handle gambling, just as some people cannot handle alcohol. The problem, unfortunately, is compounded by the attitude of our society. As we profess to admire the drinker who can "hold his liquor," we reinforce the gambler who beats the odds in Las Vegas. By glamorizing these behaviors we enable afflicted individuals to remain in denial about the destructive nature of their problem. The compulsive gambler blames circumstances and other people for the suffering occasioned by his or her affliction. One may hear excuses like: "I didn't get enough sleep; I couldn't concentrate with all the noise; I lost track of the time; I'm jinxed at this casino."

If this sounds like you or someone you love, get help. In Las Vegas there is a meeting of Gamblers Anonymous almost every night. Call 385-7732. If, like Ed, you catch something in Las Vegas and take it home with you, Gamblers Anonymous is listed in your local white pages.

Rules of the Games

SLOT MACHINES

Slot machines, including video poker, have eclipsed the table games in patron popularity. There are few casinos remaining that have not allocated more than half of their available floor space to various types of slot machines.

The popularity of slots is not difficult to understand. First, slots allow a person to enjoy casino gambling at low or high stakes. In downtown Las Vegas at the Nevada and the Gold Spike, for instance, you can play the slots for a penny a pop. Nickel slots, meanwhile, can be found in virtually every casino in town. Quarter slots are the most popular and the most common. Higher-stakes players can find machines that accept bets of $1 to $500 (high-stakes slots use special tokens instead of coins).

Second, many people like the slots because no human interaction is required. Absent in slot play is the adversarial atmosphere of the table games. Machines are less intimidating—at least more neutral—than dealers and pit bosses. Once appropriate change is obtained, a patron can sit at a machine for as long as his stamina and money last and never be bothered by a soul.

Finally, slot machines are simple, or at least ostensibly so. Although there are a number of things you should know before you play the slots, the only thing you have to know is to put a coin in the slot and pull the handle.

What You Need to Know before You Play Slot Machines

For the moment we will confine our discussion to traditional slot machines, the so-called one-armed bandits. Later we will take a look at video poker.

Starting at the beginning: All slot machines have a slot for inserting coins, a handle to pull (or button to push) to activate the machine, a visual display where you can see the reels spin and stop on each play, and a coin tray that you hope some winnings will drop into.

While most slot machines have three reels, some have as many as eight. Each reel will have some number of "stops," positions where the reel can come to rest. Reels with 20, 25, or 32 stops are the most common. On each reel at each stop (or resting position) is a single slot symbol (a cherry, a plum, an orange, etc.). What you hope will happen (when the reels stop spinning) is that three of the same symbol will line up on the pay line. If this happens, you win.

In addition to three of the same symbol on a line, many machines will pay for single cherries in the far left or far right position, two cherries together side by side, or two bells or two oranges side by side with a bar on the end.

With the old slot machines things were pretty simple. There was one coin slot, one handle to pull, and a display with one pay line. Symbols either lined up on that line or they didn't. Modern machines are much more complex. Almost all modern machines accept more than one coin per play (usually three to five). No matter how many coins the machine will take, it only requires one to play.

If you put in additional coins (bet more), you will buy one of the following benefits:

1. Payoff schedules On a certain type of machine, two, three, four, or five different payoff schedules are posted on the front of the machine above the reel display. If you study these schedules you will notice that by playing extra coins you can increase your payoff should you win. Usually the increase is straightforward. If you play two coins, you will win twice as much as if you play one coin. If you play three coins, you will win three times as much as if you play one coin, and so on. Some machines, however, have a grand jackpot that will pay off only if you have played the maximum number of coins. If you line up the symbols for the grand jackpot but have not played the maximum number of coins, you will not win. Always read the payoff schedule for a machine before you play and make sure you understand it. If you do not, ask an attendant or find a simpler machine.

Though most casino slot machines are kept in good working order, watch to make sure a section of the payoff schedule lights up for every coin you play. If you are playing a machine with four payoff schedules, the schedules should light up, one at a time, as you put in your coins. On machines where the payoff schedules do not illuminate, there will ordinarily be a light (or lights) above or below the reel display that will verify that the machine has accepted your coins. If you put in multiple coins without the appropriate lights coming on, do not play until you check things out with an attendant.

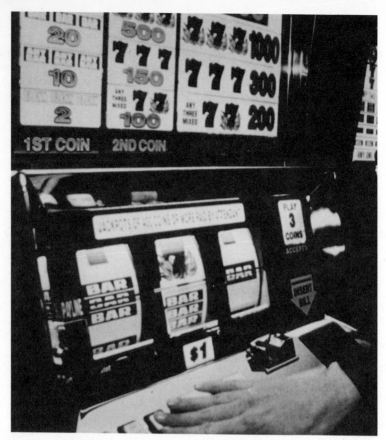

Modern multiple-coin, multiple-pay-line (nonprogressive) slot machine. (Courtesy of Las Vegas News Bureau)

2. Multiple pay lines   When you play your first coin, you buy the usual pay line, right in the center of the display. By playing more coins, you can buy additional pay lines.

Each pay line you purchase gives you another way of winning. Instead of being limited to the center line, the machine will pay off on the top, center, or bottom lines, and five-coin machines will pay winners on diagonal lines. If you play machines with multiple pay lines, make sure that each pay line you buy is acknowledged by a light before you pull the handle.

An irritating feature of many multiple-line machines are "blanks" or "ghosts." A blank is nothing more than an empty stop on the reel—a place where you would expect a symbol to be but where there is nothing. As you have probably surmised, you cannot hit a winner by lining up blanks.

Slot Machine Reels

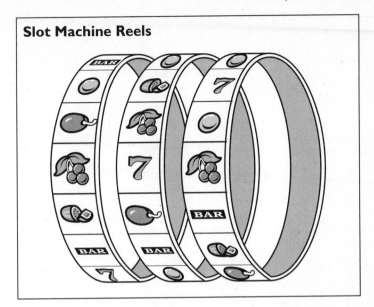

Nonprogressive vs. Progressive Slot Machines   Nonprogressive slot machines have fixed payoffs. You can read the payoff schedules posted on the machine and determine exactly how much you will get for each winning combination for any number of coins played.

A second type of machine, known as a progressive, has a grand jackpot that grows and grows until somebody hits it. After the grand jackpot has been won, a new jackpot is established and starts to grow. While individual machines can offer modest progressive grand jackpots, the really big jackpots (several thousand to several million dollars) are possible only on machines linked in a system to other machines. Sometimes an "island," "carousel," or "bank" of machines in a given casino is hooked up to create a progressive system. The more these machines are played, the faster the progressive grand jackpot grows. The largest progressive jackpots, however, come from huge multicasino systems that sometimes cover the entire state. Players have won up to $27.5 million by hitting these jackpots.

While nothing is certain in slot play, it is generally accepted that nonprogressives will pay more small jackpots. Progressives, on the other hand, offer an opportunity to really strike it rich, but they give up fewer intermediate wins. Each type of machine targets a certain player. The nonprogressive machine appeals to the player who likes plenty of action, who gets bored when coins aren't clanking into the tray every four or five pulls. The progressive machine is for the player who is willing to forgo frequent small payouts for the chance of hitting a really big one.

How Slot Machines Work

Almost all slot machines used in casinos today are controlled by micro-processors. This means the machines can be programmed and are more like computers than mechanical boxes composed of gears and wheels. During the evolution of the modern slot machine, manufacturers took a whack at eliminating the traditional spinning reels in favor of a video display, and replacing the pull handle with a button. The public rejected these innovations, however, and the spinning reels and pull handles have been retained. In a modern slot machine there is a device that computer people call a "random number generator" and that we refer to as a "black box." What the black box does is spit out hundreds of numbers each second, selected randomly (i.e., in no predetermined sequence). The black box has about four billion different numbers to choose from, so it's very unusual (but not impossible) for the same number to come up twice in a short time.

The numbers the black box selects are programmed to trigger a certain set of symbols on the display, determining where the reels stop. What most players don't realize, however, is that the black box pumps out numbers continuously, regardless of whether the machine is being played or not. If you are playing a machine, the black box will call up hundreds or thousands of numbers in the few seconds between plays while you sip your drink, put some money in the slot, and pull the handle.

Why is this important? Try this scenario: Mary has played the same quarter machine for two hours, pumping an untold amount of money into it. While she turns for a moment to buy gum from a cigarette girl, a man walks up to Mary's machine and wins the grand jackpot. Mary is livid. "That's my jackpot," she screams. Not so. While Mary bought her gum, thousands of numbers and possible symbol combinations were generated by the black box. The only way Mary could have won the grand jackpot (even if the man had not come along) would have been to activate the machine at that same exact moment in time, right down to a fraction of a millisecond.

There is no such thing as a machine that is "overdue to hit." Each spin of the reels on a slot machine is an independent event, just like flipping a coin. The only way to hit a jackpot is to activate the machine at the exact moment that the black box randomly coughs up a winning number. If you play a slot machine as fast as you can, jamming in coins and pumping the handle like a maniac, the black box will still spew out more numbers (and possible jackpots) between each try than you will have pulls in a whole day of playing.

Cherry, Cherry, Orange   The house advantage is known for every casino game except slots. With slot machines, the house advantage is whatever the casino wants it to be. In Atlantic City the maximum legal house advantage is 17%. There is no limit in Nevada. In theory a casino could program a

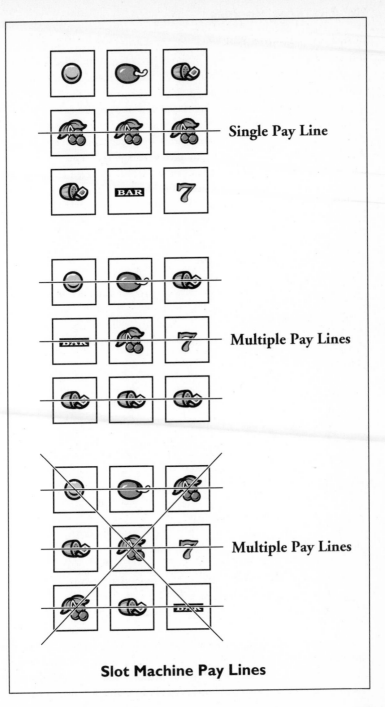

Slot Machine Pay Lines

machine to keep 50% of all the coins played. Interviews with ex–casino employees suggest, however, that the house advantage on casino slots in Las Vegas ranges from about 2.5% to 25%, with most machines giving the house an edge of between 4% and 14%.

Casinos advertise their slots in terms of payout or return rate. If a casino states that its slots return up to 97%, that's another way of saying that the house has a 3% advantage. Some casinos advertise machines that pay up to 98%, and one casino even claims to offer slots paying 101%! We're skeptical about the 98% machines, and as for the 101% machine . . . well, if you ever find it, drop us a line. Incidentally, the operative terminology is "up to," not "98%." In most casinos, only a few slots return in excess of 92%.

Slot Quest   A slot machine that withholds only a small percentage of the money played is referred to as "loose," while a machine that retains most of the coins it takes in is called "tight." "Loose" and "tight" are figurative descriptions and have nothing to do with the mechanical condition of the machine. Because return rates vary from casino to casino, and because machines in a given casino are programmed to withhold vastly differing percentages of the coins played, slot players devote much time and energy to finding the best casinos and the loosest machines. Exactly how to go about this is the subject of much discussion.

In terms of choosing a casino, there are several theories which have at least a marginal ring of truth. Competition among casinos is often a general indicator for finding loose slots. Some say that smaller casinos, which compete against large neighbors, must program their slots to provide a higher return. Alternatively, some folks will play slots only in casinos patronized predominantly by locals (Gold Coast, Palace Station, Boulder Station, Fiesta, Regent, Suncoast, Orleans, Texas Station, El Cortez, Gold Spike, Castaways, Sam's Town, Arizona Charlie's, Santa Fe Station). The reasoning here is that these casinos vie for regular customers on a continuing basis and must therefore offer extremely competitive win rates. Downtown Las Vegas is likewise cast in the "we try harder" role because smaller downtown casinos must go head to head with the Strip to attract patrons.

Extending the logic, machines located in supermarkets, restaurants, convenience stores, airports, and lounges are purported to be very tight. In these places, some argue, there is little incentive for management to provide good returns because the patrons will play regardless (out of boredom or simply because the machine is there).

Veteran slot players have a lot of theories when it comes to finding the loose machines in a particular casino. Some will tell you to play the machines by the door or in the waiting area outside the showroom. By placing the loose machines in these locations, the theory goes, the casino can demonstrate to passersby and show patrons that the house has loose slots. A more labor-intensive suggestion for sniffing out the loose machines is to hang around the casino during the wee hours of the morning when the machines are being emptied. Supposedly machines with the least number of coins in the hopper have been paying off more frequently. Or maybe these machines have just been played less often.

Of the theories for finding the loose machines in a specific casino, the suggestion that makes the most sense is to select a casino and play there long enough to develop a relationship with the slot attendants. Not as difficult as it sounds, this means being friendly and engaging the attendants in pleasant conversation. If the casino has a slot club, join up and use the club card so the slot personnel will regard you as a regular. If the attendants are responsive and kind, and particularly if you win, give them a tip. After a couple of hours, the attendants will begin to take an interest in you. Ask them candidly and forthrightly to point out a good (i.e., loose) machine. Tip them for the information and tip again if you do well on the machine. If the machine is not hitting for you, don't blame the attendant. Continue to be positive and build the relationship. In the long run, it is in your best interest, as well as in the best interest of the attendant and of the house, for the relationship to prosper. If the attendant turns you on to the loosest machine in Las Vegas, the house is still going to make money in the long run. If the force is with you, however, you might rack up a nice short-term win or at least get more play for your money.

I have had a slot manager admit to me that his nickel machines are tighter than his quarter machines and that his dollar and five-dollar machines are the loosest of all. Tight or loose, however, all slots are programmed to give the casino a certain profit over the long run. It is very unlikely, in any event, that you will play a machine long enough to experience the theoretical payoff rate. What you are concerned about is the short run. In the short run anything can happen, including winning.

Maximizing Your Chances of Winning on the Slots In any multiple-coin slot machine, as we have seen, you have a higher expectation of winning if you play the maximum number of coins. If what you actually desire to bet is 25 cents per play, you will probably be better off putting five nickels into a multiple-coin nickel slot than one quarter into a multiple-coin quarter slot. Likewise, if you are up for wagering a dollar a play, go with four coins in the quarter slot rather than $1 in the dollar slot. Never play a progressive machine unless you are betting the maximum number of coins. If you play less than the maximum on a progressive, you are simply contributing to a jackpot that you have no chance of winning. If you don't want to place a maximum bet, play a nonprogressive machine.

Slot Machine Etiquette and Common Sense

Regardless of whether you are playing a one-armed bandit, a video poker machine, or any other type of coin-operated slot machine, there are some things you need to know:

1. Obtain your change before you select a machine.

2. Realize that avid slot players sometimes play more than one machine at a time. Do not assume that a machine is not in use simply because nobody is standing or sitting in front of it. Slot players can be fanatically territorial.

3. Before you start to play, check out the people around you. Do you feel safe and comfortable among them?

4. Read and understand the payout schedule of any machine you play.

5. Check to see if the machine automatically pays coins into the tray or whether your winnings are registered on a credit meter. If your machine has a credit meter, be sure to cash out your credits before you abandon the machine.

6. If the casino has a slot club, join (this usually takes less than five minutes on-site, but can be accomplished through the mail prior to your trip). Use the club card whenever you play. When you quit, don't forget to take your club card with you.

7. Never play more machines than you can watch carefully. Be particularly vigilant when playing machines near exits and corridors. If you are asleep at the switch, a thief can dip into your coin tray or bucket and be out the door in seconds.

8. Keep your purse and your money in sight at all times. Never put your purse on the floor behind you or to the side. Leave unopened rolls of coins in your purse or pocket.

9. If you line up a winner and nothing happens, don't leave the machine. Sometimes large jackpots exceed the coin capacity of the machine and must be paid directly by the casino cashier. Call immediately for an attendant but do not wander off looking for one. While you wait, refrain from further play on the machine in question. When the attendant arrives, check his casino employee identification.

10. If the appropriate payout sections or pay lines fail to illuminate when playing multiple coins, do not leave or activate the machine (pull the handle) until you have consulted an attendant.

Slot Clubs and Frequent-Player Clubs

Most Las Vegas casinos now have slot or frequent-player clubs. The purpose of these clubs is to foster increased customer loyalty among gambling patrons by providing incentives.

You can join a club by signing up at the casino or (at some casinos) by applying through the mail. There is neither a direct cost associated with joining nor any dues. You are given a plastic membership card that very much resembles a credit card. This card can be inserted into a receptacle on certain quarter and dollar slots (including video poker machines). As long as your card is in the receptacle, you are credited for the amount of action you give that machine. Programs at different casinos vary, but in general, you are awarded "points" based on how long you play and how much you wager. Some clubs award points for both slot and table play, while other clubs confine their program to slots. As in an airline frequent-flyer program, accumulated points can ultimately be redeemed for awards. Awards range from casino logo apparel to discounts (or comps) on meals, shows, and rooms.

The good thing about slot clubs is that they provide a mechanism for slot players to obtain some of the comps, perks, and extras that have always been available to table players. The bad thing about a slot club is that it confines your play. In other words, you must give most of your business to one or two casinos in order to accumulate award points. If you are a footloose player and enjoy gambling all around town, you may never accrue enough points in any one casino to redeem a prize.

Even if you never redeem any points, however, it's still a good idea to join. Joining a club gets you identified as a gambler on the casino's mailing list. Just for joining, and without gambling that first quarter, you will be offered discounts on rooms and a variety of other special deals. If you travel to Las Vegas regularly on business, join your hotel's slot club. Membership might make you eligible for deals on rooms and food that would otherwise not be available to you.

VIDEO POKER

Never in the history of casino gambling has a new game become so popular so quickly. All across Nevada, casinos are reallocating game-table and slot space to video poker machines. More people are familiar with poker than with any other casino game. The video version affords average folks an opportunity to play a game of chance and skill without going up against professional gamblers.

In video poker you are not playing against anyone. Rather, you are trying to make the best possible five-card-draw poker hand. In the most common rendition, you insert your coin(s) and push a button marked "deal." Your original five cards are displayed on the screen. Below the screen and under each of the cards pictured are "hold" buttons. After evaluating your hand and planning your strategy, designate the cards you want to keep by pressing the appropriate hold button(s). If you hit the wrong button or change your mind, most machines have an "error" or "erase" button, which will allow you to revise your choices before you draw. If you do not want to draw any cards (you like your hand as dealt), press all five hold buttons. When you press the hold button for a particular card, the word "hold" will appear over or under that card on the display. Always double-check the screen to make certain the cards you intend to hold are marked before proceeding to the draw.

When you are ready, press the button marked "draw" (on many machines it is the same button as the deal button). Any cards you have not designated to be held will be replaced. As in live draw poker, the five cards in your possession after the draw are your final hand. If the hand is a winner (a pair of jacks or better on most quarter machines and dollar machines), you will be credited the appropriate winnings on a credit meter on the video display. These are actual winnings that can be retrieved in coins by pressing the "cash-out" button. If you choose to leave your winnings on the credit meter, you may use them to bet, eliminating the need to physically insert coins in the machine. When you are ready to quit, simply press the cash-out button and collect your coins from the tray.

You do not have to know much about poker to play video poker. All of the winning hands with their respective payoffs are posted on or above the video display. As with other slot machines, you can increase your payoffs and become eligible for bonus jackpots by playing the maximum number of coins. Note that some machines have jackpots listed in dollars, while others are specified in coins. Obviously, there is a big difference between $4,000 and 4,000 nickels.

Quarter and dollar video poker machines come in progressive and nonprogressive models. Nonprogressive machines will pay more on a full house (nine coins) and a flush (six coins) than will progressives (eight and five coins respectively). Progressives feature a grand jackpot that continues to build until somebody hits it. Nonprogressives usually feature a bonus jackpot for hitting a royal flush when playing the maximum number of coins.

In popular jargon, video poker machines are labeled according to these different payoffs as "nine/six" or "eight/five" machines. Never play a progressive (eight/five) machine unless you are playing the number of coins required to win the grand jackpot. By playing less than the maximum number of coins, you disqualify yourself for the grand jackpot while subsidizing the jackpot's growth. Plus, you get a lower return rate than you would on a nonprogressive (nine/six). Also be aware that the grand jackpot for maximum coin play on a nonprogressive can sometimes be larger than the grand jackpot on a progressive. Always scout around before you play.

It should be noted that some casinos have begun to experiment with progressive and nonprogressive ten/six and nine/seven machines. The expected value of perfect play on these machines exceeds 100%.

In addition to straight draw poker, games with jokers or deuces wild are also available at many casinos. Jokers wild machines normally pay on a pair of kings or better, while deuces wild programs pay on three-of-a-kind and up. Casinos clean up on the wild card machines because very few players understand the basic strategy of proper play.

With flawless play, the house advantage on nine/six quarter and dollar machines ranges up from about 0.5%, and for eight/five machines and wild card programs, from about 3%. On nickel video poker machines, the house advantage is about 5% to 10%.

Video Poker Strategy

Each deal in a video poker game is dealt from a fresh 52-card deck. Each hand consists of ten cards, with a random number generator or "black box" selecting the cards dealt. When you hit the deal button, the first five cards are displayed face up on the screen. Cards six through ten are held in reserve to be dealt as replacements for cards you discard when you draw. Each replacement card is dealt in order off the top of the electronic deck. The microprocessor "shuffles" the deck for each new game. Thus on the next play, you will be dealt five new and randomly selected initial cards, and five new and randomly selected draw cards to back them up. In other words, you will not be dealt any unused cards from the previous hand.

The Power of the Royal Flush   In video poker, the biggest payout is usually for a royal flush. This fact influences strategy for playing the game. Simply put, you play differently than you would in a live poker game. If in video poker you are dealt:

A♣   Q♣   10♣   A♠   J♣

you would discard the ace of spades (giving up a sure winner) to go for the royal flush. Likewise, if you are dealt:

5♠   A♠   K♠   Q♠   J♠

you would discard the 5 of spades (sacrificing a sure spade flush) in an attempt to make the royal by drawing the 10 of spades. If you are dealt:

J♥   Q♥   K♥   4♥   6♣

draw two cards for the royal flush as opposed to one card for the flush. If you are initially dealt the following straight:

7 ♣   8 ♣   9 ♣   10 ♣   J ♦

keep it on a nine/six or eight/five quarter or dollar machine. This particular hand occasions much debate among video poker veterans. The 6 of clubs or the jack of clubs would give you a straight flush, while any other club would give you a flush. Your chances of improving this hand are 9 in 47, with a 5 in 47 chance of recapturing your straight with a drawn non-club 6 or jack. It's a close call, but keeping the sure straight gets the nod (with an expected win of four coins for standing versus two and three-fourths coins for drawing). If the same situation comes up on a nickel machine, however, take the gamble and draw.

The payoff for the royal flush is so great that it is worth risking a sure winning hand. The payoff for a straight flush, however, does not warrant risking a pat flush or straight.

Other Situations   If you are dealt:

Q ♦   A ♣   4 ♥   J ♠   4 ♣

hold the small pair except when you have a chance at making a royal flush by drawing one or two cards.

But, if you are dealt:

K ♦   A ♣   4 ♥   J ♣   3 ♠

hold the ace of clubs and the jack of clubs to give yourself a long shot at a royal flush. Similarly, if you are dealt:

K ♣   A ♣   4 ♥   J ♣   3 ♠

hold the ace of clubs, king of clubs, and jack of clubs.

Straight Poker   If you are playing straight poker (no wild cards), with a pair of jacks or better required to win, observe the following:

1. Hold a jacks-or-better pair, even if you pass up the chance of drawing to an open-end straight or to a flush. If you have:

Q ♣   4 ♠   6 ♠   2 ♠   Q ♠

or

Q ♥   9 ♦   10 ♣   J ♠   Q ♣

in each case, keep the pair of queens and draw three cards.

2. Split a low pair to go for a flush. If you are dealt:

$$2 \blacklozenge \qquad 4 \clubsuit \qquad 4 \blacklozenge \qquad 8 \blacklozenge \qquad 10 \blacklozenge$$

discard the 4 of clubs and draw one card to try and make the flush.

3. Hold a low pair rather than drawing to an inside or open-end straight.

4. A "kicker" is a face card or an ace you might be tempted to hang onto along with a high pair, low pair, or three-of-a-kind. If you are dealt, for example:

$$5 \clubsuit \qquad 5 \blacklozenge \qquad 8 \spadesuit \qquad 10 \spadesuit \qquad A \heartsuit$$

or

$$J \clubsuit \qquad J \spadesuit \qquad 8 \clubsuit \qquad 7 \heartsuit \qquad A \blacklozenge$$

or

$$2 \clubsuit \qquad 2 \spadesuit \qquad 2 \heartsuit \qquad 8 \spadesuit \qquad A \heartsuit$$

hold the pair or the three-of-a-kind, but discard the kicker (the ace).

BLACKJACK

Many books have been published about the game of blackjack. The serious gamblers who write these books will tell you that blackjack is a game of skill and chance in which a player's ability can actually turn the odds of winning in his favor. While we want to believe that, we also know the casinos wouldn't keep the tables open if they were taking a beating.

The methods of playing blackjack skillfully involve being able to count all the cards played and flawlessly manage your own hand, while mentally blocking the bustle and distraction of the casino. The ability to master the prerequisite tactics and to play under casino conditions is so far beyond the average (never mind beginning) player that any attempt to track cards is, practically speaking, exhausting and futile.

This doesn't mean that you should not try blackjack. It is a fun, fast-paced game that is easy to understand, and you can play at low-minimum-wager tables without feeling intimidated by the level of play. Moreover, most people already have an understanding of the game from playing "21" at home. The casino version is largely the same, only with more bells and whistles.

In a game of blackjack, the number cards are worth their spots* (a 2 of clubs is worth two points). All face cards are worth ten points. The ace, on the other hand, is worth either 1 point or 11, whichever you choose. In this

*The correct term for the spots on playing cards is "pips."

manner, an ace and a 5 could be worth 6 points (hard count) or 16 (soft count). The object of the game is to get as close to 21 points as you can without going over (called "busting"). You play only against the dealer, and the hand closest to 21 points wins the game.

The dealer will deal you a two-card hand, then give you the option of taking another card (called a "hit") or stopping with the two cards you have been dealt (called "standing"). For example, if your first two cards are a 10 and a 3, your total would be 13, and you would normally ask for another card to get more points. If the next card dealt to you was a 7, you would have a total of 20 points and you would "stand" with 20 (i.e., not ask for another card).

It makes no difference what the other players are dealt, or what they choose to do with their hands. Your hand will win or lose only in comparison to the hand that the dealer holds.

The dealer plays his hand last. This is his biggest advantage. All the players that go over 21 points, or bust, will immediately lose their cards and their bet before the dealer's turn to play. What this means in terms of casino advantage is that while the player has to play to win, the only thing the dealer has to do is not lose. Every time you bust, the casino wins. This sequence of play ensures a profit for the casino from the blackjack tables.

We recommend that you take the time to observe a few hands before you play. This will give you the opportunity to find a personable, friendly dealer and to check out the minimum-bet signs posted at each table. They will say something like: "Minimum bet $2 to $500." This means that the minimum wager is $2, and the maximum wager is $500. If you sit down at a blackjack table and begin to bet with insufficient cash or the wrong denomination chip, the dealer will inform you of the correct minimum wager, whereupon you may either conform or excuse yourself.

A blackjack table is shaped like a half circle, with the dealer inside the circle and room for five to seven players around the outside. Facing the dealer, the chair on the far right is called "first base." The chair on the far left is called "third base." The dealer deals the cards from first base to third, and each player plays out his hand in the same order.

The best possible position is at third base or as close to it as you can get. This gives you the advantage of watching the other players play out their hands before you play.*

To buy in, find an empty seat at a table with an agreeable minimum wager and wait until the hand in progress is concluded. Though you can bet cash, most players prefer to convert their currency to chips. This is done by placing your money on the table *above* the bettor's box. Because blackjack is one of the many games in the casino in which the dealer is allowed to accept cash bets, he will assume that any money placed *in* the bettor's box is a wager.

Your dealer will take the cash, count out your chips, and push the money through a slot cut in the top of the table. Because he cannot give you change in cash, the total amount you place on the table will be converted to chips. You may at any time, however, redeem your chips for cash from the casino cashier. Once you have been given chips and have bet, you will be included in the next deal.

To confound a player attempting to count cards, many casinos deal black-jack with two to six decks shuffled together. This huge stack of cards is rendered manageable by dealing from a special container known as a shoe.

The dealer will shuffle the decks and may offer the cards to you to cut. Don't get fancy. Simply take off the top half of the deck and lay it beside the other half. Do this with one hand and never conceal the deck from the dealer. If you are playing with a large multiple deck, the dealer may offer you a plastic card stop. Place the card stop halfway or so into the deck, leaving the stop sticking out. The dealer will cut the deck at that point and put it into the shoe.

After he cuts a single deck, or puts the multiple deck into the shoe, the dealer will "burn" one or more cards by taking them off the top and putting them into the discard pile. This is yet another tactic to inhibit players from keeping track of cards dealt. Also to the advantage of the casino is the dealer's

---

*For beginning gamblers, a seat at third base can sometimes lead to an unpleasant experience. In simplest terms, the third base player, because he plays just before the dealer, can really screw things up for knowledgeable (basic strategy) bettors if he makes a dumb move. Let's say that the dealer has a 6 as his up card. An experienced player would bet that the dealer had a 10-value down card, for a total count of 16. Because the rules force the dealer to hit a count of 16, there is a high probability that the dealer will bust. Given this logic, a basic strategy player would stand on a count of 12 or higher.

A friend described the following confrontation evolving from a similar set of circumstances. A novice was seated at third base when a serious player (seated at the novice's immediate right) elected to stand with a count of 13 against the dealer's up card of 6. The novice at third base had a jack (ten count) and a 4, for a total of 14. The correct play for the novice was to stand and hope that the dealer busted. Unfortunately, however, the novice elected to take a hit, drew a 10, and busted. The dealer subsequently drew a 4 to his initial deal of a queen and a 6, and won with a total count of 20. If the novice had stood with 14 as smart play dictates, the dealer (instead of the novice) would have drawn the 10 and busted. The serious player, enraged that the novice's bad play had also caused him to lose, pounded the table, cursed the novice roundly, and told him "to take some lessons before playing with the grown-ups." The object lesson of this rather lengthy tale is not to sit at third base unless you really know what you are doing.

right to shuffle the cards whenever he pleases. Usually the dealer will deal from the shoe until he reaches the plastic stop card and then he will "break the deck," which means reshuffle and recut before dealing the next hand. In a single-deck game, the dealer will usually reshuffle about three-quarters through the deck.

Because the dealer always plays his hand last, you must develop your strategy by comparing your card count to what you assume (based on his visible card) the dealer has. The rule of thumb for most situations is to play your hand as if you know the dealer's down card has a value of ten. The principles governing when or when not to take a hit are known as "basic strategy" (summarized below in a chart). If you elect to take a hit and go over 21 (bust), you lose. If you stand with your original two cards or take a number of hits without going over 21, you can sit back and relax for a few seconds while the dealer continues on around the table, repeating the same process with the other players. When the other players finish, the dealer exposes his "down" card and plays out his hand according to strict rules. He must take a hit on any total of 16 or less, and he must stand on any total of 17 or more. When he finishes his hand, the dealer goes from third base to first, paying off each winning player and collecting chips from the losers who didn't bust.

If you have more points than the dealer, then you win. If he has more points (or if you busted), then he wins. If there is a tie, neither hand wins. When you tie, the dealer will knock on the table above your bet to indicate that the hand is a tie, or a "push." You may leave your bet on the table for the next hand, or change it.

There is a way for you to win automatically, and that is to be dealt exactly 21 points in the first two cards. This can be done with an ace and any ten-value card. Called a blackjack, or a natural, this hand is an automatic winner, and you should turn your cards face up immediately. The dealer will look to see if he ties you with a blackjack of his own; this is one of the only times a dealer will look at his cards before all the players have played. If the dealer does not have a blackjack, he will pay you immediately at three-to-two odds, so your $5 bet pays off $7.50 and you keep your original wager. If the dealer has a blackjack too, then only you and any other players at the table with a natural will tie him. The rest lose their bets, and the next round will begin.

Nothing beats a natural. If the dealer has a 4 and a 6, then draws an ace, his 21 points will not beat your blackjack. A blackjack wins over everything and pays the highest of any bet in the game.

Just as you can win automatically, you may lose just as fast. When your count goes over 21 and you bust, you must turn your cards over. The dealer will collect your cards and your bet before moving on to the next player.

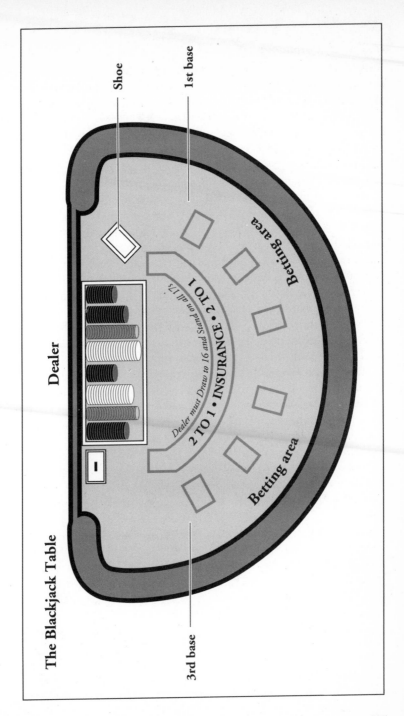

The Blackjack Table

Shoe

1st base

Dealer

3rd base

Betting area

Betting area

2 TO 1 • INSURANCE • 2 TO 1

Dealer must Draw to 16 and Stand on all 17s

Hitting and Standing

When dealing, whether from the shoe or from a single deck in his hand, the dealer will give two cards to each player. Most casinos will deal both cards facedown, though some casinos, especially those that use large multiple decks, will deal both cards faceup. There is no advantage to either method. Most players are more comfortable with the secrecy of the facedown deal, but the outcome will not be affected either way. Starting with the player at first base, the dealer will give you cards to play out your hand. After the initial deal, you have two basic options: either stand or take a hit.

If you are satisfied with your deal, then you elect to stand. If your cards were dealt facedown, slide them under the chips in the bettor's box with one hand, being careful not to touch your chips or conceal them from the dealer. If the cards were dealt faceup, wave your hand over the top, palm down, in a negative fashion, to signal the dealer not to give you another card.

Sometimes you will improve your hand by asking for another card. You signal for a hit by scratching the bottom of your cards toward you on the felt surface of the table. In a faceup game, scratch your fingers toward you in the same fashion. You may say, "Hit me," or "I'll take a hit," depending on the mood at your table but use the hand gestures also. Because of noise and distractions, the dealer may misinterpret your verbal request.

The card you request will be dealt faceup, and you may take as many hits as you like. When you want to show that you do not want another card, use the signals for standing. If you bust, turn your cards faceup right away so the dealer can collect your cards and chips. He will then go to the next player.

BASIC STRATEGY *										
The Dealer is Showing:	2	3	4	5	6	7	8	9	10	Ace
Your Total is: 4–11	H	H	H	H	H	H	H	H	H	H
12	H	H	S	S	S	H	H	H	H	H
13	S	S	S	S	S	H	H	H	H	H
14	S	S	S	S	S	H	H	H	H	H
15	S	S	S	S	S	H	H	H	H	H
16	S	S	S	S	S	H	H	H	H	H

S=Stand   H=Hit   O=Optional

*The charts reflect basic strategy for multiple-deck games. For single-deck games, a slightly different strategy prevails for doubling and splitting.

There are times when the dealer stands a good chance of busting. At these times, it is a good idea to stand on your first two cards even though the total in points may seem very low. The accompanying basic strategy chart shows when to stand and when to take a hit. It is easy to follow and simple to memorize. The decision to stand or take a hit is made on the value of your hand and, once again, the dealer's up card, and is based on the probability of his busting. Although following basic strategy won't win every hand, it will improve your odds and take the guesswork out of some confusing situations.

Basic strategy is effective because the dealer is bound by the rules of the game. He must take a hit on 16 and stand on 17. These rules are printed right on the table so that there can be no misunderstanding. Even if you are the only player at the table and stand with a total of 14 points, the dealer with what would be a winning hand of 16 points *must* take another card.

There is one exception to the rule: Some casinos require a dealer to take a hit on a hand with an ace and a 6 (called a "soft 17"). Because the ace can become a 1, it is to the casino's advantage for the dealer to be allowed to hit a soft 17.

Bells and Whistles

Now that you understand the basic game, let's look at a few rules in the casino version of blackjack that are probably different from the way you play at home.

SOFT HAND STRATEGY *										
The Dealer is Showing:	2	3	4	5	6	7	8	9	10	Ace
You Have: Ace, 9	S	S	S	S	S	S	S	S	S	S, H
Ace, 8	S	S	S	S	S	S	S	S	S	
Ace, 7	S	D	D	D	D	S	S	H	H	S
Ace, 6	H	D	D	D	D	S	H	H	H	H
Ace, 5	H	H	D	D	D	H	H	H	H	H
Ace, 4	H	H	D	D	D	H	H	H	H	H
Ace, 3	H	H	H	D	D	H	H	H	H	H
Ace, 2	H	H	H	D	D	H	H	H	H	H
S=Stand			**H=Hit**				**D=Double Down**			

*The charts reflect basic strategy for multiple-deck games. For single-deck games, a slightly different strategy prevails for doubling and splitting.

DOUBLING DOWN										
The Dealer is Showing:	**2**	**3**	**4**	**5**	**6**	**7**	**8**	**9**	**10**	**Ace**
Your Total is: 11	D	D	D	D	D	D	D	D	D	H
10	D	D	D	D	D	D	D	D	H	H
9	H	D	D	D	D	H	H	H	H	H

H=Hit   **D=Double Down**

Doubling Down　When you have received two cards and think that they will win with the addition of one and *only* one more card, then double your bet. This "doubling down" bet should be made if your two-card total is 11, since drawing the highest possible card, a 10, will not push your total over 21 points. In some casinos you may double down on ten points, and some places will let you double down on any two-card hand.

To show the dealer that you want to double down, place your two cards touching each other faceup on the dealer's side of the betting box. Then place enough in the box to equal your original bet. Now, as at all other times, don't touch your chips once the bet is made.

Splitting　Any time you are dealt two cards of the same value, you may split the cards and start two separate hands. Even aces may be split, though when you play them, they will each be dealt only one additional card. If you should happen to get a blackjack after splitting aces, it will be treated as 21 points; that is, paid off at one to one and not three to two.

Any other pair is played exactly as you would if you were playing two consecutive hands, and all the rules will apply. Place the two cards *apart from each other* and above the betting box, so the dealer won't confuse this with doubling down. Then add a stack of chips equal to the original bet to cover the additional hand. Your two hands will be played out one at a time, cards dealt faceup.

You will be allowed to split a third card if it is the same as the first two, but not if it shows up as a later hit. Always split a pair of eights, since they total 16 points, a terrible point total. *Never* split two face cards or tens, since they total 20 and are probably a winning hand.

Some casinos will let you double down after splitting a hand, but if you're unsure, ask the dealer. Not all blackjack rules are posted, and they can vary from casino to casino, and even from table to table in the same casino.

SPLITTING STRATEGY									
The Dealer is Showing: **2**	**3**	**4**	**5**	**6**	**7**	**8**	**9**	**10**	**Ace**

You Have:	2	3	4	5	6	7	8	9	10	Ace
2, 2	H	H	SP	SP	SP	SP	H	H	H	H
3, 3	H	H	SP	SP	SP	SP	H	H	H	H
4, 4	H	H	H	H	H	H	H	H	H	H
5, 5	D	D	D	D	D	D	D	D	H	H
6, 6	H	SP	SP	SP	SP	H	H	H	H	H
7, 7	SP	SP	SP	SP	SP	SP	H	H	H	H
8, 8	SP	SP	SP	SP	SP	SP	SP	SP	SP	SP
9, 9	SP	SP	SP	SP	SP	S	SP	SP	S	S
10, 10	S	S	S	S	S	S	S	S	S	S
Ace, Ace	SP	SP	SP	SP	SP	SP	SP	SP	SP	SP

S=Stand   H=Hit   SP=Split   D=Double Down

Insurance   When the dealer deals himself an ace as his second, faceup card, he will stop play and ask, "Insurance, anyone?" Don't be fooled. You're not insuring anything. All he's asking for is a side bet that he will have a natural. He must make the insurance bets before he can look at his cards, so he doesn't know if he has won or not when he asks for your insurance bets.

The insurance wager can be up to half the amount of your original bet. Place the chips in the large semicircle marked "insurance." Just as it says, it pays off two to one. If your original bet was $10 and you bet $5 that the dealer had a natural, you would be paid $10 if he actually did. Depending on your cards, you would probably lose your original $10 bet but break even on the hand. If the dealer does not have a ten-value card, you lose your $5 insurance bet, but your $10 bet still has a chance of winning.

This sounds deceptively easy. Insurance is always a bad move for the basic strategy player because the odds are against the dealer actually having a natural. You will lose this bet more often than you will win it, though the dealer may suggest it to you as a smart move. The dealer might also tell you to insure your own blackjack, though this should never be done. The odds are always against the insurance bet. When you insure your blackjack you can be paid off for it at one to one, as if it were 21 points, instead of the three to two that you would normally be paid for the blackjack. Even though you may occasionally tie with the dealer, you will more than make up for it with the three-to-two payoffs on the blackjacks you don't insure.

Avoiding Common Pitfalls

1. Always check the minimum bets allowed at your table *before* you sit down. Flipping a $5 chip into a $25-minimum game can be humiliating. If you make this mistake, simply excuse yourself and leave. It happens all the time.

2. Keep your bet in a neat stack, with the largest value chips on the bottom and the smallest on top. A mess of chips can be confusing should you want to double down, and your dealer will get huffy if he has to ask you to stack your chips.

3. Never touch the chips once the bet is down. Cheaters do this, and your dealer may assume you're cheating. It's too easy for a player to secretly up his bet once he's seen his cards or lower it if the cards are bad. Do not stack a double-down bet or split bets on top of the original bet. Place them beside the original bet and then keep your hands away.

4. Along the same lines, don't touch a hand if the cards are dealt faceup. Use the hand signals to tell the dealer that you stand or that you want a hit. *Never* move your cards below the level of the table, where the dealer can't see them. When you brush your cards for a hit, do so lightly so that the dealer won't think that you are trying to mark them by bending them.

5. Take your time and count your points correctly. The pace of the game in the casino can pick up to a speed that is difficult for a beginner. It's perfectly all right to take your time and recount after a hit. One hint: count aces as 1 first, then add 10 to your total. An ace and a 4 is equal to 5 or 15. Once you have this notion in your head, you won't make a mistake and refrain from hitting a soft hand. If you throw down an ace, a 10, and a 9 in disgust, for example, many dealers will simply pick up your cards and your bet, even though your 20 might have been a winning hand. If you are confused about your point total, do not be embarrassed to ask for help.

6. Know the denomination of the chips that you are betting. Stack them according to denomination, and read the face value every play until you know for sure which chips are which color. Otherwise you might think you are betting $5 when you are actually throwing out a $25 chip on every hand.

7. Be obvious with your hand signals to the dealer. The casinos are loud and busy, and the dealer may be distracted with a player. Don't leave any room for misinterpretation.

8. If cards fly off the table during the deal, pick them up slowly using two fingers. See number four, above.

9. Tip the dealer at your discretion if he or she has been friendly and helpful. One of the better ways to tip the dealer is to bet a chip for him on your next hand and say, "This one is for you." If you win, so does he. Never tip when a dealer has been rude or cost you money by being uncooperative. Then you should finish your hand and leave. Period.

CRAPS

Of all the games offered in casinos, craps is by far the fastest and, to many, the most exciting. It is a game in which large amounts of money can be won or lost in a short amount of time. The craps table is a circus of sound and movement. Yelling and screaming are allowed—even encouraged—here, and the frenetic betting is bewildering to the uninitiated. Don't be intimidated, however: The basic game of craps is easy to understand. The confusion and insanity of craps have more to do with the pace of the game and the amazing number of betting possibilities than with the complexity of the game itself.

The Basic Game

Because it is so easy to become confused at a crowded and noisy craps table, we highly recommend that beginning players take advantage of the free lessons offered by most of the casinos. Once you understand the game, you will be able to make the most favorable bets and ignore the rest.

In craps, one player at a time controls the dice, but all players will eventually have an opportunity to roll or refuse the dice. Players take turns in a clockwise rotation. If you don't want the dice, shake your head, and the dealer will offer them to the next player.

All the players around the table are wagering either with or against the shooter, so the numbers he throws will determine the amount won or lost by every other player. The casino is covering all bets, and the players are not allowed to bet among themselves. Four casino employees run the craps table. The boxman in the middle is in charge of the game. His job is to oversee the other dealers, monitor the play, and examine the dice if they are thrown off the table.

There are two dealers, one placed on each side of the boxman. They pay off the winners and collect the chips from the losers. Each dealer is in charge of half of the table.

The fourth employee is the stickman, so called because of a flexible stick he uses after each roll to retrieve the dice. His job, among other things, is to supply dice to the shooter and to regulate the pace of the game. When all bets are down, the stickman pushes several sets of dice toward the shooter. The shooter selects two dice, and the stickman removes the others from the table. From time to time, the stickman checks the dice for signs of tampering.

The shooter then throws the dice hard enough to cause them to bounce off the wall at the far end of the table. This bounce ensures that each number on each die has an equal probability of coming up.

The Play   When it is your turn to throw the dice, pick out two and return the other to the stickman. After making a bet (required), you may throw the dice. You retain control of the dice until you throw a 7 ("seven out") or relinquish the dice voluntarily.

Your first roll, called the come-out roll, is the most important. If you roll a 7 or an 11 on your come-out roll, you are an immediate winner. In this case, you collect your winnings and retain possession of the dice. If your come-out roll is a 4, 5, 6, 8, 9, or 10, that number becomes "the point." A marker is placed in the correspondingly numbered box on the layout to identify the point for all players at the table. In order to win the game, this number (the point) will have to be rolled again before you roll a 7.

Thus, if you roll a 5 on your first roll, the number five becomes your point. It doesn't matter how long it takes you to roll another 5, as long as you don't roll a 7 first. As soon as you roll a 7, you lose, and the dice are passed to another player.

Let's say 5 is your point, and your second roll is a 4, your third roll is a 9, and then you roll another 5. You win because you rolled a 5 again without rolling a 7. Because you have not yet rolled a 7, you retain possession of the dice, and after making a bet, you may initiate a new game.

Your next roll is, once again, a come-out roll. Just as 7 or 11 are immediate winners on a come-out roll, there are immediate losers, too. A roll of 2, 3, or 12 (all called "craps") will lose. You lose your chips, but you keep the dice because you have not yet rolled a 7.

If your first roll is 2, for example, it's craps, and you lose your bet. You place another bet and roll to come-out again. This time you roll a 5, so 5 becomes your point. Your second roll is a 4, your third is a 9, and then you roll a 7. The roll of 7 means that you lose and the dice will be passed to the next player.

This is the basic game of craps. The confounding blur of activity is nothing more than players placing various types of bets with or against the shooter, or betting that a certain number will or will not come up on the next roll of the dice.

The Craps Table

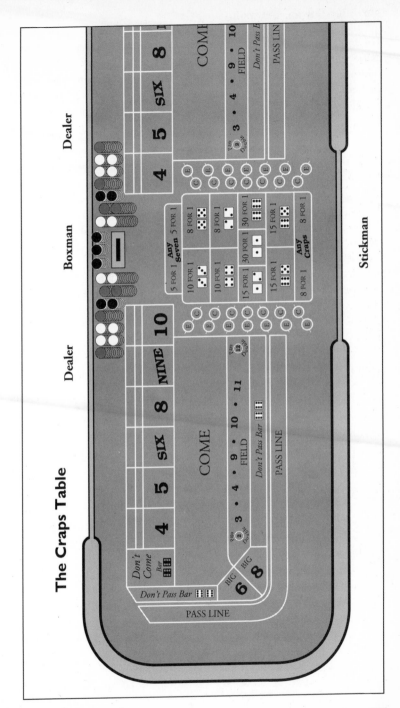

The Betting   Of the dozens of bets that can be made at a craps table, only two or three should even be considered by a novice craps player. Keeping your bets simple makes it easier to understand what's going on, while at the same time minimizing the house advantage. Exotic, long-shot bets, offering payoffs as high as 30 to 1, are sucker bets and should be avoided.

The Line Bets: Pass and Don't Pass   Pass and don't pass bets combine simplicity with one of the smallest house advantages of any casino game, about 1.4%. If you bet pass, you are betting that the first roll will be a 7 or 11 or a point number, and that the shooter will make the point again before he rolls a 7. If you bet don't pass, you are betting that the first roll will be a 2, 3, or 12, or, if a point is established, that the shooter will seven out and throw a 7 before he rolls his point number again. The two and three are immediate losers, and the casino will collect the chips of anyone betting pass. A roll of 12, however, is considered a standoff where the shooter "craps out" but no chips change hands for the "don't" bettor. Almost 90% of casino craps players confine their betting to the pass and don't pass line.

Come and Don't Come   Come and don't come bets are just like pass and don't pass bets, except that they are placed *after* the point has been established on the come-out roll. Pass and don't pass bets must be placed before the first roll of the dice, but come and don't come bets may be placed before any roll of the dice *except* come-out rolls. On his come-out roll, let's say that the shooter rolls a nine. Nine becomes the shooter's point. If at this time you place your chips in the come box on the table, the next roll of the dice will determine your "come number." If the shooter throws a six, for example, your chips are placed in the box marked with the large six. The dealer will move your chips and will keep track of your bet. If the shooter rolls another six before he rolls a seven, your bet pays off. If the shooter sevens out before he rolls a six, then you lose. If the shooter makes his point (i.e., rolls another nine), your come bet is retained on the layout.

If you win a come bet, the dealer will place your chips from the numbered box back into the come space and set your winnings beside it. You may leave your chips there for the next roll or you may remove them entirely. If you fail to remove your winnings before the next roll, they may become a bet that you didn't want to make.

Don't come bets are the opposite of come bets. A 7 or 11 loses, and a 2 or 3 wins. The 12 is again a standoff. The don't come bettor puts his chips in the don't come space on the table and waits for the next roll to determine his number. His chips are placed *above* the numbered box to differentiate it from a come bet. If the shooter rolls his point number before he rolls your number, your don't come bet is retained on the layout. You are betting

ACTUAL ODDS CHART		
Number	**Ways to Roll**	**Odds against Repeat**
4	3	2–1
5	4	3–2
6	5	6–5
8	5	6–5
9	4	3–2
10	3	2–1

against the shooter; that is, that he will roll a seven first. When he rolls seven, you win. If he rolls your don't come number before he sevens out, you lose.

The come and don't come bets have a house advantage of about 1.4% and are among the better bets in craps once you understand them.

Odds Bets When you bet the pass/don't pass, or the come/don't come area, you may place an odds bet *in addition* to your original bet.

Once it is established that the come-out roll is not a 7 or 11, or craps, the bettor may place a bet that will be paid off according to the actual odds of a particular number being thrown.

Note that the Actual Odds Chart shows the chances against a number made by two dice being thrown. For example, the odds of making a nine are three to two. If you place an odds bet (in addition to your original bet) on a come number of nine, your original come bet will pay off at even money, but your odds bet will pay off at three to two.

Because this would make a $7.50 payoff for a $5 bet, and the tables don't carry 50-cent chips, you are allowed to place a $6 bet as an odds bet. This is a very good bet to make, and betting the extra dollar is to your advantage.

To place an odds bet on a line bet, bet the pass line. When (and if) the point is established, put your additional bet behind the pass line and say, "Odds."

To place an odds bet on a come bet, wait for the dealer to move your chips to the come number box, then hand him more chips and say, "Odds." He will set these chips half on and half off the other pile so that he can see at a glance that it's an odds bet.

Craps Etiquette

When you arrive at a table, find an open space and put your money down in front of you. When the dealer sees it, he will pick it up and hand it to the boxman. The boxman will count out the correct chips and hand them to the dealer, who will pass them to you.

A craps table holds from 12 to 20 players and can get very crowded. Keep your place at the table. Your chips are in front of you, and it is your responsibility to watch them.

After you place your bets, your hands must come off the table. It is very bad form to leave your hands on the table when the dice are rolling.

Stick to the good bets listed here, and don't be tempted by bets that you don't understand. The box in the middle of the layout, for example, offers a number of sucker bets.

BACCARAT

Originally an Italian card game, baccarat (bah-kah-rah) is the French pronunciation of the Italian word for zero. The name refers to the value of all the face cards in the game: zero.

Because baccarat involves no player decisions, it is an easy game to play, but a very difficult game to understand. Each player must decide to make a bet on either the bank or the player. That's it. There are no more decisions until the next hand is dealt. The rules of playing out the hands are ridiculously intricate, but beginning players need not concern themselves with them, because all plays are predetermined by the rules, and the dealer will tell you exactly what happened.

All cards, ace through 9, are worth their spots (the 3 of clubs is worth three points). The 10, jack, queen, and king are worth zero. The easiest way to count points is to add all points in the hand, then take only the number in the ones column.

If you have been dealt a 6 and a 5, then your total is 11, and taking only the ones column, your hand is worth 1 point. If you hold a 10 and a king, your hand is worth zero. If you have an 8 and a 7, your point total is 15, and taking the ones column, your hand is worth 5. It doesn't get any simpler than this.

In baccarat, regardless of the number of bettors at the table, only two hands are dealt: One to the player and one to the bank. The object of the game is to be dealt or draw a hand worth nine points. If the first two cards dealt equal nine points (a 5 and a 4, for example), then you have a natural and an automatic winner. Two cards worth eight are the second best hand and will also be called a natural. If the other hand is not equal to or higher than eight, this hand wins automatically. Ties are standoffs, and neither bank nor player wins.

BACCARAT RULES

Player

When First Two Cards Total:

1, 2, 3, 4, 5, or 10	Draws a Card
6 or 7	Stands
8 or 9	A Natural—Stands

Banker

Having:	*Draws When Player's* *Third Card Is:*	*Does Not Draw When* *Player's Third Card Is:*
3	1, 2, 3, 4, 5, 6, 7, 9, 10	8
4	2, 3, 4, 5, 6, 7	1, 8, 9, 10
5	4, 5, 6, 7,	1, 2, 3, 8, 9, 10
6	6, 7	1, 2, 3, 4, 5, 8, 9, 10
7	Stands	Stands
8 or 9	Stands	Stands

If the hands equal any total except nine or eight, the rules are consulted. These rules are printed and available at the baccarat table. The hands will be played out by the dealer whether you understand the rules or not.

The rules for the player's hand are simple. If a natural is not dealt to either hand, and if the player holds one, two, three, four, five, or ten (zero), he will always draw a card. He will stand on a total of six or seven. A total of eight or nine, of course, will be a natural.

The bank hand is more complicated and is partially determined by the third card drawn by the player's hand. Though the rules don't say so, the bank will always draw on zero, one, or two. When the hand is worth three or more, it is subject to the printed rules.

If you study a few hands, the method of play will be clear:

First Hand   The player's hand is worth three, and the bank's is worth four. The player always goes first. Looking at the rules for the player, we see that a hand worth three points draws a card. This time he draws a 9, for a new

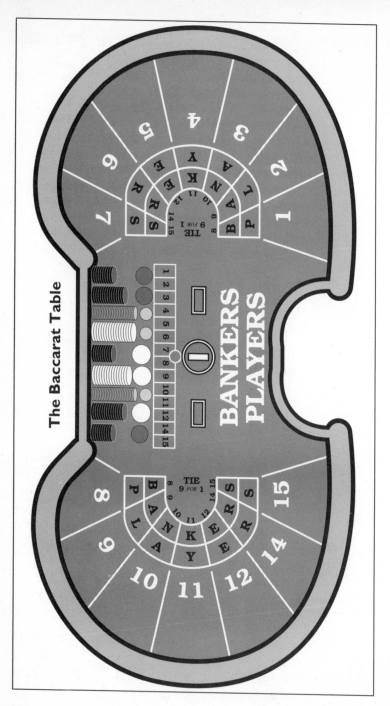

The Baccarat Table

total of 12 points, which has a value of two. The bank, having four points, must stand when a player draws a 9. The bank wins four to two.

Second Hand   The player's hand is worth six points, and the bank has two queens, for a total of zero. The player must stand with six points, while the bank must draw with zero. The bank gets another card, a 4. Player wins, six to four.

The Atmosphere

The casinos try to attract players by making baccarat seem continental and sophisticated. The section is roped off from the main casino, and the dealers are often dressed in tuxedos instead of the usual dealer's uniforms. Don't be put off by glamorous airs; everyone is welcome to play.

Because the house wants baccarat to be appealing to what they consider to be their upper-crust clientele, the table minimums are usually very high in baccarat—usually $20 to $2,000. This means that the minimum bet is $20, and the maximum bet is $2,000. Most of the players, however, will play with $25 and $100 chips.

Even the shuffle and deal of the deck is designed to perpetuate the feeling of the exotic. Elaborately cut and mixed by all three dealers, the cards are cut by one player and marked with the plastic card stop. The dealer will then separate the cards at the stop, turn the top card over, and discard, or burn, the number of cards equal to the face value of the upturned card. The cards are then placed in a large holder called the shoe.

The Play   If the game has just begun, the shoe will be passed to the player in seat number one, who is then called the bank. Thereafter, whenever the bank hand loses, the shoe is passed counterclockwise to the next player, until it reaches seat number 15, where it is passed to seat number one again.

When all bets are down, one of the three dealers will nod to the holder of the shoe, who will then deal out four cards in alternating fashion—two for the player and two for the bank.

The player's hand is passed (still facedown) to the bettor who has wagered the most money on the player's hand. He looks at the cards and passes them back to the dealer. The dealer then turns both hands faceup and plays out the game according to the rules.

The Betting   In baccarat, you must back either the player or the bank. You do this by putting your chips in the box in front of you marked "player" or "bank." Once the bets are down, the deal will begin.

The house advantage on baccarat is quite low: 1.36% on player wagers and 1.17% on bank bets. Because the bank bet has such an obvious advantage, the house extracts a commission when you win a bank bet. This is not collected with each hand, but must be paid before you leave the table.

Minibaccarat Some casinos have installed smaller baccarat tables, called minibaccarat. The dealers dress in the standard uniform and play with lower minimum bets. The games move more quickly, since there are fewer players. If you feel intimidated by baccarat, we recommend the smaller version of the game.

KENO

Keno is an ancient Chinese game. It was used to raise money for national defense, including, some say, building the Great Wall. Keno was brought to America by the thousands of workers who came from the Far East to work on the railroads during the 1800s. It is one of the most popular games in the Nevada casinos, though it is outlawed in Atlantic City.

This game has a house advantage of between 20% and 35% or more, depending on the casino—higher than any other game in Las Vegas. Too high, in fact, for serious gamblers. So if you're down to your last dollar and you have to bet to save the ranch, don't go to the keno lounge.

While keno is similar to bingo, the betting options are reminiscent of exacta horse-race betting. It is like bingo in that a ticket, called a blank, is marked off and numbers are randomly selected to determine a winner. And it is similar to exacta betting because any number of fascinating betting combinations can be played in each game. The biggest difference between keno and bingo and exactas is that in the other two, there's always a winner. In keno, hours can go by before anyone wins a substantial amount. The main excitement in keno lies in the possibility that large amounts of money can be won on a small bet.

Playing the Game

In each casino there is a keno lounge that usually resembles a college lecture hall. The casino staff sit in front while players relax in chairs with writing tables built into the arms. It is not necessary to sit in the keno lounge to play. In fact, one of the best things about keno is that it can be played almost anywhere in the casino, including the bars and restaurants. As in bingo, it is acceptable to strike up a conversation with your neighbor during a game, and because the winning numbers are posted all over the place, keno also offers the opportunity to gamble while absent from the casino floor.

Keno is one of the easiest games to understand. The keno blank can be picked up almost anywhere in any Nevada casino. On the blank are two large boxes containing 80 numbers: the top box with 1 to 40, and the bottom box with 41 to 80. Simply use one of the crayons provided with the blanks to mark between 1 and 15 numbers on the blank, decide how much you want to bet, and turn the blank in to a keno writer. The keno writer records your wager, keeping your original, and gives you a duplicate, which *you* are responsible for checking. The keno writer can be found at the front of the keno lounge. The keno runner is even easier to spot: she is usually a woman in a short skirt with a hand full of blanks and crayons. She will place your bets, cash in your blanks, and bring you your winnings. Of course, you are expected to tip her for this service.

The drawing of the winning numbers takes place in the keno lounge. When the keno caller has determined that the bets are in for the current round, he will close the betting just like the steward does at the racetrack. Then the caller uses a machine similar to those employed by state lotteries: a blower with numbered Ping-Pong balls. Ten balls are blown into each of two tubes. These 20 balls bear the numbers that will be called for the current round. The numbers, as called out, are posted on electronic keno boards around the casino. If any of the lighted numbers are numbers that you marked on your card, you "caught" those numbers. Catching four or more numbers will usually win something, depending on how many numbers you marked on your card. The payoffs are complicated, but the more numbers you guess correctly and the more money you bet, the greater your jackpot. Suffice it to say, however, that you are not paid at anything even approaching true odds. If, by some amazing quirk of fate, you win, you must claim your winnings before the next round starts or forfeit.

The Odds A "straight" or basic ticket is one where the player simply selects and marks a minimum of 1 number to a maximum of 8 to 15 numbers, depending on the casino. The ways to combine keno bets are endless and understandable only to astrophysicists. Any number can be played with any other number, making "combination" tickets. Groups of numbers can be combined with other groups of numbers, making "way" tickets. Individual numbers can be combined with groups of numbers, making "king" tickets. Then there is the "house" ticket, called different things at each casino, which offers a shot at the big jackpot for a smaller investment, though the odds won't be any better.

All of these options and the amounts that you are allowed to bet (usually from 70 cents up per ticket) will be listed in the keno brochures, which are almost as ubiquitous as the blanks. The payoffs will be listed for each type of bet and for the amount wagered. Keno runners and keno lounge personnel will show you how to mark your ticket if you are confused, but they cannot mark it for you. The only thing you really need to know about keno, however, is that the house has an unbeatable advantage.

The best strategy for winning at keno is to avoid it. If you want to play for fun (and that is the only rational reason to play), then understand that one bet is about as bad as another. Filling out a complicated combination ticket won't increase your chances of winning. If by some miracle you do win, accept the congratulations and the winnings, and then run, do not walk, to the nearest exit.

ROULETTE

A quiet game where winners merely smile over a big win and losers suffer in silence, roulette is very easy to understand. The dealer spins the wheel, drops the ball, and waits for it to fall into one of the numbered slots on the wheel. The numbers run from zero to 36, with a double zero thrown in for good measure. You may bet on each individual number, on combinations of numbers, on all black numbers, all red numbers, and many more. All possible bets are laid out on the table.

Special chips are used for roulette, with each bettor at the table playing a different color. To buy in, convert cash or the casino's house chips to roulette chips. When you are ready to cash out, the dealer will convert your special roulette chips back to house chips. If you want cash, you must then take your house chips to a casino cashier.

To place a bet, put your chips inside a numbered square or choose one of the squares off to the side. A chip placed in "1st 12," for example, will pay off if the ball drops into any number from 1 to 12. The box marked "odd" is not for eccentrics—it pays when the ball drops into an odd-numbered slot.

Roulette is fun to play, but expect to pay! The house advantage on most bets is a whopping 5.26%, and on some wagers it can be as high as 7%.

ROULETTE BET AND PAYOFF CHART	
Bet	**Payoff**
Single number	35 to 1
Two numbers	17 to 1
Three numbers	11 to 1
Four numbers	8 to 1
Five numbers	6 to 1
Six numbers	5 to 1
12 numbers (column)	2 to 1
1st 12, 2nd 12, 3rd 12	2 to 1
1–18 or 19–36	1 to 1
Odd or Even	1 to 1
Red or Black	1 to 1

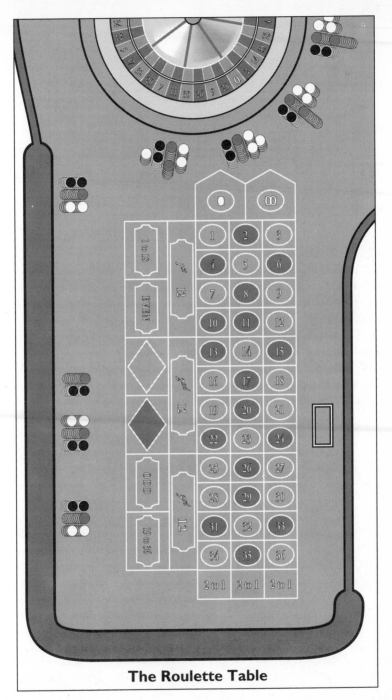

The Roulette Table

Part Four

Exercise and Recreation

Working Out

Most of the folks on our *Unofficial Guide* research team work out routinely. Some bike; some run; some lift weights or do aerobics. Staying in hotels on the Strip and downtown, it didn't take them long to discover that working out in Las Vegas presents its own peculiar challenges.

The best months for outdoor exercise are October through April. The rest of the year it is extremely hot, though mornings and evenings are generally pleasant in September and May. During the scorching summer, particularly for visitors, we recommend working out indoors or, for bikers and runners, very early in the morning. If you do anything strenuous outside, any time of year, drink plenty of water. Dehydration and heat prostration can overtake you quickly and unexpectedly in Las Vegas's desert climate. For outdoor workouts in Las Vegas comparable to what you are used to at home, you will deplete your body's water at two to three times the usual rate.

WALKING

Primarily flat, Las Vegas is made for walking and great people-watching. Security is very good both downtown and on the Strip, making for a safe walking environment at practically all hours of the day and night. Downtown, everything is concentrated in such a small area that you might be inclined to venture away from the casino center. While this is no more perilous than walking in any other city, the areas surrounding downtown are not particularly interesting or aesthetically compelling. If the downtown casino center is not large enough to accommodate your exercise needs, you are better off busing or cabbing to the Strip and doing your walking there.

If you are walking the Strip, it is about four miles from Mandalay Bay on the south end to the Stratosphere on the north end. Because the topography

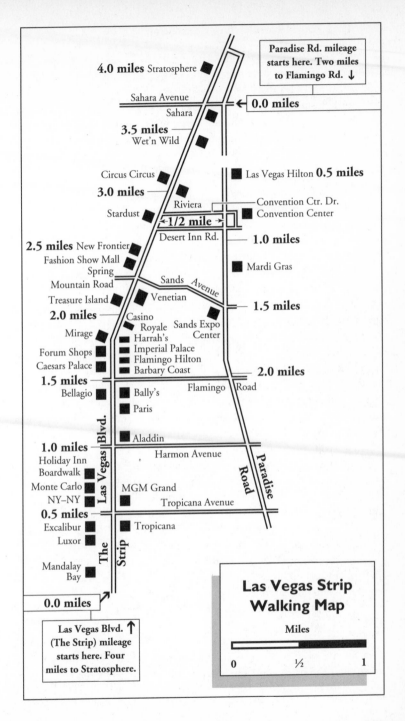

4.0 miles Stratosphere

Sahara Avenue

0.0 miles ←

Paradise Rd. mileage starts here. Two miles to Flamingo Rd. ↓

Sahara

3.5 miles
Wet'n Wild

Circus Circus

Las Vegas Hilton **0.5 miles**

3.0 miles

Riviera

Convention Ctr. Dr.
Convention Center

Stardust

← 1/2 mile →

Desert Inn Rd. **1.0 miles**

2.5 miles New Frontier
Fashion Show Mall
Spring
Mountain Road
Treasure Island

Mardi Gras

Sands Avenue

Venetian

1.5 miles

2.0 miles

Casino
Royale

Sands Expo
Center

Mirage

Harrah's

Forum Shops
Caesars Palace

Imperial Palace
Flamingo Hilton
Barbary Coast

2.0 miles

1.5 miles
Bellagio

Bally's

Flamingo Road

Paris

Las Vegas Blvd.

Aladdin

1.0 miles
Holiday Inn
Boardwalk
Monte Carlo
NY–NY

Harmon Avenue

MGM Grand

Paradise Road

Tropicana Avenue

0.5 miles
Excalibur
Luxor

Tropicana

The Strip

Mandalay
Bay

0.0 miles

Las Vegas Blvd. ↑ (The Strip) mileage starts here. Four miles to Stratosphere.

Las Vegas Strip Walking Map

Miles

0   ½   1

is so flat, however, it does not look that far. We met a number of people who set out on foot along the Strip and managed to overextend themselves. Check out our Strip walking distance map before you go, and bear in mind that even without hills, marching in the arid desert climate will take a lot out of you. Finally, carry enough money to buy refreshments en route and to take a cab or bus back to your hotel if you poop out or develop a blister.

RUNNING

If you stay on the Strip, you will have more options than if you stay downtown. Those of us who are used to running on pavement ran on the broad sidewalks of Las Vegas Boulevard South. These runs are great for people-watching also, but are frequently interrupted by long minutes of jogging in place at intersections, waiting for traffic lights to change. Our early risers would often run before 7:30 a.m. on the now defunct Desert Inn golf course. This was the best (and safest) running in town, with good footing, beautiful scenery, and no traffic. Suffice it to say, however, that course managers were less than overjoyed to see a small platoon of travel writers trotting off the 18th fairway. If you run on a golf course, stay off the greens and try to complete your run by 7:30 a.m. In addition to area golf courses, the Las Vegas Hilton and Mandalay Bay each have a jogging circuit.

If you stay downtown, you must either run on the sidewalks or drive to a more suitable venue. Sidewalks downtown are more congested than those on the Strip, and there are more intersections and traffic lights with which to contend. If you want to run downtown, particularly on Fremont Street, try to get your workout in before 10 a.m.

For those who dislike pounding the blacktop, sneaking onto golf courses, or exercising early in the morning, a convenient option is to run on the track at the university. Located about two miles east of the Strip on Harmon Avenue, UNLV offers both a regulation track and some large, grassy athletic fields. Park in the dirt lot near the tennis courts if you do not have a university parking sticker. For more information call (702) 895-3177.

A more expensive alternative is the posh Las Vegas Sporting House at 3025 Industrial Road (located directly behind the Stardust Hotel), which has both an indoor and outdoor track. The charge is a hefty $12 to 20 a day (depending on hotel), or $50 a week, but the fee includes the use of all club facilities. Call (702) 733-8999.

If you have a car and a little time, two of the better off-road runs in the area are at Red Rock Canyon, out Charleston Avenue, 35 minutes west of town. Red Rock Canyon Conservation Area, managed by the U.S. Bureau of Land Management, is Western desert and canyon scenery at its best.

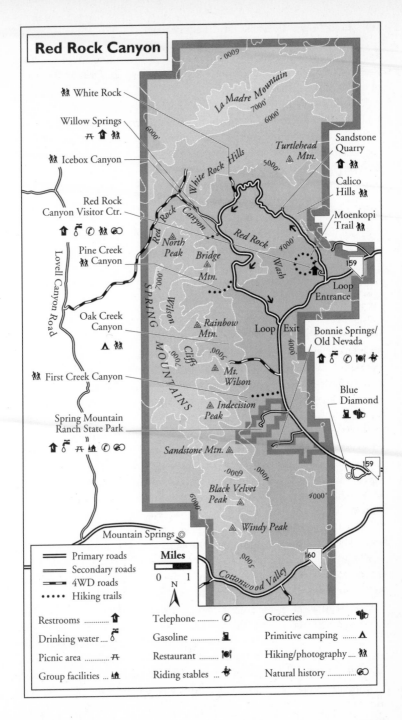

Red Rock Canyon

🚶 White Rock

Willow Springs
🛆 🛖 🚶

🚶 Icebox Canyon

Red Rock
Canyon Visitor Ctr.
🛖 💧 📞 🚶 ⚭

Pine Creek
🚶 Canyon

Oak Creek
Canyon
▲ 🚶

🚶 First Creek Canyon

Spring Mountain
Ranch State Park
🛖 💧 🛆 🏛 📞 ⚭

La Madre Mountain

Turtlehead Mtn. △

Sandstone
Quarry
🛖 🚶

Calico
Hills 🚶

Moenkopi
Trail 🚶

White Rock Hills

Red Rock Canyon

North Peak △

Bridge Mtn. △

Red Rock Wash

159

Loop
Entrance

Loop Exit

Bonnie Springs/
Old Nevada
🛖 💧 📞 🍽 🐴

Wilson Cliffs

Rainbow Mtn. △

Mt. Wilson △

Indecision Peak △

Blue
Diamond
⛽ 🍺

SPRING MOUNTAINS

Lovell Canyon Road

Sandstone Mtn. △

Black Velvet Peak △

Windy Peak △

159

160

Mountain Springs ◎

Cottonwood Valley

	Miles	
	0 ▬▬ 1	

N ⌄

══ Primary roads		
══ Secondary roads		
⊨ 4WD roads		
•••• Hiking trails		

Restrooms .... 🛖	Telephone .... 📞	Groceries .... 🎏
Drinking water .... 💧	Gasoline .... ⛽	Primitive camping .... ▲
Picnic area .... 🛆	Restaurant .... 🍽	Hiking/photography .... 🚶
Group facilities ... 🏛	Riding stables ... 🐴	Natural history .... ⚭

343

Spectacular geology combined with the unique desert flora and fauna make Red Rock Canyon a truly memorable place. Maps and information can be obtained at the visitor center, on-site.

One two-mile round trip, the Moenkopi Loop, begins and ends at the visitor center. A three-mile circuit, the Willow Springs Trail, begins at the Willow Springs Picnic Area and circles around to Lost Creek Canyon. Both routes are moderately hilly, with generally good footing. The Moenkopi Loop is characterized by open desert and expansive vistas, while the Willow Springs Trail ventures into the canyons. The Willow Springs Trail is also distinguished by numerous Indian petroglyphs and other artifacts. Both trails, of course, are great for hiking as well as for running.

Finally, if you want to hook up with local runners, you can join the Las Vegas Track Club for a weekly run to Tule Springs (north of downtown on US 95) or many other area locations. For a current schedule or additional information call the Running Store at (702) 898-7866 or the Runner's Hotline at (702) 594-0970.

SWIMMING AND SUNBATHING

Swimming, during warm-weather months, is the most dependable and generally accessible form of exercise in Las Vegas. Most of the Strip hotels and a couple of the downtown hotels have nice pools. Sometimes the pools are too congested for swimming laps, but usually it is possible to stake out a lane.

If the pool at your hotel is a funny shape or too crowded for a workout, there are pools more conducive to serious swimming at the Las Vegas Sporting House on Industrial Road, at the Las Vegas Athletic Club on Flamingo Road, and in the McDermott Physical Education Complex of UNLV.

For those who want to work on their tans in style, the Mirage, Tropicana, Mandalay Bay, Venetian, Paris, Monte Carlo, MGM Grand, Treasure Island, Caesars Palace, Rio, Las Vegas and Flamingo Hiltons, Alexis Park, Hard Rock Hotel, Bellagio, Aladdin, and Regent Las Vegas, among others, have particularly elegant facilities. Hotels with above-average pools include the Luxor, New Frontier, Riviera, Harrah's, Imperial Palace, and Sahara. If you are staying in a place where the swimming is not very interesting, try the Wet 'n Wild water theme park near the Sahara on the Strip.

Be forewarned that sunbathing in Las Vegas can be dangerous. The climate is so arid that you will not feel yourself perspiring: perspiration evaporates as soon as it surfaces on your skin. If there is a breeze, particularly on a pleasant fall or spring day, you may never feel hot, sticky, or in any way uncomfortable until you come out of the sun and discover that you have been fried.

You can really get zapped in a hurry if you do not protect yourself properly, and even those who already have a good tan need to be extra careful. We recommend using twice the block you use in nondesert areas. If in Delaware, for example, you use a SPF four lotion, use at least a SPF eight in Las Vegas. Come out of the sun frequently to check yourself, and be careful not to fall asleep in the sun for an extended period.

If you overdo it somewhat, go to a nursery and buy an aloe plant. Slice the meaty tendrils lengthwise and rub the goop from the inside all over your skin. Repeat applications until you are tolerably comfortable. This treatment also works at home with minor kitchen burns.

HEALTH CLUBS

If you can get by with a Lifecycle, a StairMaster, or a rowing machine, the fitness rooms of most major hotels should serve your needs. Fortunately, local health clubs welcome visitors for a daily ($10 to $20) or weekly ($25 to $50) fee. All of the clubs described here are coed.

The most luxurious (and expensive) club is the Las Vegas Sporting House, located close to the Strip at 3025 Industrial Road. Open 24 hours a day, the club offers racquetball, squash, tennis, basketball, volleyball, exercise equipment, and aerobics. For information and rates call (702) 733-8999.

The Las Vegas Athletic Clubs, with five locations, offer much the same activities and services as the Sporting House, though not all features are provided at each location. The Las Vegas Athletic Clubs depend more on local patronage than on visitors; their facilities are commodious but less luxurious than those at the Sports Club, and fees are at the lower end of the range. While reasonably convenient to the Strip, only the West Sahara club is within walking distance. For rates and additional information call:

Las Vegas Athletic Club
5200 W. Sahara
(702) 362-3720

Las Vegas Athletic Club
2655 S. Maryland Pkwy
(702) 733-1919

Las Vegas Athletic Club
5200 W. Sahara
(702) 364-5822

Las Vegas Athletic Club
S. Maryland Parkway at Tropicana
(702) 795-2582

Las Vegas Athletic Club
E. Flamingo at Sandhill Rd.
(702) 451-2526

The 24 Hour Fitness centers, with three locations, run an excellent aerobics program and have an extensive weight and exercise facility. While the facilities are good and the use fees midrange, the locations are a little remote for most visitors staying on the Strip or downtown.

24 Hour Fitness
S. Eastern near Sahara
(702) 641-2222

24 Hour Fitness
S. Valley View, half-
mile south of Sahara
(702) 368-1111

24 Hour Fitness
Cheyenne and Rainbow
(702) 656-7777

AEROBICS

A number of health clubs offer coed aerobics on a daily basis. Daily or weekly rates are available. For additional information, see the preceding Health Club section.

FREE WEIGHTS AND NAUTILUS

Almost all of the major hotels have a spa or fitness room with weight-lifting equipment. Some properties have a single Universal machine, while others offer a wide range of free-weight and Nautilus equipment. Hotels with above-average facilities for pumping iron are the Las Vegas Hilton, Bellagio, Venetian, Caesars Palace, Golden Nugget, Mirage, Paris, Regent Las Vegas, Monte Carlo, MGM Grand, Luxor, and Treasure Island.

For hardcore power lifters and body builders, try Gold's Gym at Sahara and Decatur, (702) 877-6966. Gold's offers daily, weekly, and monthly rates for use of its Nautilus and free weights ($10, $35, and $70 respectively). Gold's does not advertise that it is coed, but it is.

RACQUETBALL, SQUASH, AND HANDBALL

Visitors are welcome at most local racquet and health clubs. Sports Club–Las Vegas and the Las Vegas Athletic Clubs, among others, provide good court facilities. For additional information see the preceding Health Club section.

Golf

Peak season for golf in Las Vegas is October through May. The other four months are considered prohibitively warm for most golfers, and greens fees are reduced at most courses during the summer. Certain courses also have reduced rates for locals and for guests staying at hotels affiliated with the golf course. Morning tee times are always more difficult to arrange than afternoons. Call the starter one day before you wish to play. Same-day phone calls are discouraged. In summer, most courses and driving ranges stay open until at least 7:30 p.m. In winter and early spring, temperatures drop rapidly near sundown, so always bring a sweater or jacket. Las Vegas has an elevation of 2,000 feet and is considered high desert. Take this into account when making club selections.

Golf Course Ratings		
Quality rating:	★★★	Championship, challenging
	★★	Playable, suitable for all caliber golfers
	★	Preferred by beginners and casual golfers
Value rating:	1	A good bargain
	2	A fair price
	3	Not a good bargain

Note: Quality and value ratings are abbreviated as *QV Rating* in the following listings.

Important Note: Quite a few outstanding courses are not listed, including **Shadow Creek Country Club,** privately owned by Mirage Resorts, Inc., and played only by their special guests. Built at a cost of nearly $40 million and looking more like a North Carolina layout bordered by cathedral pines than a traditional desert course, Shadow Creek was named by *Golf Digest* as the finest new course in the United States in 1990. The ultimate accolade was bestowed when the same magazine listed Shadow Creek as the eighth best golf course in the United States, an unprecedented honor for a course less than five years old. **The Tournament Players Club,** open to guests of Regent Las Vegas at Summerlin is currently the host course for both the Las Vegas Senior Classic and the Las Vegas Invitational. Other than La Costa Resort, this is the only course in the United States to host both men's professional tours. The Summerlin course was designed by architect Bobby Weed with assistance from player/consultant Fuzzy Zoeller and is rated by both *Golf Digest* and *Golfweek* magazines as the second best course in Nevada, behind Shadow Creek. Many current professional athletes are members, including pitchers Duane Ward (Toronto Blue Jays), Mike Maddux (New York Mets), Greg Maddux (Atlanta Braves), and golfers Jim Colbert, Robert Gamez, and Bob May. **Canyon Gate Country Club** was designed by noted architect Ted Robinson and is a championship golf course in every sense, with lush, narrow fairways, outstanding bentgrass greens, and an eclectic scattering of fairway bunkers and mounds. Management was taken over in 1992 by the elite company ClubCorp International (CCI). Frequently ranked as one of the top five courses in Nevada, the **Las Vegas Country Club** is one of the host's

for the Las Vegas Invitational Men's PGA tournament. Beautifully conditioned, with recently planted bentgrass greens. It's not available to the public,
although a few tee times are reserved daily for high-rolling guests staying at
the Las Vegas Hilton. Eventually, **Lake Las Vegas** will be a $3.8 billion resi-
dential community surrounding a private, 320-acre lake. Its $19 million
Southshore Golf Club was designed by Jack Nicklaus, and the hilly terrain
includes a combination of manicured turf, Bermuda grass, bentgrass greens,
and desert flowers, plants, and trees. For six years **Spanish Trail Country
Club** was a host of the Las Vegas Invitational PGA tournament. This 27-hole
complex designed by Robert Trent Jones, with undulating fairways, heavy
bunkering, a number of water hazards, and fast, bentgrass greens, can play
havoc with less-than-accomplished golfers. In just its second year of operation, **Sunrise Golf Club** was a host course of the Las Vegas Invitational
PGA tournament, and Chip Beck humbled it with a 59. It was only the second time in history a player had broken 60. With 54 holes and the city's
largest driving range, Sunrise has become Las Vegas's most accommodating
and affordable private club.

Angel Park Golf Club

Established: 1989

Address: 100 S. Rampart Blvd., Las Vegas, NV 89128

Phone: (702) 254-4653
            www.angelpark.com

Status: Public/Municipal course

Tees: Palm Course
              Championship: 6,530 yards, par 70, USGA 72.6, slope 130
              Men's: 5,857 yards, par 70, USGA 69.8, slope 120
              Ladies': 5,438 yards, par 70, USGA 68.6, slope 112

             Mountain Course
              Championship: 6,722 yards, par 71, slope 128
              Men's: 6,235 yards, par 71, slope 117
              Ladies': 5,751 yards, par 71, slope 116

Fees: May 1–June 17 and September 4–30: Monday–Thursday, $130;
     Friday–Sunday, $145. June 18–September 3: Monday–Thursday, $65;
     Friday–Sunday, $85; October 1–November 30: Monday–Thursday,
     $135; Friday–Sunday, $160 (18 holes; carts included); Cloud 9 (par-
     three course), $22–25. No 9-hole rates available. Twilight rates vary
     (4 hours before sunset). Club rentals, $40–50.

Facilities: Pro shop, night-lighted driving range and 18-hole putting course, putting green, restaurant, snack bar, bar, tennis courts, and walking track nearby.

QV Rating: ★★   2

Comments   Angel Park, a good, functional golf complex, is rapidly becoming one of the most successful public golf facilities in the United States. Its courses are well designed—by Arnold Palmer, no less—and the sophisticated 18-hole putting course, complete with night lighting, sand traps, rough, and water hazards, is a popular attraction even for non-golfers. In its eight-year existence, Angel Park has matured and become lush and attractive. Both courses are crowded year-round.

Black Mountain Golf and Country Club

Established: 1959

Address: 500 Greenway Rd., Henderson, NV 89015

Phone: (702) 565-7933
         www.golfblackmountain.com

Status: Semi-private

Tees: Championship: 6,550 yards, par 72, USGA 71.2, slope 123
         Men's: 6,223 yards, par 72, USGA 69.8, slope 120
         Ladies': 5,518 yards, par 72, USGA 71.6, slope 120

Fees: Nonresidents: Weekdays, $80 for 18 holes. Weekends, $100 for 18. Seniors (over 63), $40 Tuesday and Thursday, excluding holidays. Carts mandatory on weekends and included in all fees. Club rentals, $15–30.

Facilities: Pro shop, clubhouse, driving range, putting green, restaurant, snack bar, and bar.

QV Rating: ★   1

Comments   Black Mountain is set amidst the Henderson hills, 20 minutes from the Strip. Many who prefer walking to riding play here, as it's one of the few area courses that don't require electric carts during the week. Many bunkers and unimproved areas off fairways make for tough recovery shots, but nobody said the game was supposed to be easy. A good course for beginning and intermediate golfers and juniors.

Boulder City Municipal Golf Course

Established: 1972; back 9 completed 1986

Address: 1 Clubhouse Dr., Boulder City, NV 89005

Phone: (702) 293-9236

Status: Public

Tees: Championship: 6,542 yards, par 72, USGA 70.2, slope 110
Men's: 6,120 yards, par 72, USGA 68.3, slope 103
Ladies': 5,458 yards, par 72, USGA 66.4, slope 110

Fees: $45 for 18 holes ($35 to walk); $31 for 9 holes ($25 to walk).

Facilities: Pro shop, driving range, putting green, restaurant, snack bar, and bar.

QV Rating: ★★ 1

Comments Just 20 minutes away from Las Vegas, in the one municipality in Nevada that forbids legalized gambling, this pleasant course is relaxing, accommodating to all level golfers, and just ten minutes away from Hoover Dam. Walking is permitted.

Craig Ranch Golf Course

Established: 1963

Address: 628 W. Craig Rd., North Las Vegas, NV 89030

Phone: (702) 642-9700

Status: Public

Tees: Championship: 6,100 yards, par 70, USGA 66.8, slope 105
Men's: 5,432 yards, par 70, USGA 64.6, slope 100
Ladies': 5,221 yards, par 70, USGA 67.4, slope 100

Fees: $18 to walk 18 holes, $26 to ride. $10.50 to walk 9 holes, $14.50 to ride. Club rentals, $10 ($6 for 9 holes).

Facilities: Pro shop, driving range, putting green, and snack bar.

QV Rating: ★★ 1

Comments A short public course with over 11,000 trees and perhaps the smallest greens in the state. A good course for beginning and intermediate golfers, with only one water hazard and three out-of-bounds holes.

Desert Pines Golf Club

Established: 1997

Address: 3415 E. Bonanza Rd., Las Vegas, NV 89101

Phone: (702) 366-1616
www.waltersgolf.com

Status: Public

Tees: Championship: 6,810 yards, par 71, USGA 70.4, slope 122
Men's: 6,464 yards, par 71, USGA 66.8, slope 112
Ladies': 5,873 yards, par 71, USGA 69.4, slope 116

Fees: Nonresidents: $135 for 18 holes, $85 twilight, Monday–Thursday; $165 for 18 holes, $90 twilight, Friday–Sunday and holidays (cart included).

Facilities: Pro shop, driving range, putting green, snack bar, and restaurant.

QV Rating: ★★ 3

Comments Desert Pines is a new, 6,810-yard course on Bonanza Road between Mohave and Pecos Roads. Inspired by the Pinehurst courses in North Carolina, Desert Pines' fairways and greens are flanked by trees, some already as tall as 40 feet. Instead of rough, developer Bill Walters laid down 45,000 bales of red-pine needles imported from South Carolina.

Desert Rose Golf Course

Established: 1960

Address: 5483 Club House Dr., Las Vegas, NV 89122

Phone: (702) 431-4653

Status: Public/Municipal course

Tees: Championship: 6,511 yards, par 71, USGA 69.6, slope 117
Men's: 6,135 yards, par 71, USGA 69, slope 114
Ladies': 5,458 yards, par 71, USGA 69, slope 119

Fees: Nonresidents: $69 for 18 holes on weekdays, $89 on weekends and holidays (cart included). Twilight $49 weekdays, $59 weekends. Nonresidents: $32 to walk 9 holes (before 7 a.m. or after 3:30 p.m.), $42 to ride 9 holes. Club rentals, $30.

Facilities: Pro shop, driving range, three putting/chipping greens, restaurant, banquet room, snack bar, and bar.

QV Rating: ★ 2

Comments With a name change (formerly it was Winterwood) and much moving of dirt, former PGA tour star Jim Colbert has created a functional public golf course that gets a lot of play year-round. A good course for recreational golfers, Desert Rose has fairly wide-open fairways with just a few out-of-bounds holes. Men must wear shirts with collars.

Highland Falls Golf Club

Established: 1992

Address: 10201 Sun City Blvd., Las Vegas, NV 89134

Phone: (702) 254-7010
www.suncitygolf.com

Status: Semi-private

Tees: Championship: 6,512 yards, par 72, USGA 71.2, slope 12
Men's: 6,017 yards, par 72, USGA 68.6, slope 11
Gold: 5,579 yards, par 72, USGA 67.1, slope 112
Ladies': 5,099 yards, par 72, USGA 68.2, slope 115

Fees: Nonresidents of Sun City: $125 for 18 holes, $53 after 2 p.m.

Facilities: Pro shop, driving range, one putting green, two chipping greens, luncheon area, patio for outside dining, and bar.

QV Rating: ★★   2

Comments   A testing layout designed by Hall of Famer Billy Casper's company, Casper-Nash Associates. Bentgrass greens with 328 Bermuda fairways overseeded with rye. More undulations than most desert courses, with several demanding holes. No one broke par for the first six months after opening. Schedule your tee time at least seven days in advance.

Las Vegas Golf Club

Established: 1949

Address: 4300 W. Washington Ave., Las Vegas, NV 89107

Phone: (702) 646-3003

Status: Municipal course

Tees: Championship: 6,319 yards, par 72, USGA 70, slope 112
Men's: 5,917 yards, par 72, USGA 68.1, slope 105
Ladies': 5,250 yards, par 72, USGA 69.9, slope 112

Fees: Nonresidents: $69 before noon, $49 after noon, weekdays; $89 before noon, $69 after noon, weekends. Club rentals, $20 for 18 holes.

Facilities: Pro shop, night-lighted driving range, putting green, restaurant, snack bar, bar, and beverage-cart girls who patrol the course.

QV Rating: ★   1

Comments   Popular public course and site of many local amateur tournaments. Formerly owned and managed by Senior PGA star Jim Colbert. A good course for recreational golfers, it offers fairly wide-open fairways and not a lot of trouble so play should move briskly. Tee times are always in great demand.

Las Vegas National

Established: 1961

Address: 1911 E. Desert Inn Rd., Las Vegas NV 89109

Phone: (800) GO TRY 18 or (702) 796-0013 (tee-time service and other reservations)

Status: Public (privately owned)

Tees:

Championship: 6,815 yards, par 72, USGA 72.1, slope 130

Men's: 6,418 yards, par 70, USGA 70.2, slope 121

Ladies': 5,741 yards, par 72, USGA 72.9, slope 127

Fees: $80–185.

Facilities: Pro shop, night-lighted driving range, putting green, snack bar, and bar.

QV Rating: ★★★　2

Comments　A championship course that has at one time co-hosted the Tournament of Champions, the Sahara Invitational, and the Ladies' Sahara Classic. Excellent variety of holes, with good bunkering and elevation changes uncharacteristic of a desert course. Better for intermediate and advanced golfers. No longer has any affiliation with the Sahara Hotel.

Las Vegas Paiute Resort

Established: 1995

Address: 10325 Nu/Wav Kaiv Blvd., Las Vegas, NV 89124. (US 95 between Kyle Canyon and Lee Canyon turn-off to Mount Charleston.)

Phone: (702) 658-1400

　　　www.lvpaiutegolf.com

Status: Public

Tees:　　Snow Mountain

　　　　　Tournament: 7,158 yards, par 72, USGA 73.9, slope 125

　　　　　Championship: 6,665 yards, par 72, USGA 71.2, slope 120

　　　　　Ladies' (white): 6,035 yards, par 72, USGA 74.5, slope 129

　　　　　Ladies' (red): 5,341 yards, par 72, USGA 70.4, slope 117

　　　　　Sun Mountain

　　　　　Tournament: 7,112 yards, par 72, USGA 73.3, slope 130

　　　　　Championship: 6,631 yards, par 72, USGA 70.9, slope 124

　　　　　Ladies' (white): 6,074 yards, par 72, USGA 74.8, slope 131

　　　　　Ladies' (red): 5,465 yards, par 72, USGA 71, slope 123

Fees: $145 Monday–Wednesday, $160 Thursday–Sunday, $85 twilight (seasonal); includes unlimited balls and cart.

Facilities: Pro shop, driving range, two putting greens, restaurant, snack bar, and bar with gaming.

QV Rating: ★★　2

Comments   The first of what is planned to be a 72-hole resort golf complex, the courses are Pete Dye designs, without the fangs. Director of Golf Johnny Pott, who enjoyed a fine career on the PGA tour, assures us that all caliber golfers can enjoy the course and survive.

Legacy Golf Club

Established: 1989

Address: 130 Par Excellence Dr., Henderson, NV 89014

Phone: (702) 897-2187

Status: Public (privately owned)

Tees: Championship: 7,233 yards, par 72, USGA 74.9, slope 136
Men's: 6,744 yards, par 72, USGA 72.1, slope 128
Ladies': 5,340 yards, par 72, USGA 71, slope 120
Resort: 6,211 yards, par 72, USGA 69.1, slope 118

Fees: All greens fees include mandatory carts. $135 weekdays and $150 weekends for 18 holes, no 9-hole rate. Summer rates (June 18–September 3): $65 weekdays and $90 weekends for 18 holes. Twilight rates vary (four hours before dark). Club rentals, $50.

Facilities: Clubhouse, pro shop, driving range, chipping facility, putting green, restaurant, snack bar, and bar.

QV Rating: ★★★   2

Comments   Legacy is a mixture of rolling fairways and target golf. Championship tees require long carry on tee-ball to clear desert mounding. Located at the southeastern tip of Las Vegas, Legacy has quickly become a favorite of intermediate and advanced golfers. Course plays host to a number of mini-tour professional events.

Los Prados Country Club

Established: 1985

Address: 5150 Los Prados Circle, Las Vegas, NV 89130

Phone: (702) 645-4523; pro shop, 645-5696
www.losprados–golf.com

Status: Semi-private

Tees: Championship: 5,350 yards, par 70, USGA 64.8, slope 103
Ladies': 4,474 yards, par 70, USGA 64.4, slope 104

Fees: Nonhomeowners: $45 before noon, $35 after noon, Friday–Sunday; $35 all day Monday–Wednesday. Club rentals, $20.

Facilities: Pro shop, putting green, restaurant, snack bar, and bar.

QV Rating: ★   2

Comments   Los Prados is a good course for beginners, intermediates, and families. Executive-length, with many short par-fours. Like most real estate developments in which golf is secondary to property values, the emphasis of the builders was on homesites rather than the design of the course. Not very accessible from the Strip, nearly a 25-minute drive.

Painted Desert

Established: 1987

Address: 5555 Painted Mirage Way, Las Vegas, NV 89129

Phone: (702) 645-2568 (tee-time service); (702) 645-2570 (pro shop)
        www.americangolf.com

Status: Public (privately owned)

Tees: Championship: 6,840 yards, par 72, USGA 73.7, slope 136
        Men's: 6,323 yards, par 72, USGA 71, slope 128
        Ladies': 5,711 yards, par 72, USGA 73.0, slope 127

Fees: Monday–Thursday, $130; twilight rate, $80. Friday–Sunday, $170; twilight rate, $85. Regular club rentals, $40; deluxe clubs, $50; twilight rentals half price. Twilight 1:30 p.m. until March 31, 2:30 after.

Facilities: Pro shop, driving range, putting green, snack bar, and bar.

QV Rating: ★★   2

Comments   Target course designed by renowned architect Jay Morrish, Tom Weiskopf's partner. Lush fairway landing pads and well-manicured greens, but make certain you're on target. The rough is pure waste-area. Course gets heavy traffic, primarily from intermediate and advanced golfers. A sprinkling of beginners can really slow things down on this course.

Palm Valley Golf Club (formerly Sun City Summerlin)

Established: 1989

Address: 9201-B Del Webb Blvd., Las Vegas, NV 89128

Phone: (702) 363-4373

Status: Semi-private

Tees: Championship: 6,849 yards, par 72, USGA 72.3, slope 127
        Gold: 5,757 yards, par 72, USGA 67.5, slope 119
        Men's: 6,341 yards, par 72, USGA 69.8, slope 124
        Ladies': 5,502 yards, par 72, USGA 70.7, slope 119

Fees: Nonresidents: $106 before noon, $75 after noon, weekdays; $125 before noon, $75 after noon, weekends. Carts included. Club rentals, $30.

Facilities: Pro shop, driving range, two putting greens, luncheon area, and bar. Additional facilities for members.

QV Rating: ★★   2

Comments   A demanding layout, situated in a retirement community. Rolling, wide-open terrain, heavy bunkering, and bentgrass greens. More than half of the 3,100 homes in this community have been bought, and the course will close to public play when membership fills.

The Revere at Anthem

Established: 1999

Address: 2600 Evergreen Oaks Drive, Henderson, NV 89052

Phone: (702) 259-GOLF or (877) 273-8373

Status: Public

Tees: Red: 7,143 yards, par 72, USGA 73.6, slope 139
Blue: 6,590 yards, par 72, USGA 70.8, slope 131
Black (Ladies'): 5,305 yards, par 72
White (Ladies'): 5,941 yards, par 72

Fees: Nonresidents: $150, Monday–Wednesday; $180, Thursday–Sunday.

Facilities: Fully stocked clubhouse and snack bar.

QV Rating: ★★   2

Comments   About 20 minutes from the Strip in the southeast Las Vegas Valley, this new course was designed by Billy Casper and Greg Nash. Built in a natural canyon, the course is both secluded and intimate, as well as challenging to all skill levels. Tee times, which must be reserved by credit card, can be made up to one year in advance.

Wildhorse Golf Club

Established: 1961

Address: 2100 W. Warm Springs Rd., Henderson, NV 89014

Phone: (702) 434-9000, or (800) 468-7918 (to make reservations more than one week in advance)

Status: Resort course, open to the public

Tees: Championship: 7,041 yards, par 72, USGA 74.8, slope 131
Men's: 5,911 yards, par 72, USGA 69.5, slope 121
Ladies': 5,331 yards, par 72, USGA 71.3, slope 125

Fees: Rates fluctuate and depend on time of day and day of week. Call for more specific fees. All greens fees include mandatory carts. Club rentals, $40; $55 for premium sets. Discount cards available to Clark County residents for $300.

Facilities: Pro shop, driving range, putting green, chipping green, practice traps, restaurant, snack bar, banquet facilities, and bar.

QV Rating: ★★★   2

Comments   This course has had more former names than Constantinople. The course and surrounding land were auctioned by the federal government for $16 million to the American Golf Company on April 28, 1994.

Outdoor Recreation

BICYCLING

Ask any biker in Las Vegas about the on- and off-road riding nearby and you'll probably hear two kinds of comments. First, why pedaling in the desert is such a treat: excellent surface conditions; the option of pancake-flat or hilly riding; beautiful stark scenery any time of year, and cactus blossoms in March and April; the possibility of spying raptors or jack rabbits or wild burros as you pedal; the unbelievably colorful limestone and sandstone formations . . .

Unfortunately, newcomers to desert and high-elevation biking often recall only these comments and not the "Be sure to carry—" warnings, which fellow riders usually provide after they've gotten you all revved up. So read the following and remember that bikers are subject to those very same conditions—heat and aridity—that make the desert so starkly beautiful.

Biking Essentials

1. Time of Day   Desert biking in late spring, summer, and early fall is best done early or late in the day. Know your seasons, listen to weather reports, and don't overestimate your speed and ability.

2. Clothing   Ever see someone perched on a camel? What was he wearing? Right, it wasn't a tank top and Lycra shorts. The point is protection—from the sun during the day, from the cold in the morning and evening. And if you don't use a helmet, wear a hat.

3. Sunscreen   In the desert, even well-tanned riders need this stuff.

4. Sunglasses   The glare will blind you without them.

5. Water   The first time we rode in the desert, we carried as much water as we would have used on a ride of comparable distance in the eastern United States. Big mistake. Our need for water was at least twice what it normally would be in New York or Alabama. We were thirsty the entire trip and might have gotten into serious trouble had we not cut our ride short.

You already know that you will need extra water, but how much? Well, a human working hard in 90° temperature requires ten quarts of fluid replenishment every day. Ten *quarts*. That's two and a half gallons—12 large water bottles, or 16 small ones. And with water weighing in at 8 pounds per gallon, a one-day supply comes to a whopping 20 pounds.

In other words, pack along two or three bottles even for the shortest rides. For longer rides, and particularly off-road, know ahead of time whether water is available along the way. If it is, unless it comes out of a tap, purify it. You can boil water for ten minutes and filter out the crud with a lightweight purifier (right!), or simply drop in a couple of effective, inexpensive tetraglycine hydroperiodide tablets. They're sold under the names of Potable Aqua, Globaline, Coughlan's, etc., and ought to be available at bike shops, but aren't. Check out a sporting goods store that specializes in backpacking equipment.

In the desert, the heat is dry, and you do not notice much perspiration because your sweat evaporates as quickly as it surfaces. Combine the dry heat with a little wind, and you can become extremely dehydrated before realizing it. Folks (like us) from the East tend to regard sweating as a barometer of our level of exertion (if you are not sweating much, in other words, you must not be exercising very hard). In the desert it doesn't work that way. You may never notice that you are sweating. In the desert you need to stay ahead of dehydration by drinking more frequently and more regularly and by consuming much more than the same amount of exercise would warrant in other climates. Desert days literally suck the water right out of you, even during the cooler times of the year.

6. Tools Each rider has a personal "absolute minimum list," which usually includes most of the following:

tire levers	chain rivet tool
spare tube patch kit	spare chain link
air pump	spoke wrench
allen wrenches (3, 4, 5, and 6 mm)	6-inch crescent (adjustable-end
small flat-blade screwdriver	wrench

7. First Aid Kit This too is a personal matter, usually including those items a rider has needed due to past mishaps. So, with the desert in mind, add a pair of tweezers (for close encounters of the cactus kind) and a snakebite kit. Most Las Vegas bikers have only seen snakes at the zoo or squashed on the highway, but you'll feel better if you pack one (the kit, that is) along.

Road Biking

Road biking on the Strip, downtown, or in any of Las Vegas's high-traffic areas is suicidal. Each year an astoundingly high number of bikers are injured or killed playing Russian roulette with Las Vegas motorists. If you want to bike, either confine yourself to sleepy subdivisions or get way out of town on a road with wide shoulders and little traffic.

There are a number of superb rides within a 30- to 40-minute drive from downtown or the Strip. The best is the **Red Rock Canyon Scenic Loop ride,** due west of town, which carves a 15.4-mile circuit through the canyon's massive, rust-colored, sandstone cliffs. The route is arduous, with a 1,000-foot elevation gain in the first six miles, followed by eight miles of downhill and flats with one more steep hill. One-way traffic on the scenic loop applies to cyclists and motorists alike. Although there is a fair amount of traffic on weekends, the road is wide and the speed limit is a conservative 35 miles per hour. If you park your car at the Red Rock Canyon Visitor Center, take careful note of when the area closes. If you are delayed on your ride and get back late, your car might be trapped behind locked gates.

A second ride in the same area follows State Route 159 from the town of Blue Diamond to the entrance of Red Rock Canyon Scenic Loop Drive and back again, approximately eight miles. From Blue Diamond the highway traverses undulating hills, with a net elevation gain of 193 feet on the outbound leg. In general, the ride offers gentle, long grades alternating with relatively flat stretches. Cliff walls and desert flora provide stunning vistas throughout. Traffic on NV 159 is a little heavy on weekends, but the road is plenty wide, with a good surface and wide shoulders. In the village of Blue Diamond there is a small store.

Another good out-and-back begins at Overton Beach on Lake Mead, northeast of Las Vegas, and ascends 867 feet in eight miles to the visitor center at the Valley of Fire State Park. (You can, of course, begin your round trip at the visitor center, but we always prefer to tackle the uphill leg first.) Geology in the park is spectacular, with the same red sandstone found in the cliffs and formations of the Grand Canyon. There are no shoulders, but traffic is light and the road surface is good. Since the route runs pretty much east-west, we like to schedule our ride in the afternoon so that we will have the setting sun at our back as we coast down to the lake on the return leg. Another good option is an early-morning ride with the sun at your back as you ascend and high in the sky as you return.

Dressing for a bike ride in the canyons and high country around Las Vegas is a challenge. In early December, when we rode the Red Rock loop, it was about 62° in town and about 10° cooler in the canyon. We started out in Lycra bike shorts and polypro long-sleeve windbreakers. By the time we completed the six-mile uphill, we were about to die of heat prostration. On the long, fast downhill, we froze.

Our recommendation is to layer on cooler days so that you can add or shuck clothing as conditions warrant. On warm days try to bike early in the morning or late in the afternoon and wear light clothing. Always wear a helmet and always, always carry lots of water. If you are not used to biking in arid climates, take twice as much water as you would carry at home, and drink *before* you get thirsty.

There is no place on any of these routes to get **help with a broken bike.** You should bring an extra tube and a pump and know how to fix flats and make other necessary adjustments and repairs. Water is available at Blue Diamond and at the Red Rock and Valley of Fire visitor centers, but no place else. Always replenish when you have the opportunity.

Mountain Biking

Most off-road biking in the Las Vegas area is done on jeep trails and dirt roads. In the Red Rock Canyon National Conservation Area, the Lake Mead National Recreation Area, the national forests, and the state parks, mountain bikes are not permitted (with one exception) on hiking trails. Fortunately, there are plenty of jeep trails and dirt roads.

There are several good rides in the Mount Potasi (POT-a-see) area southwest of Las Vegas, including a mostly single-track loop trail developed for mountain bike racing, and a ride over the Potasi Pass to Potasi Spring and the Potasi mine. These are fairly challenging rides over dirt roads with some long pulls. In the same area is a ride from NV 160 to the old mining town of Goodsprings. This is one of the few rides in the Las Vegas area that covers mostly level terrain. Heat, wind, and dust can be a problem on all of these rides.

In Lee Canyon of the Toiyabe National Forest, bikes are allowed on the Bristlecone Pine Trail, a five-mile mountaintop loop through a ponderosa pine and white fir forest with a 700-foot rise and fall in elevation. Tough ride at altitude, but the air is cool and the scenery is great, with spectacular views down the canyon.

In addition to the foregoing, many mountain bikers ride the scenic loop (described under Road Biking) at Red Rock Canyon National Conservation Area. See the map on page 343.

Mountain bikes can be rented from Escape the City Streets! at 8221 W. Charleston, Suite 101, on the way to Red Rock Canyon, (702) 596-BYKE. Rental fees are $24–34 for a half-day and $30–45 for a full day (range from front suspension, to full, to demo bikes) and include helmet, gloves, and water bottles. Escape the City Streets! is a good source of information on rides and provides guided tours and shuttles.

HIKING AND BACKPACKING

Hiking or backpacking in the desert can be a very enjoyable experience. It can also be a hazardous adventure if you travel unprepared. Lake Mead ranger Debbie Savage suggests the following:

> *The best months for hiking are the cooler months of November through March. Hiking is not recommended in the summer when temperatures reach 120° in the shade. Never hike alone and always tell someone where you are going and when you plan to return. Carry plenty of water (at least a half gallon per person) and drink often.*
>
> *Know your limits. Hiking the canyons and washes in the desert often means traveling over rough, steep terrain with frequent elevation changes. Try to pick a route that best suits your abilities. Distances in the desert are often deceiving. Be sure to check the weather forecast before departure. Sudden storms can cause flash flooding. Seek higher ground if thunderstorms threaten.*
>
> *Essential equipment includes sturdy walking shoes and proper clothing. Long pants are suggested for protection from rocks and cactus. A hat, sunscreen, and sunglasses are also recommended. Carry a small daypack to hold such items as a first aid kit, lunch, water, a light jacket, and a flashlight.*

Canyons and washes often contain an impressive diversity of plant life, most easily observed during the spring wildflower season. Desert springs are located in some of the canyons and support a unique community of plants and animals. They are often the only source of water for many miles around. Take care not to contaminate them with trash or other human wastes. Along similar lines, understand that desert soils are often very fragile and take a long time to recover if disturbed. These surfaces are recognizable by their comparatively darker appearance and should be avoided whenever possible.

Poisonous animals such as snakes, spiders, and scorpions are most active after dark and are not often seen during daylight hours by hikers. Speckled rattlesnakes are common but are not aggressive. Scorpion stings are no more harmful than a bee sting unless you are allergic. Black widow spiders are shy and secretive and are most often found around man-made structures. Watch where you place your hands and feet and don't disturb obvious hiding places.

The Las Vegas area offers quite a diversity of hiking options. Trips that include a choice of canyons, lakes, desert, mountains, or ponderosa pine forest can be found within an hour's drive of Las Vegas.

The Lake Mead National Recreation Area, an hour southeast of Las Vegas, offers a wide variety of hiking experiences, although there are few designated trails. Included within the NRA are Lakes Mead and Mohave, and part of the Mojave Desert. Ranger-guided hikes are offered during the winter months. The outings cover six to eight miles and are moderate to strenuous in difficulty. If you prefer to explore on your own, detailed maps and instructions to the most popular areas are available at the visitor centers. For information call (702) 293-8907.

The Red Rock Canyon National Conservation Area contains some of the most rugged rock formations in the West. Only 40 minutes from Las Vegas, Red Rock Canyon offers loop as well as out-and-back trails of varying lengths. (See map on page 343.) The short Moenkopi Loop originates at the visitor center, and it takes a little more than an hour to walk over undulating terrain in a broad desert valley. Other popular short hikes include out-and-backs to Lost Creek (three-tenths of a mile one-way), Icebox Canyon (one-and-three-tenths miles one-way), and Pine Creek Canyon (one mile one-way), leading to the ruins of a historic homestead near a running creek surrounded by large ponderosa pine trees. For additional information call (702) 363-1921.

The Toiyabe National Forest, high in the mountains 40 minutes northwest of Las Vegas, provides a totally different outdoor experience. The air is cool, and the trails run among stately forests of ponderosa pine, quaking aspen, white fir, and mountain mahogany. Hikes range in distance from one-tenth of a mile to 21 miles, and in difficulty from easy to very difficult. Most popular are the Cathedral Rock Trail (two miles round-trip), which climbs 900 feet to a stark summit overlooking Kyle Canyon, and Bristlecone, a five-mile loop that traverses the ridges above the Lee Canyon Ski Area. Though the distances of these loops are not great, the terrain is exceedingly rugged, and the hikes are not recommended for one-day outings unless you begin very early in the morning and are used to strenuous exercise at high elevations. For additional information call (702) 873-8800.

The Valley of Fire State Park, 45 minutes northeast of Las Vegas, rounds out the hiking picture. This park features rock formations similar to those found in the Grand Canyon, as well as a number of Indian petroglyphs. The *Las Vegas Advisor* compares hiking the Valley of Fire with being "beamed" onto another planet. Trails traverse desert terrain and vary from seven miles to a half-mile in length. Visitors should check in at the visitor center before they begin hiking. For more information call (702) 397-2088.

Guided Hikes and Tours

Rocky Trails (phone (702) 869-9991; e-mail: nature@rockytrails.com; www.rockytrails.com) offers guided tours to the natural sites described above as well as to Death Valley, the Grand Canyon, Bryce Canyon, and Zion National Park. Guests are picked up at their hotel and transported in modern Suburbans or vans. Lunch is included. Expeditions to the Valley of Fire, Red Rock Canyon, Death Valley, and the Grand Canyon last six to ten hours and cost $75 to $299 per adult.

ROCK CLIMBING AND BOULDERING

The Red Rock Canyon National Conservation Area is one of the top rock-climbing resources in the United States. With over 1,000 routes, abundant holds, and approaches ranging from roadside to remote wilderness, the area rivals Yosemite in scope and variety for climbers. Offering amazing diversity for every skill level amidst desert canyon scenery second to none, the area is less than a 40-minute drive from Las Vegas.

Though there is some granite and limestone, almost all of the climbing is done on sandstone. Overall, the rock is pretty solid, although there are some places where the sandstone gets a little crumbly, especially after a rain. Bolting is allowed but discouraged (local climbers have been systematically replacing bolts on some of the older routes with more modern bolts that blend with the rock). There are some great spots for bouldering, some of the best top-roping in the United States, a lifetime supply of big walls, and even some bivouac routes. Climbs range in difficulty from nonbelayed scrambles to 5.13 big-wall overhangs. You can climb year-round at Red Rock. Wind can be a problem, as can most of the other conditions that make a desert environment challenging. Having enough water can be a logistical nightmare on a long climb.

Red Rock Guide by Joanne Urioste describes a number of the older routes. Newer route descriptions can be obtained from Desert Rock Sports in Las Vegas, (702) 254-1143. Desert Rock Sports can also help you find camping and showers and tell you where the loose rock is. Offering climbing shoe rentals, the store is at 8201 West Charleston, conveniently on the way to the canyon from Las Vegas. The Powerhouse Rock Gym is next to Desert Rock Sports and offers excellent indoor climbing and showers. Guides and/or instruction are available from Desert Rock Sports or from Sky's the Limit Climbing School and Guide Service, (702) 363-4533 or (800) 733-7597. Sky's the Limit also teaches courses in winter mountaineering, avalanche awareness, and cross-country skiing. Most Sky's the Limit guides are UIAGM/IVBV/AMGA accredited and certified.

RIVER RUNNING

The Black Canyon of the Colorado River can be run year-round below Hoover Dam. The most popular trip is from the tailwaters of the dam to Willow Beach. In this 11-mile section, canyon walls rise almost vertically from the water's edge, with scenery and wildlife very similar to that of the Colorado River in the Grand Canyon above Lake Mead. There are numerous warm springs and waterfalls on feeder streams, presenting the opportunity for good side-trip hikes. Bighorn sheep roam the bluffs, and wild burros can often be seen up the canyons. The water in the river, about 53° year-round, is drawn from the bottom of Lake Mead and released downstream through the Hoover Dam hydroelectric generators.

For the most part, the Black Canyon is a scenic flatwater float. There are some easy-to-avoid rocks below Boy Scout Canyon and Ringbolt Rapids (class II with sneak route on river left) three miles into the run. Less-experienced paddlers will probably have more difficulty with whirlpools and eddies than with rapids. Headwinds coming up the canyon pose a problem for all boaters. The Black Canyon is suitable for canoes, kayaks, and rafts. The trip takes about six hours in a canoe or kayak and about three hours in a *motorized* raft.

Private (noncommercial) parties must obtain a $5 trip permit from:

Hoover Dam Canoe Lodge
P.O. Box 60400
Boulder City, NV 89006-0400
(866) 291-TOUR

Visitors can now fax the application to obtain a trip permit, and the Lodge will issue a permit two days in advance of the trip date. Only 30 private craft are allowed to launch daily, 15 at 8:30 a.m. and another 15 at 10 a.m., so apply for your trip permit early, if possible. Canoes and kayaks can be rented from Boulder City Watersport at (702) 293-7526. A commercial outfitter, Black Canyon, Inc., (702) 293-3776, operates guided, motorized raft trips and can even arrange for guest transportation from Las Vegas.

The best seasons to run the Black Canyon are the spring and fall. There is little protection from the sun in the canyon, and temperatures can surpass 110° in the warmer months. Long-sleeve shirts, long pants, tennis shoes, and a hat are recommended minimum attire year-round. Be sure to take sunscreen and lots of drinking water.

SNOW SKIING

The Lee Canyon Ski Area is a 45-minute drive from Las Vegas. Situated in a granite canyon in the Spring Mountain range, the resort provides three double chair lifts servicing ten runs. Though the mountain is small and the runs short by Western standards, the skiing is solid intermediate. Of the ten runs, seven are blue, two are black, and there is one short green. Base elevation of 8,510 feet notwithstanding, snow conditions are usually dependable only during January. Because of its southerly location and the proximity of the hot, arid desert, there is a lot of thawing and refreezing in Lee Canyon, and hence, frequently icy skiing conditions. If the snow is good, a day at Lee Canyon is a great outing. If the mountain is icy, do something else.

Snowmaking equipment allows the Lee Canyon Ski Area to operate from Thanksgiving to Easter. There is no lodging on-site and only a modest coffee shop and lounge. The parking lot is a fairly good hike from the base facility.

Skis can be rented at the ski area or from Las Vegas Ski and Snowboard Resort at the resort lodge. For information on lift tickets or snow conditions, call the ski area office at (702) 385-2SKI, and for summer event info at Lee Canyon, call (702) 593-9500.

HORSEBACK RIDING

The best place for horseback riding is Kyle Canyon in the Toiyabe National Forest northwest of Las Vegas. Quarter horses with Western saddles can be rented spring through fall for one-and-a-half- to two-hour daytime rides at $69 to $89, or for sunset dinner rides at $139. The scenery is spectacular, with mountain vistas, ponderosa pine forests, and 300,000 acres to explore. Guides are available. Advance payment and reservations are required. For information or reservations call Mount Charleston Riding Stables at (702) 387-2457.

FISHING

The Lake Mead National Recreation Area offers some of the best fishing in the United States. Lake Mead is the largest lake, with Lake Mohave, downstream on the Colorado River, offering the most diverse fishery. Largemouth bass, striped bass, channel catfish, crappie, and bluegill are found in both lakes. Rainbow and cutthroat trout are present only in Lake Mohave. Remote and beautiful in its upmost reaches, Lake Mohave is farther from Las Vegas but provides truly exceptional fishing. Bass and trout often run three pounds, and some trout weigh ten pounds or more. Willow Beach, near where the Colorado River enters the pool waters of Lake Mohave, is where many of the larger trout are taken.

Lake Mead, broader, more open, and much closer to Las Vegas, has become famous for its stripers, with an occasional catch weighing in at over 40 pounds. Bass fishing is consistently good throughout Lake Mead. The Overton Arm (accessed from Echo Bay or Overton Beach) offers the best panfish and catfish action.

Lake Mead Bait and Tackle, Boat Rental, Fuel, and Supplies	
Callville Bay Resort	(702) 565-8958
Echo Bay Resort	(702) 394-4000
Lake Mead Resort	(702) 293-2074 or (800) 752-9669 for reservations
Overton Beach Resort	(702) 394-4040
Temple Bar Resort (AZ)	(520) 767-3211
Cottonwood Cove Resort	(702) 297-1467
Lake Mohave Resort (AZ)	(520) 754-3245

Because Lakes Mead and Mohave form the Arizona/Nevada state line, fishing license regulations are a little strange. If you are bank fishing, all you need is a license from the state you are in. If you fish from a boat, however, you need a fishing license from one state and a special use stamp from the other. Fortunately, all required stamps and licenses can be obtained from marinas and local bait and tackle shops in either state.

Nonresidents have the option of purchasing one- to ten-day fishing permits in lieu of a license. Permits range from about $12 for the one-day to $24 for the seasonal and $51 for the annual, and apply to the reciprocal waters of Lake Mead and Lake Mohave only. In addition to the permit, a special use stamp costing $3 is required for those fishing from a boat, and a $10 trout stamp is necessary to take trout. In addition, a $10 stamp is available for fishing with two rods. Youngsters age 12 years and under in the company of a properly licensed, permitted, and stamped adult can fish without any sort of documentation. The best deal is the seasonal license, which costs $24 and includes the $3 stamp.

Sixteen-foot, aluminum, V-hulled fishing boats (seat five) can be rented on both lakes by the hour (about $30 with a two-hour minimum), by the half-day (four hours for about $50), or by the day (about $100). Bass boats, houseboats, and pontoon craft are also available. Rods and reels rent for about $5 for four hours or less and about $12 a day.

PLEASURE BOATING, SAILING, WATER SKIING, AND JET SKIING

Lake Mead and Lake Mohave are both excellent sites for pleasure boating, water skiing, and other activities. Both lakes are so large that it is easy to find a secluded spot for your favorite boating or swimming activity. Rock formations on the lakes are spectacular, and boaters can visit scenic canyons and coves that are inaccessible to those traveling by car. Boats, for example, can travel into the narrow, steep-walled gorge of Iceberg Canyon in Lake Mead or upstream into the Black Canyon from Lake Mohave.

First-timers, particularly on Lake Mead, frequently underestimate its vast size. It is not difficult to get lost on the open waters of Lake Mead or to get caught in bad weather. Winds can be severe on the lake, and waves of six feet sometimes arise during storms. In general, there is no shade on the lakes, and the steep rock formations along the shore do not make very hospitable emergency landing sites. When you boat on either lake, take plenty of water, be properly dressed and equipped, and be sure to tell someone where you are going and when you expect to return.

Most of the resorts listed under "Fishing" rent various types of pleasure craft and water-skiing equipment, and two of them, the Overton Beach Resort on Lake Mead and the Callville Bay Resort, rent personal watercraft. In addition, at Callville Bay on Lake Mead and Cottonwood Cove on Lake Mohave, luxury houseboats are available for rental. The boats sleep up to ten adults and have fully equipped galleys and heads. For rates and other information concerning houseboats, call (800) 255-5561 or (800) 752-9669.

Relaxation and Rejuvenation

Following a vigorous day's exercise, Las Vegas offers numerous ways to relax, including a wide choice of health spas. The spas offer everything from massage to exotic body wraps.Each spa is different but, in addition to workout equipment, these spas generally have tanning facilities, skin treatments, and steam rooms.

Most spas are open to the public, but some cater only to hotel guests. A tourist staying in one of the larger hotel-casinos should have access to on-site spa facilities. Check the following listing for phone numbers and access information

Las Vegas Health Spas	
Spas Open to the Public	
Aladdin	
The Elemis Spa at Aladdin	(702) 785-5555
AlexisPark	
Alexis Park Health Spa	(702) 796-3300

Las Vegas Health Spas (continued)

(Spas Open to the Public, continued)

Caesars Palace
The Spa at Caesars Palace   (702) 731-7776   (Sun.–Thu.)

Flamingo
Flamingo Health Spa   (702) 733-3533

Hard Rock Hotel
The RockSpa   (702) 693-5554

Harrah's
Harrah's Spa   (702) 369-5189

Hyatt at Lake Las Vegas
Spa Moulay   (702) 567-1234

Imperial Palace
Health and Fitness Center   (702) 731-3311

Las Vegas Hilton
The Spa at the Las Vegas Hilton   (702) 732-5648

Luxor
Oasis Spa   (702) 730-5724

Mandalay Bay
Spa Mandalay   (702) 632-7220

MGM Grand
The MGM Grand Spa   (702) 891-3077   (Mon.–Thu.)

Monte Carlo
The Spa at Monte Carlo   (702) 730-7596

New York–New York
The Spa at New York–New York   (702) 740-6955

Paris Las Vegas
Spa by Mandara   (702) 946-4366

Regent Las Vegas
Aquae Sulis   (702) 869-7777

Rio
The Spa at Rio   (702) 252-7779   (Mon.–Thu.)

Las Vegas Health Spas (continued)

(Spas Open to the Public, continued)

Riviera
Las Vegas Health Spas (continued)
   Executive Fitness at the Riviera (702) 794-9441

Treasure Island at the Mirage
   Treasure Island Health Spa   (702) 894-7472   (Mon.–Thu.)

Tropicana
   Tropicana Spa   (702) 739-2680

Spas for Hotel Guests Only

Bally's
   The Spa at Bally's   (702) 967-4366

Bellagio
   Spa Bellagio   (702) 693-7472

Caesars Palace
   The Spa at Caesars Palace (702) 731-7776 (Fri.–Sat.)

Four Season
   Four Seasons Spa   (702) 632-5302

Golden Nugget
   The Grand Court   (702) 385-7111

MGM Grand
   The MGM Grand Spa   (702) 891-3077 (Fri.–Sun.)

Mirage
   The Spa at the Mirage   (702) 791-7427

Rio
   The Spa at Rio   (702) 252-7779 (Fri.–Sat.)

Treasure Island at the Mirage
   Treasure Island Health Spa (702) 894-7472 (Fri.–Sun.)

The Venetian
   Canyon Ranch SpaClub   (702) 414-3600

Part Five

Shopping and Seeing the Sights

Shopping in Las Vegas

The most interesting and diversified specialty shopping in Las Vegas is centered on the Strip at the Fashion Show Mall, The Forum Shops at Caesars Palace, and the Grand Canal Shoppes at the Venetian. These three venues, within walking distance of each other, collectively offer the most unique, and arguably the most concentrated, aggregation of upscale retailers in the United States. In fairness, it should be noted that The Forum Shops and the Grand Canal Shoppes are not your average shopping centers. In fact, both are attractions in their own right and should be on your must-see list even if you don't like to shop. Both feature designer shops, exclusive boutiques, and specialty retailers. Fashion Show Mall, by comparison, is plain white bread, with no discernible theme but a great lineup of big-name department stores.

At the intersection of Las Vegas Boulevard and Spring Mountain Road, the Fashion Show Mall is anchored by Saks Fifth Avenue, May Company, Neiman Marcus, Macy's, Nordstrom, Bloomingdales', Lord & Taylor, and Dillard's, and contains 144 specialty shops, including four art galleries. There is no theme here—no Roman columns or canals with gondolas. At the Fashion Show Mall, shopping is king. And although there is no shortage of boutiques or designer shops, the presence of the big department stores defines the experience for most customers. The Fashion Show Mall is the place to go for that new sport coat, tie, blouse, or skirt at a reasonable price. The selection is immense, and most of the retailers are familiar and well known.

The Forum Shops is a *très chic (et très cher)* shopping complex situated between Caesars Palace and the Mirage. Connected to the Forum Casino in Caesars Palace, The Forum Shops offers a Roman market–themed shopping environment. Executed on a scale that is extraordinary even for Caesars,

The Forum Shops replicate the grandeur of Rome at the height of its glory. Approximately 100 shops and restaurants line an ancient Roman street punctuated by plazas and fountains. Though totally indoors, clouds, sky, and celestial bodies are projected on the vaulted ceilings to simulate the actual time of day outside. Statuary in The Forum is magnificent; some is even animatronic. A new west wing features an IMAX 3-D simulator attraction called *Race For Atlantis* (described on page 380).

The Grand Canal Shoppes are similar to The Forum Shops in terms of the realistic theming, only this time the setting is the modern-day canals of Venice. Sixty-five shops, boutiques, restaurants, and cafes are arrayed along a quarter-mile-long Venetian street flanking a canal. A 70-foot ceiling (more than six stories high) with simulated sky enhances the openness and provides perspective. Meanwhile, gondolas navigating the canal add a heightened sense of commerce and activity. The centerpiece of the Grand Canal Shoppes is a replica of St. Mark's Square, without the pigeons.

You've probably heard of doubling down in blackjack. Well, now doubling has caught on with shopping centers. The Forum Shops doubled in size in 1998 and are now in the process of expanding yet again. Retailers include Fendi, FAO Schwarz, Polo, NikeTown, and a Virgin (record) Megastore, among others. An Atlantis feature along with a giant aquarium provide some neat stuff to see for those who left all their money in the casino. Not to be outdone, the Fashion Show Mall is also doubling in size. The project, scheduled to be completed in 2003, will make Fashion Show the largest mall in Nevada.

The new Aladdin includes a 450,000-square-foot shopping and entertainment complex called Desert Passage. The venue recreates street scenes from real and imaginary North African and eastern Mediterranean towns in a shopping concourse that stretches around the periphery of the hotel and casino. The bazaars and shop facades sit beneath an arched ceiling painted and lighted to simulate the evening sky. Overall, although the replication is effective, it falls a little short of the Forum Shops but gives the Grand Canal Shoppes a run for the money. Like the Grand Canal Shoppes, Desert Passage offers primarily upscale boutique shopping, but more of it, with 144 shops and restaurants compared to the Canal Shoppes' 65.

At Paris is Rue de la Paix—31,000 square feet of upscale French boutique shopping. Modest in size by Las Vegas shopping standards, the Rue de la Paix re-creates a Paris street scene with cobblestone pavement and winding alleyways.

Another Strip shopping venue is the Showcase, adjacent to the MGM Grand. Although most of the 190,000-square-foot shopping and entertainment complex is devoted to theme restaurants, a Sega electronic games arcade, and an eight-plex movie theater, there remains space for a number of retail specialty shops.

There are two large neighborhood malls in Las Vegas, the Boulevard Mall and the Meadows. The Boulevard Mall, with 122 stores anchored by Sears, JCPenney, Marshalls, Dillard's, and Macy's, is on Maryland Avenue, between Desert Inn Road and Flamingo Road. The Meadows, featuring the same department stores (except for Marshalls), offers 73 stores spread over two levels. The Meadows is situated between West Charleston Boulevard and the Las Vegas Expressway (US 95) on Valley View.

A large discount shopping venue has materialized about five miles south of Tropicana Avenue on Las Vegas Boulevard near the Blue Diamond Road exit off I-15. A mile or so south of Blue Diamond Road on Las Vegas Boulevard is the Vegas Pointe Plaza, with a total of 50 factory-direct shops. Just north of Blue Diamond Road is a Belz Factory Outlet mall with 155 stores. Belz, like The Forum Shops, doubled its size in 1998. Promotional literature listing the individual shops at both locations is available in almost all hotel brochure racks. The easiest way to reach the outlets is to drive south on I-15 to Exit 33, Blue Diamond Road. Proceed east on Blue Diamond to the intersection with Las Vegas Boulevard. Turn left on Las Vegas Boulevard to the Belz mall, or right to the Vegas Pointe Plaza. For those without transportation, Las Vegas Citizen's Area Transit (CAT) operates a bus route that connects the various Strip and suburban shopping centers. Fare is $1.25 in residential areas and $2 on the Strip. Service is provided daily from 10:35 a.m. to 6:30 p.m. For more information on CAT, call (702) 228-7433.

About an hour southwest on I-15 in Primm, Nevada, is Fashion Outlet Mall, offering themed dining and 100 outlet stores. You'll find Williams-Sonoma, Pottery Barn, Versace, Brooks Brothers, Calvin Klein, Tommy Hilfiger, Escada, Kenneth Cole, Banana Republic, Baby Guess, LeSportsac, and Last Call from Neiman Marcus, among others. The mall is adjacent to the Primm Valley Resort and Casino.

Unique Shopping Opportunities

Wine & Liquor   Our favorite store for liquor and a decent bottle of wine is Town Pump Liquors, with five locations. In addition to a good selection of all spirits at competitive prices, Town Pump almost always offers a loss-leader bargain on good French, Italian, or California wines. The East Sahara Avenue store, in the Commercial Center, is the closest to the Strip. Though the address is listed as East Sahara, the easiest way to get there is via Karen Avenue.

Town Pump Liquors	
953 E. Sahara Avenue	735-8515
6040 W. Sahara Avenue	876-6615

1725 E. Warm Springs Road	897-9463
4410 W. Craig Road	645-9700

Art Las Vegas is a great place to shop for contemporary and nontraditional art and sculpture, with galleries in the Fashion Show Mall, The Forum Shops, and the Grand Canal Shoppes. Do not, however, expect any bargains.

Gambling Stuff As you would expect, Las Vegas is a shopping mecca when it comes to anything having to do with gambling. If you are in the market for a roulette wheel, a blackjack table, or some personalized chips, try the Gamblers General Store at 800 South Main, (702) 382-9903, or (800) 322-CHIP outside Nevada. For books and periodicals on gambling, we recommend the Gamblers Book Club store near the intersection of South 11th Street and East Charleston, (702) 382-7555.

If you have always wanted a slot machine for your living room, you can buy one at Showcase Slot Machines, 4305 South Industrial Road, (702) 740-5722. Possession of a slot machine (including video poker and blackjack) for personal use is legal in the following states:

Alaska	Minnesota	Texas
Arizona	Nevada	Utah
Arkansas	New Mexico	Virginia
Kentucky	Ohio	West Virginia
Maine	Rhode Island	

Another group of states will allow you to own a slot machine providing the machine is fairly old (how old depends on the state). In New Jersey, Pennsylvania, New York, and South Dakota, the machine must have been manufactured before 1941. In the following states and the District of Columbia, the required age falls somewhere between 20 and 42 years:

California	Kansas	New Hampshire	South Carolina
Colorado	Louisiana	New Jersey	South Dakota
Delaware	Maryland	New York	Vermont
Florida	Massachusetts	North Carolina	Washington
Georgia	Michigan	North Dakota	Washington, D.C.
Idaho	Mississippi	Oklahoma	Wisconsin
Illinois	Missouri	Oregon	Wyoming
Iowa	Montana	Pennsylvania	

In all other states the possession of any type of slot machine is illegal.

Head Rugs   The next time you go to a Las Vegas production show, pay attention to the showgirls' hair. You will notice that the same woman will have a different hairdo for every number. Having made this observation, you will not be surprised that the largest wig and hairpiece retailer in the United States is in Las Vegas. At 953 E. Sahara Avenue about five minutes away from the Strip, Serge's Showgirl Wigs inventories over 7,000 hairpieces and wigs, made from both synthetic materials and human hair. In addition to serving the local showgirl population, Serge's Showgirl Wigs also specializes in assisting chemotherapy patients. A catalog and additional information can be obtained by calling (702) 732-1015.

Ethnic Shopping   At the southwest corner of Spring Mountain and Wynn Roads is Las Vegas Chinatown Plaza with 30 outlets, (702) 221-8448. This location offers oriental theme shopping and Asian restaurants.

Authentic African products, including sculpture, art, pottery, baskets, jewelry, musical instruments, and attire, can be found at African & World Imports in the Boulevard Mall at 3680 S. Maryland Parkway, (702) 734-1900.

For Native American art, crafts, books, music, and attire, try the Las Vegas Indian Center at 2300 W. Bonanza Boulevard, (702) 647-5842. And 25 minutes north of Las Vegas in Moapa, Nevada, you'll find the Moapa Tribal Enterprises Casino and Gift Center, (702) 864-2600. Take I-15 north to Exit 75.

Zoot Suits   No kidding. For the coolest threads in town, try Valentino's Zootsuit Collection: Vintage Apparel & Collectibles at the corner of South 6th Street and Charleston. If you only want to zoot up for a special occasion, rentals are available. Call (702) 383-9555.

Baseball Cards   Finally, in the "everyone has to be someplace" category, is Smokey's Sports Cards, possibly the largest buyer, seller, and auctioneer of sports trading cards in the United States. Open seven days a week, Smokey's is at 3734 Las Vegas Boulevard South (the Strip), (702) 739-0003 (www.smokeys.com). In addition to baseball cards, Smokey's also deals in football, basketball, and hockey cards.

Seeing the Sights

Residents of Las Vegas are justifiably proud of their city and are quick to point out that Las Vegas has much to offer besides gambling. Quality theater, college and professional sports, dance, concerts, art shows, museums, and film festivals contribute to making Las Vegas a truly great place to live. In addition, there is a diverse and colorful natural and historical heritage.

What Las Vegas residents sometimes have a difficult time understanding, however, is that the average business and leisure traveler doesn't really give a big hoot. Until 1993 Las Vegas differed from Orlando and Southern California in that it did not have any bona fide tourist attractions except Hoover Dam. Nobody drove all the way to Las Vegas to take their children to visit the Guinness Book of Records exhibit. While there have always been some great places to detox from a long trade show or too many hours at the casino, they are totally peripheral in the minds of visitors. Las Vegas needs a legitimate, nongaming tourist draw, but the strange aggregation of little museums, factory tours, and mini–theme parks is not it.

In 1993 the opening of the MGM Grand Hotel and Casino and Grand Adventures Theme Park brought Las Vegas a little closer to penetrating the consciousness of the nongambling traveler, but, alas, the park was a dud. It limped along for eight years before shutting down in 2001. During the 1990s, Circus Circus opened a smaller theme park, Adventuredome, behind its main casino. For the most part, the new theme parks have made little impression on either the locals or the tourists. From 1997 through 2000, a number of Strip casinos, including Caesars Palace, the Stratosphere, New York–New York, the Sahara, and the Las Vegas Hilton opened new attractions. These attractions by and large are imaginative, visually appealing, and high-tech. Some, like the Hilton's *Star Trek* attraction, would stand out as headliners in any theme park in the country. Others, while not up to Disney or Universal Studios standards, represent a giant leap forward for Las Vegas. Clearly, the competition learned a few things from MGM Grand's theme park flop.

MGM GRAND ATTRACTIONS

In 1999, the MGM Grand opened a tri-story 5345-square-foot lion habitat that houses up to five of the big cats. The lions are on duty from 11 a.m. until 11 p.m. daily and admission is free. There is also, of course, an MGM Lion logo shop and the opportunity (for $20) to be photographed with a lion.

MANDALAY BAY ATTRACTIONS

The big draw at Mandalay Bay is the Shark Reef aquarium attraction featuring sharks, rays, sea turtles, the venomous stonefish, and dozens of other denizens of the deep playing house in a 1.3 million gallon tank. If you don't like fish, separate exhibits showcase rare golden crocodiles and pythons. Something for everybody you might say. The Shark reef audio tour is open daily from 10 a.m. until 11 p.m. Admission is about $14 for adults and

$10 for children 12 and under. Additional information is available at (702) 632-4555.

ADVENTUREDOME AT CIRCUS CIRCUS

To further appeal to the family market targeted by the MGM Grand Adventures Theme Park, Circus Circus opened a small but innovative amusement park in August of 1993. Situated directly behind the main hotel and casino, the park now goes by the name of Adventuredome. Architecturally compelling, the entire park is built two stories high atop the casino's parking structure and is totally enclosed by a huge glass dome. From the outside, the dome surface is reflective, mirroring its surroundings in hot tropical pink. Inside, however, the dome is transparent, allowing guests in the park to see out. Composed of a multilayer glass-and-plastic sandwich, the dome allows light in but blocks ultraviolet rays. The entire park is air-conditioned and climate-controlled 365 days a year.

The park is designed to resemble a classic Western desert canyon. From top to bottom, hand-painted artificial rock is sculpted into caverns, pinnacles, steep cliffs, and buttes. A stream runs through the stark landscape, cascading over a 90-foot falls into a rippling blue-green pool. Set among the rock structures are the attractions: a roller coaster, a flume ride, an inverter ride, and Chaos, a spinning amusement that hauls riders randomly through three dimensions. There are also some rides for small children. Embellishing the scene are several life-sized animatronic dinosaurs, a re-creation of an archeological dig, a fossil wall, and a replica of a Pueblo Indian cliff dwelling. There is also a small theater featuring magic and illusion. Finally, and inevitably, there is an electronic games arcade.

Adventuredome's premier attractions are the Canyon Blaster, the only indoor, double-loop, corkscrew roller coaster in the United States; and the Rim Runner, a three-and-a-half-minute water flume ride. Both rides wind in, around, and between the rocks and cliffs. The flume ride additionally passes under the snouts of the dinosaurs.

Guests can reach the theme park by proceeding through the rear of the main casino to the entrance and ticket plaza situated on the mezzanine level. Though Circus Circus has changed the admission policy so many times we have lost track, but in 2001, you could choose between paying for each attraction individually ($3–5) or opting for an all-inclusive pass ($12.95–16.95). For exact admission prices on the day of your visit, call (702) 794-3939.

BELLAGIO ATTRACTIONS

The big draw at the Bellagio was the Gallery of Fine Art Exhibition, displaying works by Paul Cézanne, Willem de Kooning, Edgar Degas, Paul Gauguin, Fernand Leger, Édouard Manet, Henri Matisse, Joan Miró, Amedeo Modigliani, Claude Monet, Pablo Picasso, Camille Pissarro, Jackson Pollack, Peter Paul Rubens, Rembrandt, Pierre-Auguste Renoir, and Vincent van Gogh. In 2000, MGM-Grand acquired the Bellagio, promptly closed the art gallery, and sold off most of the art. The gallery reopened in 2001 and now hosts traveling exhibitions. Admission for most exhibitions runs about $12. Open 10 a.m. through 10 p.m. daily, the gallery allows only a small number of viewers to tour the exhibit at any one time. On weekends reservations are recommended. Call (702) 693-7722 for ticket information.

Bellagio's free outdoor spectacle is a choreographed water fountain show presented every half-hour from 2 p.m. until midnight on the lake in front of the hotel (which stretches the length of three football fields). The five-minute production uses 1,200 fountains that blast streams of water as high as 200 feet. Almost 5,000 white lights and musical accompaniment by Sinatra, Pavarotti, and Strauss, among others, complete the picture. It's pleasant and fairy-like, but not necessarily something you should go out of your way to see.

LUXOR ATTRACTIONS

The Luxor offers two continuously running, gated (paid admission) attractions inside the pyramid on the level above the casino. Designed by Douglas Trumbull, creator of the Back to the Future ride at Universal Studios, *In Search of the Obelisk* (in the Egyptian ruins) consists of two motion simulators: A runaway freight elevator that gives you the unusual (and disconcerting!) sensation of plummeting a fair distance, and a runaway tour tram in the bowels of a subterranean world. The second attraction, a seven-story IMAX 3-D theater with a 15,000-watt sound system runs 24 hours a day and costs about $8.50.

LAS VEGAS HILTON ATTRACTIONS

In 1998, the Hilton launched an attraction called *Star Trek: The Experience*. Guests enter through a museum of *Star Trek* TV/movie memorabilia and props en route to a 16-minute "experience" that culminates in a four-minute space flight simulation ride. The Hilton ride differs from other simulation attractions (except *Race for Atlantis*) in that the field of vision seemingly surrounds the guests. Upon returning from their heroic mission to far-flung reaches of the galaxy, guests are welcomed home at the gift shop. Besides the museum, the ride, and the gift shop, *Star Trek: The Experience* includes an electronic games arcade, a restaurant, and a lounge.

Although the visuals on the simulator ride are a little fuzzy by modern standards, the overall experience (which offers several neat twists and surprises) earns *Star Trek* a first-place ranking among Las Vegas's simulator attractions. Not wanting to detract from your enjoyment of *Star Trek,* we're not going to tell you what happens. Suffice it to say that it's extremely well done, and the total experience gives most Disney or Universal attractions a good run for their money. The best times to see *Star Trek: The Experience* are on weekdays from 12:30 to 2 p.m. or after 4 p.m. If you happen to go when there is not much of a queue, take time to check out the chronological history of the universe. It's open 11 a.m. to 11 p.m. daily. Admission is $24.99, including tax ($19.99 for Nevada residents, children and seniors). You can purchase tickets three days in advance only at the *Star Trek* box office (at entrance). *Hint:* the entrance from "Deep Space Promenade" is free. For information call (702) 732-5111 or (888) GO-BOLDLY.

STRATOSPHERE ATTRACTIONS

The Stratosphere Tower stands 1,149 feet tall and offers an unparalleled view of Las Vegas, 24 hours a day. You can watch aircraft take off simultaneously from McCarran International Airport and Nellis Air Force Base. To the south, the entire Las Vegas Strip is visible. To the west, Red Rock Canyon seems practically within spitting distance. North of the tower, downtown glitters beneath the canopy of the Fremont Street Experience. By day, the rich geology of the Colorado Basin and Spring Mountains merge in an earthtone and evergreen tapestry. At night, the dark desert circumscribes a blazing strand of twinkling neon.

A 12-level pod crowns the futuristic contours of three immense buttresses that form the tower's base. Level 12, the highest level, serves as the boarding area for the High Roller, a roller coaster, and the Big Shot, an acceleration/free-fall thrill ride. Levels 11 and 10 are not open to the public. An outdoor observation deck is situated on Level 9, with an indoor observation deck directly beneath it on Level 8. Level 7 features a 220-seat lounge, and Level 6 houses an upscale revolving restaurant. Levels 4 and 3 contain meeting rooms, and the remaining levels: 1, 2, and 5, are not open to the public.

The view from the tower is so magnificent that we recommend experiencing it at different times of the day and night. Sunset is particularly stunning, and a storm system rolling in over the mountains is a sight you won't quickly forget. Be sure to try both the indoor and outdoor observation decks.

The rides are a mixed bag. The roller coaster was such a snoozer that the Stratosphere re-engineered it only two months after it opened and then closed it indefinitely because of "technical problems." When the coaster is working, it basically lumbers around the circumference of the pod. Visibility, the only thing this coaster has going for it, is limited by the tilt of the tracks, the safety restraints, and other people in the car. All sizzle and no steak, this ride only works in the press release.

Where the High Roller is hype at best, the Big Shot is cardiac arrest. Sixteen people at a time are seated at the base of the skyward projecting needle that tops the pod. The next thing you know, you are blasted 160 feet straight up in the air at 45 miles per hour and then allowed to partially free fall back down. At the apex of the ascent, it feels as if your seatbelt and restraint have mysteriously evaporated, leaving you momentarily hovering 100 plus stories up in the air. The ride lasts only about a half-minute, but unless you're accustomed to being shot from a cannon, that's more than enough.

If you're having difficulty forming a mental image of the Big Shot, picture the carnival game where macho guys swing a sledgehammer, propelling a metal sphere up a vertical shaft. At the top of the shaft is a bell. If the macho man drives the sphere high enough to ring the bell, he wins a prize. Got the picture? OK, on the Big Shot, you are the metal sphere.

The elevators to the tower are at the end of the shopping arcade on the second floor of the Stratosphere, above the casino. Tickets for the tower can be purchased at the elevator lobby (on the second floor) or at various places in the casino. The ticket line at the elevator lobby is usually shorter. Tower tickets cost about $11, including rides.

Expect big crowds at the tower on weekends. Once up top, the observation levels are congested, as are the lounge, snack bar, rest rooms, and gift shops. If you want to try the rides, expect to wait an additional 20 to 40 minutes for each on weekends. When you've had your fill of the tower and are ready to descend, you'll have another long wait to look forward to before boarding the elevator. However, if you walk down to the restaurant (you'll take the emergency staircase; ask an attendant where to find it), you can catch the down elevator with virtually no wait at all. If you must see the tower on a weekend, go in the morning as soon as the tower opens.

Another way to see the tower without a long wait is to make a reservation for the Top of the World restaurant. To be safe, reservations should be made at least two weeks in advance. When you arrive, inform the greeter in the elevator lobby that you have a dinner reservation and give him your confirmation number. You will be ushered immediately into an express elevator. The restaurant is pricey, but the food is good and the view is a knockout, and you do not have to pay the $6 tower admission. If you want to try the Big Shot or the High Roller, purchase ride tickets before taking the elevator to the restaurant. Finally, be aware that most folks dress up to eat at the Top of the World.

On weekdays it is much easier to visit the Stratosphere Tower. Monday through Thursday, except at sunset, the wait to ascend is usually short. Waits for the rides are also short. Tower hours are Sunday to Thursday, 10 a.m. to 1 a.m., and Friday and Saturday, 10 a.m. to 2 a.m. For more information call (702) 380-7777.

CAESARS PALACE ATTRACTIONS

In 1998, Caesars launched *Race for Atlantis,* an IMAX 3-D, simulator experience at The Forum Shops. Though the IMAX visuals are well done, the story line is muddled and not very compelling, and the overall experience lacks the kind of thematic continuity that makes *Star Trek: The Experience* (Las Vegas Hilton) work so well. The entrance to *Race for Atlantis* is off the rotunda at the far west end of The Forum Shops. The attraction is hyped by a free animatronic show at the Fountain of the Gods in the rotunda. The fountain show is pretty good, good enough in fact that the IMAX simulator ride (if you choose to go) is somewhat anticlimactic. If you want to experience *Race for Atlantis,* try it either before or during one of the shows at the Fountain of the Gods. Queues are at their longest just after a fountain show concludes and the crowd stacks up at the attraction.

Also at The Forum Shops you'll find a 3-D Cinema Ride, a simulation attraction featuring a haunted graveyard, a space flight, and (hold your hats!) a submarine race. This last segment is somewhat different from the submarine races my girlfriend and I enjoyed as teenagers, parked in a car on the banks of the Ohio. Other attractions at Caesars Palace include the Omnimax Theater, off the casino, where nature and travel documentaries are projected onto a six-story screen. Admission to the IMAX is $7 for adults and $5 for children ages 2 to 12. Admission to *Race for Atlantis* is $10 for adults, $8.50 for seniors, and $8.00 for students and Nevada residents. Hours are 10 a.m. to 11 p.m. Sunday to Thursday, 10 a.m. to 12 a.m. Friday and Saturday. For more information, call Caesars at (702) 731-7110.

MIRAGE AND TREASURE ISLAND ATTRACTIONS

Not only are the Mirage and Treasure Island attractions of top quality, they are also free. The two biggies are the pirate battle at Treasure Island and the exploding volcano at the Mirage. The pirate battle takes place every 90 minutes, weather permitting, beginning at 4 p.m., with the last performance at 10 p.m. (11:30 p.m. on warm-weather-month Fridays and Saturdays). As you face Treasure Island, the pirate ship is on your left, and the British man o' war enters on the right. The best vantage points are on the rope rail facing the man o' war. If you want to relax with a drink before the show, try the terrace bar right behind where the British dock. On weekdays, claim your spot 15 to 20 minutes before show time. On weekends, make that 35 to 45 minutes. If you do not insist on having a *perfect* vantage point, you can see most everything just by joining the crowd at the last minute. If you are short, or have children in your party, it's probably worth the effort to arrive early and nail down a position by the rail.

The volcano at the Mirage goes off about every 15 minutes from dusk until midnight, if the weather is good and the winds are light. In the winter, when it gets dark earlier, the volcano starts popping off at 6 p.m. Usually, because of the frequency of performances (eruptions?), getting a good, rail-side vantage point is not too difficult. If you want to combine the volcano with a meal, grab a window table at Trilussa, the second-floor restaurant in the Casino Royale across the street. Dinner here costs $15 to $25, though, so these are not cheap seats.

The Mirage also has some of Siegfried and Roy's white tigers on display in a well-executed, natural habitat exhibit. In addition to the tigers, the Mirage maintains a nice dolphin exhibit. Both are open weekdays, 11 a.m. to 7 p.m., and weekends, 10 a.m. to 5:30 p.m (the Secret Garden tigers retire at 3:30 p.m., however). The exhibit costs $10 except on Wednesdays when it's $5, because only the dolphins are on show. (Children ages 10 and under get in free.) For the price of admission you can also take in the Secret Garden next to the dolphin habitat, and a small zoo with Siegfried and Roy's white and Bengal tigers, white lions, an Indian elephant, and more. For more information about Mirage call (702) 791-7111. For more information about Treasure Island call (702) 894-7111.

PARIS LAS VEGAS ATTRACTIONS

The big draw at Paris is, of course, the 540-foot-tall replica of the Eiffel Tower. Requiring ten million pounds of steel and over two years to erect, the Las Vegas version is a little more than half the size of the original. Just below the top (at 460 feet) is an observation deck accessible via two ten-passenger glass elevators. It costs a stiff nine bucks to ride, but that's just the beginning of the story. You must first queue up to buy tickets. Your ticket will show a designated time to report to the escalator (that's right: *escalator*. You must take an escalator to reach the elevators). If you're late you'll be turned away and there are no refunds. The escalator will deposit you in yet another line where you'll wait for the elevator. The elevators run from 10 a.m. until 1 a.m. except when it's raining.

Though all this hopping from line to line is supposed to take 5 to 20 minutes, we found 40 to 60 minutes more the norm. Here's the rub. The observation deck holds less than 100 persons and once someone gets up there they can stay as long as they want. Hence, when the observation deck is at max capacity, nobody can go up unless someone comes down. Because the tower affords such a great view of Bellagio across the street, gridlock ensues several times nightly while people squeeze on the observation overlong to watch Bellagio's dancing-waters show. If accessing the observation platform seems like too much work, take the separate elevator that serves the restaurant and bar on the 11th floor of the tower. You don't need reservations to patronize the bar, but you must be nicely dressed, i.e., jackets recommended for men and absolutely no jeans, T-shirts, tank tops, or sandals. The bar is open nightly from 5 p.m. until midnight.

SAHARA ATTRACTIONS

The newly renovated and expanded Sahara has its own entry in the raging simulator ride craze. Called Speedworld, the attraction draws its inspiration from Indy car racing. You can elect to drive an Indy car in an interactive simulated race, or alternatively, you can strap in as a passive passenger for a 3-D, motion-simulator movie race. The interactive racecars respond exactly like a real racecar to braking, acceleration, and steering control. You can even choose between driving a manual or automatic (recommended) transmission. Your race pits you against other drivers and lasts about eight minutes.

There are several racecourses to choose from, ranging from an easy oval to a simulated Grand Prix course through the streets of Las Vegas. You start by choosing a racecourse and then proceed to a video orientation briefing where you learn how to get into the car, adjust the seat and steering wheel, turn on the engine and work the transmission, accelerator, and brakes. While none of the above is especially complicated, most people require a little coaching or assistance when they actually get into their car.

Once your race begins, driving the course at high speed demands intense concentration. If you have a simulated crash, you will be directed to the simulated pits for repairs. The visuals on the screen in front of your car are reasonably good, but come at you at numbing speed. If you are sensitive to motion sickness, the Indy car simulator will leave your stomach spinning.

In our opinion, you need to race once just to understand how everything works. After you get the hang of it, you will enjoy the experience more and also be more competitive. Start out on a simple course with an automatic transmission and work up to more demanding courses. After each race you will be given a computer generated report that tells how you finished, as well as provides some comparative information on your general performance. Each race you drive costs $8, while the 3-D movie costs $5.

Speed, the roller coaster at the Sahara, opened in June of 2000. You race down 1,350 feet of track, including one 360-degree loop and a harrowing 224-foot climb straight up a tower. From the tower's top, you'll roll *backwards* back to the starting point. The round trip takes 48 seconds. Special electromagnetic fields slingshot riders from zero to 40 mph and again from 35 to 70 mph in two seconds flat. Yikes! Speed is flat out the fastest roller-coaster in town, and open from 11 a.m to 11 p.m. every day. Rides cost about $8 each, but for exact prices, call (702) 737-2111 on the day you go.

VENETIAN ATTRACTIONS

Like New York–New York down the Strip, it can be argued that the entire Venetian is an attraction, and there's a lot to gawk at even if you limit your inspection to the streetside Italian icons and the Grand Canal Shoppes. But there's more. The Venetian is host to the first Madame Tussaud's Wax Museum in the United States. Covering two floors and 28,000 square feet, the museum is about half the size of the original London exhibit. Approximately 100 wax figures are displayed in theme settings. Some, like Frank Sinatra and Tom Jones, were central to the development of the entertainment scene in Las Vegas. The museum is opens daily at 10 a.m. Admission is about $13.

A WORD ABOUT STRIP ROLLER COASTERS

There are now four roller coasters on the Strip. After careful sampling, we have decided that, although shorter, the Canyon Blaster at Adventuredome offers a better ride than the more visually appealing Manhattan Express at New York–New York. The Canyon Blaster is tight and oh-so-smooth. The Manhattan Express, on the other hand, goes along in fits and starts, all of which are jerky and rough. It does, however, provide a great view of the Strip as it zips in and out of the various New York–New York buildings.

Speed lives up to its name, but is overpriced at $8. The other coaster, the High Roller at the Stratosphere is a dud.

FREE STUFF

Two other "attractions" worthy of your consideration are the Fremont Street Experience and the Rio's Masquerade in the Sky. The Fremont Street Experience is an electric light show produced on a futuristic canopy over the Fremont Street pedestrian concourse downtown. Shows begin at dusk and run about once an hour through 11 p.m. on weekdays and midnight on weekends. The show at the Rio is a sort of musical Mardi Gras parade complete with floats, acrobats, musicians, and dancers, all circling the casino suspended from a track on the ceiling (who thinks this stuff up?). Both shows are free. A third free attraction is the water and laser show at Sam's Town. This production, staged four times daily, combines animatronic birds and animals with choreographed fountains and laser effects in a show about the West. Outdoor productions at Bellagio, Treasure Island, and the Mirage (all described earlier) are also free of charge.

REALLY EXPENSIVE THRILLS

If you're really flush, you can (with an instructor beside you) fly an authentic World War II fighter and engage in a mock dogfight. Cost is $190 to

$590 for 15 minutes to an hour at North American TopGun at the Boulder City Airport. For information call (702) 294-8778. For $99 and up you can go about the same speed a foot off the ground at the Richard Petty Driving Experience. Here you can get behind the wheel of a 600 horsepower NASCAR Winston Cup style stock car. The Driving Experience is located at the Las Vegas Motor Speedway. Call (702) 643-4343 for additional information.

Other Area Attractions

The local visitor guides describe nearby attractions and sites pretty honestly. If you have children, try the **Scandia Family Fun Center** (phone (702) 364-0070) for miniature golf and the **Lied Discovery Museum** (phone (702) 382-5437) for a truly rewarding afternoon of exploration and enjoyable education. Right across the street from the Lied is the **Las Vegas Natural History Museum** (phone (702) 384-3466). The **Wet 'n Wild** water theme park (phone (702) 737-3819) may be the best place in Las Vegas for teens and is also good for preschoolers. Look for Wet 'n Wild discount coupons in the local visitor guides.

Adults who wax nostalgic over vintage automobiles should check out the **Auto Collection at the Imperial Palace** (phone (702) 731-3311) where more than 200 antique and historically significant vehicles are on display. Part of a much larger collection, these automobiles are rotated periodically to keep the exhibit fresh. Seeing the collection is well worth the admission price of $6.95, $3 for seniors and children under 12, though discount coupons are readily available in the local visitor guides and at the Imperial Palace casino.

The Liberace Foundation and Museum (phone (702) 798-5595) on East Tropicana Avenue is one of Las Vegas's most popular tourist attractions. Housed in multiple buildings connected by a parking lot, the exhibit chronicles the music, life, and excesses of Liberace. Though possibly the most professionally organized and well-presented celebrity museum in the United States, it's definitely more fun if you are a Liberace fan.

Adjacent to the MGM Grand is the **Showcase,** a shopping, dining, entertainment venue with a giant Sega arcade, an eight-screen movie complex, and the World of Coca-Cola—a 150-foot coke bottle housing two elevators.

NATURAL ATTRACTIONS NEAR LAS VEGAS

In the Mexican Pavilion of Epcot at Walt Disney World, tourists rush obliviously past some of the most rare and valuable artifacts of the Spanish colonial period in order to take a short, uninspired boat ride. Many Las Vegas visitors, likewise, never look beyond the Strip. Like the Epcot tourists, they are missing something pretty special.

Las Vegas's geological and topographical diversity, in combination with its stellar outdoor resources, provides the best opportunities for worthwhile sight-seeing. So different and varied are the flora, fauna, and geology at each distinct level of elevation that traveling from the banks of Lake Mead to the high, ponderosa pine forests of Mount Charleston encompasses (in one and a half hours) as much environmental change as driving from Mexico to Alaska.

Red Rock Canyon, the Valley of Fire, the Mojave Desert, and the Black Canyon of the Colorado River are world-class, scenic attractions. In combination with the wet summits of the Spring Mountains, they comprise one of the most dramatically diversified natural areas on the North American continent. So excuse us if we leave coverage of the Guinness World of Records Museum to the local visitor's guides.

Driving Tours

For those who wish to sample the natural diversity of the Las Vegas area, we recommend the following driving tours. The trips begin and end in Las Vegas and take from two hours to all day, depending on the number of stops and side trips. The driving tours can very conveniently be combined with picnicking, hiking, horseback riding, and sight-seeing. If you have the bucks ($70–200 per person depending on the package), we also recommend taking one of the air/ground tours of the Grand Canyon.

1. Mount Charleston, Kyle Canyon, Lee Canyon, and the Toiyabe National Forest *4 to 6 hours*

If you have had more than enough desert, this is the drive for you. Head north out of Las Vegas on US 95 and turn left on NV 157. Leave the desert and head into the pine and fir forest of the Spring Mountains. Continue up Kyle Canyon to the Mount Charleston Inn (a good place for lunch) and from there to the end of the canyon. Backtracking a few miles, take NV 158 over the Robbers Roost and into Lee Canyon. When you hit NV 156, turn left and proceed to the Lee Canyon Ski Area. For the return trip to Las Vegas, simply take NV 156 out of the mountains until it intersects US 95. Turn south (right) on US 95 to return to Las Vegas. If you start feeling your oats once you get into the mountains, there are some nice short hikes (less than a mile) to especially scenic overlooks. If you are so inclined, there is also horseback riding, and there are some great places for picnics.

2. Red Rock Canyon Scenic Loop *1½ to 3 hours*

Red Rock Canyon is a stunningly beautiful desert canyonland only 20 minutes from Las Vegas. A scenic loop winds among imposing, rust-red, Aztec sandstone towers. There is a visitor center, as well as hiking trails and picnic areas. With very little effort you can walk to popular rock-climbing sites and watch the action. From Las Vegas head west on Charleston Boulevard (NV 159) directly to Red Rock Canyon. The scenic loop is 13 miles (all one-way), with numerous places to stop and enjoy the rugged vistas. The loop road brings you back to NV 159. Turn left and return to town via Charleston Boulevard.

3. Lake Mead and the Valley of Fire   *5 to 8 hours*

This drive takes you to the Lake Mead National Recreation Area and Valley of Fire State Park. How long the drive takes depends on how many side trips you make. If you plan to visit Hoover Dam during your visit, it will be convenient to work it into this itinerary. The same is true if you wish to tour the Ethel M (as in Mars bars) Chocolate Factory and Cactus Garden.

Head south out of Las Vegas on US 95/93 (detour west on Sunset Road to visit the Chocolate Factory and Cactus Garden), continuing straight on US 93 to Boulder City. From Boulder City continue to the Hoover Dam on US 93 (if desired) or turn left on the Lakeshore Scenic Drive (NV 166) to continue the drive. Travel through the washes and canyons above the lake until you reach the Northshore Scenic Drive (NV 147 and NV 167). Turn right, continuing to the right on NV 167 when the routes split. If you wish, you can descend to the lake at Callville Bay, Echo Bay, or Overton Beach. If you are hungry, Callville Bay and Echo Bay have restaurants and lounges. Overton Beach has a snack bar, but Echo Bay has the best beach.

Near Overton Beach, turn left to NV 169 and follow signs for Valley of Fire State Park. Bear left on NV 169 away from Overton. Valley of Fire features exceptional desert canyon scenery, a number of panoramic vistas, unusual and colorful sandstone formations, and Indian petroglyphs. A short two-mile scenic loop makes it easy to see many of the valley's most interesting formations. If you have time, take the road past the visitor center and climb to the Rainbow Vista overlook. From here a new highway accesses some of the most extraordinary terrain in the American Southwest. After the loop (and any other detours that interest you), continue west on NV 169 until it intersects I-15. Head south to return to Las Vegas.

Hoover Dam

Hoover Dam is definitely worth seeing. There is a film, a guided tour, and a theater presentation on the Colorado River drainage, as well as some static exhibits. All are well done. Try to go on a Monday, Thursday, or Friday. Arrive no later than 9 a.m., and do the tour first. After 9:30 or so, long lines form for the tour, especially on Tuesdays, Wednesdays, Saturdays, and Sundays.

Other than chauffeured transportation, there is no advantage in going to Hoover Dam on a bus tour. You will still have to wait in line for the tour of the dam and to see the other presentations. If you are the sort of person who tours quickly, you probably will have a lot of time to kill waiting for the rest of the folks to return to the bus.

The Canyons of the Southwest

Las Vegas tourist magazines continue to claim Bryce Canyon (400 miles round-trip) and Zion Canyon, Utah (350 miles round-trip), as well as the Grand Canyon, Arizona, as local attractions. We recommend all of the canyons if you are on an extended drive through the Southwest. If your time is limited, however, you might consider taking one of the air day tours that visit the canyons from Las Vegas. Running between $100 and $400 per passenger, the excursions follow one of two basic formats: air only, or air and ground combined. Some tour companies offer discounted fares for a second person if the first person pays full fare. Also, discount coupons are regularly available in *Today in Las Vegas,* distributed free of charge in most hotels.

Almost all canyon tours include a pass over Lake Mead and Hoover Dam. The trip involving the least commitment of time and money is a round-trip flyover of one or more of the canyons. A Grand Canyon flyover, for example, takeoff to touchdown, takes about two hours. While flying over any of the canyons is an exhilarating experience, air traffic restrictions concerning the Grand Canyon severely limit what air passengers can see. Flying over the other canyons is somewhat less restricted. If you want to get a real feel for the Grand Canyon particularly, go with one of the air/ground excursions. The Grand Canyon is many times more impressive from the ground than from the air.

The air/ground trips fly over the Grand Canyon and then land. Passengers are transferred to a bus that motors them along the rim of the canyon, stopping en route for lunch. Excursions sometimes include one or more of the other major canyons in addition to the Grand Canyon, and they last from seven to ten hours. Many flights offer multilingual translations of the tour narrative.

All of the aircraft used will feel very small to anyone accustomed to flying on big commercial jets. Most of the planes carry between 8 and 20 passengers. The captain often performs the duties of both flight attendant and pilot. Each passenger usually has a window, though some of the windows are pretty small. Cabin conditions for the most part are Spartan, and there is not usually a toilet on board.

Because small aircraft sometimes get bounced around and buffeted by air currents, we recommend taking an over-the-counter motion-sickness medi-

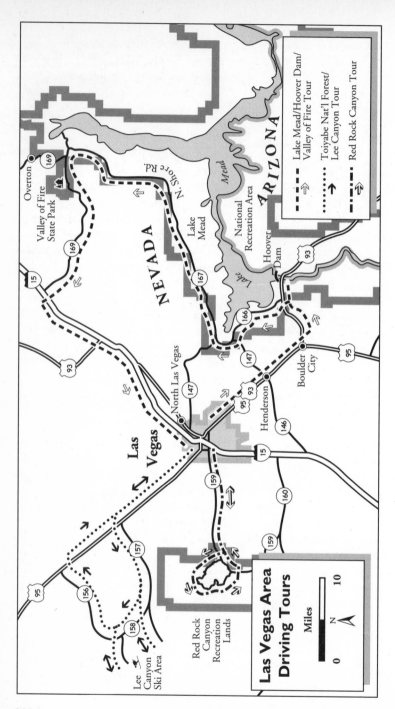

Las Vegas Area Driving Tours

Miles

0   N   10

Lake Mead/Hoover Dam/
Valley of Fire Tour

Toiyabe Nat'l Forest/
Lee Canyon Tour

Red Rock Canyon Tour

NEVADA

ARIZONA

Las Vegas

Overton

Valley of Fire State Park

N. Shore Rd.

Lake Mead

Mead

Lake Mead National Recreation Area

Hoover Dam

North Las Vegas

Boulder City

Henderson

Lee Canyon Ski Area

Red Rock Canyon Recreation Lands

cation if you think you might be adversely affected. The other thing you want to do for sure is to relieve your bladder *immediately* before boarding. If you go on an early-morning excursion, take it easy on the coffee and juice during breakfast.

Part Six

Dining and Restaurants

Dining in Las Vegas

The Las Vegas dining scene has undergone a major revolution over the past five years. In an effort to attract customers in an increasingly competitive market, casino owners have literally scoured the country for famous, big name restaurants, convincing the proprietors to open a branch in Las Vegas. Michael Mina (Aqua) has opened NOBHILL, replacing Gatsby's at MGM Grand. Wolfgang Puck has added Cili at the posh Bali Hai Golf Club, which is open to the public on the strip. Delmonico Steak House was imported from New Orleans; Spago and Pinot from Los Angeles; Morton's from Chicago; The Palm, Smith & Wollensky, Nobu, Aureole, and Le Cirque from New York; Aqua from San Francisco; Olives from Boston; China Grill and Red Square from Miami; Chinois from Santa Monica; and Star Canyon from Dallas. Celebrity chefs such as Julian Serrano (Picasso at the Bellagio) and Maurizio Mazzon (Canaletto at the Venetian), arriving with the regularity of Swiss trains, have opened scores of additional new restaurants. Upscale chains like Lawry's and Ruth's Chris are likewise well represented. Pacing the famous eateries and acclaimed chefs is theme dining—so-called concept restaurants like Harley Davidson Café, Blue Note Jazz Club and Café, House of Blues, Planet Hollywood, Hard Rock Café, Rainforest Café, . . . and the list goes on. There's also been a proliferation of brew pubs, seven at last count, with four located in casinos. Suffice it to say you can now eat high on the hog, in theme heaven, or cry in your beer all over Las Vegas.

But, of course, you always could. And today, if you want to avoid the expense-account joints or sense-assaulting themed eateries, Las Vegas offers some of the best local, independent restaurants found anywhere, as well as trendy new off-the-strip fine dining. Wild Sage Café in Green Valley is a great example.

Much improved in response to all the imported culinary talent, these local restaurants offer ethnic diversity, exceptional food, and great value. They're easy to get to by cab or car, most don't require reservations a month in advance, and offer ample parking. Conversely, the majority of the swish new restaurants need advance notice for reservations. You must guarantee your reservation with a credit card number, and if you don't show up a fee is charged. If you must cancel a guaranteed reservation, the restaurant will not charge you—as long as you call to cancel in advance.

If this practice seems unreasonable, consider this: There is an emerging breed of diner who will make reservations all over town when they don't quite know what they or their date will want for dinner. On the night in question, they don't show or bother calling to cancel, and the umpteen stiffed restaurants are left with empty tables—ones you could have reserved if the marauding diner had had to leave a card number to show his good intentions.

Subsidized Dining and the Free-Market Economy

There are two kinds of restaurants in Las Vegas: those that are an integral part of a hotel-casino operation, and those that must make it entirely on the merits of their food. Celebrity-run restaurants and gourmet rooms in the hotels are usually associated with the casinos. Their mission is to pamper customers who are giving the house a lot of gambling action. At any given time, many of the folks in a hotel restaurant are dining as guests of the casino. If you are a paying customer in the same restaurant, the astronomical prices you are charged help subsidize the feeding of all these comped guests. Every time you buy a meal in one of these places, you are helping to pay the tab of the strangers sitting at the next table.

This is not to say that the hotel restaurants do not serve excellent food or offer the best of service. On the contrary, some of the best chefs in the country cook for hotel-casino gourmet rooms. The bottom line, however, if you are a paying guest, is that you are taking up space intended for high rollers, and the house is going to charge you a lot of rent.

What has changed in the hotel restaurant scene is the arrival of the celebrity chefs. They have created a demand for fine dining totally independent of their restaurant's relationship with the host hotel and casino. Expressed differently, before the advent of the big-name chefs, hotel restaurants catered primarily to the guests of the hotel and the patrons of the casino. These hotel restaurants, though excellent, provided convenience first and operated within the context of the casino's relationship with its customers. Generally speaking, and with a few exceptions, nobody went out of their way simply to dine in these places. Today, celebrity run restaurants have immense drawing power, and patrons will haul themselves all the way across town just to have dinner in one of them. And although they still cater to high rollers and hotel guests, they function much more like an independent restaurant than did the hotel gourmet rooms of old.

Restaurants independent of casinos work at a considerable disadvantage. First, they do not have a captive audience of gamblers or convention-goers. Second, their operation is not subsidized by gaming, and third, they are not located where you will just stumble across them. Finally, they not only compete with the casino gourmet rooms, but also go head-to-head with the numerous buffets and bulk-loading meal-deals that casinos offer as loss-leaders to attract the less affluent gambler.

Successful proprietary restaurants in Las Vegas must offer something very distinct, very different, and very good at a competitive price, and must somehow communicate to you that they are offering it. Furthermore, their offer must be compelling enough to induce you to travel to their location, forsaking the convenience of dining in your hotel. Not easy.

All of this works to the consumer's advantage, of course. High rollers get comped in the gourmet rooms. Folks of more modest means can select from among the amazing steak, lobster, and prime rib deals offered by the casinos, or enjoy exceptional food at bargain prices at independent restaurants. People with hardly any money at all can gorge themselves on loss-leader buffets.

In many ways, Las Vegas restaurants are the culinary version of free-market economy. The casinos siphon off the customers who are willing to pay big bucks for food and feed them for free. This alters the target market for the independents and serves to keep a lid on their prices. Independents providing exceptional quality for such reasonable charges ensure in turn that buffets and meal-deals stay cheap. Ah, America, what a country!

So Many Restaurants, So Little Time

Dining options in Las Vegas, as noted above, have been shaped by the marketing strategies of the casinos. Before a gambler can wager any money, the casino has to get him through the front door. If what it takes are $3 steaks, buffets, and dollar shrimp cocktails, that's what the casino does. For those more attracted to eating than to gambling, this is a great boon to mankind.

While there are hundreds of restaurants in Las Vegas, you will be able to sample only a handful during your stay. But which ones? Our objective in this section is to point you to specific restaurants that meet your requirements in terms of quality, price, location, and environment. No beating around the bush.

BUFFETS

Buffets, used by the casinos to lure customers, have become a Las Vegas institution. Like everything else, they come and go, but on average there are

Buffet Speak	
Action Format	Food cooked to order in full view of the patrons
Gluttony	A Las Vegas buffet tradition that carries no moral stigma
Groaning Board	Synonym for a buffet; a table so full that it groans
Island	Individual serving area for a particular cuisine or specialty (salad island, dessert island, Mexican island, etc.)
Shovelizer	Diner who prefers quantity over quality
Fork Lift	A device used to remove shovelizers
Sneeze Guards	The glass/plastic barriers between you and the food

around 40 to choose from. The majority of casinos operate their buffets at close to cost or at a slight loss. A few casinos, mostly those with a more captive clientele (like the Las Vegas Hilton, the Mirage, and Caesars Palace), and the new breed of upscale spreads (Bellagio, Paris) probably make money on their buffets. Café Lago, the new 24-hour "resort café" located in Caesar's Palace("coffee shop" is no longer hip) also serves up a buffet.

Almost all of the buffets serve breakfast, lunch, and dinner, changing their menus every day. Prices for breakfast range from under $4 to $10. Lunch goes for $6 to $14, with dinner ranging between $7 and $27. Because most buffets operate as an extension of sales and marketing, there is not necessarily any relationship between price and quality.

At breakfast, relatively speaking, there is not much difference between one buffet and the next (exceptions are the standout breakfast buffets at the Orleans, Paris, and Bellagio). If your hotel has a breakfast buffet, it is probably not worth the effort to go somewhere else. When it comes to lunch and dinner, however, some buffets do a significantly better job than others.

If you are looking for upscale gourmet-quality food and a large variety to choose from, head straight for our top four buffets. If you're hankering for well-seasoned meats and vegetables, ethnic variety, and culinary activity, the other six will suffice nicely.

Our top choice of Las Vegas buffets is Sam's Town Firelight Buffet. The buffet room is gorgeous and well laid-out; the two identical serving lines are long enough that there's rarely a wait to get to the food. The quantity, variety,

Buffet	Quality Rating	Last Year's Ranking
Las Vegas's Ten Best Buffets		
1. Sam's Town Firelight Buffet	98	not ranked
2. Aladdin Spice Market Buffet	98	not ranked
3. Bellagio Buffet	97	1
4. Paris Le Village Buffet	95	not ranked
5. Rio Carnival World Buffet	93	9
6. Reserve Grand Safari Buffet	92	4
7. Orleans French Market Buffet	91	6
8. Main Street Station Garden Court Buffet	90	3
9. Fiesta Festival Buffet	89	5
10. Sunset Station The Feast	85	10

and quality, of the selections are top-notch, even better than you'd expect from a new Las Vegas superbuffet. And best of all, the prices, especially for lunch, are extremely reasonable.

Sam's Town, Aladdin, Paris, Rio, Fiesta, Texas and Sunset Stations, Main Street Station, Reserve, Harrah's, Paris, Orleans, and Bellagio all have the new-style "superbuffets." The Rio started the craze in 1993 with its huge room, action cooking, and separate serving islands for a vast variety of ethnic choices: American, Italian, Chinese, Mexican, and Mongolian barbecue, along with sushi, fish and chips, pizza, steak (you pay extra), burgers, franks, salads, and desserts. Aladdin includes an excellent Middle Eastern station, the only one in town.

The Fiesta buffet is not as sprawling and various as the Rio's, but it has a monster rotisserie for barbecuing every kind of flesh known to man, specialty Cajun and Hawaiian selections, and Las Vegas's first and only coffee bar, serving espresso, cappuccino, and latte. Texas Station introduced a chili bar with nine selections and cooked-to-order fajitas; it also has good barbecue, Chinese, Italian, and lots of pizza. Paris has a made-to-order crepe station.

Bellagio is the most expensive superbuffet—and is worth every penny. The quality, quantity, and variety of food is unsurpassed in Las Vegas history. Seafood galore, bread warm from the oven, creative salads, gourmet entrées, perfect vegetables—this joint has it all. Even at $10.95 for breakfast, $13.95 for lunch and $22.95 for dinner, the Bellagio buffet barely breaks even. For the money, we like lunch here better than dinner.

Main Street Station is the only superbuffet downtown, served in one of the most aesthetically pleasing buffet rooms in town. The buffet room at The Regent Las Vegas is also stunning and has a great view to boot. Main Street's cuisine has a distinct Hawaiian emphasis, which is where most of its patrons come from. The Reserve has wood-fired pizza, a Mongolian grill, and a daily seafood island.

The Mirage Buffet is the Strip's version of the good Golden Nugget Buffet downtown, with a few extras such as plentiful smoked fish and lox, peel-and-eat shrimp, mussels, snow crab legs, action Italian, and separate Mexican and Chinese serving areas. Also, it opens at 3 p.m. and is uncrowded until about 5:30 p.m.

Harrah's buffet gets an A for effort, a B for quality, and a C for value. Mandalay Bay's buffet is expensive and odd; it's small, congested, and slow —there's something off about it. But Treasure Island, Palace and Boulder Stations, MGM Grand, and Luxor are tried-and-true; you won't go wrong at any of these.

The new buffet at Paris is an interesting set-up for Las Vegas buffets. The different buffet stations represent different regions of France, and the dining room has several intimate dining nooks and a view as well. Best of all, there's virtually no waiting! You check in with the host or hostess, they tell you when a table will be available, take your name, and you are free to explore until the designated time. When you return, a table is actually ready!

As a footnote, Bellagio, Main Street Station, Paris, Aladdin, Sam's Town. Regent Las Vegas, the Flamingo, Caesars Palace, the Mirage, the Golden Nugget, Sunset Station, the MGM Grand, and Treasure Island provide the most attractive settings for their buffets. The buffets at the Rio, Fiesta, Regent Las Vegas, Orleans, and Texas, Palace, Sunset and Boulder Stations are the favorites of Las Vegas locals.

A number of casinos have very acceptable, though not exceptional, buffets. Not worth a special trip if you are staying or playing elsewhere, these buffets are just fine if you happen to be at the hotel in question when you get the urge to go to the trough. Alphabetically, they are:

Seafood Buffets

Several casinos feature seafood buffets on Friday and sometimes on other days. The best of the seafood buffets are the Rio's Village Seafood Buffet and The Flamingo's Paradise Garden (both daily), Fiesta's seafood night (Wednesday), and the Fremont's Seafood Fantasy (Wednesday and Friday).

The Rio's seafood buffet is the most expensive buffet, but the quality and variety of this piscatory repast are unbelievable, even for Las Vegas. Check it out: small lobster tails (dinner), peel-and-eat shrimp, Dungeness crab legs, Manila steamers, and oysters on the half-shell; seafood salads, chowders, and

Mongolian grill; plus Italian, Mexican, and Chinese dishes, along with fried, grilled, broiled, breaded, blackened, beer-battered, and barbecued preparations. And if you have even a millimeter of stomach space left after the main courses, the dessert selection is outstanding.

The Flamingo began serving all-you-can-eat cold king crab legs, cold steamed clams and mussels, and several seafood entrées in early 2000. At the Fiesta's Wednesday night seafood buffet, you can gorge on all the steamed and fried clams, mussels, oysters, snow crab legs, peel-and-eat shrimp, seafood gumbo, and baked, stir-fried, broiled, grilled, and wokked fish you can cram in. And if you still have some room, grub down on the barbecued meats and poultry, Mongolian grill, coffee, and desserts. The Fremont's Wednesday and Friday Seafood Fantasy isn't quite as extensive or expensive as the Fiesta's, but its quality and popularity are almost as strong.

Buffet Line Strategy

Popular buffets develop long lines. The best way to avoid the crowds is to go Sunday through Thursday and get in line before 6 p.m. or after 9 p.m. If you go to a buffet on a weekend, arrive extra early or extra late. If a large trade show or convention is in town, you will be better off any day hitting the buffets of casinos that do not do a big convention business. Good choices among the highly ranked buffets include Texas Station, Fiesta, Main Street Station, Palace Station, Boulder Station, Silverton, Showboat, the Fremont, and Reserve.

Some restaurants now use pagers to let diners know when their table is available. This gives you a bit more freedom to roam around while you wait, but many pagers have a fairly small range. Even better, you'll never wait for a table at Paris' buffet. You check in and they'll tell you a specific time to return to be seated—and they usually peg it dead on the money.

CHAMPAGNE BRUNCHES

Upscale, expensive Sunday champagne brunches with reserved tables, imported champagne, sushi, and seafood are making an impact on the local brunch scene. Although there are a plethora of value-priced champagne brunches, the big-ticket feasts attract diners who are happy to pay a higher tab for fancy food and service and reservations to avoid a wait. In general, the higher the price of the brunch, the better the champagne served. Bally's and the MGM serve decent French champagne; California sparkling wine is the norm at the others. Reservations are accepted at all of the following.

- **Sterling Brunch,** Bally's Steakhouse (702) 739-4111
  The Sterling Brunch was the first of its kind. At $69.95 per person (plus tax), it's also the most costly, but there's no shortage of diners who love it,

even at double its original price. The lavish selection of foods includes a host of breakfast items, freshly made sushi, real lobster salad, raw and cooked seafood, caviar, and French champagne. Pheasant and rack of lamb appear regularly. The dessert selection is awesome. Entrée selections change weekly. Available: 9:30 a.m.–2:30 p.m.; reservations are required.

- **Grand Champagne Brunch at the Brown Derby,** MGM Grand (702) 891-3110 (after 9 a.m.)
  A complete seafood bar, filet mignon, prime rib, and rack of lamb are regular features. Eggs Benedict and omelets are prepared to order. There are more than 50 items and desserts. Adults, $39.95 per person (plus tax); children ages 5–12, $19.95; children under age 5 dine free. Available: 9 a.m.–2:30 p.m.

- **The Steak House,** Circus Circus   (702) 734-0410
  Elaborate ice carvings and decorative food displays are a tribute to the chef's cruise line background. Featured are many breakfast items, steak and seafood, entrées, and salads. Adults, $21.95 (all-inclusive); children ages 6–12, $10.95. Three seatings: 9:30 a.m., 11:30 a.m., and 1:30 p.m.

- **Gospel Brunch,** House of Blues, Mandalay Bay   (702) 632-7777
  "Praise the Lord and pass the biscuits!" This is the most raucous and joyous Sunday brunch in town. A five-member group belts out the gospel tunes, and the food is soulful as well: fried chicken, skillet cornbread, jambalaya, turnip greens, made-to-order omelets, ham and prime rib, bagels and lox, smoked salmon, and banana bread pudding. Adults, $32.95; children ages 7–11, $16.95. Two seatings at 10 a.m. and 1 p.m.

- **Garduno's Margarita Brunch,** Fiesta Hotel   (702) 631-7000
  There's no way Jose that even hearty eaters could down everything on this generous Mexican-style buffet. Colorful decor, margaritas galore, and strolling mariachis make for happy dining. An omelet station, fajita station, peel and eat shrimp, crab legs, and fresh oysters as well as 15 or more Mexican specialties, including enchiladas, beef machaca, beef and chicken taquitas, chili and tacos. Salads and desserts, both Mexican and American. Come early or prepare to wait. Adults, $11.99 per person; children ages 3–8, $8.99. Available: 10 a.m.–3 p.m.

Bally's Sterling Brunch, though quite expensive, is by far the best brunch in town and, in our opinion, a fair value for the money ($69.95) if you are a big eater. Circus Circus has an excellent Sunday brunch in the $20 range. Other good brunches include Caesars Palace (which often features Bananas Foster), the Fiesta (serving Mexican specialties and substituting margaritas for champagne to correspond with the southwest theme), Bellagio, and Golden Nugget.

MEAL-DEALS

In addition to buffets, many casinos offer special dining deals. These include New York strip, T-bone, and porterhouse steaks, prime rib, lobster, crab legs, shrimp cocktails, and various combinations of the foregoing, all available at give-away prices. There are also breakfast specials.

While the meal-deals generally deliver what they promise in the way of an entrée, many of the extras that contribute to a quality dining experience are missing. With a couple of notable exceptions, the specials are served in big, bustling restaurants with the atmosphere of a high school cafeteria. Eating at closely packed formica tables under lighting bright enough for brain surgery, it is difficult to pretend that you are engaged in fine dining.

Our biggest complaint, however, concerns the lack of attention paid to the meal as a whole. We have had nice pieces of meat served with tired, droopy salads, stale bread, mealy microwaved potatoes, and unseasoned canned vegetables. How can you get excited about your prime rib when it is surrounded by the ruins of Pompeii?

Deke Castleman, coauthor of this book and writer for the *Las Vegas Advisor* doesn't believe that discount dining is about food at all. He writes,

> *Of course you're entitled to your opinion, and I'll fight to the death for your right to express it. But 'quality dining experience' is not really what Las Vegas visitors, IMHO ('in my humble opinion,' in Netspeak), are looking for when they pursue a $3 steak, a $4.95 prime rib, or a $9.95 lobster. To me what they're after is twofold: A very cheap steak, prime rib, or lobster and damn the salad, vegetable, and Formica; and to take home a cool story about all the rock-bottom prices they paid for food.*

Finally, it's hard to take advantage of many of the specials. They are offered only in the middle of the night, or alternatively you must stand in line for an hour waiting for a table, or eat your evening meal at 3:30 in the afternoon. In restaurants all over town, in and out of the casinos, there is plenty of good food, served in pleasant surroundings, at extremely reasonable prices. In our opinion, saving $5 on a meal is not worth all the hassle.

Because Las Vegas meal-deals come and go all the time, it is impossible to cover them adequately in a book that is revised annually. If you want to stay abreast of special dinner offerings, your best bet is to subscribe to the *Las Vegas Advisor*, a monthly newsletter that provides independent, critical evaluations of meal-deals, buffets, brunches, and drink specials. The *Las Vegas Advisor* can be purchased by calling (800) 244-2224. If you are already in town and want to pick up the latest edition, single copies are available at the Gamblers Book Club store at 630 South 11th Street, (702) 382-7555.

Steak Though specials constantly change, there are a few that have weathered the test of time. Our favorite is the 16-ounce porterhouse steak dinner at the Redwood Bar & Grill in the California, (702) 385-1222. A complete dinner, including relish plate, soup or salad, and steak with excellent accompanying potatoes and vegetables, can be had for about $13 excluding drinks, taxes, and tips. What's more, it is served in one of the most attractive dining rooms in Las Vegas. The porterhouse special, incidentally, does not appear on the menu. You must ask for it.

There's a great 16-ounce T-bone served in the coffee shop of the Gold Coast 24 hours a day for $7.95, (702) 367-7111. This big slab is accompanied by soup or salad, potatoes, onion rings, baked beans, garlic bread, and a glass of draft beer. For $7.95 this would be a deal *without* the steak.

Little Ellis Island, attached to the Super 8 motel on Koval Lane near East Flamingo Road, serves an excellent $4.95 steak dinner complete with crunchy rolls, salad, baked potato, and garlic bread. It's available 24 hours, but it's not on the menu, so you have to ask for it. The Hard Rock Hotel has a steak and shrimp special served 24 hours in the coffee shop for $5.95, (702) 693-5000.

Prime Rib The most readily accessible and one of the best prime rib specials in a town full of prime rib specials is available at the San Remo's Ristorante del Flori coffee shop, (702) 739-9000. They offer a generous piece of meat, accompanied by good sides. The special is available 24 hours a day, and the restaurant is rarely crowded. Downtown, the Lady Luck has a good prime rib special for $8–12, available 4–10 p.m. in the coffee shop, (702) 477-3000. Up the block at the California, you can get the smaller cut of meat during the same hours for $5.95.

For $5 or $6 more you can dine in comparative luxury with much less effort at Sir Galahad's at the Excalibur, (702) 597-7777. The prime rib is excellent and served tableside in huge slabs accompanied by fresh salad/soup and excellent side dishes, including Yorkshire pudding. There is no hassle about getting a table if you arrive by 6:30 p.m.

Another good prime rib and crab leg special, when available, is at Bally's ($12.50), (702) 739-4111. Jerry's Nuggett on Las Vegas Boulevard in North Las Vegas has a trio of prime rib meal deals for $8.95, $12.50, and $23 (for the biggest piece of roast beef you've ever seen), (702) 399-3000.

Lobster and Crab Legs   Lobster and steak (surf & turf) combos and crab leg deals appear regularly on casino marquees around Las Vegas. Pasta Pirate at the California serves the best all-around shellfish specials, (702) 385-1222. Unfortunately, they are on-again, off-again. When on, they alternately feature a steak and lobster combo, a lobster dinner, or a king crab dinner, all for $11–13, not including tax or gratuity. Entrées are served with soup or salad, pasta, veggies, garlic bread, and wine. The setting is relaxed and pleasant. Reservations are accepted.

In addition to the Pasta Pirate, an excellent crab special for $14.95 is routinely offered in the Mediterranean Room at the Gold Coast, (702) 367-7111. Another good one is the king crab and steak special served for $18.95 at Roberta's at El Cortez, (702) 385-5200. Though El Cortez is not the fanciest joint in town, the total restaurant experience is not a drawback, either: Roberta's is the best bargain gourmet room in town.

The perennial favorite of the steak and lobster deals (which tend to be of lesser quality than steak, prime rib, and crab leg meal-deals) is found at Island Paradise Café at the Stardust ($9.95), (702) 732-6111. Beware of buffets advertising lobster. Buffet lobsters have the consistency of rubber and have been known to leap tall buildings in a single bounce.

Shrimp Cocktails   Shrimp cocktails at nominal prices are frequently used to lure gamblers into the casinos. Usually the shrimp are small (popcorn shrimp) and are served in cocktail sauce in a tulip glass. The best and cheapest shrimp cocktails can be found at the Golden Gate, a small downtown casino, which has been serving this special for more than 45 years. Other contenders are the Four Queens, Arizona Charlie's, and the Lady Luck.

Pasta and Pizza   The Pasta Palace at Palace Station regularly runs half-price specials on excellent pasta entrées, and the Pasta Pirate at the California offers some of the best designer pasta dishes in town. As far as pizza is concerned, the best play is to hit up pizza "satellite" outlets (fast-food counters attached to the Italian restaurants) at Boulder Station and Sunset Station for a quickie slice. You can also get a good slice of New York–style pizza at Toscana's at the Rio.

Breakfast Specials   Our favorite breakfast deal is the huge ham and eggs special at the Gold Coast. One of the best breakfasts you will ever eat, it would still be a bargain at three times the price. Other worthwhile breakfast deals include steak and eggs at the Frontier, Arizona Charlie's, and the San Remo (24 hours), and the ham and eggs breakfast at the Horseshoe (4 a.m.–2 p.m.) and the breakfast buffets at Regent Las Vegas and The Orleans.

NEW/ALREADY IN PLACE/ SOON TO OPEN RESTAURANTS

New entries in the ever-burgeoning dining race include many that are not profiled. These are just a little taste. If they survive and maintain their quality, they'll be profiled in next year's edition.

In 2001, the Brennan family opened a **Commander's Palace** at the Aladdin. This is New Orleans at it's best, and we sincerely hope the Sunday brunch here becomes a tradition to equal that of it's eastern kin. Young Brad Brennan has moved with his family to Las Vegas to oversee the addition. New York's **Blue Note** will also open a new eponymous restaurant at the Aladdin—and we're certain the food will be top notch.

In a different take on old names opening new restaurants, Aureole's Charlie Palmer has opened **Charlie Palmer Steak** with the Four Seasons. We have exceedingly high expectations, since the is the first time, ever, that the Four Seasons has partnered a restaurant.

Although no longer with the restaurant, Nicholas Nickolas (founder of Nick's Fishmarket) has opened **Bones,** a rib joint, at the former site of the Vito's Italian in the Orleans hotel. The Cheesecake Factory has opened a new concept restaurant, **Café Lux,** at the Venetian. The concept? Big menu, reasonable prices, and fine cheesecake on the dessert menu. Nothing to scoff at there.

The Restaurants

OUR FAVORITE LAS VEGAS RESTAURANTS

We have developed detailed profiles for the best restaurants (in our opinion) in town. Each profile features an easily scanned heading that allows you, in just a second, to check out the restaurant's name, cuisine, Star Rating, cost, Quality Rating, and Value Rating.

Star Rating The Star Rating is an overall rating that encompasses the entire dining experience, including style, service, and ambiance in addition to the taste, presentation, and quality of the food. Five stars is the highest rating possible and connotes the best of everything. Four-star restaurants are exceptional, and three-star restaurants are well above average. Two-star restaurants are good. One star is used to denote an average restaurant that demonstrates an unusual capability in some area of specialization—for example, an otherwise unmemorable place that has great barbecued chicken.

Cost Our expense description provides a comparative sense of how much a complete meal will cost. A complete meal for our purposes consists of an entrée with vegetable or side dish, and choice of soup or salad. Appetizers, desserts, drinks, and tips are excluded.

Inexpensive	$14 and less per person
Moderate	$15–30 per person
Expensive	Over $30 per person

Quality Rating On the far right of each heading appear a number and a letter. The number is a Quality Rating based on a scale of 0–100, with 100 being the highest (best) rating attainable. The Quality Rating is based expressly on the taste, freshness of ingredients, preparation, presentation, and creativity of food served. There is no consideration of price. If you are a person who wants the best food available, and cost is not an issue, you need look no further than the Quality Rating.

Value Rating If, on the other hand, you are looking for both quality and value, then you should check the Value Rating, expressed in letters. The value ratings are defined as follows:

A	Exceptional value, a real bargain
B	Good value
C	Fair value, you get exactly what you pay for
D	Somewhat overpriced
F	Significantly overpriced

Location Just below the address is a zone name and number. This zone will give you a general idea of where the restaurant described is located. For ease of use, we divide Las Vegas into five geographic zones:

Zone 1	The Strip and Environs
Zone 2	Downtown
Zone 3	Southwest Las Vegas
Zone 4	North Las Vegas
Zone 5	Southeast Las Vegas and the Boulder Highway

If you are staying downtown and intend to walk or take a cab to dinner, you may want to choose a restaurant from among those located in Zone 2. If you have a car, you might include restaurants from contiguous zones in your consideration. (See pages 14–18 for detailed zone maps.)

Other Information If you like what you see at first glance when you scan a particular restaurant's heading and location, you might move on to read the rest of the profile for more detailed information.

OUR PICK OF THE BEST LAS VEGAS RESTAURANTS

Because restaurants are opening and closing all the time in Las Vegas, we have tried to confine our list to establishments with a proven track record over a fairly long period of time. Newer restaurants (and older restaurants under new management) are listed but not profiled. Those newer or changed establishments that demonstrate staying power and consistency will be profiled in subsequent editions. Also, the list is highly selective. Noninclusion of a particular place does not necessarily indicate that the restaurant is not good, only that it was not ranked among the best in its genre. Note that some restaurants appear in more than one category.

The Best Las Vegas Restaurants

Name	Star Rating	Price Rating	Quality Rating	Value Rating
Adventures in Dining				
Emeril's (New Orleans)	★★★★½	Very Exp	95	B
8-0-8 (Hawaiian/French)	★★★★	Expensive	93	C+
Marrakech (Moroccan)	★★★	Moderate	86	B
American				
Aureole	★★★★★	Expensive	98	C
Spago	★★★★★	Mod/Exp	96	C
Olives	★★★★	Mod/Exp	95	B
Neros	★★★★	Expensive	90	C
Brown Derby	★★★★	Mod/Exp	87	C
Range Steakhouse	★★★½	Expensive	93	B
Hugo's Cellar	★★★½	Expensive	89	B
Redwood Bar & Grill	★★★½	Moderate	89	A
Grape Street	★★★½	Inexp/Mod	87	A
Red Square	★★★½	Expensive	87	C
Rainforest Café	★★★½	Moderate	86	B
Lawry's The Prime Rib	★★★½	Expensive	85	C
Magnolia Room	★★★½	Moderate	85	A
Top of the World	★★★½	Expensive	85	C
Wolfgang Puck Café	★★★½	Moderate	85	B
Wild Sage	★★★	Mod/Exp	89	B
Harley-Davidson Café	★★★	Moderate	85	C+
Kathy's Southern Cooking	★★★	Inexp/Mod	85	A
Asian/Pacific Rim				
Malibu Chan	★★★★	Mod/Exp	90	C
China Grill	★★★★	Mod/Exp	89	B

The Best Las Vegas Restaurants (continued)

Name	Star Rating	Price Rating	Quality Rating	Value Rating
Barbecue				
Sam Woo Bar-B-Q	★★★	Inexpensive	89	A
Brazilian				
Samba Grill	★★★★	Moderate	90	A
Rumjungle	★★★½	Mod/Exp	87	C
Brewpub				
Barley's	★★★	Inexpensive	86	A
Triple Seven Brewpub†	★★★	Inexp/Mod	85	A
California-Continental				
Drai's	★★★★½	Exp	96	B
Chinese				
(see also Dim Sum)				
Fortunes	★★★★	Mod/Exp	93	C+
Noodles	★★★½	Moderate	93	B
Peking Market	★★★½	Moderate	87	B
Chang	★★★	Moderate	85	B
Chungking East	★★	Inexpensive	85	A
Chinese/French				
Mayflower Cuisinier	★★★★½	Mod/Exp	94	B
Chinois	★★★★	Mod/Exp	96	A
Continental/French				
Picasso	★★★★★	Expensive	98	C
Renoir	★★★★★	Very Exp	98	C
Napa	★★★★★	Expensive	95	C
Buccaneer Bay Club	★★★★½	Mod/Exp	96	B
Andre's	★★★★½	Expensive	90	C
Fiore	★★★★	Mod/Exp	95	C
Michael's	★★★★	Very Exp	93	D
Mon Ami Gabi	★★★★	Mod/Exp	90	B
Seasons	★★★★	Very Exp	90	D
Isis	★★★½	Expensive	90	C
Pinot Brasserie	★★★½	Mod/Exp	89	C
Swiss Café	★★★½	Moderate	89	B
Café Nicolle	★★★½	Moderate	88	B
Pamplemousse	★★★½	Expensive	87	C
Burgundy Room	★★★½	Mod/Exp	85	B

† No profile

The Best Las Vegas Restaurants (continued)

Name	Star Rating	Price Rating	Quality Rating	Value Rating
Creole/Cajun				
Commander's Palace	★★★★	Expensive	90	C
Voodoo Café and Lounge	★★★½	Mod/Exp	85	C+
Cuban				
Florida Café	★★★½	Inexp/Mod	85	A
Dim Sum (see also Chinese)				
Chang	★★★	Moderate	85	B
Mirage Noodle Kitchen†	★★★	Moderate	85	B
Eclectic				
Cheesecake Factory	★★★½	Moderate	89	A
Greek				
Magnolia Room	★★★½	Moderate	85	A
Tony's Greco Roman†	★★★	Moderate	81	B
Indian				
Shalimar	★★★½	Mod/Exp	86	C
Italian				
Terrazza	★★★★½	Expensive	95	C+
Piero's	★★★★½	Expensive	92	C
Stefano's	★★★★	Mod/Exp	94	C
Trattoria del Lupo	★★★★	Mod/Exp	91	B+
Antonio's	★★★★	Mod/Exp	90	B
Manhattan	★★★½	Mod/Exp	92	B
Ristorante Italiano	★★★½	Expensive	91	C
Mortoni's	★★★½	Mod/Exp	90	B
Anna Bella	★★★½	Inexp/Mod	89	A
Bootlegger	★★★½	Moderate	89	A
Ferraro's	★★★½	Mod/Exp	89	C
North Beach Café	★★★½	Moderate	89	A
Sazio	★★★½	Moderate	89	A
Bertolini's	★★★½	Moderate	88	B
Olio	★★★½	Mod/Exp	88	C
Fellini's	★★★½	Mod/Exp	87	A
Venetian	★★★½	Mod/Exp	87	B
Circo (Osteria Del)	★★★½	Mod/Exp	86	B
Magnolia Room	★★★½	Moderate	85	A
Il Fornaio	★★★	Mod/Exp	87	B

† No profile

The Best Las Vegas Restaurants (continued)

Name	Star Rating	Price Rating	Quality Rating	Value Rating
Japanese (see also Sushi)				
Shintaro†	★★★★	Mod/Exp	94	B+
Noodles	★★★½	Moderate	93	B+
Tokyo	★★★½	Moderate	85	B
Fuji	★★★	Inexp/Mod	84	B
Latin American				
Bohemias	★★★½	Moderate	89	B+
Lobster				
Alan Alberts	★★★½	Expensive	89	C+
Lobster House†	★★★½	Expensive	89	C+
Rosewood Grille	★★★½	Expensive	88	C+
Mediterranean				
Olives	★★★★	Mod/Exp	95	B
Mexican/Southwestern				
Coyote Café	★★★★	Mod/Exp	90	B
Garduno's Chili Packing Co.	★★★½	Inexp/Mod	89	B
Star Canyon	★★★½	Mod/Exp	89	B
Viva Mercado's	★★★½	Moderate	86	A
Ricardo's	★★★½	Moderate	85	B
Lindo Michoacan	★★★	Moderate	84	A
Middle Eastern				
Habib's	★★★½	Moderate	88	C
Haifa (Kosher)†	★★★	Moderate	85	B
Jerusalem (Kosher)	★★½	Inexp/Mod	80	B
Moroccan				
Marrakech	★★★	Moderate	86	B
Persian				
Habib's	★★★½	Moderate	88	C
Prime Rib				
Sir Galahad's	★★★½	Moderate	89	A
Redwood Bar & Grill	★★★½	Moderate	89	A
Lawry's The Prime Rib	★★★½	Expensive	85	C
Seafood				
Aqua	★★★★★	Expensive	98	C
Buzios	★★★★	Expensive	93	B

† No profile

The Best Las Vegas Restaurants (continued)

Name	Star Rating	Price Rating	Quality Rating	Value Rating
Kokomo's	★★★★	Expensive	93	C
The Tillerman	★★★½	Mod/Exp	87	C
Pasta Pirate	★★★½	Moderate	86	A
The Broiler	★★★	Moderate	85	A
Steak				
Prime	★★★★½	Expensive	96	C
Delmonico	★★★★	Very Expensive	95	C
Ruth's Chris Steak House	★★★★	Expensive	94	C
Kokomo's	★★★★	Expensive	93	C
Samba Grill	★★★★	Moderate	90	A
The Palm	★★★★	Very Expensive	85	C
Alan Alberts	★★★½	Expensive	89	C+
Morton's	★★★½	Very Exp	89	C
Redwood Bar & Grill	★★★½	Moderate	89	A
Rosewood Grille	★★★½	Expensive	88	C+
The Steak House	★★★½	Moderate	86	B
Billy Bob's Steakhouse	★★★	Mod/Exp	88	B
Yolie's [†]	★★★	Moderate	86	B
The Broiler	★★★	Moderate	85	A
Binion's Ranch Steakhouse	★★★	Moderate	82	B
Sushi (see also Japanese)				
Chinois	★★★★	Mod/Exp	96	A
Makino Sushi Restaurant	★★★★	Inexp/Mod	95	A
Teru Sushi	★★★½	Mod/Exp	89	C
Tokyo	★★★½	Moderate	85	B
Hamada of Japan [†]	★★★	Mod/Exp	84	C
Thai				
Lotus of Siam	★★★½	Mod/Exp	95	A
Noodles	★★★½	Moderate	93	B+
Vietnamese				
Noodles	★★★½	Moderate	93	B+
Pho Chien	★★★½	Inexp/Mod	89	A
Rooms with a View				
Eiffel Tower Restaurant [†]	★★★★	Very Exp	93	C
Top of the World	★★★½	Expensive	85	C
VooDoo Café and Lounge	★★★½	Mod/Exp	85	C+

[†] No profile

MORE RECOMMENDATIONS

The Best Bagels

Bagel Oasis   9134 West Sahara Avenue (702) 363-0811
The best bagels in town, New York–style; baked fresh daily; large selection.

Harrie's Bagelmania   855 E. Twain Avenue (at Swenson) (702) 369-3322
Baked on the premises; garlic and onion among the choices.

The Best Bakeries

Albina's Italian Bakery   3035 East Tropicana Avenue in the Wal-Mart
   Center (702) 433-5400
Classic Italian pastries; baba au rhum, with and without custard; Italian and
American cheesecakes; wide variety of cookies.

Great Buns   3270 East Tropicana Avenue (at Pecos) (702) 898-0311
Commercial and retail; fragrant rosemary bread, sticky buns, and apple loaf
are good choices. Regularly add new items.

Tintoretto at The Venetian, Italian Bakery   Canal Shops at
   The Venetian Hotel (702) 414-3400
International breads, cakes, and cookies. Charming European design and a
patio perfect for people-watching.

The Best Brewpubs

Barley's Casino and Brewing Company   4500 East Sunset Road,
   Suite 30, Henderson (702) 458-2739
Reminiscent of old Las Vegas, Barley's features a small casino, attractive
decor, and comfort foods galore.

Gordon Biersch Brewpub   3987 Paradise Road (Hughes Center)
   (702) 312-5247
Upbeat brewery restaurant with contemporary menu and surprisingly good
food at reasonable prices.

Holy Cow!   2423 Las Vegas Boulevard, South (702) 732-2697
A trilevel barn-styled bar with comical cow decor. They also feature 24-hour
food service.

Monte Carlo Pub & Brewery   Monte Carlo (702) 730-7777
Located adjacent to the pool area in a faux-warehouse setting, this new
brewpub offers six different beers and affordable food options. The beer is
brewed right on the premises. Eighteen different pizzas are available, as well
as sandwiches, pastas, and more.

Triple Seven Brewpub 200 North Main Street (Main Street Station) (702) 387-1896
Late-night happy hour with bargain brews and food specials. Open 24 hours.

The Best Burgers

Kilroy's 210 South Buffalo Dr. (at West Charleston) (702) 363-4933
Half-pound burgers, choice of 15 toppings.

Lone Star
1290 East Flamingo Road (702) 893-0348
1611 South Decatur Boulevard (702) 259-0105
210 Nellis Boulevard (702) 453-7827
3131 North Rainbow (702) 656-7125
Cheese, Bubba, Texas, Mexi, or Willie half-pounders on a toasted onion bun.

Champagne Café 3557 South Maryland Parkway (702) 737-1699
Classic half-pounder with creative toppings.

Tommy's Hamburgers 2635 East Tropicana Avenue (702) 458-2533
Good eat-in or carry-out burgers.

The Best Delis

Bagelmania 855 East Twain (at Swenson) (702) 369-3322
Breakfast and lunch only. Full service bagel bakery and deli. On Tuesdays buy bagels by the dozen at half price.

Samuel's Deli 2744 North Green Valley Parkway, Henderson (702) 454-0565
Full-service deli, bakery, and restaurant. Home cooking and giant matzo balls.

Siena Deli 2250 East Tropicana Avenue (at Eastern) (702) 736-8424
Italian spoken here: everything Italian and homemade. Excellent bread baked fresh every morning. Siena bakes bread for many of the area's Italian restaurants. Local favorite for Italian grocery items.

Stage Deli The Forum Shops at Caesars (702) 893-4045
Las Vegas branch of New York's famous pastrami palace; enormous menu runs gamut of Jewish specialties, including triple-decker sandwiches named for celebrities, and 26 desserts. Open wide—the sandwiches are skyscrapers.

The Best Espresso & Dessert

Café Nicolle 4760 West Sahara Avenue Suite 17 (at Decatur) (702) 870-7675
Sidewalk café west; cooling mist in summer.

Café Sensations   4350 East Sunset Road (east of Green Valley Parkway)
  (702) 456-7803
Scrumptious variety of baked goods, casual food, sandwiches, salads.

Coffee Pub   2800 West Sahara Avenue Suite 2A (702) 367-1913
Great breakfast and lunch location, imaginative menu.

Jitters Gourmet Coffee
  2457 East Tropicana Avenue (at Eastern) (702) 898-0056
  2295 North Green Valley Parkway (702) 434-3112
  8441 West Lake Mead Boulevard (Summerlin location)
  (702) 256-1902
Many varieties of coffees; homemade muffins; sandwiches, brownies, truffles.
Popular local hangout.

La Piazza   Caesars Palace (702) 731-7110
Caesars' bakers create pies, cakes, and cookies to eat in or take out.

Spago   The Forum Shops at Caesars (702) 369-6300
Wolfgang Puck's pastry chef creates imaginative and sinful creations. Available all day in the café and at dinner in the dining room.

Starbucks Coffee Houses   Many area locations.

Tintoretto at The Venetian   Canal Shops at The Venetian,
  (702) 414-3400

Palio   Bellagio, (702) 693-8160
Cafeteria-style coffee house with scrumptious pastries and casual eats—
quiche, salads, and sandwiches.

The Best Oyster & Clam Bars

Buzios   Rio (702) 252-7697
Oyster stews, cioppino, shellfish, and pan roasts. Table service or oyster bar.

Emeril's   MGM Grand (702) 891-1111

The Best Pizza

Bootlegger   7700 South Las Vegas Boulevard (702) 736-4939
Great selection; crispy, tender, homemade crust.

California Pizza Kitchen   Mirage (702) 791-7111
Trendy—even offers low-cal versions without cheese. No take-out service.

Metro Pizza　　1395 East Tropicana Avenue　(702) 736-1955
Fast service, generous with the cheese. Try the Old New York with thick-sliced mozzarella, plum tomatoes, and basil. Thick Ragu-style tomato sauce topping.

Spago　　The Forum Shops at Caesars　(702) 369-6300
Wolfgang Puck's regular specials include spicy shrimp, duck sausage, and smoked salmon with dill cream and golden caviar. Other toppings change frequently.

Venetian　　3713 West Sahara Avenue　(702) 876-4190
Old-time Las Vegas favorite; pizza with greens and olive oil (no cheese) is a popular item.

The Best Soup & Salad Bars

Paradise Garden Café　　Flamingo Hilton　(702) 733-3111
A good display at lunch; a large choice of seafood added at dinner.

Souper Salad
　　2051 North Rainbow　(702) 631-2604
　　4022 South Maryland Parkway　(702) 792-8555
　　Moderate prices, many combinations, shiny clean, and inexpensive.

Restaurants with a View

Circo　　Bellagio, (702) 693-8150
Circo (full name Osteria Del) is adjacent to its pricier sister, Le Cirque. Tuscan fare with a view of Lake Como and Paris' Eiffel tower.

Eiffel Tower Restaurant　　Paris (702) 948-6937
Fancy French food in a drop-dead gorgeous setting that towers over the strip. This is one spectacular view.

Picasso　　Bellagio (702) 693-7223
Highly original food and glorious original artwork by Picasso. As good as it gets (since you can't eat in the Louvre!).

VooDoo　　Rio Hotel and Casino　(702) 252-7777
At the top of the new Rio tower, VooDoo offers the mystique of New Orleans, a complete view of the city, Cajun/Creole cooking, and late-night lounge.

ALAN ALBERTS ★★★ ½

		QUALITY
Steak/Lobster	Expensive	**89**

	VALUE
Epicenter Plaza, North of the MGM Grand; (702) 740-4421	**C+**

Strip   Zone 1

Customers: Tourists, locals	Friendliness rating: ★★★★★
Reservations: Accepted	Parking: Lot
When to go: Any time	Bar: Full service
Entrée range: $18–35	Wine selection: Excellent
Payment: VISA, MC, AMEX, CB, DC, JCB	Dress: Business attire, informal
Service rating: ★★★★★	Disabled access: Ground floor

Dinner: Every day, 5–11:30 p.m.

Setting & atmosphere: This self-named "vintage steakhouse" features beveled glass, fine wood paneling, and photo walls showcasing celebrities and stars of the glory days of Old Las Vegas. The dining room has comfortable, easy-to-get-into booths and expert, flattering lighting.

House specialties: Prime Angus steaks and jumbo lobsters; a flavorful culotte steak seldom found elsewhere; crab cakes; osso buco; a 26-ounce rib eye; veal and lamb chops.

Other recommendations: Grilled salmon on garlic spinach; oysters Rockefeller; delectable desserts, especially the tiramisu.

Summary & comments: Tucked away in the corner of a strip mall, Alan Alberts is a pleasant surprise. Lobsters are fairly priced—choose one from the live tank. Average weight is 2½ pounds. Portions are generous. A meal could be made from a combination of appetizers.

ANDRE'S ★★★★ ½

		QUALITY
Continental/French	Expensive	**90**

	VALUE
401 S. 6th St.; (702) 385-5016	**C**

Downtown   Zone 2

Monte Carlo Hotel; (702) 798-7151
Strip   Zone 1

Customers: Tourists, locals	Payment: VISA, MC, AMEX, DC
Reservations: Necessary	Service rating: ★★★★
When to go: Early or late	Friendliness rating: ★★★½
Entrée range: $20–40	Parking: Street, valet

Bar: Full service
Wine selection: Excellent

Dress: Sport coat, dressy
Disabled access: Ramps

Dinner: Monday–Saturday, 6–9:30 p.m.

Setting & atmosphere: Country French decor in a converted former residence in a historic part of the city. Elegant European decor at the Monte Carlo.

House specialties: Menu changes with the seasons. Sea scallops with duck foie gras, black truffle, and port wine en papillote; marinated salmon tartare with cucumber salad; Maryland blue crab cakes with citrus beurre blanc, escargot garlic butter; rabbit loin with spinach fettuccini Dijon; pavé of veal sautéed with morel mushrooms; variety of unusual fresh fish with imaginative sauces; filet of pork tenderloin stuffed with sun-dried fruit and nuts, served with apricot sauce. Soufflés and pastries.

Other recommendations: Ask if you can tour Andre's extensive wine cellar; vintages date back to 1830. The daily specials, especially the fish.

Summary & comments: Owner-chef Andre Rochat is mostly in the kitchen of the Monte Carlo. He makes frequent forays into the dining room to visit with guests. He honors special requests if given 24-hour notice. Spectacular winemaker dinners (Thursday nights) several times a year. Ask to be put on the mailing list. Downtown location is closed the month of July.

Honors & awards: *Wine Spectator* Award of Excellence; *Travel/Holiday* magazine award for many years; Ambassador Award of Excellence through 1987 (discontinued); DiRoNA Award.

ANNA BELLA ★★★ ½

		QUALITY
Italian	Inexpensive/Moderate	**89**
		VALUE
3310 South Sandhill Rd. at Desert Inn Rd.; (702) 434-2537		**A**

Southeast   Zone 5

Customers: Locals
Reservations: Suggested all week
When to go: Any time
Entrée range: $11.95–18.95
Payment: VISA, MC, AMEX, DC
Service rating: ★★★★

Friendliness rating: ★★★★★
Parking: Shopping-center lot
Bar: Full service
Wine selection: Modest
Dress: Casual
Disabled access: Ground floor

Dinner: Tuesday–Sunday, 4:30–10 p.m.

Setting & atmosphere: A charming neighborhood restaurant with flower-bedecked booths, pink tablecloths, soft lighting, and a caring staff.

House specialties: Homemade ravioli filled with wild mushrooms (not on the menu, but frequently available); fettuccine with fresh salmon in vodka sauce; cannelloni alla Romano; pollo alla Tony; osso buco; capellini gamberi puglia.

Other recommendations: The flavorful homemade soups; a generous bowl or a green salad comes with entrées. Veal marsala; linguini with clams in a red or white sauce (try the pink sauce made from a mix of both); the classic angel hair pasta with fresh tomato sauce, garlic, basil, and olive oil.

Summary & comments: Anna Bella is a real find. The owners are always there, the service is friendly and caring, and the food is affordable for even modest budgets. Daily specials allow the chef to offer seasonal seafood and higher-end Italian dishes. Service can be slow at times, but be patient. The wait staff is small, and most of the delicious food is cooked to order.

ANTONIO'S ★★★★

Italian	Moderate/Expensive	QUALITY
		90
		VALUE
Rio, 3700 W. Flamingo Rd.; (702) 252-7777		**B**
Strip Zone I		

Customers: Locals, tourists	Parking: Lot, valet, garage
Reservations: Suggested	Bar: Full service
When to go: Any time	Wine selection: Excellent
Entrée range: $17–48	Dress: Informal, slacks and collared
Payment: VISA, MC, AMEX, DC, D	shirts for men
Service rating: ★★★★★	Disabled access: Through casino
Friendliness rating: ★★★★★	

Dinner: Friday–Tuesday, 5–11 p.m. Closed Wednesday and Thursday.

Setting & atmosphere: Marble accents, fresh flowers, elegant table appointments, and expert lighting highlight the comfortable dining room; domed ceiling replicates the sky. Enjoy drinks and Italian coffees before or after dinner in the comfortable lounge.

House specialties: The chef's appetizer of the day; vitello al marsala, veal scallops with porcini mushrooms and marsala wine, a superior version of the classic dish; osso buco, the traditional braised veal shank, is presented à la the Rio chef. Daily specials such as oven-roasted pork loin with apricot port wine demi-glacé.

Other recommendations: Lobster sautéed with delicate lobster sauce over capellini; pollo all'aglio e rosmarino. There's a small patio outside with its own moderately priced menu of soups, salads, and a dozen pastas. Cioppino. Tiramisu, the classic mascarpone cheese–based dessert.

Summary & comments: There are nice touches at Antonio's. A fruity olive oil for dunking is offered instead of butter—the imported breadsticks are habit-forming; a complimentary liqueur is offered "to thank you for dining at Antonio's." A small private dining room for up to 12 is available. This attractive restaurant is a local favorite.

AQUA ★★★★★

		QUALITY
Seafood	Expensive	**98**
		VALUE
Bellagio; (702) 693-7223		**C**

Strip   Zone I

Customers: Tourists, locals
Reservations: A must
When to go: Avoid convention times
Entrée range: $29–49; five course tasting, $75
Payment: All major credit cards
Service rating: ★★★★★

Friendliness rating: ★★★★★
Parking: Valet, garage
Bar: Full service
Wine selection: Extensive
Dress: Casual elegance
Disabled access: Ground floor

Dinner: Every day, 5:30–11 p.m.

Setting & atmosphere: Elegant yet relaxed decor with rich woods and fabulous fabrics. Window tables overlook the pool. Aqua is located away from the Bellagio restaurant corridor. The walk through the amazing Botanical Gardens is glorious—bring a camera.

House specialties: Appetizers: a superb tartare of ahi tuna; a selection of chilled shellfish; sea scallops and domestic foie gras; black mussel soufflé. Entrées: Miso-glazed Chilean sea bass; porcini-crusted turbot; the comforting Maine lobster pot pie. An old fashioned root beer float, Aqua-style, served with warm chocolate-chip cookies or the Grand Marnier crème caramel for a memorable finish.

Summary & comments: This San Francisco transplant wins raves for service, food, and decor. It's not easy to get a reservation if you're not staying at Bellagio, but it's worth any effort it takes to get one.

AUREOLE

★★★★★

American	Expensive	QUALITY **98**
		VALUE **C**

Mandalay Bay; (702) 632-7401
Strip Zone 1

Customers: Tourists, locals
Reservations: Required
When to go: Any time
Entrée range: $55–75 prix-fixe
  menus; 6-course tasting menu,
  $95; a la carte menu $9–39 in
  lounge area only
Payment: All major credit cards

Service rating: ★★★★★
Friendliness rating: ★★★★★
Parking: Valet, garage
Bar: Full service
Wine selection: Outstanding
Dress: Casual elegance
Disabled access: Elevator

Dinner: Every day, 6–11 p.m. lounge open (serving food) 5 p.m–1 a.m.

Setting & atmosphere: A one-of-a-kind, four-story wine tower dominates the entrance to this exceptional restaurant. There are three dining rooms and the separate Swan Court with just 14 tables—all have a view of the waterfall and live swans.

House specialties: Roasted duck pot-au-feu with foie gras; spiced tuna tartare; lobster chowder with grilled prawns; sautéed veal mignon with blue cheese lasagna; citrus-basted chicken; roasted pork Saltimbocca.

Other recommendations: Thyme-roasted filet mignon; Colorado lamb chop with red onion rings. Desserts are scrumptious; homemade chocolates are served with coffee.

Summary & comments: The wine tower is unique—the bottles are accessed by black-clad females who hoist themselves up to the various levels to remove the bottles. It's quite a show and a great photo op. Another wine first is Aureole's wine e-book, which enables patrons to order their favorite dinner wines in advance. All dining rooms offer prix-fixe menus only, with an a la carte menu available in the lounge and bar area. Several multi-course tasting menus are available.

BARLEY'S

★★★

Brewpub	Inexpensive	QUALITY **86**
		VALUE **A**

Town Center, 4500 E. Sunset, Green Valley; (702) 458-2739
Southeast Zone 5

Customers: Locals, tourists
Reservations: Parties of 8 or larger

When to go: Any time
Entrée range: $5.95–16.95

Payment: VISA, MC, AMEX, DC, D
Service rating: ★★★½
Friendliness rating: ★★★★★
Parking: Town Center lot
Bar: Full service

Wine selection: Fair
Dress: Casual
Disabled access: Ramp, ground
floor

Hours: *Brewer's Café:* Sunday–Thursday, 7 a.m.–10 p.m.; Friday and Saturday, 7 a.m.–11 p.m.
Pizza Parlor: Sunday–Thursday, 10 a.m.–11 p.m.; Friday and Saturday, 11 a.m.–12 a.m.
Bar menu: 24 hours, breakfast served 11 p.m.–7 a.m.

Setting & atmosphere: Housed in the trendy Town Center in upscale Green Valley, Barley's is reminiscent of Old Las Vegas. With a small casino as the anchor, Barley's offers popular foods at modest prices. The brewery is the high point of the casino with gleaming stainless steel tanks. You can enter directly into the Brewer's Café without going into the casino. Dine on the outdoor patio facing one of the center's most popular attractions, the interactive fountain—it's wonderful entertainment. The decor features an open ceiling, wood floors, and attractive, comfortable seating.

House specialties: Comfort foods galore. Grilled vegetable lasagna in a rich marinara sauce; wood-roasted chicken breast; charbroiled, honey-glazed pork chops; man-sized sandwiches with great steak fries; large soft pretzels with lager mustard and pepper Jack cheese sauce; Barley's original barley soup; smoked barbecued brisket sandwich in the bar; Barley's signature beef barley soup.

Summary & comments: Generous amounts of food for the money. Entrées include endless trips to the small soup and salad bar; it costs an additional $2.95 with sandwiches and other items. The Pizza Parlor also serves sausage and meatball heros. Barley's regularly runs out of the popular brews, so plans are under way to increase the capacity for brewing the frothy drink. Pastas are sometimes overcooked; ask for them al dente. On Thursdays, this casual eatery dons tablecloths and candlelight. Even the servers dress up for this weekly bit of gastronomy. Gourmet specials change weekly. Dinner prices are moderate.

BERTOLINI'S		★★★ ½
Italian	Moderate	QUALITY 88
The Forum Shops at Caesars Palace; (702) 735-4663 Strip Zone 1		VALUE B

Customers: Tourists, locals
Reservations: For large groups only
When to go: Always busy, especially
  Friday and Saturday evenings
Entrée range: $9.95–24.95
Payment: VISA, MC, AMEX, DC, JCB
Service rating: ★★★

Friendliness rating: ★★★★
Parking: Hotel garage, valet
Bar: Full service
Wine selection: Good
Dress: Informal, casual
Disabled access: Ground floor

Lunch & dinner: Sunday–Thursday, 11 a.m.–midnight; Friday and Saturday, 11 a.m.–1 a.m.

Setting & atmosphere: The restaurant's beautifully decorated interior offers peaceful respite from the lively action of the dining patio. A colorful mural decorates one wall. There is a display of antipasto, a mesquite-fired pizza oven, an open kitchen, and a gelateria. Butcher paper–covered tables and crayons for doodling.

House specialties: Focaccia and pizza made in a wood-burning oven. Carpaccio di manzo; insalata di pollo con pasta; gorgonzola and fontina pizza with roasted potatoes and rosemary; rigatoni with sausage ragout, tomato sauce, and mozzarella; angel hair pomodoro. Homemade ice cream as well as cakes, espresso, and cappuccino in the gelateria.

Other recommendations: Salad with homemade mozzarella, tomatoes, and basil oil; prosciutto and smoked mozzarella with fig jam crostini and sun-dried tomato vinaigrette; roasted garlic, fresh spinach, béchamel, and mozzarella pizza; lasagna. Any of the new dishes, especially crusted chicken Romano with Gorgonzola sauce and the fazzoletto con funghi— a "handkerchief" of pasta enfolding spinach and ricotta cheese in a delicate wild mushroom sauce. Cappuccino crème brûlée.

Summary & comments: The Sidewalk Café outside Bertolini's overlooks the Forum's bustling scene and the Roman fountain. It's an ideal spot for photos. The fountain can be noisy, but no one seems to mind—it's so pretty. Table turnover is good, but even with a busy day's wait, time goes quickly.

BILLY BOB'S STEAKHOUSE & SALOON ★★★

Steak	Moderate/Expensive	QUALITY
		88
		VALUE
		B

Sam's Town, Boulder Highway; (702) 456-7777
Southeast   Zone 5

Customers: Locals, tourists
Reservations: Suggested
When to go: Any time

Entrée range: $15–48
Payment: VISA, MC, AMEX, DC, D
Service rating: ★★★★

Friendliness rating: ★★★★
Parking: Valet, lot, garage
Bar: Full service

Wine selection: Good
Dress: Come as you are
Disabled access: Through casino

Dinner: Sunday–Thursday, 5–10 p.m.; Friday and Saturday, 5–11 p.m.

Setting & atmosphere: Stroll through the lovely climate-controlled park to Billy Bob's. The critters that chirp and peep are lifelike robotics; the trees and lush foliage are real. Mosey into the Western-themed Billy Bob's for a taste of the Old West and some mighty fine grub.

House specialties: Beef is king at Billy Bob's: steaks and prime rib. The 28-ounce rib-eye is a huge favorite. Entrée prices include soup or salad and a selection from the potato bar. Desserts serve four to six. The Grand Canyon chocolate cake could serve a small army. The foot-long eclair is a dessert lover's fantasy.

Summary & comments: Prepare to eat as if you were heading out for a day on the range. The setting and the prices make Billy Bob's a popular choice. At prime times, even with a reservation, there might be a wait. Have a drink in the saloon. After dusk, enjoy the laser light show complete with original music and a lifelike wolf who shows up on the mountain top.

BINION'S RANCH STEAKHOUSE ★★★

		QUALITY
Steak	Moderate	82
		VALUE
Binion's Horseshoe Hotel; (702) 382-1600		B

Downtown   Zone 2

Customers: Locals, tourists
Reservations: Recommended
Entrée range: $30–54
Payment: VISA, MC, AMEX, CB,DC, D
Service rating: ★★★★
Friendliness rating: ★★★★
Parking: Garage, valet

When to go: Avoid late-night crowds
  for steak special
Bar: Full service
Wine selection: Good
Dress: Casual
Disabled access: Elevator

Dinner: Every day, 6–10:30 p.m.

Setting & atmosphere: Western decor, friendly service, and large portions. Ten-gallon hats, fancy boots, and Levis are very much in evidence.

House specialties: Prime rib roasted in rock salt; 20-ounce porterhouse. Entrées are accompanied by soup or salad and ample servings of rice pilaf or baked potato.

Other recommendations: Prime New York steak; half chicken with honey Dijon sauce; broiled spring lamb chop.

Entertainment & amenities: Dramatic panoramic view from top floor of hotel.

Summary & comments: The late Benny Binion believed in good food and large portions. The restaurant maintains his philosophy. One of the best buys in town.

BOHEMIAS		★★★½

Latin American	Moderate	QUALITY
		89

		VALUE
2550 Rainbow; (702) 253-6274		**B+**
Zone 3		

Customers: Locals	Service rating: ★★★½
Reservations: Suggested for dinner	Parking: Lot
When to go: Anytime	Bar: Full service
Entrée range: $16.95–24.95	Wine selection: Limited
Payment: VISA, MC, AMEX, D	Dress: Casual
Friendliness rating: ★★★★★	Disabled access: Ground floor

Lunch: Daily, 11 a.m–4 p.m.

Dinner: Sunday–Thursday, 4–10 p.m.; Friday & Saturday, 4–11 p.m.

Setting & atmosphere: South-of-the-Border decor, peach colored stucco walls and curtained windows are warm and inviting. On weekends, when Flamenco dancers perform, diners are transported to Spain via a restaurant in a strip mall in Las Vegas.

House specialties: Such specialties as Spanish tapas, Argentinian empanadas, Brazilian feijoada (a zesty stew), are typical menu items. Sandwich Marinero, a terrific triple decker, fresh salmon and bacon combo is served on a plate-size homemade bread. Paella Valenciana, a bed of saffron rice filled with clams, mussels, calamari, shrimp, langostino, choriza, chicken and pork. Bistec Gaucho, a New York strip marinated in chimichurri sauce, charbroiled—wonderful flavors; guacamole, prepared tableside; ceviche tropical, scallops marinated in coconut and mango juices atop a fruit salsa. Not to be missed—the irresistible Dulce de Leche Mousse served in a double martini glass. The caramel mousse covers warm, glazed bananas.

Summary & comments: Have a pisco Rita or a mojitos or a caipirinha, the Brazilian sensation made with cachaca. These heady Latin cocktails liven up any meal. A fruity sangria is available by the glass or by the pitcher. Lunch prices are very reasonable; sandwiches are not offered at night. Bohemias is thoroughly enjoyable, even when service is slow. Flamenco dancers perform Thursday through Saturday beginning at 7 p.m. Reservations are advised.

BOOTLEGGER ★★★½

		QUALITY
Italian	Moderate	**89**
		VALUE
7700 S. Las Vegas Blvd.; (702) 736-4939		**A**

Strip   Zone I

Customers: Locals, some tourists
Reservations: Accepted
When to go: Any time
Entrée range: $10–28
Payment: VISA, MC, AMEX, DC, D
Service rating: ★★★★

Friendliness rating: ★★★★★
Parking: Shopping-center lot
Bar: Full service
Wine selection: Large
Dress: Informal
Disabled access: Ground floor

Lunch & Dinner: Tuesday–Friday, 11 a.m.–11 p.m.; Saturday and Sunday, 4 p.m–11 p.m; Monday, closed. Tavern open 24 hours.

Setting & atmosphere: Turn-of-the-century decor, Italian style. Wonderful ancestral portraits decorate the walls. The full bar overlooks an informal dining room with fireplace. Two additional dining rooms offer comfortable banquettes, which are original to the previous location. The booths were relocated in the new location at the request of sentimental longtime patrons of Bootlegger. Twenty-two-hundred-square-foot tavern offers round-the-clock drinking opportunity and a late-night menu.

House specialties: Complimentary homemade appetizer panettis (small bread puffs) tossed with garlic, oregano, and oil, served with tomato-basil sauce. Homemade breads. Seafood diavolo; veal saltimbocca à la Blackie; and veal Lorraine with fresh mushrooms in a cream and wine sauce, named for the owners. Varied pasta menu; vegetarian menu; pizzas; and calzones. Biscuit tortoni and tartufo.

Other recommendations: The seafood dishes are very good.

Summary & comments: This venerable Italian restaurant is owned by Nevada's current Lieutenant Governor. The joint swings on the weekends with impromptu jamming by such Las Vegas stalwarts as Sonny King. While the menu may change with the new digs, we think the quality will remain consistent with tradition. A politician's reputation may depend upon it, after all . . .

THE BROILER ★★★

Steak/Seafood	Moderate	QUALITY
		85

		VALUE
Boulder Station, Boulder Hwy. and Desert Inn Rd.; (702) 432-7777		A
Southeast Zone 5		

Customers: Locals, tourists
Reservations: Suggested
When to go: Any time
Entrée range: $16.95–42.95
Payment: VISA, MC, AMEX, DC, D
Service rating: ★★★★

Friendliness rating: ★★★★★
Parking: Valet, lot
Bar: Full service
Wine selection: Fair
Dress: Casual
Disabled access: Through casino

Dinner: Sunday–Thursday, 5–10 p.m.; Friday and Saturday, 5–11 p.m.

Setting & atmosphere: Comfortable, relaxed dining room with greenery, an exhibition kitchen, and a handsome soup and salad bar. Desert decor with style. A refrigerated showcase at the entrance displays the day's fresh fish and meat selection.

House specialties: Fresh seafood, steaks, and prime rib. All entrées include the soup and salad bar, a choice of potatoes or rice, and vegetable or cole slaw. Fish selections are mesquite-grilled or broiled, baked, or sautéed. Most earn the American Heart Association heart symbol for being low cholesterol. Nonfat dressings and sour cream are available, too. Chicken, marinated in herbs and garlic, cooked on the rotisserie. Sunday brunch is a fine value. Included are the soup and salad bar, dessert, and table service for the entrées.

Summary & comments: Reservations should be made for dinner and Sunday brunch.

BROWN DERBY ★★★★

American	Moderate/Expensive	QUALITY
		87

		VALUE
MGM Grand; (702) 891-7300		C
Strip Zone 1		

Customers: Tourists, locals
Reservations: Requested
When to go: Any time except concerts or boxing matches
Entrée range: $25–45
Payment: VISA, MC, AMEX, CB, DC, D, JCB

Service rating: ★★★★★
Friendliness rating: ★★★★★
Parking: Valet, garage
Bar: Full service
Wine selection: Very good
Dress: Casual
Disabled access: Ground floor

Dinner: Every day, 5:30–10:30 p.m.

Setting & atmosphere: A reincarnation of the original Brown Derby, a Hollywood icon of the elite of filmdom since the 1920s. MGM Grand bought the name, photographs, artifacts, and recipes from the owner, who was the consultant for the restaurant. There's a good bit of nostalgia and many memories of Hollywood, in the days when it was HOLLYWOOD and the only things known about a star's private life were the stories concocted by the studio flacks.

House specialties: The Brown Derby mixed grill; the original Cobb salad; Mr. Derby beef Wellington; chateaubriand or rack of lamb for two; orange-roasted half duckling; grilled Pacific salmon.

Other recommendations: Brown Derby–style Caesar salad; lump crab meat cakes; the iced seafood assortment appetizer; "Meet Me at the Derby" ice cream cake; the old-fashioned baked apple dumpling redolent with cinnamon and brown sugar.

Summary & comments: Sit in the Oscar room with its marvelous photographs and feel like a star. Most of the Brown Derby recipes have been adapted well. The acclaimed grapefruit cake still needs work, but this throwback to the Hollywood that was is a fine dining choice.

BUCCANEER BAY CLUB		★★★★½
		QUALITY
Continental	Moderate/Expensive	**96**
		VALUE
		B

Treasure Island; (702) 894-7111
Strip   Zone 1

Customers: Tourists, locals; hotel guests get preference	D, JCB
	Service rating: ★★★★
Reservations: Accepted 7 days in advance	**Friendliness rating:** ★★★★★
	Parking: Garage, valet
When to go: Avoid peak hours	**Bar:** Full service
Entrée range: $20–36, higher for lobster	**Wine selection:** Small, but good
	Dress: Sport jacket, informal
Payment: VISA, MC, AMEX, DC,	**Disabled access:** Elevator

Dinner: Every day, 5–10:30 p.m.

Setting & atmosphere: Exotic decor and accessories gathered from all parts of the world. Restaurant overlooks the Pirates Village and Buccaneer Bay, scene of the "fight to the finish" sea battles between the British ship *Britannia* and the pirates' *Hispaniola*. It's a fierce, colorful encounter with dialogue to match.

House specialties: Pyramid of fresh salmon fillets atop a mound of mashed potatoes and fresh vegetables; Buccaneer clams casino; oysters (topped with smoked salmon and hollandaise); lobster bisque under a puff-pastry dome. Bay Club combination—filet mignon au poivre, breast of chicken Oscar. Pirate's Plunder—chocolate treasure chest filled with coconut rum mousse, white chocolate treasure map, and devil's rock cake. Menu changes seasonally.

Other recommendations: Smoked salmon Napoleon; lobster ravioli; escargot in brioche; osso buco; veal Florentine; prime rib; Chilean sea bass with fruit salsa. Chocolate Frigate—pair of chocolate ships filled with frozen chocolate and walnut parfaits topped with coconut cookie sails.

Summary & comments: The menu, geared to the pirate theme, changes seasonally. Some dishes listed above may not be available. The rousing sea battle takes place every hour and a half from 4 p.m. to 11:30 p.m. Diners experience the fun without the din and smoke. Request a window table for best view. Who wins the battle? It's a surprise, mateys!

BURGUNDY ROOM

★★★½

Continental	Moderate/Expensive	QUALITY
		85
		VALUE
		B

Lady Luck Hotel; (702) 477-3000
Downtown   Zone 2

Customers: Locals, tourists	**Friendliness rating:** ★★★★★
Reservations: Suggested	**Parking:** Valet, garage, and lot
When to go: Any time	**Bar:** Full service
Entrée range: $18–53	**Wine selection:** Good
Payment: VISA, MC, AMEX, CB, DC, D	**Dress:** Informal
Service rating: ★★★★	**Disabled access:** Ground floor

Dinner: Thursday–Monday, 5–11 p.m.

Setting & atmosphere: Plush and intimate; sculptures add to the decor of this attractive dining room.

House specialties: Fillet of beef Wellington; veal Oscar; double-cut lamb chops. Chateaubriand and rack of lamb for two carved tableside. Porterhouse. Excellent prime rib.

Other recommendations: Salmon Monte Carlo; supreme of chicken Angelo; veal picante; flaming desserts.

Summary & comments: A moderately expensive gourmet room with a good selection of entrées and fine service in downtown Las Vegas. Overflow diners are seated in the adjacent dining room. The service and food are the same.

BUZIOS ★★★★

		QUALITY
		93
Seafood	Expensive	VALUE
		B

Rio; (702) 252-7697
Strip   Zone 1

Customers: Locals, tourists
Reservations: Recommended for dinner
When to go: Any time
Entrée range: $15–60
Payment: VISA, MC, AMEX, DC, D
Service rating: ★★★★

Friendliness rating: ★★★★
Parking: Valet, lot, covered garage
Bar: Full service
Wine selection: Very good
Dress: Casual
Disabled access: Through casino

Lunch & Dinner: Every day, 11 a.m.–11 p.m.

Setting & atmosphere: This popular seafood restaurant is a magnet to local business types. The new section has been cleverly added so that the original ambience is intact. The decor includes massive alabaster chandeliers and flowering plants suspended from the canvas-tented ceiling. Walls of glass allow a beautiful view of the sandy beach and pool. A comfortable counter à la Grand Central Station attracts diners who like to watch the seafood being prepared in the individual high-pressure steam kettles. The counter is a good choice for quick meals.

House specialties: Buzios offers a selection of fresh oysters from Canada, Maine, and Washington State; clams; shrimp; and many hot seafood appetizers. Fish soups and stews such as bouillabaisse and cioppino; huge bowls filled with a savory assortment of denizens of the deep. Rockefeller-style prawns, clams, or oysters; lobsters from Japan, Finland, Great Britain, Germany, Iceland, and The Netherlands; a selection of fresh fish flown in daily. The irresistible Rio breads, baked in their own bakery in a European open-hearth oven, accompany all dishes. They're wonderful when used to mop up the broth from the fish soups and stews. Endless baskets are provided.

Other recommendations: Seafood salads and Louis; pastas with seafood; the chicken and shrimp combination glazed with a tarragon and honey sauce; any preparation with Chilean sea bass.

Summary & comments: Buzios, named for a small Portuguese fishing village, is the Rio's version. All entrées include a choice of salad or soup. On weekends and during conventions, even with reservations, there is sometimes a short wait for a table. Don't fret. For seafood afficionados Buzios is worth a brief delay. Or sit at the oyster bar; the savory pan roasts are quickly prepared.

CAFÉ NICOLLE

★★★½

Continental	Moderate	QUALITY
		88
4760 W. Sahara Ave.; (702) 870-7675		VALUE
Southwest Zone 3		B

Customers: Locals
Reservations: Strongly suggested
When to go: Any time
Entrée range: $6.95–29.95
Payment: VISA, MC, AMEX, DC
Service rating: ★★★★

Friendliness rating: ★★★★
Parking: Shopping-center lot
Bar: Full service
Wine selection: Excellent
Dress: Informal, casual
Disabled access: Ground floor

Lunch & dinner: Monday–Saturday, 11 a.m.–11 p.m.; Sunday, closed.

Setting & atmosphere: Restaurant and European-style outdoor café with cooling overhead mist in summer and heat lamps in winter. Bright, cheerful interior on two levels, with cozy corners for intimate dining.

House specialties: Spinach pie; variety of egg dishes; calamari appetizer; osso buco with wine sauce; blue crab cakes; Atlantic salmon cakes. Scallops Nicolle baked with white wine, paprika, and light butter sauce; lamb chops à la Grecque; filet mignon with béarnaise sauce. Same menu all day and evening, plus lunch and dinner specials on blackboard.

Other recommendations: Selection of salads including garlicky Caesar with garlic bread. Selection of pastas such as penne arrabbiata. Variety of fresh seafood. Spicy veal stew with fettuccini; chicken Française; daily specials. Entrée and dessert crêpes; tiramisu; pecan pie. Cappuccino; espresso; caffe latte.

Entertainment & amenities: Live entertainment nightly except Sunday in the bar-lounge area.

Summary & comments: This is a longtime local restaurant with a strong local following.

CHANG

★★★

Chinese/Dim Sum	Moderate	QUALITY
		85
Gold Key Shopping Center, Strip and Convention Center Dr.		VALUE
(702) 731-3388		B
Strip Zone 1		

Customers: Locals, tourists
Reservations: Suggested

When to go: Any time
Entrée range: $7.95–28.95

Payment: VISA, MC, AMEX, CB, DC
Service rating: ★★★★
Friendliness rating: ★★★★★
Parking: Shopping-center lot

Bar: Full service
Wine selection: Fair
Dress: Casual
Disabled access: Ground floor

Lunch & dinner: Every day, 10 a.m.–midnight

Dim Sum: Every day, 10 a.m.–3 p.m.

Setting & atmosphere: Chang's is filled with Chinese art and artifacts, artistic sand-blasted glass, live plants, comfortable booths, and many lazy Susan tables for large parties.

House specialties: Excellent assortment of dim sum, including the seldom-seen-here Chinese cruller. The sizable dim sum menu offers items not available elsewhere such as the large, steamed shark's fin dumpling served in a bowl. Bite into it over the bowl, for the delicious dumpling contains not only bits of seafood and mushrooms, but also shark's fin soup. New dumplings include sweet rice enclosed in a steamed bun and piquant Chinese sausage spiral-wrapped in flaky pastry. Peking-style pork cutlet (called Mandarin here); jumbo crystal prawns; half or whole steamed chicken with ginger sauce; crispy beef—a spicy dish of shredded beef; and eggplant Szechuan cooked with ground pork and red chili peppers are all fine choices.

Summary & comments: Chang shines during the day when owner Hing is on the premises. She is friendly and helpful and never minds answering questions, even when the restaurant is busy. Service in the evening is friendly, but reserved. Special dishes are always available for Chang's Asian customers. Adventurous eaters are welcome to ask what's available.

CHEESECAKE FACTORY	★★★½

		QUALITY
Eclectic	Moderate	89
		VALUE
The Forum Shops at Caesars Palace; (702) 792-6888		A

Strip   Zone I

Customers: Tourists and locals
Reservations: For large parties only
When to go: Any time
Entrée range: $7.95–17.95
Payment: VISA, MC, AMEX, DC, D
Service rating: ★★★★

Friendliness rating: ★★★★★
Parking: Valet, garage, lot
Bar: Full service
Wine selection: Fair
Dress: Casual
Disabled access: Ground floor

Lunch & dinner: Monday–Thursday, 11:15 a.m. (after the first Atlantis show)–11:30 p.m.; Friday and Saturday, 11:15 a.m.–12:30 a.m; Sunday, 10:15 a.m.–11:30 p.m.

Setting & atmosphere: Patio dining that's perfect for people-watching. The Egyptian-themed dining room has impressive brick red pillars that reach from the first floor to the second-floor dining room; the ceiling is a series of exquisite murals; lush foliage thrives among the cheesecakes.

House specialties: American and ethnic specialties—Vietnamese shrimp rolls; quesadillas; a terrific selection of appetizers, pizzas, and meal-size salads, especially the Beverly Hills pizza salad, Chinese chicken salad, and herb-crusted salmon salad. Chicken Madeira is a most requested dish. The monster Factory Burrito Grande, filled with chicken, cheese, rice, onions, and peppers, and topped with guacamole, salsa, and sour cream accompanied by black beans and rice; fresh lump meat crab cakes or grilled skirt steak; jumbo hamburgers or omelets; scrumptious desserts in addition to the scrumptious cheesecakes—at least 30 or more flavors.

Summary & comments: The eclectic menu is so large it's spiral-bound. Portions are more than generous. Share a dish rather than forego the cheesecake. This is no time to order the light version—opt for the real thing and share it. Not to be overlooked is the huge, warm apple dumpling topped with billows of whipped cream. True believers order it with two scoops of vanilla ice cream.

CHINA GRILL ★★★★

Asian	Moderate/Expensive	QUALITY
		89
Mandalay Bay; (702) 632-7777		VALUE
Strip Zone 1		B

Customers: Locals, tourists	**Friendliness rating:** ★★★★★
Reservations: Accepted	**Parking:** Valet, self
When to go: Any time	**Bar:** Full service
Entrée range: $25–35	**Wine selection:** Excellent
Payment: All major credit cards	**Dress:** Casual
Service rating: ★★★★	**Disabled access:** Ground floor

Dinner: Every day, 5:30–11 p.m.

Setting & atmosphere: Highly original furnishings and lighting and contemporary art and accessories make a dramatic statement at China Grill. It all works.

House specialties: Lamb spareribs in a spiced plum sauce; duck pancakes; sake-cured salmon rolls; mahi mahi with those amazing lobster mashed potatoes; Shanghai lobster; sizzling whole fish; lobster pancakes.

Other recommendations: Oriental antipasto; crispy duck with caramelized black vinegar sauce; grilled 38-ounce porterhouse steak with a kimchi dressing; China Grill banana split—enough for a crowd.

Summary & comments: Unlike its New York original, the sound level here allows conversation. The comfy lounge is a fine place for relaxing. Food portions are sized to be shared. Dishes arrive as cooked, not all at once, but it's not a problem unless you don't want to share.

CHINOIS		★★★★
		QUALITY
Chinese/French	Moderate/Expensive	96
		VALUE
The Forum Shops at Caesars Palace; (702) 737-9700		A
Strip Zone I		

Customers: Locals and tourists	**Parking:** Valet, garage, lot
Reservations: Recommended	**Bar:** Full service
When to go: Avoid conventions	**Wine selection:** Excellent
Entrée range: $16–30	**Dress:** Casual
Payment: VISA, MC, AMEX, DC, D	**Disabled access:** Ground floor and
Service rating: ★★★★½	elevator
Friendliness rating: ★★★★★	

Lunch & dinner: Every day, 10:30 a.m.–10:30 p.m.

Setting & atmosphere: Enchanting Asian decor by Barbara Lazaroff, the wife-partner of Chinois owner Wolfgang Puck. All the Asian art and artifacts are from her own private collection. Steps on the dramatic staircase to the upstairs banquet and party room are emblazoned with bits of wisdom in English and Chinese. A waterfall trickles down the stone wall. Both the café and dining room blaze with ribbons of color that, according to Lazaroff, "energize the viewer."

House specialties: Hog Island oysters on the half shell; satays; noodles; wok-charred salmon; incredible short ribs; and crispy sesame-crusted pork loin. The sushi bar area includes table seating—sushi selection is extensive and excellent. The menu includes many signature dishes from Puck's Chinois on Main in Santa Monica, California—Shanghai lobster, whole sizzling catfish, and grilled Mongolian lamb. A small vegetarian menu is now available, and the chef will adapt other dishes upon request. Service is family style. Entrées are sized to share. Asian-influenced desserts are by the award-winning Spago pastry chef. Have one of the cold premium sakes served in a wine glass, but sip slowly—this is heady stuff.

Summary & comments: Chinois is another winner for Puck. The view is wonderful, but it can be noisy when the Trojan horse across the way at FAO Schwarz speaks his piece. The outdoor patio is a fine place for people-watching.

CHUNGKING EAST ★★

Chinese buffet	Inexpensive	QUALITY
		85

		VALUE
2710 E. Desert Inn Rd.; (702) 693-6883		A
Southeast Zone 5		

Customers: Locals	Friendliness rating: ★★★½
Reservations: No	Parking: Lot
When to go: Any time	Bar: None
Entrée range: $5.95–9.95	Wine selection: None
Payment: VISA, MC, AMEX, DC, D	Dress: Informal
Service rating: ★★★	Disabled access: Ground floor, ramp

Lunch: Every day, 11:30 a.m.–5 p.m.
Dinner: Every day, 5–9 p.m.

Setting & atmosphere: Simple but comfortable; pleasing and clean.

House specialties: Pan-fried dumplings; seaweed soup (drop in some won tons); crisp Chinese fried chicken; spicy bean curd; Singapore noodles; Kung Pao chicken; sweet and sour pork chops; a variety of vegetables; noodle dishes; fried rice.

Other recommendations: Chinese doughnuts and small custard tarts for dessert.

Summary & comments: A large number of items are available at lunch and dinner. The dinner selection includes more seafood and meat dishes; there are more dumplings and vegetables at lunch. The food is always fresh and hot. Cooking is ongoing, so you might have a short wait if a dish is empty—it will quickly be replaced. Buffet cooking stops 15 minutes before each session ends. Latecomers get a 25% discount. For a reasonable, tasty, quick meal, it can't be beat.

CIRCO (OSTERIA DEL) ★★★½

Italian	Moderate/Expensive	QUALITY
		86

		VALUE
Bellagio; (702) 693-8150		B
Strip Zone 1		

Customers: Tourists, locals
Reservations: Recommended
When to go: Any time
Entrée range: $25–36
Payment: All major credit cards
Service rating: ★★★★

Friendliness rating: ★★★★
Parking: Valet, garage
Bar: Full service
Wine selection: Excellent
Dress: Dressy casual
Disabled access: Through casino

Lunch: Every day, 11:30 a.m.–2:30 p.m.

Dinner: Every day, 5:30–10:30 p.m.

Setting & atmosphere: Circo is a delight. At once whimsical and vibrant, the decor is pure fun. Booths, tables, and hideaway corners with a view of the fountains are wonderful. Linger over an espresso and enjoy the action in this homespun but chic haven.

House specialties: Pizzas and homemade focaccia breads; home-style Tuscan food inspired by Egidiana Maccioni, matriarch of the New York family that owns the popular Le Cirque and Circo; papardelle with a Chianti–braised duck sauce and wild mushrooms; grilled hanger steak with caramelized onions and steak fries; satisfying Tuscan fish soup with lobster, prawns, calamari, monkfish, clams, and mussels. Half orders are a good starter.

Other recommendations: Napoleon of grilled portobello mushroom layered with zucchini, crispy potato, goat cheese, and green tomatoes—a vegetarian's dream come true. The sensational desserts.

Summary & comments: This elegant Italian restaurant is not as grand as the adjacent Le Cirque, but it's every bit as inviting, and there's super views of the fountain from most tables. Mario Maccioni, son of the founders, directs both restaurants.

COMMANDER'S PALACE		★★★★
		QUALITY
Creole/Cajun	Expensive	90
		VALUE
Desert Passage at the Aladdin; (702) 892-8272		C
Strip Zone 1		

Customers: Locals, tourists
Reservations: Suggested
When to go: Anytime
Parking: Valet, garage
Payment: All major credit cards
Bar: Full service

Wine selection: Very good
Dress: Upscale casual
Disabled accent: Ground floor
Service rating: ★★★★
Friendliness rating: ★★★★

Hours: Lunch daily & Sunday brunch, 11 a.m.–2:30 p.m.

Dinner: Daily, 6–11 p.m.

Entrée range: $24–37; 7-course tasting menu, $75

Setting & atmosphere: Like the original in New Orleans, Commander's Palace is handsome and large, yet at the same time intimate. Divided into spacious dining rooms that flow naturally into one another, the size is minimized. Locals favor the wine room with its candle-lit fireplace and wine walls. The very southern garden room is just right for the ladies who lunch.

House specialties: Tasso shrimp Hemican, flash-fried and coated with Crystal hot sauce beurre blanc; the trio of small cups filled with real turtle soup, murky, wonderful gumbo and a soup of the day; pan roasted gulf oysters with a confit of artichokes; Creole seasoned filet mignon, grilled and served over a warm smashed potato; lamb chops so thick and tender; grits and goat cheese that will make a believer out of any non-grits type; Louisiana Pecan-crusted gulf shrimp. Any of the desserts, but especially the Creole bread pudding soufflé with a heady bourbon sauce; tiny French Quarter Beignets, dusted with powdered sugar, served with a café au lait dipping sauce. The price fixed Sunday Jazz Brunch, a toe-tapping delicious event.

Summary & comments: Brad Brennan, the youngest working member of the illustrious New Orleans restaurant family, is always available to chat about New Awlins. Service can sometimes be slow, but the food is always pleasing. Don't expect Café Diablo made tableside. The fire department wouldn't allow it, so there's an exhibition dessert station where diners may gather to watch the lames. The shortest way to reach CP is through the Aladdin casino. It's a long walk through Desert Passage.

COYOTE CAFÉ   ★★★★

Southwestern	Moderate/Expensive	QUALITY
		90
MGM Grand; (702) 891-7349		VALUE
Strip Zone 1		**B**

Customers: Tourists	**Service rating:** ★★★★
Reservations: Suggested in Coyote's Grill Room	**Friendliness rating:** ★★★★
When to go: Any time	**Parking:** Valet, garage, lot
Entrée range: Café, $5–35; Grill Room, $17–32	**Bar:** Full service
	Wine selection: Limited
	Dress: Casual
Payment: VISA, MC, AMEX, CB, DC, D	**Disabled access:** Ramps, elevator

Open: *Café:* Every day, 8:30 a.m.–11 p.m.; *Grill Room:* every day, 5:30–10 p.m.

Setting & atmosphere: Mark Miller's original Southwestern decor. Two dining rooms: one is an all-day café; the Grill Room is for dinner only. Paintings of corn, beans, squash, and chiles cover the walls.

House specialties: Sweet corn soup with poblano chiles and cilantro; grilled buttermilk corn cakes; spicy crab cake with tomato-basil salsa; coriander-rubbed ahi tuna; "cowboy" Angus rib chop with fire-roasted salsa, black beans, and spicy onion rings. Sour lemon bread pudding with fresh berries; chocolate truffle cake with bittersweet chocolate sauce.

Other recommendations: Chilled yellow tomato gazpacho; cold poached Maine lobster; Coyote's vegetarian plate; Texas Hill Country lemon-crusted venison with ragout of lima beans, artichokes, and roasted tomatoes. Entrées change seasonally. Desserts change seasonally, too. All are imaginative and scrumptious.

Summary & comments: Mark Miller has defined Southwestern cuisine in his own expert style. He uses blue corn, a variety of hot and sweet peppers, and spices to greatest advantage. None of the dishes are palate searing. Those who like a lighter touch of heat should tell the server. The moderately priced café has a new margarita bar and menu. Both are value priced.

DELMONICO ★★★★

		QUALITY
Steak	Very Expensive	**95**
		VALUE
		C

Venetian Hotel; (702) 414-3737
Strip   Zone 1

Customers: Tourists, locals	**Friendliness rating:** ★★★★★
Reservations: A must	**Parking:** Valet, garage
When to go: Avoid conventions	**Bar:** Full service
Entrée range: $23–36	**Wine selection:** Excellent
Payment: VISA, MC, AMEX, DC, D	**Dress:** Upscale resort wear
Service rating: ★★★★½	**Disabled access:** Ground floor

Lunch: Every day, 11:30 a.m.–2 p.m.

Dinner: Sunday through Thursday, 5:30–10:30 p.m.; Friday and Saturday, 5:30–11 p.m.

Setting & atmosphere: Expert lighting sets off the handsome decor highlighted with rich woods and fine fabrics. A separate cigar lounge and bar adjoins the dining room.

House specialties: Dry aged beefsteaks; lobsters from the live tank and fresh fish; roasted, double-cut pork chop with walnut-glazed sweet potatoes; New Orleans–style veal picatta with Louisiana crawfish vegetable slaw; the side dishes—especially the addictive truffle oil-and-Parmesan homemade potato chips.

Other recommendations: Grilled creole rack of lamb; baked oysters casino; grilled smoked-salmon flatbread with Maytag white cheddar cheese; Caesar salad, served table-side for two; cornmeal-fried Alabama rock shrimp with mixed greens, avocado, and remoulade dressing.

Summary & comments: It's not surprising that owner Emeril Legasse has infused the menu with strong Creole influences. Getting a reservation for prime dinner hours is not easy, but if you're willing to dine late or early you may get lucky. (Even with a reservation diners must confirm by 3 p.m. on reservation day.) A private kitchen table is open to those who order a tasting menu, with an optional wine-pairing offered. The full menu is available at the bar.

DRAI'S ★★★★½

California-Continental	Expensive	QUALITY
		96

		VALUE
Barbary Coast Hotel; (702) 737-0555		**B**
Strip Zone I		

Customers: Locals and tourists	Parking: Valet
Reservations: Requested	Bar: Full service
When to go: Any time	Wine selection: Very good
Entrée range: $18–28	Dress: Upscale casual or business
Payment: VISA, MC, AMEX	attire
Service rating: ★★★★½	Disabled access: Ramp
Friendliness rating: ★★★★★	

Dinner: Sunday–Thursday, 5:30–10 p.m.; Friday and Saturday, 5:30–11:30 p.m.

Setting & atmosphere: Drai's features a cutting-edge contemporary dining room designed by the owner, Los Angeles restaurateur Victor Drai. The handsome lounge is designed like a library in a grand home. Filled bookcases cover one wall. The pattern on the faux leopard skin banquettes is repeated on the china and gift tins of cookies. Live plants somehow thrive in the soft lighting of the lounge and the dining room. It's all very appealing. Original art, mostly nudes, are on every wall. A private elevator in the casino transports diners to the lower level, where Drai's is located.

House specialties: A large variety of fresh fish and seafood (expertly cooked), including soy-glazed Chilean sea bass, delicate escolar, and Lake Superior whitefish; in season, jumbo langoustine, prepared a variety of ways;

calf's liver cut into strips, sautéed with balsamic vinegar and roasted shallots; grilled free-range chicken with roasted garlic and crispy, perfectly cooked french fries; the house signature mashed potatoes in three flavors; briny Willipa Bay oysters from the Northwest; the irresistible chocolate soufflé— order when ordering dinner to avoid a delay.

Other recommendations: Rich, creamy soups made without dairy products; terrine of foie gras; frog legs; the vegetarian selection; the whitefish in phyllo dough appetizer.

Summary & comments: Drai's is a gorgeous new addition to the Barbary Coast. Wednesday through Saturday Drai's becomes an after-hours nightclub—cool and crowded.

8-0-8		★★★★
		QUALITY
Hawaiian/French	Expensive	93
		VALUE
Caesars Palace; (702) 731-7110		C+
Zone 1		

Customers: Locals & tourists	Bar: Full service
Reservations: Accepted	Wine Selection: Good
When to go: Anytime	Dress: Casual
Entrée range:	Disabled access: Ground floor
Payment: All major credit cards	Service rating: ★★★★
Parking: Valet, garage, lot	Friendliness rating: ★★★

Hours: Sunday, Monday and Thursday, 5:30–10:30 p.m.; Friday and Saturday, 5:30–11 p.m.

Setting & atmosphere: This newest Caesars dining gem was conceived by Hawaii's premiere chef, French transplant Jean-Marie Josselin. The small dining room and bar glow with special lighting (flattering to everyone). The island influence is everywhere, in the furnishings and appointments. Yet it's not hokey—it's relaxing and lovely.

House specialties: Josselin has created an a la carte menu of original specialties with his own island twist. A chilled seafood platter includes seasonal fish and seafood—a typical variety includes Kumamoto oysters, sashimi, sesame poke, shrimp, lobster, and clams (market price). The deconstructed ahi roll is as gorgeous as it is delicious—fusion cooking at its best. Wok stirred fried lobster, porcini-crusted ahi, miso-crusted Chilean sea bass; any of the terrific appetizers. Desserts are choice. More masterful fusion.

Summary & comments: Caesars continues to update and revamp this veteran hotel. 8-0-8 is just one of the new eateries scheduled to open. It's trendy without being chichi, the food and setting are wonderful. Josselin shows up frequently and is always friendly.

EMERIL'S NEW ORLEANS FISH HOUSE	★★★★½	

Contemporary New Orleans	Very Expensive	QUALITY
		95
MGM Grand; (702) 891-7777		VALUE
Strip Zone 1		B

Customers: Locals, tourists
Reservations: Strongly suggested
When to go: Nonconvention times
Entrée range: $18–50; prix fixe $65
Payment: VISA, MC, AMEX, DC, D
Service rating: ★★★★★

Friendliness rating: ★★★★★
Parking: Valet, lot, covered garage
Bar: Full service
Wine selection: Excellent
Dress: Upscale casual
Disabled access: Through casino

Lunch: Every day, 11 a.m.–2:30 p.m.

Dinner: Every day, 5:30–10:30 p.m.

Oyster Bar/Café: Every day, 11:30 a.m.–10:30 p.m.

Setting & atmosphere: "A bit of New Orleans" is the way award-winning chef-owner Emeril Lagasse describes his beautiful restaurant. The main restaurant is comfortable and handsome with fine appointments and accessories. The separate courtyard dining room is French Quarter pretty with a faux balcony and louvered shutters. Masses of real plants and a stone floor complete the illusion.

House specialties: The five- to eight-course "tasting" dinner is a fine way to sample small portions of many dishes, prix-fixe at $65; some are special recipes being considered for the menu. Emeril's lobster cheesecake with Creole-spiced tomato coulis; the house Louisiana Choupiquet caviar; the "lobster dome," a whole lobster shelled and served with roasted potatoes, onion marmalade, and lobster sauce and covered with a puff pastry dome; Louisiana campfire steak served on a cedar plank on a bed of country-style mashed potatoes and drizzled with warm rémoulade and Emeril's homemade Worcestershire sauce.

Summary & comments: Emeril's is an exciting restaurant that personifies the "new Las Vegas." The food and service are a tribute to Emeril's concern for his diners.

Honors & awards: Emeril's is the recipient of many dining awards including: "Best Southeast Regional Chef"—The James Beard Foundation; "One of the Top 25 Chefs in the Country"—*Food & Wine* magazine; "American Express Fine Dining Hall of Fame"—*Nation's Restaurant News.*

FELLINI'S		★★★½

		QUALITY
Regional Italian/Provençal	Moderate/Expensive	87
		VALUE
5555 W. Charleston Blvd.; (702) 870-9999		A

Southwest   Zone 3

Customers: Locals and visitors	Friendliness rating: ★★★★★
Reservations: Suggested	Parking: Lot
When to go: Any time	Bar: Full service
Entrée range: $9.95–26.95	Wine selection: Good
Payment: VISA, MC, AMEX, D	Dress: Upscale casual
Service rating: ★★★★½	Disabled access: Ground floor

Dinner: Monday–Thursday, 5–10 p.m.; Friday and Saturday, 5–11 p.m.

Setting & atmosphere: Inviting decor and lighting, comfortable seating, fresh flowers, a European-style dessert table, and congenial management that welcomes everyone as if they were longtime friends.

House specialties: Warm spinach salad served in an edible Parmesan cheese basket; bouillabaisse (when available); arrabbiata con melanzane (penne pasta in a spicy sauce with grilled eggplant); New Zealand and California mussels in a tomato and white wine sauce; bistecca Fiorentina (the famous steak of Florence); Tuscan-style grilled chicken breast with little pillows of polenta.

Other recommendations: The breads and desserts (all made on the premises); homemade contuccini (small biscotti), served with a glass of Italian dessert wine, Vin Santo—dunk the hard cookies in the wine, as they do in Tuscany.

Summary & comments: Fellini's chef-partner Chaz LaForte spent four years in Tuscany refining his skills. He frequently comes out of the kitchen to talk with diners. Live piano music is played at just the right level. Fellini's has a strong local following. Free limousine service is offered; just ask for it when making a reservation.

FERRARO'S RESTAURANT & LOUNGE ★★★½

		QUALITY
Italian	Moderate/Expensive	**89**
		VALUE
		C

5900 W. Flamingo Rd.; (702) 364-5300
Southwest   Zone 3
1916 Village Center Circle; (702) 562-9666
North   Zone 5
2895 N Green Valley Pkwy.; (702) 450-5333
North   Zone 5

Customers: Locals
Reservations: Suggested, required
   on weekends
When to go: Any time
Entrée range: $12.95–32
Payment: VISA, MC, AMEX, DC, D
Service rating: ★★★★

Friendliness rating: ★★★★★
Parking: Lot
Bar: Friendly, fully stocked
Wine selection: Good
Dress: Informal, casual
Disabled access: Two-level dining

Flamingo Road:
   Lunch: Monday–Friday, 11 a.m.–2 p.m.
   Dinner: Monday–Sunday, 5:30–10:30 p.m.

Village Center Circle:
   Open: Monday–Friday, 11 a.m.–10 p.m.; Saturday, 4–10 p.m.; Sunday,
   12–8 p.m.

Green Valley Parkway::
   Lunch: Monday–Friday, 11:30 a.m.–2 p.m.
   Dinner: Monday–Saturday, 5–10 p.m.; Sunday, 5–9:30 p.m.

Setting & atmosphere: Classic Roman-style dining room with white
walls, columns, and recessed lighting. Handsome black carpeting has pink
highlights that are reflected in the table appointments.

House specialties: Panzerotti, a family recipe (potato croquettes with roasted
peppers), and Manila clams in tomato-sauce appetizers. Penne amatriciana;
osso buco in burgundy sauce with fettuccini; fresh seafood; linguini Portofino;
Rosalba's tiramisu and Godiva passion liqueur desserts. Bread made daily in
the pizza oven. Plate-size pizzas are available at Stratosphere.

Other recommendations: Light menu includes chicken with honey-
mustard sauce and bow-tie pasta; shrimp with risotto; bow-tie pomodoro;
grilled halibut; plus rustica salad, a meal in itself. Carciofo ripieno (arti-
choke stuffed with seasoned bread crumbs, garlic, butter, and wine); pasta e
fagioli; veal and lamb chops. Pistachio passion dessert.

Entertainment & amenities: A musician plays piano in the lounge.

Summary & comments: Ferraro's continues to serve southern Italian fare with some northern Italian specialties. The Green Valley (at Sunset and Green Valley Parkway) and Summerlin locations serve more contemporary Italian fare and the prices are lower. An added attraction at the Summerlin location is the excellent outdoor dining and a spectacular view that can be seen from some tables. Request a seat with a view when you call for reservations.

FIORE		★★★★
		QUALITY
Continental	Moderate/Expensive	95
		VALUE
Rio; (702) 252-7777		C

Strip   Zone I

Customers: Tourists, locals	**Friendliness rating:** ★★★★★
Reservations: Suggested	**Parking:** Lot, garage, valet
When to go: Any time except during conventions	**Bar:** Full service
	Wine selection: Excellent
Entrée range: $22–48	**Dress:** Dressy, informal
Payment: VISA, MC, AMEX, DC, D	**Disabled access:** Ground floor
Service rating: ★★★★½	

Dinner: Thursday–Monday, 6–11 p.m. Closed Tuesday and Wednesday.

Setting & atmosphere: Handsome exhibition kitchen filled with cookware. Elegant table appointments. Climate-controlled cigar terrace for smokers. A fine selection of cigars.

House specialties: Dill and grappa-cured salmon with blinis; limestone lettuce with marinated shiitake mushrooms, lemon avocado oil; charred tuna carpaccio; Dungeness crab cake with diablo sauce; breast of quail salad; Moroccan-spiced chicken in phyllo. The menu changes every seven to ten days, so specialties are always changing.

Other recommendations: Pizzas from the wood-burning ovens; any of the nightly rotisserie offerings, including roast lamb; hand-carved New York strip; duck or chicken; whole salmon (portioned). Different woods used for grilling include cherrywood, almond, olive, and mesquite. Edible flowers garnish dishes; Dom Perignon tops sorbets (doused tableside by captain). Twenty fine wine selections by the glass.

Summary & comments: Fiore is a departure from the Rio's usual moderately priced restaurants. There is much that's new and exciting here; menu changes are constant.

FLORIDA CAFÉ   ★★★½

Cuban	Inexpensive/Moderate	QUALITY
		85

VALUE
A

Howard Johnson Hotel, 1481 Las Vegas Blvd. S.; (702) 385-3013
Strip   Zone 1

Customers: Cuban community, locals,
  HoJo guests
Reservations: No
When to go: Any time
Entrée range: $5–12
Payment: VISA, MC, AMEX, DC
Service rating: ★★★½

Friendliness rating: ★★★★
Parking: Lot
Bar: Wine and beer
Wine selection: Small
Dress: Casual
Disabled access: Yes

Breakfast: Every day, 7–11 a.m.

Lunch: Every day, 11 a.m.–4 p.m.

Dinner: Every day, 4–10 p.m.

Setting & atmosphere: Colorful Cuban paintings adorn the walls, but it's still a coffee shop at heart.

House specialties: Cuban-American food at value prices; cuban breakfast eggs, stuffed potatoes, sweet plantains, and toast; croquettes; corn ramales; fresh seafood; real Cuban sandwiches, pressed thin in a special grill. All entrées include side dishes.

Other recommendations: Classic arroz con pollo, chicken with yellow rice; marinated leg of pork; cuban pizzas; the many Cuban desserts. A meal could be made from the a la carte side dishes.

Summary & comments: Very little English is spoken here, but the staff is accommodating and the menu descriptions are clear.

FORTUNES   ★★★★

Chinese	Moderate/Expensive	QUALITY
		93

VALUE
C+

Rio; (702) 247-7923
Strip   Zone 1

Customers: Locals and tourists
Reservations: Requested
When to go: Any time
Entrée range: $12.95–market price
Payment: VISA, MC, AMEX, DC, D
Service rating: ★★★★★

Friendliness rating: ★★★★★
Parking: Valet, garage, lot
Bar: Full service
Wine selection: Excellent
Dress: Upscale casual
Disabled access: Elevator

Dinner: Tuesday–Saturday, 6–11 p.m.

Setting & atmosphere: A stunning restaurant designed for the Rio's Chinese clientele. Walls of the hall leading to the dining room are lined with museum-quality Chinese art and artifacts. Additional artworks are in the dining rooms. The main dining room is splendid, with rich woods and magnificent fabrics and appointments. Three private dining rooms are equally beautiful. Opulent and posh it may be, but there is no dress code.

House specialties: Live seafood from a huge tank in the kitchen; the jumbo freshwater Santa Barbara shrimp, with heads and tails, are split, seasoned, and flash-fried—even the shells are edible; real squab, minced and served in trimmed lettuce cups; whole Peking duck, sliced at the table; Chinese cabbage rolls, a complex version of a usually simple dish, filled with roast duck, abalone, black mushrooms, and transparent noodles; Chef Choi's lemon chicken, a tasty version that is not breaded or fried, with a light, not overly sweet lemon sauce.

Other recommendations: Crispy crab claws; sautéed clams with noodles; Mongolian beef; salt and pepper pork chops; Cantonese roast duck; Chinese broccoli with oyster sauce; the house special Yang Chow fried rice; spicy Singapore noodles with curry.

Summary & comments: Not content to have just one new Asian restaurant, Mask (serving Chinese, Thai, and Japanese), the Rio has added the authentic Fortune. It's an experience dining here, but it's not at all intimidating. Order the live seafood and the bill will rise considerably. The Santa Barbara shrimp are worth the extra cost. Order two as an appetizer, but ask about the price first. Prices for the live seafood are not listed on the menu.

FUJI		★★★
		QUALITY
Japanese	Inexpensive/Moderate	**84**
		VALUE
3430 E. Tropicana Ave.; (702) 435-8838		**B**
Southeast Zone 5		

Customers: Locals	**Friendliness rating:** ★★★★
Reservations: Accepted, required on weekends	**Parking:** Large lot
	Bar: Beer and wine only
When to go: Any time	**Wine selection:** Fair
Entrée range: $7.50–16.50	**Dress:** Informal, casual
Payment: VISA, MC, AMEX, DC, JCB	**Disabled access:** Ground floor
Service rating: ★★★★	

Lunch: Tuesday–Friday, 11:30 a.m.–2 p.m.

Dinner: Tuesday–Sunday, 4:30–10 p.m; closed Monday

Setting & atmosphere: Small family-style restaurant with two teppan tables, booths, and traditional seating.

House specialties: All the basic Japanese fare is available: sushi, tempura, sukiyaki, teriyaki. Combination dinners also available.

Other recommendations: Tall or large diners will find a table more comfortable than the small booths.

Summary & comments: Moderate prices, a caring staff, and good food make Fuji a popular local dining option. Children are treated like honored guests.

GARDUNO'S CHILI PACKING CO. ★★★½

Mexican	Inexpensive/Moderate	QUALITY 89
		VALUE B

Fiesta Hotel; (702) 631-7000
Northwest   Zone 4

Customers: Locals, tourists	Friendliness rating: ★★★★
Reservations: Not accepted	Parking: Valet, lot
When to go: Any time	Bar: Full service
Entrée range: $6.95–18.95	Wine selection: Good
Payment: VISA, MC, AMEX, DC, D	Dress: Informal
Service rating: ★★★★	Disabled access: Ground floor

Brunch: Sunday, 11 a.m.–3 p.m.

Lunch & dinner: Sunday, 10 a.m.–3 p.m., 4–10 p.m.; Monday–Thursday, 11 a.m.–10 p.m.; Friday and Saturday, 11 a.m.–11 p.m.

Setting & atmosphere: Colorful, appealing Mexican decor with many plants and beautiful artifacts. This large restaurant has been cleverly divided, making it more intimate.

House specialties: Hatch chiles, grown only in the Mesa Valley of New Mexico, are used exclusively. Baskets of fresh sopaipillas accompany entrées. The honey on the table is for pouring over the puffy pillows of dough. Spicy chili verde served in a huge bowl. Guacamole prepared tableside; fresh avocadoes are mashed, then lime juice, spices, chiles, and seasonings are added to your taste. Tortillas are handmade the old-fashioned way. Posole soup rich with hominy, pork, and red chiles. Any of the fajitas. The red snapper served with adobe corn cake.

Summary & comments: This is the first venture out of New Mexico for the Garduno restaurant family. The food is authentic and good. Daily lunch specials are large enough to be an early dinner. The Sunday margarita brunch is a fine value and a good way to get to know the Garduno style of Mexican cooking.

GRAPE STREET		★★★½

		QUALITY
American bistro and wine bar	Inexpensive/Moderate	87
		VALUE
Summerhill Plaza, 7501 W. Lake Mead Blvd.; (702) 228-9463		A
North Zone 4		

Customers: Locals

Reservations: Accepted

When to go: Any time

Entrée range: $7.95–23.95

Payment: VISA, MC, AMEX

Service rating: ★★★★

Friendliness rating: ★★★★★

Parking: Lot

Bar: Wine and beer

Wine selection: Excellent

Dress: Informal

Disabled access: Ground floor

Lunch & dinner: Sunday and Tuesday–Thursday, 11 a.m.–10 p.m.; Friday and Saturday, 11 a.m.–11 p.m. Dinner specials available from 4 p.m.

Setting & atmosphere: The 90-seat dining room has brick walls, polished concrete floors, hand-forged wrought-iron tables and chairs (they're available for sale), a counter that faces the kitchen, and a wine bar. Adjacent to the dining room is the wine cellar sales room and a take-out counter. Grape Street is a very homey place with a San Francisco feel.

House specialties: Any of the daily specials; the grilled goat cheese and portobello mushroom "Philly" sandwich; the exceptional chopped salad; any of the entrée-sized salads; linguine with Brie; the plate-sized pizzas with creative toppings, or make up your own; the tapas appetizer (roasted garlic and vegetables, Greek meatballs, olives, and goat cheese); the salmon burger.

Other recommendations: The reasonably priced dinner specials served after 4 p.m., which include a house salad and side dishes; the succulent rack of lamb includes English-style mint sauce; chocolate fondue with fruit and cake for dipping, big enough for two.

Summary & comments: Grape Street is a delightful, informal eatery with caring owners. An outdoor patio seats 50. It's always busy. At least 50 wines are always available by the glass. Wines from the cellar are available with meals for just $5 over the retail price. The take-out counter sells pâtés, imported cheeses, and a variety of prepared dishes that would be ideal for a picnic. Live music every Thursday night includes everything from Flamenco to jazz to steel drums to folk and acoustic.

HARLEY-DAVIDSON CAFE   ★★★

American Road Food	Moderate	QUALITY
		85

		VALUE
Strip at Harmon; (702) 740-4555		C+

Strip   Zone I

Customers: Mostly tourists	Entrée range:
Parking: Garage and lot	Dress: Casual
Bar: Full service	Disabled access: Ground floor
Wine selection: Fair	Payment: All major credit cards
Reservations: Accepted	Service rating: ★★★½
When to go: Anytime	Friendliness rating: ★★★★½

Hours: Daily, 10 a.m.–midnight

Setting & atmosphere: Hog heaven for Harley fans. This place is a kick. It's home to Harley-Davidson memorabilia, past, present and future, including one-of-a-kind H-D bikes and famous movie bikes. A special section celebrates a Las Vegas entertainment legend, Ann-Margret. A 15,00 pound H-D Heritage Softail Classic Bike bursts through the café's facade. What a sight!

House specialties: Harley Hog sandwich, Carolina pulled pork covered in barbecue sauce with two sides; a chunky chicken pot pie overflowing with a pastry crust; would you believe a veggie wrap—grilled veggies in a sundried tomato wrap; the café's homestyle meatloaf, a thick slab covered in brown gravy; barbecued baby back ribs. Sweet things, too—Reese's chocolate peanut butter pie topped with chocolate ice cream a warm chocolate chip Toll House cookie swimming in hot chocolate sauce with a scoop of English toffee crunch ice cream.

Summary & comments: The adjacent, fully-loaded merchandise store, is a treasure of Harley-Davidson merchandise. Be patient, there's usually a line of fans waiting to get their turn. the store is open daily, 9 a.m.–11 p.m. Have fun, you hear.

HABIB'S   ★★★½

Persian/Middle Eastern	Moderate	QUALITY
		88

		VALUE
Sahara Pavilion, 4750 W. Sahara Ave.; (702) 870-0860		C

Southwest   Zone 3

Customers: Locals, tourists	Payment: VISA, MC, AMEX
Reservations: Accepted	Service rating: ★★★
When to go: Any time	Friendliness rating: ★★★★
Entrée range: $10.95–21.95	Parking: Shopping-center lot

Bar: Beer and wine

Wine selection: Poor

Dress: Casual

Disabled access: Ground level

Lunch: Monday–Saturday, 11:30 a.m.–3 p.m.

Dinner: Monday–Saturday, 5–10 p.m.

Setting & atmosphere: Located in the restaurant corridor of a popular neighborhood shopping center, this attractive, small restaurant has gained a loyal local following. A mist-controlled outdoor patio allows for al fresco dining even in warm weather. The area is filled with beautiful plants.

House specialties: Middle Eastern appetizers and salads; chicken, ground beef, and beefsteak kabobs; many Persian specialties.

Other recommendations: Tabbouleh salad, so fresh the parsley tastes just-picked; the eggplant appetizer, borani; hummus; torshi, a mixture of pickled, aged vegetables; zereshk polo, a seasoned chicken breast kabob prepared with barberries and fragrant spices that are then mixed with rice.

Summary & comments: Habib's menu is not large, but it is filled with exotic, delicious dishes that, except for the Middle Eastern starters and salads, have unfamiliar names. The wait staff is happy to explain the food to the best of their ability. At least two of the special Persian dishes listed separately on the menu are available each day. Habib's is the only Persian restaurant in Las Vegas; the Middle Eastern dishes are a concession to his sizable following of Middle Eastern customers. Photos of the dishes are included with the menu, enabling diners unfamiliar with the cuisine to see what the finished dish looks like. A selection of American dishes has been added, giving Habib's a broader base of diners.

HUGO'S CELLAR ★★★½

		QUALITY
American	Expensive	**89**
		VALUE
Four Queens Hotel; (702) 385-4011		**B**
Downtown Zone 2		

Customers: Locals, tourists

Reservations: Strongly recommended

When to go: Any time but Friday and Saturday

Entrée range: $26–52

Payment: VISA, MC, AMEX, DC, D

Service rating: ★★★★

Friendliness rating: ★★★★★

Parking: Indoor garage, valet

Bar: Full service

Wine selection: Very good wine list

Dress: Informal, tie and jacket suggested

Disabled access: Elevator to cellar

Dinner: Every day, 5:30–11 p.m.

Setting & atmosphere: Unique cellar location, comfortable lounge, warm bar, and gracious hostess. Booths provide privacy; noise at minimum. Cozy cocktail lounge serves pâté, cheese, crackers, and very large drinks.

House specialties: Variety of breads including lavosh crackers, warm French bread. Waiter creates salad of choice from selection on the cart wheeled to your table. Steaks and prime rib; duck flambé anise; snapper en papillote with shallots and white wine; medallions of lobster with white wine, crushed red pepper, sun-dried tomatoes, and mushrooms.

Other recommendations: Appetizer for two of beef tenderloin medallions; marinated swordfish, breast of chicken, and jumbo shrimp cooked at the table on sizzling granite slab. Imaginative preparations of veal and chicken; rack of lamb Indonesian.

Entertainment & amenities: Hostess presents a fresh rose to female guests. Sorbet is served in a miniature cone. Chocolate-dipped fruits with whipped cream are presented before dessert order is taken.

Summary & comments: A most popular downtown restaurant. On weekends the Cellar is packed. Expert wine steward to assist you with selection. Don't let the little cone of sherbet served between courses throw you—it's a house signature. A consistent local favorite, in spite of too-high prices.

IL FORNAIO ★★★

		QUALITY
Italian	Moderate/Expensive	**87**

		VALUE
New York–New York; (702) 740-6969		**B**
Strip Zone 1		

Customers: Tourists, locals	Friendliness rating: ★★★★★
Reservations: Suggested for dinner	Parking: Valet, garage
When to go: Any time	Bar: Full service
Entrée range: $9.50–25	Wine selection: Small, but good
Payment: VISA, MC, AMEX, CB, JCB	Dress: Informal
Service rating: ★★★★	Disabled access: Ground floor

Hours: Everyday, 8:30 a.m.–12 a.m.

Setting & atmosphere: Upscale, upbeat contemporary decor. Rich woods and natural stone and marble accents. Dine on the outdoor patio with a view of the flowing brook and people-watch as you dine. Faux trees add an almost real touch of nature.

House specialties: Carpaccio with shavings of Italian cheese, capers, and baby arugula; Tuscan tomato and bread soup; the meal-sized salad of mixed greens, rotisserie chicken, apple wood-smoked bacon, and shaved Parmesan;

the selection of thin-crusted pizzas baked in the wood-fired oven. Eat at the bar and watch as they're assembled and baked. The herbed chicken roasted on the wood-burning rotisserie and served with vegetables and roasted potatoes; the 22-ounce certified Angus porterhouse marinated in olive oil and rosemary, served with Tuscan white beans and sautéed spinach; the remarkable breads, baked on the premises, served with all meals.

Other recommendations: Any of the homemade pastas, especially the ravioli filled with spinach, Swiss chard, pine nuts, and basil, with baby artichokes; grilled fresh salmon; veal scallopini with baby artichokes and lemon; elbow macaroni with chicken breast, fresh broccoli, and sun-dried tomatoes.

Summary & comments: The success of New York–New York has brought an enormous amount of business to Il Fornaio. Dine during off hours for the most relaxing experience. Patio dining is the most requested. It can be noisy, so opt to dine in the lovely dining room. Take home the remarkable Il Fornaio European breads. They're sold in Il Fornaio's retail bakery/coffee house just a few doors from the restaurant.

ISIS		★★★½
		QUALITY
Continental	Expensive	**90**
		VALUE
Luxor; (702) 262-4773		**C**
Strip Zone 1		

Customers: Tourists, locals	Friendliness rating: ★★★★★
Reservations: Suggested	Parking: Lot, valet
When to go: Any time	Bar: Full service
Entrée range: $18–70	Wine selection: Excellent
Payment: VISA, MC, AMEX, DC, D	Dress: Dressy, informal
Service rating: ★★★★★	Disabled access: Elevator

Dinner: Thursday–Monday, 5:15–10:45 p.m.; closed Tuesday and Wednesday

Setting & atmosphere: Exact replicas of the statues guarding the entrance to the pharaohs' tombs dramatically flank the entrance to Isis. Glass-enclosed Egyptian artifacts separate the comfortable booths. A statue of Isis is the focal point of this lovely dining room.

House specialties: Poached oysters over creamed spinach with a touch of Pernod; baked shrimp filled with crab and mushroom duxelle; Sonoma greens with warm goat cheese and walnut dressing; beef Wellington; lobster tail en croute with seafood mousse and white zinfandel sauce. Baked Egypt (pyramid-shaped baked Alaska); specialty coffees, Ramses' Torch and Flaming Sceptor.

Other recommendations: Grenadine of veal loin sautéed with sorrel and dry vermouth sauce; Red Sea sesame chicken with lobster tahini; seafood ravioli in chive and lobster sauce. Dahibeyeh Delight (barge-shaped chocolate mousse with raspberry filling).

Entertainment & amenities: Romantic harpist performs at restaurant's entrance.

Summary & comments: Unusual menu cover decorated with illustrations of Egyptian stone carvings is just one of the original touches at Isis.

JERUSALEM ★★½

Middle Eastern/Glatt Kosher	Inexpensive/Moderate	QUALITY 80
		VALUE B

Plaza de Vegas, 1305 Vegas Valley Dr. (East of Maryland Pkwy.)
 (702) 696-1644
Southeast   Zone 5

Customers: Locals and tourists	Friendliness rating: ★★★★
Reservations: No	Parking: Lot
When to go: Any time	Bar: None
Entrée range: $9–22	Wine selection: None
Payment: VISA, MC	Dress: Casual
Service rating: ★★★	Disabled access: Ground floor

Lunch & dinner: Sunday–Thursday, 11 a.m.–9 p.m.; Friday, 10 a.m.–3 p.m.; closed Saturday

Setting & atmosphere: Beautiful it isn't, but it's clean. Tables are large, and there are always extra chairs for the large parties who find their way to Jerusalem, the best of the few kosher restaurants in Las Vegas.

House specialties: Middle Eastern and European traditional dishes: falafel; tabbouleh; Israeli salads; deli sandwiches; matzo ball soup; kabobs of ground beef; shwarma; schnitzel of chicken breast; stuffed grape leaves and stuffed cabbage; chicken or beef shashlik; Israeli-style sautéed beef or chicken with pine nuts on a bed of hummus; tilapia, trout, and spicy Moroccan fish.

Other recommendations: On Sundays only, cholent—the long-cooked meat and bean Sabbath (shabbas) casserole; phull medamess for vegetarians.

Summary & comments: Owner Rachel does catering from an adjacent store. With 24-hour notice, she'll make special dishes. Some inconsistencies exist in the food pricing, but it's mostly a good value. Portions are large.

KATHY'S SOUTHERN COOKING ★★★

		QUALITY
American	Inexpensive/Moderate	85
		VALUE
6407 Mountain Vista St.; (702) 433-1005		A

Southeast   Zone 5

Customers: Locals
Reservations: Suggested, especially for groups of 6 or more
When to go: Any time
Entrée range: $8–22.50
Payment: VISA, MC, AMEX, D
Service rating: ★★★★

Friendliness rating: ★★★★
Parking: Shopping-center lot
Bar: Wine and beer only
Wine selection: Limited (house wine)
Dress: Informal
Disabled access: Ground floor

Lunch & dinner: Tuesday–Thursday, 11 a.m.–8:30 p.m.; Friday and Saturday, 11 a.m.–9:30 p.m.; Sunday, 1–7:30 p.m. Same menu. Closed Monday.

Setting & atmosphere: Casual, down-home dining room with 46 seats. One wall is painted with a mural of a paddle wheeler on the Mississippi River.

House specialties: Gumbo; catfish; "gravy dinners"—smothered pork chop, steak, or chicken with rice or mashed potatoes, slabs of cornbread, and a side dish from a selection of black-eyed peas, red beans and rice, greens, and more.

Other recommendations: Oxtails; shrimp Creole; barbecued beef and spareribs; étouffé, sweet-potato pie. Kathy's spareribs are huge, with a zesty sauce that will make you tingle. Hearty, wholesome fare.

Summary & comments: The owners of this family operation, Kathy and Felix Cook, present authentic selections from Mississippi and Louisiana kitchens "like Mama used to make." Comfortable, with a "you all" kind of friendliness. Park in shopping center and walk through to Mountain Vista Street (no access from shopping center).

KOKOMO'S ★★★★

		QUALITY
Seafood/Steak	Expensive	93
		VALUE
The Mirage; (702) 791-7111		C

Strip   Zone 1

Customers: Tourists
Reservations: Required; high rollers and hotel guests get preference;

reservations available 7 days in advance
When to go: Any time

Entrée range: $35–60 (à la carte)

Payment: VISA, MC, AMEX, DC, D

Service rating: ★★★★★

Friendliness rating: ★★★★

Parking: Lot (long walk), valet

Bar: Full service

Wine selection: Good choices

Dress: Casual

Disabled access: Ramp

Dinner: Every day, 5–10:30 p.m.

Setting & atmosphere: Magnificent tropical decor. Waterfalls, streams, lush foliage, orchids and other exotic flowers. South Pacific on the Strip. Tables well spaced for privacy.

House specialties: Red onion soup with Monterey Jack and Parmesan cheeses. Shaved fried onions; steaks; chops and ribs; grilled rib-eye with sautéed red onions and tricolor pepper sauce. Crème brûlée; peanut butter cheesecake; chocolate mousse; and bread pudding.

Other recommendations: Orange roughy caprice; veal and salmon combo; baked oysters in a smoked-salmon crust; sea bass Montego; lobster Mediterranean-style; grilled Polynesian swordfish; broiled breast of chicken basted with honey mustard; extra-thick lamb chops. English trifle; marshmallow brownie cheesecake; apple torte with cinnamon ice cream; taco shell delight; raspberries with Grand Marnier crème; chocolate sinful pâté with pecan brandy sauce.

Summary & comments: Imaginative chefs and decor combine to create a memorable lunch or dinner in this romantic room. Peaceful and romantic, Kokomo's is a sleeper. One of the best-kept secrets in town.

LAWRY'S THE PRIME RIB		★★★½

American	Expensive	QUALITY
		85
		VALUE
		C

4043 Howard Hughes Pkwy.; (702) 893-2223

Strip   Zone 1

Customers: Locals, tourists

Reservations: Requested

When to go: Any time but convention times

Entrée range: $20–30

Payment: VISA, MC, AMEX, CB, DC, D, JCB

Service rating: ★★★★★

Friendliness rating: ★★★★★

Parking: Valet, lot

Bar: Full service

Wine selection: Good

Dress: Business attire

Disabled access: Ground floor

Dinner: Sunday–Thursday, 5–10 p.m.; Friday and Saturday, 5–11 p.m.

Setting & atmosphere: Elegant but not intimidating, Lawry's reflects the founder's philosophy that a restaurant should be "believable, understandable and appeal to all." The dramatic "silver" carts brought to the table, so the beef can be carved as you watch, are actually made of hammered stainless steel. A handsome separate bar is a fine place for before- or after-dinner drinks.

House specialties: Prime rib, and not much else, has kept diners happy since the original Lawry's The Prime Rib opened in Beverly Hills, California, in 1938. All prime rib dinners include a spinning salad bowl, Yorkshire pudding, mashed potatoes, and whipped cream horseradish. Four cuts of prime rib are offered. Add twin lobster tails to a prime rib dinner for an additional $12.95.

Other recommendations: The fresh fish of the day—expertly prepared in the kitchen, accompanied by seasonal vegetables; the nostalgic creamed spinach or creamed corn. The selection of homespun desserts, especially the deep-dish apple pie with caramel sauce and the coconut banana cream pie.

Summary & comments: How can a restaurant survive that's devoted almost exclusively to prime rib in a town filled with inexpensive prime rib deals? Very well indeed. Lawry's Las Vegas opened with a rush that's never stopped. For prime rib devotees, it's the ultimate luxurious temple of beefdom.

LINDO MICHOACAN		★★★

		QUALITY
Mexican	Moderate	**84**
		VALUE
2655 E. Desert Inn Rd.; (702) 735-6828		**A**
Southeast Zone 5		

Customers: Locals	**Friendliness rating:** ★★★★
Reservations: Suggested	**Parking:** Lot
When to go: Any time	**Bar:** Full service
Entrée range: $8.95–17	**Wine selection:** Good
Payment: VISA, MC, AMEX, D	**Dress:** Casual
Service rating: ★★★★	**Disabled access:** Ground floor

Lunch & dinner: Monday–Wednesday, 11 a.m.–10 p.m.; Thursday–Sunday, 9 a.m.–11 p.m. Same menu day and evening with lunch specials.

Setting & atmosphere: Cozy storefront, neighborhood cantina with wood-paneled walls and a brick bar. Decor includes Mexican wall hangings—a woven rug, guitar and serape, and posters of the picturesque (lindo) region of Michoacan on the southern coast of Mexico.

House specialties: Mexican cactus with onions, cilantro, tomatoes, and jalapeños; chicken broiled and served with cactus, or simmered in a Spanish orange sauce; large selection of seafood. Menudo (tripe soup) is served on Saturday and Sunday. Milanesa con papa (breaded steak with potatoes). Flan Tio Raul.

Other recommendations: Monday–Friday, $6.25 lunch buffet, served until 3 p.m.; Saturday and Sunday, $6.95 brunch buffet, served from 11 a.m. to 3 p.m.; margarita with Cointreau; combination platters.

Summary & comments: The entrance is not impressive, but the good food is. Lindo Michoacan presents an amazing variety of more than 100 appetizers and entrées, all authentic, a good bet for Mexican food enthusiasts. When busy, the chef is sometimes careless with food presentation, but it always tastes good.

LOTUS OF SIAM		★★★½
Thai–Nissan	Moderate/Expensive	**QUALITY** 95
Commercial Center, 953 E. Sahara Ave.; (702) 735-3033 Strip Zone I		**VALUE** A

Customers: Locals & visitors	Friendliness rating: ★★★★★
Reservations: Not required	Parking: Lot
When to go: Any time	Bar: No
Entrée range: $6.95–14.95; market price	Wine selection: No
Payment: VISA, MC	Dress: Casual
Service rating: ★★★★	Disabled access: Ground floor

Lunch: Monday–Friday (buffet and menu), 11:30 a.m.–2:30 p.m.
Dinner: Every day, 5:30–9:30 p.m.

Setting & atmosphere: Attractive, though modest, decor; teak tables and comfortable chairs. Thai paintings and accessories.

House specialties: Beef jerky, Nissan style—crisp yet tender marinated beef served in a spicy sauce. Nam kao tod—minced, tart sausage mixed with crispy rice, ginger, peanuts, and lime juice. Green papaya salad with or without crab; salmon Panang—charbroiled fresh salmon, served Thai-style with a creamy curry sauce.

Other recommendations: long-grained sticky rice steamed and served in small bamboo baskets; the generously sized satays. Ask the owner to design a special menu of Issan dishes for your party.

Summary & comments: The Issan specialties featured here come from the Northwestern corner of Thailand, bordering Laos. These dishes are both hotter and more highly seasoned than most Thai food, but the chef/owner will temper the heat to suit your taste. Gentle, caring service and exceptional, if little-known, Thai dishes make Lotus of Siam a fine choice when you've jostled through quite enough surf-n-turf buffets, thank you. Service can be slow, especially on the weekends.

MAGNOLIA ROOM   ★★★½

	QUALITY
Italian/Greek/American Moderate	85
	VALUE
	A

Jerry's Nugget Casino; (702) 399-3000
North Las Vegas   Zone 4

Customers: Locals and tourists	Friendliness rating: ★★★★
Reservations: Required	Parking: Valet, lot
When to go: Any time	Bar: Full service
Entrée range: $15–25	Wine selection: Small
Payment: VISA, MC, AMEX, DC, D	Dress: Casual
Service rating: ★★★½	Disabled access: Ground floor

Dinner: Wednesday–Saturday, 3–10 p.m.; Sunday, 2–9 p.m.; Monday and Tuesday, closed.

Setting & atmosphere: The newly revamped Jerry's Nugget made a leap into fine dining with the beautifully decorated Magnolia Room. Warm woods, floral fabrics, and other design touches are a far cry from the Jerry's Nugget of the past. This comfortable room offers a lot for the money.

House specialties: The Greek appetizer (spinach pie, stuffed grape leaves, and mini-souvlaki); Magnolia's salad; linguine with seafood; chicken breast Marsala; Greek lemon chicken; the 18-ounce Black Angus porterhouse steak; prime rib, a thick, thick cut; salmon on a bed of spinach and other vegetables, baked in parchment. Desserts: baked Alaska; the Greek custard wrapped in phyllo dough with citrus honey sauce, Galatoboureko; Magnolia's signature bread pudding; chocolate soufflé with a choice of chocolate sauce or crème Anglaise (order with dinner). The early bird dinners are a fine value.

Summary & comments: The Magnolia Room is a real find. The food is not epicurean, but it doesn't pretend to be. An earlier attempt to "get fancy" didn't work. Expect good food, inviting surroundings, and generous portions at reasonable prices. Entrée price includes a choice of soup or spinach, Caesar, or house salad.

MAKINO SUSHI RESTAURANT ★★★★

Japanese	Inexpensive/Moderate	QUALITY
		95

		VALUE
Renaissance Center, Decatur near Flamingo; (702) 889-4477		A
Southwest Zone 3		

Customers: Asian community, locals
Reservations: No
When to go: Any time
Entrée range: Fixed buffet price
Payment: VISA, MC
Service rating: ★★★★

Friendliness rating: ★★★★
Parking: Large Lot
Bar: Wine and beer (license due any day)
Dress: Casual
Disabled access: Ground floor

Lunch: 11:30 a.m.–2:30 p.m. Monday–Friday, $12.99; 11:30 a.m.–3 p.m. Saturday, Sunday, and holidays, $13.99.

Dinner: 5:30–9 p.m. Monday–Thursday, $20.95; 5:30–10 p.m. Friday; 5–10 p.m. Saturday; 5–9 p.m. Sunday and holidays, $21.95. Seniors (65 & older) with ID get a 20% discount at dinner only. Youngsters under five-feet tall are half-price.

Setting & atmosphere: Simple, pleasant Japanese decor. The dining room is surrounded by food stations. The food stations are captivating, especially the sizeable sushi, sashimi, and nigiri sushi area.

House specialties: More than 40 varieties of sushi made as you watch (a supply is always ready) by a cadre of sushi chefs who work nonstop. More than 12,000 pieces of sushi are made most days. Hot and cold salads, some include seafood. A remarkable selection of hot seafood and Japanese specialties including roast chicken, noodle dishes, sukiyaki, and much more. The food selections change daily. The largest selection is at dinner when mountains of snow crab legs, shrimp, and other pricey seafood are added. Mikino offers a spectacular selection of fresh fruits and desserts. The almond cookies, more like French sugar cookies, are exceptional.

Summary & comments: If you enjoy serving yourself, Makino is a fantastic deal. You'll not find a more appealing array of foods. Salads and desserts are presented on white porcelain platters. Everything is appealing and tasty. This is no ordinary buffet. Before making your choices take the time to walk all of the stations. It would be nigh impossible to taste all of the foods, so hone in on your favorites. Except for the array of sushi the food is put out in small amounts and replaced as needed. The sushi alone is worth more than what it costs for this no-limits Japanese feast.

MALIBU CHAN ★★★★

		QUALITY
Pacific Rim	Moderate/Expensive	90

VALUE
C

Promenade Center, 8125 West Sahara; (702) 312-4267
Southwest   Zone 3

Customers: Locals
Reservations: Suggested for prime
    times
When to go: Any time
Entrée range: $10–25 (changes with
    menu)
Payment: VISA, MC, AMEX, D

Service rating: ★★★★
Friendliness rating: ★★★★★
Parking: Lot
Bar: Full service
Wine selection: Good
Dress: Upscale casual
Disabled access: Yes

Dinner: Everyday, 5 p.m.–2 a.m.

Setting & atmosphere: Colorful, high-energy, California-style café and sushi bar with contemporary art and decor. An open kitchen gives some diners a view of the action.

House specialties: Generously sized starters (a few could be a light meal), salads, and entrées. Among the favorites are the garlic shrimp pizza; chicken wings laced with Thai sweet-soy glaze; Tokyo ravioli pot stickers; and live Manilla clams. The rack of lamb is basted with sesame, soy, and ginger; scampi Asia is a new twist on the Italian classic.

Other recommendations: Sesame-crusted salmon with Thai cucumber salsa; seared duck breast; basil–lemon grass shrimp; Chilean sea bass with a potato crust; the excellent sushi.

Summary & comments: This high-powered local hangout serves very good, albeit pricey, food and sushi. The happy hour sushi menu (served 11 pm. until closing) is a terrific value. Though the sushi menu is shorter during this time, prices are considerably less.

MANHATTAN ★★★½

		QUALITY
Italian	Moderate/Expensive	92

VALUE
B

2600 E. Flamingo Rd.; (702) 737-5000
Strip   Zone 1

Customers: Locals, tourists
Reservations: Suggested
When to go: Any time
Entrée range: $12.95–49.95
Payment: VISA, MC, AMEX, CB, DC, D
Service rating: ★★★★★

Friendliness rating: ★★★★
Parking: Valet, large lot
Bar: Full service
Wine selection: Good
Dress: Informal
Disabled access: Ground floor

Lunch: Everyday, 11:30 a.m.–2 p.m.
Dinner: Everyday, 5 p.m.–1 a.m. (same hours for restaurant and lounge).

Setting & atmosphere: Manhattan carries on the tradition of Old Las Vegas with tuxedoed captains, deep booths that afford privacy, and personal service. The entrance is highlighted with an etched-mirrored wall portraying the Manhattan, New York, skyline, a vaulted ceiling, and other designer touches. Lighting is designed to make everyone look their best. The music of Frank Sinatra, Tony Bennett, Nat King Cole, and Ella Fitzgerald is kept at a soothing, nonintrusive level.

House specialties: Scampi P.J.; carpaccio of salmon; salad Caprese served country-style on a bed of roasted peppers; pasta alla Mary Macaluso (the owner's mother's recipe); the pastas with seafood; New York steak Florentine; the 22-ounce, double-cut, fully trimmed veal chop; rib-eye steak with garlic mashed potatoes and portobello mushrooms.

Other recommendations: The antipasto Manhattan, a selection of marinated and grilled vegetables, assorted meats and cheeses, and a wonderful chunky homemade caponato; the rich homemade ice cream served almost soft—have it with seasonal berries.

Summary & comments: A separate bar and lounge features a late-night menu with appetizers, hamburgers, steak sandwiches, and other casual fare. The dining room menu is also available. Dining hours are flexible. If reservations warrant, the staff will accommodate by remaining open later, so call ahead. In spite of the tuxedoed captains, Manhattan is, like its management, casual and relaxed.

MARRAKECH ★★★

		QUALITY
Moroccan	Moderate	**86**
		VALUE
3900 Paradise Rd.; (702) 736-7655		**B**
Strip Zone 1		

Customers: Tourists, locals
Reservations: Suggested; required on weekends

When to go: After 6:30 p.m. for belly dancers; busy during conventions

Entrée range: 6-course complete dinner, $26.95

Payment: VISA, MC, AMEX, CB, D

Service rating: ★★★★

Friendliness rating: ★★★★

Parking: Shopping-center lot

Bar: Full service

Wine selection: A Moroccan red and French white by the glass or bottle; Mondavi and Jordan, plus imported wines

Dress: Informal, casual

Disabled access: Ground floor

Dinner: Every day, 5:30–11 p.m.

Setting & atmosphere: Simulated desert tent with servers in native garb. Brass tables, floor pillows, and benches for seating maintain the illusion. Diners eat with their hands.

House specialties: Shrimp scampi; harira soup; Moroccan-style chicken in light lemon sauce; flambé lamb brochette. Multi-course fixed-price dinner, which does not include couscous. Pastilla, a flaky chicken pie, normally a dinner course, is served for dessert at Marrakech.

Entertainment & amenities: Belly dancers undulate and undulate, pausing only to have greenbacks thrust into their costumes.

Summary & comments: Las Vegas version of Moroccan food in an Arabian Nights setting. Belly dancing is competent but often intrusive. It's not authentic, but it's fun.

MAYFLOWER CUISINIER ★★★★½

		QUALITY
Chinese/French	Moderate/Expensive	**94**
		VALUE
		B

4750 W. Sahara Ave.; (702) 870-8432

Southwest   Zone 3

Customers: Locals, some tourists

Reservations: Suggested

When to go: Any time

Entrée range: $12.95–21.95

Payment: VISA, MC, AMEX, DC, D

Service rating: ★★★★

Friendliness rating: ★★★★½

Parking: Shopping-center lot

Bar: Full service

Wine selection: Upscale

Dress: Casual to semi-dressy

Disabled access: Ground floor

Lunch: Monday–Friday, 11 a.m.–2:30 p.m.

Dinner: Monday–Thursday, 5–9:30 p.m.; Friday and Saturday, 5–10:30 p.m.; Sunday, closed.

Setting & atmosphere: Two-level, 100-seat dining room; tastefully decorated in pink with contemporary black lacquer accents and handsome wall hangings. Choose from the main-level dining room or the more private mezzanine, or dine on the mist-cooled patio.

House specialties: Roast duck salad with plum vinaigrette; roast duck and goat cheese quesadilla with salsa topping; chicken pot-stickers with peanut-basil sauce; grilled lemongrass chicken salad; Cornish game hen à la Chinoise; grilled tenderloin of beef with Mongolian sauce; Mayflower shrimp in pineapple-apricot sauce with scallion noodles.

Other recommendations: Ginger chicken ravioli with scallion-Szechuan sauce; hot and sour soup; Mongolian grilled lamb chops with cilantro-mint sauce; grilled ahi tuna with Dijon-lime sauce; stir-fried chicken in plum wine with lychee nuts. Imaginative desserts that change seasonally.

Summary & comments: Owner-chef Ming See Woo and manager Theresa, her daughter, created this fine cross-cultural restaurant. The new bar is ideal for a pre-dinner drink. An excellent fusion of Chinese and other cuisines.

MICHAEL'S ★★★★

Continental	Very Expensive	QUALITY
		93
Barbary Coast Hotel; (702) 737-7111		VALUE
Strip Zone 1		D

Customers: Tourists, locals	Service rating: ★★★★★
Reservations: Difficult, but starts tak- ing reservations at 3:30 p.m.	Friendliness rating: ★★★★★
	Parking: Parking garage, valet
When to go: Whenever you can get a reservation	Bar: Full service
	Wine selection: Excellent
Entrée range: $37–75, a la carte	Dress: Sport coat, dressy
Payment: VISA, MC, AMEX, CB, DC, D	Disabled access: Small staircase

Dinner: Every day, two seatings at 6 and 6:30 p.m., 9 and 9:30 p.m.

Setting & atmosphere: Comfortable chairs in intimate table settings. Deep carpeting and romantic lighting create a luxurious room in the rococo style of early Las Vegas.

House specialties: Rack of lamb bouquetière; live Maine lobster; veal chop Florentine; fresh Dover sole.

Other recommendations: Shrimp cocktail served atop an igloo of ice, illuminated from within. All meats are prime.

Entertainment & amenities: Complimentary petits fours, chocolate-dipped fruits, and fancy fresh fruits are presented after dinner.

Summary & comments: If you're staying at a Strip hotel, the casino can help with a reservation. Early diners have a better chance of securing a table than those who like to dine at prime time. The menu (strictly à la carte) is a high-priced view of the Las Vegas of yesteryear.

MON AMI GABI		★★★★
		QUALITY
French Steakhouse	Moderate/Expensive	90
		VALUE
Paris Hotel; (702) 944-GABI		B

Strip   Zone I

Customers: Tourists, locals
Reservations: Requested for dining
  room, not accepted for patio
When to go: Any time
Entrée range: $15.95–28.95
Payment: VISA, MC, AMEX, DC
Service rating: ★★★★

Friendliness rating: ★★★★
Parking: Garage, valet
Bar: Full service
Wine selection: All French wines
Dress: Upscale casual
Disabled access: Yes

Lunch: Every day, 11:30 a.m.–3:30 p.m.

Dinner: Sunday–Thursday, 5–11 p.m. Friday and Saturday, 5 p.m.–12 a.m.

Setting & atmosphere: Handsome brasserie with black leather booths and tables. The main dining room leads to a wonderful, plant-filled patio and a marvelous sidewalk café with a view of the Strip.

House specialties: Steak frites, thin-sliced steak and French fries; an excellent selection of seafood and hors d'oeuvres; many hot seafood appetizers; the daily special listed on the blackboard; filet mignon and New York strip are among the regular steak selections.

Other recommendations: Crepes; salads; omelettes and sandwiches served at lunch; plates of seafood, le coquillage, including mussles gribiche (mussles with caper mayonnaise).

Entertainment & amenities: The restaurant is child-friendly, accepts take-out requests, and features banquet dining with fixed-price gourmet meals.

Summary & comments: Mon Ami is a charming dining place. everyone wants to dine at the sidewalk café, but you'll have to come early to get a table (there are no reservations for the café). The frites are curly fries, not steak fries, but they're crisp and good, so what if they're not authentic? Everything else is right on the mark. And for those whose dinner isn't complete with a good bottle of wine, a separate list of fine reserve wines has just been added.

MORTONI'S

★★★½

Italian, California-style	Moderate/Expensive	QUALITY
		90

		VALUE
		B

Hard Rock Hotel; (702) 693-5000
Strip   Zone 1

Customers: Hotel guests, tourists, locals

Reservations: Recommended

When to go: Any time but concert time

Entrée range: $25–35

Payment: VISA, MC, AMEX, DC, D, JCB

Service rating: ★★★★
Friendliness rating: ★★★★
Parking: Valet, lot
Bar: Full service
Wine selection: Good
Dress: Casual chic
Disabled access: Ground floor

Dinner: Sunday, Monday and Thursday, 6–10 p.m.; Friday and Saturday, 6–11 p.m.; Tuesday and Wednesday, closed.

Setting & atmosphere: Enter through a massive door that is a work of art; the decor is understated and elegant. Lighting is soft and subdued, enhancing both the food and the diner. In a hotel with a music theme, of course there is music in the dining room. Be assured that it is not intrusive and is not hard rock, but it can be loud at times.

House specialties: Bisteca con funghi, a 20-ounce rib-eye with a bone that would have satisfied Elvis; clams and mussels steamed in wine with garlic; double-cut pork chops; veal Milanese, a chop pounded wafer-thin, breaded, and fried; pasta and risotto selection includes choices ideal for vegetarians; plate-size pizzas; chocolate paradise, fresh berries with mascarpone cheese, tiramisu, or the fine cookie selection for dessert. All entrées include generous portions of roasted potatoes and fresh vegetables, along with arugula salad—the spicy green is so perfect it looks just-picked. The steaks are first marked on the grill, then finished in the high heat of the wood-burning oven.

Summary & comments: Only natural ingredients and organic produce are used at Mortoni's. The menu is small but choice, offering a full selection of dishes. The Hard Rock Hotel transcends generations; it should be experienced by everyone, regardless of age.

MORTON'S

★★★½

Steak	Very Expensive	QUALITY
		89

		VALUE
		C

400 East Flamingo Rd.; (702) 893-0703
Strip   Zone 1

Customers: Tourists, locals
Reservations: Recommended, especially during conventions
When to go: Any time
Entrée range: $19.95–34
Payment: VISA, MC, AMEX, DC, CB
Service rating: ★★★★
Friendliness rating: ★★★

Parking: Shopping-center lot, garage, valet
Bar: Attractive, full service
Wine selection: Excellent
Dress: Business casual
Disabled access: Same level as parking lot

Dinner: Monday–Thursday, 5:30–11 p.m.; Friday and Saturday, 5–11 p.m; Sunday, 5–10 p.m.

Setting & atmosphere: Men's club atmosphere, with paneled boardroom (for large parties), polished oak barroom, and comfortable booths.

House specialties: Black bean soup. Whole onion bread brought to table. Porterhouse steak; New York sirloin steak; rib-eye steak; double filet mignon; whole Maine lobster; shrimp Alexander. Huge strawberries with sabayon sauce.

Other recommendations: Appetizer of broiled sea scallops wrapped in bacon, apricot chutney; double-cut prime rib; lamb chops; swordfish steak; lemon-oregano chicken. Shrimp Alexander as an appetizer.

Entertainment & amenities: Storage lockers for regular guests' wines.

Summary & comments: Branch of Chicago-based steakhouse. Entrance from outside Fashion Show Mall. Appetizers, salads, entrées, desserts all served in large portions. Everything à la carte, including side dishes. The dessert soufflés are a specialty but are disappointing. Stick to selections from the pastry tray or the gorgeous fresh berries. Cigar smoking is encouraged in the dining room. Prime steaks, but a less than prime attitude.

NAPA	★★★★★
Contemporary French cuisine Expensive	QUALITY
	95
	VALUE
	C

Rio; (702) 252-7777
Strip   Zone 1

Customers: Locals, tourists
Reservations: Requested
When to go: Any time
Entrée range: $28–53
Payment: VISA, MC, AMEX, DC, D
Service rating: ★★★★★

Friendliness rating: ★★★★★
Parking: Valet, garage, lot
Bar: Full service
Wine selection: Outstanding
Dress: Business attire
Disabled access: Elevator

Dinner: Tuesday–Saturday, 6–11 p.m.

Setting & atmosphere: Napa has an enlightened mission, one whole-heartedly endorsed by Rio founder Tony Marnell and the mostly male executive staff: to create an ambience specifically for women. The enchanting dining room is elegantly appointed and filled with art. Men enjoy the inviting room as much as the women.

House specialties: Maryland lump crab cake appetizer; Maui onion soup with truffle dumplings, served in a Maui onion; Maine diver scallops with black truffles; wood-grilled Maine monkfish, studded with garlic; marinated breast of chicken roasted in a salt crust. Dishes change frequently.

Other recommendations: A large baked potato filled with Louisiana crayfish and lobster coral sauce; wood-grilled veal chop with truffled potato gnocchi; chicken pot pie; the selection of desserts.

Summary & comments: Celebrity chef Jean-Louis Palladin, formerly of the Watergate restaurant in Washington, D.C., works in an exhibition kitchen that can be viewed from the front tables. Napa's wine list includes 250 wines by the glass. A grand circular staircase joins Napa to the superb Wine Cellar Tasting Room. A grand tasting adventure at modest prices. As of mid-2001, though, Palladin has been off duty; his return is wished, but uncertain.

NEROS		★★★★
Contemporary American	Expensive	**QUALITY** 90
Caesars Palace; (702) 731-7731		**VALUE** C
Strip Zone 1		

Customers: Tourists, locals	**Friendliness rating:** ★★★★★
Reservations: Requested	**Parking:** Valet, garage, lot
When to go: Any time except convention times	**Bar:** Full service
	Wine selection: Excellent
Entrée range: $22–49	**Dress:** Business attire
Payment: VISA, MC, AMEX, CB, DC, D	**Disabled access:** Ground floor
Service rating: ★★★★★	

Dinner: Every day, 5:30–11 p.m.

Setting & atmosphere: Softly lit, with comfortable booths and tables, Neros is a fine example of understated elegance.

House specialties: Cut-to-order steak tartare with toasted brioche, waffled potato chips, and a garnish of pansies; pan-seared foie gras with 100-year-old balsamic vinegar; roasted beet and wild green salad; smoky vidalia onion soup with herbed goat cheese crouton; glazed, whole roasted Sonoma squab with parsnip puree; grilled swordfish with pan-fried risotto cakes.

Other recommendations: Pan-roasted free-range chicken atop truffled mashed potatoes; rack of Colorado lamb with creamy Parmesan polenta; grilled Pacific salmon with French de Puy lentils; the splendid desserts, especially the delectable fallen chocolate soufflé.

Summary & comments: This one-time steak house took on new life under former Chef Mario Capone, formerly of Biba restaurant in Boston. He was one of the bright young chefs who was fast making Las Vegas a culinary destination. Cheers and best wishes to the new chef.

NOODLES		★★★½
		QUALITY
Chinese/Japanese/Thai/Vietnamese	Moderate	93
		VALUE
Bellagio; (702) 693-7111		B+

Strip   Zone 1

Customers: Tourists, locals	Friendliness rating: ★★★★
Reservations: No	Parking: Valet, lot
When to go: Any time	Bar: Full service
Entrée range: À la carte $5.95–27	Wine selection: Good
Payment: All major credit cards	Dress: Casual
Service rating: ★★★★	Disabled access: Ground floor

Hours: Sunday–Thursday, 11 a.m.–11 p.m.; Friday and Saturday, 11 a.m.–2 a.m.

Setting & atmosphere: Follow the marble floor with Chinese brass inlays that represent bits of Asian wisdom into this wonderful eatery. There's an open kitchen, a wall of artifacts, and the hustle and bustle of an authentic noodle kitchen.

House specialties: Oodles of slurpy, authentic noodle dishes from China, Vietnam, Thailand, and Japan and authentic Hong Kong–style barbecue dishes, reasonably priced. There's a long list of appetizers and many different teas.

Summary & comments: Noodles is small, only 88 seats, so it's tough to get in at prime times, but it's open long hours so you're bound to get in sometime. This is a favorite stop for Bellagio's Asian clientele. Find the Baccarat bar, and you'll find Noodles

OLIO

★★★½

		QUALITY
Contemporary Italian	Moderate/expensive	**88**
		VALUE
MGM Grand; (702) 891-7775		**C**
Strip Zone I		

Customers: Locals, tourists
Reservations: Suggested for dining
  room

When to go: Avoid convention times
Entrée range: $15–25
Payment: All major credit cards

Parking: Valet, garage
Bar: Separate lounge & bar, full ser-
  vice
Wine selection: Good
Dress: Business casual

Disabled access: Ground floor, few
  steps to upper dining room
Service rating: ★★★½
Friendliness rating: ★★★★

Hours: Lunch and dinner, Sunday–Thursday, 11 a.m.–midnight; Friday
and Saturday, 11:30 a.m.–2 a.m.

Setting & atmosphere: Olio is a showcase for owner John Tunney's imagination. There are many parts to Olio. Two dining rooms on two levels, a
smashing fireplace divides the bar from the dining rooms. A long antipasto
bar fronts the entrance on one side; on the other is an out-of-this-world
gelato bar attended by silver-clad pretty women. A private screening room
is available for parties. Each section has it's own upbeat, decor. Don't like the
furniture in the screening room? The owner will change it!

House specialties: Dishes from the antipasto bar; crispy, crunchy calamari;
Alaskan crab cakes; Chilean seabass perched atop velvety mashed potatoes;
the butterflied, lightly breaded veal chop that covers the plate; osso buco
Marsala; any of the pastas or the ravioli of the day; grilled portobello mushroom salad. Any of the daily fresh fish. Desserts such as the upside-down polenta cake with sour cream gelato or the Olio take on tiramisu—it may not
look like classic tiramisu, but it sure is good.

Summary & comments: Olio has so much going it can make you gaga.
Prices are moderate at the antipasto bar, more costly in the dining rooms.
Check out the wine deal at the antipasto bar—imbibe unlimited quantities
of a good Chianti for a reasonable fixed price. The screening room is wild.
Everything from old movies to sporting events. Olio's bar hours are at the
whim of of the guests. You stay, they'll pour.

OLIVES ★★★★

		QUALITY
American/Mediterranean	Moderate/Expensive	95

VALUE **B**

Bellagio; (702) 693-7223
Strip   Zone I

Customers: Tourists, locals
Reservations: Accepted
When to go: Any time
Entrée range: Lunch, $13–25; dinner,
  $25–40
Payment: All major credit cards
Service rating: ★★★★

Friendliness rating: ★★★★★
Parking: Valet, garage
Bar: Full service
Wine selection: Eclectic
Dress: Casual
Disabled access: Ground floor

Lunch: Every day, 11 a.m.–3 p.m.

Dinner: Every day, 5–11:30 p.m.

Setting & atmosphere: Intricate mosaic tiling, a sculpted wood ceiling, an open kitchen, and an outdoor patio with a view of the lake.

House specialties: The menu changes regularly but always includes a risotto with a wild mushroom ragu; the signature butternut squash tortellini with brown butter, sage, and Parmesan cheese; the savory spit-roasted chicken on a crisp mashed potato cake; individual pizzas with a flatbread-like crust; and grilled sirloin with shiitake glaze. Typical of the daily specials is the pan-seared, maple-glazed Hudson Valley foie gras.

Other recommendations: Cod cake with lobster rémoulade and Boston baked beans; chocolate falling cake; roasted banana tiramisu; any of the wonderful sandwiches served only at lunch.

Summary & comments: Olives at Bellagio bears no resemblance to the Boston original, but it does have the same warmth and expert staff; many are from the Boston Olives. These Olives veterans have re-created the essence and spirit of the original. Try for a terrace table, but don't be disappointed if it's not available. Everyone wants one.

THE PALM ★★★★

		QUALITY
Steak	Very Expensive	85

VALUE **C**

The Forum Shops at Caesars Palace; (702) 732-7256
Strip   Zone I

Customers: Tourists, locals
Reservations: Recommended
When to go: Any time
Entrée range: $16–95
Payment: VISA, MC, AMEX, CB, DC
Service rating: ★★★★

Friendliness rating: ★★★★★
Parking: Parking garage, valet
Bar: Extensive, full service
Wine selection: Very good
Dress: Business casual
Disabled access: Ground floor

Lunch: Every day, 11:30 a.m.–4 p.m.
Dinner: Every day, 11:30 a.m.–10:30 p.m.

Setting & atmosphere: Colorful caricatures of local notables as well as nationally known entertainers cover walls. Antique wall boasts reproductions of some of the original 1920s artwork from the first Palm in New York.

House specialties: Monday Night Salad, named for football fans who frequent the Palm Too in New York (lettuce, onion, pimento, tomato, and anchovy); Raju salad. Jumbo lobsters; clams and shrimp Posillipo; cottage fries and fried onions. The 38- to 40-ounce New York strip for two can easily serve three. Steak à la Stone; veal martini; outstanding lump-meat crab cakes—broiled, not fried. Excellent hash brown potatoes.

Other recommendations: Veal; lamb and pork chops; pastas; blackened breast of chicken.

Entertainment & amenities: Celebrity-watching is the entertainment.

Summary & comments: Caters to celebrities, with drawings of many entertainers and local movers and shakers on the walls. The Palm suffers from the "good news, bad news" Las Vegas malady—too much business. Avoid the banquet room in back. It's noisy and drab; the service is careless. Stick to your guns and insist on a table in the dining room. Tables in the front are least noisy.

PAMPLEMOUSSE   ★★★½

Continental/French	Expensive	QUALITY
		87
		VALUE
		C

400 E. Sahara Ave.; (702) 733-2066
Strip   Zone 1

Customers: Locals, tourists
Reservations: Required
When to go: Avoid conventions
Entrée range: $17–27
Payment: VISA, MC, AMEX, DC, D
Service rating: ★★★★★

Friendliness rating: ★★★★★
Parking: Street, lot
Bar: Beer and wine only
Wine selection: Excellent
Dress: Upscale casual
Disabled access: Ground floor

Dinner: Tuesday–Sunday, 6–10 p.m.; Monday, closed.

Setting & atmosphere: Country French. Attractive wine cellar at entrance to dining room. Restaurant has no menu; waiters recite the day's offerings and describe each dish.

House specialties: Duckling dishes; medallions of veal prepared with baked apples; special seafood dishes in season—mussels, monkfish, salmon; assorted desserts, all delicious.

Other recommendations: Dinner begins with a fine assortment of fresh vegetables (crudités) served from a handsome basket with an individual crock of house vinaigrette.

Summary & comments: Waiters will give prices when reciting menu only if asked. Ask, so there are no surprises when the check arrives.

PASTA PIRATE		★★★½

		QUALITY
Seafood/Pasta	Moderate	86
		VALUE
California Hotel; (702) 385-1222		A

Downtown   Zone 2

Customers: Locals, tourists	Friendliness rating: ★★★★
Reservations: Suggested	Parking: Garage, valet
When to go: Any time	Bar: Full service
Entrée range: $10–40	Wine selection: Adequate
Payment: VISA, MC, AMEX, DC, D	Dress: Casual
Service rating: ★★★★	Disabled access: Ground floor

Dinner: Every day, 5:30–11 p.m.

Setting & atmosphere: Small restaurant with waterfront motif featuring tin walls, a brick floor, fishnets, neon signs, and an open kitchen.

House specialties: Pasta and seafood; Alaskan king crab legs; scampi; baby lobster tails; and marinated sesame lobster brochettes. A glass of wine is included with all entrées.

Other recommendations: Filet mignon with prawns; live Maine lobster; rigatoni Romano; cavatelli with broccoli; penne Diana; Cajun tuna.

Entertainment & amenities: Piano player entertains between bar and dining room entrances, 6–11 p.m.

Summary & comments: The Pasta Pirate offers an imaginative menu at moderate prices. Consistently good food and prices.

PEKING MARKET   ★★★½

Chinese	Moderate	QUALITY
		87

		VALUE
Flamingo Hilton; (702) 733-3111		B
Strip Zone 1		

Customers: Tourists, locals	Friendliness rating: ★★★★★
Reservations: Suggested	Parking: Valet, garage
When to go: Any time	Bar: Full service
Entrée range: $10–30	Wine selection: Good
Payment: VISA, MC, AMEX, CB, DC, D	Dress: Informal
Service rating: ★★★★★	Disabled access: Ground floor

Dinner: Friday–Tuesday, 5:30–11 p.m.; Wednesday and Thursday, closed.

Setting & atmosphere: Contemporary Chinese decor with traditional, authentic art and antiques. Each dining area is a treasure with teakwood walls, silk fabric accents, and other decorative enhancements. The upholstered booths are plush and comfortable. Table linens are moiré embossed. A captivating saltwater aquarium is on view at the entrance.

House specialties: Seafood dishes with shrimp, lobster, and crab; orange peel beef; Peking duck, available without advance notice; lop chung fried rice; five spice monkfish; Peking Market chow mein with tender pieces of squid.

Other recommendations: Well-priced family-style dinners for two or more diners; Chinese chicken salad; pot stickers; Peking Market's signature flambéed dessert, prepared tableside—warm crispy pudding topped with vanilla ice cream and a heady sauce made from caramelized sugar, coconut and pineapple juices, and Triple Sec.

Summary & comments: Peking Market has posh new decor, an expanded staff for better service, and an extensive menu of regional Chinese dishes.

PHO CHIEN   ★★★½

Vietnamese	Inexpensive/Moderate	QUALITY
		89

		VALUE
3839 West Sahara; (702) 873-8749		A
Southwest Zone 3		

Customers: Asians and locals	Service rating: ★★★½
Reservations: No	Friendliness rating: ★★★★★
When to go: Any time	Parking: Lot
Entrée range: $5.25–9.50	Bar: No
(complete dinner); lobster at	Wine selection: No
market price	Dress: Casual
Payment: VISA, MC	Disabled access: Ground floor

Lunch & dinner: Monday, Tuesday, Thursday, and Friday, 10:30 a.m.–9 p.m.; Wednesday, 10 a.m.–4 p.m.; Saturday and Sunday, 10:30 a.m.–10 p.m.

Setting & atmosphere: New owners have cleaned up this storefront Vietnamese restaurant, but it's no beauty. The owner provides the friendly atmosphere and speaks understandable English. Come for the food, not the setting—though very clean, your surroundings will be rather spare.

House specialties: Sautéed shrimp and spareribs; Vietnamese egg rolls; noodle soup with steak and brisket; curried chicken with steamed rice; beef satay with rice or egg noodle soup; beef with lemon grass.

Other recommendations: Charbroiled pork and vegetable rolls; grilled shrimp wrapped with sugar cane; the selection of noodle soups.

Summary & comments: The food is far prettier than the premises, and it's very good. This is not capital "D" dining, but if you're in the mood for a delicious, inexpensive meal served quickly, this is the place.

PICASSO		★★★★★
		QUALITY
French with Spanish influence	Expensive/Very Expensive	**98**
		VALUE
Bellagio; (702) 693-7223		**C**

Strip Zone I

Customers: Tourists, locals	Service rating: ★★★★★
Reservations: A must	Friendliness rating: ★★★★★
When to go: Any time you can get a reservation!	Parking: Valet, self
	Bar: Full service
Entrée range: Prix fixe only, $79.50 or $89.50	Wine selection: Excellent
	Dress: Casual elegance
Payment: All major credit cards	Disabled access: Elevator

Dinner: Thursday–Tuesday, 6–9:30 p.m; Wednesday, closed.

Setting & atmosphere: Arguably the most beautiful dining room in Las Vegas. A treasure of original Picasso artworks adorn the walls. The flower displays throughout the restaurant are exquisite. A wall of windows gives most tables a full view of the dancing fountains.

House specialties: Selections on both the five-course degustation and the four-course prix fixe change regularly according to the whim of the chef. The warm lobster salad, sautéed foie gras, roasted Atlantic turbot, and seafood sausage—a plump casing filled with chunks of seafood—appear often. The roasted pigeon (squab) is outstanding. Chef Julian Serrano, formerly of Masa's in San Francisco, sometimes offers a sensational amuse bouche (entertainment for the mouth), a tiny potato pancake topped with crème fraîche and osetra caviar. It's worth asking for—beg if you have to.

Summary & comments: This exceptional restaurant (one of only two five-star restaurants in Las Vegas) is grand yet unpretentious. Allow enough time to enjoy the experience. After dinner have a drink on the terrace. Where else but in Las Vegas can you have a view of Lake Como as well as one of the Eiffel Tower!

PIERO'S ★★★★½

Italian	Expensive	**QUALITY** 92	
355 Convention Center Dr.; (702) 369-2305 Strip Zone 1		**VALUE** C	

Customers: Locals, tourists, conventioneers

Reservations: Required

When to go: Any time

Entrée range: $20–40 (higher for lobster)

Payment: VISA, MC, AMEX, DC, D

Service rating: ★★★★½

Friendliness rating: ★★★★½

Parking: Valet, lot

Bar: Full service

Wine selection: Excellent

Dress: Business casual

Disabled access: Ground floor

Dinner: Every day, 5:30–9 p.m.

Setting & atmosphere: Many softly lit booths and alcoves for guests desiring privacy. There are two private dining rooms for 12 to 20 people; a banquet room that can accommodate up to 250; a piano bar; and a much larger kitchen. The excellent wait staff specializes in Old World–style service.

House specialties: Osso buco Piero; zuppa di pesce, a seafood "soup" filled with lobster, clams, mussels, shrimp, calamari, and scallops; whole roasted kosher chicken as good or better than Mama used to make; any dish with Provimi veal; the Italian pastas with French-influenced sauces; the 25-ounce New York steak; stone crab claws or cakes of Maryland blue crab, in season.

Summary & comments: Celebrities and sports figures always make their way to Piero's, as do Las Vegas power brokers, who consistently dine here. Dom Perignon, Cristal, Grand Cordon champagnes and $400 bottles of Montrachet are the norm at Piero's. Owner Freddy Glusman divides his time between Piero's and his new Piero's Trattoria.

PINOT BRASSERIE ★★★½

		QUALITY
French	Moderate/Expensive	89

VALUE
C

Venetian Hotel; (702) 414-8888
Strip   Zone 1

Customers: Locals, tourists
Reservations: Requested at dinner
When to go: Avoid conventions
Entrée range: $10–20 (lunch);
$24–market price (seafood) (dinner)
Payment: VISA, MC, AMEX, DC, D

Service rating: ★★★★
Friendliness rating: ★★★★½
Parking: Valet, garage
Bar: Full service
Wine selection: Good
Dress: Upscale casual (dinner)
Disabled access: Ground floor

Lunch: Every day, 11:30 a.m.–3 p.m.

Dinner: Sunday–Thursday, 5:30–10 p.m.; Friday and Saturday,
5:30–10:30 p.m.

Setting & atmosphere: Authentic French brasserie decor, with comfortable booths and tables. The owners scoured flea markets and design centers in Paris to achieve this warm and inviting atmosphere. Everything from the lamps to the beautiful wood façade (rescued from an old hotel) are authentic.

House specialties: Fresh seafood—the shellfish platter for two is especially terrific, as are the steamed mussels with shallots, garlic, and wine; traditional french onion soup gratinée with a thick crust of melted cheese; rotisserie pork rack with pommes Anna; pan-seared breast of duck; and cote du boeuf for two—a hearty grilled beef chop with roasted portobello mushrooms, roasted potatoes, onion rings, and red wine shallot sauce.

Other recommendations: The daily plat du jour (plate of the day) that could be a classic cassoulet, lamb shank pot-au-feu, bouillabaise, grilled veal chop, or a Sunday surprise, known only to the chef (for adventurous diners only). The desserts are scrumptious—order the chocolate soufflé when you place your entrée order.

Summary & comments: A small café outside the Brasserie is a fine place to people-watch and enjoy a casual meal. They serve seafood, appetizers, sandwiches, salads, and some entrées—but it's plenty to choose from. Seafood is not inexpensive here, but this is a rare Las Vegas occurrence of truly getting what you pay for, just expect the higher tab. As in France, meals are a leisurely occurrence at Pinot, especially so if the restaurant is busy, but with such carefully chosen surroundings and lush food, you might gladly while away an entire day here, anyway.

PRIME ★★★★½

Steakhouse	Expensive	QUALITY
		96
Bellagio; (702) 693-8484		VALUE
Strip Zone I		**C**

Customers: Tourists, locals	Friendliness rating: ★★★★★
Reservations: Requested	Parking: Valet, self
When to go: Avoid convention times	Bar: Full service
Entrée range: $20–market price	Wine selection: Excellent
Payment: All major credit cards	Dress: Casual elegance
Service rating: ★★★★★	Disabled access: Elevator

Dinner: Every day, 5:30–11 p.m.

Setting & atmosphere: Dazzling chocolate and powder-blue carpets and wall hangings in a setting seldom seen for a steakhouse—it's gorgeous. In keeping with Bellagio's fine arts policy, there's plenty of original art to view here. Have a drink at the elegant bar and take it all in.

House specialties: Prime, aged steaks and seafood; herb-crusted rack of lamb; roasted rib eye steak for two; caramel-roasted pork loin. A choice of a variety of sauces.

Summary & comments: Prime is on the lower level of the shopping corridor beside Picasso. Both restaurants get their share of lookers, but the staff keeps them from disturbing diners. It's hard to resist this rare steakhouse.

RAINFOREST CAFÉ ★★★½

American	Moderate	QUALITY
		86
MGM Grand; (702) 891-8580		VALUE
Strip Zone I		**B**

Customers: Tourists and locals	Friendliness rating: ★★★★
Reservations: No	Parking: Valet, garage
When to go: Any time	Bar: Full service
Entrée range: $9.99–30	Wine selection: Good
Payment: VISA, MC, AMEX, CB, DC, D	Dress: Casual
Service rating: ★★★	Disabled access: Through casino

Breakfast: Every day, 8–10:15 a.m.

Lunch & dinner: Every day, 10:30 a.m. until closing: Monday–Thursday and Sunday, until 11 p.m.; Friday and Saturday, until midnight

Setting & atmosphere: Whimsical and wonderful—a faux tropical paradise with live birds, animatronic animals (elephants, leopards, gorillas), and butterflies. The retail shop, designed to entice kids, includes a talking tree that's home to a slinky, talking python, Julius Squeezer, and there's a pond filled with scary alligators. The café is a marvel of simulated and natural effects.

House specialties: Amazon flatbreads that look suspiciously like pizzas; meat loaf; fried chicken; barbecued ribs; kid's choices; chicken pot pie; vegetable lasagna.

Other recommendations: Daily fish special; mini–hot dogs on mini-buns; chicken tidbits; pastas; selection of wild desserts; exotic spirited and non-spirited beverages.

Summary & comments: Themed restaurants are very common in Las Vegas, but Rainforest Café has better food than most, and a wonderful theme. Ask about the free safari tours. However, calling the Rainforest Café for information can be a maddening experience. To get a real person, defeat the long, long taped litany of information by pushing 0. Per Rainforest Café's instructions, the café cannot be accessed through the MGM switchboard.

RANGE STEAKHOUSE		★★★½
		QUALITY
American	Expensive	**93**
		VALUE
Harrah's; (702) 369-5000		**B**

Strip   Zone I

Customers: Locals and tourists	**Friendliness rating:** ★★★★★
Reservations: Requested	**Parking:** Valet, lot
When to go: Avoid conventions	**Bar:** Full service
Entrée range: $18.95–market price	**Wine selection:** Very good
Payment: VISA, MC, AMEX, DC	**Dress:** Upscale casual
Service rating: ★★★★	**Disabled access:** Elevator

Dinner: Sunday–Thursday, 5:30–10:30 p.m.; Friday and Saturday, 5:30–11:30 p.m.; bar open until 2 a.m.

Setting & atmosphere: Enter the glass-enclosed elevator to the second floor, and the adventure begins. The blue sky turns to sunset by the time the restaurant comes into view. Range's tiered dining room (three levels) affords every table a splendid view of the Strip. The decor is a fine mix of rough-hewn wood and polished copper and brass with splashes of forest colors.

House specialties: Steaks; slow-roasted prime rib; veal, beef, pork, and lamb chops; the signature swordfish; lobster, shrimp, and Alaskan king crab legs; free-range chicken; a bone-in filet mignon. Signature dishes are marked on the menu with the Range brand.

Summary & comments: Harrah's has undergone a dramatic change. No sign of the former hotel remains. The Range is a prime example of the direction the hotel has taken. An elegant lounge and bar serves light snacks. An ideal spot for viewing the action on the Strip.

RED SQUARE		★★★½

American/"Russian"	Expensive	QUALITY
		87
Mandalay Bay; (702) 632-7777		VALUE
Strip Zone 1		**C**

Customers: Locals and tourists	Parking: Valet, garage
Reservations: Suggested on weekends	Bar: Full service
When to go: Anytime	Wine selection: Vodka's the drink
Entrée range: $19–36	here
Payment: VISA, MC, AMEX, DC	Dress: Casual
Service rating: ★★★★	Disabled access: Ground floor
Friendliness rating: ★★★★	

Dinner: Every night, 5:30 p.m.–midnight; bar open Sunday–Thursday until 2 a.m. and until 4 a.m. Friday and Saturday

Setting & atmosphere: More American than Russian, this comfy dining room with "Russian inspired" decor and a large bar with a top that's partly a slab of ice is neat.

House specialties: Updated Russian classics: Stroganoff; chicken Kiev and caviar; rack of lamb; crab and arugula angel hair pasta; Chilean sea bass.

Other recommendations: The frozen-ice bar offers more than 100 frozen vodkas and infusions, plus martinis and Russian-inspired cocktails.

Summary & comments: Another winning concept from the China Grill creators. There are some dining limits, ask when you make your reservation.

REDWOOD BAR & GRILL ★★★½

	QUALITY
American/Prime Rib Moderate	89
	VALUE
	A

California Hotel.; (702) 385-1222
Downtown   Zone 2

Customers: Tourists, locals
Reservations: Suggested
When to go: Early evening
Entrée range: $12.95–40.95
Payment: VISA, MC, AMEX, DC, D
Service rating: ★★★★

Friendliness rating: ★★★★★
Parking: Hotel lot and valet
Bar: Full service
Wine selection: Good
Dress: Informal
Disabled access: Ground floor

Dinner: Every day, 5:30–11 p.m.

Setting & atmosphere: Country English furnishings and a fireplace make for comfortable dining. A quiet room where service is efficient and gracious.

House specialties: Caesar salad; steak Diane; chicken with apricot sauce. Porterhouse steak special: 16 ounces for $12.95 includes soup or salad, potatoes, vegetable, dessert.

Other recommendations: Soup du jour such as seafood chowder; Australian lobster tail; fresh fish; roast prime rib; veal Oscar; steak and lobster.

Entertainment & amenities: Piano music nightly.

Summary & comments: Excellent value. Prime rib portion is succulent, generous, and cooked as ordered. Although part of a locally owned group of five hotels, the Redwood Bar & Grill maintains its cozy individuality in both decor and service. Outstanding value.

RENOIR ★★★★★

	QUALITY
French/American Very Expensive	98
	VALUE
	C

Mirage; (702) 791-7111
Strip   Zone 1

Customers: Locals and visitors
Reservations: A must
When to go: Whenever a reservation
   is available
Entrée range: $35–80
Payment: VISA, MC, AMEX, DC
Service rating: ★★★★★

Friendliness rating: ★★★★★
Parking: Valet; garage
Bar: Full service
Wine selection: Excellent
Dress: Jackets required for men
Disabled access: Ramp

Dinner: Tuesday–Sunday, 6–10 p.m.; closed Mondays.

Setting & atmosphere: Exquisite silk fabrics, brightly colored tapestries, and rich wood are a perfect foil for Renoir and art by other French impressionist painters. A most romantic setting.

House specialties: A superb braised shortrib without a drop of fat served with a red wine sauce you won't believe; slow-baked salmon; cream of lobster soup with wild mushrooms and lobster fricassee; Napoleon of house-smoked salmon with ahi tuna and osetra caviar.

Other recommendations: Cave Creek escargots with roasted garlic ravioli; tenderloin of veal; a five-course tasting menu; any one of the irresistible desserts.

Summary & comments: Flawless food and service in a divine setting, yet it's not terribly pretentious. A genuinely welcoming staff adds to the charm and your comfort level. Overall, Renoir offers a high-ticket meal, but then it *is* exceptional dining.

RICARDO'S		★★★½

Mexican	Moderate	QUALITY
		85
4930 W. Flamingo Rd.; (702) 871-7119		VALUE
Southwest Zone 3		**B**

2380 E. Tropicana Ave.; (702) 798-4515
Southeast   Zone 5

MGM Grand; (702) 736-4970
Strip   Zone 1

Customers: Locals	Friendliness rating: ★★★★
Reservations: Accepted	Parking: Lots at all locations
When to go: Any time	Bar: Full service
Entrée range: $5–16	Wine selection: Good
Payment: VISA, MC, AMEX, CB, DC, D	Dress: Informal, casual
Service rating: ★★★	Disabled access: At all locations

Lunch & dinner: Same menu day and evening, all locations.

At West Flamingo Road: Friday–Saturday, 11 a.m.–11 p.m.; Monday–Thursday, 11 a.m.–10 p.m.

At East Tropicana Avenue: Monday–Thursday, 11 a.m.–10 p.m.; Friday–Saturday, 11 a.m.–11 p.m.

At MGM Grand: Every day, 11 a.m.–11 p.m.; until 2:30 a.m. Fridays and Saturdays (with entertainment)

Setting & atmosphere: Attractive Mexican decor at each location, especially nice at the MGM Grand.

House specialties: Good selection of appetizers to complement margaritas. Chimichanga ranchera; enchiladas rancheras; chicken picado; sizzling camarones al diablo; steak cilantro verde. A separate taco bar is an added feature at the MGM Grand.

Other recommendations: Albondigas soup, thick with vegetables; taco-enchilada combinations; chili Colorado; chili relleno; burritos. Lunch buffet at West Flamingo and East Tropicana locations Monday–Saturday from 11 a.m.–2 p.m.—all you can eat for $6.75.

Summary & comments: Although all the restaurants are operated by the same owners, each restaurant has its own distinctive flavor and specials. The MGM Grand branch is colorful and fun.

RISTORANTE ITALIANO		★★★½
		QUALITY
Italian	Expensive	**91**
		VALUE
Riviera Hotel; (702) 734-5110		**C**
Strip Zone 1		

Customers: Tourists, some locals	Parking: Garage lot, valet
Reservations: Recommended	Bar: Full service
When to go: Any time	Wine selection: Good choice of both
Entrée range: $12–40	reds and whites
Payment: VISA, MC, AMEX, CB, DC, D	Dress: Business casual
Service rating: ★★★★	Disabled access: Casino level
Friendliness rating: ★★★★	

Dinner: Friday–Tuesday, 5:30–10 p.m.; Wednesday and Thursday, closed.

Setting & atmosphere: Soft lighting highlights Italian Mediterranean murals. Richly upholstered booths line the walls.

House specialties: Pasta rolls with ricotta cheese, spinach, prosciutto, and mozzarella baked in a mushroom cream sauce; vermicelli salsa bella vista; melanzane al caprino; costolete di vitello and gorgonzola. Ristorante special dessert—grilled eggplant stuffed with mascarpone cheese, rolled in pistachio nuts, heated and topped with liqueur-flavored sauce.

Other recommendations: Squid-ink lasagna layered with salmon mousse and scallop mousse, spinach, and ricotta served in creamy pink sauce; rack of lamb roasted with fresh garlic, rosemary, and mustard; breast of chicken saltimbocca; sautéed swordfish on a bed of fettuccini with olives, sun-dried tomatoes, capers, and white wine sauce with herbs; vermicelli tutto di mare alla ristorante.

Summary & comments: Opened in 1975, the Ristorante is a favorite of many of the stars who have appeared at the hotel. Menu includes contemporary dishes as well as a good classic Italian selection. A private dining room, which is warm and inviting, is available for small parties.

ROSEWOOD GRILLE ★★★½

Lobster/Steak	Expensive	QUALITY
		88

3339 Las Vegas Blvd., S.; (702) 792-9099	VALUE
Strip Zone 1	C+

Customers: Tourists	Service rating: ★★★★
Reservations: Strongly recommended	Friendliness rating: ★★★★
When to go: Any time	Parking: Lot behind restaurant
Entrée range: $18.50–29.50,	Bar: Full service
higher for lobster and stone crab	Wine selection: Excellent
Payment: VISA, MC, AMEX, DC, D,	Dress: Informal
JCB	Disabled access: Ground floor

Dinner: Every day, 4:30–11:30 p.m.

Setting & atmosphere: Muted lighting, large booths, seating for 200. This always-busy restaurant still retains its Old World charm.

House specialties: Live Maine lobster in humongous sizes. Dinner includes salad and potatoes.

Other recommendations: Lobster and steak combination; beef chop; beef-eaters brochette; scampi; stone crabs; broiled salmon Charlotte; tournedos Scandia; lobster ravioli; chicken with strawberries in Cointreau. Strawberries with Dom Perignon for two; café Mozart.

Summary & comments: Restaurant stocks a week's supply of large and extra-large lobsters (up to 25 pounds). Price (three-pound minimum) changes with the market. Lobster prices are typically $17–22 per pound, depending on availability.

RUMJUNGLE ★★★½

Brazilian rodizio/nightclub	Moderate/Expensive	QUALITY
		87

Mandalay Bay; (702) 632-7408	VALUE
Strip Zone 1	C

Customers: Boomers and Gen-Xers
Reservations: Suggested for dinner
When to go: Anytime
Entrée range: $25–36 (rodizio, $36)
Payment: VISA, MC, AMEX, DC, D
Service rating: ★★★½
Friendliness rating: ★★★★★

Parking: Valet, garage
Bar: Full service
Wine selection: Small
Dress: No overly funky clothes, no
  hats. A blazer or collared shirt
  must be worn with jeans.
Disabled access: No

Dinner: Monday–Thursday, 5:30–11 p.m.; Friday and Saturday, 5:30 p.m. to last seating (usually 9 p.m.)

Setting & atmosphere: Wild jungle-like setting with soaring ceilings, an open fire pit, and a wall of fire. This place really rocks, though dinner hours are less frenetic.

House specialties: Unlimited quantities of meat, fish, and poultry with many accompaniments and sauces for a fixed price. The cost is about half the adult price for kids ages 12 and under.

Other recommendations: À la carte appetizers—Jamaican spiced chicken skewers; coconut shrimp; jerk spiced chicken wings and bahamian conch fritters; Honolulu Caesar salad; banana leaf seabass; baby back pork ribs.

Summary & comments: There are so many rules and restrictions here, you need a guide to get you through without mishap. On weekends, parties of eight or more have two hours in which to dine. There is a cover charge after 11 p.m. Still, rumjungle is a cool spot for the younger (but over 21) set who find the dancing fire wall and pulsating dance floor a kick.

RUTH'S CHRIS STEAK HOUSE ★★★★

Steak	Expensive	QUALITY
		94
		VALUE
		C

3900 Paradise Rd.; (702) 791-7011
Strip   Zone 1
4561 W. Flamingo Rd.; (702) 248-7011
Southwest   Zone 5

Customers: Tourists, locals
Reservations: A must
When to go: Nonconvention times
Entrée range: $18.95–65
Payment: VISA, MC, AMEX, DC, D, JCB
Service rating: ★★★★★

Friendliness rating: ★★★★★
Parking: Lot
Bar: Full service
Wine selection: Excellent
Dress: Informal
Disabled access: Ground floor

Lunch: *Paradise:* Monday–Friday, 11 a.m.–4:30 p.m.
Dinner: *Paradise:* Every day, 4:30–10:30 p.m.; *Flamingo:* 4:30 p.m.–3 a.m.

Setting & atmosphere: Plush with dark cherry woods and beveled glass windows. Comfortable cocktail lounge.

House specialties: Prime steak, cooked to order and served sizzling with butter (steaks may be ordered dry).

Other recommendations: Besides excellent steaks, the restaurant offers veal chops, lamb chops, fresh salmon, and an outstanding variety of potatoes and vegetables. The Lyonnais and hash brown potatoes are addictive.

Summary & comments: Wine selection includes Dom Perignon and Louis Roederer Cristal, in the $100- to $300-per-bottle category. Ruth's Chris serves only prime beef. The check for two, however, can be steep; everything is à la carte, but portions are large enough to be shared. There is no service charge for sharing. The new Proprietor's Reserve private dining room can seat up to 45. There's a new, attractive garden room at the Paradise location. A late-night supper menu is available at the Flamingo location along with entertainment from 10 p.m.—mostly jazz, some pop classics.

SAM WOO BAR-B-Q   ★★★

Chinese Barbecue	Inexpensive	QUALITY
		89

		VALUE
Chinatown Mall, 4215 Spring Mountain Rd.; (702) 368-7628 Southwest Zone 3		A

Customers: Asian community, locals, tourists	Friendliness rating: ★★★½
	Parking: Large lot
Reservations: No	Bar: None
When to go: Any time	Wine selection: None
Entrée range: $4.50–8.95	Dress: Anything goes
Payment: Cash only	Disabled access: Ground floor
Service rating: ★★★½	

Lunch & dinner: Every day, 10 a.m.–5 a.m. Take-out barbecue shop: Every day, 10 a.m.–10 p.m.

Setting & atmosphere: Enter Sam Woo and enjoy the sights of meats and whole ducks hanging from hooks in the glass holding case. To the left is the popular take-out barbecue counter; to the right, a spacious good-sized restaurant. No frills, but pleasant.

House specialties: Any of the barbecued foods—roast pork, spare ribs, duck, and chicken; the Sam Woo combination plate is an exceptional value—the large platter is heaped high with roast and barbecued pork, roast duck, and chicken. Vegetable dishes are outstanding and inexpensive. The extensive menu is filled with an interesting selection of dishes, including hot pots that are cooked at the table.

Summary & comments: Very little English is spoken here, but the menu is in English. Service is good but can be brusque when the restaurant is busy. Take it in stride. Sam Woo is one of the best values in a town filled with them.

SAMBA GRILL		★★★★
Brazilian steakhouse	Moderate	**QUALITY** 90
		VALUE A

Mirage; (702) 791-7111
Strip   Zone 1

Customers: Locals, tourists	Friendliness rating: ★★★★★
Reservations: Recommended	Parking: Valet, garage
When to go: Any time	Bar: Full service
Entrée range: Prix fixe, $28.95; à la carte, $20–40	Wine selection: Good
	Dress: Dressy casual
Payment: All major credit cards	Disabled access: Ground floor, ramp
Service rating: ★★★★	

Dinner: Every day, 5:30–10:15 p.m.(last seating)

Setting & atmosphere: Vibrant colors and colorful booths and appointments capture the theme of this Brazilian steakhouse. Remember Fiesta chinaware? The same palette of colors is found here.

House specialties: The Rodizio Experience: unlimited servings of marinated meats, poultry, and fish for a fixed price. Dinners include a bottomless bowl of Samba salad, side dishes of creamed spinach, black beans and rice, fried bananas (plantains), Cuban-style potatoes, and a basket of authentic Brazilian breads. À la carte selections include the side dishes.

Other recommendations: À la carte appetizers, especially Nuestra duck tamales and awesome coconut prawns; freshly made juices by the glass or pitcher—mango, passion fruit, grapefruit, and orange. The delectable rice pudding laced with fresh pineapple, and a huge banana split for two that could easily serve four.

Summary & comments: The jewel-like bar is a nice place for a drink and appetizers. Samba Grill is a terrific new restaurant with prices right out of Old Las Vegas.

SAZIO		★★★½

Italian	Moderate	QUALITY
		89

		VALUE
Orleans Hotel, Valley View and Arville; (702) 948-9501		**A**
Southwest Zone 3		

Customers: Locals, visitors	Payment: All major credit cards
Reservations: Accepted	Parking: Valet, garage, lot
When to go: Anytime	Bar: Full service
Friendliness rating: ★★★★★	Wine selection: Limited
Service rating: ★★★★	Dress: Casual
Entrée range: $8.95–14.95	Disabled access: Ramp

Lunch: Daily, 11 a.m.–4 p.m.

Dinner: Daily, 11 a.m.–11 p.m.

Setting & atmosphere: Large framed "paintings" in the style of Andy Warhol dominate the various dining rooms. Featured are likenesses of local movers and shakers. Retro ceiling lights cast beams of color. Comfortable booths circle the rooms; stylish chairs and tables, complete the sleek design.

House specialities: Spit-roasted loin of pork, lightly seasoned with rosemary and garlic; spit-roasted chicken Diablo, brushed with hot mustard, herbed bread crumbs and a peppercorn sauce add more zip. Sicilian Caprese salad— generous slices of tender, fresh mozzarella and roasted peppers Siciliano, topped with garlic bread crumbs—the roasted peppers can be ordered separately; Tuscan-style mussels, a generous portion for a small price; swordfish picatta, topped with lemon, herbs and capers is another tasty dish. Apple crumble à la mode and the chocolate lovin' spooncake for dessert. (Desserts are the only weakness on the menu.)

Summary & comments: Sazio is a terrific value. Food may be ordered solo, sized for one person, or grandioso, family-style platters that can easily satisfy three to four eaters. Solo portions are equally generous, especially the spit-roasted pork. Wines are priced right, too. This is Old Las Vegas revisited. Nothing fancy, just good tasty food at affordable prices, in a most pleasant setting.

SEASONS		★★★★

Continental	Very Expensive	QUALITY
		90

		VALUE
Bally's; (702) 739-4111		**D**
Strip Zone 1		

Customers: Tourists	Friendliness rating: ★★★★
Reservations: Required	Parking: Valet, hotel lot
When to go: Any time	Bar: Full service
Entrée range: $20–60	Wine selection: Excellent
Payment: VISA, MC, AMEX, DC, D	Dress: Sport coat, dressy
Service rating: ★★★★	Disabled access: Ramps

Dinner: Tuesday–Saturday, 6–11 p.m.; Sunday and Monday, closed.

Setting & atmosphere: Marie Antoinette would have been at home in this exquisite room.

House specialties: Fresh fish prepared in imaginative ways; roast duckling Grand Marnier; lobster in light crayfish sauce with smoked salmon mousse.

Other recommendations: Seasonal appetizers such as sea scallops on a bed of spinach with pine nuts and pear vinegar. Grilled chicken breast in hazelnut sauce; chateaubriand bordelaise for two with cabernet sauvignon sauce and potato soufflés. Strawberries Romanoff; crème brûlée; seasonal coffees.

Summary & comments: Bally's featured gourmet room. Menu reflects today's demand for lighter, healthier dining. Menu changes four times a year to include seasonal specialties. A new French chef is making waves with the menu; it's lighter and more varied.

SIR GALAHAD'S ★★★½

		QUALITY
Prime rib	Moderate	**89**
		VALUE
		A

Excalibur; (702) 597-7777
Strip   Zone I

Customers: Tourists, locals	When to go: Less crowded weekdays
Reservations: Suggested	Entrée range: $17–40
Payment: VISA, MC, AMEX, DC, D	Bar: Full service
Service rating: ★★★★	Wine selection: Good
Friendliness rating: ★★★★	Dress: Casual
Parking: Large lot, valet, garage	Disabled access: Elevators

Dinner: Sunday–Thursday, 5–10 p.m. (last seating); Friday and Saturday, 5–11 p.m. (last seating)

Setting & atmosphere: English castle; wait staff in costume of days of King Arthur. Prime rib served from large, gleaming steel and copper cart. Sliced to order by skilled carvers tableside.

House specialties: Prime rib, prime rib, and prime rib served with beef barley soup or a garden salad, plus mashed potatoes, creamed spinach, and whipped cream horseradish.

Other recommendations: Appetizers such as mushrooms Cliffs of Dover. Chicken à la reine; fresh fish of the day.

Summary & comments: Prime rib plus Yorkshire pudding, creamed spinach, mashed potatoes, and beef barley soup or green salad is a very hearty meal. Top it off, if you can, with English trifle or mud pie.

SPAGO		★★★★★	
American	Moderate/Expensive	**QUALITY**	96
The Forum Shops at Caesars Palace; (702) 369-6300		**VALUE**	C
Strip Zone 1			

Customers: Tourists, locals	Service rating: ★★★★
Reservations: Recommended for dinner; not accepted for lunch	Friendliness rating: ★★★★★
When to go: Any time except during busy conventions	Parking: Garage, valet
	Bar: Full service
Entrée range: $16–25 in the café; $25–36 in the dining room	Wine selection: Excellent
	Dress: Informal, casual
Payment: VISA, MC, AMEX, DC, D	Disabled access: Ground floor

Lunch & dinner: *Café:* Every day, 11 a.m.–11 p.m.
Dinner: *Restaurant:* Every day, 6–9:30 p.m.

Setting & atmosphere: There are two separate dining rooms. The casual café offers a fine bird's-eye view of The Forum Shops from the comfort of a European-styled sidewalk setting. The restaurant inside is an eclectic mix of modern art, wrought iron, and contemporary tables and chairs and booths. Each Sunday in the café from about 2:30 p.m. to 6:30 p.m., a jazz band entertains. A private banquet room is available for parties up to 100. A small private room within the restaurant can seat up to 20.

House specialties: *Café*—Wolfgang Puck's signature pizzas; imaginative sandwiches on homemade bread; salads; pastas; and frequently, a super-tasty meat loaf with port wine sauce, grilled onions, and garlic potato puree. *Restaurant*—exquisite appetizers; pastas; grilled veal chop with dried cherry-wild rice and sage hollandaise; big-eye tuna with couscous; salmon encrusted with almonds and ginger. Menus in the café and restaurant change daily. Desserts are sensational.

Summary & comments: Wolfgang Puck's first venture outside California is an instant success. Puck surrounds himself with the best staff, the best ingredients, the best of everything. One caveat—on very busy nights the dining room noise level can make conversation difficult, but the people-watching is terrific.

STAR CANYON		★★★½
		QUALITY
Southwestern	Moderate/Expensive	**89**
		VALUE
Venetian Hotel; phone (702) 414-3772		**B**

Strip   Zone 1

Customers: Tourists, locals
Reservations: Required for dinner
When to go: Any time except during conventions
Entrée range: $22–65
Payment: VISA, MC, AMEX, DC, D
Service rating: ★★★★

Friendliness rating: ★★★★★
Parking: Garage, valet
Bar: Full service
Wine selection: Good
Dress: Business casual
Disabled access: Ground floor

Breakfast: Every day, 8–11 a.m.

Lunch: Every day, 11:30 a.m.–2:30 p.m.

Dinner: Sunday–Thursday, 5:30–10 p.m.; Friday and Saturday, 6–11 p.m.

Setting & atmosphere: Texas through and through. The handsome dining room has a "branded" ceiling, open kitchen, and many fine appointments, but it's relaxed and comfortable. Previous owner Stephan Pyles, a home-grown Texan, was one of the first to showcase the dishes of the southwest. Let's hope the new owner carries on the tradition.

House specialties: The Texas-style breakfasts (and the traditional break-fasts) with such southwestern specialties as cowboy omelettes and Star Canyon Benedict with chipolte mayonnaise; salads that are meals—try the Texas gulf coast crab and marinated bean salad with ruby red grapefruit; or the clayuda—a flour tortilla Texas pizza. At dinner, have a fried green tomato salad or a zesty tamale tart.

Other recommendations: Bone-in cowboy rib eye with pinto bean–wild mushroom ragout; oak-smoked prime rib; spit-roasted chicken; or fennel-crusted salmon. For dessert, try the award-winning Heaven and Hell cake.

Summary & comments: Everything from omelettes to barbecued beef sandwiches to wood-roasted Maine lobster gets equal attention. Be adventur-ous—watch the chefs at work by requesting a table near the open kitchen.

THE STEAK HOUSE   ★★★½

		QUALITY
Steak	Moderate	86

	VALUE
Circus Circus; (702) 734-0410	B

Strip   Zone 1

Customers: Locals, tourists
Reservations: Required
When to go: Weekdays
Entrée range: $17–46; $10.95 for
   children, $21.95 for adults
   (brunch)
Payment: VISA, MC, AMEX, CB, DC, D

Service rating: ★★★★
Friendliness rating: ★★★★
Parking: Garage, lot, valet
Bar: Full service
Wine selection: Good
Dress: Informal
Disabled access: Ramps

Brunch: Sunday, 9:30 a.m.–3:30 p.m.

Dinner: Monday–Friday, 5–11 p.m.; Saturday, 5 p.m.–midnight

Setting & atmosphere: Wood-paneled rooms. The small dining room is
decorated like a manor-house library. A mesquite-fired broiler in center of
main room creates a cozy atmosphere. Glass refrigerator case displays over
3,000 pounds of aging meat.

House specialties: Thick steaks; black bean soup; giant baked potato.

Other recommendations: Shrimp, crab, and lobster cocktails; Caesar salad;
grilled chicken.

Summary & comments: Consistently high quality and service. Don't be
fooled by the children running around the lobby. Inside the Steak House,
the atmosphere is adult and the food is wonderful. Plan ahead to dine here.
Reservations are a must.

STEFANO'S   ★★★★

		QUALITY
Southern Italian	Moderate/Expensive	94

	VALUE
Golden Nugget; (702) 385-7111	C

Downtown   Zone 2

Customers: Tourists, locals
Reservations: Required
When to go: Nonconvention times
Entrée range: $15–30
Payment: VISA, MC, AMEX, CB, DC, D
Service rating: ★★★★

Friendliness rating: ★★★★
Parking: Garage, valet
Bar: Full service
Wine selection: Very good
Dress: Sport coat
Disabled access: Elevators

Dinner: Sunday–Thursday, 6–10:30 p.m.; Friday and Saturday, 5:30–10:30 p.m.

Setting & atmosphere: A bright room with hand-decorated cabinetry, custom tile and Venetian chandeliers. Italian murals grace the walls.

House specialties: Agnolotti, fresh mussels; veal scallopini Stefano (with prosciutto, asparagus, and mozzarella); chicken Sorrentino; osso buco; veal chop with porcini mushrooms and mascarpone cheese.

Other recommendations: Roasted peppers; carpaccio; cioppino; capellini frutti di mare; fresh fish; daily specials. Chocolate pasta with vanilla ice cream, almonds, strawberries, and honey sauce; crème brûlée; tiramisu.

Entertainment & amenities: The staff breaks into classical Italian songs throughout the meal. You will, too.

Summary & comments: Dishes presented with flair. A happy dining experience.

SWISS CAFÉ		★★★½
		QUALITY
European	Moderate	89
		VALUE
3250 E. Tropicana Ave.; (702) 454-2270		B

Southeast   Zone 5

Customers: Locals, conventioneers	$15.95–24.95 (dinner)
Reservations: A must at dinner, not accepted for lunch	Payment: VISA, MC, AMEX
When to go: Early lunch; weeknights, dinner	Service rating: ★★★
	Friendliness rating: ★★★★★
Entrée range: $8–13 (lunch);	Parking: Shopping-center lot
Bar: Full service	Dress: Informal
Wine selection: Fair	Disabled access: Ground floor

Lunch: Monday–Friday, 11 a.m.–2:30 p.m.

Dinner: Monday–Saturday, 5–10 p.m.

Setting & atmosphere: Swiss collectibles fill the restaurant; pepper mills, antique kitchenware, and plants make for a charming Old World setting.

House specialties: Duck salad; schnitzel, a variety of veal dishes; nightly specials; Veal Zurich, scallopini with herb sauce; steak Diane prepared with a New York strip; tournedos in the style of the Café de Paris; duck with orange or raspberry sauce. Sauces are well seasoned. Entrée price includes salad and a vegetable medley; handmade apple strudel, baked by a Viennese friend of the owners.

Other recommendations: The newly added steaks, pork chops, and veal chops.

Summary & comments: Chef-owner Wolfgang and his wife-partner, Mary, welcome everyone. The affable couple have a devoted local following. Specials change daily and are listed on a blackboard.

TERRAZZA ★★★★½

Italian	Expensive	QUALITY
		95

	VALUE
Caesars Palace; (702) 731-7110	C+
Strip Zone 1	

Customers: Tourists and locals	Friendliness rating: ★★★★★
Reservations: A must	Parking: Valet, garage
When to go: Avoid conventions	Bar: Full service
Entrée range: $17–36	Wine selection: Excellent
Payment: VISA, MC, AMEX, DC, CB, D	Dress: Business attire
Service rating: ★★★★½	Disabled access: Ground floor

Dinner: Every day, 5:30–10:30 p.m.

Setting & atmosphere: Italian rustic design carried throughout the various dining rooms, each with its own unique decor. Terrazza's design is open and inviting. An outdoor patio for warm weather dining gives a splendid view of the new Palace Tower and the grand swimming pools. A wood-burning pizza oven, visible from the entrance, is as beautiful as the dining rooms.

House specialties: Fat, homemade pappardelle pasta with wild mushrooms and truffle oil; risottos that change each day; rack of lamb, Roman-style; a succulent pan-fried veal chop; thin, crisp focaccia filled with robiola cheese and drizzled with truffle oil; seared salmon with a light mustard sauce. Desserts: Triestine-style chocolate mousse with zabaglione; warm mascarpone tortine with coffee ice cream; Italian blood orange flan with pear, Barolo, and assorted berries.

Other recommendations: Any of the seasonal daily specials.

Summary & comments: Terrazza in the new Palace Tower has replaced the older Primavera. The main dining room is adjacent to Terrazza's lounge, where diners may have a before-dinner drink and a variety of pizzas and focaccia. Restaurants in the Palace Tower offer elegant dining away from the din of the casino.

TERU SUSHI ★★★½

		QUALITY
Sushi	Moderate/Expensive	**89**
		VALUE
		C

700 E. Sahara Ave.; (702) 734-6655
Strip   Zone I

Customers: Asian community, locals, tourists
Reservations: Not necessary
When to go: Any time
Entrée range: $6–30
Payment: VISA, MC, AMEX
Service rating: ★★★½

Friendliness rating: ★★★½
Parking: Street and lot
Bar: None
Wine selection: Minimal
Dress: Casual
Disabled access: Ground floor

Dinner: Monday–Saturday, 5–11 p.m.; closed Sunday.

Setting & atmosphere: Small store-front restaurant with a large sushi bar. A restaurant in the true tradition of sushi. Servers are kimono-clad. Japanese screens and art add a little bit of color.

House specialties: Sushi is king. Everything from sea urchin to flying fish–egg sushi is available. With the small dishes and combination plates, including a side of tempura or chicken teriyaki, diners can create a traditional Japanese meal. Two sushi combination plates and a beautiful sashimi combination. Teru Sushi specializes in seasonal fresh fish and vegetable dishes. The soft-shelled crab is a delight. Udon or soba noodles, usually eaten at the end of the meal.

Summary & comments: Sushi-quality fish is the best, and here it is priced accordingly. Portions are Japanese-style—small. It takes many dishes to satisfy hearty appetites and can be costly. The selection at Teru Sushi is excellent.

THE TILLERMAN ★★★½

		QUALITY
Seafood	Moderate/Expensive	**87**
		VALUE
		C

2245 E. Flamingo Rd.; (702) 731-4036
Southeast   Zone 5

Customers: Tourists, locals
Reservations: Requested
When to go: Early evening
Entrée range: $19–49
Payment: VISA, MC, AMEX, DC, D
Service rating: ★★★★

Friendliness rating: ★★★★
Parking: Lot
Bar: Full service
Wine selection: Excellent
Dress: Informal, casual
Disabled access: Ramp

Dinner: Sunday–Thursday, 5–10 p.m.; Friday and Saturday, 5–11 p.m.

Setting & atmosphere: Attractive, airy main dining room with balcony seating. Hanging plants, wood paneling, beautiful live trees. Menu presented on scroll. Servers memorize orders without taking any notes. Ten to 15 fresh fish listed daily.

House specialties: Seafood fresh from California, the Gulf of Mexico, the Atlantic. Pacific salmon, Chilean sea bass, Florida snapper.

Other recommendations: Prime steaks; Tillerman pasta Portofino. Fresh homemade pastries.

Summary & comments: One of the most popular Las Vegas seafood restaurants. A new owner has made many improvements. For the first time since opening, the Tillerman accepts reservations.

Honors & awards: *Wine Spectator* Award of Excellence for many years.

TOKYO		★★★½

Japanese/Sushi	Moderate	QUALITY
		85
Commercial Center, 953 E. Sahara Ave.; (702) 735-7070		VALUE
Strip Zone 1		**B**

Customers: Locals, tourists
Reservations: Accepted
When to go: Any time
Entrée range: $11.75–24.95
Payment: VISA, MC, AMEX, DC, D, JCB
Service rating: ★★★★

Friendliness rating: ★★★★
Parking: Large lot
Bar: Full service
Wine selection: Fair
Dress: Informal, casual
Disabled access: Ground floor

Dinner: Every day, 5–10 p.m.

Setting & atmosphere: Newly decorated interior—tatami room, sushi bar.

House specialties: Small hibachi grills for those who wish to cook their own dinner. Shabu shabu also available.

Other recommendations: Combination, special, and deluxe dinners, all modestly priced; a wide selection is available.

Summary & comments: A family-run restaurant—very popular with the locals. Tokyo has been enlarged to include party and catering facilities.

TOP OF THE WORLD ★★★½

		QUALITY
American	Expensive	85

		VALUE
		C

Stratosphere Tower:; (702) 380-7711
Strip   Zone 1

Customers: Tourists, locals	Friendliness rating: ★★★★
Reservations: Required	Parking: Valet, garage, and lot
When to go: Any time	Bar: Full service
Entrée range: $25–50	Wine selection: Excellent
Payment: VISA, MC, AMEX, DC, D	Dress: Dressy casual
Service rating: ★★★★★	Disabled access: Elevator

Dinner: Sunday–Thursday, 6–11 p.m.; Friday and Saturday, 6 p.m.– midnight.

Setting & atmosphere: Without question, Top of the World offers the most beautiful view of the city. The restaurant revolves as you dine, giving a panoramic spectacle of the surrounding mountains. The dining room is handsomely designed with inlaid tables, fine woods and brass, and copper accents. There are no bad tables.

House specialties: San Francisco–style cioppino; chicken quesadilla soup; char-broiled portobello mushrooms with Marsala demi-glace; Sonoma Valley rack of lamb; Santa Fe–style rotisserie chicken.

Other recommendations: Tequila-lime shrimp, served on a bed of linguini; almond-crusted salmon; the towering vacherin dessert; the signature bread pudding made with egg bread.

Summary & comments: The food is secondary to the view, which is simply spectacular, but the food is very good. Arrive before sunset and watch one of the best free shows. Be aware there is a $15 food minimum. It's an easy amount to reach in this strictly à la carte room. The fine service and the view enhance any meal.

TRATTORIA DEL LUPO ★★★★

		QUALITY
Italian	Moderate/Expensive	90

		VALUE
		B+

Mandalay Bay; (702) 740-5522
Strip   Zone 1

Customers: Locals, tourists
Reservations: Suggested
When to go: Anytime
Entrée range: $11–16 (lunch)
    $18–38 (dinner)
Payment: All major credit cards
Service rating: ★★★★

Friendliness rating: ★★★★★
Parking: Valet, garage
Bar: Full service
Wine selection: Good
Dress: Dressy casual
Disabled access: Through casino

Hours: Lunch: 11:30 a.m.–5 p.m.

Dinner: 5–11 p.m. Sunday–Thursday; Friday and Saturday 5 p.m.–midnight

Setting & atmosphere: Designed by the renowned restaurant specialist, Adam Tihany, Lupo features laid-back Italian rustic decor with vaulted ceilings, an open exhibition kitchen and a handsome bar for imbibing or dining as the centerpiece of the dining room.

House specialties: Prosciutto-wrapped monkfish with artichokes peas and fava beans, seared Tuscan-style porterhouse steak with caramelized fennel and lemon. The marvelous breads and pizzas; homemade charcuterie, pastas grilled fish and meats. Heavenly desserts.

Summary & comments: Yet another winner for Wolfgang Puck. Executive chef Mark Ferguson came to Lupo from Spago after a tour of Italy. His spin on such classic dishes as the Tuscan porterhouse is super. The bar attracts local brokers who like nothing better than to observe the scene from the lofty barstools. Noisy and energetic, Lupo is a cool dining place.

VENETIAN		★★★½
Italian	Moderate/Expensive	**QUALITY** 87
3713 W. Sahara Ave.; (702) 876-4190 Southwest Zone 3		**VALUE** B

Customers: Locals, tourists
Reservations: Accepted
When to go: Any time
Entrée range: $12–35
Payment: VISA, MC, AMEX, DC, D
Service rating: ★★★★★

Friendliness rating: ★★★★★
Parking: Large lot
Bar: Full service
Wine selection: Outstanding
Dress: Casual, informal
Disabled access: Ground floor

Open: Every day, 24 hours (dinner, 4–11 p.m.).

Setting & atmosphere: This landmark eatery changed owners a few years ago, at which time they lightened the decor and updated the dining room.

House specialties: Specialty homemade breads such as bruschetta, garlic, and tomato-and-mozzarella. Hearty dinners with a good selection of pastas.

The grilled veal chop is a favorite. Unique to the Venetian, and very popular, are the sautéed greens and the pork neckbones marinated in wine. Chilled roasted eggplant; pasta with cream sauce and lemon zest.

Other recommendations: The baked halibut, shrimp à la pizzaiola, and shrimp à la bianco are excellent, as are the veal scallopini picante, pizzaiola, and marsala; and the chicken cacciatore and chicken breast dore. The early dining menu, served nightly from 4 p.m. to 6 p.m., is moderately priced.

Summary & comments: Portions are generous, and the menu is extensive. Longtime diners are hoping it remains that way. Some changes in the menu are inevitable, but nothing major. All the favorite dishes remain; many new ones have been added, including a selection of steaks and chops.

VIVA MERCADO'S ★★★½

		QUALITY
Mexican	Moderate	**86**
		VALUE
6128 W. Flamingo Rd.; (702) 871-8826		**A**

Southwest   Zone 3

Town Center (adjacent to Barley's Sunset); (702) 435-6200
Southeast   Zone 5

Customers: Locals
Reservations: Accepted
When to go: Any time; the lunch
 hour is very busy
Entrée range: $7.95–18.95
Payment: VISA, MC, AMEX, D
Service rating: ★★★★★

Friendliness rating ★★★★★
Parking: Shopping-center lot
Bar: Full service
Wine selection: Good
Dress: Casual
Disabled access: Ground floor

Lunch & dinner: Same menu day and evening, all locations.

At West Flamingo Road: Sunday–Thursday, 11 a.m.–9:30 p.m.;
Friday–Saturday, 11 a.m.–10:30 p.m.

At Town Center: Sunday–Thursday, 11 a.m.–9:30 p.m.;
Friday–Saturday, 11 a.m.–10 p.m.

Setting & atmosphere: Friendly, cozy restaurants. The decor is wall-to-wall Mexican, with hats, serapes, and posters everywhere.

House specialties: Chili relleno—roasted, peeled peppers filled with Monterey Jack cheese; turf and surf (tierra y mare); carnitas; carne asada; and a fillet of roughy à la Mexicana. Lunch specials from 11 a.m. to 2 p.m., $5.25; Saturday and Sunday sangria brunch from 11 a.m. to 3 p.m.

Other recommendations: Broiled breast of chicken in a variety of styles; New York steak with stir-fried cactus, onion, garlic, cilantro, and chili verde strips. Siesta Dining, 2–5 p.m., Monday through Friday, when the chef prepares a number of items such as enchiladas, burritos, tacos, tostadas, tamales, and chili rellenos for $6.95, and invites diners to create their own combinations from any two of the above; served with sopa de fideo (angelhair pasta in a chicken broth), rice, and refried beans.

Summary & comments: The owner created a number of the entrées. In keeping with today's healthier lifestyle, he cooks exclusively with canola oil. Upon request, cheese can be eliminated from any dish.

VOODOO CAFÉ & LOUNGE ★★★½

Creole/Cajun	Moderate/Expensive	QUALITY 85
		VALUE C+

Rio Hotel; (702) 252-7777
Strip   Zone 1

Customers: Tourists and locals	Parking: Valet, garage, lot
Reservations: Suggested	Bar: Full service
When to go: Any time	Wine selection: Excellent
Entrée range: $12–37.95	Dress: Sportscoat or dress shirt with collar for men; no shorts
Payment: VISA, MC, AMEX, DC, D	
Service rating: ★★★★	Disabled access: Elevator
Friendliness rating: ★★★★★	

Hours: Every day, 5–11 p.m.

Setting & atmosphere: Voodoo decor, black walls accented with splashes of color, comfortable booths and tables, and a spectacular view from atop one of the city's tallest buildings. With its location west of the Strip, the view of the action is the absolute best.

House specialties: Crawfish and blue crab cakes; frog legs d'Armond; baked oyster sampler with Rockefeller, Bienville, and tasso toppings; spicy, boiled Louisiana crawfish; VooDoo gumbo; the house salad with cane syrup vinaigrette; fresh tuna Napoleon; soft shell crab Lafayette.

Other recommendations: Cajun rib eye; catfish Bayou Teche (pan-fried catfish topped with crawfish étouffée); a seafood plate of cornmeal-crusted fried oysters, shrimp, crawfish, and catfish.

Summary & comments: It took a while for VooDoo to hit its stride, but now this colorful eatery and late-night hangout offers some very tasty food. The lounge features bartenders who do tricks while mixing drinks. In the past they performed flaming tricks, tossing the fiery libations from glass to glass, but those spoilsports at the fire department put out their fire.

WILD SAGE CAFÉ ★★★

		QUALITY
Contemporary American	Moderate Expensive	**89**

		VALUE
600 West Warm Springs, (McKaren Shopping center); (702) 944-7243		**B**

Need Zone

Customers: Locals	Parking: No valet
Reservations: A must for dinner	Bar: Beer and wine
When to go: Any time	Wine selection: Good
Entrée range: $12.50–21	Dress: Casual
Payment: VISA, MC, AMEX, D	Disabled access: Yes
Service rating: ★★★	
Friendliness rating: ★★★	

Brunch: Saturday and Sunday, 10 a.m.–3 p.m.
Lunch: Monday–Friday, 11 a.m.–3 p.m.
Dinner: Sunday–Thursday, 5–9:30 p.m.; Friday and Saturday, 5–10 p.m.

Setting & atmosphere: Contemporary art and furnishings, comfortable, laid back, and friendly surroundings.

House specialties: Menus change frequently, but don't miss any of these signature dishes: House-smoked salmon on a crisp potato gallette; sautéed crab cakes with field greens; morel mushrooms in a spinach crepe; thick, wild mushroom soup; or the old fashioned meatloaf served with mashed potatoes, gravy, and onions.

Other recommendations: Whole rack of baby lamb; free range chicken with risotto cake; roasted duckling with wild rice and cherry-port sauce. At brunch try the crispy banana fritters with raspberry sauce. The house-prepared-corned-beef reuben on homemade rye or grilled portobello mushroom sandwich are both fine choices at lunchtime. The daily specials are where they'll first introduce items slated for future regular menus.

Summary & comments: Owned by Spago alumni, these young chefs really know how to cook. Service can be slow, but that's because most items are cooked to order, so be patient. Expect to wait for a table at lunchtime unless you make a reservation.

WOLFGANG PUCK CAFÉ ★★★½

		QUALITY
American	Moderate	**85**

		VALUE
MGM Grand; (702) 891-3019		**B**

Strip   Zone 1

Customers: Tourists, locals
Reservations: Not accepted
When to go: Any time
Entrée range: $6.95–24.95
Payment: VISA, MC, AMEX, DC
Service rating: ★★★

Friendliness rating:★★★★
Parking: MGM lot
Bar: Full
Wine selection: Wide variety
Dress: Casual
Disabled access: Yes

Breakfast, lunch & dinner: Sunday–Thursday, 8 a.m.–11 p.m.; Friday and Saturday, 8–1 a.m.

Setting & atmosphere: Designed by Wolf's partner-wife, designer Barbara Lazaroff. Cheerful, attractive, with posters, tiled walls, and an open kitchen.

House specialties: Appetizers such as Chinois chicken salad with spicy honey-mustard dressing; roasted corn chowder with jalapeño cream. A variety of pizzas, including barbecued chicken with tomatoes and julienned red onion; smoked salmon with red onion and fresh dill cream; Barbara's fettuccini with shrimp, fresh vegetables, and tomato curry sauce; Grandma Puck's linguini with chicken Bolognese; Wolf's meat loaf with port wine sauce and garlic mashed potatoes. Apple tarte tatin (caramelized apples on puff pastry with whipped or ice cream).

Other recommendations: Mixed green salad with herb and goat cheese crostini; vegetable spring rolls with orange cabernet glaze; fried calamari with cilantro aioli. Calzone with mozzarella, sweet roasted peppers, sautéed spinach, wild mushrooms, roasted garlic, and thyme; rotisserie barbecued chicken with garlic mashed potatoes, french fries, or Caesar salad. Vanilla or chocolate crème brûlée.

Summary & comments: When busy, as it usually is, service can be slow, and food quality inconsistent. Sidewalk café design allows diners to watch people in the MGM Grand's casino.

Other Books to Read

Bass, Thomas. *Eudaemonic Pie*. Houghton Mifflin, 1985. The fascinating story of physicists from the University of California–Santa Cruz who invent a computer to beat the casinos at the game of roulette. A hilarious, true-life adventure.

Castleman, Deke. *Las Vegas*. Compass American Guides, 1999. A well-written guide to Las Vegas and its environs. This book is long on anecdote and history. If you take only one other book to Las Vegas, take this one. A very enjoyable read. Castleman has also authored an excellent guide to the entire state of Nevada.

Dalton, Michael. *Blackjack, a Professional Reference*. Spur of the Moment Publishing, 1992. A sourcebook for professionals and serious recreational players.

Demaris, Ovid, and Ed Reid. *Green Felt Jungle*. Trident Press, 1963. When first published, this was a highly sensational exposé of Las Vegas—its mobsters, rackets, and prostitution. Lively reading. . . .

McGervey, John D. *Probabilities in Everyday Life*. Ballantine Books, 1986. Although this book covers much more than gambling, it also deals with the odds of winning at casino games. It identifies the faulty logic and misleading statistics that can lead to bad debts. Recommended reading.

Nestor, Basil. *The Unofficial Guide to Casino Gambling*. Hungry Minds, 2001. Every game has an optimal strategy. So, if you want to win more, this is the book to check out first.

Orkin, Mikael. *Can You Win?* W. H. Freeman and Company, 1991. A discussion of the real odds for casino gambling, sports betting, and lotteries, including winning strategies and computer odds.

Rubin, Max. *CompCity: A Guide to Free Las Vegas Vacations*. Huntington Press, 1994. A practical and often hilarious guide to taking advantage of every possible comp and freebee.

Silberstang, Edwin. *The Winner's Guide to Casino Gambling*. Signet, 1980. The basic primer on casinos in simple, easy-to-understand language. A difficult subject made simple and fun.

Thorp, Dr. Edward O. *The Mathematics of Gambling*. Gambling Times, 1984. Thorp's book *Beat the Dealer* changed casino blackjack forever. In this book, he turns his attention to baccarat, roulette, and other games.

Vinson, Barney. *Casino Secrets*. Huntington Press, 1997. Breezy, entertaining, anecdotal gambling instruction and insider guide to Las Vegas casinos.

Index